Rebirth of a Nation
WALES 1880–1980

KENNETH O. MORGAN

OXFORD UNIVERSITY PRESS
UNIVERSITY OF WALES PRESS
1982

Oxford University Press, Walton Street, Oxford OX2 6DP

London Glasgow New York Toronto
Delhi Bombay Calcutta Madras Karachi
Kuala Lumpur Singapore Hong Kong Tokyo
Nairobi Dar es Salaam Cape Town
Melbourne Auckland

and associates in
Beirut Berlin Ibadan Mexico City Nicosia

First published by the Clarendon Press 1981
First issued as an Oxford University Press paperback 1982

British Library Cataloguing in Publication Data

Rebirth of a nation: Wales 1880–1980.
—(Oxford paperbacks)
1. Wales—History
I. Title
942.9'082   DA722
ISBN 0-19-821760-9

Printed in Great Britain by
Richard Clay (The Chaucer Press) Ltd
Bungay, Suffolk

TO THE MEMORY OF MY FATHER,

DAVID JAMES MORGAN (1894–1978)

PREFACE

In this book I have tried to describe the main features of the history of Wales from 1880 down to the present day. I have sought to discuss the political, constitutional, economic, social, religious, intellectual, literary, cultural, and sporting aspects of the period. In a few areas (notably science and technology) I am woefully ignorant, but it seemed to me right to concentrate on what I know best and what most engages my attention. At any rate, I hope that no serious distortion results. This is the final volume of the projected new History of Wales series. It follows the style laid down there, notably in trying to appeal to the general reader and in cutting down footnotes and technical appendices. At the same time, I hope that it may be regarded as a distinct study in its own right of a crucial phase of the evolution of modern Wales.

Perhaps inevitably, this is an academic study and something more. It is the product of over twenty years of research, writing, and meditation on modern Welsh history, a period that spans the whole of my adult life. It is also the beneficiary of the remarkable surge of interest in Welsh history in schools, colleges, and universities, in academic journals and in the media. I hope the bibliography makes clear how much I owe to the scholarly labours of other workers in the field. At the same time, it has proved impossible to eliminate entirely personal overtones. In this connection, it may assist the reader to know a little of my own background. I was born in England; I went to a secondary school in London, and to university in Oxford. For the past thirteen years I have earned my living in Oxford, a city of which I am very fond. At the same time, it has never occurred to me that I am anything other than Welsh. I was brought up in a Welsh-speaking home. I spent much of my childhood and early youth in north and mid-Wales. The accident of employment later sent me to Swansea for eight very happy years as a university lecturer, as a result of which I got to know south Wales equally well. The one area of Wales with which I was relatively unfamiliar until the 1970s was the north-east. As it happens, the good fortune of marriage has since enabled me to make good that deficiency. My own family tree illustrates some of the themes underlying this book. My grandfathers were both mid-Wales working men, one a blacksmith in north Cardiganshire, the other a fisherman in Merioneth. My parents, like many others of their generation, found the schoolteaching profession an escape route during the lean years and eventually moved to teach in state schools in London. And I, in Gwyn A. Williams's imperishable phrase, 'withered into an historian', though one who retains his Welsh commitment. This book is, then both a detached scholarly work and also a personal account of values that I mostly cherish and a nation that I love. How much the book gains or suffers from this inescapable personal dimension must be left to readers and reviewers to judge.

A work such as this must rest in part on the enormous stimulus I have gained from friends and advisers in Wales and elsewhere. My manuscript has been much improved by the expertise on linguistic and literary matters of Professor D. Ellis Evans of Jesus College, Oxford. I am also indebted to Prys Morgan of Swansea and Walford Davies of Aberystwyth for other advice on literary and cultural themes. Among those who have greatly helped me with source material are Owen Edwards, Controller of the BBC in Wales; Meic Stephens of the Welsh Arts Council; D. Emrys Jones, secretary of the Welsh Labour Party; Gareth Wyn Evans of the University of Wales Registry; and Sidney Tongue, chief executive officer of Wrexham−Maelor Borough Council. Throughout the past twenty-four years, the staff and officers of the National Library of Wales, Aberystwyth, have been endlessly helpful and considerate; it has been truly a home from home for me, as for many others. I am also very grateful to Vernon Bogdanor of Brasenose College for help on the devolution issue, to Ross McKibbin of St. John's College, Oxford, and Henry Pelling of St. John's College, Cambridge, for assistance on social and political aspects, to the Rt. Hon. Lord Cledwyn of Penrhos for valuable advice on recent politics, and to Neil Kinnock MP for some stimulating comments on economic policies and themes. I have also much benefited from innumerable conversations with academic friends in Wales over the years. Particular mention must be made of Ralph Griffiths, Peter Stead, David Howell, Neville Masterman, Gareth Jones, and the late Alun Davies of Swansea; my old friend, Ieuan Gwynedd Jones, Beverley and Llinos Smith, John Davies, Peter Madgwick and Owen R. Jones of Aberystwyth; Cyril Parry of Bangor; Professors Gwyn A. Williams and Gwynedd Pierce, and David Smith of Cardiff; and Alan Butt Philip of Bath. They will not all accept all of my judgements, but my understanding and enjoyment of modern Wales have been much enhanced by their friendship.

I am also much indebted to Ivon Asquith of the Oxford University Press and John Rhys of the University of Wales Press for the patience and kindness that they have shown me. Once again, it has been a joy to have a book published by the presses of the two universities in which I have spent my entire career. The Provost and Fellows of The Queen's College gave my Celtic obsessions every help, notably a sabbatical year during which this book was written. Pat Lloyd (who happens to be Welsh) once again typed out a lengthy and untidy manuscript with her usual cheerfulness and efficiency. I have Mrs Glenys Bridges of Swansea to thank warmly for the maps.

The final acknowledgements are the most profound of all. Professor Glanmor Williams read the whole manuscript as editor, and made many valuable suggestions. I am also deeply indebted to him, both for his professional advice and for innumerable acts of personal kindness, far beyond the call of duty, over the past twenty years and more. My wife Jane has, as always, been an untiring and utterly dependable source of encouragement, reassurance, and inspiration. In addition, she has drawn my attention to many printed sources for modern Welsh history, and helped redress many (though probably not all!) of my prejudices. My mother has given unstinting encouragement to my writing and research throughout my career. Finally, I must mention my late father, who lived through eighty-four of the years chronicled here, who helped greatly with the research into Welsh materials, and who embodied many of the best qualities of the land to which he was deeply devoted. I particularly hope that he would have liked this book.

KENNETH O. MORGAN

The Queen's College, Oxford
1 January 1980

CONTENTS

1. The counties of Wales (to 1973).

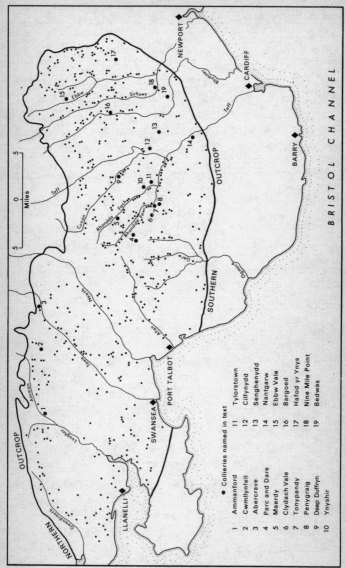

2. The collieries of the South Wales coalfield in 1913.

- Collieries named in text

1 Ammanford	11 Tylorstown
2 Cwmllynfell	12 Clfrynydd
3 Abercrave	13 Senghenydd
4 Parc and Dare	14 Nantgarw
5 Maerdy	15 Ebbw Vale
6 Clydach Vale	16 Hafod yr Ynys
7 Tonypandy	17 Hafod yr Ynys
8 Penygraig	18 Nine Mile Point
9 Deep Duffryn	19 Bedwas
10 Ynyshir	

PART I

THE REAWAKENING
1880 – 1914

CHAPTER 1

WALES IN THE EIGHTIES

The idea of Wales in later Victorian Britain was a singularly ill-defined one. To one local bishop in 1886, Wales was no more than a 'geographical expression', as Italy had been to Metternich.[1] It bore the same relationship to the England of which it formed a part as did the Highland zone to the rest of Scotland. In the 1880s, as far as most British people were concerned, the land beyond Offa's Dyke still was viewed as a semi-civilized, picturesque survival, much as George Borrow had depicted it in *Wild Wales* in the mid-fifties. It lay shrouded in the swirling mountain mists of that Celtic twilight which Matthew Arnold had invented in the course of his lectures as Professor of Poetry at Oxford in 1867. To adopt the terms of that notorious entry in the *Encyclopaedia Britannica*—in which were encapsulated all the humiliation and the patronizing indifference which helped to launch the modern nationalist movement in the principality—'for Wales, see England'.

Wales, it seemed, existed on a lower stratum from England, Scotland, or even Ireland. It belonged to prehistory. It was still cast in the druidic mould, where Borrow claimed to have discovered it. This attitude, especially among the English, truly died hard. Years later in 1919, in a passage on the Paris peace conference which was widely thought to be brilliant in perception as well as in literary panache, John Maynard Keynes described Lloyd George as 'a goat-footed bard, a half-human visitor to our age from the hag-ridden magic and enchanted woods of Celtic antiquity'. Lloyd George, so Keynes concluded—and here he was surely commenting on the nature of Welsh society generally as well as on the special qualities of this Celtic Prime Minister—was 'rooted in nothing'.[2] It was truly a world that this fellow of King's, with his entrées into Bloomsbury and Whitehall, never knew, let alone understood. But, even as late as 1919, ignorance of 'the unspeakable Celt' was fashionable, almost the conventional wisdom.

It is true that the years since the early 1860s had seen something of a sea-change in the attitudes adopted towards matters Welsh amongst sections of the Liberal *literati* and high intelligentsia. Matthew Arnold retained his full meed of naïve dogmatism about the divergent ethnic and cultural characteristics of the Saxon and the Celt: the Celt (ironically in the light of future

---

[1] Bishop Basil Tickell Jones, charge to St. David's diocese, 1886.
[2] J. M. Keynes, *Essays in Biography* (London, 1933, new ed., 1961), pp. 35–6.

developments) he claimed to be ineffectual in practical business, in politics, and the art of government, and to be in a state of eternal revolt against 'the despotism of fact'.[3] But he did manage to convey a more intelligent and kindly appreciation of the literary roots and value of Celtic culture. He helped to combat postures such as those struck by Delane, the editor of *The Times*, in 1866, who viewed the Welsh language as 'the curse of Wales',[4] an obstacle to the march of intellect, prosperity, and progress. In due course, a chair of Celtic Studies was founded at Oxford in 1877 as Arnold himself had demanded. A far more powerful and articulate Liberal ideologue, William Ewart Gladstone, also helped inspire a new and more sympathetic awareness of the historical value of Welsh culture, and of Wales as a society. At the national *eisteddfod* at Mold in Flintshire in 1873, in a speech delivered while he was Prime Minister he spoke warmly of 'the ancient history, the ancient deeds and the ancient language' of the principality.[5] He also introduced a political note: he referred to newspaper articles written by the Welsh radical MP, Henry Richard, member for Merthyr Tydfil, which had first opened his eyes to the unjust treatment of the legitimate claims of Wales by successive British governments. When Gladstone addressed the national *eisteddfod* again, at Wrexham in 1888, his speech was, significantly for the time, much more outspokenly political in content. He called for the more whole-hearted recognition of the Welsh language by the Church and, by implication, the British government.

By the 1880s, then, the concepts of Wales and Welshness were beginning to assume a more coherent form. Nevertheless the overriding impression left, even by sympathizers such as Arnold and Gladstone, was of a land whose concerns were still largely of interest to folklorists and antiquarians. Arnold himself thought that the death of the Welsh language was inevitable and perhaps in some ways desirable. Gladstone's emphasis, by contrast to his treatment of Irish questions, was on the culture and traditions that had unified Welshmen centuries ago rather than on those political, economic, and social conflicts that were tearing them apart in the 1880s. Meanwhile, in terms of hard information obtainable from blue books, practical action through legislation or administrative devolution, or informed concern with its contemporary difficulties, Wales remained as neglected and isolated as ever. Indeed, 'neglected Wales' was a favoured theme for journalists in the eighties. Along with the Mabinogion, with Owain Glyndŵr, with the druidic bards whose traditions were allegedly commemorated annually at the national *eisteddfod*, Wales belonged to the ages. The modern phase of Welsh history, one which spans the hundred years from the 1880s to the late 1970s, is, therefore, an attempt to dispel the primordial Celtic twilight with the contemporary Welsh reality. It is an

[3] Matthew Arnold, *On the Study of Celtic Literature* (London, 1867), pp. 99–102.

[4] *The Times*, 8 September 1866

[5] Ibid., 20 August 1873.

essential facet of the rediscovery of modern Britain, a conscious, sustained effort to propel an important section of the British Isles out of prehistory. It is a process of education and enlightenment which, a hundred years on, is still very far from complete.

Even in the 1880s, however, there were some hard facts which could be gleaned to help reduce these twilit legends to earthy reality. The nature of the population and the demographic structure of Wales were by now reasonably well established. According to the census returns of 1881, the counties of Wales—technically twelve, but with Monmouthshire increasingly coming to be regarded as an intrinsic part of the principality − contained 1,577,000 people. This represented a sharp increase of over 150,000 since the last census returns in 1871. The growth points of this population, however, were highly localized. Much of the increase came in Glamorgan, whose population rose from 405,798 to 518,383; this was an increase of 27 per cent in the decade, the third largest recorded in Britain.[6] The urban areas of the major towns of Cardiff (with a population of 106,164 in 1881) and of Swansea (with 93,001) showed the most striking increase, along with the Pontypridd registration district, which included the Rhondda coal-mining region that was now expanding so dramatically. Conversely, the upland districts around Merthyr Tydfil and Aberdare showed a fall in population during the decade 1871−81. This illustrated the relative decline in their iron production and the magnetic pull of the mining valleys to the south. Monmouthshire (6.7 per cent) and Carmarthenshire (9.7 per cent) also showed a growth in population during the decade: this was almost wholly due to the expansion of the coal industry in the western valleys of Monmouthshire and in Carmarthenshire east of the Gwendraeth valley on the perimeter of the coalfield. In the north-east of Wales, the increase of 7.4 per cent in the population of Denbighshire in the previous ten years, and of 5.2 per cent in that of Flintshire showed the recent growth of coal mining there, in the industrial belt between Wrexham and Holywell. The population statistics, indeed, were testimony to the growth and buoyancy of industrial Wales. Even the more distant and fragmented slate-quarrying industry of north-central Caernarvonshire and the Ffestiniog area of north Merioneth was relatively thriving at this period. These two counties also showed a sharp rise in population during the 1871−81 period, largely for this reason.

On the other hand, rural Wales was already showing the familiar indices of declining opportunity, low investment, and an excess of labour, especially for young males. In the ten years up to 1881, Breconshire, Radnorshire, and Montgomeryshire in mid-Wales, Pembrokeshire and Cardiganshire on the western seaboard, all showed a fall in population during the decade, while that of Anglesey was static. These counties were all left increasingly with a

[6] *Census of England and Wales, Vol. IV. General Report,* Parl. Papers 1883, lxxx (C. 3797), pp. 583 ff.

surplus of old men and of unmarried girls in their demographic structure. In Cardiganshire, apart from the general problem of the precarious base of upland dairy farming, there was the additional factor of the collapse of the small lead- and silver-mining industries in the Ystwyth and Rheidol valleys in the hinterland of Aberystwyth, as a result of American and other competition. Throughout the next decade, this contrast between a rapidly expanding population in the industrial valleys and urban centres of the south, and of decline and depression in most of the rural counties of mid- and north Wales became more and more pronounced. Indeed, in the 1880s, with the collapse of farm prices leading to new poverty in the countryside, the flight of population from rural Wales, especially amongst young farm labourers, became more emphatic. In the period 1881–91, according to the census returns, population was to fall in eight out of thirteen Welsh counties, even by as much as 11.68 per cent in Montgomeryshire. Already much of the land bore the appearance of what a later generation would term 'a depressed area'.

Much of this rural exodus was to the major cities of England, as was the case with the migration from the countryside of southern Ireland. The 1891 census recorded that over 228,000 Welsh natives were now resident in England: this probably underestimated the actual total. By the eighties, London, Birmingham, Middlesbrough, Manchester, and Birkenhead all had sizeable Welsh immigrant colonies. The milk-dairying trade of London owed much to the emigration of tenant farmers and labourers from Cardiganshire and elsewhere in mid-Wales: wags would claim that they turned for help, in their provision of milk to the metropolis, to another product of Welsh enterprise in an earlier age—London's supply of water. There were articulate and powerful groups of business and professional Welshmen who congregated in London. The movement for a Welsh national university began with London-based men like Sir Hugh Owen in the sixties. The campaign for Welsh home rule (*Cymru Fydd*) received powerful stimulus from these *emigrés* in the eighties, and from the formation of a 'Union' of London Welsh societies in Fetter Lane chapel in March 1889. By the eighties, there were many influential Welsh-language chapels to serve as assemblies for the people of the diaspora—Methodist like Jewin, Charing Cross, and Shirland Road; Independent like King's Cross and Radnor Walk; Baptist like Castle Street, just behind Oxford Circus, later patronized by the Lloyd George family. Paddington station, surrounded by a myriad of small hotels, became a point of arrival for the Welsh in London almost as evocative as Boston for the American Irish. Even more important than London in the world of the emigrant was Liverpool. By the eighties, it had become a kind of auxiliary capital for north Wales, with a rich array of chapels, newspaper houses, and cultural institutions. It spawned a major publishing house, the Brython Press, while the *Liverpool Daily Post* by the turn of the century had become in effect the daily newspaper of north Wales. Several leading figures in Welsh national life in the twentieth century were proud and self-conscious products of the Liverpool Welsh community, including the historian and essayist R. T. Jenkins, the scholar Idris Foster, the shipowner Sir R. J. Thomas, and that brilliant, angular representative of the spirit of nationalism, the *littérateur* Saunders Lewis.

Welsh men and women, of course, migrated much further afield than London or Liverpool. The 1890 census recorded that over 100,000 Welsh natives were resident in the United States, largely in New York state and in the mining and steel-producing areas of Ohio, Pennsylvania, and West Virginia. Many of the Mormons who followed Brigham Young to Utah were of Welsh stock. There was a Welsh-language monthly, *Y Drych*, published at Utica, New York. Emigrants journeyed even further to South Africa, to Australia, and New Zealand. A small but significant group of a few thousands ventured to the wilds of Patagonia in the southern part of the Argentine, seeking their version of Zion in the wilderness.

On the other hand, this kind of worldwide dispersal of population is true of Ireland, too. What differentiates the history of modern Wales from that of modern Ireland in terms of demography is that the vast bulk of the displaced emigrant population of rural Wales found alternative employment and secure prospects within Wales itself. It was to the mining valleys and the coastal ports of the south in their own native land that the preponderant mass was drawn. Professor Brinley Thomas has shown that in the sixty years 1851–1911, a net loss of 388,000 people from the rural areas was balanced by an inward migration of 366,000 into the Glamorgan–Monmouthshire–Carmarthenshire coalfield. Until the mid-nineties, the vast bulk of it came from rural Wales.[7] This was a far more significant feature of the movements of Welsh population than the overseas migration across the Atlantic or the Pacific, of which much was later made when welcoming 'exiles' home, amidst much sentimentality, to the national *eisteddfod*. It certainly counted for much more than the small community marooned in the Chubut valley in Patagonia, whose desperate struggles to survive at all belied the glowing hopes (and somewhat dubious prospectuses) offered by Michael Daniel Jones and other pioneers of emigration in the sixties. The dominant fact of Welsh emigration is that so much of it found new domicile within Wales. This helped perpetuate and develop the native culture and language in the industrial and urban communities of the south. The consequences were long-lasting, even after the turn of the century when migration from England began to swamp that from the Welsh hinterland, and the potential anglicizing effects of industrialization became clearer. Until that time, the flow of young Welsh people finding their way south, often for a season only but usually more permanently, through the new railways, by horse-and-cart, frequently on foot, served to keep the Welsh nation recognizably alive and intact.

[7] Brinley Thomas, 'Wales and the Atlantic Economy', *Scottish Journal of Political Economy* (November 1959), pp. 169 ff.

The land, after all, was riven by so many divisions of geography and geology. It was dominated physically by vast, almost impenetrable mountain uplands, with an unrewarding, unproductive soil. Its communities were small and scattered. Until the eighties, Wales was mainly a land of hamlets and villages rather than of towns. Its structure in some ways still reflected the early territorial divisions of the Middle Ages. Gwynedd and Clwyd, Dyfed and Powys, Morgannwg and Gwent were psychological realities in the eighties, long before the names were resurrected in order to popularize the new local government boundaries in 1973. The completion of the basic Welsh railway network in the third quarter of the nineteenth century (apart from some local lines in the southern valleys to transport coal to the ports) while providing new access to markets for Welsh farmers and manufacturers, only partially broke down these physical and psychological barriers. The main south Wales line through to Fishguard in northern Pembrokeshire; that in north Wales along the coast to Holyhead in Anglesey; the Cambrian railways taking tourists to Aberystwyth and the Cardigan Bay coast and a supposed 'Welsh riviera'; the mid-Wales line intersecting at the non-existent town of Moat Lane and opening up such holiday resorts as the spa of Llandrindod Wells—all of these were largely designed to link the various parts of Wales with the markets and urban centres of England, rather than with each other. Progress from north Wales to the far south was almost as laborious still as it had been for George Borrow. Shrewsbury or even London was a more convenient rendezvous. The same principle applied to the major roads of Wales. These were in any case a byword for their primitive inadequacy in the late-nineteenth century. Some roads even disappeared, like the old drovers' trails over the roof of the mountain heartland, casualties (like the trade of the drovers themselves) of the competitive pressures of the railways. In general, transport and the communications network served to divide the Welsh people from each other still further.

And yet, despite all this, despite these forces for separatism within their society, the Welsh people retained their identity and their elements of unity. The land remained in many respects more integrated than Scotland or Ireland. The barriers between highland and lowland Wales were more negotiable than those north of the border, while there was emphatically nothing that resembled a Welsh Ulster. Industrialization and urbanization, as has been seen, served to reinforce the unity of Wales. The growth of new towns, the new bourgeoisie that they produced, made a modern Welsh national movement possible. It has here in the major towns that the chapels, the newspapers, the *eisteddfodau*, and the choral festivals flourished above all. If there was an outstanding cradle of the national revival in modern Wales, it may be found not in the sparsely populated countryside, even though it was from here that men like Owen M. Edwards and John Morris-Jones were to come, but amidst the grimy iron-works and winding-shafts of the working-class metropolis of Merthyr Tydfil.

In terms of economic growth, a good deal of Wales in the eighties was distinctly dynamic, as will be noted later. But the social and political super-structure was very different. Despite the dramatic expansion of industry and the explosive growth of population in the industrial south and east, much of Wales, most characteristically in the more isolated rural areas, was cast in a highly traditional mould. In its social structure and its fabric of political leadership, the land was still, to use Henry Richard's journalistic shorthand, a 'feudal' one, a place where, in his words, clansmen struggled for their chief tains as they had done for centuries past.[8] Henry Richard was emphasizing here the ascendancy of landed families at parliamentary elections. But in a much broader sense the dominance of aristocratic families were writ large on Welsh society in the later nineteenth century as it had been since the age of the Tudors. In rural Wales, there were great dynasties such as the Penrhyns in Caernarvonshire; the Wynns of Wynnstay in Denbighshire, Montgomery-shire and Merioneth; the Powis family in eastern Montgomeryshire; the Pryses of Gogerddan, the Vaughans of Trawscoed, and the Powells of Nanteos in Cardiganshire; the Cawdors of Golden Grove in Carmarthenshire and Pembrokeshire; along with, in the industrial regions, the Butes in Glamorgan, the Beauforts and the Morgans of Tredegar in Monmouthshire. These were amongst the major dynasts. Indeed, Wales was remarkable for the preponderance of large landed estates. Over 60 per cent of the princi-pality, as recorded in the 'new Domesday book' compiled by John Bateman in 1873, consisted of estates of over 1,000 acres.[9] These estates were in the hands of only 571 landowners, a mere 1 per cent of the total of those owning land in some form. Beneath these great families lay a whole nexus of smaller land-owners and squireens, bound together by marriage and by commercial and social intercourse. Over most of Wales, these landowners still exercised a massive, almost unchallenged authority. Most of them boasted of their ancient Welsh lineage and antiquity, going back to the age of the Princes—even though such names as Bute and Cawdor and Londonderry testified to the extent of Scottish or Anglo-Irish penetration. A landlord like Sir Watkin Williams Wynn controlling a domain of 148,000 acres from Wynnstay, near Wrexham, took pride in his cordial relations with his tenants, most of whom had occupied their farms on a family basis, generation after generation. Tenant farmers at Wynstay held festivities for days to celebrate the Wynn heir's coming of age in 1848.[10] Over a century later, affectionate regard for 'Old Sir Watkin' was still a powerful folk-memory in rural Montgomeryshire.

[8] Henry Richard, *Letters on the Social and Political Condition of Wales* (London, 1867), p. 80.

[9] John Bateman, *The Great Landowners of Great Britain and Ireland* (London, 1876).

[10] Cf. Jane Morgan, 'Denbighshire's *Annus Mirabilis*: the County and Borough Elections of 1868', *Welsh History Review*, vol. 7, No. 1 (June 1974), p. 66.

At the start of the eighties, the relations of these great landowners with rural society in Wales were very different in tone from the conflict that marked the Irish countryside at the same period. There were, as yet, no land leagues, no boycottings, no agrarian 'plans of campaign' in rural Wales. At the quarter sessions as justices of the peace, as patrons of local churches and protectors of chapel leases, often as father figures at local *eisteddfodau*, the authority of the great landlords was implicit, in accord with an understood and respected tradition of social hierarchy and deference. For all that, the ascendancy of the gentry, relatively unoppressive though it might be, was hard to reconcile with a dynamic, rapidly-changing society, stirred not only by industrial expansion but increasingly by political radicalism and cultural nationalism. The rule of the gentry was complicated by broad changes in the social structure. In the coalfield, the gentry often turned entrepreneur, or else allied to newer entrepreneurial families, as the Llewellyns, landlords of Penllergaer, had united with the Dillwyns, industrialists of Swansea. Landowners took a major part in the industrial development of towns such as Cardiff and Neath. New industrial or commercial dynasties, long-established like the Guests of Merthyr, newer ones like the Corys in Cardiff or the Davieses of Llandinam in the Rhondda, were making their own bid for social power. Long before the 1880s, boroughs such as Swansea in south Wales had their own middle class of substantial commercial and trading families, bankers, merchants, and the like, who dominated local government. In smaller county towns in the rural areas, like Caernarfon, Aberystwyth, Carmarthen, or Brecon, a new middle-class élite of small businessmen, shopkeepers, solicitors, journalists, and nonconformist ministers was pressing for a growing control of municipal life. But blanketing their efforts, until the democratic revolution of the eighties, was the omnipresent dominance of the landed gentry, enveloping government, local justice, and local society in what was largely a small-town, small-scale frontier world.

Nevertheless, there were signs of a massive change. Over the countryside as a whole, these mighty landlords were increasingly divorced from the overwhelming bulk of the population over whom they maintained their ascendancy, in terms of language, religion and, finally, political outlook. Soon, the stresses between a static framework of landlord ascendancy and the pulsating forces of social and political democracy were becoming almost insupportable. By the eighties, the signs of the coming explosion were everywhere apparent. Welsh landlords, usually benevolent, often bewildered, men who had long prided themselves on their harmonious relations with their hereditary tenants, now became the popular scapegoats for a vast upsurge of democratic protest. From Lloyd George to Gwynfor Evans, every major figure in Welsh radical politics was to base his crusade, at least in part, on a mass hostility towards the domination of the landlords. They became targets for radicals and for nationalists as well; it seemed almost providential that an unexpectedly ferocious attack on the value of Welsh culture in the 1950s should be delivered by the elderly dynast, Lord Raglan.[11] Penrhyn Castle, Nanteos, Wynnstay, Golden Grove, Picton Castle, and the rest, landmarks of an immemorial style of rural life and of the ascendancy of the *plas* dating from at least Henry VIII's Act of Union, now became beleaguered outposts of a new form of English and Anglican dominance over the countryside. They became almost as hated in their turn as Harlech or Conway castles had been, amidst a very different social order, centuries before.

The political structure that this landowning ascendancy reflected was no less in tension with the social and economic realities of Wales in the eighties. There had been symptoms, long before the passage of the Reform Act of 1867, that the Welsh-speaking nonconformist majority of the nation were pressing for a more appropriate and less anachronistic political order. There had been abortive campaigns by nonconformists such as Richard Davies in the Caernarfon Boroughs election of 1852 and by David Williams for Merioneth in 1859. Even more significant, after the latter election there took place some evictions of tenant farmers who had voted Liberal in Merioneth. Among those evicted were the uncle of Tom Ellis, the future Liberal member for the county, and the mother of Michael Daniel Jones, a widow. Many years later, before the royal commission inquiring into the Welsh land question in 1894, Tom Ellis was to testify to the 'thrill of horror' that these evictions had caused in the Welsh countryside and to the radical backlash that they released among the hitherto pacific nonconformist peasantry.[12] The martyrology and the demonology of the Welsh radical tradition, without which no left-wing crusade can survive, were being created. Significantly, they originated in the remoter rural areas of the land, but they retained its validity and their appeal in the industrial valleys of the south. 'There is a spirit of vassalage amongst the tillers of the soil', declared a Cardiganshire Liberal, a Methodist ironmonger, in 1894, evoking the memories of evictions thirty years earlier;[13] but it was industrial and urban toilers who responded with equal passion. Truly, here was a folk memory that refused to die. Lloyd George made much electoral capital out of it during his campaigns for the 'People's Budget' in 1910. 'It awoke the spirit of the mountains, the genius of freedom that fought the might of the Normans. . . . The political power of landlordism was shattered as effectively as the power of the Druids.'[14]

According to received tradition, it was the great expansion of the electorate in 1867 and the 'great election' of that *annus mirabilis*, 1868, which saw a decisive thrust away from this traditional pattern of political authority.

[11] Lord Raglan, 'I take my Stand', *Wales* (October 1958).
[12] *Evidence to the Welsh Land Commission*, vol. 1, Parl. Papers 1894 (C. 7439), qu. 16,912.
[13] Ibid., vol. iii, Parl. Papers, 1895, xl (C. 7661), qu. 47,489 (evidence of J. M. Howell).
[14] Speech at Queen's Hall, 23 March 1910.

Undoubtedly, the election results in 1868 were remarkable enough. There was the defeat of a Douglas-Pennant, the scion of Penrhyn, in Caernarvonshire, and of the Vaughans of Trawscoed in Cardiganshire. There was the election of twenty-three Liberals as against only ten Conservatives in Wales. Most striking of all there was the return of three nonconformists including the famous radical pacifist, Henry Richard, 'the apostle of peace', in the highly democratic two-member constituency of Merthyr Tydfil, at the expense of Henry Austen Bruce, Gladstone's Home Secretary. But the transformation in 1868 was only a partial one. Twenty-four of the thirty-three Welsh MPs were still landowners; most of the Liberal members returned were undeniably Whiggish; the bulk of the Welsh electorate, let alone the Welsh people, remained unrepresented. Nor did the new Welsh Liberal MPs have much to show for their efforts, as far as Wales was concerned, in the 1868–74 session of parliament. The first motion on behalf of the disestablishment of the Church in Wales, moved by Watkin Williams, a barrister who sat for Denbigh District, failed ignominiously. Gladstone himself spoke strongly against it, and denied that the circumstances that had promoted disestablishment in Ireland were paralleled at all in Wales.

At the general election of 1874, the tide turned back somewhat. There was a swing towards Toryism and older forms of authority, accompanied by a good deal of political coercion, the new Ballot Act notwithstanding. There was a net gain of four seats by the Conservatives; nineteen Liberals (twelve representing borough seats) and fourteen Conservatives were returned. The reversal was most pronounced in the country constituencies, conspicuously in those counties, Carmarthenshire, Cardiganshire, and Caernarvonshire, where intimidation and eviction had been most prevalent in the aftermath of 1868. In all of these, Conservative landowners were again returned to Westminster. Most striking of all, the Hon. George Douglas-Pennant, the heir to the Penrhyn estates, defeated a Liberal opponent in Caernarvonshire. The Conservative vote was buoyant in northern parts of the county, around Bangor and in the quarrying region around Bethesda and Llanberis where Penrhyn's was 'the prevailing interest'. An election which stuck a significantly different theme was that in Merthyr Tydfil where a Labour candidate, Thomas Halliday of the Amalgamated Association of Miners, polled nearly 5,000 votes. But it was evident that much of Wales was still enmeshed in the 'feudal' politics which Henry Richard had denounced in the press eight years earlier.

But the next general election, that of 1880, offered clear signs that political authority in Wales was beginning to change hands. No part of Britain responded more passionately to the radical crusade heralded by the agitation against the 'atrocities' committed by the Turks in Bulgaria, and by Gladstone's Midlothian campaign. Wales responded even more warmly to the transcendent personality of Gladstone himself, the squire of Hawarden,

married to a Welsh wife, and increasingly as attuned to Welsh national sentiment as he was to Polish or Italian. Gladstone's portrait flourished on the
walls of farm labourers' or miners' cottages, a symbol of the new religion of
the cult of Hawarden. There were nine Liberal gains in 1880. In all, twenty-
nine of the thirty-three Welsh seats fell into Liberal hands, with only a few
anglicized border seats along the marches resisting the Liberal tide. The
majority of these Welsh MPs were no longer landowners, but industrialists
and manufacturers, or else barristers and solicitors. The law retained in full its
appeal as a step-ladder for the aspiring bourgeois politician in Wales, as in
Scotland. Significantly, at least eight of the Welsh MPs now were nonconformists. One election, in particular, captured the imagination of the
land. This was the contest in Montgomeryshire. Here, Stuart Rendel, an
Englishman, an Anglican, even (astonishingly enough for the land of the
pacifist, Henry Richard), an arms manufacturer, defeated the massive
influence of the Wynns of Wynnstay in a memorable contest. It was notable
that Rendel polled most strongly in the mainly Welsh-speaking and nonconformist areas of western Montgomeryshire, rather than in towns such as
Welshpool in the east where Powis Castle and Wynnstay exerted their
traditional influence. Here and elsewhere, the demise of the Welsh gentry,
Tory and Whig, was clearly discernible in the quality of politics in the early
eighties, as it was in the new energy and cohesion of the Welsh Liberal MPs in
the House of Commons, in pressing for educational and temperance reform,
and in raising the issue of the disestablishment of the Church in Wales. Yet
these were only portents. Wales, even more than most parts of Britain, was
still far from being a democracy. Politically and socially, much of the land
remained in slumber. The gentry and their clerical associates still ruled the
quarter sessions and the parish as they had done for centuries past.

This pattern of social and political leadership resulted in Welsh society reveal-
ing a massive and growing gulf between an anglicized largely English-
speaking and English-educated gentry class and the vast majority of the
population, rural and industrial. Truly Wales now consisted of two nations (in
Disraeli's usage), although there remained important bridges between them.
It meant also that modes of cultural and national self-expression in Wales
were in special respects popular ones. The culture was a people's culture (if
not really a 'peasant culture' as it has sometimes been defined). This was in
stark contrast to the position in Scotland where the romantic myths of Sir
Walter Scott still retained their appeal, and where great landowners still
claimed to reflect national and patriotic endeavour, as they had done long
before the time of the Jacobite risings. Culture in Wales emerged from below,
from the tenant farmers and labourers on their smallholdings in the rural
areas, from the striving self-made bourgeoisie in the smaller towns, from the
slate-quarrying villages of Caernarvonshire and Merioneth and the mining

villages of Denbighshire, and most of all from the frontier communities of the industrial valleys in the south, populated to a great extent, as has been seen, by immigrants from the Welsh hinterland.

This popular, democratic quality of Welsh culture was most evident in the dominant feature of Welsh social life in the eighties, and for a generation to come, namely the nonconformist chapels. Nonconformity had swept through most of rural Wales in the earlier nineteenth century, in the wake of the population explosion there after the end of the Napoleonic wars, as village names such as Bethesda, Carmel, Nebo or Zion bore witness. It was surging on into the industrial valleys of the coalfield simultaneously with the industrial process itself. Places like Merthyr Tydfil, Aberdare, Neath, and Llanelli were, by the eighties, citadels of dissent, their ministers and deacons a new élite of popular leadership. Swansea, where elaborate celebrations had taken place in 1862 to commemorate the bicentenary of the establishment of Congregationalism, was commonly known as 'the Mecca of Nonconformity'. The religious census of 1851 had shown that the nonconformist chapels claimed over 80 per cent of those at worship on the census Sunday. There had been further growth since then, not least following the impact of the religious revival of 1859 whose influence radiated outwards from the small hamlet of Treddôl in north Cardiganshire where it had begun. By the eighties, indeed, the nonconformist bodies were far more flourishing and socially ambitious than in the revivalist years at the turn of the century. Denominations now set aside development funds for building programmes, and employed professional architects to embellish or rebuild their chapels. In place of the austerity of style favoured by nonconformist chapels in the earlier part of the century, echoing the meeting-house or conventicle tradition of the puritan fathers of the seventeenth century, chapels were now often imposing structures, with elaborate façades and theatrical, almost Baroque, interiors. They reflected High Gothic, Baroque, Regency, or even Moorish styles. The massive new chapels built in such towns as Aberystwyth, Caernarfon, and Swansea in the sixties and seventies illustrate this process clearly. The mid-Victorian 'battle of the styles' affected the Welsh chapels, too. It lent them almost a kind of 'high church' image which confirmed the increasingly self-confident character of the free churches in Wales.

Since the mid-century, it is true, the Anglican Church in Wales had also undergone something of a renaissance. Bishop Alfred Ollivant in the diocese of Llandaff and Bishop Connop Thirlwall in St. David's diocese stimulated a new programme of church building and renovation, of the promotion of church or 'National' elementary schools, and of general evangelization. Thirlwall, an Englishman like so many Welsh bishops, even learnt to speak the people's language. In 1870 Gladstone had made the spectacular gesture of appointing a Welsh-speaking Welshman, Joshua Hughes, to the see of St. Asaph. As luck would have it, Hughes was an indifferent scholar and an undistinguished prelate; but the appointment of a Welsh-speaking bishop for the first time since the reign of Queen Anne caused something of a stir. For all that, spokesmen for the Anglican Church remained acutely conscious that theirs was a minority Church, even though one by law established. It was certainly not established in the hearts of the great majority of the Welsh people. With barely 20 per cent of worshipping Welsh men and women claimed as Anglican communicants, the possibility of the four Welsh dioceses undergoing the same fate as the Irish Church which Gladstone had disestablished in 1869 was an increasingly real one. At the annual Church Congress held at Swansea in 1879 (significantly the first time that this body had ever met in Wales), Dean H. T. Edwards of Bangor created a sensation by asserting openly what many churchmen had long accepted tacitly, that the nonconformists formed the vast majority of the Welsh people. Dean Edwards claimed that over a million of the population habitually spoke in Welsh (an extrapolation from the 1871 census by the statistician, E. G. Ravenstein). Of these, declared the Dean, 800,000 were nonconformists.[15] Wales, claimed Gladstone at this time, was 'a nation of nonconformists', though he was cautious in pursuing the political implications of this, notably the need for disestablishment of a minority Church.

Some of the statistics presented by the nonconformists themselves, including such books as the Revd Thomas Rees's celebrated history of dissent in Wales, suggested a somewhat less glowing picture. One striking statistic that emerged from the figures of the nonconformist bodies, though seldom emphasized by them, was that the census of religion in 1851 had also shown that nearly half the population of Wales did not attend a place of worship at all. The growth of an industrial, urban society since 1851 suggested that the hold of all religious bodies over working-class society was increasingly tenuous. By the mid-eighties, such nonconformist newspapers as the Methodist *Goleuad* and the Independent *Tyst*, together with the new quarterly, *Y Geninen*, were speaking of symptoms of decline or of loss of momentum amongst the Welsh nonconformist bodies in the face of industrialization, secularization, and new scientific schools of biblical criticism. The last major religious revival, the transatlantic efforts of Moody and Sankey notwithstanding, had been as long ago as 1859. Nevertheless, the crude figures of chapel membership remained impressive enough. In 1882 it was recorded by the yearbooks of the four main denominations that their members totalled 352, 249 in all, with a larger number of 'adherents' claimed as a kind of penumbra around the solid core of chapel members. The denominational picture and its geographical distribution were clear enough. The largest denomination was the Calvinist Methodist, usually termed simply 'the Methodists' or *Yr Hen Gorff*, the historic church of Whitefield, Howell

---

[15] *Report of the Nineteenth Annual Meeting of the Church Congress, 1879* (London, 1880), pp. 354–8.

Harris and Williams of Pantycelyn in the previous century, with 122,107 members. It was most strongly rooted in the most Welsh parts of rural Wales, in Anglesey, Caernarvonshire, Merioneth, and Cardiganshire along the western fringe. A close second were the Congregationalists, the 'Independents' or *Annibynwyr* in the traditional usage, especially strong in south Wales, notably in Carmarthenshire and in Glamorgan, with 116,218 members. Third came the Baptists with 81,378 members; their main strength lay in the south and west, in Pembrokeshire, Glamorgan, and Monmouth. The smallest of the big four were the Wesleyan Methodists or 'Wesleyans', with 32,146. They were the most anglicized of the four main bodies and were strongest in Flintshire and around Cardiff. There were some smaller sects. The Unitarians flourished, as for two centuries past, along the Teifi valley in southern Cardiganshire and northern Carmarthenshire. There were Quakers in Glamorgan, notably in Swansea, Neath, and Cardiff; and there were a handful of Campbellite Baptists, notably the redoubtable Richard Lloyd in Llanystumdwy, Lloyd George's famous shoemaker uncle. But it was the four largest denominations which counted.

They predominated in a way that transcended the bleak (and often unreliable) evidence provided by annual yearbooks and sessional returns. They dictated the quality of life of a whole society. It was their ministers who became eloquent popular tribunes—the 'big guns' (to adopt a later style), like Thomas Jones, enthroned at Libanus, Morriston, and later at Walter Road, Swansea; Herber Evans at Salem, Caernarfon; Evan Jones at Moriah in the same town; John Thomas ministering to the diaspora at Great Crosshall Street, Liverpool. There were younger men rising fast, like John Williams of Brynsiencyn, Anglesey (b. 1855) and Elfed Lewis, of Conwyl Elfed, Carmarthenshire (b. 1860). Some leading Welsh preachers, Hugh Price Hughes or later J. D. Jones, for instance, were exports to tabernacles in England; but most stayed in their native land. Some were products of Welsh, Scottish, or even American theological seminaries, and even gained spurious transatlantic doctorates. Many were from an uncultured rustic background, as in the case of the colourful David Rees, from Bronant, north Cardiganshire, a former shoemaker. Thomas Jones was once a collier; Herber Evans began life as a draper's assistant. These men were essentially populist (*gwerinol* in the Welsh term) in style of life and in rhetoric. They enjoyed a natural, spontaneous relationship with their congregations, not only in delivering fiery, fundamentalist sermons on Sundays but also in popular lectures on such figures as John Penry, Oliver Cromwell, or (a recent new favourite) David Livingstone, on whom the formidable Independent divine, Kilsby Jones, orated affectingly. The big four denominations supplied almost all these ministerial tribunes. They also dominated much of the Welsh newspaper and periodical press, with the Methodist weekly, *Y Goleuad*, published at Dolgellau, the Independent *Tyst* published at Caernarfon, and the Baptist *Seren Cymru*, based on Carmarthen, the most influential. By the eighties, the barriers between the various sects still survived, though largely on a social rather than a theological basis. There were sometimes barriers within denominations, too, as in the Independents' 'battle of the two constitutions' between 1879 and 1885, with Michael Daniel Jones and the Revd John Thomas as the leading protagonists. Otherwise, the Baptists' insistence on total immersion or the Methodists' organizational structure based on an itinerant pastorate were less distinctive or significant than they had been forty or fifty years earlier. For practical purposes, in furthering the social and cultural values of local communities, increasingly in acting as the voices of social and political protest against the dominance of the clergy and the landed gentry, the chapels spoke largely as one. They formed almost a kind of unofficial established religion, the more so since, through vigorous publicists such as Thomas Gee of Denbigh, the Methodists had since 1868 decisively shaken off their traditional reluctance to participate in political activity.

The influence of the nonconformist chapels upon modern Wales will always generate controversy. Without doubt, the impact of a peculiarly sombre Sabbatarian puritanism stifled many aspects of the national genius. The chapels frowned on cultural experiment, especially in literature or the dramatic arts. They were largely immune to new currents of thought, hermetically sealed by the pressures of the Welsh language. Darwinian biology, the 'higher criticism' of modern biblical scholarship, the 'new theology' at the turn of the century made scant impact on the chapels, their denominational assemblies or *cyrddau mawr*, their *sêt fawr* of respectable middle-class shopkeepers or Lib-Lab artisans each Sunday. Nonconformity interacted closely with a ferociously zealous temperance movement: the Good Templars and the Blue Ribbon movements produced much excitement in the seventies and eighties, while 'taking the pledge' became almost a rite of civic initiation for young schoolboys. At its worst, Welsh nonconformity helped generate tensions, frustrations and fantasies, feelings of subconscious guilt, and sexual deprivation. They were outlined in devastating fashion at the time of the First World War by the short stories of Caradoc Evans with their piercing, merciless exposures of rural and small-town puritan hypocrisy and the religion of responsibility.[16] The world of sectarian bitterness between church and chapel, perhaps even between chapel and chapel, portrayed vividly by Huw Evans in *Cwm Eithin* with reference to the early decades of the century, was an unappealing one. Ministers in the eighties, men like the Revd Evan Jones of Moriah, Caernarfon, seemed even more intransigent in their moral rectitude and political partisanship than had been their predecessors a generation earlier. This rampant sectarianism was a monument to the parochial animosities of the chapel ethos, of which Thomas Gee was

[16] Notably in *My People* (1915).

perhaps the most aggressive spokesman, rather than to the bland, complacent superiority affected by the Church of England in Wales.

In important respects, then, Welsh nonconformity restricted and stunted the national growth. Yet in many other ways, too, it must surely have enabled a poor, isolated, semi-feudal community to reach out for new aspirations and to fulfil itself the more completely. With all its limitations, nonconformity was responsible for almost every significant and worthwhile aspect of social and cultural activity in late nineteenth-century Wales. The preacher-poet had become a national symbol of cultural vitality (later supplanted by the professor-poet). The astonishingly rich local community life, the choral festivals, the 'penny readings', *eisteddfodau* in abundance, the wide range of Welsh- and English-language publications, much of the educational provision afforded in Sunday schools or in chapel-dominated Board elementary schools after the passage of the Forster Act in 1870, more ambitious institutions such as the 'college by the sea' founded on the coast at Aberystwyth in 1872—the first higher education institution created in Wales apart from the exclusively Anglican college at Lampeter—all these were the creations of the chapels. More important still, the chapels lent to the Welsh national movements of the *fin de siècle* a focus for collective aspiration and action, opportunities for democratic leadership and for social mobility, most of all a self-confidence and a passion for popular education and improvement which represent much of the best of modern Wales. Ultimately, one suspects, the 'big guns' of the pulpit gained their mass appeal not from the theological or the literary content of their fiery sermons but from the populist impact of their own personalities. They were accessible embodiments of that relatively classless ethos valued by Welsh-speaking people which the concept of *y werin* (the common folk) only misleadingly conveys. Below the veneer of upper-class ascendancy maintained by the landed gentry at so many levels in the eighties, the Welsh democracy was a thriving and creative one. It was its nonconformist leadership and ideology that largely made it so.

Equally, cultural life in the eighties was flourishing and vigorous. The national *eisteddfod* enjoyed great prestige as a folk festival of the arts. It had safely survived the insults of *The Times* in the 1860s. Scholarly attacks on the historical authenticity of the *gorsedd* and its bardic ritual, such as those delivered by John Morris-Jones in 1896, still lay some years off. The reputation of the national festival was exceptionally high, and the cultural life of ordinary people in Wales exceptionally rich. That cultural life was focused on two art forms almost exclusively, music and literature, especially poetry. There was very little drama in Wales, partly the result of the puritanism of the chapels, more of the lack of large towns to support dramatic productions. Welsh opera was primitive, with Joseph Parry's *Hywel a Blodwen*, laced with sentimental ballads, the most popular specimen of it. The visual arts in Wales, painting, sculpture and the like, were virtually non-existent. The *eisteddfod* ignored them, while the Royal Cambrian Academy was an English survival concerned with painting, which dated from the 'picturesque' phase of the Richard Wilson era a hundred years earlier. Appropriately, its headquarters was a country house in Conway. Welsh architecture was equally uninspired, although some features of house design were not without interest. Such innovation as there was in architecture in Wales came from the more imaginative members of the gentry, as in Burges's Gothic fantasies constructed for the eccentric third Marquess of Bute at Cardiff Castle and at Castell Coch, on a hill above Tongwynlais. Chapel architecture, too often with heavy, derivative façades and lifeless forms, was what most of the rest of Wales had to offer, and inevitably so.

But there was always music. Even in the eighties, the Welsh blessed their Creator for their being a musical nation, and for the *eisteddfod* and choral festivals which encouraged this blessed faculty. Yet the musical gift had its limits. There were no Welsh orchestras or concert halls, no traditions in instrumental music other than the omnipresent harp or the antiquated *crwth*. There was no significant Welsh composer other than the tireless Joseph Parry, the first Professor of Music at the College of Aberystwyth in 1872, later vividly recalled in Jack Jones's novel, *Off to Philadelphia in the Morning*. Parry was also a passionate popular educator and a notable figure in the *eisteddfod*, which was partly why the Aberystwyth council dismissed him after a few years. For the rest, Welsh composers invariably found their main inspiration in the composition of hymns. John Ambrose Lloyd, a Liverpool-based composer, became celebrated for his hymn 'Eifionydd' rather than for his collection of secular ballads. Joseph Parry finally achieved immortality with the mournful hymn, 'Aberystwyth'. Welsh music, in fact, was populist, chapel-based and essentially choral. The growth of the *cymanfa ganu* in the middle decades of the century, the musical inspiration provided by the chapels, the central role given to choral music at local *eisteddfodau*, gave a massive stimulus to popular choirs, with all the communal rivalry involved. As in mid-Victorian England, Welsh music flourished above all on the great oratorio. Handel and Haydn in particular formed the staples of Welsh musical creation—and became popular Christian names as a result. The requiems of Brahms and Verdi, and later on Dvořák's *Stabat Mater*, became intensely popular in this most Protestant of societies. From 1881, in fact, music played an even more central part in the national *eisteddfod*; the standard of musical performances there steadily improved, and the rivalry between the major choirs in industrial and rural Wales, and between conductors such as Harry Evans of Dowlais and John Williams of Caernarfon, became essential features of eisteddfodic life. In the twentieth century, spontaneous upsurges of song at rugby internationals, with hymns still the staple diet, kept this popular form of musical involvement going at a time when the choral aspects of the *eisteddfod* and its 'blue ribbon' choral contests were somewhat falling into decline. By the eighties, the legend of *gwlad y gân* (the land of song) was firmly established, indeed unshakeable, even amongst the tone-deaf. The spread of the simple Tonic Solfa system of notation, published by Joseph Parry in *Y Cerddor Cymreig* from 1861 onwards, made the subtleties of choral singing accessible to ill-educated and musically unsophisticated people, and added enormously to the cultural enrichment of community life. Ieuan Gwyllt's new hymn book of 1863 was actually produced in Tonic Solfa notation. In 1883 a new popular monthly appeared, *Cerddor y Cymry*, edited by 'Alaw Ddu' (W. T. Rees). On the other hand, it must be said that this musical tradition was still a limited one, instinctive and inspirational rather than geared to an advance of cultural and aesthetic standards.

Much the same could probably be said of Welsh literature at this time. It was almost entirely produced in the Welsh language, generally believed to be spoken habitually by at least three-quarters of the population and in almost all the rural hinterland away from the English border. Certainly the religious and cultural expression of the nation came almost universally through the medium of Welsh. But in the early eighties, the Welsh linguistic and literary world showed some of the limitations as well as the strengths of a simple popular tradition. Welsh poetry was still caught up almost exclusively in a natural lyrical style. 'Ceiriog' (John Ceiriog Hughes, 1832–87), whose poetry was much influenced by old Welsh melodic airs, was perhaps the most celebrated representative of it. There was alive at least one notable Welsh novelist, Daniel Owen, once an apprentice tailor, whose 'Autobiography of Rhys Lewis' appeared in the magazine *Y Drysorfa* in chapter form between 1882 and 1884 and was published as a book in 1885. This, like Owen's later works, *Enoc Huws* (1891) and *Gwen Tomos* (1894), the latter published a year before his death, derive their strength as a series of character sketches drawn from village life in the countryside, somewhat loosely strung together in anecdotal form. They are simple evocations of the enclosed, chapel-dominated, small-town world that the author knows at first hand. They do not reveal either the technique or the universality of appeal of the great novelist; Owen is no Welsh Balzac or Dickens. In literature, as in music, Welsh culture retained a primitive, unsophisticated quality. Even the spelling and grammar of Welsh as a literary medium were uncertain: indeed, his stylistic roughness was thought to be an attractive feature of Daniel Owen's writing. This was not surprising as Welsh remained largely a medium of daily conversation; it was taught neither in elementary schools as an authorized subject under the school code (here, the taboo of the 'Welsh not' retained its appeal), nor in the new 'college by the sea' in Aberystwyth. When the first lecturer in the Welsh language was appointed to a higher education institution, John Morris-Jones to Bangor in 1889, he had at first no students to teach. When they did begin to trickle in, they were lectured to on their native tongue in the English language.

What can be said, however, is that Welsh in the 1880s was securely based in terms of daily intercourse—far more so than Irish, Gaelic in the Scottish Highlands, or Breton in Brittany. Whatever its aesthetic or technical limitations, it had a clear capacity for growth—and as a medium for a significant mode of cultural expression, not merely as a peasant patois. It was very widely spoken. It was intimately associated with the dominant institutions of the land, the chapels which were overwhelmingly Welsh in their forms of service. It was transcendent at the *eisteddfod*, now revitalized by the creation of the 'National Eisteddfod Association' in 1880. Henceforth, winning poems, successful in gaining the 'chair' or 'crown' for their bards, would be widely circulated. Successful poets such as 'Dyfed' or 'Pedrog' would become, for a time, national celebrities.

Most important of all, Welsh was the language of contemporary argument and discussion. It was buoyant in the newspaper and periodical press. In 1866 it had been calculated that there were five quarterlies, twenty-five monthlies and eight weeklies published in the Welsh language.[17] Wales more than most places benefited from the financial freedom afforded by the repeal of the stamp duties in 1855 and of the excise duty on paper in 1861. There had been steady expansion since then. Notable journals appeared such as *Tarian y Gweithiwr*, the miners' weekly, at Aberdare in 1875, and *Y Genedl Gymreig*, another weekly, at Caernarfon in 1877. Many of these publications were from the start highly political; some of them proved to have only a brief existence. But a quarterly like *Y Traethodydd,* founded by Lewis Edwards of Bala in 1845, provided an important vehicle, on the pattern of the great English and Scottish literary reviews, for philosophic, literary, and theological discussion and debate in the Welsh language. It notably raised the standard of literary composition. This kept the quality of discourse in Welsh, at least at the level of the *literati* and the chapel-based intelligentsia, potentially at a high level. Works such as Thomas Gee's *Gwyddoniadur* or encyclopaedia, published in ten volumes between 1856 and 1879, had a wide circulation. Another major literary quarterly, *Y Geninen*, edited by John Thomas ('Eifionydd'), was to be launched in 1883. The main problem for Welsh literature, and indeed for other art forms, was how to continue to raise its cultural and aesthetic standards without sacrificing its popular, democratic appeal. It was the effort to create a bridge between Welsh men and women of all classes and of widely differing levels of education that was to provide the life work of Owen M. Edwards later on.

Welsh popular culture in the eighties was thriving and outgoing, not simply an exotic growth treasured by esoteric groups of intellectuals. But it was

[17] Henry Richard, *Letters,* p. 36.

undermined in its quality, as was much else in Wales, by the essential poverty, even backwardness, of much of the nation. The achievements of the Welsh people in cultural and religious terms were gained in the face of their environment and their material circumstances. Despite the expansion of industry in the south, in 1880 Wales had still the air of a colonized society, on the periphery of the great metropolitan civilization. It was notably poorer in economic resources than was England, or indeed Scotland. Its towns were mostly small and scattered. The quality of its civic life was restricted: Cardiff was no Edinburgh or Athens of the west. Government statistics illustrated this graphically. In 1875–6, the counties of England produced a mean tax on income of £15 7s. a head. In Wales, it was only £12, and a mere £8 4s. in Cardiganshire. Most of the Welsh counties consisted largely of barren, unproductive mountainous upland, criss-crossed by small, precarious family tenant farms. Their average size in 1875 was only forty-seven acres. Many Welsh counties, as has been seen, were losing population. Rural industries such as the woollen industry of Montgomeryshire or the lead-mining of north Cardiganshire were in rapid decay. Many old country fairs had lost their standing. In grimmer terms still, rural Wales provided six of the leading ten counties in England and Wales in terms of the incidence of deaf-mutism, with Anglesey, Merioneth, and Cardiganshire the first three on this sombre list. In terms of certified imbecility, rural Wales supplied five of the first eight counties, too. In each case, these tragic figures were a comment on the poverty and social isolation of life in upland mountain regions. The statistics for such health services as there were, for working-class housing, for child malnutrition, for illness in maternity, and for adult tuberculosis suggested a far more gloomy picture for Wales than for England.

More generally, the popular stereotype seemed to be of the Welshman sunk in brooding, deferential inferiority before the aggressively self-confident, public-school-trained Englishman he encountered in business or in the courts, or as tourists at the spas of mid-Wales or the golf courses of Harlech or Aberdyfi. If Taffy was a thief, as legend had it, he was indubitably a penitent thief. Symbolically, the first international rugby match between Wales and England was played at Blackheath in 1881. The English won overwhelmingly over a scratch team of opponents by seven goals and six tries to nil. Even at rugby, it seemed, the poor Welsh had much to learn from the master race that lived beyond Offa's Dyke.

In one respect above all the contrast between aspiration and achievement, between popular vitality at the grass roots and enervation at the institutional level, was most pronounced. This was in the sphere of education. Long before 1880 the passion of poor Welsh country families for education was most marked. Already the yearning for elementary and perhaps higher education as an avenue for upwardly mobile Welsh children to become schoolteachers or perhaps ministers—then as later the classic escape routes from rural or industrial poverty—was widely noted. And yet, despite the traditions of Griffith Jones's circulating schools, despite the efforts of the Sunday schools on the Sabbath and of mechanics' institutes the rest of the week, the educational provision in Wales was lamentably low. The Educational Commisioners who reported in their 'blue books' in 1847 were best remembered for their ignorant attacks on the Welsh language as an obstacle to culture and enlightenment. The 'treachery of the blue books' passed down in folk memory, as a kind of Welsh Drogheda. Less vividly recalled were the commissioners' well-founded comments on the low educational standards and, indeed, illiteracy prevalent throughout Wales. In the 1880s, by comparative standards, there had been little enough progress since 1847. The impact of the Board Schools set up in Forster's Act of 1870 was just beginning to be felt.

At any level above the elementary, Wales was remarkably ill provided for. The departmental committee under Lord Aberdare, appointed by Gladstone to inquire into Welsh secondary and higher education, reported in 1881 that only 1,540 children in Wales enjoyed any kind of grammar-school education, with a further 2,946 at private and proprietary schools such as Llandovery College, Christ College at Brecon, Howell's school at Denbigh, and Friar's School at Bangor. Education charities in Wales yielded a total of £14,281.[18] Nonconformists, the vast majority of the population, were especially badly catered for. There were none on the representative boards of the Howell's schools at Llandaff or Denbigh, for example. Beyond the secondary level, there was St. David's College, Lampeter, essentially a training college for Anglican ordinands, with the right to transfer to an incorporated MA at Oxford or Cambridge. There was the 'Normal' training college for teachers founded by Hugh Owen at Bangor beside the Menai Straits in 1858, a kind of alternative working-class university which extended its sights far beyond a narrow course of instruction in education alone. There were a number of Meyricke awards for schoolboys available for Jesus College, Oxford, though these were under challenge from the new principal, the Englishman Dr Harper. Most interesting of all, there was the new 'college by the sea' at Aberystwyth. But in 1880 its future was still precarious, its debts still considerable in the absence of any assistance from the government. The quality of its student entrants, many of whom failed to stay the course, others returning from the portals of Aberystwyth to resume mundane careers as farm labourers or shop assistants, was far below what could reasonably be considered to be university standard. Broadly speaking, the Aberdare Committee sympathetically but convincingly recorded that most Welsh children had no educational opportunity at all, above the most elementary

---

[18] *Report of the Committee appointed to inquire into the condition of Higher Education in Wales,* Parl. Papers, 1881, xxxiii, p. xvi. There is a good digest of this Report in *Y Traethodydd* (1881), pp. 473 ff.

level. They were doomed to the same routine of mindless manual work of their parents and grandparents. By implication, the quality of Welsh life, its leadership in the professions, in the arts, in commerce and industry, even within the circumscribed world of the nonconformist pastorate, remained diminished.

And yet Wales at the dawn of the eighties was on the threshold of mighty changes. A 'new Wales' was about to be forged, far more decisively than the 'new South' allegedly created in the agrarian southern States of America after the end of the civil war in 1865. Education itself pointed the way forward. The Aberdare Committee, a body appointed after much effective agitation by Welsh MPs in the House of Commons and some useful lobbying on Gladstone by Stuart Rendel, called for dramatic changes. It demanded a new network of secondary schools, run by popularly-elected governing bodies. It called for government funds to supplement the local rates levied by the local authorities, on a pound for pound basis. It urged, above all, two new institutions of higher education of university calibre, one in north Wales, one in the south. The old vision of a 'University of Wales', actively promoted by Welsh patriots in London and elsewhere since the sixties, was now attaining tangible form. In other ways, too, the nation was poised for a massive advance, some the product of external legislative or economic enterprise, some of it the result of the spontaneous combustion of the Welsh themselves. Politically, the election returns were now spelling out unmistakably the end of an old order. The Reform and Redistribution Acts of 1884–5 were about to reinforce them, and to make Wales a democracy and a stronghold of popular radicalism. In economic terms, the industrial south was surging ahead to new levels of growth, illustrated by the prolonged expansion of the mining industry in the Rhondda and the opening up of new pits in western Monmouthshire and eastern Carmarthenshire. The passage of the Barry Docks Bill through parliament in 1884 was itself the portent of a new economic order, with Wales as the entrepôt for a world market, dominant in finance capitalism and in the export trade of the British staple industries, coal, tinplate, and steel above all. The material base essential for a wider educational and social renaissance was being fashioned anew. In the cultural field, the period from the eighties has always been viewed, rightly, as 'a great awakening', in which new standards would be set in relation to the innate strength of the language, the quality of its poetry and imaginative prose writing, and the impact of its popular appeal. On a different level of patriotic endeavour, the Welsh Rugby Union had been founded in 1881, with founding clubs ranging from Cardiff to Haverfordwest. Revenge over the dominant English here, too, would not be far off.

Potentially, then, Wales in the eighties was no longer a kind of stagnant backwater, placidly dominated from within by an impoverished and unimaginative gentry class. Some of the old leaders of an older generation of national protest were passing away now. The journalist William Rees ('Gwilym Hiraethog') died in 1883, the publicist Samuel Roberts ('S.R.') of Llanbrynmair in 1885. But a new world, the world of Tom Ellis and Lloyd George, of 'Mabon' and D. A. Thomas, of John Morris-Jones and Owen M. Edwards, was breaking through. The eighties in Wales proved to be, more than in any other region of Britain, a major turning-point in a special sense. They provided the springboard for an age of national growth, dynamism and prosperity unknown since the union with England under the Tudors—and certainly without parallel since. Caught up in the heady turmoil of late-Victorian imperialist England, but safely detached from it too, colonized, 'neglected', impoverished Wales took its first conscious steps out of pre-history and the fantasies of the 'twilight' towards a new era of modernity and fulfilment.

CHAPTER 2

THE LIBERAL ASCENDANCY

The Welsh are, and have long been, an intensely political nation. And it was in the sphere of politics that the reawakening of the national energies in the period between the early eighties and the dawn of the new century was most emphatic. A generation later, for instance in the periodical *Wales* between 1911 and 1914, journalists would look back with awe on the years after 1880 as an epoch of extraordinary national achievement in politics.[1] There was the prominence of Welsh political leaders symbolized by the triumphs of David Lloyd George; new legislative and departmental recognition of the needs of Wales; the emergence of a distinctly Welsh 'radical' style in politics, less bitter and less strident than the nationalist movement in Ireland, but in its quieter fashion perhaps the more effective. It is, then, in politics, at Westminster and in Wales, at national and constituency level, that the transformation of Victorian Wales was most dramatic. Through politics, the greatest impact of Welshness upon the British consciousness was effected.

What gave colour and form to politics in this period, and enhanced its Welsh national characteristics, was the overwhelming ascendancy of the Liberal Party. It was more pronounced here than in any other part of the British Isles. Wales became, and was to remain for a hundred years, a unique stronghold of the British left. When the Labour Party largely supplanted the Liberals after 1922, heralding a period of Labour ascendancy that endured until the 1970s and perhaps beyond, this aspect of Welsh politics became the more emphatic. But it was in the late-nineteenth century that the roots lay.

Until the eighties, Welsh politics had been largely predictable and unexciting. In the principality, as has been seen, the traditional dominance of the landed gentry survived, with many of its features intact, even after the dramatic events of the election of 1868. At Westminster the Welsh made little impact. Their members of parliament were ineffective, wrote Stuart Rendel later, 'almost in an inferior category, a cheaper sort of member'.[2] The growing coherence and vigour of the Welsh MPs during the seventies and in the lead-up to the general election of 1880 produced neither a clear statement of national priorities nor any agreed strategy on how to achieve them. Some MPs

[1] F. E. Hamer, 'Twenty-Five Years of Welsh Nationalism', *Wales* (June 1913), pp. 86–9.
[2] *The Personal Papers of Lord Rendel* (London, 1931), p. 313.

had their own special causes which they promoted with some effect. George Osborne Morgan, a barrister who sat for Denbighshire, was concerned with the burial acts; Hussey Vivian, an industrialist who represented Swansea District, pressed for intermediate education; Henry Richard, the member for Merthyr, advocated international peace. But they had no collective policy that made any nationwide impact. Compared with the Irish, whose own Nationalist Party under the formidable chairmanship of Charles Stewart Parnell had become by 1880 a crucial element at Westminster, compared even with the Scots who managed, with their aristocratic patronage, to extract a secretaryship of state for Scotland in 1885, the influence and reputation of the Welsh were feeble indeed.

After 1880, however, the position changed dramatically and conclusively. Long before the end of that decade, it was clear that Welsh politics had been totally transformed in tone and in substance. The roots of this will be examined later: they lay deep in the substructure of society, where a yawning gulf opened up between the anglicized gentry and the largely nonconformist, Welsh-speaking majority, comprehending industrial and rural Wales alike. The immediate impetus, however, lay in the crucial impact of franchise reform. The Reform Act of 1884, coupled with the redistribution of constituencies in 1885, had a massive effect on Welsh politics. That Act may have been conceived in terms of the 'high politics' of manoeuvring between Gladstone, Salisbury, and other party leaders in London. The Celtic 'fringe', apart from Ireland, may have played only a minor part in their calculations. But the result was to make possible a new kind of politics in Wales. The enfranchisement of the householder in the counties made Wales something resembling a political democracy for the first time. Not only the rural labourer and tenant farmer, but also the industrial miner, tinplate and steel worker now received the vote. The Welsh county vote rose from 74,936 to 200,373. The impact on rural counties such as Anglesey and Merioneth was emphatic. Even more striking was the transformation of industrial Glamorgan and Monmouthshire. Glamorgan was turned from a two-member constituency with only 12,785 voters in 1880 into five new county divisions, with a combined electorate of 43,449. Especially in the case of the Rhondda division, overwhelmingly working-class voters dominated the electorate. Again, Monmouthshire, a two-member constituency with only 7,609 voters in 1880, was turned into three new constituencies with a total electorate of 31,541. As in England, many restrictions on the working-class male voter still survived—of course, women remained totally unenfranchised. Registration requirements, the disfranchisement of younger sons and categories of lodgers, above all the disqualification of voters who had received the aid of the poor law still survived. This last had special impact on unemployed workers or, for instance, on the miners out of work as a result of the six-months' coal stoppage of 1898. Keir Hardie in Merthyr was but one candidate in 1900 who lost several thousand votes on this account.[3] In Britain as a whole, barely 60 per cent of adult males had the vote. The percentage must have been smaller in Wales, with its large working-class population. Even so, the change in the quality of the Welsh electorate, far more strikingly than in 1867, was beyond dispute.

The redistribution of seats changed the face of politics also. Five small borough seats were abolished—Beaumaris, Cardigan, Haverfordwest, Radnor, and Brecon—a great blow to the Whig gentry. Some of the 'contributory' boroughs that survived had undeniably small electorates—Montgomery, Denbigh, Pembroke, Carmarthen, Flint, and also Caernarfon Boroughs, the latter the future seat of David Lloyd George, and destined, no doubt for that reason, to survive all electoral changes until 1950. While an extra member was given to the town division of Swansea, the great port and commercial centre of Cardiff, with almost 100,000 inhabitants in 1890, returned only one member until 1918, the same as the scattered country towns of the rural borough seats. But the general effect, nevertheless, was to create in Wales as in England a large preponderance of distinctively working-class single-member constituencies: Merthyr Tydfil survived as the sole two-member seat in Wales. Furthermore, while England returned roughly one member per 54,000 of the population, Wales had a ratio of one per 45,342. The preponderance that the Conservatives demanded to maintain the representation of rural England also worked to the advantage of the voters of Wales—and of Scotland and Ireland which were also over-represented in strict numerical terms. During the devolution debates in the 1970s, nearly a century later, it was noted that Wales and Scotland still returned, proportionally, more MPs to Westminster than did England. In the mid-1880s, with a far larger electorate, with a new structure of county and borough constituencies, with a favoured position in terms of representation, Wales lay ready for the radical, Liberal take-over of its politics which inevitably followed.

The results of these structural changes were most clearly observed at the level of parliamentary elections between 1885 and 1906. The overwhelming majority of constituencies in Wales, industrial and rural, were impregnably Liberal, election after election, particularly in the most intensely Welsh parts of the land. Only in the anglicized fringe—south Monmouthshire, the vale of Glamorgan, the dockyards of Pembrokeshire in the south; Radnorshire, Montgomery Boroughs and Denbigh Boroughs along the English border; very briefly in Caernarfon Boroughs in the far north-west of Gwynedd (largely owing to cathedral influence in Bangor)—did the Conservatives put up an effective challenge and retain any strength. In addition, Cardiff and to a lesser extent Swansea, with their large, heterogeneous electorates, were hard to organize and therefore uncertain in their allegiance. Curiously, this pattern

[3] *Lancashire Daily Post*, 26 September 1900.

of enduring Conservative strength along the periphery of Wales continued well into the twentieth century. The seats captured by the Conservatives in the principality in the general elections of 1970 and 1974 repeated a pattern that would have been instantly recognizable to Gladstone and Salisbury. In the Welsh heartland, Conservatism, uniquely identified with Englishness and with the 'unholy Trinity' of the bishop, the brewer, and the squire, stood little chance.

In the election of November 1885 this pattern revealed itself. It was the first fought under the new constituency arrangements and on the new, enlarged electorate. The protection afforded by the 1872 Ballot Act was now widely understood. In the event, the Liberals won thirty seats out of thirty-four. Fourteen of these thirty members, at least, were nonconformists. They included such worthies as Alfred Thomas (East Glamorgan), president of the Welsh Baptist Union, and John Roberts (Flint District), chairman of the Methodist Association of North Wales and a zealot for temperance. There were some famous victories over the gentry to record. In Eifion (North Caernarvonshire), Bryn Roberts, a Methodist barrister and a loyal Gladstonian, defeated Ellis Nanney, Lord Penrhyn's estate agent, by over 2,000 votes. In a celebrated contest in East Denbighshire, Sir Watkin Williams Wynn, 'Old Sir Watkin' whose dynasty had held the county since the days of the Jacobite uprising in 1715, was defeated by 393 votes by Osborne Morgan. Even the Wynns of Wynnstay, cocooned within their 28,000 acres of land in the constituency, could not escape the democratic hurricane.

This pattern was confirmed, though marginally less decisively, in the general election of July 1886. This came after the schism in the Liberal Party and the defeat of the first Irish Home Rule Bill as a result of Liberal defections in the Commons. There were weakening divisions in the Liberal ranks in Wales, too. The Conservatives now managed to capture six seats in Wales, and recorded gains in the borough constituencies of Pembroke, Monmouth, and Caernarfon. In addition, there were three Liberal Unionists elected. Two of them, however, the veteran Sir Hussey Vivian (Swansea District) and the even more venerable C. R. M. Talbot (Mid-Glamorgan) rejoined the Gladstonian fold immediately after the polls. Elsewhere, the Liberals held on to twenty-five of the thirty-six Welsh seats, precariously at times, with Osborne Morgan clinging on to East Denbighshire in the face of a renewed Wynn challenge, by twenty-six precious votes.

The years 1886 to 1892 were a period of glowing promise for the Welsh Liberals. Not only were they gaining in confidence and parliamentary strength. They counted for far more in the counsels of the Liberal Party which since 1886 had been increasingly dependent on its Celtic support in Wales and Scotland. Land reform, education, temperance, church disestablishment all made spectacular progress. Welsh disestablishment actually appeared in second place on the Liberals' Newcastle Programme of 1891. The consequences were writ large in the general election of July 1892. While Gladstone and the Liberals fared less well in Britain generally and gained only a small majority that rested on Irish support, in Wales the Liberal ascendancy was more overwhelming than ever. Thirty-one out of the thirty-four seats were won, most of them by huge majorities. Only three border seats were left in Tory hands. Nine of the Liberal majorities were over 2,000 while in the radical stronghold of Merthyr Tydfil the two Liberal candidates, D. A. Thomas and Pritchard Morgan, swamped a Unionist barrister by the margin of 9,500 votes, the largest majority in the British Isles. With the thirty-one Welsh Liberals in theory holding the balance in the Commons since Gladstone's administration had a majority of only forty, the prospects of progress on the major Welsh demands were encouraging indeed.

In fact, the Liberal government, particularly during the premiership of Rosebery in 1894–5, petered out ignominiously. There was open conflict at the top between Rosebery and Harcourt, divided counsels in the party over the priorities now that Irish home rule had again failed to get through parliament, and marked internecine warfare in Wales itself after the nationalist experiment of the *Cymru Fydd* movement. There were those who argued that the freelance activities of one or two backbench Welsh Liberals, notably Lloyd George and D. A. Thomas, during the committee stage of the Welsh disestablishment bill, had really been the cause of the government's resignation in June. Its majority had fallen to only two on 20 June and this was said to have been the undoing of the administration rather than the relatively trivial defeat on the 'cordite' vote the next day. These quarrels were reflected at the polls. The Liberals suffered also from renewed agricultural depression in rural areas, and from depressed trade in some industrial constituencies, notably in the south Wales tinplate industry where heavy unemployment had been caused by the McKinley tariffs imposed in the United States. As a result, the Unionist vote rose in Wales in July 1895; six seats were gained, including Cardiff and Swansea Town, Pembroke, and Carmarthen Boroughs. In all, the Conservatives won nine seats—the best performance in a Welsh election in the entire period between 1880 and 1924. Many Liberals got home with much reduced majorities. In Montgomeryshire, Rendel's successor, Arthur Humphreys-Owen, an Anglican landowner though in many ways a zealous radical, scraped in by twenty-seven votes.

But the Liberal dominance in Wales was far too overwhelming to be seriously undermined by the unique combination of disadvantageous circumstances of 1895. At the 'khaki' election of October 1900, held during the South African War, while Liberalism elsewhere was struggling, the Liberals of Wales made three net gains and restored their tally of seats to twenty-eight. This was achieved in spite of the moribund character of local Liberal Associations between 1895 and 1900, Cardiganshire, Gower and Merthyr Tydfil being notable examples. The strength of Welsh Liberalism rested on social and cultural factors, not on the techniques of the organization men. Radnorshire, Swansea Town, Carmarthen Boroughs and, most prized of all, Cardiff were recaptured, while Monmouth Boroughs were lost, to Dr Rutherfoord Harris, an associate of Cecil Rhodes. However, this last contest was an exception that proved the rule. Wales swung back to Liberalism in 1900 because, in short, the Liberal Party was the party of Wales. There is little evidence to support the view, sometimes offered, that sympathy for the Boers in South Africa, another little Calvinist nation battling against English imperialism, swayed the Welsh voters. Most Welsh Liberals were sympathetic to imperialism, or at least not hostile. The victor at Cardiff, Sir Edward Reed, was a passionate supporter of the Boer War. The 1900 'khaki election' in Wales was a strange affair, with some uncontested seats, and many of the normal issues in the background. But the basic pattern of Liberal domination, somewhat interrupted in 1895, was amply confirmed.

The years after 1900 saw the Liberal tide, reinforced by Labour or 'Lib-Lab' consciousness amongst miners and other industrial workers in the south, flow ever more strongly. It was entirely predictable that the next general election of January 1906, fought under the auspices of a new Liberal government under Campbell-Bannerman, largely on the hallowed themes of free trade, church schools, temperance, and the rights of labour against a background of anti-imperialism, would see Welsh Conservatives swamped everywhere. So it proved. Even in that halcyon year of landslide Liberal victories, the Welsh performance was extraordinary. All thirty-four seats fell to the Liberals, save only for the second seat in Merthyr Tydfil which was gained by Keir Hardie for the Labour Representative Committee, in tandem with the friendly Liberal coalowner, D. A. Thomas (who still headed the poll). Everywhere, Welsh Conservatives were wiped out. They lost Cardiff by over 3,000 votes, South Glamorgan (Conservative since 1895) by over 4,000. South Monmouthshire witnessed the defeat of the Morgan family of Tredegar (at the hands of a Roman Catholic landowner) after an almost continuous tenure of the seat since 1659. From Lloyd George's comfortable majority in Caernarfon Boroughs in the north (the first time that his seat ceased to be a marginal one) to the return of four miners as 'Lib-Labs' in industrial constituencies ranging from Gower to West Monmouthshire, the Liberal triumphs were irresistible. Indeed, the results in January 1906, exaggerated though they were, may serve as a comment on twenty years of domination by a party and a tradition to whose values the electorate subscribed with greater unanimity than in any other region of the British Isles.

These, then, were decades of overwhelming Liberal achievement. They were marked, too, by growing cohesion and organization among the different segments of the party in the principality. By the eighties, Liberal Associations of varying degrees of effectiveness had sprung up in constituencies from Anglesey to Cardiff. It was inevitable that there should be growing pressure to unify them. After the elections of 1886, demands by Stuart Rendel and other MPs for a great nationwide organization in Wales chimed in with pressure by Schnadhorst and the Liberal central organization in London for stronger links between constituency and central Liberalism. After some discussion on a possible Mid-Wales Federation, a new step forward came in the winter of 1886–7 with the creation of the Liberal Federations of North and of South Wales, with secretaries at Wrexham and at Merthyr respectively. Their main importance was in the period 1886–95 when these regional federations became rallying points for the nationalist demands of the *Cymru Fydd* movement associated with Lloyd George and others. Thereafter, they petered out somewhat. They served as a useful piece of organizational machinery and an annual platform for the faithful, but in no sense as the basis of a separatist Welsh political movement.

More significant and more interesting by far was the emergence of a Welsh Parliamentary Party, apparently on the lines of Parnell's Irish Nationalists. This kind of development had always been resisted by Henry Richard and the older type of Liberal whose ties lay with English and cosmopolitan radicalism generally. Stuart Rendel, an Englishman warmly sympathetic to Welsh national causes, was also very reluctant to promote an idea which might lead Liberalism into nationalism or separatism. But the rising tide of national sentiment now led him to see the necessity for a Welsh parliamentary organization, if only to forestall the most extreme nationalism of *Cymru Fydd*. More positively, almost all the younger members returned in or after the general election of 1886 saw a Welsh Party as essential to create discipline and lend unity to the various Welsh demands. So it was that in December 1888, significantly just after Henry Richard's death, Stuart Rendel was elected chairman of a new 'Welsh Parliamentary Party', with two Glamorgan members as whips. Proposals were agreed for joint balloting by the Welsh members on private MPs' motions each session, and for lobbying techniques to put pressure on the major party leaders. The Welsh Party, no doubt, aroused expectations that it could not fulfil. Rendel, the close confidant and admirer of Gladstone, was never a man to lead the Welsh Party into an independent position. His successors as chairman, George Osborne Morgan (1894–7) and Sir Alfred Thomas (1897–1910), were both elderly, unimaginative, and conformist. The Liberal whips could sleep quietly at nights if the Welsh were in the hands of such men as these. By the First World War, the Welsh Party was a familiar target for ironic scorn as its repeated, and always ineffectual, threats of revolt against the party leadership carried no conviction. Nevertheless, the formation of a Welsh Party was an important factor in ensuring the growing recognition and primacy of the Welsh Liberal demands. It helped to underline the similarities as well as the differences between the national movements in Wales and Ireland. Its very existence, and the undeniably powerful mandate that its members received at the polls in

Wales, demonstrated in the clearest fashion that Celtic revolt lay nearer Westminster than simply across the Irish Sea. Even if separatism in Wales was relatively muted, even if demands for home rule were seldom voiced, nevertheless on issues affecting the Church, tithe, education, land and other questions, the Welsh were able to set out their own register of grievances and of protest against centuries of domination by an alienated squirearchy. By 1914, however tedious and repetitive many of its demands, the Welsh Party had several successes to record—certainly far more than the Scots in the same period. Under its auspices, such men as Tom Ellis and Lloyd George first rose to national prominence. The Welsh Party is a useful index not only of the transformation in Wales at this period but of the wider political and social dissolution affecting Victorian Britain at the end of the century. As such, it deserves to be taken very seriously.

Beneath and beyond this formal façade of electoral triumph and of parliamentary organization by Welsh Liberalism, the spirit and tone of the nation's politics were vastly different after 1886. There were new men, new issues, new currents of protest and challenge surging through Welsh society as a whole.

The new leaders who emerged in politics after 1886 are highly evocative of the changes that affected the nation at this time. Older political figures—men like Henry Richard, Lewis Llewelyn Dillwyn, Hussey Vivian, Osborne Morgan—adherents of the ancient tenets of the Manchester School and the Liberation Society, men who thought in a British Liberal rather than a Welsh national context, were passing away. A new generation of talented young politicians was taking their place. There was Tom Ellis, returned for Merioneth in 1886 and destined to become Liberal chief whip in 1894. Ellis was a figure of immense charm and romance. His tragically early death in 1899 in his fortieth year added to the legends that will always surround his name. He was a nationalist of a complex kind. He was the son of a tenant farmer from Bala, that cradle of rural protest, the home of Lewis Edwards and the Revd Michael Daniel Jones. He was brought up amidst folk memories of the political evictions of 1859 and 1868. He went up to Aberystwyth college in the early eighties, then caught up in the heady emotion of a national revival. But at this crucial moment in his life, Ellis moved on to New College, Oxford, where, even though an unsuccessful student, he was deeply influenced by the Idealism of T. H. Green, the quasi-socialism of Arnold Toynbee, and perhaps the social imperialism of Ruskin. He later became the admirer of Cecil Rhodes, whom he met in Cape Colony. There was in Ellis always a tension between involvement and detachment as far as Welsh nationalism was concerned—involvement, through Bala and Aberystwyth, the Methodist chapels and a profound love of Welsh poetic traditions; detachment, which came from Oxford and Westminster and made Ellis a social imperialist and the friend of such as Asquith, Haldane, and even the Fabians. There was a tension also between an earthy realist, at home in perusing rental returns and blue books, and a visionary, almost mystical prophet of the national soul. After 1890, after a visit to Luxor in Egypt which deeply stirred his imagination, Ellis's prophetic faith in 'the Wales that was to be' reached new heights. He seemed to embody the spririt of Mazzini and of Thomas Davis, with something of Ruskin and Toynbee as well. When Ellis became a junior whip in 1892, it caused widespread disappointment. Some patriots wrote of him as 'grasping the Saxon gold'.[4] For all that, his impact upon Welsh political and cultural life between 1886 and 1892 was unique. Through his speeches, even more through his attractive, magnetic personality, 'burning with a peculiar intensity',[5] he gave Welsh politics a passionate vision, an intensity and depth which transcended party and sectarian conflict and ennobled the life of the nation as a whole.

Tom Ellis was a rare and gifted spirit. But there were other talented young men rising up in politics at this time. Samuel Evans, 'a lawyer on the make' in the words of one critic,[6] was a powerful advocate of Welsh nonconformist causes after his return to the House of Commons for mid-Glamorgan in 1890. In time, he was to attain high judicial office. Before that, a rakish private life somewhat conflicted with sound Congregationalist dogma. But he was undoubtedly a formidable spokesman for the new Wales. So, too, was Ellis Griffith, an eloquent Methodist barrister, elected for Anglesey in 1895, whose failure to attain Cabinet office still seems a great mystery. There was William Jones, a schoolmaster and member for Arfon; the 'silvery tones' of his lilting and beguiling oratory caught the fancy of *Punch*. There was Herbert Lewis, an honourable, peaceful man of Flintshire, who fought the good fight for educational and other reform, and who also stuck to Lloyd George through thick and thin, 'coupon election' and all, from 1892 to 1922. Very significantly, there was D. A. Thomas, member for Merthyr Tydfil from 1888 to 1910. He was really most preoccupied with his industrial concerns as a coalowner and proprietor of the Cambrian Collieries. But he was also a formidable political spokesman for the distinctive mercantile, Anglo-Welsh world of the commercial south-east, and for the Cardiff Chamber of Commerce in particular.[7] It was he who helped launch the *Cymru Fydd* movement in 1892. By insisting on the special interests of South Wales in opposition to the Welsh-speaking hinterland in 1896, he largely killed it. He was friendly with his fellow Merthyr member, the socialist Keir Hardie, after 1900, and sympathetic to social reform. Yet he had also become by 1910 the

    [4] J. Arthur Price to J. E. Lloyd, 14 October 1892 (Bangor Univ. Library, Lloyd Papers, MS 314, f. 449).

    [5] J. A. Spender, *Sir Robert Hudson: a Memoir* (London, 1930), p. 24.

    [6] Rendel to A. C. Humphreys-Owen, 10 December 1895 (Nat. Lib. of Wales, Glansevern MSS, 672).

    [7] Cf. Kenneth O. Morgan, 'D. A. Thomas: the Industrialist as Politician', *Glamorgan Historian* iii (1966), pp. 33-51.

hated 'Czar of the coalfield', the dynast of the Cambrian combine and the owners of the collieries at Tonypandy at the time of the riots. Thomas was an original and interesting politician, whose talents were politically wasted until in 1916 Lloyd George buried the hatchet and set him to reorganize local government and then the food supplies. Here he proved to be a brilliant success, in some ways the man who really won the war.

The most celebrated of all these newcomers, of course, was David Lloyd George, returned by eighteen votes for the Caernarfon Boroughs constituency in April 1890. He was then only twenty-seven, yet his political career was already lengthy and controversial. In 1885 he had been considered for the Liberal nomination in Merioneth. The following spring he almost joined Joseph Chamberlain's Liberal Unionists and all his life remained agnostic about the purist Gladstonian arguments for Irish self-government. After 1886, he was heavily involved in local politics as a vigorous young country solicitor was wont to be—the Anti-Tithe League, the Llanfrothen burial dispute, the new Caernarvonshire county council where he became the 'boy alderman', ventures with a newspaper syndicate in Caernarfon with his Labour nationalist friend, D. R. Daniel. By the time he entered the House, Lloyd George had several chapters of political activity behind him. Even then, he was a widely admired and widely distrusted figure. His brand of Welsh nationalism was very different from that of Tom Ellis. Whereas Ellis's gentle visions were shot through with cultural and literary values, Lloyd George's ideology was wholly and narrowly political. He represented the spirit of equality just as Ellis reflected that of liberty. He was obsessed with the social ascendancy of the clergy and the squirearchy, and pursued these demons throughout his career. He was an untypical figure in Welsh politics. He took less concern than did most Welsh members in higher education or the university movement. He had scant interest in literature or the aesthetic aspects of Welsh culture. He rebelled against the gloomy puritanism of the chapels and the petty snobberies of the 'glorified grocers' and 'beatified drapers' on the deacons' bench.[8] He remained a kind of free-thinker in religion, as in politics and finance.

For all that, Lloyd George emerged after 1890 as the most formidable of all the spokesmen for the new radical Wales. In the parliament of 1892—5 he took the lead in pressing for government action on Welsh disestablishment, and in trying to organize the *Cymru Fydd* League on a national basis. In the years of opposition after 1895, when he ascended a wider, British and imperial stage, he was also zealous in resisting concessions to the landed gentry over agricultural rating in 1896, and to the church schools by putting them on the rates after 1902. Further, by linking the narrowly nonconformist protest against rate aid for denominational schools with the wider objective of a Welsh

[8] Lloyd George to his wife, 10 June 1890: Kenneth O. Morgan (ed.), *Lloyd George: Family Letters, 1885—1936* (Oxford and Cardiff, 1973), p. 28.

national council for education to which all sects and parties could subscribe, he showed the range of his political genius—his rare capacity to push on beyond the world of the mundane and to transcend petty party conflict with national or supra-national aspirations. In Wales as in Britain as a whole, Lloyd George was at once the committed radical and the statesmanlike architect of the supra-party approach; he was the partisan and the coalitionist, the man of Limehouse and the wartime leader, fused into one mercurial whole. With all his limitations, many of them imposed on themselves by his uncritical, over-adulatory supporters in Wales, Lloyd George did more than any other man to make Wales a political reality and a political fact. He gloried in the fact that, throughout his life, he was manifestly a foreigner in English politics, the unmistakable, immediately identifiable unknown soldier of the Welsh *gwerin*. It was not the least remarkable feature of his extraordinary public career.

Tom Ellis, Sam Evans, Ellis Griffith, William Jones, Herbert Lewis, D. A. Thomas, Lloyd George, and others—these were the type of new member and new leaders that Wales threw up in this period, with powerful young journalists, publicists, and activists backing them up in the constituencies. They made the Welsh presence felt in politics as never before—far more so than English carpet-baggers like Sir William Harcourt or Reginald McKenna. If much credit should go to the enigmatic Englishman, Stuart Rendel, who made the Welsh Parliamentary Party effective in organizational terms, the main impetus and passion undoubtedly came from the turbulent, dynamic new Wales that these new men represented.

The issues that governed Welsh politics were new, too, and their parameters much more closely defined. Temperance, education, tithes, land reform, devolution, above all, the transcendent issue of the disestablishment of the Church—these were the stuff of Welsh politics in these decades, at a time when Welsh politics, almost as much as Irish, became dominated by purely local issues and national concerns.

Temperance was a theme naturally congenial to the nonconformist Welsh. The Blue Ribbon movement swept the land in the seventies; 'taking the pledge' became for chapel boys what the Bar Mitzvah was for Jews. Even if the Welsh Liberals never quite achieved local option, let alone the more severe forms of prohibitionist licensing restriction that temperance enthusiasts demanded, there was one major achievement. This was the Welsh Sunday Closing Act of 1881, a measure endorsed by Gladstone himself, and a legislative landmark which survived into the later twentieth century. It was constitutionally significant in being the first distinctively Welsh act of parliament. By imposing the Sunday closure of public houses in Wales, in response to an orchestrated pressure by Welsh nonconformists, it was for the first time applying a distinct legislative principle for Wales, as distinct from England. It was pronounced for the first time by parliament that Wales had a separate political identity. The effectiveness of the Welsh Sunday Closing Act was debated by licensing victuallers and nonconformist partisans over the years thereafter. After it was extended to Monmouthshire as well in 1921, the debate over the moral or social worth of Sunday Closing became the more intense. With all its flaws and lack of logic (after all, hotels and clubs remained open on Sunday, just the same), the Welsh Sunday Closing Act of 1881 was a notable political milestone, a testimony to the identity of the nation.

Another area where politics showed results was education. In part, this question was commendably non-partisan. The passage of the Welsh Inter-mediate Education Act of 1889, introduced by Rendel and other Welsh members, owed much to the sympathy of the Conservative government of Salisbury and to its education minister, Sir William Hart-Dyke. It imple-mented the main recommendation of the Aberdare committee on higher education eight years earlier. By the First World War, Wales was covered with a network of a hundred 'county' secondary schools, and had a secondary education system notably in advance of that of England. It was educationally disadvantaged no longer. The creation of Welsh university colleges, at Bangor and Cardiff in 1883–4, and the rescue of the 'college by the sea' at Aberystwyth with a government grant in 1885 will be discussed in a later chapter. This was also a non-party issue at bottom. Even though the new Welsh colleges, and the University of Wales that they combined to form in 1893, were strongly coloured from the outset by the ethos of Liberal non-conformity, higher education really was a cause that appealed to men and women of goodwill of all parties and of none.

Elementary education, however, was very different: it raised the very essence of 'the religious difficulty'. In Wales, given its religious complexion, it was inevitable that the near-monopoly of church 'National' schools and the existence of about three hundred 'single school areas' where church schools ministered for the needs of largely nonconformist populations, should produce especial acrimony. Lloyd George was himself one rebellious product of such a school, in Llanystumdwy; Owen M. Edwards, less rebellious, was another in Llanuwchllyn. Some recompense was found in the dominance of nonconformity in the new Board schools created after 1870. It was notable that in Wales, 62 out of 320 School Boards in 1889 had no religious instruction, while almost all had no religious examination. Even so, the position of the church schools was a long-standing Liberal grievance in Wales; attempts to bolster up their finances with aid from public funds, let alone the rates, were inevitably controversial.

The Education Bill of 1896, an abortive measure as it proved, aroused passionate opposition in Wales. Members like Lloyd George, Sam Evans, and Tom Ellis were vehement in their hostility. The Balfour Act of 1902, which placed all schools, 'provided' and 'non-provided' alike, on the local rates, caused a massive revolt amongst Welsh nonconformists and local authorities. By the start of 1904 almost all the Welsh county councils were refusing to administer the Act—or, rather, were proposing to operate it only on condition that the church school managers met their terms over denominational instruction, over the abolition of religious tests for teachers and over bringing the management of the schools under public control. It was clearly an illegal position to adopt, as much so as that taken up by the Labour council at Clay Cross in the early 1970s. This 'Welsh revolt', however, was a very effective one, far more so than the nihilistic 'passive resistance' towards the Education Act adopted by individual nonconformists in England. It was a strategy conceived by Lloyd George, at first a sympathizer with the Act, who now saw in the strength of nonconformity in Wales and the Liberal dominance on all its county councils a unique instrument with which to effect basic changes in the system of elementary education—and also to harass the Tory government. He combined the Welsh 'revolt', as has been seen, with an attempt to secure a broader objective of a national council of education, no doubt also destined to be under Liberal control. When the Unionist government fell from office in December 1905, the impasse in relation to the Welsh schools was as total as ever. Several Welsh councils had been declared in default by the Board of Education and faced legal sanctions as a result of their refusal to operate a legally passed parliamentary statute. The very robustness of the Liberal protest over education emphasized the centrality of sectarian questions in giving impetus and passion to the Liberal ascendancy and its demands.

Welsh Liberalism had also, to some degree, an economic objective. This applied solely to the rural areas, and was an attempt to remedy the poverty and insecurity of Welsh tenant farmers, much on the lines of the measures demanded by Michael Davitt's Land League in Ireland. Indeed, the very similarities between the Welsh land protests and the agrarian disturbances in southern Ireland alarmed men like Stuart Rendel by tending to emphasize unduly the separatist, near-revolutionary character of the Welsh national movement. 'It is not the Irish case over again.'[9] The land agitation welled up in full force after 1886. This was in part a result of the deepening depression in the countryside and the fall in farm prices. In part too, of course, it was a result of the new political ascendancy of the Liberals and the new prominence of agrarian populists such as Tom Ellis. One bold diagnosis offered came from the Revd E. Pan Jones, Mostyn, a socialist who called, on Henry Georgian lines, for the taxing of land values and even for the nationalization of land, in journals like *Y Werin* and *Cwrs y Byd*.[10] But this was a minority view, even if one with its influence on Lloyd George. A Welsh Land League formed at Rhyl

[9] Gladstone to Rendel, 12 November 1892 (BL, Gladstone Papers, Add. MSS, 44549, f. 39).

[10] Cf. Peris Jones-Evans, 'Pan Jones—Land Reformer', *Welsh History Review*, vol. 4, No. 2 (December 1968), pp. 143–60.

in late 1886 embodied the majority opinion; it was under the presidency of the formidable preacher-publisher, Thomas Gee of Denbigh. The main demands followed the 'three Fs' implemented in the 1881 Irish Land Act—a massive reduction in rental (i.e. 'fair rents'), security of tenure for tenant farmers, compensation for improvement and for disturbance, and above all a land court to adjudicate on rents. It was a programme designed to appeal to tenant farmers who owned their own tools and stock, potential peasant proprietors on the French pattern—or the Irish, after 1905. It had nothing to offer agricultural labourers, a large but politically unrepresented class, though one just beginning to find a voice now through such journalists as J. O. Thomas ('ap Ffarmwr') in Anglesey.

Two parliamentary debates inaugurated by Tom Ellis in 1888 and 1892 gave new momentum to the Welsh land campaign. In the latter, Gladstone himself intervened. Hedging his remarks with characteristic Delphic ambiguity, he committed himself to 'a thorough, searching, impartial and dispassionate inquiry' into Welsh agriculture and its problems.[11] When he became Prime Minister in 1892 he appointed a royal commission on Welsh land which conducted its inquiries between 1893 and 1895. Here, the old Liberal demands for the compulsory fixing of rents by a land court, security of tenure, and compensation for unexhausted improvements were endlessly rehearsed by witnesses. The old animosity towards landowners (and their agents) as a class came through time and again. Many were the bitter references to the eviction and coercion of Liberal tenants in 1859 and 1868, a generation ago. In fact, as will be seen in the next chapter, the commission and the Welsh land agitation generally produced very little. By 1900 little was heard of it. The Land Commission produced two diametrically opposed reports in 1896, one reflecting the views of the six Liberal members, the other the pro-landlord attitudes of the three Unionists. There was now a Unionist government in power; inevitably, no action on Welsh land would follow. In any event, by the turn of the century, conditions on the land were improving. Prices were more stable, employment on the land rose again, the idea of a land court began to lose its appeal for Welsh Liberals. More generally, the landlords had put up a stout defensive action before the Land Commission and managed to show how exaggerated were many Liberal complaints of the rapacity and vindictiveness of landlords and the alleged severity of the rents they imposed. The land question, in fact, was largely social rather than economic for most Liberals, and short-term in impact. Its importance lay really in underlining the basic character of Welsh Liberalism as a revolt against a static, hierarchical social order which political and economic change was making anachronistic. As Lloyd George's later career was to show, anti-landlord sentiment retained much of its currency in Welsh and English circles down to 1914. But its urgency had long since passed away.

[11] *Parl. Deb.*, 4th ser., ii, p. 985 (16 March 1892).

Closely connected with the land question was that of tithe. Here was an issue which brought together dislike of the landowners with resentment at the Anglican Church. In the years after 1886, fuelled by the land agitation and by the depression in agriculture, protests against the payment of tithe to 'an alien Church' spread amongst farmers in mid- and north Wales. There were riots in such peaceful, remote communities as Llangwm and Mochdre in Denbighshire: the militia had to be called in. At Mochdre, fifty civilians and thirty-four policemen were injured after scuffles at distraint sales. Many contemporaries, Liberal as well as Unionist, looked with alarm at the tithe disturbances in Wales. They seemed to be a clear echo of violent agrarian troubles in Ireland and the crofting districts of the Scottish highlands. In the event, the Salisbury government passed in 1891 a Tithe Rent Charge Act which made tithe payable by the owner, not the occupier of land. This tended to bury the tithe question by merging it with payment of rent; it would remove the clergy from the front line of confrontation over the payment of tithe, and would transfer the odium to the landlords. Welsh Liberals, headed by Sam Evans, Tom Ellis, and Lloyd George in the House, denounced the Tithe Rent Charge Act as a subterfuge which left on one side the real issue of the payment of an antiquated charge to an alien Church to which the vast majority of the population did not adhere. In fact, though, the tithe question was effectively settled from that time on, and little was heard of it after 1892. Its importance was rather in giving a sharper edge to the overriding issue which obsessed Welsh Liberals during these years of social tension—the establishment of the Anglican Church in Wales.

Church disestablishment and disendowment were, in fact, the cornerstone of the programme advanced by the triumphant Liberals after 1885. It is highly significant of the essential difference between Irish and Welsh nationalism that the Irish concentrated their major effort on separation and home rule, whereas the central passion of the Welsh was disestablishment, an issue that left the Union and the basic political fabric of the United Kingdom quite untouched. Political exclusion in Ireland, religious equality in Wales—such were the cries of these very different national movements. Small wonder that Tom Ellis, let alone Lloyd George, never came close to playing their oft-proclaimed role as 'the Parnell of Wales', any more than Saunders Lewis was to become the Welsh de Valera.

Until 1885, disestablishment had been conceived in Wales largely in terms of English Liberationism. Church and State should be separated on principle, in all countries; national distinctions had nothing to do with it. But after 1885, this traditional view, the attitude of older men such as Henry Richard and Lewis Dillwyn, became an anachronism. Thereafter, disestablishment and disendowment were urged by Welsh Liberals on largely national grounds— on the distinct history and religious complexion of Wales, and on the fact that the Welsh MPs had received a mandate for disestablishment at the polls, election after election. Conversely, Conservatives were forced to deny the case for Welsh nationality, rather than take their stand on the higher ground of defending the establishment on principle. Not until the dawn of a new century, through the lead of such patriotic churchmen as Bishop John Owen of St. David's, a Welsh-speaking native of Llŷn in Caernarvonshire, was it argued more effectively that historically and, increasingly, in contemporary terms, the Church was just as Welsh in spirit and outlook as were the non-conformist chapels, themselves seventeenth-century imports from England. After disestablishment was finally achieved in 1920, the Welsh Church became increasingly fervent in its commitment to Welsh nationality and devolution, a concept that for much of the previous century its leaders had denied. No longer would Welsh bishops dare to proclaim, as Bishop Basil Jones of St. David's had done in 1886, that Wales was but a 'geographical expression'.

The battle for disestablishment aroused fierce controversy after 1886. The evidence that the Welsh Church was showing some sign of awakening from its slumbers and that the rate of growth of nonconformity was slowing down made Welsh Liberals all the more passionate. A series of motions between 1886 and 1892 effectively drew the attention of the House of Commons to the central arguments on behalf of Welsh disestablishment and its intimate relationship to the nationhood of Wales. Further, the growing importance of the Celtic nations within the Liberal Party materially helped their cause. At the Nottingham conference in 1887, the National Liberal Federation formally adopted Welsh disestablishment as a major item on its programme. Leading Liberals like Harcourt, Morley, Spencer, and Rosebery committed themselves to the principle. On the Newcastle programme in October 1891, that Magna Carta of 'faddism', disestablishment in Wales and Scotland came second in priority only to Irish home rule. More striking still, Gladstone himself, a devout Anglican and an opponent of Welsh disestablishment back in 1870, now declared himself in favour of it. In 1891 he spoke out ringingly in favour of the separation of Church and State in Wales: 'the nonconformists of Wales were the people of Wales'.[12] When he became Prime Minister in 1892, action on the Welsh Church question was most earnestly expected.

In fact, action came only in half-hearted, indirect fashion. A Welsh Church Suspension Bill, designed to suspend the creation of new vested interests in the four Welsh dioceses as a preliminary to disendowment, was introduced in early 1893 and later withdrawn. There were rumbles of disappointment amongst the Welsh MPs, and Lloyd George, D. A. Thomas and two other Liberals led a brief revolt against the party whip in April–May 1894. When Rosebery succeeded Gladstone as Prime Minister, however, a Welsh Disestablishment Bill duly followed, introduced by Asquith as the Home Secretary. It provided a model for the later bills of 1909 and 1912–14. The

[12] *Parl. Deb.*, 3rd ser., cccl, p. 1265 (20 February 1891).

Church would be disestablished in the thirteen Welsh counties, and its endowments, notably tithe and glebe, would be secularized and largely handed to the county councils for social and charitable purposes. This bill petered out in the 1894 session, but a successor passed its second reading in the House by 44 votes on 1 April 1895. It was still enmeshed in the committee stage when the Liberal government fell from office in June.

The next ten years of Unionist government predictably saw no action on Welsh disestablishment. The question, like that of land, seemed to lose its urgency. The Church in Wales continued to progress; the Welsh chapels were riven by more self-doubt. Many wondered how much concern a time-worn issue like disestablishment really aroused among the industrial workers of south Wales, by comparison with basic economic issues of wages, employment, and unionization. Even so, the return of a Liberal government in December 1905 confirmed that Welsh disestablishment, even if somewhat jaded, remained an albatross that the Liberal leadership could not shake off. Throughout the twenty years from 1885, in fact, it symbolized the sectarian essence of Welsh Liberalism, that democratic yearning for social, civic, and religious equality which the establishment of a minority Church largely propped up by an unpopular landowner class appeared to deride. Liberalism and disestablishment were inseparable throughout this period. It comprehended all other issues—temperance reform, church schools, the land agitation, tithe. It certainly aroused much more passion than did anything that resembled Welsh home rule or even modest forms of devolution. There was a mild National Institutions Bill introduced by Alfred Thomas in 1892 which proposed, among other things, an elected assembly and a Secretary of State, but it fell flat. The *Cymru Fydd* controversy surrounding Welsh home rule came and went in 1894–6, with Welsh Liberalism as bound to its English counterpart and the central Liberal leadership as ever. Disestablishment symbolized the Welsh desire for a place in the sun. It was, perhaps, an unappealing symbol in some ways. The sectarian malice of ministers and bishops, journalists and publicists, the denominational rancour of men like Thomas Gee and Bishop A. G. Edwards of St. Asaph divided and diffused the national energies. It undoubtedly blunted the impact of the Christian message, and diverted the churches from collaboration on social reform, education, or evangelization. In Wales, even more than in England, the ecumenical spirit was hard to detect between 1885 and 1905. Small wonder that by 1905 Lloyd George was anxious to bury the disestablishment question and direct the national attention towards higher objectives of social and economic reconstruction. But even he could not shake off his past. As long as Wales remained dominated by the real memories and the partial reality of the traditional clerical and land-owning authority, so long would disestablishment capture the hearts and minds of politically active Welshmen.

This programme, these men, dominated Welsh politics in the period. They made the land politically news as never before. In the parliament of 1886–92, Welsh backbenchers were active in putting new heart into the divided Liberal Party by raising effective protests on the Church, land, tithe, and education. In the parliamentary sessions of 1892–5, Welsh issues loomed larger than ever. Even if no action resulted on Welsh disestablishment, Gladstone and Rosebery were forced to bow to local pressure on a range of questions. There was the Welsh Land Commission in 1892, a University of Wales in 1893, Tom Ellis aspiring to high office in a Liberal government. Ten years later, when the Liberals returned to power, Welsh priorities still loomed prominently in their programme, even if the mix was somewhat different from 1895. The very presence of Lloyd George was testimony to the power of Welsh Liberalism in pushing its demands forward, by protest and persistence, if not through outright rebellion. It was, in its way, an impressive chronicle of peaceful achievement for a national minority, long neglected. Welsh Liberalism had indeed advanced far since 1885.

Throughout these twenty years, the Liberal ascendancy was quite unshakeable. Every crisis was safely negotiated, with Liberalism stronger than ever as a result. There were three main periods of danger for the Liberals in this period—the schism over Irish home rule in 1886; the *Cymru Fydd* crisis in 1894–6; and the South African War in 1899–1902. Each was surmounted; none left the kind of division that, for instance, Irish home rule or imperialism left amongst the Scottish Liberals. The Irish home rule schism of 1886 brought problems for Liberals in Wales as elsewhere.[13] There were prominent defectors from Gladstonian ranks, mainly on grounds of sympathy for Protestant Ulster, and detestation of Irish Catholicism. Some leading Welsh Liberals veered towards Liberal Unionism; seven Welsh Liberal MPs voted against the second reading of Gladstone's Irish Home Rule Bill in June 1886. The celebrated publicist, Thomas Gee, editor and publisher of *Baner ac Amserau Cymru*; the eminent Methodist theologian, the Revd J. Cynddylan Jones; the barrister-critic, T. Marchant Williams; even the young Caernarvonshire solicitor David Lloyd George—all flirted with Liberal Unionism. And yet, the Liberal Unionist revolt soon crumbled away. Only one Liberal Unionist sat for a Welsh seat when parliament reassembled after the 1886 election, and he (Cornwallis-West, member for West Denbighshire) was defeated at the next election. The industrialist and millionaire, David Davies of Llandinam, for all his money and his Methodism, was narrowly defeated in Cardiganshire by W. Bowen Rowlands, a Gladstonian barrister who actually became later on a Roman Catholic. Liberal Unionists in Wales found the going hard after that. *Yr Undebwr Cymreig*, a Unionist monthly edited by H. Tobit Evans, collapsed in December 1890, at the time of the O'Shea-Parnell divorce scandal, ironically enough. In the 1892 general election,

[13] Cf. Kenneth O. Morgan, 'The Liberal Unionists in Wales', *National Library of Wales Journal*, xvi, No. 2 (Winter 1969), pp. 163–71.

Joseph Chamberlain put up a string of eight nonconformist Unionist candidates in Wales. Each was slaughtered at the polls. Liberal Unionism disappeared from Welsh history. Loyalism, the appeal of Gladstone, the enduring appeal of the old radical causes, folk memories of 1868—all these transcended other values for most Welsh voters.

The *Cymru Fydd* crisis of 1894–6 was potentially more damaging. The roots of the *Cymru Fydd* movement were basically cultural and literary as will be explained in Chapter 4. But it is relevant to note here that in 1894–5 the Cymru Fydd League came near to capturing the organizational base of Welsh Liberalism and turning it in an overtly nationalist direction. Lloyd George became the chief apostle for the idea of a Welsh Liberal Party that should be basically distinct from that of England, and the precursor of Welsh self-government on the same lines as that promised for Ireland. In April 1895 the Cymru Fydd League formally merged with the North Wales Liberal Federation. But the Liberals of the South Wales Federation were a more difficult proposition. Their dominant figure, and a formidable force in south Wales life was a coalowner MP, D. A. Thomas, president of the SWLF and the voice of those commercial, mercantile, anglicized Welshmen or immigrant Englishmen in Swansea, Barry, Cardiff, and Newport who refused to bow down to pressures from the rural hinterland. Lloyd George devoted much artifice in the autumn of 1895, after the Liberals' electoral defeat, to a well-orchestrated campaign among Liberal Associations in the valleys to secure their adherence to *Cymru Fydd* also. He found the going hard. The men in the south (the *hwntws*) seemed to be very different animals from the Welsh-speaking nonconformists he knew in north Wales. They were sunk, he complained to his wife, in a 'morbid footballism'.[14] At the crucial meeting of the SWLF at Newport in January 1896, there was a massive verbal brawl; Lloyd George was howled down; the south Walians asserted loudly that the cosmopolitan population of the south, the southern coal ports in particular, would never submit to Welsh domination. In embryo, that cultural and social division that paralysed every movement for self-government in Wales from the 1880s to the 1970s was clearly foreshadowed. *Cymru Fydd* disappeared. The Welsh National Liberal Council formed in 1897 was only an organizational shell. Even this aroused some bad feeling as to whether it was another attempt to repeat the divisive tactics of *Cymru Fydd*. For all that, the divisions provoked by the *Cymru Fydd* movement did not prove long lasting. There was simply not the pressure for separatism in Wales to lead to the kind of friction, for instance, between Parnellites and anti-Parnellites in Ireland, let alone between Orange and Green in Ulster. Cardiff, Swansea, and Newport were no Welsh Ulster: after all, there was no Welsh Home Rule League, nothing comparable to Sinn Fein. By the end of 1897, the Welsh Liberals had quietly buried their own civil war. Lloyd George was working

14 Lloyd George to his wife, 19 November 1895 (*Family Letters*, p. 91).

again in effective harmony with his south Wales colleagues. The old values of the years since 1868 were again comfortably in command.

The final crisis for Welsh Liberalism in these years was the South African War. Wales was far from being as united in favour of the Boer cause as has sometimes been alleged.[15] In fact, Lloyd George, Herbert Lewis, and other 'pro-Boers' were in a small minority, and faced hostility and even violence in their constituencies. Prominent Welsh Liberals like Ellis Griffith or Brynmor Jones were ardent imperialists, as was much of the Welsh press in both languages. The relief of Mafeking aroused much enthusiasm. If an apostle of *Cymru Fydd* such as Beriah Gwynfe Evans, an ardent nationalist, could embrace the imperialist cause, it must run deep in Wales. In fact, as has been seen, their divisions during the 1900 'Khaki' election did not obstruct the further advance of the Welsh Liberals. They recorded a net gain of three seats; the pendulum swung back to Liberalism even amidst the jingoism of a war election. The later stages of the Boer War, when attention concentrated on the 'methods of barbarism' employed in British concentration camps in the Transvaal and the anti-guerrilla strategy pursued on the Rand, rather than on the philosophy or morality of empire, rallied almost all Welsh Liberals to the cause. An anti-war radical like Lloyd George gained new prestige and acceptance. The years after 1902 saw the division between pro-Boer and imperialist in Wales forgotten, amidst the unifying effects of the 'revolt' against the 1902 Education Act, the defence of free trade, and the protection of free labour against 'Chinese slavery'. In 1900, as in 1895 and 1886, Welsh Liberalism was far too coherent and internally secure to be fundamentally rent apart by a particular crisis. Indeed, Edwardian Wales was to witness the Liberal ascendancy even more overwhelmingly dominant than in the Victorian era.

Welsh Liberals, in this period, can therefore be discussed largely in terms of Liberal politics. It is Liberal MPs, Liberal journalists, Liberal ideologues who are interesting and who dominate the scene. It is worth speculating, however, on the possible alternatives to this Liberal domination. Welsh Conservatism counted for relatively little in the 1885–1905 period, even though there was a Conservative government for sixteen of those twenty years. Nor has Welsh Conservatism found its historian since, no doubt because Welsh historians tend to the political left as readily as American historians swear allegiance to the Democratic Party. As has been noted, Conservatism retained most strength in the anglicized periphery, along the marcher borderlands with England, and amidst the docks and cities of the far south. In Cardiff, Welsh Conservatism was particularly assertive. Indeed, the Cardiff *Western Mail*, edited by Lascelles Carr until 1901, was an effective newspaper, much more

---

[15] Cf. Henry Pelling, 'Wales and the Boer War'; Kenneth O. Morgan, 'Wales and the Boer War—A Reply', both in *Welsh History Review*, vol 4, No. 4 (December 1969), pp. 363–80.

lively than its local Liberal rival, the *South Wales Daily News*. It gave special prominence to Welsh happenings and issues. It featured articles by such patriotic Liberals as 'Mabon' and 'Cochfarf', bards both. Elsewhere in Wales, in the mining valleys and in most of the countryside, Conservatism was in eclipse. It was indelibly associated with the old social order. The landed gentry, struggling hard to survive now, were the staples of their local organization in much of Wales, the Penrhyn family in Caernarvonshire, the Powis family in Montgomeryshire, the Wynns in Denbighshire, the Cawdors in Carmarthenshire, and so on. In Cardiganshire, the disarray and impoverishment of such families as the Lisburnes of Trawscoed and the Powells of Nanteos go far to providing a sufficient explanation of the feeble, antiquated character of those remnants who upheld the tattered banner of Cardiganshire Toryism, in election after disastrous election. The gentry had also a difficult relationship with the Anglican Church, forced into Tory postures by the Liberal pressure for disestablishment and for the abolition of tithe. Bishop A. G. Edwards of St. Asaph and, from 1897, Bishop John Owen of St. David's became, in effect, vigorous spokesmen for lay Conservatism on clerical issues. But the Anglican Church in Wales was never that monolithic, nor indeed partisan. After 1903, Bishop Edwards became unexpectedly friendly with his old adversary and dialectical sparring partner, Lloyd George, in trying to work out a 'concordat' over denominational education. Bishop Owen himself had Liberal antecedents and maintained friendly relations with leading Liberals. With the Church ambivalent and the gentry in full retreat, Welsh Conservatism simply lacked any firing power; its inevitable identification with English as well as Anglican attitudes doomed it to electoral calamity. At no stage during this period did Wales enjoy real two-party politics, nor did Welsh Toryism at any time present an enduring challenge to the domination of nonconformist Liberals.

A much more searching and dangerous challenge loomed up in the late 1890s in the valleys of the south. Socialism had been a feeble plant in Wales until this period. There was a branch of the Fabian Society in anglicized Cardiff, but, in general, cultural and geographical isolation kept the ideas of Webb and Shaw, the crusades of Hardie, Blatchford, and Morris well removed from the Welsh scene. But after the massive six-months' coal stoppage of March–September 1898, a new political force took root. Several branches of the Independent Labour Party were formed at Merthyr Tydfil, Briton Ferry, Swansea, and other places in the south, and at Wrexham in the industrial north-east. Keir Hardie toured the coalfield and devoted much space in his *Labour Leader* to extolling the potential socialistic qualities of the Celt.[16] In the general election of 1900, Hardie was nominated as Labour Representation Committee candidate for Merthyr, by the local trades council. He was

---

[16] *Labour Leader*, 28 May, 16 July, 10 September 1898.

handicapped by the fact that he was also candidate for Preston in Lancashire, and by the opposition that his vigorously pro-Boer views aroused. The Welsh collier, after all, had done very well out of the war. On the other hand, Merthyr enjoyed a unique place in the pantheon of British radicalism, dating from the martyrdom of Dic Penderyn in 1831 and the election of Henry Richard in 1868. More important, the two sitting members, D. A. Thomas and the virulently imperialist Pritchard Morgan, were hopelessly at odds, and Thomas, even though a coal-owning capitalist, was fully prepared to lend unofficial assistance to the socialist Hardie. With the support of Thomas's voters, Hardie was elected as junior member for Merthyr. Another remarkable contest took place in Gower or West Glamorgan, an intensely Welsh constituency of miners and tinplate workers. Here an Englishman, John Hodge of the Steel Smelters' Union, almost defeated a Liberal employer. He won the support of such eminences as the famous Baptist preacher, the Revd Gomer Lewis of Capel Gomer, Swansea. Given Gower's traditions, the result there is almost as remarkable as Hardie's victory in Merthyr.

In the years after 1900, partly because of the charismatic appeal of Hardie's personality, partly because of the radicalizing pressures of growing class conflict in the coalfield and the formation of the South Wales Miners' Federation, the ILP made much headway in south Wales. By 1905 the party claimed twenty-seven branches in south Wales, with Merthyr, Aberdare, Briton Ferry, and the Swansea valley particularly fruitful areas.[17] In the heart of the anthracite coalfield, at Ystalyfera in the upper Swansea valley, the weekly *Llais Llafur* spread the gospel of socialism through the aggressive (and occasionally libellous) editorship of D. J. Rees. In Merthyr, the ILP was to found its own publishing house. In Swansea, a Labour member of the town council, David Williams, was elected in 1898; by 1900 there were five Labour men on the council. In a series of local elections in south Wales, for county and town councils, for Boards of Guardians and (up to 1902) for School Boards, Labour candidates, usually ILP men, were frequently successful. Merthyr became a particularly rewarding town both for the Labour Representation Committee, comprehending socialist societies and the trade unions, and for the overtly socialist ILP. At Merthyr in the municipal elections of November 1905, all twelve Labour candidates were returned, eleven of them miners, and a miner, Enoch Morrell, was elected mayor. Even in north Wales, Liberals were encountering a new challenge from Labour. Herbert Lewis had to move from Flint Boroughs to Flintshire because 'Labour difficulties threaten the unity of the Party'.[18]

Without doubt, by 1905 the threat of the ILP to Liberal pretensions in much of south Wales was a serious one. But in Wales, as in much of the rest of

[17] *Thirteenth Annual Conference Report of the Independent Labour Party*, 1905, pp. 60 ff.

[18] J. Herbert Lewis to Stuart Rendel, 19 September 1903 (N.L.W., Rendel Additional MSS, 108).

Britain, the ILP was still a struggling party, fighting a hard battle against traditional Liberal values and influences. Even in Merthyr itself, Hardie found the going hard. He was never to head the poll there, but always came second to the Liberals. His local organization was precarious, and morale amongst constituency workers often low: one of his party workers, H. T. Hamson, was to tell Ramsay MacDonald, the secretary of the LRC, in June 1903 of the difficulties facing the ILP in Merthyr. In 1905, J. Watt wrote to MacDonald that the LRC in Cardiff was 'in a thoroughly unsatisfactory state'.[19] In 1906, a last-minute Liberal opponent took 7,000 votes from Hardie and gave the Merthyr Labour Party an unpleasant shock. Hardie was to remain the only ILP member elected in Wales down to the First World War. The Independent Labour Party had many warm qualities that appealed to the Welsh. Its chapel-style ethos, its evangelistic crusading, its insistence on the moral rather than the material aspects of the socialist gospel all chimed in well with the character of the Welsh voters, above all in Welsh-speaking areas. It appealed even to some nonconformist ministers and to students of the 'new theology' school in theological colleges at Bala and Aberystwyth. But the challenge of the ILP to the Liberal ascendancy was still a fringe one in 1905, and its implications were hard to define. The branches of the party in the Swansea and Ogmore valleys, in Briton Ferry, Merthyr, and parts of west Monmouthshire were active but localized. Most trade unionists kept aloof from them. They did not as yet form an organization that would seriously disturb the pattern of Welsh politics as it had endured since 1885.

These years of Liberal rule provided evidence of the social roots of much of Welsh politics at this period. A self-contained, small-town middle-class élite was crystallizing and reaching out for power at all levels. The personnel of local Liberal Associations in places as far apart as Cardiganshire and Merthyr Tydfil conveys the same tale—a class of shopkeepers, merchants, doctors, journalists, nonconformist ministers, and (omnipresent at this period) solicitors as the vanguard of grass-roots Liberalism, with a fringe of commercial and manufacturing magnates in Cardiff, Swansea, and South Glamorgan (the last an overspill from Cardiff and dominated by shipping owners such as Henry Radcliffe and T. W. David). The ruling élite of Cardiganshire came from much the same men from the mid-eighties until after the First World War—Peter Jones, Aberystwyth coal merchant; J. M. Howell, Aberaeron ironmonger; D. C. Roberts, Aberystwyth timber merchant; Morgan Evans, Aberaeron farmer; C. M. Williams, Aberystwyth draper; Thomas Levi, minister of Tabernacle Methodist chapel, Aberystwyth, nonconformists to a man, embodied the social and political revolution which had penetrated the Cardiganshire countryside. They were truly the

[19] H. T. Hamson to Ramsay MacDonald, 10 June 1903 (Transport House, LRC letter files, 9/172); J. Watt to Ramsay MacDonald, 13 November 1905 (ibid., 27/344).

new conquerors. The Liberals' thirty-seven members on the first Cardigan-shire county council elected in 1889 included thirteen tenant farmers, eleven small businessmen and shopkeepers, four ministers, two surgeons, and (to cater for unsuccessful surgeons?) one stone-mason. Merthyr Liberalism had less of a continuous history to record, since the local association went into eclipse some time after 1890 after the feud between the two sitting Liberal members, D. A. Thomas and Pritchard Morgan. But those who emerged from the shadows in 1909 to re-form the Merthyr Liberal Association (in effect, a preliminary to fighting Labour and Keir Hardie for the second seat) were much the same personnel as twenty years earlier, W. Rees Edmunds, solicitor, the Revd Jacob Jones, minister of Bethesda Independent chapel, D. M. Richards, Alderman D. W. Jones and so on.[20] Men such as these, diluted by working men in very few instances, formed the bedrock of Welsh Liberalism.

There were some other elements in the mix, also. There were pockets of friendly Whiggish landowners, such as Lord Kensington in Pembrokeshire and (from 1904) Lord Stanley of Alderley in Anglesey.[21] There were a few committed radical squires such as Arthur Humphreys-Owen of Glansevern, Montgomeryshire. Welsh journalists wrote affectingly of the patriarchal relations enjoyed with their Liberal tenants by the Williams family of Castell Deudraeth in north-west Merioneth, which produced two Liberal MPs. In a few constituencies in the south, working men were active in some numbers. The classic case was the Rhondda, where 'Mabon', William Abraham, the secretary of the Cambrian Miners' Association was nominated and elected by the local association in 1885, in opposition to a young coalowner. As it turned out, Mabon was an inactive politician, decidedly cautious in outlook and as committed to the Welsh, nonconformist, quasi-nationalist values of the Liberal ascendancy as was Tom Ellis himself. Mabon's eminence as a conductor of choirs at the *eisteddfod*, his prominence as a Methodist lay preacher and deacon at Nazareth Chapel, Ton Pentre, above all his fine tenor voice which quelled industrial discontent and brought his bardic celebrity, spoke volumes on his political attitudes. He epitomized conformist Lib-Labism in its Celtic form. For the rest, the Welsh Liberal world was one run by a series of small, locally-based, self-perpetuating middle-class élites, linking the world of municipal government, local politics, the chapels, and unofficial social leadership in a democratic, face-to-face community.

Welsh Liberalism can be examined at many levels. One is its journalism. The period from the 1880s was a golden age for the radical journalist, with its immense array of local newspapers and periodicals. Welsh politics as much as Irish demonstrated the power of the printed word. Many leading Welsh Liberals first emerged to prominence as contributors to the press, Lloyd

[20] *Merthyr Express*, 21 August, 23 October 1909.
[21] *North Wales Observer and Express*, 1 January 1904.

George and Llewelyn Williams prominent among them. The newspaper press is therefore a vital aid in understanding the structure and the essence of the Liberal movement.

In north-east Wales, Liberalism can be defined in part in terms of the orbit of Thomas Gee of Denbigh. Born in 1815, he was decidedly a veteran by the late eighties, but still inexhaustibly active. He was powerful on the platform, leader of the Welsh Land League, an unflagging protagonist for disestablishment, above all editor of the influential weekly, *Baner ac Amserau Cymru*, as he had been since 1859. Through this intensely political journal he poured out a weekly stream of highly prejudiced but trenchant comment on issues of the day. Always to the left in politics, he flirted for a while with republicanism. His apparent deviation from Gladstonianism at the time of the Irish home rule schism in 1886 was a great shock; by 1887 he was happily back in the fold, drawing the maximum of parallels between the agrarian situations of Wales and of Ireland. The strength of the *Baner* lay in the quality of its news coverage: it contained the cream of political intelligence, for overseas as well as for Welsh affairs. It was broad-minded enough to open its columns to Archdeacon David Howell of Wrexham, a staunch Liberal as it happened. Thomas Gee serves as the link between the mid-Victorian world of S. R. and Lewis Edwards, and the neo-nationalism of Lloyd George and Tom Ellis. His death in 1898, shortly after that of the other Grand Old Man, Mr Gladstone, marked a great divide in the odyssey of Welsh Liberalism. The *Baner* was never quite the same newspaper again.

In north-west Wales Liberalism focused on Caernarfon, where there were several notable Liberal newspapers. The *Herald Cymraeg* and the *Carnarvon and Denbigh Herald* gradually became more local in outlook as the century drew to its close. *Y Genedl Gymreig* had a more cosmic outlook; north Wales was its parish, if not the whole of the principality. Lloyd George was one of its early columnists. It went through many managerial changes until in 1892 it had appointed as its managing editor Beriah Gwynfe Evans, a passionate Independent in religion and an even more passionate nationalist. He was close to Lloyd George throughout the *Cymru Fydd* controversy. In 1895 he left to serve as secretary of the Cymru Fydd League. Later he was to appear as one of Lloyd George's many hero-worshipping Welsh biographers. Evans's lengthy career was to link the nationalism of the nineties with the more modest growth of Plaid Cymru thirty years later. In fact, he was to join Plaid Cymru soon after its foundation and just before his death in 1927.

In mid-Wales, Liberalism to some degree reflected the world of John Gibson, a pugnacious Lancastrian who walked from Oswestry as a young man to take charge of the *Cambrian News* at Aberystwyth. He acted as its first editor from 1873 and remained so until his death during the First World War. He had a curious career. He was outstandingly ignorant of the Welsh language even in so Welsh an area; his marriage was an unhappy one, and his temperament neurotic. He wrote pathetically to Rendel in 1904 of how 'everything drifts'.[22] His journalistic style was *sui generis*—highly quarrelsome with an endless series of vendettas directed against local worthies, Liberal and non-Liberals alike, on various public authorities. In *Leeks and Daffodils* Thomas Jones was to observe that 'every public man in the counties of Cardigan and Merioneth lived in fear of being dipped in [Gibson's] inkpot'.[23] But Gibson was no mere devotee of the parish pump. He linked up the local concerns of the Cardigan Bay coast with the wider Welsh world. By 1904 the newspaper's circulation (after a reduction in price to 1*d*.) had risen to 7,000. Gibson was in his way a warm-hearted man, who believed in great causes. He became a particular supporter of Lloyd George, even during the Boer War which aroused so much controversy in Liberal ranks. In his scornful puncturing of the inflated pretensions and humbug of rectors and gentry and the local shopocracy, in his fierce attachment to local democracy and libertarian values, John Gibson (knighted by Lloyd George in 1915, just before his death) reflects a good deal of the best as well as a little of the worst of Welsh Liberalism in its era of greatness.

Elsewhere, in industrial Wales especially, local journalists and editors did not operate with such a distinct degree of influence. The *Merthyr Times*, the *Cambria Daily Leader* of Swansea, the *Rhondda Leader* were useful vehicles for Liberal propaganda without making any wider impact. Mention must be made, however, of the *South Wales Daily News*, the Cardiff Liberal daily, and the rival of the Tory *Western Mail*. It fought the good fight for Liberalism until its demise in 1928. But significantly it always found the going harder and the circulation more difficult to keep up than did its Conservative counterpart. This may have been due to the special flavour imparted by its Scottish proprietors, the Duncans, who tended to measure their distance from the wider Welsh scene. They gave little prominence to cultural or educational affairs. The *Daily News* was also, quite simply, less fun to read than was the other Cardiff daily. The Duncans, wrote one Welsh critic, J. O. Jones, possessed a 'Scottish dullness of comprehension'.[24] For all that, the *Daily News* remained an invaluable source for the historian, a unique commentary on the bourgeois élite, Conservative as well as Liberal, who dominated the civic life of Cardiff at its greatest period of expansion. It is also valuable for the quasi-American ethnic ghettos that underlay Cardiff politics. The *Daily News* was basically an honest paper, if dull, and it did the Liberal cause valiant service over three generations. The distinction between its style, though, and that of a newspaper like the *Genedl* in Caernarfon speaks volumes on the cultural and social gulfs that existed within the Welsh Liberal coalition.

[22] John Gibson to Stuart Rendel, 8 January 1904 (Nat. Lib. of Wales, Rendel Additional MSS, 195).

[23] Thomas Jones, *Leeks and Daffodils* (Newtown, 1942), p. 13.

[24] J. O. Jones, 'The National Awakening in Wales, IV. In its Relation to the Press', *Young Wales* (December 1895), p. 284.

Liberalism permeated Welsh life at every point during this period. Every major transformation of Welsh life owed something to it. The most buoyant staple industries of the south and of north-east Wales, coal, shipping and tin-plate above all, had strong affiliations with Liberalism and free trade. With D. A. Thomas in coal, Henry Radcliffe in shipping, Lord Glantawe in tinplate, the Manchester creed of economics would inevitably dominate those export-minded industries. The chambers of commerce of Swansea, Cardiff, and Newport tended to reflect Liberal attitudes also. Joseph Chamberlain's campaign in 1903–5 on behalf of tariff reform and preferential import duties made scant headway in south Wales, save perhaps within the steel industry. Again, the growth of public education in this period was closely associated with this Liberal domination that blanketed Welsh life. The new 'county schools', their headmasters and teachers, the managers on county education committees, the inspectors appointed by the Liberal-dominated Central Welsh Board after 1896 were products of the Liberal upsurge since the 1868 election. These schools were undenominational; they were concentrated widely in the small towns of rural Wales (seven in Cardiganshire alone, a further seven in Merioneth). By definition, they provided avenues of advancement and of social mobility for the offspring of the heirs of 1868; perhaps, too, they provided cradles of cultural indoctrination. Fanning outwards through the Normal college at Bangor and the University colleges of Aberystwyth, Bangor, and Cardiff, they raised a new generation of educated, professional leadership. They were to perpetuate the values of Liberal Wales for a new generation and a new century.

The Liberal world was a highly local one. It was, therefore, natural that local government, with all the spectrum of authority and patronage involved, should become a particularly crucial citadel of Liberalism. The new county councils created by the Local Government Act of 1888 showed more strikingly in Wales than in any other part of Britain the new transition to democracy. The landed gentry who had dominated the countryside for centuries as justices of the peace were routed in an immense social revolution. They were almost totally wiped out by the new nonconformist middle class. In north Wales in the local government elections in January 1889, 175 Liberal councillors were returned out of 260; in south Wales, the figures were 215 out of 330. Only Brecknockshire, with its heavily anglicized eastern region, stayed in Conservative hands and that by a narrow margin. In district after district, representatives of the gentry were in full and disorganized retreat. In Cardiganshire, squire Lloyd of Bronwydd lost to a humble farmer at Troed-yr-aur; Waddingham of Hafod was defeated by the local postmaster at Devil's Bridge; Bonsall of Cwm, Clarach, was routed by a coal merchant at Bow Street, one William Morgan, the grandfather of the later first Labour MP for the county. There were only a few exceptions. In Llanystumdwy, Lloyd George's home village, Ellis Nanney (Lord Penrhyn's agent and Lloyd

George's electoral opponent in 1890 and 1892) was elected. This Liberal dominance over local government and, therefore, over a whole range of local services and sources of patronage endured for over thirty years. In February 1904, in the county council elections held at the height of the furore over the 1902 Education Act and the 'revolt' against it, every council in Wales, including Radnor and Brecon which had been previously Unionist, returned Liberal majorities. In all, 639 Liberal councillors were elected as against 157 Conservatives: in Merioneth, the Liberals gained a majority of 52 to three. In matters of high controversy, as in matters of parochial concern, watch committees, magistracies, road maintenance and drainage, the Liberal domination was ever present. The Liberals were usually well organized: they caucused amongst themselves for aldermanships, coronerships, and chairmanships of vital committees. They turned on Tory lord-lieutenants for appointing so few nonconformists as magistrates. This, indeed, was a more remarkable portent than the victories of Liberalism in parliamentary contests, an index of the way in which political life in Wales had responded so completely to social and cultural change.

The ideology of these Liberals, journalists, councillors, and propagandists, has already been made clear. It was infused with the spirit of social equality and of civil libertarianism, modified always by the ethic of middle-class chapel respectability. The values of nonconformity lay close to the surface of the Liberal ascendancy. Only a relatively few ministers, however, participated directly in politics: the journalistic activities of the Revd Thomas Gee caused a few frowns. The return to parliament for East Carmarthenshire in 1912 of the Revd Josiah Towyn Jones, an Independent 'big gun' of howitzer proportions, was distinctly unusual. It was with social, municipal and, indirectly, with religious issues that Liberals were concerned and from which they drew their life force. On economic questions, they had little new to say beyond the hallowed tenets of the Manchester school. Indeed, it is noticeable that in Welsh-language periodicals especially, say the *Traethodydd* or the *Geninen*, economic themes (other than aspects of the land question as it impinged on rents or prices) were seldom discussed. On industrial questions, the Welsh Liberals were invariably silent. Rather was it assumed that Liberalism in Wales as elsewhere united all the productive classes, middle and working class, against an anachronistic feudal order. The Liberal ethic presupposed the harmony of classes, a co-operative ethic to unite middle-class enterprise and working-class solidarity, always infused by the democratic memories of the world of 1868. New ideas on economic and financial questions, the ideas of the socialists or the 'new unions' or the 'fair traders' or the tariff reformers, new trends in Marshallian economics or neo-Hegelian philosophy, even the industrial or social implications of the 'new theology' advocated by R. J. Campbell in the early years of the new century—these found few echoes in Welsh Liberal gatherings or periodicals. The Welsh were distinctly Old Liberals and old theologians. Social critics in the pulpit such as Revd David Adams of Talybont,[25] the Revd J. Cynddylan Jones of the Bible Society, Rhondda Williams who eventually migrated to England, were few indeed, and usually gave up in despair in the face of conservative-minded congregations. Not until after 1908 did Liberal Associations or denominational assemblies devote time or effort to a serious examination of issues of class tension or social reform in terms relevant to an industrial community. The struggles of the coalfield were viewed from the perspective of the rural hinterland, from which after all so many of the valley populations had migrated and to which they were instinctively attached. The essentially rural quarrymen of the Penrhyn slate quarries, locked in fierce combat with a feudal landowner, Lord Penrhyn, from 1896 to 1903, aroused more lasting sympathy in Welsh Liberal circles than did the more pervasive and damaging struggles between workers and capitalists in the industrial valleys.

This failure to articulate a social or economic philosophy might be thought of as a serious weakness of Welsh Liberalism. It could be seen as undermining Liberal strength in the face of the growing militancy of the labour movement and the challenge of socialism after 1900. In fact, it is clear that the complacency of Welsh Liberalism was well justified. Its insistence on the older values, its ignoring of new currents of social thought, made it well equipped to keep the Liberal world sound and coherent. Indeed, down to 1914, at a time when Liberalism in England was in many ways suffering from fundamental difficulties in the face of labour, socialism, and syndicalism, Liberalism in Wales remained secure. Its very strength in Wales made the New Liberalism apparently the less necessary. Lloyd George could remain an Old Liberal in Wales, even though a New Liberal in England.

More dangerous was the evident reluctance of largely middle-class Liberal Associations to adopt working men as candidates. After all even Lib-Labs of the Mabon type were liable to be tarred with the ILP or socialist brush. The outspoken attacks of Keir Hardie on the chapels and on Welsh Liberalism, despite his dependence on Liberal votes at election times, made 'labour' candidates the more suspect. There was growing difficulty every time a parliamentary seat in south Wales fell vacant. There were problems in South Glamorgan in 1903 and in West Monmouthshire in 1904. In each case, miners' agents of decidedly Lib-Lab outlook, William Brace and Tom Richards, respectively the vice-president and secretary of the South Wales Miners' Federation, presented themselves to the local Liberal associations. In each case, there was immense difficulty with the local mercantile élite. Only after intense pressure by Herbert Gladstone, the Liberal chief whip, and by prominent Welsh Liberals outside the constituencies—and only after Brace and Richards had assured their respective associations of their unimpeach-

[25] Cf. E. Keri Evans and W. Pari Huws, *Cofiant y Parch David Adams* (Liverpool, 1924), pp. 143–5.

able Liberal credentials—did they receive the nomination. In time, each was elected as a Lib-Lab member of parliament.

This intransigence from local Liberal bodies was to bode ill for the future. In 1910–14, there were to be increasingly bitter conflicts between Liberals and Labour candidates in a variety of south Wales constituencies. But for the present it did not seem to matter. The Labour movement in Wales, even its more militant ILP fringe, seemed happy enough to be accommodated within the Liberal tabernacle. The Welsh labour movement, be it local activists such as D. J. Rees in the *Llais Llafur* offices in Ystalyfera, parliamentary candidates such as Brace and Richards, trade-union leaders such as Mabon, seemed to subscribe in full to the old Liberal nonconformist ethos. For them, too, the call of community was more powerful than the pull of class. It was noticeable that in the 1906 election the addresses of the Lib-Lab candidates were even more nationalist and suffused with Welsh issues than were those of the average Liberal. Keir Hardie himself, while tending to decry 'the little Bethel mentality of Wales for the Welsh',[26] paid his full meed of recognition to the old Welsh causes. He was zealous for disestablishment and even more for disendowment, for repeal of the 1902 Education Act, for temperance and land reform. In his eccentric way, he claimed to be a Welsh home ruler. He wanted the land of Wales to belong to the people of Wales; socialism for him meant power being brought closer to the people, not a vast bureaucratic leviathan of state control as was urged by the German Social Democrats. He was respectful to the Welsh language. His newspaper, the *Merthyr Pioneer*, founded in 1911, had a vigorous Welsh language-content with its editor the noted socialist bard and rebellious Independent minister, the Revd Thomas Nicholas of Glais, near Swansea. Hardie even learnt the Welsh national anthem, and indeed struck firmer roots in Wales than he had ever done during his earlier controversial career in Lanarkshire and Ayrshire in his native Scotland. With even Keir Hardie paying obeisance to the radical past and all its puritan, evangelical overtones, with Welsh Labour an essential product of the Sunday school, the village choir, the brass band, and all the rich panoply of village life, the values of Welsh Liberalism remained impregnable. After the concluding of the electoral 'entente' between the Liberal whip, Herbert Gladstone, and Ramsay MacDonald for the Labour Representation Committee, in 1903, the organizational difficulties between Liberals and Labour greatly diminished. Welsh Liberalism evidently contained multitudes, sufficient to include most of working-class Wales as well.

The very strength and tactical effectiveness of Liberalism in Wales at this time made its impact upon a wider British public the more emphatic. In 1885, the Welsh were still a deferential, largely silent fringe of the Gladstonian coalition. By 1905, things were very different. Party leaders, more reluctantly

[26] *Merthyr Pioneer*, 14 March 1914.

the London press, paid court to Welsh political concerns and even to aspects of Welsh cultural nationalism, in a manner unthinkable prior to the 1884 Reform Act. Gladstone himself helped pave the way. Here as elsewhere he proved supremely flexible, capable of sensitive response to an overwhelming tide of popular pressure. As a high Anglican, as the squire of Hawarden, as one committed to inegalitarianism and the rights of private property, as an Oxford man devoted to ancient usages and time-honoured traditions, he was an odd figure to be cast into the maelstrom of Welsh radical politics. Often, notably during the agitation for Welsh land reform or during nonconformist attacks on the Clerical Discipline Bill in 1892, he showed his alarm. His last major action while an MP was to break his pair in favour of the Welsh Disestablishment Bill during the committee stage in June 1895, because of that measure's treatment of cathedrals and churchyards. But on issue after issue, he swallowed his words, and progressed in understanding. The change was seen in the intense sympathy he showed towards Welsh education, the inter-mediate schools, the Welsh colleges, the financial plight of Aberystwyth, the charter of the national university. On Sunday Closing, even on the land question, he was by 1890 far more responsive to Welsh Liberal pressure than would have been thought conceivable twenty years earlier. On Welsh disestablishment, he danced a typically complicated gavotte, with many periods of ambiguity and even of silence. Without question, the direct attack launched on the Established Church and its ancient endowments (far more directly so than in the case of the disestablishment of the separate Church in Ireland in 1869) alarmed him deeply. The fact remained that from 1891 onwards he voted and worked for Welsh disestablishment and helped the cause materially on its way.

The pressures on him were various. His personal friendship with Stuart Rendel must have helped greatly. So, too, did his politician's awareness of where the votes lay, and the importance of Wales and Scotland in bolstering up his party now that the majority in England alone had disappeared. More than that, however, Gladstone's outlook shows that the dominating influence upon him, in Wales as in Ireland, Italy, or Bulgaria, was the mighty force of nationalism. More sensitively and more passionately than any other figure in political life, he responded to the cries of struggling nationhood. Disestab-lishment gained its ultimate validity because of the clear expression of opinion in Wales that the Church was an alien one, anti-national in spirit and out of touch with the aspirations of the vast majority of the worshipping population. By affirming the reality and the validity of Welsh national consciousness, Gladstone helped—and helped deliberately—to impel Wales towards a new era in its history.

Less articulately and perhaps less passionately, all other Liberal leaders came to echo the Gladstonian refrain. The erastian Harcourt, the rationalist Morley, the languid aristocrat Rosebery all sang the praises of the Welsh national genius at this period with more or less conviction. By 1905, there was a new generation of Liberal leaders, not all so besotted with Wales. The imperialists, Grey and Haldane, viewed Welsh nationality with incomprehension. In 1904, Grey heard with amazement a local bard declaim at Caernarfon a lengthy eulogistic ode in praise of Lloyd George.[27] Asquith regarded Wales with some hostility. He well recalled the freelance behaviour of Lloyd George and other Welsh members in June 1895 when he was striving to pilot the Welsh Disestablishment Bill through the Commons on a wafer-thin majority. He was indignant at the role Lloyd George played in helping to undermine the government. 'Peter was a Celt,' Asquith sardonically observed of this latter-day betrayal. On another occasion—'I would sooner go to hell than to Wales'.[28] Nevertheless it was to Wales rather than across the Styx that most Liberal leaders must venture if they wished to keep their coalition afloat. Particularly in the prominence accorded to disestablishment, Welsh issues and Welsh personalities loomed large in the Liberal Party down to the First World War.

The Conservative or Unionist Party, whether headed by Salisbury or Balfour, necessarily played a more hostile role at this time. Joseph Chamberlain's early sympathy for liberationism in Wales at the time of the Unauthorized Programme in 1885, turned into sour rejection, though he still voted for Welsh disestablishment until 1895 and retained a nonconformist outlook on educational matters in 1902. On land and tithe questions, Conservative spokesmen were as implacable as on the Church. Too often they turned to a general dismissal of Welshness in general and Welsh culture in particular. There was a lobby of marcher squires, headed by Stanley Leighton, the member for Oswestry, which made a practice of ridiculing all things Welsh. Welsh poetry was stigmatized as consisting of 'bardic fragments',[29] Welsh literature as being of interest solely to archaeologists, and so forth. And yet, by 1905, perhaps stimulated by the success of the Tory *Western Mail* in anchoring itself firmly even in Liberal south Wales, the Unionists showed a much more sensitive appreciation of aspects of nationhood than they had done in the past. In 1905 it was Balfour's government which authorized the creation of a Welsh national library and museum, and accorded city status to Cardiff—the latter admittedly probably a political move with an election coming up. Perhaps even Unionists understood, as a man like the Anglo-Catholic nationalist, J. Arthur Price, tried to tell them, that Welsh nationality was deeply, instinctively traditional, backward-looking and conservative, reaching back to the organic religious community of the middle ages long before factories and chapels divided the land.

This greater prominence of Wales in Britain politics owed much to a more

[27] Keith Robbins, *Sir Edward Grey* (London, 1971), p. 112.
[28] Roy Jenkins, *Asquith* (London, 1964), p. 505.
[29] *Parl. Deb.*, 3rd ser., cccxxiii, p. 482 (7 March 1888).

intelligent understanding on the part of Britain politicians, from Gladstone downwards. It helped ensure that Wales did not go the same violent route as Ireland: perhaps Welsh home rule was indeed killed by kindness. But the main reason for the success of the Welsh causes lay in the vitality and strength of its Liberal core, and in the extraordinarily able leaders that it threw up. Stuart Rendel, an Englishman of course, led the way in making the Welsh Parliamentary Party tactically effective. Tom Ellis added to a gift for visionary inspiration that deeply stirred his countrymen an ability to beguile his contemporaries in London by charm and persuasion. The other Welsh members played their parts, as did the Welsh press and the shock troops of the pulpit. By 1905, above all, Lloyd George had become the decisive catalyst for Welsh Liberalism as for English. His opposition to the Boer War had given him new stature in British politics and made him a serious contender for Cabinet office when the Liberals returned to power. His involvement in the Welsh 'revolt' against the 1902 Education Act had strengthened his radical base in his homeland, while the prospect of inter-party collaboration on behalf of a national council for education enhanced a growing reputation for constructive statesmanship. Lloyd George was an outsider in Welsh politics in 1905, even more than before. His cosmopolitan mode of life, his travels to the French Riviera, the Alps, or Biarritz, his penchant for the company of self-made journalists and businessmen, his growing friendship with the aristocratic renegade Winston Churchill, all suggested a growing gulf between Lloyd George and his prosaic countrymen—and perhaps between the ambitious MP in London and his placid Methodist wife rooted in Criccieth. But he needed his nation as much as it needed him. They both now stood at a crucial watershed. In 1905, he served as his people's champion, the symbol of twenty years of achievement in Wales and of the promise of much more to come.

CHAPTER 3

ECONOMIC PROGRESS AND SOCIAL CONFLICT

The Welsh economy from the early eighties to the first decade of the twentieth century presented a picture of astonishing contrast. In no part of Britain was the divide between rural and industrial society more pronounced. The mountainous farming regions which dominated most of north and central Wales, beyond the Brecon Beacons, were sunk in depression from the 1870s, seemingly as impoverished and insecure as ever. Those scattered pockets of industry dispersed throughout rural Wales, copper mining in Anglesey, lead mining in north Cardiganshire, woollen manufacturing in Montgomeryshire and Merioneth, were in steady decay. They were victims of the superior strength of industrial England and of overseas competitors, brought ever nearer by the growth of railways within Britain itself and by steamship services across the oceans. Small ports on the western seaboard, places like Portmadoc, Barmouth, Aberdyfi, Borth, and Newquay which once flourished from the seagoing trade with Scandinavia, the Iberian peninsula, and north America, were in gradual decline as the railways cut into the coastal trade. For the same reason, the shipyards in a small town like Penhelig on the Dyfi estuary, bustling and active in the mid-century, had by 1880 almost ceased to operate.

By contrast, industrial Wales, above all the mining valleys of the south, was swept along in intense, almost uncontrolled expansion. Economically, as well as politically and culturally, south Wales had reached the point of take-off. In the years from 1880 to 1914 it was amongst the most buoyant growth centres in the world for industrial production, and for manufacturing and commerce. Only the Ruhr in Germany and the industrial sectors of the eastern United States rivalled south Wales as a centre of heavy industry. Above all, coal was enthroned as king in Wales during these years. The ports of Cardiff and, only to a slightly lesser extent, Newport, Barry, Port Talbot, Swansea, and Llanelli, were where he held court. At no period was Wales with its heavy industry more central to the performance of the British economy and the international ramifications of its finance, investment, capital outflow, and export trade.

It is, then, the continued surging growth of the Welsh coal industry, largely in the south from the Gwendraeth and Amman valleys in Carmarthenshire on the west of the coalfield, to the Rhymney and Sirhowy valleys in Monmouthshire in the east, with fringes of growth in north-east Wales in the Wrexham/Rhos district and in southern Pembrokeshire between Milford Haven and Saundersfoot, that most spectacularly illustrates this extraordinary economic explosion. The exploitation of the bituminous, 'house', or 'steam' coal seams of Glamorgan and Monmouthshire was already far advanced by the eighties. The great majority of pits had already been sunk. Their waste tips and winding shafts already towered above sprawling mining communities from Ammanford in the west to Pontypool in the east. The character and social culture of Welsh mining villages had long since crystallized. But the growth potential of the Welsh coal industry was still far from exhausted.

Production of coal of different types soared from 16 million tons in the early seventies, to 30 million in 1891, and on to 56.8 million in 1913, when the coal industry reached its zenith. In 1913 south Wales supplied over one-fifth (19.7 per cent) of the entire coal production of the British mines, and, with nearly 30 of its 56 million tons of coal produced going for export, almost one-third of the entire world exports in coal of all types. Welsh collieries numbered 485 in 1913, of which 323 were located in Glamorgan alone.[1] The labour force in the Welsh mines amounted to well over a quarter of a million men. With occasional discontinuities, such as the fall in production and employment resulting from the six-months' coal dispute of 1898 which involved almost 100,000 workers, the growth of the Welsh coal industry throughout this period was relentless.

There were some areas of the industry in which this continued expansion was especially pronounced in the thirty years before the First World War. In the heart of the coalfield in central Glamorgan, the Rhondda valleys maintained their extraordinary rate of growth since the first pioneering efforts of David Davies of Llandinam in the mid-sixties. Indeed, the presence of Davies was still a dominant one twenty years later. In 1887 he formed the Ocean Coal Company, with an initial share capital of £800,000, to consolidate his various colliery enterprises. Producing over a million and a half tons annually, the Ocean combine was second only to Powell Duffryn as a producer of steam coal. Between 1885 and 1913, coal output in the Rhondda Fawr and Rhondda Fach increased by 73 per cent, from over 5,500,000 tons to over 9,600,000. The number of miners working in the Rhondda in the same period rose from 25,000 to over 41,000. Major new collieries were opened up even in these highly developed valleys between 1891 and 1914, at Clydach Vale, Penygraig, and Tonypandy in the Rhondda Fawr, and Maerdy, Ynyshir, and Tylorstown in the Rhondda Fach.[2] At the cost of low productivity, primitive standards of mechanization and much social hardship and physical injury and illness for a cheap and steady expanding labour force,

---

[1] G. M. Holmes, 'The South Wales Coal Industry, 1850–1914', *Trans. Hon. Soc. Cymmrodorion* (1976), p. 183.
[2] E. D. Lewis, *The Rhondda Valleys* (Cardiff, 1959), pp. 91–3, 103–4.

Rhondda's coal led the Welsh and British economies to new peaks of expansive growth.

Elsewhere in the bituminous coalfields of central and eastern Glamorgan and western Monmouthshire, there was a constant picture of expanding production in existing pits. Such giant companies as Powell Duffryn in the Cynon valley near Aberdare were already well established, and there were not many new accessible seams to be opened up. In the mining valleys of Monmouthshire, in fact, there was some contraction, partly due to a declining demand for house coal. Monmouthshire's total of working pits fell from 153 in 1875 to 102 in 1913. But there was a totally different segment of the coalfield which was throbbing with new life after 1880. This was the anthracite field of the Swansea valley and eastern Carmarthenshire, bounded by the Vale of Neath on the east and the Gwendraeth on the west. Anthracite, with its high proportion of pure carbon and its durable and smokeless qualities, was increasingly in domestic and commercial demand. From the 1880s onwards, the Welsh anthracite industry showed immense capacity for growth, and claimed an increasing share of the production and profits of the coal export trade. The output of Welsh anthracite increased almost threefold from 1,676,128 tons in 1895 to 4,778,114 tons in 1913. Small communities such as Brynamman, Ammanford, Gowerton, Pontardawe, Ystalyfera, and Glynneath suddenly mushroomed into sizeable industrial centres. Their tone was very different from the more rugged mining communities to the east. The anthracite towns were marked by sedate standards of Lib-Lab Welsh respectability; semi-detached houses built for owner-occupiers became the norm instead of the ribbon development of company-housing development prevalent in much of the bituminous coalfield. Swansea achieved new life as an industrial port. It became the centre for the anthracite coalfield, as surely as did Cardiff and Barry for steam coal. Coal shipments exported from Swansea rose from 900,000 tons in 1880 to 3,500,000 in 1913.[3] In the first decade of the new century, new anthracite pits were sunk every year. The western coalfield began to approach the levels of the coalfield of central and eastern Glamorgan in its expansion and prosperity.

On the eve of the First World War, therefore, the Welsh coal industry presented an extraordinary pattern of prolonged success. The nature of this success was not in doubt; to some degree, it was unique to the region. More than any other sector of the British coal industry, that in Wales was geared to export. In 1901, it was recorded that south Wales, with 18 million tons, exported 46 per cent of the coal shipped from British ports, compared with 26 per cent from the Tyneside ports, 17 per cent from Scottish ports, and 10 per cent from Hull, Grimsby, and Goole. There were, therefore, furious protests, by Chambers of Commerce and by trade-union leaders in April 1901

[3] D. T. Williams, *The Economic Development of Swansea and of the Swansea District to 1921* (Cardiff, 1940), p. 149

when Hicks-Beach's budget imposed an export tax on coal. It was urged that this would have a detrimental effect on smaller Welsh mines and would lead to French and Italian manufacturers turning to Belgium and elsewhere for cheap fuel. Partly as a result of this, the coal tax was shortly rescinded. Shipments of coal overseas continued to mount. By 1911, exports from Welsh ports had risen to over 25 million tons, with France, Italy, Egypt, the Argentine, and Brazil, in that order, the major customers. The fine burning qualities of Welsh anthracite and house coal made it much in demand for domestic and commercial use in Europe and in South America. Welsh steam coal was also much used by foreign railways and, above all, as bunker coal in worldwide merchant and naval vessels. The staid pages of Professor H. S. Jevons's *magnum opus* on the British coal trade, written at the start of the First World War, were a paean of praise for the almost limitless potential of Welsh and British coal in world markets.[4] In fact, the upward curve of demand for coal served to mask a declining market for Welsh coal in domestic industry and manufacturing, as the British iron and steel industry, for instance, entered a period of prolonged stagnation from the early eighties. Indeed, from 1896 onwards, Welsh coal that was exported steadily outstripped that produced for home consumption.

The effects of this change in the pattern of demand were writ large on the future history of south Wales in terms of employment and labour costs. More than any other section of the British coal industry, south Wales was sensitive to overseas competition. Its coalowners, therefore, were peculiarly cost-conscious; the precarious nature of the export trade had to be weighed along with the high-cost, labour-intensive nature of mining in south Wales due to its peculiar geological and other physical difficulties. Productivity fell from 309 tons per man year in 1883 to only 222 in 1912, at a time when industrial efficiency in the United States and Germany was rising rapidly. The heady, carefree expansion of the Welsh coal industry in this period was deceptive. Its workforce was peculiarly vulnerable to slumps in trade; exports, prices, and wages were unusually cyclical in character. It was not surprising, therefore, that south Wales, more than any other sector of the mining industry in Britain, should, after the turn of the century, become the major centre for industrial conflict between cost-conscious, inefficient employers and an inflated workforce with a low rate of productivity. But these days of potential difficulty still seemed very remote. Only a few percipient observers, such as D. A. Thomas, the Liberal MP for Merthyr who began a new career as the owner of the Cambrian collieries in the Rhondda from 1895, could detect problems ahead in fluctuations of world trade, the shrinking of markets, and the fall in the return from coal freights.[5] There was also the longer-term

    [4] *South Wales Daily News*, 24 April 1901; H. S. Jevons, *The British Coal Trade* (London, 1915).
    [5] D. A. Thomas, 'The growth and direction of our Foreign Trade in Coal during the last Half Century', *Jnl. of the Royal Statistical Society* lxvi (1903).

possibility of growing competition from rival fuels such as oil. The frenetic boom quality of expansion in the coal industry, and the physical and structural problems that underlay it, served to colour the later explosion of working-class militancy with a unique bitterness and to provide the mining valleys with a history and a legend all their own.

There were other important features of industry in south Wales in these years, apart from coal. The Welsh iron and steel industry, for instance, was an important one, thriving on local supplies of limestone and coking coal. Local iron-ore of the right quality, however, was in short supply, and south Wales depended heavily on supplies from Spain and elsewhere as the local ore was too phosphoric. The major change now was the transition from iron to steel. Many of the giants of the old iron-making days early in the century were now defunct. The iron-works of Plymouth and Penydarren in the Merthyr area, for instance, closed for ever in the seventies. The Rhymney plant was dismantled in 1890 and the company turned to coal production. The royal commission inquiring into the trade depression in 1885–6 received graphic evidence from the ironmakers as to the depressed state of the Welsh iron industry in the face of competition from larger and more modernized American and German producers.[6] However, south Wales was able to adapt to the opportunities afforded by the Siemens process of open-hearth steel manufacture. This gave Welsh iron and steel plants new life; by the First World War, steel produced by the Siemens process far outstripped Bessemer steel.

A general change of long-term sociological, as well as economic, significance was the movement of steel production from the inland valleys down to the coast. In 1891 the historic Dowlais works was moved to Cardiff on the East Moors site, far nearer to coastal outlets. The old works at Dowlais became less and less significant; it was near to closure by 1911, despite a poignant appeal by Keir Hardie to George V on behalf of 'sweated Dowlais'.[7] The old blast-furnaces at Blaenavon and Ebbw Vale were closed down in 1911. There was now a clear contrast between steel-making concerns on the coast, modernized and often caught up in amalgamation between companies, and stagnation in the upland heads of the valleys. The Guest, Keen Company mopped up steel-works from Cardiff to Port Talbot, while Lysaghts of Newport took over a new plant in the Orb Works. The secular process of movement of steel-making from the valleys down to the coast was to continue remorselessly thereafter until it was quite unexpectedly reversed in 1938 when a new strip-mill was opened in Ebbw Vale.

There was much buoyancy in these coastal works, and in the major steel industry which grew up in north-east Wales also, on Deeside in Flintshire and around Wrexham after 1885. In that year, a continuous steel-making plant,

---

[6] *Second Report of the Royal Commission on the Depression in Trade and Industry*, Parl, Papers, 1886, xxi (C. 4715), Appendix A.

[7] *Merthyr Pioneer*, 29 July 1911.

with the first Siemens open-hearth steel furnace in Britain, was built at Brymbo, Wrexham, by a descendant of the Darby family of Coalbrookdale. In addition, John Summers and Sons built an open-hearth steel works and bar mill at Shotton, near Hawarden. The rolling of sheet steel began there in 1896. After 1909, John Summers also built a steel-making plant for producing its own steel bars. A further steel plant with eight furnaces and a bar mill was to be established during the war in 1917-18. Shotton and Brymbo were to remain major elements in the British steel industry until the 1970s and to turn Deeside and Wrexham into a major centre of industry. Overall, though, the Welsh steel industry was somewhat precarious, with much antiquated plant, as vulnerable to foreign competition as the coal industry appeared impervious to it.

More dynamic in the field of metallurgical production was the tinplate industry. Since the fifties, it had been centred on western Glamorgan and eastern Carmarthenshire and around Swansea Bay. By 1880, there were six tinplate mills in Llanelli alone, five each in Pontardulais, Morriston, and Briton Ferry, and others in Port Talbot, Neath, Pontardawe, and Gorseinon.[8] The growth of Siemens-process steel manufacture in south Wales gave considerable stimulus to the independent tinplate firms after 1880. Side by side with the west Wales anthracite industry, tinplate displayed considerable capacity for expansion, not least with the growing demand for tin in the canning of food and for petroleum containers. In 1891, tinplate production reached 586,000 tons, of which well over half was exported, most of it to the United States. The McKinley tariff of 1891 imposed by the American government had, therefore, a calamitous effect upon Welsh tinplate manufacture. There was a collapse in the export trade, many pack mills closed down, and severe unemployment resulted in the Swansea valley area. But after the turn of the century, these difficulties had largely been overcome. New markets had been discovered in the Far East and South America; new openings had been discovered such as the use of tinplate mills for making 'blackplate' or galvanized steel sheets. The demand for tin for canning mounted impressively. In 1912, the Welsh tinplate industry recorded a peak production of 848,000 tons of plate. Swansea, as the major port for the export of tinplate as well as of anthracite, reached new peaks of prosperity. The tonnage of tin, terne, and black plates exported from there rose from 209,400 tons in 1902 to 330,350 in 1912. New works were built along the coastal belt between Port Talbot and Llanelli. Firms such as Richard Thomas at Gorseinon and Gilbertsons at Port Talbot flourished with the upsurge of the trade cycle from about 1901. Richard Thomas Ltd, in particular, notably expanded their ownership of tinplate mills in the early years of the century. Here again, then, was an industry where south Wales dominated the British scene. The tinplate industry was overwhelmingly a west Wales one. It brought new wealth, new

[8] W. E. Minchinton, *The British Tinplate Industry* (Oxford, 1957), pp. 34-5.

population, and cultural vitality to this section of the industrial region. Respectable, chapel-going owner-occupiers settled comfortably into their bay-windowed houses. Towns like Pontardulais and Gorseinon found new vigour, while the religious and cultural life of Morriston, with celebrated preachers like the Revd J. J. Williams of Tabernacle chapel, and later institutions like Morriston Orpheus Choir, resounded throughout the land.

In other areas, too, metallurgical industry was flourishing in south Wales, notably in the hinterland of Swansea. Although the old copper industry, so dominant in the previous century, was now in acute decline, non-ferrous metal production in the Swansea region continued to expand. By 1913 there were seven zinc-smelting works in such areas as Landore and Llansamlet. The Swansea spelter works had eleven zinc furnaces with an output of seven tons of spelter each per day. Meanwhile in 1902 Mond Nickel, the largest nickel works in the world, was established at Clydach. Here again was a new, technologically advanced giant of heavy industry bestriding the coalfield. It was to bring with it the impact of the personality of Sir Alfred Mond, heir to the Mond—Brunner chemical combine, with mixed consequences for commercial and for political life.

Industry, however, was not wholly confined to the coalfield of the south. Apart from the smaller coalfield around Wrexham and Rhos in the north-east of Wales, extending as far north as the Point of Ayr colliery in Flintshire, and the growing iron and steel industry of Deeside, there was another interesting element in the Welsh industrial scene. This lay in the far north-west, deep in the heart of the mountainous Gwynedd. Here was the slate-quarrying industry, centred in north and eastern Caernarvonshire in the domain of Lord Penrhyn around Llanberis, Bethesda, and the Nantlle valley, and in the north of Merioneth around Blaenau Ffestiniog, with small pockets to the south in Abergynolwyn in south Merioneth and around Corris in the Dyfi valley. At its peak, the Welsh slate industry employed 16,000 men. Quarries such as the Penrhyn, Dinorwic, Dorothea, and Oakley were major employers of labour and the largest slate quarries in the world. The demand for Welsh hard slate for the roofs of housing was still very buoyant in the eighties; indeed, the year 1889 was to see the peak of production. Thereafter, Welsh slate entered a more chequered period. Exports of slate had given new vitality to such coastal ports as the new creation of Port Dinorwic, to Portmadoc in southern Llŷn, and to Aberdyfi. From Aberdyfi, for instance, 5,000 tons of slate were exported annually from the quarries of Corris, Aberllefenni, and Bryneglwys until the early years of the twentieth century. Portmadoc, where the young Lloyd George began work as a solicitor in 1884, was a bustling little place of nearly 5,000 people, busy with the export of slate transported from Ffestiniog by the narrow-gauge railway. But then the industry declined. There was a severe depression in the export trade and steady fall in the domestic British building industry, partly as a result of dearer money which slowed down construction. More ominously for the long term, the development of tiles and other cheaper, roofing materials cut into the demand for slate.

For all that, the Welsh slate industry was still of much economic importance as the century reached its close. The South African War boosted demand, as did programmes of new housing and slum clearance in London, Birmingham, Liverpool, and Glasgow. The year 1898 was another peak: the Penrhyn quarries made a record profit of £133,000.[9] The story was an erratic one thereafter. In 1909, there were still 13,000 quarrymen at work in Welsh quarries. Thereafter, there were severe unemployment and cutbacks in trade and wages. Stocks of unwanted Welsh slate piled up on the quayside at Port Dinorwic. Even so, it is worth recalling that the picture of the north Wales slate industry at this period, so affectionately recalled in the novels of T. Rowland Hughes in the 1940s,[10] was by no means one of unrelieved poverty and economic decline. The problems of the slate industry lay rather in social factors, in the paternalistic, almost feudal approach of landowners such as Lord Penrhyn and their agents, in the role of sub-contractors in undercutting local workmen, and in the immense barriers placed to frustrate the growth of trade unions. These led to a sharp deterioration in industrial relations throughout the quarrying community. But in narrowly economic terms, the slate industry brought new wealth into a barren mountainous area and made its contribution to a general picture of industrial growth.

As important as the bare facts of the growth of industry was the expansion of the infrastructure of transport and other services to link this industry up with wider markets. It was this growth in services, above all, that buoyed up the enormous advance of the ports of Cardiff, Swansea, Barry, and Newport. The port of Cardiff continued to grow in this period to accommodate the thriving export trade in coal. The Roath Docks were opened in 1887, the Queen Alexandra Docks twenty years later. Extensions of a major kind were also made in the dock and port facilities of Newport, Llanelli, and Port Talbot. The Port Talbot New Dock, opened in 1898, imported ores and timbers for local smelting and mining industries, as well as exporting anthracite, tinplate, and other metals. Swansea, which experienced a vast surge of prosperity in these years through the overseas coal trade as well as tinplate, opened up a new King's Dock between 1904 and 1909, while the older Prince of Wales and North Docks were considerably widened. Here again, the boom in exports led to a vast expansion of foreign shipments and to considerable local prosperity. The most dramatic new development of all, however, was the opening of a totally new dock at Barry under the aegis of David Davies of Llandinam, and John Cory, to by-pass the congested facilities of Cardiff docks and the charges inflicted by the third Marquess of Bute. By 1889 the new Barry docks had

---

[9] Jean Lindsay, *A History of the North Wales Slate Industry* (Newton Abbot, 1974), p. 255.
[10] See below, p. 250.

opened and were linked by rail with the mines of the Rhondda fifteen miles to the north. Barry docks steadily expanded over the next twenty years and proved a formidable competitor to Cardiff, its more established rival. In 1913, Barry actually outstripped Cardiff as the major coal-exporting entrepôt, not just in Wales but in the world.

Linked with these massive developments in the ports of south Wales, the railway network, both for passenger and for freight traffic, built up steadily. There were 'statutory' services run by the Great Western Railway and the Taff Vale Railway among others to carry workmen, together with subsidized 'contract' lines run for the private colliery companies. By 1913, indeed, the south Wales railway system was one of immense sophistication and complexity with a myriad of local lines linking outlying parts of the coalfield with urban centres and coastal ports. Coal from the Rhondda, for instance, was shipped not only from Barry, via the main railway lines from Hafod and Porth, but also from Swansea via the Afan valley and Briton Ferry, from Cardiff along the Taff Vale Railway and the Bute docks complex, and even from Newport where the newly-formed Pontypridd and Caerphilly railway company carried the coal of the Rhondda Fawr to the Alexandra Docks at the mouth of the Usk. The result was a rapid growth in the coastal ports, Newport, Cardiff, Barry, and Swansea. They had absorbed many English and Irish immigrants long before 1850. A marked divergence in their social structure from the inland industrial valleys was increasingly apparent. It was a divergence that was to have cultural implications as the coastal ports became more anglicized and cosmopolitan, and political ones as well. The *Cymru Fydd* crisis of 1894−6, for instance, was to show up the very different political outlook towards home rule prevalent in the coastal seaboard compared with the rural and industrial hinterland. The mining valleys were homogeneous, intensely Welsh centres of manufacturing and extractive industry. The coastal ports, by contrast, generally lacked an industrial base. Their workers were mainly employed in servicing and in transporting the mineral products of the valleys. Not until the Dowlais works moved to East Moors, for instance, could Cardiff be said to have any significant pocket of industrial production. It was very noticeable that the ports of south Wales, unlike those of the Tyne-Tees region in north-east England or Belfast in northern Ireland, developed no shipbuilding industry, despite the immense importance of shipping in the economic life of Newport, Cardiff, Barry, and Swansea. The result was that the coastal fringe of south Wales tended to follow a very different path, distinct in its responses to economic fluctuations from the vast mass of the coalfield. Industrial and commercial growth, in many ways the economic salvation of Wales, was also in longer perspective the key to a new, more disturbing source of national division—the gulf between the Welsh and the Anglo-Welsh.

The divergence of outlook between the valleys and the coastal ports, however, was intermittent. Many of its cultural and political consequences lay in the future. In the perspective of the years up to 1914, it is perhaps the unity of the coalfield and its integrated character that is most striking. Entrepreneurs were able to take a more cosmic view of its economic potential, transcending the parochial boundaries of valleys and individual communities. The role of David Davies and John Cory in linking up Rhondda coal mining with the facilities of the various Welsh ports is particularly instructive here. The main battles with land-owning magnates such as Bute or Beaufort in obtaining long leases for the expansion of railways, collieries, or docks had been fought and won by the eighties. Legacies still remained in the pattern of urban development, notably the prevalence of leasehold housing (usually on 99-year leases) in Cardiff, Swansea, and Newport. In Cardiff, well under 10 per cent of its houses were owned by their occupiers prior to 1914, while some of the leasehold property, notably the drab terraces of Butetown in the dockside area, was notoriously dilapidated and squalid. But the impact of the Bute family upon the economic life of Cardiff and south-east Wales was now more indirect than before 1868. This may have been partly the result of the curious personality of the third Marquess of Bute, who focused his vagrant mind upon the Gothic fantasies of Castell Coch and on eccentric forms of religion. The defeat of the Bute interest in 1884, when the Barry Docks Bill was passed, as a clear portent of rivalry to the Bute docks in Cardiff, was a symbol of dynastic decline. Industrial Wales had now fallen into the hands of a thrusting, expanding class of manufacturers, shippers, exporters, merchants, and brokers who linked together the various strands of its economic life. Cardiff, Swansea, and Newport became almost regional capitals, their mercantile élite the new conquerors of the second, more lasting phase of the industrial development of south Wales. They served as the apex of a vast industrial population, still predominantly Welsh in origin, but with a character and a bilingual, bicultural tradition of its own.

In this expanding coalfield, a distinctive form of society, far more settled than the frontier settlements of the earlier nineteenth century, was being created. No longer was it the 'Samaria' of industrial Britain as excited demagogues had once proclaimed.[11] By the early years of the twentieth century, this society was becoming as clearly demarcated in its class and cultural aspects as was that of rural Wales. On a remote social pinnacle were the coalowners who bestrode this world like so many colossi. In the early nineteenth century, most Welsh pits had been small in scale. The majority of coalowners then had been Welshmen, often nonconformist, who lived locally and enjoyed a close, paternalistic relationship with their workers. Often they would attend the same chapels or patronize the same local eisteddfodau. Invariably, they came to share the same Gladstonian Liberal faith. But by the eighties, the growth in the scale of operations of the mining industry had

[11] Gwyn A. Williams, The Merthyr Rising (London, 1978), p. 21.

elevated the coalowner to new heights. The founding of the Coalowners' Association of South Wales in 1873—admittedly, a relatively weak body to which never more than 80 per cent of coalowners belonged[12]—confirmed the new cohesion and capacity for self-defence of the new capitalist class. The growth of great combines—Powell Duffryn, Lewis Merthyr, David Davies's Ocean Company, D. A. Thomas's Cambrian Combine, formed in the Rhondda area from 1895 (after his political disappointments over *Cymru Fydd*)—these betokened a new growth of vertical and horizontal combination in the coal industry. By the first decade of the century, south Wales, with its fine steam coal and its involvement with the export trade, was more marked than any other coalfield in Britain for its oligopolistic or cartelized structure of ownership. As a result the titans who ran these new combines became more and more remote from the mining communities. The old class collaboration was coming to a rapid, violent end.

The great majority of the coalowners, unlike the Crawshays, Guests, and other ironmasters in the past, were undeniably Welsh by birth; most of their share capital seems to have been local in origin rather than drawn from the public capital market. But their Welshness often ended there. Sir William T. Lewis, later Baron Merthyr of Senghennydd, formerly manager of the Bute collieries, now the head of mighty industries including much of Cardiff docks as well as collieries galore in the Rhondda, Cynon, and Rhymney valleys, lived in almost baronial splendour. His attitude towards the Welsh coal industry was scarcely less feudal than was that of Lord Penrhyn towards the slate-quarrying industry. Lewis's company had built up most of the miners' terrace houses in the neighbourhoods; the mining villages became virtually company towns on the model of the United States. Lewis was truly a Welsh 'robber baron' on the Texan scale. He ruled the Coalowners' Association in autocratic fashion. When D. A. Thomas in 1897 proposed an imaginative scheme for controlling output and prices by a combined scheme for restricting the production of each company to a fixed amount each year, Lewis had it thrown out. The household gods of the laws of supply and demand, free from collective control or social responsibility, continued to hold sway. D. A. Thomas himself was an industrial, as well as a political rebel. But he, too, lived very affluently in Llanwern, a large late-seventeenth-century house set in wooded parkland in southern Monmouthshire. This aristocratic mode of life was emulated by other industrialists, such as the Vivians of Singleton Park, on the west of Swansea, and the Gilbertsons, the tinplate and steel family, in Port Talbot. Some coalowners lived significantly well away from the coalfield and grew culturally and geographically more distant from their workforce. The Corys and the Nixons lived in squirearchical style in the Vale of Glamorgan. John Cory built Duffryn House, another Gothic edifice with fine gardens, and

[12] Cf. L. J. Williams, 'The Coalowners of South Wales, 1873–80: Problems of Unity', *Welsh History Review*, vol. 8, No. 1 (June 1976), pp. 75–93.

served as lord of the manor of St. Nicholas. These coalowners were now involved much more directly in the shipping and mercantile world of the coastal ports than in the heavy industry on whose productive growth their enterprises basically depended. Newer coalowners tended to be essentially salesmen, exporters and entrepreneurs, skilled in commerce and investment rather than in mining techniques, and remote from the daily working life of the coalfield. The gap was filled by a new breed of managers and overseers in the valleys. Many of them lived in a very grand style also, such as William Jenkins, the manager of the Ocean collieries, 1871–1915, and E. M. Hann, general manager of the Powell-Duffryn collieries and leader of the Rorke's Drift stand in defending the Aberdare pits against an embittered workforce in November 1910. It was the managers who took the major industrial decisions and who bore the brunt of social injustice.

There was emerging a more integrated middle class in the valley towns and villages also—a new group of small businessmen, shopkeepers, solicitors, journalists, and sometimes more affluent workmen such as checkweighmen. They occupied superior terrace houses with bay windows, put up by property investors and speculative builders cashing in on the new prosperity of the valleys.[13] Owner-occupation became more widespread, and with the increased operation of building societies the power of the mortgage was felt in the land. This new middle class was usually central to the activities of the Liberal Party in south Wales, and increasingly hostile towards the growth of trade unions with their new emphasis on socialism and on international considerations of class loyalty rather than Welsh considerations of community. These men were also central to the evolution of new organs of local and municipal government, to provide essential services for the new valley communities, and to build up a new network of local patronage and control. As in other industrial regions, south Wales showed a rapid transformation in its fabric of local government, with economic growth as its motor. The spread of public education after the passage of the Forster Act in 1870 also had a powerful effect in building up a new middle class in this industrial society. By the end of the century, education had helped markedly in increasing social mobility and in providing a new generation of literate young people, many of whom were admittedly to migrate to the ports of the coastal fringe or across the border to England. South Wales was a stronghold of the Board school. Under its aegis, pupil teaching centres were set up in several mining areas and new higher grade schools were established as a result. The foundation of so many 'county' or publicly-maintained secondary schools in Wales after the passage of the Intermediate Education Act in 1889 was also to impose a powerful stamp on the quality of life in the valleys by the turn of the century.

[13] Cf. Philip N. Jones, *Colliery Settlement in the South Wales Coalfield, 1850 to 1926* (Hull, 1969), pp. 41 ff.

The village schoolmaster, in Wales as in France, was outstripping the village pastor as local leader, spokesman, and public critic.

But the outstanding consequence of the industrial society in south Wales—and this is true, on a smaller scale, of the mining communities of north-east Wales and of Pembrokeshire also—was the creation of a rich but raw working-class world. Under the impact of the industrial expansion that has been described, the influx of population into the mining valleys was enormous. By 1891, the population of the Rhondda was already over 127,000; the population of the port of Cardiff in 1911 stood at 182,259. The entire Welsh coal-field was absorbing population, much of it young able-bodied working men, at a rate without comparison in the United Kingdom, and indeed was a magnet for immigrants surpassed in the world by the United States alone. Until the 1890s, as has been seen, the bulk of this immigration came from rural Wales, with cultural legacies in the chapels, local *eisteddfodau* and choral festivals, and newspapers. Increasingly thereafter, the majority of migrants came from England, especially from neighbouring counties in the west of England. Many young colliers followed the route taken by Frank Hodges from Lydney, Gloucestershire, or by Arthur Cook from Wookey in Somerset. Many were to follow them, too, in rejecting the old Welsh values with their chapel-based, Lib-Lab ethos. This vast new population was accommodated, somehow, in the straggling, winding settlements of terrace housing along the face of the mining valleys, so characteristic of south Wales. Every valley became an unsightly, sprawling settlement.

By most criteria it was a harsh, rough world in which this population lived. Long before 1914, south Wales lagged behind most parts of Britain in terms of sub-standard working-class housing, in urban overcrowding, in its health and hospital services, in the indices of industrial disease among workers, poverty and ill-health among the old, malnutrition and disease among children. Welsh local authorities built a mere 776 dwellings between 1890 and 1909. The figures for infant mortality were particularly shocking. In 1911, the five major boroughs of south Wales showed a death rate of 380 children per 1,000 born.[14] Most of the literature has, understandably, focused on the mining valleys and their social deprivation, on the valleys of Swansea and Neath, of Ogmore and Garw, of Rhondda and Cynon, of Taff, Rhymney, and Ebbw. But it is worth noting that among the most extreme pockets of social decay were poorer areas of Cardiff and Swansea. Splott and Butetown in Cardiff became a byword for rough picaresque working-class life in the raw, as vividly as Merthyr's 'China' (still in existence in the 1890s) had been generations earlier. The Irish communities of Cardiff, living mainly in Adamsdown, and of Swansea located in Brynmelin-Greenhill, both long established, were also noticeably impoverished in their social and welfare amenities. Merthyr Tydfil itself, along with ancillary communities like Dowlais and Cyfarthfa, was marooned like

[14] Thomas Jones, *Welsh Broth* (London, 1952), p. 126.

some aged industrial whale, at the head of the valleys. It was already somewhat left behind by the new industry as its iron-works steadily closed down and its workers sought employment in the Rhondda or in the docks of Cardiff or Barry. The new Welsh working-class world, that 'American Wales' of teeming peoples and of mass, cosmopolitan immigration later depicted by Sir Alfred Zimmern, was a poorly-endowed one, with social revolution an ever-present threat.

For all that, it was a society with its own richness and satisfying qualities of life. The valley world that one perceives from newspapers of the time or, for instance, from Thomas Jones's autobiographical account of the Rhymney valleys in the eighties, was in many ways a thriving one, with new wealth constantly pumped in through the agency of the mining industry. One aspect of this is the surprisingly high degree of owner-occupation in the Rhondda and other areas of the Glamorgan and Monmouthshire coalfield which could run to over 50 per cent of all houses there. A major factor here was the spread of building clubs or societies in south Wales, eighty-six in number in Glamorgan by the nineties, with annual receipts of over £350,000.[15] Some of the new terrace housing provided by colliery companies, such as David Davies constructed at Ton Pentre and Treorchy, was in advance of its time, though, to set against this, were innumerable jerry-built terraces put up by speculative builders and private contractors, with a total absence of urban planning or amenity provision in so bleak a landscape.

The nonconformist chapels continued to spread, and multiplied throughout the coalfield: Morriston with its Gothic tabernacles came to rival Caernarfon as a Mecca for dissent. Welsh migrants substantially built up the Welsh-language religious life of Cardiff in this period, while the Cardiff Cymmrodorion and Cambrian Society, dominated by such men as Beriah Gwynfe Evans, Professor T. F. Roberts (from 1883 to 1891), and the carpenter-bard Edward Thomas ('Cochfarf'), became powers in the land. In the valleys, *eisteddfodau*, friendly societies, working men's institutes, choral festivals and *cymanfaoedd canu*, 'penny readings', local theatricals and operatic societies (the last patronized by Adelina Patti who lived at Craig-y-Nos above Swansea)—all these by-products of popular folk culture flourished more richly than ever before or since. It might be added that the world of the public house, in some ways a source of degradation and violence, of domestic strain and physical deterioration, was also one of vigorous community life, of political debate and of spontaneous musical activity. The Welsh pub like the Welsh chapel, which it rivalled, provided (except on Sundays) an always available escape route from the harshness of industrial squalor and exploitation. New leisure activities emerged to quicken the pulses of Welsh working men and to provide their offspring with an alternative to the Sunday school

[15] Thomas Jones, *Rhymney Memories* (Llandysul, new ed. 1970); John Davies, *The Bute Estate*, chapter V (Cardiff, 1980).

outing. Boxing became a spectacular attraction in many Welsh towns, much to the scandal of local nonconformist ministers. A Welsh professional pugilist, Tom Thomas of the Rhondda, became in 1909 the first holder of a Lonsdale belt. Rugby football, originally introduced into the valleys by sporting missionaries, muscular Christians from the few Welsh public schools such as Llandovery and Christ's, Brecon, became a powerful focus for village or valley loyalty. By the turn of the century, there were thriving rugby teams in most south Wales towns, and powerful ones in Cardiff, Newport, and Swansea. The Welsh team soon established the capacity to beat the English. The 'triple crown' was first won in 1893, and was captured a further six times between 1901 and 1912, truly a 'golden age' for that rugby which the Welsh working class increasingly patronized.

In many ways, then, this new industrial world was a satisfied one, content with itself, happy with the new wealth that was enriching its community life as well as its pockets. It was not, in general, a world that questioned fundamentally the values that held it together. If there was one dominant creed that pervaded the social, religious, cultural, political, and even sporting life of the coalfield it was the 'Lib-Lab' ethos, by which working men acquired pride in their own social advancement but also identified with a wider Welsh community in which relationships were stable and traditions perceived and understood. If there was one symbolic figure who characterizes this society from the eighties until perhaps about 1904–6, say until the religious revival of those years, it was William Abraham, 'Mabon', the secretary of the Cambrian Miners' Association and later first president of the South Wales Miner's Federation.[16] He was a canny bargainer, but one deeply committed to class collaboration and social harmony. His influence pervaded most of the coalfield. He was a lay preacher, a fluent speaker and writer in Welsh, the possessor of a fine tenor voice which he used to placate audiences of unruly or discontented miners by striking up a popular hymn. He embodied in his sturdy frame the solid virtues of Gladstonian Lib-Labism in its Welsh incarnation. Appropriately, the miners' holiday inaugurated in 1888 and held on the first Monday of each month was termed 'Mabon's Day'. Passenger trains, taking miners and their families down to the coast, for instance on the Taff Vale Railway, bore the lettering 'M.D.' to commemorate this folk festival. The abolition of Mabon's Day after the six-months' coal stoppage of 1898 was not only an error of monumental, if characteristic stupidity by the coalowners. It marked the end of an era in the coalfield in which the values of Welshness, of nonconformity, of class harmony and identification with the valley community would be rapidly eroded by new imperatives of class struggle and industrial conflict. Ethical priorities would be supplanted by economic, and Mabon's world brought crashing down.

[16] See Eric Wyn Evans, *Mabon* (Cardiff, 1959).

As the century drew to its close, the economic progress of industrial Wales became increasingly to be challenged by the other main theme of the period— social conflict. In the eighties, the coalfield still maintained a precarious peace, or at least cold war. The Amalgamated Association of Miners, led by Thomas Halliday, which had led a rapid growth of unionism in the early seventies and had resulted in strikes and growing militancy, had petered out after 1875. A new arrangement for determining wage levels was instituted throughout the coalfield, the Sliding Scale of 1875, under which five employers and five miners' representatives sat as a joint committee. The chairman was Sir William T. Lewis; the vice-chairman, appropriately for this symbol of industrial partnership, was 'Mabon'. Under this scheme, wages were linked to the selling price of coal; a change of 1s. a ton in price would involve a change of 7½ per cent in wages. This system lasted, with modifications, until 1898, in the face of mounting criticism, not least of the autocratic, Carnegie-type methods of Sir William Lewis, 'the last of the industrial barons' as he was called.[17] The system never worked satisfactorily for the miners even after a renegotiation in 1880 basing the system on the price levels of 1879. Employers had an incentive to over-produce or under-sell; wage levels fluctuated violently; audits were infrequent. It is, among other things, a tribute to the influence of Lib-Labbery and to the modest impact of 'new unionism', let alone socialism in Wales, that the Sliding Scale lasted for so long. It is also a testimony to the parochialism and fragmentation of the miners, who were organized in eight small local unions, of which only three, according to Sidney Webb's findings in 1893, possessed their own independent funds.[18] The remainder were essentially company unions. Only 45,000 out of 120,000 miners in south Wales in the early nineties were organized in unions at all; only a small fraction of these were members of the Miners' Federation of Great Britain. Meanwhile, Mabon stoutly resisted strikes or any form of industrial resistance, even when the Welsh coalowners opposed the implementation of the eight-hour day principle in their collieries. The pressure for industrial confrontation and a new system of wage bargaining was somehow contained.

After 1898, the pressure exploded. South Wales became the cockpit for industrial conflict and class bitterness without parallel in the British Isles. By 1908 when the Miners' Federation of Great Britain affiliated to the Labour Party, after a solid vote in favour by the south Wales men, 'Mabonism' lay in the dust. Class war seemed rampant throughout much of the coalfield. Since so much of the emphasis here has, understandably, been placed on developments in the coal industry, it is worth spelling out that trade unionism grew rapidly and encountered similar industrial and legal obstacles in other

[17] Viscountess Rhondda (ed.), *The Life of D. A. Thomas, Viscount Rhondda* (London, 1921), p. 118.
[18] British Library of Political Science, Webb Collection, section A, vol. xxvi, ff. 155–205.

industries also. The 'new unions' made some impact amongst unskilled workers in south Wales after 1889 and established new branches among dockers and general labourers at Swansea, Cardiff, and Newport. Trades councils, often with socialist members, were set up there, and in Merthyr, Aberdare, Briton Ferry, and elsewhere. By 1900, the Merthyr and Dowlais trades council claimed to represent 7,000 workers and was geared to fight district elections. By April 1902, the Cardiff trades council had 4,000 members and ran its own distinctly socialist monthly periodical, the *Labour Pioneer*. It also had two members on the local authority, John Chappell and John Jenkins. The Cardiff council, with the unions represented including the Plumbers, the Painters, the Railway Servants, the Shop Assistants, the Iron Founders, the Electricians, the Iron and Steel Dressers, the Class Teachers, the Plasterers, the Engineers, the Upholsterers, the Bricklayers, the Boilermakers, the Enginemen, the Bakers, the Masons, Shipwrights, and Coal Trimmers, was a mirror of the extraordinary diversity of trades in Wales's largest town.

At first, the influence of the new unions was of brief duration: they found it hard to maintain continuity of membership and a reliable financial basis among shifting groups of unskilled workers; the trades councils, too, remained relatively dormant for a time. But they survived into the new century to act as the spearhead of a new working-class militancy. It was the trades councils of Merthyr and Aberdare that invited Keir Hardie to become the Labour parliamentary candidate for Merthyr boroughs in 1900. Of the new union branches, the dockers' union at Swansea organized by James Wignall proved to be a lasting growth; the young Ernest Bevin was to spend some time as organizer there after the turn of the century. In Merthyr and Swansea were formed, too, branches of the Workers' Union for the unskilled labourer, with Matt Giles, formerly an employee of Fry's Cocoa, as its organizer.[19] The Swansea branch numbered 500 by 1908, mainly lead and spelter workers. Railway workers in Cardiff, Barry, Tondu, and elsewhere also expanded their membership; from 1897 the general secretary of the Amalgamated Society of Railway Servants was a Welshman, Richard Bell of Merthyr Tydfil. Indeed, it was in south Wales that the struggle for the unions' defence of the right to strike without financial penalty took place, in the historic strike on the Taff Vale Railway in 1900.[20] The resultant decision in the House of Lords was a disaster for the railwaymen. They were found liable for £23,000 payment in damages to the company; the whole right to strike seemed to be in jeopardy. But the militancy of the Welsh railway workers was not diminished. Another Welshman, J. H. Thomas of Newport, was to rise to prominence after 1905 and to spearhead the demand for industrial unionism

[19] Stan Awbery, *Labour's Early Struggles in Swansea* (Swansea, 1949), pp. 55–6; Richard Hyman, *The Workers Union* (Oxford, 1971), pp. 26–7.

[20] Records of Taff Vale Case, Modern Records Centre, University of Warwick Library.

on the railways. He became secretary of the new National Union of Railwaymen in 1913. In several industries after the turn of the century, there were
clear signs of industrial conflict. Even the traditionally quiescent unions of the
tinplate workers, riven amongst themselves between the Steel Smelters and
the Tin and Sheet Millmen, were showing new signs of aggressiveness,
especially as new prosperity returned to the Welsh tinplate industry with the
revival of trade after 1901. The joint wage conciliation board for the industry,
set up in 1899, was frequently under fire. More generally, the new energy of
trades councils, their vigour in promoting their members on to school boards,
burial boards, boards of guardians, and the like, betokened a new challenge
for power by labour throughout south Wales. By 1900, for instance, the
Swansea Trades Council had elected representatives on every public body in
the town.

It was not only the industrial south which illustrated the new mood. In
1896, the Welsh-speaking quarrying community became the centre of a major
industrial struggle which caught the imagination of the Welsh, and indeed the
British public. In that year, relations between the struggling North Wales
Quarrymen's Union and the autocratic Lord Penrhyn and his agent, E. A.
Young, finally broke down. There had been labour troubles before—
dismissals and wage reductions; problems affecting the *rybelwr* or unskilled
'rubble man'; a lock-out in 1885−6 which cost the quarrymen about £10,000 in
union funds. The basic problems always concerned recognition of the union.
Lord Penrhyn and Young simply refused to negotiate with the Quarrymen's
Union or its secretary, W. J. Williams about minimum wages, or the sub-
letting of quarry work to the non-unionized scab workers of outside contractors. In September 1896, after demands for a standard daily wage, a minimum
wage of 4s. 6d. and an apprentices' poundage award had been dismissed and
some workmen suspended, a lock-out began which lasted over a year. Feeling
ran high throughout the Caernarvonshire quarries; but in 1897 the men had
to return to work virtually on Penrhyn's dictated terms. The old grievances
remained, culminating with orders by Penrhyn in 1900 that union payments
were not to be collected in his quarries. More men were suspended, the Chief
Constable of Caernarvonshire had to call in the militia, and a historic struggle
began which lasted from November 1900 until November 1903.

Despite the support of the TUC, of the Labour Representation Committee, of some Liberal MPs including Lloyd George (after some delay), and
of a public fund organized by the *Daily News*, the poorly-paid quarrymen
faced inevitable and crushing defeat. Their humiliation was total. Wages of
over £360,000 had been lost; yet the basic problem of union recognition had
not been solved at all. The irony was that the Welsh-speaking quarrymen
were supremely committed to the values of Lib-Labism and of class harmony.
Their secretary for a time was W. J. Parry of Coetmor, a prominent Liberal
nonconformist trained in accountancy and once involved in a newspaper

syndicate with Lloyd George.[21] It was notable that Parry, a supremely non-revolutionary bourgeois, should be the victim of a celebrated libel action brought by Lord Penrhyn whom he had accused of personal responsibility for the death-rate among his workers and of industrial tyranny in general. Even more than Mabon in the coalfield, Parry symbolized the old view of industrial relations. Yet even he was swept along unwillingly in the currents of industrial warfare now. His legal defeat in the courts proved to be a moral victory. The *Morning Leader* denounced Penrhyn as 'the autocrat of Bethesda'. The travails of the quarrying community, their heroism and solidarity in the face of Penrhyn's autocratic pretensions, made a powerful impact on the labour movement throughout the land. Here, as in the railway workshops and docks of south Wales was a harbinger of new social cleavage, as fundamental to the Wales of the twentieth century as was the Lib-Lab ethic of harmony to that of the nineteenth.

But, of course, it was the Welsh miners, a labour force now over 150,000 strong, who led the way. Economic and structural factors told steadily against the maintaining of the quasi-peace that endured in the coalfield until 1898. The inexorable growth of combination and of cartelization militated continuously against peaceful industrial relations. As it happened, an attempt to rationalize the wage and price system of the coal industry materially helped on this process. As has been seen, D. A. Thomas's plan for an agreed control of output by all the coalowners to avoid wasteful competition was frustrated by Sir William T. Lewis and his Coalowners' Association. Lewis's stipulation that 95 per cent of the coalowners should agree to Thomas's scheme before it was implemented doomed it from birth. The result was twofold. Competition between cost-conscious coalowners became all the more ruthless. And Thomas himself turned to build up the massive oligopoly of the Cambrian Combine, a new phase in the growth of combination amongst the Welsh coal-owners. Thomas, a benevolent employer and an advocate of industrial partnership with a strong social conscience, became the agent of a still more bitter period of industrial relations. For many years, there had been growing pressure against the strait-jacket of the Sliding Scale. The growing labour force; the geological difficulties of the mining industry with frequent faults in seams and often appalling pit explosions such as that which killed 250 miners in the Albion Colliery, Cilfynydd, in 1894; the high-cost, labour-intensive nature of the coal industry made conflict over wages almost inevitable. In September 1897, the miners' leaders gave six months' notice that the Sliding Scale agreement would be terminated. Instead, they demanded a 10 per cent wage increase and a basic minimum wage. In retaliation the coalowners, headed by Lewis, suspended negotiations in February. By March, 100,000 miners were out of work in a lock-out which lasted for six months.

The coal stoppage of 1898 was a powerful divide in the industrial, social,

[21] See J. Roose Williams, *Quarryman's Champion* (Denbigh, 1978).

and eventually political history of south Wales and of the nation generally. Truly, '1898 was the 1868 of the coalfield'.[22] From March to the end of September, valleys and villages were thrown on to their own resources, as wages were no longer paid. Soup kitchens and emergency feeding schemes were in operation; poverty was widespread. A national appeal was organized by the cocoa magnate, George Cadbury, via the *Daily News*. More significant as a testimony to the nationwide impact of the Welsh miners' dispute, Keir Hardie visited south Wales and wrote some powerful articles in the *Labour Leader* on conditions there. Several ILP branches sprang up in the valleys, and the ILP newspaper, *Llais Llafur* of Ystalyfera, circulated more widely. The miners' lock-out aroused intense passion at a time when British trade unionists generally were alarmed at the hardening attitudes of employers in the engineering and other trades towards trade unions, and the apparent introduction of the anti-union methods of the American trusts. It was noticeable that the south Wales Liberal MPs, eventually vocal on behalf of the Welsh-speaking quasi-rural quarrymen of Bethesda, were silent in the face of industrial strife in their own valleys. Here indeed was a portent of industrial warfare far more fundamental to their assumptions and their style of life.

The coal stoppage was a complete victory for the owners. The men had to return to work, dispirited, starving, with none of their objectives attained. The hated Sliding Scale was to remain until 1902. Poor Mabon had himself the humiliating task of informing his men of the abolition of the monthly holiday that bore his name. But the capitalists' victory was a pyrrhic one. The temper of industrial protest quickened throughout the entire coalfield. The old mood of harmony died away. The completeness of their defeat shook the Welsh miners into new class unity. The appeal of the Miners' Federation of Great Britain, previously sustained by only a few lonely pioneers such as William Brace, suddenly became compelling. On 11 October 1898, less than a month after the end of the coal dispute, the South Wales Miners' Federation—the old 'Fed' destined to last until the Second World War throughout industrial defeat and recovery—was founded. By the end of 1899, it claimed over 104,000 members. Mabon was its president, Brace its vice-president. It was clear that their Lib-Lab outlook was under fire from their rank and file in many areas, When in early 1899, the SWMF affiliated to the Miners' Federation of Great Britain, the Welsh emerged as its largest section numerically, as well as ideologically the most aggressive.

The old fabric of industrial peace was disappearing. In 1900 and 1901, the Federation led a series of 'stop days' on which the miners were ordered to stop work for a period of twenty-four hours. The purpose of this was partly to restrict output, partly to protest against recent reductions in basic wage rates under the Sliding Scale. In December 1902, the new strength of the Miners'

---

[22] Kenneth O. Morgan, *Wales in British Politics, 1868–1922* (Cardiff, new ed. 1980), p. 204.

Federation showed itself in a further challenge to the existing system of wage settlements. The Sliding Scale now disappeared for ever, and was replaced by a new system governed by a joint conciliation board, including maximum and minimum wage provisions based on a rate 30 per cent above that of the 1879 standard, and arbitration procedures for wage settlements. This new agreement also lapsed, amidst much acrimony, in 1905 and a further settlement was signed between the Federation and the coalowners on 3 December of that year. This was clearly no more than a truce. The Miners' Federation in south Wales, with membership now standing at over 120,000 and funds of £160,000 in reserve, was poised to join with its comrades in other British coalfields in a new, militant push towards a nationwide minimum wage.

But the pace of change in collective wage bargaining was less rapid than a wider ideological and political upheaval now wrenching the entire coalfield into new directions. It was most pronounced in the valleys of Monmouthshire and eastern Glamorgan, with their heavy influx of migrants from England, but the Rhondda was also becoming a pace-setter, as were some of the pits in the anthracite coalfield of west Wales. In the north-east, Wrexham and Rhos had their own branches of the ILP, while Edward Hughes was busily building up the Miners' Federation membership there, too.[23] There was a growing sense of change as Mabon's style of Lib-Labbery was undermined by doctrines of class war, and ideas of socialist transformation gained increasing hold. The growth of the ILP in south Wales in the period from 1898 to 1905 encouraged this movement, as did the spectacular victory of Keir Hardie in the general election of 1900 at Merthyr Tydfil. But it was industrial pressures that underlay the new upheaval. A powerful intellectual challenge and sense of ideological liberation were emerging to sever the ties with the old Lib-Lab outlook. Men like Mabon were on the run, as younger militants, usually Welsh like Vernon Hartshorn in Maesteg or Charles Stanton in Aberdare, urged the older groups of leaders to 'move on or move out'.[24] Ironically, this new challenge was given new force by movements deeply related to the fabric and traditions of south Wales. The branches of ILP, the tutorial classes of the Central Labour College after 1909, owed much to the village democracy and educational traditions of the Welsh Sunday school. Many young workers, native miners like Noah Ablett in Porth or James Griffiths in Ammanford, immigrants like Frank Hodges in the Garw valley and Arthur Cook in the Rhondda, were deeply stirred by the religious revival of 1904−6.[25] Inspired by the young Welsh evangelist, Evan Roberts, and radiating outwards from its place of origin at Loughor on the Carmarthenshire−Glamorgan

[23] R. K. Mathias, 'The Records of the National Union of Mineworkers in North Wales', *Annual Report* of Clwyd County Archivist, 1976 (Hawarden, 1977).

[24] *Merthyr Express*, 17 October 1909, reporting a speech by Stanton.

[25] Cf. Frank Hodges, *My Adventures as a Labour Leader* (London, 1925); 'A. J. Cook', in Joyce M. Bellamy and John Saville (eds), *Dictionary of Labour Biography*, vol. iii (London, 1976), p. 38.

boundary, it galvanized many militant young miners with a sense of a new social apocalypse, a belief in overwhelming, almost total change.

In addition, there was detectable an ethnic, perhaps generational, change as new English migrants into the coalfield brought in new attitudes and new values. From 1905 onwards, it was obvious that Mabon and his colleagues on the executive committee of the SWMF were under fire from aggressive young militants. Many pithead branches of the union were under the control of new and fiery miners' agents, whose authority was considerable, given the de-centralized nature of the SWMF. More and more prominence was being given, especially in the Rhondda and Aberdare valleys, for a new recognition of the views of the rank-and-file miner, and a change in the style of union leadership which was seen as merely bolstering up a corrupt, capitalist order. By the end of 1905, therefore, south Wales showed an entirely different industrial climate from that prevalent ten years earlier. It was already a cauldron for new doctrines of social and economic revolution, already in the militant vanguard of the working class in Britain generally. The new industrial economy would continue to progress but it would be against a background of social conflict that was to generate increasing momentum, in peace and then in war.

But the general overall verdict on the character of industrial Wales in the early years of the century must still be a positive one. By most tests, south Wales was a highly prosperous, expanding region. It was a pioneer for industrial and commercial progress without a rival in the United Kingdom. Indeed, the very growth of trade unionism and the new self-confidence of the miners and other industrial workers were in themselves testimony to the greater prosperity that afforded men the scope to question their economic and political environment. Erratic though the process might be, the Welsh coalfield showed an overall pattern of full employment and of rising wages. After a downturn of trade in 1907, the picture of industrial growth resumed. The indices of wages, the range of urban and cultural institutions in the valleys are a sign of economic advance, in marked contrast to the grey, intro-spective mood of depression that cast its shadow over south Wales in the inter-war years. The entrepôts of the mining industry, the ports of Cardiff, Newport, Barry, and Swansea also illustrated the prosperity that coal and other heavy industry had brought to south Wales and its people. The well-stocked shops of Cardiff and Swansea, the growing expenditure on drink, gambling, sport, and other forms of popular recreation, were evidence of the advance of an industrial population clawing its way successfully out of poverty. Towns such as Neath, Pontypridd, Llanelli, Pontypool also showed a steady growth in this period, both in terms of population and in terms of their civic life and public amenities. In the north-east, Wrexham with its coal-mining, tanning, brick-making and steel manufacture, also presented a scene of vitality and prosperity. At the cost of a barely hidden environmental decay and despite the insecure, febrile character of the coal industry's expansion in these golden years, the Welsh industrial base was a strong and growing one. The foundation for the political advance and cultural flowering of Wales in the early twentieth century was the new prosperity brought to it by industry and trade, in such marked contrast with the peasant poverty and insecurity of most of Ireland. Here alone was one vital factor to explain why Wales, unlike Ireland, seemed most unlikely to pursue the path of separatism and exclusion. In economic terms, within the framework of an imperial commercial and fiscal system, Wales at the dawn of a new century basked in its place in the sun.

In rural Wales, of course, the pattern and the priorities were very different. The prosperity of the industrial coalfield was achieved to some degree by siphoning off the male youth and some of the material resources of an already depressed and impoverished countryside. For many years after 1880, indeed, rural Wales—virtually the whole of the land north of the Brecon Beacons and west of the Vale of Clwyd—was more disastrously than ever cast into desperate poverty. Some of this was endemic in the basic character of agriculture in Wales. As has been shown, it was largely a land of small upland farms, tenanted by livestock or dairy farmers on largely unrewarding soil. The arable sector was extremely small: little wheat could be grown. Bryner Jones later wrote that the Welsh were by nature 'stockmen rather than ploughmen'. Only in a few areas did richer soil permit a more varied and profitable form of agriculture—the Vale of Clwyd in Denbighshire, the Vale of Aeron in Cardiganshire, southern Pembrokeshire, the Vale of Glamorgan south and east of Bridgend. Nearly 90 per cent of land in Wales was occupied by small-scale tenant farmers; most holdings amounted to less than fifty acres. Farm labourers were fewer per farm than in England and most were outdoor. With land hunger so prevalent, farmers commonly had to borrow up to a third of the purchase money or else take out mortgages on severe terms. While there were major landowners such as the Wynns of Wynnstay or the Cawdors of Golden Grove, the majority of Welsh estates ranged between 100 and 1,000 acres. There was, as there had been for decades, a low margin of profitability for landowners; agricultural technique was relatively backward; capital input was at a consistently low ratio. Most landowners and their agents seemed more concerned to maintain amicable relations with their tenants, most of whom had been settled on their farmsteads for generations, rather than strike out boldly for agricultural improvement or innovation. In fact, as has been seen, the landlords were increasingly unsuccessful in this endeavour as differences in religion, language, and political outlook between them and their tenants poisoned relations in rural society and added an ideological edge to very real financial problems. The legends of 1868 and of the political evictions that followed became the stock-in-trade of Welsh radicals such as Thomas Gee and coloured the minds of two generations to come. Lloyd George faithfully stoked up the flames of agrarian protest as he rose to political prominence. This endemic social warfare embittered still further a countryside caught up in impenetrable economic difficulties.

The agricultural depression of the eighties and early nineties made matters distinctly worse, though perhaps more so for landowners than for their tenants as rental returns fell steadily in Wales throughout this period. How crucial the agricultural depression really was for Welsh farmers is debatable. Its major impact came for the wheat-growing farmers of southern and eastern England, undermined by competition from the American mid-West, from Argentina and the Russian steppes. The livestock and dairy farmers of rural Wales were less directly affected: indeed, they may even have benefited as the cost of animal feeding stuffs fell throughout the period. The Welsh land market remained active throughout the eighties as land hunger kept up capital values.

Even so, it is evident that the blight of depression was felt in upland Wales also. The price of dairy and livestock products spiralled downwards. Store cattle fell 20 per cent in price between 1877−80 and 1894−7, fattened sheep and pigs by 18 per cent. Returns from the land fell in consequence. Wales recorded a drop in annual land values of 6.1 per cent between 1879 and 1894, according to Schedule A income tax assessment, without taking into account rent abatements by sympathetic landlords. Some tenants had to leave their holdings or were given notice to quit.[26] Many farm labourers were laid off and took refuge in the collieries of the south. Many marginal holdings in mountainous areas were returned permanently to grassland on grounds of economy. The population of eight counties fell in the decade 1881−91, with the impact most shattering in mid-Wales in Montgomeryshire and Radnorshire where farm labourers were drawn away to the industrial opportunities of south Wales or the English Midlands. The bustling Radnorshire countryside around Clyro of which the Revd Francis Kilvert had been the gentle chronicler became rapidly denuded of population. In Cardiganshire, population also fell sharply, with the additional problem, as has been noted, of the collapse of the lead industry in the Ystwyth and Rheidol valleys and a shattering fall in the population there. Places like Dylife and Yspytty Ystwyth became ghost villages, just like silver-mining communities in the Rocky Mountains. By the nineties rural Wales was, or seemed to be, caught up in inexorable economic difficulties. Its poverty and insecurity were in mocking contrast to the glossy prosperity of the neighbouring counties in the industrial south. And always there was the undercurrent of political tension. Young Liberal spokesmen like Tom Ellis were quick to blame what they claimed was a general pattern of exploitation and of exorbitant rents on the unsympathetic and ignorant attitudes of absentee Tory landlords and their sycophantic agents.

[26] David W. Howell, *Land and People in Nineteenth-Century Wales* (London, 1977), p. 56.

When the Liberals returned to office under Gladstone in July 1892, some kind of action to alleviate the grievances of rural Wales, and especially of the tenant farmer, was inevitable. After some dispute within the ranks of the Welsh MPs as to whether a select committee or the more public and elaborate form of a royal commission were appropriate, a royal commission was appointed, as was noted in the previous chapter. It began its inquiries in May 1893. Its nine members, under the chairmanship of Lord Carrington, included six who may be characterized as broadly Liberal, and three who were Unionist, headed by Lord Kenyon. The atmosphere of the commission was anything but dispassionate. It was from the start charged with the whiff of gunfire. The commission sat for two and a half years, calling 1,086 witnesses whom it examined in various parts of Wales. Of these, 516 were tenant farmers; significantly, a mere twenty-one were farm labourers.[27] Without doubt, then, the grievances of Liberal farmers were given the fullest airing. Indeed, the findings of the commission as a whole, partly because of the labours of its admirably zealous secretary, Daniel Lleufer Thomas, provided a marvellous conspectus of rural life in the period, from which historians may still derive enormous enlightenment.

Witness after witness on the Liberal side repeated the standard demands for a Welsh version of the 'three Fs' granted in Ireland in 1881 under Gladstone's Irish Land Act. There would be a land court to provide for the compulsory fixing of rents, security of tenure and compensation for improvements. Witnesses constantly laid emphasis on the social and cultural gulf between landlords and tenants; capricious and unfeeling agents were roundly condemned. By contrast, landlords and their agents denounced Liberal 'agitators' and claimed that estates were well managed and rents kept within moderate bounds. They pointed out the long, hereditary tenancies of most Welsh family farms, a tribute to the harmonious relations on the land over the decades. Instead of a land court to interfere with freedom of contract, there should be state assistance to depressed landlords through rural credits or rating reform. On the whole, landlords came out of their baptism of fire pretty well. Through such expert advisers as the barrister J. E. Vincent their case was effectively presented, not least in demolishing Liberal claims that rents had risen exorbitantly during the years of depression. It was shown clearly that there had frequently been abatements of rent of up to 20 per cent during the bad years. Many other Liberal allegations, notably a clutch advanced with more passion than accuracy by the aged Thomas Gee, were successfully exploded. The Report was published in 1896 when the Liberals had already fallen from power. It was a damp squib and no one seriously expected the demands for a land court, predictably put forward by the Liberal majority report, to be implemented. On the whole, the Land Commission had the salutary effect of clearing the air, and of reducing many of the charges made

[27] *Report of the Royal Commission on Welsh Land*, 1896 (C. 8242), p. 7.

about Welsh agrarian conditions to sober reality. The main theme that emerged was that the land question was basically social, not economic, the product of a growing cultural alienation between owners and occupiers. It merged almost naturally into an industrial conflict like the lock-out of the Penrhyn quarrymen, with the autocratic landlord of Penrhyn Castle involved in each case. If the economic circumstances on the Welsh land improved, then the social difficulties that accompanied them might be diminished.

In fact, after the issuing of the majority and minority reports of the Land Commission in 1896, the rural scene became less bleak. Partly, as has been noted, this was the result of the very appointment of the commission in the first place Its tales of oppression and exploitation by wicked landlords tended to recede into a very distant past, if indeed such allegations were not shown to be totally fictitious. The land question ceased to be a major source of controversy after 1897 when the Liberals brought up an abortive Land Tenure Bill. The main provision of this was to set up a Land Court under a judge appointed by the Board of Agriculture to fix fair rents and reasonable conditions of tenancy for five years. This bill, ironically, was introduced by M. Vaughan Davies, the Liberal member for Cardiganshire and the squire of Tan-y-bwlch, whose malpractices towards his own tenants had been censured by the land commissioners.[28] His bill was inevitably swamped by the Unionist majority in the Commons and no major debate again took place until after the Unionists themselves fell from office in December 1905.

It is clear, in fact, that a good deal of the agitation against 'landlordism' in the Welsh press lost its force in subsequent years. The volumes of the Welsh Land Commission remained on library shelves, unheeded and perhaps unread. By 1903 a leading Welsh Liberal, Llewelyn Williams, the son of a tenant farmer from Llansadwrn who had given evidence to the Land Commission in 1894, could argue against the basic concept of a land court.[29] Although a lawyer himself, Williams urged that it could turn Wales into 'a litigating Hades', while landowners could evade the terms of a court's findings by claiming bonuses to make up the difference between the judicially-enforceable rent and the real competitive rent as assessed in market terms. Williams's most cogent argument, though, was one that appealed with increasing force to Liberals after the turn of the century, committed as they were to a democratic society in which property would be more widely diffused. A land court, he claimed, would merely confirm the state of dependent tenancy. Welsh farmers, like medieval peasants, would become *adscripti glebae*—'once a tenant, always a tenant'. Farmers' spokesmen now looked with more enthusiasm on the peasant proprietorship already established in France or Scandinavia, or indeed on the farm-purchase provisions

<hr />

[28] *Parl. Deb.*, 4th ser., xlix, pp. 817 ff. (19 May 1897); Land Commission, *Report*, p. 307.
[29] Llewelyn Williams, 'The Needs of Wales: Land Law Reform', *Young Wales,* Jan.–March 1903.

of the Ashbourne and Wyndham Acts in Ireland between 1885 and 1903, under which occupiers in Ireland were given indirect assistance to purchase their holdings. They sought a similar happy outcome in Wales. A 'green revolution' which could by-pass the issue of landlordism, expand the small occupying freeholder class and end the degrading servility of dependent tenancy now became a pressing objective. This began to take place after 1910 with the gradual break-up of many estates in Merioneth and in Denbighshire. A totally new priority now engaged Welsh land reformers, though one achieved only in the aftermath of a world war.

The main reason, though, why the Welsh land question appeared less depressing and less urgent is that, to some degree, the countryside began to share in a little of the prosperity enjoyed by the industrial and urban communities of the south. Indeed, the industrial expansion had a direct impact on the Welsh country areas, as has been shown, since the continuing attraction of the mines and factories of south Wales for young farm labourers and some sons of tenant farmers, too, relieved the pressure of excess population upon the scanty resources of rural Wales. Conditions on the land, in any case, showed some improvement, as the worldwide agricultural depression began to lift and such radical farmers' revolts as the American Populist movement began to collapse. After 1900, the prices for dairy farmers started to rise, without reaching the heights of the early 1870s. With more money circulating in rural areas, landlords were able to invest more capital in modernization and improvement schemes, introducing such labour-saving machinery as hay-mowers, and importing seed varieties and artificial fertilizers to improve crop yields. Welsh agriculture became generally more capital-intensive, with fruitful results in such areas as the Vale of Glamorgan. Although still backward by comparison with many other parts of Britain, agriculture in Wales was by 1910 becoming increasingly profitable. Hill farmers, for instance, were turning successfully to the production of liquid milk; those in north Wales found ready markets in the coastal resorts such as Llandudno and Rhyl, and in Liverpool. The population of Welsh rural areas was more concerned with the productive efficiency of agriculture as an integrated economic unit than with the divisive effects of class conflict.

Despite the agricultural depression, therefore, rural Wales showed signs of social and economic advance in the first decade of the century. Its upland farms were less precarious in their finances. County towns, especially marketing centres like Cowbridge, Carmarthen, Lampeter, Brecon, Welshpool, and Denbigh, were more thriving. Their shops, banks, and chapels seemed better endowed, their civic buildings in better repair. The census returns reflected this growing confidence. The fall in the population of rural Wales in the 1881—91 period was arrested; the population employed on the land actually rose in the decade 1901—11, the only increase recorded between 1851 and the later twentieth century. New sources of income such as that from the growing tide of tourism to coastal resorts also pumped in new wealth to Welsh rural areas. They themselves were beginning to share in the social and cultural amenities of the towns of the south. Of course, many of these amenities were brought that much nearer by the growth of railways before 1914, and by the advent of the motor car afterwards.

In general, life in the Welsh countryside seems less isolated and culturally deprived than that in France for the same period as depicted by Professor Eugen Weber. In Wales the peasants had already been turned into Welshmen. In particular, there was the extraordinary impact on rural society of the 'county schools' founded in the years after 1889, which flourished especially in the rural counties. In counties like Caernarvonshire, Anglesey, Merioneth, and Cardiganshire, opportunities for mobility and improvement for the sons—and, to a growing extent, the daughters—of farmers and small shopkeepers in the country areas of Wales were immense. An increasing number of them could proceed to higher education institutions like Bangor Normal College, for prospective school teachers, or to Aberystwyth or to other colleges of the expanding and maturing University of Wales. For their elders, there were the fruits of progress to be enjoyed also. The world of magistrates' benches and county councils beckoned with increased beguilement. The economic attacks on the landowner may have been too often inaccurate and misconceived. But the social gulf in opportunity and in status which underlay Wales's peaceful land war had been real enough. With democratically-elected county and parish councils, staffed largely by nonconformist sons of the country areas, replacing the justices of the peace in every county in the land, the gentry were in manifest retreat. The hierarchies and class distinctions of rural Wales were gradually being levelled out. Not only was rural Wales somewhat more prosperous by 1910 than it had been in 1880: its prosperity was now increasingly underpinned by the state, with assistance from the central government to the young through aid to the secondary schools and to the old by pensions and insurance. The countryside was, in general, more self-confident, less defensive and parochial, more aware that it, too, had its share in the Welsh boom that marked the economic developments of these years.

This revival of the rural communities, even if only partial, was important for the future of the national movement at the turn of the century. It meant that the rural areas could supply some of the reality, as well as the myths, of the new Wales, and could play a self-respecting and expanding part within it. The Welsh country areas were much more involved in the political and cultural renaissance of the new century than was the rural community of other European nations. They never resembled the *mezzogiorno* of southern Italy. They never served just as a colonized area of primary production supplying cheap food and cheap labour for the metropolitan market. Rural Wales, and its little towns, kept many of the national institutions, notably the chapels, in full and vigorous life. At the same time, the traditions of the countryside persisted to colour the values of the new Wales that were emerging. The ideal of *y werin* that underlay the rhetoric of so many Welsh Liberals in this period was a profoundly rural concept, an idealization of peasant democracy and country craftsmen, a celebration of the timeless traditions and rhythms of the countryside. Men like Owen M. Edwards, appointed chief inspector of schools in Wales in 1907, gave this new currency in shaping the outlook of a new generation of schoolchildren. The very ideal of *Cymru Fydd* was of a small-scale, familiar, rural world, in contrast to the twentieth century, with its mass structures, its impersonality and its centralization. Legend had much to do with building up this ideal. So too did the strength of indigenous rural institutions such as the chapels, where pulpit oratory so often identified the simple values of the Old Testament with realities of the Welsh countryside. Preachers and poets (or perhaps preacher-poets such as Elfed) sang the virtues of the rural existence, and of closeness to nature and the sustaining force of mother earth.

But the triumph of the ideal of *y werin* could not rest solely on legend and imagination. The partial economic recovery of the country areas had some- thing to do with it, too. There was also the restoration of rural dignity. The insecure, barren countryside, of which Thomas Gee had been the embattled champion each week in *Baner ac Amserau Cymru* was becoming something of a legend in its turn. When Thomas Gee died in 1898, something of the old vision of rural poverty and conflict passed away with him. There was to be no Thomas Gee in the twentieth century, while the growth of such occasional movements as the agricultural labourers' movement under 'ap Ffarmwr' in the nineties showed that rural Wales contained more class divisions than the philosophy of an older generation of radical publicists had ever conceived. This, indeed, was what 'Brutus' the Anglican satirist, David Owen, had argued long ago. The rural revival in Wales should certainly not be exagger- ated, but it was a part of the economic and cultural progress of the new century, just as was the more obvious expansion of heavy industry and manufacturing in the coalfield.

For all its major pockets of poverty, therefore, especially in the rural areas, Wales on the whole manifested many of the signs of a boom region throughout this period. Many of the difficulties inherited from the past were being over- come. The extremes of insecurity in the countryside were passing away. Older pockets of obsolescent industry in the steel and tinplate industries were being superseded though the slate industry of the north-west remained as pre- carious as before. New classes were being thrown up, a new bourgeois élite in the towns, a new cadre of managers, agents, shippers, and brokers in the ports of the south, to provide leadership for a new society. Most of the Welsh industries were almost unbelievably successful. The advance of the coal industry seemed relentless and inexhaustible. The Rhondda alone showed an almost unshakeable capacity to expand. To the west, the full potential of the anthracite industry was far from wholly tapped: Professor Jevons even urged that south Wales could acquire a near-monopoly of world trade. The docks and port facilities of Swansea, Barry, Cardiff, and Newport were throbbing with activity. The west Wales tinplate industry was showing the capacity to fight out of recession, to adapt to new market conditions and to find new outlets overseas. The steel industry was also expanding, with the new monolith of Guest, Keen as its symbol. In the countryside, wealth and to some degree population were being maintained. In later generations, there were those who could see the signs of future division in the evolution of the Welsh economy at this period. The gulf between the dynamic industrial world of the coalfield and the static order of the countryside, and between both and the Anglo-Welsh mercantile complex of Cardiff and south-east Wales were seen as future sources of discord that would separate Welshman from Welshman, interpose economic values in place of cultural, and fatally confuse the response of the Welsh people in the assessment of their relationship with their English neighbours. Every major Welsh political movement in the past hundred years, from *Cymru Fydd* in the 1890s down to Plaid Cymru in the 1970s found difficulty in reconciling its industrial and rural wings. Invariably, the Welsh language has appeared to be the main source of division and of the gulf between divergent societies.

But in the perspective of the Wales of the early 1900s, it was the opportunities not the dangers presented by industrial growth that presented themselves most forcibly. A man like Owen Edwards, himself a product of the remotest *cefn gwlad* of rural Merioneth, rejoiced in the new industry and technology of the south, and hoped that the craft traditions and skills of the people would be adapted to this new technical order instead of being frozen in the modes of the past century.[30] Edwards urged that the schools of Wales pay more heed to industrial, technical, and commercial instruction. It would be a mistake to soak the minds of schoolchildren solely in literary or theological subjects, and in traditions of bookish learning on the model of English grammar schools that were at variance with the inclinations of the native genius. The growing national self-confidence of Wales at this time was rooted in prosperity and in economic change. Paradoxically, the very gulf between capital and labour looming up in the coalfield was testimony to the growing vitality of industrial Wales with mass trade unions confronting oligopolistic employers, William Brace confronting D. A. Thomas, each of them convinced of his Welshness and his certainty in defending Welsh values. The strength of a militant South Wales Miners' Federation in the wider world of British trade unionism was paralleled by the confidence and aggressiveness

[30] J. R. Webster, 'Welsh Secondary Education and Society, 1800-1918' (unpublished University of Wales Ph.D. thesis, 1959), pp. 530-3.

of coalowners, shippers, and manufacturers in south Wales towards the wider world of British capitalism. Each was testimony to the affluence of Wales. With the political order in rapid transformation and the economic base apparently so secure, the material conditions were present for a new and more dynamic definition of Welsh values and national consciousness. Thus it was that political democracy and economic progress led on inexorably to a wider cultural renaissance, with each feeding on the other. They lent a new glow to the fires of nationality, and it is to this that we must now turn.

CHAPTER 4

THE NATIONAL REVIVAL

A sense of nationality is as old as the Welsh themselves. There were echoes of it even in the writings of Gildas before the time of Bede. The differences between themselves and the English who had conquered them was a constant theme in Welsh poetry and prose throughout the Middle Ages. Giraldus Cambrensis gave it forceful expression in resisting attempts in the twelfth century to impose Anglo-Norman centralization upon the native Welsh Church. The same theme was voiced again during the Owain Glyn Dŵr rebellion in the early fifteenth century. In subsequent centuries, it remained vigorously alive, materially helped by the advance of literacy. The translation of the Bible and other devotional literature into Welsh; the rise of indigenous forms of religious observance through the growth of Welsh-language non-conformity; the work of antiquarians and scholars in the eighteenth century such as the Morrisian circle in Anglesey; even the bardic fantasies of Iolo Morganwg conceived in the Vale of Glamorgan during the period of the French revolution wars—all these helped to keep alive a sense of Welshness and of the validity of the native culture.

This sense of a national identity gained new momentum in the early and middle decades of the nineteenth century. The expansion of industry and the growth of new towns, the internal colonization of the industrialized areas of their own land by Welsh-speaking migrants gave new urban and institutional direction to the native culture. It was the industrial towns of south Wales, and the expanding smaller towns of the rural north and west—Merthyr, Ponty-pridd, and Swansea; Caernarfon, Aberystwyth, and Carmarthen—that provided the main agencies by which Welsh national consciousness was to flourish. It was here in the towns that the chapels, the newspapers, the *eisteddfodau*, and the choral festivals helped to give the awareness of being Welsh a new depth during the industrial era. Side by side with the growth of industry came the equally explosive growth of religious nonconformity, through the Methodists, Independents, and Baptists above all. This gave further impetus to popular involvement in Welsh cultural and religious experience. By the early 1880s, a sense of Welsh nationality and of national distinctiveness within the wider framework of the United Kingdom was present as never before. It was not merely the academic concern of remote scholars and antiquarians. It was a living element in the daily experience of the

Welsh people.

But this national emotion remained vague and unfocused. It could hardly be claimed that the Welsh, until the last quarter of the nineteenth century, possessed anything that resembled an articulated or coherent view of nationalism. The contrast with the history of Ireland at the same time was stark indeed. Attempts to give Welsh culture in the early nineteenth century a more self-consciously national quality had been the work of small literary coteries. They were usually drawn from the Anglican gentry, people such as the eccentric and venerable Lady Llanover and other patrons of a revived folk culture and folk dress, or else through 'literary clergy' or 'clerical patriots' like Walter Davies (*Gwallter Mechain*). If the nineteenth century in Europe was an era of nationalism, this was slow to manifest itself in Wales. Certainly, the writings of the nationalist prophets Giuseppe Mazzini of Young Italy and Thomas Davis of Young Ireland made some impact in Wales, notably amongst young patriots such as Tom Ellis while he was a student at Aberystwyth college in the late seventies and early eighties. The idea of Young Wales was a self-conscious attempt to provide an echo of these foreign movements. The national revolt of Kossuth in Hungary in 1848 aroused much sympathy in Wales, and Kossuth later addressed a demonstration there.[1] William Rees in *Yr Amserau* hailed Kossuth as the harbinger of a new era of national liberation. The Anglican judge, Arthur Johnes, launched a public appeal on behalf of Hungarian, Polish, and Italian refugees. More, he drew indirect parallels between the national predicament of the Hungarians and of the Welsh. But in general it was clearly the radicalism rather than the nationalism of Mazzini and Kossuth that appealed to Welsh Liberals. It merely reinforced their sense of possessing a dual identity, British as much as Welsh. By 1853 the excitement of the Kossuth agitation had spent itself. Few indeed in Wales saw their nation as one oppressed or rightly struggling to be free. On the contrary, the benefits of association with the wealth and authority of England and the empire seemed overwhelming. It was in part a response to this lack of nationalist ferment within his own land that impelled the Revd Michael Daniel Jones in 1865 to embark on his romantic exploit of founding a Welsh-speaking community in the Chubut valley in the wastes of Patagonia in the southern Argentine, as far away as possible from the contamination of England's imperialistic impact. Michael Daniel Jones was one of the very few who took the nationalist example of Kossuth literally. For almost all the rest of his countrymen, nationalism was an exotic plant, a creed for export only.

The Welsh until the eighties in fact betrayed all the symptoms of what Marx called unhistoric nationalism. They were akin to the forgotten ethnic sub-cultures of central or south-eastern Europe, the Ruthenes or the Croats for

[1] See Marion Henry Jones, 'Wales and Hungary', *Trans. Hon. Soc. Cymmrodorion*, 1968, part I, esp. pp. 11–23.

instance, rather than the English or the French. They possessed many attributes of national identity. They had undeniably their own language, spoken by a clear majority of the population at a time when Gaelic in Scotland and Erse in Ireland were manifestly in retreat and spoken only by remote crofting or peasant communities on the coastal fringes of the Hebrides or Galway. The Welsh, too, had an overall ethnic homogeneity, and a continuous history as a distinct race, inhabiting a separate geographical area of the British Isles, for over thirteen hundred years, ever since they were cut off from their fellow-Brythons in Cornwall and Cumbria in the sixth century. Even in the late nineteenth century, the Celt and Saxon were easily distinguished, though not in the ways that Matthew Arnold imagined. The Welsh retained their own legends, their own folk memories and songs, a sense of shared experience and suffering over the centuries, with myths in abundance from Arthurian days down to the cultural renaissance of the eighteenth century. After 1856, thanks to Evan James, a weaver from Pontypridd, the Welsh even possessed the dignity of their own national anthem. But the land of their fathers still lacked for most Welsh men and women the essential attributes to turn a static sense of national consciousness into a more dynamic sentiment of nationalism.

Politically, the principality had never possessed a unity of its own. The fragmentation of the various princedoms in the Middle Ages, prior to conquest by Edward I in 1282 contrasted sharply with the political unity of the Kingdom of Scotland until union with England in 1707. Wales had in any case been merged into the central and local governmental structure of England since the reign of Henry VIII and was constitutionally indistinguishable from the various regions of England. The fragmentation of Wales had continued into the industrial age. The spread of railways, and later of roads, linked the various parts of Wales up with the markets of England rather than with each other. It was almost as difficult to travel directly from the Menai Straits to the Bristol Channel as it had been six centuries earlier. The growth of industry highlighted still further the economic and social contrasts between the industrial complex of the coalfield of Glamorgan and Monmouth, and the sparsely-peopled hinterland of north and central Wales. There was no focus for national life. Gatherings of Welshmen concerned with trade, education, or politics tended to meet in England—in Shrewsbury or elsewhere in the marches, or, most conveniently in London, far more emphatically the capital of Wales until the 1880s than was any local town. Administratively, too, Wales possessed no specific institutions of its own. The last of them, the Courts of Great Sessions had been abolished in 1830. The Welsh fabric of local government, of education, of law and justice was coterminous with that of England. Welsh lawyers and schoolteachers made their way in English legal circuits and grammar schools. There was nothing that resembled the proud national distinctiveness of the educational and legal system in Scotland or the establishment of the presbyterian Kirk of Scotland.

Above all, Wales had failed to evolve the kind of social leadership that had generated national emotion elsewhere. The Welsh gentry, unlike the Scottish, were more and more divorced from the aspirations of the bulk of the people. The gentry might have Welsh names. They might trace their ancestry back, as could Lord Penrhyn, to the age of the princes hundreds of years earlier. They might claim, amongst the Tudor and Jacobean gentry, names such as Sir John Wynn of Gwydir who had pioneered Welsh cultural consciousness and patronized the arts and antiquities of their native land. By the later nineteenth century, the Welsh gentry were thoroughly anglicized, Anglican in religion, English in speech and usually in educational background (if any), totally removed from the democratic and national aspirations of the vast mass of the Welsh people in rural and urban areas alike. There was no parallel with the Scottish aristocracy, those flowers of the forest, Sutherlands, Argylls, and the like, which traced a proud native tradition back beyond the Jacobites to earlier centuries of proud independence from England. There was certainly no Welsh Walter Scott to endow Welsh history with the same veneer of aristocratic legend and honour. If Welsh national consciousness had to find a voice, it must certainly discover it at different levels in the social hierarchy.

Nor had Wales evolved the kind of self-conscious, educated, sophisticated middle class that had enabled Scottish self-awareness to flower anew in the ages of the enlightenment. There was no parallel to the glories of Hume, Robertson, and Adam Smith, to the men of letters and the literary periodicals of Georgian Edinburgh and the Scottish age of reason. After all, until the mid-nineteenth century there were no Welsh towns. Merthyr Tydfil, the largest until the 1860s, was still a rough, raw frontier settlement, consisting largely of uneducated colliers and ironworkers. Cardiff until the sixties was no more than a large village, with the parochial atmosphere of one, rather than a city with the international consciousness of Edinburgh, Glasgow, or Aberdeen. Aberystwyth college was hardly a Welsh St. Andrews. There was no indigenous Welsh middle class, no university, no literate or educated élite of civilizing intellectuals, the very engine of national consciousness in other countries. Welsh culture was in a remarkably healthy condition, but it still bore the hallmarks of a peasant culture, unsophisticated in expression, unconnected with any philosophy of nationhood. When Arnold, Gladstone, and other well-wishers extolled the distinctive literature and traditions of Wales from 1870 onwards, when Gladstone paid such gestures as appointing Welsh-speaking bishops to the see of St. Asaph in 1870 and to Llandaff in 1882, they were still viewing Wales as an attractive antique survival whose cultural distinctiveness would eventually disappear with the march of imperial progress and educational advance. Wales even to them, and surely to the vast bulk of the English, was in essence a somewhat more exotic outlying region of Britain rather than another nation, another Yorkshire or Norfolk rather than a Scotland, let alone an Ireland.

The vast majority of Welshmen, pathetically enough, appeared to share this view. This was partly the result of centuries of government by England, partly of the sense of inferiority of any poor, remote territory cut off from the major social, economic, and cultural developments that transformed Britain in the industrial and imperial age. Even the growing impetus of religious and political change in the mid-sixties failed to produce any coherent sense of Welsh nationhood. Nor were there any local theorists of nationality to provide one, either in the *Volksgeist* version or any other. The radical spokesmen of the *werin*, William Rees, S.R. of Llanbrynmair, Thomas Gee, and the like were basically Manchester-School little Englanders of a standard mid-Victorian type. Even for them, the prevailing attitude, mirrored faithfully in reference books and encyclopaedias, was still 'for Wales—see England'.

From the early 1880s, all this began to change. Dramatic transformations swept through the land which added up to a kind of national renaissance. The very sense of national identity acquired a new, robust vitality, the consequences of which still reverberated in Wales nearly a hundred years later. In retrospect, it may seem to have been almost inevitable that Wales should share in the national currents of the time. That sense of consciousness and of historic identity which fired so many European peoples in the later nineteenth century, from Finland to Serbia, which inspired patriotic poetry and saga, which coloured the music of Liszt, Dvořák, Smetana, and later Sibelius, inevitably seeped through, even to geographically and culturally isolated Wales. Further, the very proximity of Wales to England, itself apparently the major obstacle to Welsh self-assertiveness, helped on some of the processes of national renewal as it did in Ireland. The progress of political liberation and of franchise reform, especially after 1884, gave a new edge to the Welsh sense of enforced inequality within the framework of the United Kingdom. It gave hostility to the establishment of the Church of England a nationalist as well as a purely religious or liberationist aspect. Economic expansion provided the coalfield, and indirectly other parts of the principality, with a new prosperous mercantile and professional class such as it had previously lacked, new wealth to invest, a thriving industrial population to participate in the cultural opportunities of economic growth. It would be improbable, given the vigour of native Welsh culture, if these wider transformations did not have a profound impact upon Welshmen's consciousness of themselves, of their dignity and identity, and their sense of separateness from their Anglo-Saxon neighbours. It might be a much more peaceful process than in Ireland. For all the poverty and insecurity in the Welsh countryside, there was not the same sense of class exploitation which fuelled the Irish land campaigns. There was, sociologically and organically, less sense of exclusion from the English system. But a peaceful revolution is no less valid than a violent one, and the Welsh renaissance of the late nineteenth and early twentieth century had revolutionary potential enough. In the anxious debates over Welsh and Scottish devolution in the later 1970s, the transformation of late-Victorian Wales was still casting its long shadow.

In many ways, the new renaissance expressed itself at the most popular grass-roots level. The Welsh language in some ways proved more vigorous than ever in the years after 1880. In crude numerical terms, the language may not have been as secure as local patriots imagined. The census of population in 1891 was the first to provide data on the Welsh language. Its findings (which may have underestimated the total, admittedly) showed that only 54.4 per cent of the adult population of Wales and Monmouthshire (898,000 in all) spoke their native language. The censuses of 1901 and 1911 were to show a proportion falling below 50 per cent even if the absolute total of the Welsh-speaking or bilingual population continued to grow until the First World War. Already, in the industrial, urban complex of Glamorgan and Monmouth especially, the social conformity, the immigrant working population, the centralizing pressures of modern industrial technology were having a marked effect on the speaking of Welsh, even in places as distinctively Welsh as the Rhondda or Ogmore valleys. Here and elsewhere, English alone was the language of business, commerce, and administration. For all that, the Welsh language was in most ways in buoyant condition at this time. Writing and publishing in Welsh flourished as never before. The Land Commissioners recorded the enormous variety of weekly, monthly and quarterly publications in Welsh, together with nationally-conscious English-language journals such as *Cymru Fydd* (published in 1888–91) and *Young Wales*, which appeared between 1895 and 1903. Welsh-speaking Wales was a more literate, intellectually lively, and sophisticated land than ever before. Further, the language had new status and protection. In 1885 a group of cultural patriots, headed by the omnipresent Beriah Gwynfe Evans, founded a Society for the Utilization of the Welsh Language. Its objectives were distinctly less ambitious than those of the Welsh Language Society of the 1960s. It sought to promote the use of the composition, grammar, and translation of Welsh in schools and its adoption as a recognized school subject, in elementary schools in the first instance, accepted under the Board of Education code and eligible for financial assistance.[2] Leading members of the Society included Archdeacon Griffiths of Neath, Principal Viriamu Jones of Cardiff, Thomas Gee, Dr Isambard Owen, and T. Marchant Williams, representing most parties and denominations. Membership soon rose to nearly a thousand. As a result Welsh became not only more prestigious but also more academically and culturally secure, especially when it came to be widely taught in the new 'county' schools as well.

[2] *Baner ac Amserau Cymru*, 13 January 1886; Beriah Gwynfe Evans, 'The Welsh Language in Education', *Welsh Review* (March 1892), pp. 507–13.

This increased standing for the Welsh language was, as always, closely linked with the progress of the nonconformist chapels which were much linked with this popular renaissance of the native culture. In some ways, these were less encouraging years for the four main nonconformist bodies. They became aware of a diminishing impact, especially in the industrial coalfield where younger men and women in particular preferred the new wealth and leisure opportunities of increasing affluence to a stern Sabbatarianism, or in some cases the secular faith of socialism to the puritanism and fundamentalism offered by chapel pulpits. The major denominations also faced severe structural difficulties, with over-expansion in rural areas with populations that were falling or else in decaying centres of industrial towns leaving problems of unused plant and spare capacity—and also of growing indebtedness. By 1908 chapel debts had soared to £668,429 and it was much harder than in the past to interpret this as a sign of ambition and vitality. Membership was no longer rising so fast—indeed, in 1900 the Baptists, Independents, and Wesleyans had actually to report an actual drop in membership compared with 1899.

Nevertheless, these sources of long-term difficulty did not undermine the new life that the chapels gained from the new cultural vitality associated with the Welsh language. More than any other institution in Wales, the chapels were popular focuses for social and cultural activity in the Welsh tongue. Of the 434,000 members of the four major denominations in 1900, well over 300,000 attended Welsh-language chapels. For the Calvinist Methodists, strong in north and west Wales, the proportion was higher still. Ministers and lay preachers were deeply involved with the new surge of cultural vigour and the national consciousness that followed from it. A new nationally-minded quarterly like the *Geninen* founded in 1883, was strongly nonconformist in outlook, tone, and editorial policy. Preacher-poets of high literary talent like Silyn Roberts, Elfed Lewis, or Puleston Jones, added to the association between chapel life and the advance of the native culture. By 1904, too, there were signs that the ministers were preaching to enlarged congregations once again. After a decade of some struggle, the revivalist movement associated with Evan Roberts provided a massive, if temporary, impulse to the membership of the big four denominations. Chapel membership of these four rose from 463,000 in 1903 to 549,000 at the end of 1905, according to the chapels' own figures, with a swelling penumbra of 'adherents' also claimed by them. In the coalfield especially, evangelistic, messianic Protestant revivalism had immense impact, particularly in offering young miners and steelworkers a new spiritual and social vision in contrast with the harshness of the realities of industrial life. The temperance movement won thousands of new recruits. For a moment, the nature of the Welsh as 'a nation of nonconformists', in Gladstone's words of 1891, was amply confirmed. In their turn, the chapels responded to a growing sense of nationhood and national pride.

Associated with the popular press and the chapels was the new status of the national *eisteddfod*. Since its reorganization in 1880–1, this annual festival of the arts had gone from strength to strength, as was shown by the recognition provided, for instance, by Gladstone when attending the Wrexham *eisteddfod* in 1888. More than any other institution, the *eisteddfod*, now meeting alternatively in north and south Wales, provided a powerful stimulus for the literature and the cultural identity of Wales. In part, this was the result of a new professionalism in the direction of this essentially amateur festival, as the role of men like (Sir) Vincent Evans, secretary of the Eisteddfod Association and editor of its publications since 1881, illustrated. The authority of arch-druids like 'Clwydfardd' (David Griffiths) and 'Hwfa Mon' (Rowland Williams, an ex-carpenter and Independent minister) was considerable, not least in giving status to the traditional strict-metre poetry. The choral competitions, in particular, provided a great encouragement to local pride in one's village or valley, not least with their elements of north–south rivalry. The culminating Blue Ribbon contest between male-voice choirs at the end of the *eisteddfod* week became major celebrations of Welshness, expressed in passionate song with massive emphasis. Many conductors became celeb-rities, such as Harry Evans of Dowlais, conductor of the Merthyr Tydfil male-voice choir and later of the Liverpool Welsh choral union.

Above all, the *eisteddfod* gloried in its literary activities, especially the strict-metre verse contests for crown or chair each year. There is some evidence that, in strictly literary or aesthetic terms, the standards of *pryddest* and *awdl* were somewhat pedestrian despite the fame of such *eisteddfod* winners as 'Pedrog' (the Independent minister, the Revd John Owen Williams). In *Cymru*, John Morris-Jones offered caustic comment on the poor quality of the language and of the style of verse displayed at the national *eisteddfod*. There was criticism, too, of the bogus, folksy pageantry that sur-rounded its ceremonial, and of 'Hwfa Mon' for retaining his faith in the authenticity of the bardic past in the face of all scholarly evidence to the contrary.[3] This ceremonial owed its origin largely to Iolo Morganwg's liter-ary forgeries a hundred years earlier: some observers saw it as detracting from the dignity and artistic validity of the festival. Yet here, too, was a nationwide institution which could only benefit from the growing national cultural aware-ness and add to it. In 1902 a celebrated ode, 'Ymadawiad Arthur' (the passing of Arthur), won the chair at the Bangor festival. It was the work (written under the pseudonym of 'Tir-na-n'Og') of Thomas Gwynn Jones, a self-taught journalist on *Y Faner* in Denbigh and, politically, a strong partisan of the Independent Labour Party. His favourite journalist was Robert Blatch-ford of the *Clarion*. Although he was previous little known as a poet, Gwynn

[3] John Morris-Jones, *Cymru* (1896) and introduction to G. J. Williams, *Iolo Morganwg a Chywyddau'r Ychwanegiad* (Cardiff, 1926).

Jones's *awdl* has generally been viewed as marking a new departure in the literary standards of the *eisteddfod*—apparently to the surprise of its author.[4] It won the warm commendation of Morris-Jones, the main adjudicator, for its beauty of style and economy of phrase. Gwynn Jones's importance for Welsh literature can hardly be overstated. A historian may also note the powerful current of nostalgic nationalism that suffuses Jones's writing of the death of Arthur, so typical of the time, and so potent a stimulus to cultural experiment. Under the impetus of Gwynn Jones's achievement, the *eisteddfod* underwent a marked revival, with the emergence of distinguished younger poets like Silyn Roberts and W. J. Gruffydd in winning its major competitions. It became again of cultural as well as of social importance. It became central to an important new departure, a rich flowering of romantic, lyric poetry which gave Welsh literature a rare quality in the early years of the century. Clearly, through the new vitality and artisitic quality of the *eisteddfod,* the cultural nationalism had solidity and depth, as well as transient emotion. The sense of national pride welled up all the more strongly.

The chapel and the *eisteddfodau* operated to a large extent at a popular level. They were folk gatherings in which literary and artistic standards were often seen as incidental. But, at a more profound level too, the cultural life of the nation, its language and literature were making impressive advances. More than almost anywhere else in Europe, Wales was undergoing a massive revival in its cultural expression. In part, this resulted from the new inherent strength, in purely structural and technical terms, of the language itself. This was the work in large measure of one remarkable pioneer, John Morris-Jones. He was an Anglesey man, born in 1864, a product of Friars' School, Bangor and then of Jesus College, Oxford. He was appointed lecturer in Welsh at the University College of North Wales, Bangor, although at first his was purely a research appointment since he had no pupils to teach. His impact on the cultural maturing of Wales was considerable. His concern was always with purity of language, correctness of grammar, and dignity of style. He was alarmed that Welsh literature bore the hallmarks, the weaknesses as well as the strengths, of a peasant culture. The novels even of Daniel Owen were full of linguistic crudities and errors, though some felt that they added substantially to the charm of the works. In 1893, Morris-Jones produced a powerful scholarly work *Welsh Orthography*, which was to go far to strengthen and purify the language by making its spelling uniform and its linguistic forms consistent. His major interest was always in the linguistic components of the culture, and in his years at Bangor he worked devotedly at the refinement of the language. His major work, *Welsh Grammar: Phonology and Accidence* (1913) was a highly technical and erudite piece of scholarship, which provided detailed comparison of the relationship of grammar in Welsh to that of other European languages. Its very complexity caused some popular

[4] David Jenkins, *Thomas Gwynn Jones* (Denbigh, 1973), pp. 126–32.

bewilderment and even disappointment. The present writer's great-grandfather is said to have remarked, 'Good Lord—algebra', when first confronted with a book from which so much had been hoped. Certainly, Morris-Jones had less concern with the everyday vernacular of his own time. But, austerely academic though it might be, his work on grammar had a wider impact in providing the language with a new prestige, by analysing its phonology and morphological process in detail and with much clarity, and with constant respect for the traditional 'classical' standards of the poetry of an earlier age. Indirectly, he helped the language acquire much of the robustness necessary to adapt it to the requirements of twentieth-century creative literature. He also stimulated later works of comparative and historical analysis, and of phonological and etymological study. His work, wrote W. J. Gruffydd, provided Welsh with a 'body',[5] with that skeletal framework of technique without which Welsh literature might have followed Basque, Provençal, and Breton into mere *patois*.

Morris-Jones had his more purely literary interests, too. Although basically a linguist, he could turn his pen to poetry with powerful effect, when he chose. His *awdl*, 'Cymru Fu, Cymru Fydd', written for the 1892 *eisteddfod* was a remarkable evocation of the springs of national identity. Not for nothing was he a staunch nonconformist Liberal, closely identified with the new national emphasis in Welsh higher education. His 'Salm i Famon' (Hymn to Mammon) in 1894 was a slashing satire of the philistinism and commecialism which, in his view, was debasing the quality of much of Welsh life (notably in the south, no doubt). His main contribution to Welsh literary culture, however, lay through the *eisteddfod*, whose druidic rites he mercilessly criticized. Beginning with the Llandudno *eisteddfod* in 1896, his adjudications of the poems entered for the prize competitions were major landmarks in literary criticism, and a powerful stimulus to the *pryddestau* of the new romantic poets of the younger generation. To up-and-coming young poets like Thomas Parry-Williams, Morris-Jones was a transcendent figure before 1914. At the *eisteddfod*, Morris-Jones proved himself to be not merely a remote scholarly *érudit* but an accessible people's professor, anxious to communicate new and higher literary standards to the writers of Wales and, through them, to diffuse an improved grasp of aesthetic and cultural standards throughout the whole of society. Through men like him were forged links between the academics of the universities of Wales and Oxford, and the new popular renaissance of *y werin*. Morris-Jones was a great educator and a great communicator. The renewed vitality of Welsh life, cultural and social, in the new century, in the face of the centralizing pressures of an anglicizing or americanizing world owes much to his mighty efforts.

Morris-Jones's career, incidentally, illustrates a different element that was important in the life of Wales at the time. Until 1893 there was no national

[5] *Wales* (December 1912), p. 648.

university and necessarily there was difficulty in creating the kind of intellectual élite which could provide a spur to cultural renewal and national pride. To some extent, the University of Oxford filled the gap. The links between Wales and Jesus College, Oxford, had always been close. Attempts by principal H. D. Harper of Jesus to diminish the Welshness of the college by emasculating the Meyricke awards had been frustrated, after much national protest, in the early eighties. Now the Welshness of Oxford received powerful new impetus. There was a distinguished Welshman *in situ* there in the person of John Rhŷs, appointed Professor of Celtic Literature at Oxford in 1877 and later bursar and principal of Jesus College, a kind of Welsh revenge on the wretched Harper. Rhŷs's work was highly specialized and lacking totally in popular appeal. He was a philologist and ethnologist *par excellence*. His major work was on Welsh folklore and aroused little general interest; it has not always survived academic criticism in later years. Indeed, Rhŷs himself frequently changed his mind and often set up some new theory only to demolish it with a later one. Still, he was an outstanding pioneer in his work on language, folklore, even religion, which still retains its value. Further, as an inspiration to talented young Welsh undergraduates at Jesus and other colleges, Rhŷs's personality was an important influence.

In May 1886, there was founded a new society of Welsh-speaking undergraduates at Oxford, *Cymdeithas Dafydd ap Gwilym*. Its seven founder members included John Morris-Jones, Owen M. Edwards (of whom much more, shortly), the eminent philologist, Edward Anwyl, the preacher-poet John Puleston Jones, and the scholar-publicist, Daniel Lleufer Thomas.[6] By the end of the year, they had been joined by three more Welsh Oxonians, including the politician, author and patriot, W. Llewelyn Williams who was at Brasenose. The impact on Welsh life of so distinguished and closely-knit a coterie at the leading university in Britain was immense. The members of the Dafydd ap Gwilym felt themselves to be a cultural élite. Almost a hundred years later, Welsh students at Oxford (now of both sexes) who joined the 'Dafydd', preserving many of the rituals and customs of their Victorian predecessors, still felt membership of their society to be a badge of rare distinction. It inspired a passionate sense of pride in their native land. Men like Morris-Jones, Owen Edwards, and the rest were to spread the gospel of cultural awakening, nurtured at first in the alien cloisters and halls of Oxford, later diffused throughout their native land. Other young Welshmen of intellectual distinction were subsequently to follow them. Young writers like Thomas Parry-Williams and W. J. Gruffydd also took the path to Oxford and created in their turn new legends of the Welsh farm boy made good and scaling the heights of scholarly distinction. That Owen Edwards should be a Brackenbury Scholar of Jowett's Balliol was exciting enough in itself. Oxford for Wales was a cultural, perhaps spiritual inspiration, not a political one. The Dafydd was, and remained, strictly non-political. We are not thinking in terms of, say, the impact of the London School of Economics on the political left and the 'third world' in the years after 1920. But the passion of the exile was added to the questing spirit of the late-Victorian intellectual in making the impact of *fin-de-siècle* Oxford upon the Welsh consciousness a powerful and lasting one.

More widely than the small circles of the Dafydd and its members, Welsh literature began to flourish mightily after 1900. As has been seen, Gwynn Jones's *awdl* in 1902 provided an inspiration for many poets, and for a great flowering of mainly romantic lyric poetry, some of it, however, in the Georgian vein. There were folk poets of the old style, notably the socialist and secularist R. J. Derfel ('Derfel') who wrote profusely until his death in 1905. Two young poets, however, provided work of more enduring value. Indeed, they combined in 1900 to produce a new volume of poetry, *Telynegion*, published at Bangor. They were R. Silyn Roberts, a Methodist minister and an ardent propagandist for the ILP who was also a staunch disciple of Morris-Jones, and W. J. Gruffydd, at this time a young student at Jesus College, and, like Roberts, a native of the Caernarvonshire quarrying community. This volume was lyric in tone and form; it consisted in part of translations from Wordsworth, Heine, and even Catullus. It was indicative of the new mood, however, that the preface should dedicate the book to the Welsh *werin* and express the hope that the book 'should be a drop in the flood of the new literary life of Wales'. Neither poet was strictly a nationalist. Silyn Roberts was an ethical, fraternal socialist of internationalist outlook. Gruffydd was in essence a radical Liberal of somewhat critical and even misanthropic stance. As an educationalist by instinct, Gruffydd strongly disliked Lloyd George's tactics in leading the Welsh county councils in resistance to the Balfour Education Act of 1902, and wrote a powerful indictment of this policy in the *Christian World*. In his memoirs, *Hen Atgofion*, thirty years later, Gruffydd still held to the gravamen of his charges. In 1906 he then produced on his own a remarkable volume of poems, *Caneuon a Cherddi*, again published at Bangor. This works shows great maturity and complexity of theme and expression. In part, it reflects the influence of Gruffydd's growing friendship with T. Gwynn Jones. What is more relevant here than the purely literary qualities of the poetry, mostly written in sonnet form, is its evocation of the simple folk life of the Welsh peasantry, such as the Old Quarryman or the Crofter of Tyn-y-Mynydd, expressed in idiosyncratic terms but still reflecting the folk consciousness of the national renaissance. Gruffydd continued to be a significant figure in Welsh literary circles: he added depth to his work by his academic research as an assistant lecturer in Welsh at the University College, Cardiff. There, in the fullness of time, he was to be elevated to a chair, a further testimony to the influence of the poet-professor class. Through the work of Gwynn Jones, Roberts, Gruffydd, and others, enormous new reserves of creativity were released. Younger poets, usually expounding the usual traditional rural themes (and often from rural communities themselves) were coming forward in their turn. The poem, *Yr Haf* (Summer), by R. Williams Parry at the Colwyn Bay national *eisteddfod* in 1910 heralded in the clearest fashion the coming of a new generation of literary craftsmen. Poetry, rather than novels, short stories or the drama, proved to be the popular form of communicating the new cultural movements to a wider and increasingly educated public. And, as Gwyn Jones has remarked, a renaissance of poetry implied a renaissance of thought.

At a different literary level, the writing of Welsh history first began seriously in these years. The pioneer here, without any doubt, was John Edward Lloyd, born in Liverpool in 1861 who read history at Aberystwyth and at Lincoln College, Oxford, in the eighties. He was a vigorous Liberal and partisan of *Cymru Fydd*, friendly with Tom Ellis, Llewelyn Williams, and other patriots of the period. After a period at Aberystwyth, he was appointed lecturer in history (not yet in Welsh history) at Bangor, where he was later to serve as secretary, registrar, and professor. Lloyd began a new era in the serious study of Welsh medieval history. Indirectly, he was to add to the historical traditions and public remembrances which every national movement needs to sustain itself. His history of Wales before the Edwardian conquest, published in two volumes in 1913, was a mammoth enterprise of scholarship which still holds the stage as the major work in its field. It was sober, unpolemical, and scholarly in approach. Even so, Lloyd wrote with clear sympathy for Wales under the princes before the English yoke descended in 1282. The impression left on the reader is that the Edwardian conquest was a massive tragedy, an imperialist invasion of a small, vigorous, self-conscious nation. The impact is the more striking for the absence of any didactic note. Llewelyn the Great in particular emerges as a heroic figure for his 'patriotic statesmanship' in resisting the Norman invader. 'No man ever made better or more judicious use of the native force of the Welsh people for adequate national ends.'[7] Lloyd's later and smaller book on the Glyn Dŵr rebellion of the early fifteenth century (based on his Ford lectures at Oxford) is more clearly nationalist in tone. Lloyd's life was that of the scholar. He served his college at Bangor for over forty years as teacher, scholar, and administrator. He lacked populist appeal. Even so, his dedicated academic work, infused throughout with patriotic devotion, laid another foundation for the growing sense of historic identity, which younger scholars like William Rees were to take further after the First World War. Significantly enough, the main emphasis was always on pre-conquest Wales, when the nation retained its political independence, rather than on the years of union with and

---

[7] J. E. Lloyd, *A History of Wales from the Earliest Times to the Edwardian Conquest* (London, 1911), vol. ii, p. 693.

colonization by England, when Wales subsided into being a fringe society, perhaps a region, certainly not a distinct nation. The study of post-conquest Wales, especially for the industrial era, was really the achievement of less passionate, more detached (though not necessarily better) historians in the years after 1945.

The work of scholars like Morris-Jones, poets like Gruffydd, historians like Lloyd, needed above all to be communicated to the *werin* that they extolled. Bridges had to be built to make this cultural renaissance one capable of being grasped by ordinary working men and women on the farm, at the quarry-face or down the pit. This crucial act of popular transmission was the work of one last central figure in this cultural explosion, Owen M. Edwards, the great popular educator of Welsh-speaking Wales and perhaps the most powerful single personal influence upon the generation up to 1914. Edwards hailed from an upland farm near Llanuwchllyn, above Bala Lake in Merioneth. He was born in 1858, a year before his near neighbour, Tom Ellis. He shared with him the passion and the humiliation of the common people after the political evictions in the Bala region following the general elections of 1859 and 1868. Edwards went to a Church of England 'National' school, although himself a staunch Methodist. He studied at Aberystwyth college in the eighties, and worked briefly under the philosopher Edward Caird, at Glasgow in 1883–4. But the turning-point for him as for other Welsh intellectuals, was his time at Oxford. He was a highly successful (if elderly) Brackenbury history scholar at Balliol in 1884–7, the very heyday of the imperial élite that Balliol was supposed to be offering to a grateful world. In 1887, Edwards was appointed Fellow in Modern History at Lincoln College and remained there until 1907.

But the Oxford don was always consumed with a sense of wider mission to educate and civilize the Welsh *werin* with which he identified, in literary and indeed in national values. There is every evidence that Edwards was a conscientious, sympathetic, and successful history tutor, though his historical writings on Machiavelli and the like (including a survey work on Wales) were romantic and seldom of high quality. His main concern was to provide for the Welsh people popular forms of communication that could spread a secure, living culture throughout the nation as a whole. Thus he founded a remarkable series of periodicals at his own expense, the monthly *Cymru*, a popular literary magazine for the ordinary reader in 1891; an English-language equivalent, *Wales*; a more academic production, *Y Llenor*; and most influential of all on the younger generation, *Cymru'r Plant*, the first-ever magazine for schoolchildren. Until it disappeared in 1927, *Cymru'r Plant* had an extraordinary influence upon the literary and artistic sensibilities of Welsh boys and girls. Throughout, it was infused with passionate love of the nation, even though this was always cultural rather than political in emphasis. Edwards also produced a wide range of translations, short stories, and travel books, communicating in easy form the charms of Brittany or Italy to Welsh readers, and by implication celebrating the peasant values of rural Welsh communities with which these European societies could so easily be identified. Owen M. Edwards (more simply, 'O.M.') thus set the cultural horizons for an entire generation, giving them good, correct popular Welsh to read and new values to cherish. He also gave warm encouragement, especially in the red-covered *Cymru*, to obscure 'rustic' authors who would otherwise have remained silent and unknown.

Edwards was always concerned to involve himself more directly in the life of Wales than merely as an Oxford don writing for his people at a distance. In 1897 he was bitterly disappointed when the Central Welsh Board turned him down as chief inspector of the Welsh 'county' schools and chose instead the more pedestrian Owen Owen, a former headmaster at Oswestry and a fierce Liberal partisan. In a curious episode, Edwards served as Liberal MP for Merioneth in 1899–1900, following the death of Tom Ellis; at the same time, he retained his fellowship at Lincoln. He owed his nomination to the quarrymen of Ffestiniog and Corris. He hated politics and never addressed the House. However, in 1907 he came back to Wales as chief inspector of schools under the aegis of the new Welsh department of the Board of Education. This was in many ways an unhappy departure for him. He clashed bitterly and repeatedly with the Central Welsh Board, which had rejected him ten years earlier. He felt that the Board, dominated by middle-class Liberal county councillors, had a narrow, stultifying, examination-bound view of education, of little benefit to the Welsh or to anyone else. His annual inspector's reports often included harsh criticism of the methods of the Board. More positively, they called for syllabus reform, for new subjects technical as well as literary, appropriate for the talents and traditions of the children of Welsh men and women. Despite all the quarrelling, Owen Edwards did valiant work as chief inspector as well as author. His visitations to Welsh schools, when he could discourse on European history, literature, and philosophy over a wide range, were memorable for the children who experienced them. He had a genius for communication to the young, and for quiet encouragement of the raw talents of the sons and daughters of the Welsh working class. More generally, Edwards's remarkably magnetic personality, angular and difficult though he could sometimes be, captivated his generation. Through that personal appeal and the popular writings that reflected it, he inspired a popular renaissance as few men in modern Europe have done. W. J. Gruffydd reflected on the varying contributions of Morris-Jones and 'O.M.' to Welsh literary life. If Morris-Jones supplied literature with its 'body', in terms of a tough, technical linguistic discipline, Edwards more importantly provided it with its 'soul',[8] with those spiritual qualities and that divine passion without which any culture will wither and die.

[8] *Wales* (December 1912), p. 648.

These intellectual and literary currents were given new momentum because Wales after 1900 possessed the kind of intelligentsia, the kind of educated, literary élite that it had previously lacked. The fact that this élite was so closely enmeshed with the daily concerns of the people, through chapels, *eisteddfodau*, and popular publishing, made its influence all the more lasting.

Thus it was that the surging national awareness within Wales at the turn of the century, most pronounced of all in poetry and imaginative literature, was intimately linked with the growth of public education. Indeed, the growth of a system of education, at the higher levels above all, came in Wales to acquire national overtones reminiscent of the Scottish educational system. Whereas national education in a country like France was deliberately used to enforce centralization, to crush the separate identities of Gascons, Provençals, Bretons, and the like, in Wales public education served to promote diversity, and, to some extent at least, reinforce and enrich a sense of local and national awareness.

The elementary and secondary schools systems, of course, were closely involved with the development of public education in England after the passage of Forster's Act of 1870. At the elementary level, some of the voluntary schools achieved astonishing academic success like the British school at Talybont, north Cardiganshire, under the inspired headship of an Englishman, T. H. Kemp, who trained a generation of pupil teachers and whose pupils achieved great things in the London matriculation.[9] But neither the voluntary schools, National or British, nor the newly-founded Board schools had much inherent connection with the culture and traditions of the Welsh. Indeed, men like Owen M. Edwards were to attack the Board schools for superimposing on their pupils a largely alien range of studies, narrowly literary and mathematical, which did not relate to the daily experience of the Welsh people. The gradual admission of Welsh as a recognized school subject made only a partial difference. For all that, it was clear by the turn of the century, especially after the implementation of free elementary education in 1891, that more and more young Welsh people were at least literate and numerate enough to participate at some level in their country's national expansion.

A powerful difference was made, too, by the growth of secondary education after the passage of the Intermediate Education Act of 1889. By 1900, every county in Wales had passed schemes for 'county' schools, partly supported by the rates, and had had them approved by the Board of Education. This was accomplished in the face of religious antagonism between churchmen and nonconformists, and of some delaying tactics by representatives of St. David's College, Lampeter, an Anglican institution. By 1902, there were 95 'county' schools in Wales, which provided a network of opportunity and instruction superior to that of England. Under an amendment supported by

[9] P. B. Ballard, *Things I Cannot Forget* (London, 1937), pp. 147–51.

the Welsh Party in the House of Commons in December 1902, the Welsh 'county' schools were brought under the same administrative framework as the elementary schools, 'provided' and 'non-provided', and run by the same elective county education committees. On the eve of war in 1914, Wales could claim 117 recognized secondary schools, of which only six were private, while 99 were 'county schools' established under the 1889 Act. Clearly, there now existed the basis of a Welsh educated class, culturally aware, more intellectually sophisticated, poised to supply political, social, and cultural leadership in the new century. Some of the expectations attached to these new schools were perhaps unduly inflated. Lloyd George in 1905 welcomed Lewis School, Pengam, near Bargoed, as an institution that could become 'the Eton of Wales'. Just as the public schools of England, such as Eton and Winchester, turned out 'the English idea of a perfect English gentleman', so the new secondary schools here would 'produce the higher type, the ideal of a Welsh gentleman, not dependent on rank, wealth and birth or blood (hear, hear)— but upon character and attainments, the real type which would stand for the ideal Welshman in all parts of the world'.[10] It was a curious gloss on his supposedly democratic or egalitarian outlook. But it is clear that the new educational provision at the post-elementary levels had powerful cultural and national, even perhaps nationalist, implications. New ranges of professional opportunities were being opened up for Welsh boys, and to some extent girls. Many of them were to become schoolteachers and headmasters and headmistresses in their turn, to transmit cultural and patriotic values to new generations of Welsh pupils. Certainly, social and educational mobility was a significant fact in the new Welsh renaissance.

The most emphatic example of the new relation between national awareness and the educational system, however, came at the level of post-school education. Apart from St. David's College, Lampeter, which remained an Anglican preserve largely concerned with the training of ordinands, there were by 1885 three major institutions which served as focuses for national and educational aspiration. Two of them were direct products of the recommendations of the Aberdare Committee in 1881. They were the University College of South Wales and Monmouthshire founded in Cathays Park, Cardiff, in 1883, and the University College of North Wales, established at Bangor in 1884. The attachment of regions of Wales to the new colleges shows that they were meant to have far more than purely local or civic responsibility. But both Bangor and Cardiff were somewhat indirectly connected with the new patriotic movements of *Cymru Fydd*. Both were to some degree products of the demand for a new technical, trained class in Wales to run the new commerce and industry, and to enable Welsh graduates to respond to the cultural and social priorities of the British system. The work of eminent

<hr />

[10] *Western Mail*, 21 September 1905. I am indebted to Dr Ralph A. Griffiths, himself a distinguished product of Lewis School, Pengam, for this reference.

scholars such as Ker, Seth, and Burrows at Cardiff or the philosopher Henry Jones at Bangor transcended national or ethnic boundaries. The first principal of Cardiff, John Viriamu Jones, was a man of extraordinary intellectual brilliance, a distinguished scientist who held senior appointments when only in his mid-twenties; he was also closely associated with the Liberal/nonconformist background of the new national reawakening. His father was a famous nonconformist minister at Swansea; his brothers, David Brynmor Jones and Leif Jones (popularly known as 'Tea Leaf Jones' through his passion for temperance) became Liberal MPs. But the college at Cardiff soon came to reflect the cosmopolitan, mercantile concerns of the anglicized southeastern parts of Wales. The college at Bangor had as its first principal Sir Harry Reichel, an Ulster Tory, to the consternation of local radicals; its links with north Wales tended to be squirearchical rather than populist, with figures like Lord Kenyon prominent on its council. On the other hand, with the appointment of John Edward Lloyd as lecturer in Welsh history in 1892 and of John Morris-Jones as Professor of Welsh in 1894, the national characteristics of Bangor became far more identifiable, and Reichel strove to encourage them.

It was, however, the third Welsh college which was always most directly associated with the new currents in Welsh life, the 'college by the sea' at Aberystwyth founded on the seafront in a disused railway hotel in 1872. Aberystwyth had survived many setbacks. There was the departure of some members of staff, such as the celebrated composer, Joseph Parry, whose evangelism on behalf of musical instruction upset some members of the local council. There was a serious fire which demolished much of the old building. Most serious, there was a risk of total financial collapse, since there was no government grant of £4,000 a year such as had attended the launching of Bangor and Cardiff. In 1882, in fact, Gladstone had approved the awarding of a £4,000 grant to Aberystwyth but this was promptly transferred to Bangor when the college there was founded the following year. Many argued that Aberystwyth had no purpose, and that Wales had no need for as many as three new institutions of higher education. Only after intensive lobbying by Stuart Rendel, Henry Richard, and other Welsh MPs did Gladstone very reluctantly agree to extend an annual grant to Aberystwyth as well, at first of only £2,500. Then it was raised by the new Conservative administration of Salisbury to the full £4,000 on the same basis as Bangor and Cardiff.[11] Even so, the 'college by the sea' had to struggle hard for survival.

By then, however, Aberystwyth was already firmly impressing itself on the social and national consciousness of the Welsh people in a manner unique in the educational world. Its first principal, Thomas Charles Edwards, was a man of powerful personality, the scion of a famous Methodist radical family

[11] Rendel to Thomas Charles Edwards, 25 August 1885, in T. I. Ellis (ed.), *Letters of Thomas Charles Edwards* (Aberystwyth, 1952–3), p. 239.

from Bala. There had been a massive subscription campaign which led to a high degree of popular commitment to the success of Aberystwyth, largely orchestrated by Sir Hugh Owen in the later seventies. Some of the legends about the 'pence of the poor' that surrounded the popular support for Aberystwyth may be somewhat inflated. By far the largest contribution to the new college came from the capitalist David Davies of Llandinam: he was to resign in disgust from the college council in 1886 after the principal, Thomas Charles Edwards, failed to support him in the Cardiganshire election when Davies stood as a Liberal Unionist.[12] But the popular view of Aberystwyth as the 'people's college' is not wholly mythical. There were over 100,000 contributions to Aberystwyth of under half a crown, mostly from poor working people. The 'University Sunday' (*Sul y Brifysgol*) on which chapels donated some of their funds became a widely-supported occasion. The inspiration that Aberystwyth evoked among countless miners, quarrymen, and farm labourers, like the popular involvement for the new land-grant colleges in the American mid-West, cannot be cynically disregarded.

This popular enthusiasm was reflected in the early 1880s with the emergence in Aberystwyth of powerful new currents of national fervour. A new generation of talented young students came there, mostly from humble homes—future politicians like Tom Ellis and Ellis Griffith, scholars like John Edward Lloyd and T. F. Roberts (later Aberystwyth's second principal), the barrister, T. Marchant Williams. They testified to the kind of ability residual in the hitherto untapped *pays réel* of nonconformist Wales and to its growing national awareness. Aberystwyth products figured prominently among the first generation of secondary-school headmasters appointed to the new 'county schools' after 1896. The 'A.C.C.' of which Tom Ellis was a member in 1883 was a precursor in Aberystwyth of the kind of nationalist and intellectual student society of which the Dafydd ap Gwilym at Oxford was soon to become a more celebrated example. More than any other institution in Wales, Aberystwyth enjoyed its own organic relationship with the Welsh people and their social culture. It was a vision given eloquent expression by Tom Ellis as warden of the Aberystwyth Guild of Graduates, when urging that new efforts be made to preserve literary and archival records in Wales. Indeed, the Guild of Graduates became a powerful national pressure-group: in the twentieth century, it was often to have a strongly nationalist tone. The first two wardens were those two symbolic patriots, Tom Ellis and Owen M. Edwards. Aberystwyth thus offered its own Celtic version of the American 'Wisconsin idea', its own passionate vision of populist culture, integrated with the society that gave it birth, steeped with the folk nationalism of *Cymru Fydd*, the Wales that was to be.

The kind of emotion kindled first at Aberystwyth, and always latent at Bangor and Cardiff too, provided an immense stimulus to the ideal of a

[12] J. B. Rogers to Thomas Charles Edwards, 19 August 1886, ibid., p. 259.

national university. This had been foreshadowed rather vaguely in the recommendations of the Aberdare Committee. Now, fired by the example of other provincial or civic universities springing up in other parts of Britain, the vision of a university of Wales became a powerful symbol of national identity. In January 1888 the Cymmrodorion Society, a formidable pressure-group of mainly London-based intellectuals and businessmen, convened a conference under the chairmanship of Professor John Rhŷs as a result of which an application was made to the Lord President of the Council for a university charter. In November 1891, another conference, this time at the familiar venue of Shrewsbury in the Welsh marches, decided in favour of a teaching rather than merely an examining university—that is, one that would teach and confer degrees on its own students. The issue somewhat hung fire until Gladstone returned as Prime Minister in 1892. He acceded to the views of his minister for education, Arthur Acland, a warm-hearted friend of Wales who lived in Caernarvonshire and was intimate with Tom Ellis and other young nationally-minded Welshmen. Owen M. Edwards was appointed as commissioner to lay information before the government as to the practicability of a federal university, comprehending Bangor, Aberystwyth, and Cardiff. There was also St. David's College, Lampeter, deeply suspicious of the Liberal nonconformist hue of the movement for Welsh higher education. Bishop Jayne of Chester, a former principal of Lampeter, led the attack. He claimed that St. David's College was being victimized by 'aggressive and intolerant denominationalism' in Wales. [13] In practical terms, it was obvious that Lampeter would never agree to the scheme being proposed for a national university, and progress had to continue without the assistance of the men at Lampeter. In January 1893 another conference at Shrewsbury formally agreed that a federal university be set up, with a teaching and not merely an examining system. Three representatives, headed by Dr Isambard Owen, then drafted a charter which was approved by the Privy Council and laid before parliament.

The only real stumbling-block concerned the future of Lampeter, whose inclusion in any future scheme for a university had been recommended by the Aberdare Committee. On 29 August 1893 the House of Lords carried a motion that the royal assent be withheld from the university charter until Lampeter was included. This would have delayed it more or less indefinitely. Fortunately, Gladstone simply ignored this motion. After all, the charter did contain a reservation clause which would enable Lampeter to enter the university as another constituent college if it chose to do so. The door was not closed for ever. In fact, no such moves occurred until the 1960s when the inability of Lampeter to obtain grants through the University Grants Committee made its financial problems virtually insoluble. Not until 1972 when the sectarian passions of the previous century had evaporated, was Lampeter brought in to join the other Welsh colleges in a federal system and

[13] *Parl. Deb.*, 4th ser., House of Lords, xvi, pp. 1316 ff.

enabled to participate more fully in the educational and national life of Wales, as the Aberdare Committee had prescribed and patriotic churchmen at the time had expected.

At the end of 1893, the University of Wales formally received the royal assent. In 1896 it came into being on a federal basis. Its chancellor was the Prince of Wales, after the death of the first nominee, Lord Aberdare. A government grant of £20,000 was grudgingly extracted from Harcourt, the Liberal Chancellor of the Exchequer, in 1894, while a further £50,000 was raised by voluntary appeal. Viriamu Jones of Cardiff became its first vice-chancellor and immediately launched schemes to integrate the university with the teaching and inspection of the secondary schools. From the start, the University of Wales had powerful national overtones. The vast bulk of its students, over 90 per cent until well after the First World War, came from Wales, many from relatively humble or poor homes. There were close links built up with the county school system; later on, the growth of extension or extra-mural teaching through such men as Robert Richards at Bangor (later a Labour MP) and Herbert Morgan at Aberystwyth established intimate contact between the constituent colleges and ordinary working people. The university's teaching and research programmes were increasingly geared to Welsh themes, with the presence of such men as Morris-Jones and Lloyd at Bangor, Edward Anwyl at Aberystwyth, and W. J. Gruffydd at Cardiff.

Above all, the university served as a powerful symbol of popular achievement and of national status. In no other area of Welsh life, transcending political and sectarian barriers, was national pride more genuinely manifested. As late as 1964-6, politicians who sought to break up the federal structure of the national university and reduce it to a congeries of obscure local institutions found that the national emotions within Wales were proof against such ill-considered activities. The university always had critics of its internal mechanisms. Its federal system meant a great deal of duplication of meetings and correspondence, with the university registry in Cardiff a relatively weak directing agency. In March 1905, Llewelyn Williams, an apostle of *Cymru Fydd*, launched a vigorous attack on the university in the *New Leader*. He claimed that it was run by a narrow professional class, that it was too detached from the 'county schools' and not much more than a mere examining body. He also complained that the university was not sensitive enough to Cymric idiosyncrasies and had failed to become a 'people's university' deriving its inspiration from native democratic institutions. These views were debatable. But it can certainly be said that Welsh education, like the nation generally, was centrifugal in tendency, always prone to fragmentation. Not until after the First World War were there bodies such as the University of Wales Press and the Board of Celtic Studies to bring together the research conducted into history, law, literature, language, and archaeology in the various colleges. In terms of teaching and the planning of syllabuses, the individual colleges sought independence rather than academic collaboration. The Haldane Commission on the University of Wales which reported in 1918 in some ways denationalized it still further. Nevertheless, the strength of the new university as a unique focus for popular aspiration was generally accepted. 'The history of learning in Wales, of which the new University is a symbol and a manifestation, is not merely the history of a movement or of a phase of national activity. It is the history of the nation itself.'[14] This romantic, somewhat exaggerated conclusion, drawn from the official history of the University of Wales, published in 1905, remained and remains largely true, generations later.

The university was soon to be followed by other badges of cultural and national distinctiveness. In 1905, shortly before its fall from office, the Unionist government under Balfour sanctioned a national library of Wales, to be established at Aberystwyth. This owed much to the land purchased for it by the munificence of Stuart, now Lord Rendel. It owed more to the remarkable collection of manuscripts accumulated by the doctor-antiquarian, Sir John Williams, which were destined for the library if it were set up in Aberystwyth. Four years later, the library came into being, located in the Assembly Rooms, an attractive regency house in the centre of the town. It was much boosted by the deposit of the remarkable collection of the Peniarth manuscripts that Dr Williams had handed over to the library. The first national librarian, John Ballinger, formerly head of the free library at Cardiff, rapidly built up the nascent national library into a major centre for research into Welsh antiquities, history, and literature; it was later to acquire copyright status. Conversely, by an astute political balance, the new national museum was to be located in Cardiff where a handsome neo-Baroque building was shortly to be constructed on the southern side of Cathays Park.

If these developments owed something to the benevolent attentions of the Unionist government, the bipartisan aspect of Welsh culture was shown in 1907 when the new Liberal government under Campbell-Bannerman set up a Welsh department in the Board of Education. There had been pressure for a Welsh educational council for several years. Lloyd George had tried hard between 1903 and 1905 to divert the argument away from the low road of the sectarian 'revolt' against the Balfour Education Act to the higher ground of administrative devolution to promote Welsh education, elementary and secondary, which would unite Welshmen of all denominations. He established contact with prominent churchmen like the Bishop of St. Asaph and Lord Kenyon, and even with the Roman Catholic Bishop of Menevia. Lloyd George's genius for coalition and compromise was already amply displayed. After a further attempt at an agreement over a council early in 1906, when Lloyd George was now President of the Board of Trade in the now Liberal government, a Welsh Council of Education (with admittedly vague powers and financial provision) was included in Birrell's abortive Education Bill of 1906. This measure was intended to allay nonconformist grievances against the Balfour Act; inevitably, it passed the Commons easily but foundered in the Lords. In some ways this may have saved Lloyd George some public embarrassment. He had interfered a good deal in Birrell's bill, and to no great effect. The nature of the new Council was most imprecise. At one stage, a kind of Minister for Welsh Education was proposed, and then promptly struck out of the bill as soon as there was public criticism.

As a consolation for the failure to obtain an education council, in February 1907 the new Welsh department was set up. Its first secretary was a Flintshire solicitor, A. T. Davies; he was a strong Liberal active in the revolt against the Balfour Education Act, as Unionist critics did not fail to point out. As has been noted, Owen M. Edwards was appointed as the first chief inspector of schools. As an experiment in administrative devolution, the Welsh department of the Board of Education is of much interest. Although co-ordinated with the English educational system, the Welsh department was able to look at the specific needs of Welsh education as a whole, and to weigh up the different needs of primary, secondary, and extra-mural education. It was also able to give much encouragement to the Welsh language in schools and, well before 1914, to ensure that Welsh language and literary courses were added to the curricula of Welsh schools and training colleges. It shows how education and national consciousness were intimately related, and, of course, soon led to further experiments in devolution in other departments of central government. It suggests how the national renaissance, most apparent in the literary and cultural spheres, was having a constitutional and administrative impact (one later to be followed up in the fields of health insurance, agriculture, and public health), cementing the Welsh people more firmly together, differentiating them more distinctly from the English, and reinforcing a thriving sense of nationality.

The developments so far described were mainly cultural and educational. To turn national consciousness into nationalism in the fullest sense, however, a political aspect was also necessary. It must now be examined how far the cultural nationalism of these years attained political form, how far this new, more self-confident Wales followed its neighbour across the Irish Sea by advancing towards a demand for some form of political separatism.

It is clear that a good deal of the nationalist emotion of the period between 1880 and 1907 was profoundly apolitical. The leading figures in the cultural and literary renaissance were scarcely political, certainly not separatist. Morris-Jones urged that literature would flourish the more successfully if it was purged of a political or didactic quality. Owen M. Edwards was very briefly a Liberal MP, but it is clear that literary and educational questions absorbed almost the whole of his attention, even (or perhaps especially) when he was a backbench MP. Political nationalists, in the sense of being advocates of some version of Welsh home rule, were rare indeed. One such was Robert Ambrose Jones, 'Emrys ap Iwan'. He was an eccentric figure since he was sympathetic to Roman Catholicism and an ardent admirer of French culture who felt distaste for the narrow horizons of Calvinist Wales. There was also Michael Daniel Jones, the pioneer of the Patagonian settlement, with his bitter hatred of all things English. For the rest, Welsh radicals were essentially British Liberals rather than Celtic nationalists. When Joseph Chamberlain raised the issue of Welsh home rule in 1886 under the framework of 'home rule all round', it was obviously an attempt to divert attention from home rule for Ireland alone, and to wean Welshmen away from their attachment to Gladstonian Liberalism, since the demand for Welsh home rule scarcely existed at all.

In the years after 1886, the spirit of *Cymru Fydd* advanced steadily into the political field. Some of its partisans deplored the attempt to over-politicize the Welsh national movement. For instance, there was Llewelyn Williams, fresh from the Dafydd ap Gwilym at Oxford who embarked on a journalistic career and tried to run first the Barry *Star* and then the Swansea *Daily Post* on nationalist lines. He told the historian J. E. Lloyd how 'sordid' modern Irish nationalism had become, by comparison with the Young Ireland movement of the 1840s. 'That is not the sort of "nationalism" I should like to see in Wales—a nationalism divorced from everything except politics.'[15] More and more Welsh politicians, however, seemed to be convinced that the logical culmination of the new movement surging throughout their nation was to create a movement for Welsh home rule on the same lines as Irish.

This was particularly the view of Tom Ellis, who felt that only by pushing for self-government would the Welsh have truly 'a national programme and a national party'. Ellis's nationalism was fortified by his student years at Aberystwyth, by his attraction to neo-hegelian Idealism while at Oxford, and by his awareness of the new political forces he beheld in Wales when elected for Merioneth in 1886 and became the more intense and visionary. His passion for Wales reached new heights during a visit to Africa for the sake of his health in 1890 (Ellis was a consumptive and never physically robust). Here he witnessed the archaeological splendours of Luxor on the Nile and discussed the concept of imperial federation with Cecil Rhodes in South Africa, Rhodes himself being an enthusiast for Irish home rule on imperial grounds. On his return, Ellis delivered a famous speech at Bala in September 1890 in which he appealed openly for a Welsh parliament. Along with close friends such as D. R. Daniel and W. J. Parry in Caernarvonshire, Ellis formulated a new concept of nationhood, in which the history, traditions, social culture, literature, and political institutions of his people would be organically linked.

[15] Llewelyn Williams to John Edward Lloyd, 21 September 1894 (UCNW Bangor, Lloyd Papers, MS 314, f. 592).

The spirit of Wales, and of its village life, he argued, was a collective one, rather than individualist. It had animated the pioneer socialist, Robert Owen of Newtown. Wales was the land of '*cyfraith*, *cyfar*, *cyfnawdd*, *cymorthau* and *cymanfaoedd*',[16] a land of social co-operation and of associative effort, predestined to act as a collective whole.

Ellis's visions were too ethereal to make much impact, however, even upon his own Bala constituents. As the *Cymru Fydd* movement became more narrowly political and enmeshed in the politics of Welsh Liberalism, he and *Cymru Fydd* gradually parted company. But the pressure for some form of Welsh separatism expressed in political terms continued to mount. An influential new monthly journal appeared between 1888 and 1891, *Cymru Fydd*, under the editorship of the radical patriot, T. J. Hughes, 'Adfyfr'. While largely rehearsing the standard Liberal demands for disestablishment, education, temperance and land reform, it also called powerfully for Welsh self-government. Significantly enough, this seemed to be taking *Cymru Fydd* into wrong channels, in the view of some observers. In June 1889 Owen M. Edwards and R. H. Morgan jointly replaced 'Adfyfr' as editor of the periodical, and it henceforth became much more cultural and literary in emphasis. The previous editorial policy was attacked by R. H. Morgan for being too censorious, rancorous, and 'narrow in scope'.[17] Still, the appearance of such a periodical at this time, openly advocating separatism, was a striking portent. Among other things, it served to give the contemporary campaigns for the reform of the tithe system or disestablishment of the Church a more overtly nationalist colouring. This view was advocated with much fervour by an interesting man, J. Arthur Price, an Anglo-Catholic barrister and a Tory turned Liberal. He saw the disestablishment of the Welsh Church not in sectarian terms but rather as an attempt to restore the old organic community of the Middle Ages before puritanism and sectarianism divided the nation. There was, at the same time, pressure for the newly-formed Liberal Federations of North and South Wales to amalgamate and perhaps to form some kind of parallel to the Home Rule League in Ireland.

The climax came with the growth of a Cymru Fydd League after 1886. As with so many other nationalist movements, this was the work initially of *emigrés*. The first branch was formed in London in 1886 and the second at Liverpool in 1887. There was no branch in south Wales at all until one was set up at Barry, under the aegis of Llewelyn Williams, in 1891. The main emphasis of these early branches was almost entirely cultural and literary; but by 1890 a new note could be detected. *Cymru Fydd* sympathizers in Liberal ranks were calling for Welsh home rule and for official Liberalism in Wales to be transformed into a movement for self-government very much on

---

[16] Thomas Edward Ellis, 'The Memory of the Kymric Dead', *Speeches and Addresses by the late T. E. Ellis M.P.* (Wrexham, 1912), p. 22.
[17] *Cymru Fydd*, June 1889, p. 273.

the lines of current developments in Ireland, the kind of transition that had led from Isaac Butt to that of Charles Stewart Parnell. In the North Wales Liberal Federation, the young Lloyd George and associates such as R. A. Griffiths became spokesmen for *Cymru Fydd* and for making home rule part of the Liberal platform.[18] The election of Lloyd George to parliament as MP for Caernarfon Boroughs in April 1890 gave this narrower, more politicized version of *Cymru Fydd* a formidable and compelling parliamentary voice. Men such as Ellis and Price were somewhat in the shadows as *Cymru Fydd* pressed on beyond purely cultural concerns and seemed likely to challenge, and even to capture, the formal machinery of the Liberal Party in the principality. It was the kind of development that Stuart Rendel, in striving to make the Welsh Liberalism effective within the wider umbrella of nationwide party, had always dreaded.

After the return of the Liberal government in 1892, with its majority of forty theoretically dependent on the goodwill of the Welsh Liberal Parliamentary Party of thirty-one, the fortunes of *Cymru Fydd* expanded dramatically. Branches of the League mushroomed all over north and mid-Wales and in parts of the southern coalfield. There was widespread support for Lloyd George and three other Welsh members when they briefly rejected the Liberal whip in April–May 1894 because of the apparent refusal of the Rosebery government to give the first priority to a Welsh disestablishment bill. Lloyd George now evolved his own scheme, along with nationalistic churchmen such as the Revd R. Edmonds Jones, the warden of Bangor Divinity School, for a compromise over the question of endowments. He aimed to get all-party agreement on behalf of a self-governing Church within a self-governing Wales.[19] In fact, though, the Rosebery government soon yielded to pressure and introduced its Welsh Disestablishment Bill in May.

In August 1894 a national Cymru Fydd League was formed at Llandrindod Wells, to amalgamate on a federal basis the different segments of Welsh Liberalism. Its national organizer was Beriah Gwynfe Evans, until recently editor of *Y Genedl Gymreig* at Caernarfon. With Lloyd George as its inspiration, the new league now seemed to be sweeping all before it in Welsh political life. A new magazine was launched in January 1895 under the title of *Young Wales*, to promote the cause. Its editor was J. Hugh Edwards, Aberystwyth graduate, former Independent minister and later to be a Liberal MP and Lloyd George's biographer on more than one occasion. Finally, in April 1895, at a time of great crisis for the Liberal government, the Cymru Fydd League formally merged with the North Wales Liberal Federation, at a meeting at Aberystwyth.

But the main decision would clearly rest with the South Wales Liberal Federation, which represented most of the population, wealth, and pro-

---

[18] Minutes of the North Wales Liberal Federation (NLW), especially *sub* 25 February 1890.
[19] Bishop of St. Asaph to Principal John Owen, 16 February 1895 (Bishop John Owen MSS).

ductive capacity of the nation. Here, there were mounting difficulties. Under the chairmanship of the coalowner, D. A. Thomas MP, the SWLF had formerly taken the lead in advocating the cause of *Cymru Fydd*. But this was always subject to the view that Glamorgan and Monmouth, the most populous counties in Wales, should have their own independent position demarcated. There had been trouble on this issue twice already. It first arose over discussions on the representative basis of the elected assembly proposed in Alfred Thomas's National Institutions Bill in 1891. It came up even more sharply in 1894 when D. A. Thomas proposed a national council which would allocate the secularized tithe between the counties of Wales when the Church was disestablished and disendowed. He urged his fellow south Wales Liberals that under the scheme of secularization of church property proposed by Lloyd George and the men from the north, Glamorgan and Monmouth would be treated most unjustly. Instead of gaining up to £20,000 which was its due, for social and cultural purposes such as hospitals, libraries, art galleries, and the like, the great town of Cardiff would receive 'only a few paltry hundreds'. Glamorgan would receive only £26,000 instead of the £90,000 to which it was entitled.[20] Because of this, negotiations broke down between north and south Wales over the proposed council for allocating church endowments. Indirectly, a permanent wedge was driven between D. A. Thomas and Lloyd George which was to have profound consequences for the entire home rule movement.

South Wales had already been giving much trouble to the *Cymru Fydd* campaign. It was clear that the south, or more especially the ports of Swansea, Barry, Cardiff, and Newport on the southern seaboard, diverged in outlook from the rest of the principality. Llewelyn Williams was depressed by the anti-nationalist tone of Swansea—'a howling wilderness of Philistinism'—and of Barry, 'a large, rapidly-growing town, intent on nothing but money-making'. Cardiff, he added, was 'already lost to Welsh nationalism'.[21] All were deeply suspicious of the domination likely to be exercised over their cosmopolitan, anglicized mercantile population by the Welsh-speakers in the more sparsely-populated hinterland. This gulf, as marked in the *Cymru Fydd* campaign in the 1890s as in the debate prior to the referendum on devolution in 1978–9, proved quite unbridgeable. When a Cymru Fydd League, or 'Welsh National Federation' was formed at Aberystwyth on 18 April 1895 under the chairmanship of the aged Thomas Gee, it was noted that the South Wales Liberal Federation was totally unrepresented, even though a south Walian, Alfred Thomas, MP for East Glamorgan, was tactfully elected president of the new organization. D. A. Thomas continued to brood, resentfully, in Cardiff. He was told, in fact, by a Flintshire Liberal that even the North Wales Liberal

[20] D.A. Thomas to 'Gronow', 3 October 1894 (NLW, D. A. Thomas MSS).
[21] Llewelyn Williams to Tom Ellis, 19 February 1892 (NLW, Ellis Papers, f. 2134); Llewelyn Williams to Edward Thomas, 6 April 1893 (Cardiff Public Library, Cochfarf Papers).

Federation 'was far from being in love with the Cymru Fydd movement'.[22] This was especially so in anglicized areas of north-east Wales such as Ruthin, Mold, and Wrexham; only packed meetings and a doctored newspaper press were whipping up the agitation. This correspondent added, 'The whole movement from the beginning on is a beautifully arranged attempt to boss Welsh people, and to call themselves a National Federation seems profoundly absurd'.[23]

After the fall of the Liberal government in June, relations between Lloyd George's Cymru Fydd League and D. A. Thomas's South Wales Liberal Federation rapidly reached a point of crisis. The *Cymru Fydd* movement now attempted to penetrate south Wales. Lloyd George, backed up by the veteran Gee in the *Baner*, continued his campaign by means of speeches and carefully-placed journalistic articles and press interviews. In the autumn of 1895 he launched a personal crusade to win over south Wales to adherence to *Cymru Fydd*. The rather obvious stratagem that he pursued was a series of lectures in the valleys on the ostensible subject of Llywelyn the Great, in his eyes, a thirteenth-century apostle of *Cymru Fydd*. He had some success in the Rhondda at such places as Ferndale, Tonypandy, and Treherbert, and Rhondda Liberals were apparently won over, despite the cautious attitude of Mabon himself;[24] Merthyr also seemed likely to be captured, despite D. A. Thomas being its MP, not least because the patriotic socialist 'ap Ffarmwr' edited the *Merthyr Times*. Lloyd George himself seemed to have been in a very disorientated mood at this period in his life. The downfall of the Liberal government, the failure to obtain Welsh disestablishment, the apparent disintegration of the post-Gladstonian Liberal Party, presented a very different world, one with new opportunities for minority groups such as the Welsh to break free from the traditional strait-jacket of Westminster politics. A new urgency could be injected into purely Welsh issues—the Church, temperance, education and so forth—that they would never receive at Westminster, given the basic structure of national party politics. More than at any time in his kaleidoscopic career, Lloyd George felt temporarily detached from the British scene. He was pre-eminently now the Welsh outsider, striving to forge a new instrument by which to dominate and to advance his own nation.

The crisis came at the Newport meeting of the South Wales Liberal Federation. This was a disaster. The pretensions of *Cymru Fydd* and of Lloyd George, the claims of political nationalism, were blown to atoms. The meeting was badly prepared, and undoubtedly packed with delegates hostile to *Cymru Fydd*—'the Newport Englishmen' of whom Lloyd George angrily wrote to his wife.[25] The largely commercial and mercantile delegates from

[22] Fred Llewellyn Jones to D. A. Thomas, 21 June 1895 (NLW, D. A. Thomas MSS).
[23] Fred Llewellyn Jones to D. A. Thomas, 5 June 1895 (ibid.).
[24] *South Wales Daily News*, 27 November, 3, 4 December 1895.
[25] Lloyd George to his wife, 16 January 1896 (*Family Letters*, p. 94).

south-east Wales were in no mood to listen to a plea for separatism originating from the remote fastnesses of the Welsh-speaking rural north and west. Robert Bird, an amiable man, a moderate-minded Wesleyan businessman from Cardiff, declared that Liberalism was more important than Welshness. The cosmopolitan population of south-east Wales would never submit 'to the domination of Welsh ideas'. Alfred Edmunds of Merthyr asserted that 'Glamorgan and Monmouth were not to be dictated to by the isolated county of Caernarvon'.[26] A crucial motion to merge the SWLF with the Cymru Fydd League, moved by the Independent minister, H. Elfed Lewis, was defeated by 133 votes to 70. Lloyd George tried to keep his spirits up afterwards. He appealed to the anti-Cardiff mood of Swansea delegates—'West Wales is with us'.[27] But his defeat was complete, one of the very few irreversible setbacks he suffered in his otherwise dazzlingly successful career prior to 1916. He himself was shouted down. The meeting turned into a bear-garden, with Liberal hurling abuse at brother Liberal in a manner unthinkable in the heyday of party unity after 1885. The unreal nature of the Cymru Fydd League was manifest. It was an artificial construct of packed committees and pliant newspaper editors, not a genuinely popular movement for home rule. By the end of 1896 *Cymru Fydd* was in ruins. The gulf between north and mid-Wales on the one hand, and mercantile, industrial south Wales on the other seemed alarming and gaping, and Liberals strove to patch it up by dropping the entire campaign for home rule. Lloyd George himself had decided that it was as a British Liberal not a Welsh nationalist that his future was to lie. He never chanced his arm as a Welsh separatist again at any time in his career.

In subsequent years, Welsh home rule receded from the limelight. Indeed, genuine proposals to overhaul and to strengthen the organizational structure of Liberalism had to be advanced very warily in case they became a pretext for reviving something that might resemble the ill-fated Cymru Fydd League. In February 1898 Lloyd George experienced much difficulty in establishing a Welsh National Liberal Federation, to co-ordinate the activities of the north and south Wales Liberals. Cardiff and Newport remained incurably hostile, and Lloyd George had to make many concessions, notably the elimination of non-elective members of the new body. The 'wire-pulling' of *Cymru Fydd* continued to rankle. Tom Ellis died prematurely in April 1899, still a revered figure in the principality, the epitome of the 'cottage-bred boy', but already distanced from some of the national forces for national self-expression in Wales, the more so since he had been acting as Liberal chief whip in London from 1894 onwards. Meanwhile Lloyd George and D. A. Thomas, two of the most gifted figures in Welsh Liberal circles, remained bitter enemies until 1916, each recalling the fratricidal divisions of *Cymru Fydd*, each prone to recall, with different interpretations, the response of industrial and mercan-

---

[26] *South Wales Daily News*, 17 January 1896.
[27] Lloyd George to his wife, 18 January 1896 (*Family Letters*, p. 94).

tile south Wales to the *Cymru Fydd* movement. Not until Lloyd George served as President of the Board of Trade in 1905–8 did he make his peace with the industrialists of the south. Then it was that the editor of the Tory *Western Mail* actually invited him to stand, unopposed, as Liberal candidate for the city of Cardiff.[28] But this was a different, less parochial Lloyd George.

Not for many years did another movement designed to promote political nationalism make any headway. This came in 1910 and was the work of a middle-aged iron manufacturer from Middlesbrough, though originally from Denbighshire, E. T. John. He returned from years in the industrial world of Teesside to become Liberal MP for East Denbighshire in December 1910. With the aid of Beriah Gwynfe Evans, still active in promoting Welsh home rule as fifteen years earlier, John advanced schemes for Welsh self-government as part of a wider framework of imperial devolution. A single-chamber Welsh legislature would be established, to deal with domestic issues, including power over local taxation. John also founded his own Welsh National League. It seemed at this time that current proposals for some kind of devolution settlement as a compromise alternative to the impasse over home rule for Ireland in 1910–12 might give some assistance to pressure for Welsh home rule. It appeared to gain support from imperial federalists such as F. S. Oliver and the *Round Table* group.[29] John even went so far as to introduce his own private member's Welsh Home Rule bill in the Commons in March 1914 and it received a formal first reading.

But this was obviously a dead letter. John himself, an earnest, deeply sincere but desperately dull middle-aged industrialist, had little charisma and no personal following. After 1906, the attraction for Welshmen of adherence to the British Liberal Party was more potent than ever, especially now that Lloyd George was such a dominating figure in the government. Apart from Beriah Gwynfe Evans, a few churchmen of nationalist outlook like J. Arthur Price, and a handful of others, E. T. John found no support at all. Long before 1914, it was obvious that Welsh political separatism, in such striking contrast to the vitality of cultural nationalism, was quite moribund.

The Welsh renaissance, then, remained firmly cultural and literary above all. It did have political by-products as well. The demand for church disestablishment, as has been seen, chimed in with the growing recognition that the Welsh were a distinct nation with their own culture, and might be reasonably expected to have views on running their own institutions and social arrangements, no less than the Scots and Irish—not to mention the English. Welsh education, as has been noted, had acquired distinctly national overtones, confirmed by the creation of the Welsh department of the Board of Education in 1907. The same could apply in the future to Welsh agriculture, which also

[28] Lloyd George to his wife, 31 July 1907 (ibid., p. 147).
[29] See articles by Oliver in *The Times*, 20 October–2 November 1910, written under the pseudonym of 'Pacificus'.

had many distinct features, while the Sunday Closing Act of 1881 was a potent of specifically Welsh legislation distinct from measures passed for England alone. But that was as far as it went. In Wales, unlike Ireland, the supreme objective was equality not exclusion—equality within the framework of the United Kingdom and the empire, recognition of the distinct social and cultural needs of Wales without disturbing the overall governmental system, let alone breaking away from it. Most of the Welsh were content with their dual identity, which stressed their Britishness as well as their Welshness, which encouraged their growing influence and importance within an expanding empire and a thriving system of manufacture, trade, and enterprise, rather than put it all to risk by severing Wales from England and letting it sink or swim on its own.

In addition, there had emerged clear signs of political and cultural divergence between north and mid-Wales and the southern coalfield which helped to undermine attempts to create national unity. Even in the Welsh-speaking north, demands for Welsh separatism was largely artificial. Lloyd George was immune to many of the cultural and literary impulses that underlay the *Cymru Fydd* movement at its inception; he lacked the broad cultural vision of a man like Tom Ellis. He saw his new creation, in 1894 at least, in narrowly political terms, as a lever to affect substantial political change and to transform the balance of power within the Liberal party. It bore little relation to a broader conception of nationalism conceived for a whole society. He never supplied any kind of blueprint of the self-governing Wales that he claimed to desire. In fact, it seems scarcely conceivable that the ambitious young backbencher with a hearty contempt for the parochialism and puritanism of chapel-going society, and with a 'juggernaut' of ambition driving him on, would cut himself off from the central sources of power so irrevocably. The disenchantment with the British political system that shaped his outlook in the later months of 1895 did not last long. Probably the most that he would have demanded would have been some kind of modified devolution along the lines of the Labour government's proposals for Wales and Scotland advanced in 1976–9. In any event, after the traumatic crisis at Newport in January 1896, his interests moved on. He would fight for a losing cause, but never for a lost one. He was never one for slogging, meaningless trench warfare either in politics or in military strategy. The hopes and visions of Welsh home rule were well and truly lost thereafter for three generations. The centralizing pressures of the Liberal Party after 1896, like those of the Labour Party after 1922, suppressed pressures for separatism in Wales as they did in Scotland. Only in a very different political world in the later 1960s, when the appeal of national political parties, like other sacred cows of British life, seemed to weaken, and Englishness seemed less obviously the key to prosperity and civilization, did the demand for Welsh self-government became vocal once again. Even then, it was only a minority of Welshmen who responded as the referendum of 1979 was to show; the majority, especially in the south-east, were as apprehensive of domination by the Welsh-speaking hinterland as the Cardiff businessmen had been in 1896. Welsh home rule had always been the cry of a minority. In 1900 that minority was so small and shattered in morale that separatism was stillborn.

If the test of a nationalist movement is Ireland, then the Welsh national renaissance of the period from 1880 to 1910 must appear highly unsatisfactory. Welsh nationalism was political only to a limited degree, and scarcely at all separatist then or later. But the major significance of Welsh historical development in the hundred years from 1880 lies in the fact that its fortunes and impulses have been radically different from those of southern Ireland. If Wales has not to date enjoyed any viable form of self-government, neither has it experienced or sought the trauma of conflict and civil war. In the period after 1880, the peaceful quality of the Welsh national movement seemed to most contemporaries its outstanding feature. It emphasized the aspects of the nation and its culture that were most enduring; it played down social, class, and sectarian differences; it stressed the qualities and values that brought most Welsh people together. It had extraordinary achievements to show in linguistics, in imaginative literature, in historical scholarship, in popular culture as transmitted by Owen M. Edwards and the newspaper press. There were institutional symbols in the National Museum and Library, above all in the glorious achievement, against all the odds, of a national university, a dream since the age of Glyn Dŵr, now a vigorous reality. By 1910, Wales seemed more thriving and more aware of its national potential than at any period in its chequered history. In the peaceful world that it was hoped the new century would bring, civilized by the liberal ethic, there seemed no valid reason why this steady progress should ever come to an end.

Above all else, this cultural reawakening brought an immense surge of self-confidence, which transformed the quality of life at every level. Wales was defensive and anxious no longer. The native language, which in the later twentieth century was to become a token of precarious survival and cultural attenuation, seemed in 1910 more vigorous than ever before. The fact that a smaller proportion of the Welsh people spoke it did not arouse much concern at this time—49.9 per cent in 1901, only 43.5 (of whom 35 per cent were bilingual) in 1911. The linguistic and literary attributes of that language had never been stronger. Further, the numbers of those who spoke their native language were steadily increasing. In 1911, the total reached 977,366: surely they would be able to cymricize the immigrants into the towns and cities of the south and north-east. If Welsh *emigrés* to England were added, then the total of Welsh speakers would reach well over a million. Further, they were using their language for a wider range of contemporary purposes political and administrative as well as literary and academic. Welsh national consciousness, it appeared, had broken free of the shackles of the 'unhistoric nationalities'. It bore witness to achievements in scholarly and institutional terms that the Slav peoples of eastern Europe, for instance, had frequently failed to attain by 1914. Many of these achievements, it should be added, owed much to the benevolence and growing enlightenment of politicians and civil servants in England who saw the recognition of Welsh culture as a way of shoring up the United Kingdom, not of undermining it on the Irish model. The national renaissance, then and later, gave the Welsh people legitimate pride. It extended to a politically liberated, economically prosperous people new cultural horizons. It created a nation less tormented, more secure, more at peace with itself and a wider world.

CHAPTER 5

THE EDWARDIAN HIGH NOON

Edward Gibbon, at the start of his epic history, looked back on the Age of the Antonines as the period when the human race was most happy, cultivated, and prosperous. It was ruled by emperors 'severe to themselves, indulgent to the imperfections of others, just and beneficent to all mankind'.[1] A historian with a more modest province, the history of Wales in the recent period, may perhaps look back on the Edwardian era from about 1905 down to the coming of war in 1914, as Wales's Antonine Age, a period when the economic prosperity, national awareness, and political creativity of the Welsh people were most effectively deployed for the benefit of themselves and their neighbours. Almost all the literature of this era, the periodicals, the daily press, the memoirs, the social commentaries, the devotional and scholarly works, provide testimony to the golden glow of optimism and hope that characterized this happy generation. Only occasionally amongst the intelligentsia at least, in diaries or in the private correspondence of individualists such as the Anglo-Catholic nationalist J. Arthur Price does one encounter a note of pessimism or foreboding. This buoyant national confidence sometimes reached absurd levels. The full range of Darwinian organic biology, as related to the comparative cultural qualities of different races, was deployed in extolling the Welsh rugby victory over the all-conquering New Zealand 'all blacks' at Cardiff Arms Park in December 1905. Here at last, in the view of some sentimental observers, Matthew Arnold's analysis of the superior intuitive qualities of the Celt in contrast to the more prosaic virtues of the steadier Saxon, had found its ultimate fulfilment.[2] Periodical articles on 'Wales and the World' painted a picture of growing worldwide recognition of the political importance and cultural significance of the Welsh. The political elevation of 'Billy' Hughes, born in Llansanffraid-ym-Mechain, to become Labour premier of Australia in 1915, even more absurdly the selection of Charles Evans Hughes, the son of a native of Tredegar, to become Republican candidate for the presidency of the United States in 1916 were later thought to provide further evidence of the international impact of the Welsh.

[1] Edward Gibbon, *The Decline and Fall of the Roman Empire,* vol. i (Everyman ed.), p. 78.
[2] Theodore Watts-Dunton's introduction to 1906 edition of Borrow's *Wild Wales*, pp. xxii–xxiii.

The eyes of the world, it was claimed, were increasingly focused upon gallant little Wales, and still the wonder grew.

New heights of bathos were scaled in 1911 with the investiture of the young Edward as Prince of Wales. It was a quaint, if picturesque ceremony at Caernarfon Castle on a brilliantly sunny day, like its sequel, the investiture of Prince Charles in July 1969. The specific ritual, supposed to recall the original proclamation of the son of Edward I at Caernarfon in the late thirteenth century was largely devised by the bizarre combination of Bishop A. G. Edwards of St. Asaph and David Lloyd George, Chancellor of the Exchequer (now firm friends). In terms of the real Wales of 1911, the Caernarfon investiture was a grand irrelevance. For all that, it undoubtedly focused national and international attention upon Wales and its people. In return, there was a flood of emotional and patriotic self-congratulation in the periodicals and newspapers of the principality. Even a critic as sardonic as W. J. Gruffydd was temporarily moved by this national euphoria. In the journal *Wales*, he extolled the particularly Celtic qualities exemplified above all in the cultural missionary work of Owen M. Edwards and the political drive and dynamism of David Lloyd George. 'The spirit of modern Wales is as fertile in songs of action as in plans of social reform.'[3] To many Edwardians, then—and the term can be extended beyond Edward VII's death in May 1910 to span the whole era up to August 1914—the Welsh had absorbed the qualities of the Greeks and of the Romans as well. They were cultural innovators, intellectuals, and educators. They were also businessmen, planners, and social engineers. They were as active in the dockyards of Cardiff as in the choral festivals of Caernarfon. The future beckoned with seemingly unlimited promise.

Despite the sentimentality, and even the plain foolishness, of some of these national claims, despite the already dated Darwinian emphasis with which they were often presented, there are solid grounds, nevertheless, for seeing Edwardian Wales as a land of especial achievement and success. In the first place, the material prosperity of the nation reached new peaks of affluence. South Wales in particular seemed to be swept along on a tidal wave of economic expansion. Of course, this prosperity did not by any means apply to the whole of Wales. The slate-quarrying industry in Gwynedd, for instance, entered a depressed phase after the turn of the century, particularly after the unsatisfactory ending of the three-year-old Penrhyn quarry strike in November 1903. Markets were falling away, there was renewed depression in the domestic building industry which reduced the demand for Welsh slate, there was a formidable new competitor in the imported tiles used for roofing material. Lloyd George himself, whose constituency included many quarrymen, inadvertently helped depress the slate industry still further when his

[3] *Wales*, June 1911, p. 83.

Budget of 1909 (technically the Finance Act of 1910), by inflating the price of land due for valuation, led to a fall in the number of new houses being built. The encouragement offered by the Board of Education by the use of slates in school instruction was very modest compensation. The working week was reduced in the quarries of Penrhyn and Llechwedd; by 1913, widespread poverty was reported throughout the Nantlle valley, with the labour force contracting sharply.

Again, Welsh agriculture remained in comparative terms poor and under-capitalized, despite the marginal recovery since 1900. The sub-committee of the Welsh Party, under the chairmanship of Sir Alfred Mond, which reported in July 1914 again spelt out the insecurity and want of resources of tenant farmers. The improvement in the economic base of Welsh farming since the turn of the century had evidently only been a modest affair. More serious, the Welsh National Memorial Association, launched by David Davies MP, the heir to the Llandinam estate, in September 1910 with a donation of £125,000, drew stark attention to the inadequate housing, malnutrition, and low standards of hygiene in Welsh rural areas. In particular, tuberculosis was more prevalent in rural Wales than in other parts of the United Kingdom: the six worst-affected counties, Anglesey, Caernarfon, Merioneth, Cardigan, Pembroke, and Carmarthen, were all Welsh, and all largely rural in character.

Despite these grim facts, the overwhelming conclusion to be drawn about most of Welsh economic and social life in the years up to 1914 was that it was exceptionally thriving. The surging economic success of the industry and commerce of the south Wales coalfield meant opportunities of employment and a diffusion of wealth throughout the whole of the principality to some degree. By 1913, the south Wales coal industry was at its zenith. Its workforce included over a quarter of a million miners. It was emphatically the largest and most prosperous coalfield in Britain, probably in the world. By 1913, exports of Welsh coal, steam and bituminous coal from Cardiff, Barry, and Newport, anthracite from Port Talbot, Swansea, and Llanelli, were running at almost thirty million tons, about 40 per cent of the entire coal exports of the United Kingdom. With Britain claiming about four-fifths of the world carrying trade, according to the statistical calculations of D. A. Thomas (which Jevons later largely confirmed), it could be said that south Wales products constituted about a third of the coal exports of the world. The domestic heating of eastern and central Europe, the railways of France, Italy, Brazil, and Argentina, above all the oceanic steam-driven carrying fleet of the world, all rested to a great degree on the expanding production and aggressive marketing of Welsh coal. The pits of south Wales, for all their labour troubles and low productivity (partly geological in origin, partly due to the resistance of management and men to improved machinery such as modernized coal cutters), were booming. The valleys of the Cynon and the Rhondda, Ogmore and Garw, Swansea and Neath, Taff and Sirhowy, Rhymney and Ebbw were alive with the pulsating growth that resulted from the limitless demands for coal.

Nor was it coal alone that was surging ahead. As had been seen, the tin-plate industry of west Wales showed new buoyancy after the turn of the century, especially through the sheeting of galvanized steel. By 1914 it was clear that the tinplate mills of western Glamorgan and eastern Carmarthen-shire had freed themselves from 'the curse of McKinley', those immense tariffs put up in the United States from 1891. They were again expanding rapidly with newer technological resources and increased capital investment. Welsh steel was also prospering, in compensation for the depressed state of the old iron industry at Dowlais and elsewhere. From East Moors in Cardiff to Shotton in Deeside, Welsh steel production was booming. In 1909 John Summers notably expanded the Shotton works with a vast new steel-manufacturing plant for the making of steel bars.

With heavy industry so thriving, Welsh commerce and shipping flourished equally. The Edwardian era was a golden age for Newport, Barry, Swansea, and above all Cardiff. The chambers of commerce of those major ports were manned by aggressive, self-confident entrepreneurs, men such as Cory, Nicholl, and Radcliffe, well aware of the pivotal importance of their mer-cantile citadels in the British and the world economy. The docks of Cardiff, especially the Bute Docks and the Roath basin, were immensely active—indeed, unable to keep up with the demands imposed on them by the freight of coal and other minerals from the valleys. Barry had surged ahead since 1889 with its rail links with the Rhondda; by 1913 it had actually outstripped Cardiff in the tonnage of coal exported, free on board. The new King's Dock at Swansea was fully stretched with the handling of tin sheet and anthracite. The return, both in contributions to the invisible exports which sustained the British economy (shipping, insurance, broking, investment, and the like) and to the immediate affluence of the south Wales region was immense.

Inevitably, the social structure and the very quality of life in south Wales began to respond to this economic success and the new consumer affluence. Cardiff, designated the capital city of Wales in 1905, began to look like a metropolis by 1914. It was the Mecca for the working-class citizens of the colonized valleys to the north who came to the big city to marvel at great departmental stores like Howells, and to worship at its chapels and sporting stadia. Its industrial population included Germans, Italians, Spaniards, Somalis, Indians, and Chinese. By 1914, Cathays Park in the centre of the city was ringed with an impressive display of Baroque buildings, Cardiff City Hall and the National Museum (completed in 1927) to the south, the Law Courts and Glamorgan County Hall to the west (with the 'Temple of Peace' to join them in 1938), the University College to the east. Lanchester and Rickards's City Hall, with its dome crowned by an enormous Welsh dragon, was a particularly celebrated example of Edwardian Baroque, Austrian and

French in inspiration as well as English. If Cardiff was not yet the Athens of the west, it certainly exhibited some of the style and dignity of civic status. Its growing middle class, expanding with the progress of commerce and shipping in the port of Cardiff, began to settle in new bourgeois suburbs, assisted by the growth of municipal bus and tram services which enabled them to live at some distance from their place of work in the central dockside areas. The Roath Park district around the lake had by 1914 become a haven for aspiring Cardiff bourgeois and it has remained one ever since. Cardiff also subscribed to the 'city beautiful' movement, associated with disciples of Morris and Norman Shaw, Mackintosh and Voysey. There were public-utility societies in Wales concerned with building houses that were well established before 1914. The most notable of them were the Welsh Town Planning and Housing Trust, of which David Davies MP was the president, and Welsh Garden Cities Ltd, a purely commercial body. In addition, there was the South Wales Garden Cities and Town Planning Association, which merged with another body to form the Welsh Housing and Development Association in 1916.

The most striking legacy of these bodies was the institution of the new garden suburb of Rhiwbina to the north of Cardiff. It was founded on a co-operative basis, under which tenants would in effect become investors, by the Rhiwbina Garden Village Society, registered in 1912. It was very much on the lines of the Hampstead Garden Suburb or Bedford Park in London, and inspired by much the same kind of emphasis on planned open development. By 1914 it had built seventy houses in Rhiwbina, but its operations were then suspended by the war. A further impetus was to be given by the Addison Housing Act in 1919. Rhiwbina was intended as a mixed community largely for workers and the lower middle class. Its leading figures included Professor H. S. Jevons and Edgar L. Chappell, later secretary of the Welsh Housing Association and an ardent socialist and campaigner for the ILP. But Rhiwbina rapidly became, like its London counterparts, not a socially diverse community at all, but a peaceful leafy refuge for bankers, accountants, and professors in their Voysey-style 'English houses'. The same eventually held true for other 'garden cities' or 'garden suburbs' in Wales, such as that launched at Barry in 1915, or that founded by Wrexham Tenants Ltd at Acton Park (and originally intended largely for miners from Gresford colliery) on the east of Wrexham in 1913. The latter had completed 245 houses by the end of 1915. There were also small local schemes at Llanidloes and Machynlleth. After the war, there was the Burry Port Garden Suburb to provide houses for employees at the ordnance factory at Pembrey. But all these, like Rhiwbina, were additions to middle-class suburbia. Further away from the grimy city centre of Cardiff, there were further middle-class oases at Gwaelod-y-Garth and Radyr, where the leading figures of the academic community of the University College at Cardiff tended to migrate. And the grandest citizens of all, the tycoons of trade and industry like the Cory family, fled to the rural pastures of the Vale of Glamorgan, to become aspirant gentry in their turn, socially and geographically distant from the sooty valleys, overcrowded dockyards, and overworked dockers who brought them their profits.

The new middle-class world of Cardiff (which contrasted ironically with Welsh claims to be a classless society in contradistinction to their English neighbours) was paralleled elsewhere. In Swansea, middle-class enclaves spread westwards from the centre of the old town, along Ffynone and Brynmill, taking in Cwmdonkin Drive in the Uplands (where Dylan Thomas was born to a schoolteaching family in 1914), along towards West Cross, Mumbles, and the delights of the Gower peninsula. Barry and Newport also produced their own professional or mercantile élite, though the wealthy of Barry often chose the stately villadom of Penarth with its gardens and pier as their place of refuge. In the smaller towns of the rest of Wales, bankers, wealthier shopkeepers and migrant *nouveaux riches* also made their settlements. Places like Tenby in Pembrokeshire, Aberdyfi in Merioneth, Colwyn Bay, Llandudno, and Rhos-on-Sea along the north Wales coast became fashionable for the retired wealthy middle class including a growing number of retired public schoolmasters, judges, and businessmen from England. There were, in the university towns, enclaves of academic villadom, often imposing in size and sometimes attractive in architectural style, in the College Road area of Bangor and towards the Menai Bridge, and along Llanbadarn and St. David's roads in Aberystwyth. This was where the growing middle class lived. Often they took vacations somewhere else. Many seaside resorts became popular, Tenby, Llandudno, Rhos, and especially Aberystwyth with its lengthy new promenade, golf course, and growing importance as a marketing and academic centre. It was sometimes hailed as the 'Biarritz of Wales'. By 1914 it had ten large hotels on the seafront, innumerable boarding houses, and such attractions as the large Pavilion built for entertainments on the mid-Victorian pier.

Alternatively, this middle class—and many working-class people as well, especially unmarried young men and women anxious for life partners—migrated for their summer holidays to the fashionable spas of mid-Wales. If one town in Wales more than any other exhibited the affluence and success of Edwardian Wales, it was Llandrindod in Radnorshire, renamed Llandrindod Wells in the 1890s. Until the middle of the century, it had been only a small hamlet with a few boarding houses to accommodate those wishing to partake of the water from the mineral springs. But after the coming of the railway in 1865, by means of the mid-Wales line from Shrewsbury to Swansea, Llandrindod experienced an extraordinary boom in its popularity. By 1912 its population was recorded as 2,779: in 1921 it was to reach a peak of 4,596. During the season, more than 100,000 people would visit it. Apart from the traditional attraction of the waters, sulphurous, chalybeate, saline, and magnesium, Llandrindod offered a vast range of genteel family entertain-

ment—golf, bowls, and boating in the day time, *soirées*, palm court orchestras, and dances in the evening. Above all, there was an endless panorama in
its parks and small streets; it was a Welsh Cheltenham, Harrogate, even
Marienbad, where the socially aspiring could see and be seen. Llandrindod's
hotels, such as the Metropole, Glanusk, and Gwalia, with their Baroque
ornamentation, glass chandeliers, elaborate mirrors, and oriental carpeting,
were clients of the new prosperity, not least for the mercantile élite of south
Wales and the Liverpool and London Welsh. It was also the ideal centre for
the innumerable conferences and committees that the Liberal ascendancy
generated. Truly for Llandrindod Wells, and to a lesser extent Llanwrtyd
Wells and Builth Wells along the Wye, Edwardian Wales was a halcyon age of
Regency-type splendour and gaiety.

There was, then, a growing middle class in Wales able to display its
affluence in conspicuous consumption and ostentatious leisure—literally
keeping up with the Joneses, in fact. There were, as has been seen, swelling
crowds of manufacturers, shippers, and merchants in south and north-east
Wales, together with the academics, bankers, and small businessmen of the
north and west. Their ranks were being afforced all the time with the growth
of an educated class through the spread of the county schools, and the further
expansion of the university colleges and of Bangor Normal and other training
colleges at Cardiff, Carmarthen, and Caernarfon. The schoolteaching profession, in English as well as Welsh schools, was rapidly becoming a Welsh
preserve, an obvious escape route for the socially and intellectually ambitious
young, yet one that could retain them for employment within their own native
communities. Welshmen became prominent in the National Union of
Teachers, like Tom John, a Rhondda headmaster and president of the NUT
in 1905. By 1914, the prestige of senior schoolmasters and headmasters and
headmistresses in Wales was high, in part due to the expanding operations of
the Central Welsh Board. Those school heads who served on the Central
Board's executive at its foundation, like Tom John, Dr George Turpin of
Swansea Grammar School, and Miss Collins of Cardiff High School for Girls,
became respected public figures.

The legal profession was also steadily expanding. Of course, Welsh
barristers usually had to make their way on English circuits, though there
were recorderships and county court judgeships to tempt them back to Wales.
Barristers loomed large in Welsh Liberal circles, as such names as Ellis
Griffith, David Brynmor Jones, Llewelyn Williams, and Samuel T. Evans
indicate. It was also a nation of endlessly busy solicitors, a profession that
expanded enormously with the new demands and opportunities of the county
councils and other organs of local and central government. Men like Alfred
T. Davies, once a solicitor in Liverpool, then first secretary of the Welsh
department of the Board of Education in 1907, or Evan R. Davies, who rose
from being town clerk of Pwllheli to entering Lloyd George's private

secretariat in 1919, showed the potential upward mobility for an industrious, obedient country solicitor. Welsh doctors also expanded in number, their profession shortly to be enhanced by the founding of the Welsh School of Medicine in Cardiff: its early progress, however, was complicated by internal dissensions in Cardiff over the creation of a medical faculty. The doctor-politician Christopher Addison was asked by Lloyd George in June 1914 to disentangle the position regarding a grant from the Treasury. 'They are at sixes and sevens there', Addison recorded in his diary.[4] However, Lloyd George's National Health Insurance Act of 1911, with its generous capitation fees and stimulus to preventive medicine, was a further incentive for Welsh general practitioners to develop their practice, even in less fashionable, thinly-populated country areas or in the mining valleys of the south.

Finally, there was now a discernible Welsh bureaucracy: periodicals wrote enthusiastically of 'administrative Wales'. There were the growing staffs of the new county councils which markedly changed the pattern of employment in such towns as Caernarfon, Holyhead, Aberystwyth, and Carmarthen. There were openings in central government such as the new department of the Board of Education founded in 1907, and later the Welsh Council of Agriculture, with Professor Bryner Jones of Aberystwyth as commissioner, set up in 1912. A notable new departure was the creation, in 1912, of a special Welsh commission to administer the new National Health Insurance Act, a measure of devolution by Lloyd George which Braithwaite and other civil servants in Whitehall much resented. As in other parts of Britain, the Welsh National Insurance Commission became a major entrée for able young Welshmen into the government service. Lloyd George was to make use of many of its recruits when he expanded the organs of central government after becoming Prime Minister in December 1916; a veritable Welsh Mafia was in the making. Sir T. J. Hughes, formerly active on the Glamorgan county council, served as its first chairman from 1912 to 1920 and became a powerful figure in public life. More important still in the long term was his secretary, a relatively little-known economics lecturer from Queen's University, Belfast, Thomas Jones of Rhymney. He had moved back to Wales in 1910 to take up the secretaryship of the Welsh National Memorial Association formed to combat tuberculosis and ill-health generally; he had forged a firm alliance with David Davies MP of Llandinam. As secretary of the National Insurance Commission from January 1912, he proved immensely capable, despite such difficulties as rivalry with Lloyd George's 'darkly ambitious' secretary, John Rowlands. After 1916 'T.J.' was to move into the new Cabinet secretariat under Sir Maurice Hankey and to become the very prototype of the 'fluid person' in central government, the model of the bureaucratic Welshman.[5]

A new range of professional, managerial Welshmen now moved almost

[4] Christopher Addison, Four and a Half Years (London, 1934), vol. i. p. 18 (16 June 1914).
[5] Thomas Jones to his wife, 12 December 1916 (NLW, Thomas Jones Papers).

effortlessly along with him to dominate the new expanding worlds of government and its myriad of committees with which Wales was saturated. Men like Alfred T. Davies and Evan R. Davies have already been referred to. Most characteristic of all, perhaps, was Percy Watkins, the son of an auctioneer in Llanfyllin, Montgomeryshire, who began life as a reporter on the *Oswestry Advertiser*. He was to move on to become first secretary of the Central Welsh Board in 1896; secretary to the West Riding Education Committee in 1903; registrar of the University College, Cardiff, in 1910; assistant secretary to the Welsh Insurance Commission in 1912; finally, secretary of the newly-created Welsh Board of Health from 1919 to 1925. He occupied a variety of niches in Welsh public service, every one of them highly influential. His marvellously evocative memoirs, *A Welshman Remembers* (1944) provide a superbly documented, delicately restrained commentary on the rise of the new *apparatchik* in the administrative cadres of Wales. In this and other ways, then, the new economic affluence of Wales had its social counterpart in the new professional and administrative classes, the true conquerors of the social revolution that found its fulfilment in Edwardian Wales.

In addition to economic affluence and professional advancement, it was also a time of increasingly passionate national awareness. As has been seen in the previous chapter, the Edwardian years marked a climax in an intense cultural renaissance. The impact of men like Morris-Jones and Owen M. Edwards was all-pervasive. Morris-Jones's influence on standards of literary craftsmanship and linguistic precision was now vast indeed. In 1911 he began a new literary periodical, *Y Beirniad* (The Judge), an interesting title with its evocations of the adjudications at the national *eisteddfod*. Here, new critical standards were to be set for literary and linguistic studies. Poets like Thomas Gwynn Jones, Silyn Roberts, and W. J. Gruffydd were at the height of their powers, advancing beyond simpler styles of lyricism in their poetry. In 1910, it became clear that another major poet had arrived to join them, R. Williams Parry, yet another product of rural Caernarvonshire. His prize-winning *awdl*, *Yr Haf*, (Summer) at the Colwyn Bay *eisteddfod* has always been considered a masterpiece of technical craftsmanship. In 1912, another, still younger poet emerged, Thomas Parry-Williams, who hailed from Rhyd Ddu in the same small community in rural Caernarvonshire as Williams Parry to whom he was distantly related. Parry-Williams actually captured both the crown and the chair at the Wrexham *eisteddfod* in 1912, a feat he was to repeat at Bangor three years later. His writings were suffused with the rural nostalgia for *y werin* current in so much Welsh literature at the time. *Y Ddinas* (the city) was a fierce condemnation of the squalor, cruelty, and immorality of the city (Paris being specifically referred to) and a celebration of the purer, decent qualities of the small rural community. Equally heartening, other forms of literary expression were also being used in the Welsh language—the short story, the extended novel—while, through the person of J. O. Francis, the first significant native drama was written, albeit in English.

How many people benefited from these artistic creations, how many actually read these poems is very hard to determine. One knows that they sold and published well, and that their authors became for a time nationwide celebrities. The more academic *Beirniad*, however, sold no more than 1,000 copies. Most Welsh people rejoiced in the existence of distinguished, creative writers in their midst, drawn from the humbler ranks of rural society. It must markedly have stimulated the national pride so redolent of these golden Edwardian years. But national pride could exist at other, less rarefied levels as well. The popular press was full of optimistic national confidence in all respects. One interesting example of this was the new monthly, *Welsh Outlook*, started up by the initiative of Thomas Jones in the autumn of 1913. It was a tribute to his lifelong association with the cultural and national mainsprings of his native land, as well as with high politics in London. The 'fluid person' had the heart, soul, and passion of a patriot. As a student of the industrial scene, he was particularly concerned by the signs of class conflict in the coalfield, and anxious to divert his countrymen to higher, national values that would draw them all together. His periodical first appeared in January 1914 and was shortly to be overtaken by the First World War, even though it continued publication until the end of 1933. It provided a powerful intellectual conspectus of the major developments in politics, literature, religion, social thought and action, from a relatively non-partisan standpoint. It provided a platform for such earnest commentators on the human condition as the Revd Gwilym Davies, a Baptist minister in Carmarthenshire. He had been recently the founder of the 'Welsh School of Social Service', a kind of Cymric version of the nonconformist 'forward movements' in England. Daniel Lleufer Thomas, another characteristic Edwardian, was to serve as its chairman from 1911 to 1923. *Welsh Outlook* was mildly, benevolently nationalistic. It preached a kind of gradualist devolution while always indicating the gulf that lay between Welsh aspirations and Irish. Its editors included such constructive patriots as Edgar Chappell, Watkin Davies (later one of Lloyd George's biographers), and T. Huws Davies, editor, poet, and publicist, destined to end up administering the secularized temporalities of the Church. The tone of *Welsh Outlook*, evangelistic and infused with *gravitas*, was captured in its title-page on which the biblical phrase rang out— 'where there is no vision, the people perish'.

The vision of most working people, however, was probably focused on other, less intellectual symbols of national pride. The Welsh in the Edwardian age may well have been a musical nation, perhaps a religious one as well. Beyond doubt, they were and have remained a sporting nation with a fierce commitment to national success. Professional boxing was one activity with

⁶ J. O. Francis, 'The New Welsh Drama', *Wales*, November 1913, pp. 6–8.

much appeal in the valleys: no doubt, the monetary rewards that were offered to hungry, physically tough young Welsh fighters made the Welsh coafield a natural breeding-ground for aspiring pugilists. As it happened, south Wales produced some of the outstanding performers in the British prize ring in this era. 'Freddie Welsh' (Frederick Hall Thomas from Pontypridd, the son of an auctioneer) won the British light-weight championship in 1909; in 1914 he defeated an American to become light-weight champion of the world. His zest for his profession was inexhaustible; in 1907 he knocked out three opponents in one day. Jim Driscoll, a Cardiffian of Irish parentage, won the British bantam-weight championship in 1910 and the European championship two years later. He had already won the world title and retired undefeated after four years' tenure in 1913. Driscoll became a legendary exponent of the classical style of so-called 'self-defence'. The most celebrated of all was to be Jimmy Wilde, born at Quaker's Yard in 1892 but usually associated with Tylorstown, Rhondda, fly-weight champion of the world in 1916 and probably the most skilful and successful British boxer there has ever been. In his career, he lost only four contests out of 864. The Welsh credentials of these boxers were in no doubt. In time, they even figured alongside the preachers, poets, and professors recorded in Welsh biographical dictionaries. On the other hand, there was immense distaste in Welsh nonconformist circles at the fame gained by men who achieved eminence through physical violence and the deliberate inflicting of injury on fellow men. The Welsh indeed, a peaceful people, have always been ambivalent about the boxing successes of their countrymen. The other side of boxing was always there to be recorded—Jim Driscoll down and out financially, wandering around the pubs of London penniless after his retirement, and dying at forty-four; Jimmy Wilde retiring with a fortune of £70,000, almost all of which was promptly lost for him; and, of course, hundreds or thousands who ended their days of involvement with the 'noble art' as unknown punch-drunks, mental and physical wrecks.

A much less controversial and overwhelming popular source of national sporting esteem was rugby football. In the Edwardian era, the reputation of the Welsh for unique skill at rugby, especially in the finer points of attacking open half-back and three-quarter play, was firmly established. Indeed, the Welsh were the first to play with four three-quarters to assist in fluid running play. After the first humiliating defeat by England, the Welsh rugby team defeated the other nations with regularity. In the 'golden age' between 1900 and 1912, the 'Triple crown' was won six times in twelve years. It was very much a south Wales game, dominated by Newport, Cardiff, and Swansea, with Neath, Aberavon, Llanelli, and Pontypool also emerging as first-class sides. Most of Wales was not rugby territory at all and took pride rather in the success of Welsh soccer players such as the Morriston tinplate worker, Billy Meredith, a celebrated outside-right for Manchester City and a man of extraordinary speed and skill who played for Wales in forty-five international matches.

But the success of Welsh club sides, and above all, the triumphs of the Welsh international fifteen made rugby in south Wales a game apart. Early heroes such as the Newport three-quarter Arthur Gould were commemorated with civic monuments. The Edwardian years threw up a golden generation of gifted rugby backs. Their greatest day of glory came on 16 December 1905, with the legendary defeat of the unbeaten New Zealand 'all blacks' by 3–0. Two of the Welsh heroes of that day were born in England; the captain and centre-three-quarter, Gwyn Nicholls, was from Gloucestershire while Bert Winfield, the full-back and his brother-in-law, came from Leicester. But most of the Welsh backs were indisputably Welsh-speaking natives, notably the famous Swansea scrum-half Dickie Owen. So, too, were other noted performers such as Percy Bush, Billy Trew, Rhys Gabe, Willie Llewelyn, and Dr 'Teddy' Morgan, who scored the winning try against the New Zealanders. Morgan, a highly-qualified medical practitioner who played side by side with miners and tinplaters, illustrates the role of rugby as a social solvent as distinct from its upper-class image in most of England. Most of these sporting heroes fitted naturally into their valley backgrounds even during these years of dazzling success for Welsh teams. When they retired, they usually remained in every sense sober citizens and accepted their new oblivion with modesty and good grace. Rugby was, and remains, an attractive aspect of the national identity of Wales. On the other hand, it was also a harmless safety-valve for national sentiment. Welsh identity, so easily asserted in pounding the Saxon on the rugby field, was too easily diverted, in the view of more serious nationalists, from the quest for national independence. Rugby and investitures, the bread and circuses of the populace, became a peaceful therapy to suppress embarrassing political aspirations. Then and later, most of the Welsh were content to have it that way. They rejoiced in their rugby skills, made no protest, and asked few questions.

The Welsh in the Edwardian years, then, drew secular inspiration from the sporting arena. More ethereal stimulus then, as before, came from the remarkable religious vitality of the land, to which mass sport often seemed a rival. For the nonconformist chapels, as for other institutions in Welsh life, the Edwardian years were a halcyon period, too, one viewed with nostalgia and affection in the difficult years after 1918. In 1906 the chapels were still at flood tide, still reeling with the inspiration of the religious revival associated with Evan Roberts since November 1904. For over eighteen months, chapel life all over Wales was galvanized by spontaneous Bible readings and prayer meetings and revivalist passion. Chapel membership boomed. In 1906, the four main denominations recorded a peak membership of 549,000. Evan Roberts himself, a strange mystical figure of doubtful sanity at the end, had become a major national influence, one to whom even Lloyd George had to pay obeisance. When Roberts observed seven days of silence in March 1905, that silence seemed to resound throughout Wales. The impact of the revival proved somewhat transient. Indeed, at the time it aroused some alarm amongst ministers for its revolutionary, almost anarchistic impact upon chapel congregations and denominational organization, and the way it drew attention away from pulpit preaching. By 1908 newspapers were recording that the main impulse of the revival in purely religious terms had been exhausted. Evan Roberts himself announced that he was 'quite run down'; his presence at a religious convention at Bangor in mid-April 1906 passed almost unnoticed. From 1907 he gave himself almost exclusively to a ministry of intercessory prayer. During his later years, he became a recluse and lived obscurely in Cardiff from 1930 until his death in 1951.

In 1908, a Caernarfon newspaper conducted two surveys of attendance at places of worship, one on a bitterly cold Sunday in January, the second on a glorious warm, sunny day in July.[7] Each showed the same pattern—that in this centre of religion, with its twenty-two places of worship including five large Methodist chapels, only about one in eight of the population of over 9,000 attended church or chapel on Sunday. The figures were higher for Sunday evening than for the morning, which the newspaper surmised might have something to do with the weekend entertainment at Caernarfon's thirty-eight public houses. Most disturbing, the attendance of children at Sunday school showed a distinct fall compared with the past. What the revival had done was to provide countless men and women with new hope and comfort in the face of brutalizing material conditions. The cause of temperance in particular made immense advances, as the Baptist *Seren Gomer* noted in 1905.[8] Social life became that much gentler and more civilized. Debts were paid; family feuds were healed overnight. But much of the inspiration was purely secular in terms of social communalism or even socialism. Certainly the Independent Labour Party was one beneficiary of the revolutionary impact of the revival; the political and social impulses of young men like Frank Hodges and James Griffiths were quickened accordingly. By 1914 all the main denominations were again recording annual decreases in membership. In all, 26,000 members had been lost in the six years since the revival passed its peak.

Later religious writers, like Ambrose Bebb and R. Tudur Jones, were to find the revival 'lamentable rather than creative'.[9] But still the Evan Roberts revival did give the Welsh chapels a temporary impetus, unique in the western world. Their association with the new national movement in the cultural and eisteddfodic fields provided more. On the eve of war in 1914, the institutional solidity of the chapels permeated Welsh life more than ever, outside perhaps

[7] *Carnarvon and Denbigh Herald*, 31 January, 7 February, 10 July 1908.
[8] *Seren Gomer*, March 1905, p. 63.
[9] R. Tudur Jones, *Hanes Annibyniaeth Cymru* (Swansea, 1966), p. 237.

of the major conurbations of Cardiff, Newport, and the south-east. Popular preachers such as the Revd John Williams of Brynsiencyn, Anglesey (Methodist) and the Revd Josiah Towyn Jones of Ammanford, Carmarthenshire (Independent) enjoyed a vast prestige and influence over their congregations. Towyn Jones indeed had higher aspirations still. In July 1912 he was elected MP for East Carmarthenshire, though it soon became obvious that his talent for emotional oratory was insufficient to make any noticeable impact on the laconic House of Commons.

Between 1906 and 1910 a royal commission sat to inquire into the condition of the various religious bodies in Wales, as a preliminary to possible disestablishment of the Church. Its picture, from the nonconformist standpoint, was a somewhat mixed one. It provided further evidence of the renewed vigour of the Church of England, whose communicants in 1906 had risen to 193,000, one-quarter of the whole. A younger bishop, John Owen of St. David's, a Welsh-speaking former Methodist from the heart of Llŷn in Caernarvonshire, was having a powerful effect, both in strengthening the educational and other institutions of the Church and in providing a new sense of pride in Welshness among traditionally Anglo-centric Welsh churchmen. The royal commission also provided ample evidence of the way in which political conflict vitiated collaboration between the Church and nonconformists, for instance in the temperance movement. The conduct of the commission itself was itself proof of this atmosphere of religious warfare amongst Christians of mutual ill-will. One commissioner, Sir Henry Jones, later recalled, 'Such an atmosphere of distrust, suspicion and pious malice I never breathed before or since'.[10] In April 1907 three of the nonconformist commissioners, Jones himself, Samuel Evans MP, and Principal Fairbairn of Mansfield College, Oxford, resigned in protest at the obstructive tactics of the chairman of the commission, a prickly Anglican, Judge Vaughan Williams. Even after this, the commission finally presented a series of reports in 1910, with little common ground between its members, a fair testimony to the climate in which it had conducted its inquiries.

Still, the reports did offer incontestable evidence of the residual strength of the chapels in Wales. Indeed, that strength was being reinforced because the doctrinal barriers between the denominations were now relatively minor, save for the Baptist belief in total immersion. This was confirmed by the founding in 1906 of an annual Free Church Convention for Wales, as many nonconformists had long demanded. The Methodists, it was noted, were beginning to abandon their traditional system of itinerant ministers in favour of the more settled pastorate of the Independents.[11] In general, the picture

[10] H. J. Hetherington, *Life and Letters of Sir Henry Jones* (London, 1924), vol. 2, p. 95.

[11] Evidence to the Royal Commission appointed to inquire into the Church and other Religious Bodies in Wales, vol. 2 (Cd. 5433), qu. 13,834; vol. 4 (Cd. 5435), qu. 37,866 (Parl. Papers, 1910, xv, xvii).

that came through was one of religious bodies still self-confident and aggressive, well-endowed through voluntary contributions, above all strongly rooted in those parts of north and west Wales and the mining valleys that were most Welsh in speech and outlook. Much pride was taken in the Revd Evan Jones, Caernarfon, elected as the first Welsh president of the National Free Church Council in 1909. If Edwardian Wales was a time of prosperity and national awareness, the chapels, with all their limitations of puritanism and parochialism, were a part of that process.

Above all, Edwardian Wales was a land of relative political peace. Edwardian England is usually thought of as riven by political and social bitterness—the People's Budget and the Parliament Act; the suffragettes and the syndicalists; Irish home rule and National Insurance; personal scandals such as Lloyd George's involvement in the Marconi affair. Some authors have claimed to detect a 'strange death' of Liberal England at this time, long before 1914. In Wales, by contrast, Liberalism was without doubt very much alive. Its very strength throughout most levels of Welsh life, the very feebleness of the Tory challenge gave a unity and a peace to Welsh politics which are most striking. It might be added, too, that some of the themes that agitated Edwardian England were less powerful in Wales. The suffragettes, for instance, made relatively little headway in the principality. More than most parts of Britain, nonconformist Wales was a sternly patriarchal society which believed that a woman's place was in the home and in chapel, certainly not in the polling-booth, even though Lloyd George and many other Welsh Liberals voted for women's suffrage in the House. When suffragettes interrupted a speech by Lloyd George when he was opening a village hall in his home community of Llanystumdwy in 1910, and again when they interrupted proceedings at the Wrexham national *eisteddfod* in 1912, they met with no sympathy and scant mercy. Stewards battered them with Old Testament fervour. Social and religious equality might be honoured in Wales. Sexual equality was not, despite the steady entry of Welsh girls to the schoolteaching and other professions. The first branch of the Women's Institute movement was not established in Wales until 1915, with one founded at Llanfairpwll in Anglesey, though the movement later grew rapidly.

Liberalism in Wales was at this period overwhelmingly strong. In the general election of January 1906, as was seen in Chapter 2, the Liberals captured every seat in the principality, save for Keir Hardie's return as junior member for Merthyr Tydfil—and he was the beneficiary of second votes from Liberal electors. Everywhere, the Unionists were routed, usually by huge majorities, from Cardiff to Caernarfon Boroughs. Nor did this Liberal tide show much sign of ebbing thereafter. By-elections at East Denbighshire in 1906 and at Pembrokeshire in 1908 saw huge Liberal majorities virtually unimpaired. Nor was there much recession in the two general elections of January and December 1910 in which the Liberal Party nationally lost much of its impetus and lost, too, its overall majority. In January 1910, national fervour for Liberalism, fanned anew by the People's Budget, was almost as great as in 1906. The combined Liberal–Labour vote was assessed at 260,876 as against 121,521 Unionist votes. In 1906, the estimated totals had been a rough 200,000 to 111,000. Two marginal border seats, Denbigh District and Radnorshire, were lost to the Unionists. But, in general, Liberal enthusiasm at the grass-roots was as overwhelming as before. The People's Budget attracted much support, both for its duties on the 'unearned increment' of landlords, urban and rural, and for being the 'first Welsh budget', the handiwork of Lloyd George himself. Attacks on the Chancellor for his alien, Welsh qualities were foolishly made by Unionist peers. Archbishop Cosmo Lang alluded to 'that mysterious possession affecting the Celtic temperament which is called the "hwyl" which makes the speaker say he knows not what, and excites the audience they know not why'.[12] These criticisms merely added to the determination of Liberals in Wales.

In December 1910, the second election of that year, called to endorse the Asquith government's Parliament Bill, the Liberal strength in Wales remained basically undiminished. Radnorshire was won back, but Denbigh District and now Montgomery District, another border marginal, were lost to the Unionists. More damagingly in the long term, the great cosmopolitan port of Cardiff was lost to the younger son of the Marquess of Bute, Lord Ninian Crichton-Stuart, later to be killed in the war. The signs of Liberal decay had been evident in Cardiff since 1907 when the Liberals lost, permanently as events were to show, their majority on the city council. Otherwise the general pattern of Liberal domination was easily confirmed, as it was in the by-election at East Carmarthenshire in July 1912, called at a time of general unpopularity for the Liberal government in most parts of Britain. The memories of 1868, the strength of nonconformity in the north and west, and of Labour in the south, the growing awareness of national identity which was so closely associated with Liberalism at all levels—all these added to the residual dominance of Liberalism in Wales and its largely monolithic hold over political and intellectual life.

The Welsh Parliamentary Party played a more passive role in these years than it had done in the heyday of Tom Ellis and the young Lloyd George between 1886 and 1895. Its chairman until 1910 was the elderly Sir Alfred Thomas, later Lord Pontypridd, a businessman, a Baptist, and a bachelor. He was succeeded by Ellis Griffith (Anglesey), a far more brilliant figure and a successful barrister, and then by Sir David Brynmor Jones (Swansea District), yet another political lawyer from Wales. It was hard for them to make the Welsh Party very assertive in the House, with the government's comfortable majority, nor did they really try. Welsh Liberalism more generally seemed to be entering upon a kind of silver age. With Lloyd George, Herbert Lewis,

[12] Quoted in J. Hugh Edwards, *Life of David Lloyd George* (London, 1913), vol. iv, p. 126.

Reginald McKenna, and Samuel Evans in the government, many of the more effective members had been siphoned off; D. A. Thomas was mainly interested in his collieries and retired from political life in 1910. There was a tranquil quality about the Welsh Party now—quiet businessmen like Sidney Robinson and John Hinds, earnest solicitors like Ellis Davies, totally obscure figures like Vaughan Davies, the odd exotic like Sir Alfred Mond—returned for Swansea Town in January 1910 despite anti-Semitic onslaughts from his Tory opponents who placarded Swansea with posters that ridiculed his Germanic accent and proclaimed 'Vales for the Velsh'. In the constituencies, Liberalism largely slumbered without effective challenge. The National Liberal Council, formed in 1898, was an annual conference, nothing more, certainly not an echo of the separatist aspects of the Cymru Fydd League. Even so, there were still distinguished figures in politics to draw attention to the grievances and needs of Wales. There was, in particular, Llewelyn Williams, member for Carmarthen Boroughs from 1906 to 1918, an ardent patriot, successful barrister, historian, novelist, man of letters, a cultivated and gifted man. His failure to gain government office after 1906 is a mystery, as (until 1912) is that of Ellis Griffith.

Above all, there was Lloyd George. His relationship to Welsh Liberalism was a somewhat ambivalent one at this period. He lived largely in England now, and was increasingly estranged from his wife, firmly based at Criccieth. He golfed at Walton Heath, he holidayed on the French Riviera. His associates were newspaper tycoons, self-made businessmen, adventurers he met in the clubs and political underworld of London. He was under fire at times for neglecting Welsh interests. In the summer of 1907 there was a threatened 'revolt' against the government by nonconformists because of the failure to introduce a Welsh disestablishment bill. Lloyd George managed to quell the protests with an adroit display of patriotic oratory at Cardiff—though his friendly relations with one of the leading rebels, the veteran Revd Evan Jones of Caernarfon, also helped. Lloyd George, one may surmise, was somewhat bored with Welsh issues now, with his mind soaring on, not only to social reform and reconstruction, but also to dreams of inter-party coalition as outlined by him to the Liberal and Unionist leaders in London in the autumn of 1910. In 1906, the Archbishop of Canterbury, Randall Davidson, was told that he was anxious to see disestablishment and disendowment settled quickly.[13] They were a time-worn legacy of the past which got in the way of progressive legislation and purposive action now. For all that, he remained the personification of Welshness at the highest pinnacles of politics. His home at 11 Downing Street was a very Welsh one, down to its famous cook, Sarah; certainly it was Welsh in speech. He retained some close ties with Criccieth and especially with his venerable Uncle Lloyd. His annual address to the national *eisteddfod* on Thursdays was 'Lloyd George's day', a national

[13] G. K. A. Bell, *Life of Archbishop Davidson* (London, 1935), vol. i, p. 504.

occasion in the life of Wales. He was by his very presence in the Cabinet a symbol of what a 'cottage-bred boy' could achieve and, by extension, of what poor little Wales itself could attain by its own talent and determination. *From Village Green to Downing Street* by J. Hugh Edwards, an early biography of the Chancellor published in 1908, made much of the folk-hero image. It extolled the country boy who had trod the primrose path, Horatio Alger-like, from Llanystumdwy to Westminster, bearing the hopes and dreams of his nation with him. As long as Lloyd George remained the central dynamic figure of British political life, the claims of Wales would not be forgotten.

Those claims varied somewhat in their fortunes in these years. The old controversies that surrounded education, temperance, and land reform somewhat petered out, and by 1914 were far less potent than ten years earlier. The Welsh revolt against the Balfour Education Act gradually subsided after the Liberals returned to office in 1906. One last echo came in the Oxford Street school case in Swansea, *The Board of Education* v. *T. J. Rice and others*, in 1909. The local authority was found in default by the House of Lords, and the Board of Education censured for its misuse of quasi-judicial adminstrative powers. An effort to remedy the nonconformist grievances on rate-aided education, especially over church schools, foundered when Birrell's Education Bill of 1906 was rejected by the House of Lords. Further bills, introduced by first McKenna and then Walter Runciman in 1908, also failed, through the usual denominational obstacles, as did a compromise measure brought forward by Bishop Edwards of St. Asaph in the House of Lords in the same year. It was clear now, in fact, that the church schools no longer formed a prime political issue for most Welshmen. Indeed, to wave sectarian banners over the schooling of the nation's children seemed in ironic contrast to the bipartisan achievements in setting up the new 'county' schools and the new University of Wales. Most local authorities by 1914 were administering the Balfour Act quietly enough. In fact, their control over the management and financing of the 'non-provided' church schools was greater than had been anticipated. In addition, a steady transfer of church schools to the local authorities was taking place. In 1903, there had been 926 state elementary schools, as against 800 Anglican. By 1913, the respective totals were 1,218 and 649. Secularism and shortage of cash were winning the nonconformists' battle for them, and quietly enough.

Temperance again had lost its capacity to inflame opinion. The failure of the government's licensing bill in the Lords, which contained some special provisions of a semi-prohibitionist kind in Wales, aroused some temporary protest. But here again was an 'Old Liberal' issue of scant concern to a new reform-minded generation. The failure to extend the Welsh Sunday Closing Act to Monmouthshire also aroused little discussion, even though the Inter-mediate Education Act had firmly included Monmouthshire as a part of Wales once again.

Equally, the Welsh land question had lost much of its urgency since the days of Thomas Gee (whose fine biography by T. Gwynn Jones appeared in 1913). This was partly through the relative improvement in the countryside compared with the years prior to 1900. By March 1914, the Liberal MP, Ellis Davies (Eifion), was casting doubt on the general diagnosis of the Welsh Land Commission in 1896.[14] He disputed that there was any marked difference now between Wales and England in the average size of a holding. The old nostrums of a land court and a judicially-fixed rental had lost their point. Instead, attention was focused on the land as a productive enterprise. New capital, long-term credits for tenant farmers, co-operative credit associations now seemed more urgent. So, too, did a minimum wage and improved housing for farm labourers, so long a neglected class. The problems of Welsh land increasingly seemed economic and technical, rather than social and sectarian. The Council of Agriculture set up in 1912 was a body of farmers and agriculturists, chosen without partisan distinction. Nationalists called for a Welsh Board of Agriculture, but in vain.

The supreme test for the vitality of Liberalism in the Edwardian era would come with the success or failure of the cause of church disestablishment. If the battle could not be won now, with a government majority of over 300 and Lloyd George himself in the Cabinet, then nonconformists would indeed despair. In fact, progress was cautious and erratic. The appointment of a royal commission in 1906 to inquire into the religious bodies in Wales was rightly regarded by many as a delaying measure by the government, to sweep a complex and embarrassing issue on one side. For the next three years, there was no government action to take disestablishment and disendowment in Wales any further. Nonconformists muttered indignantly at the irresolution of the government, but in general the official view that the Lords blocked the way for Welsh and other reforms was accepted. In April 1909 Asquith did introduce a Welsh disestablishment bill at last. It was much on the lines of that of 1895, save that a national council in Wales was to administer the secularized endowments after disestablishment. But it was obvious that this bill was introduced only as a token to placate the Welsh members. It carried its first reading by 172 votes (Unionists taking the unusual step of dividing the House at this stage), but then was lost to view. For the next two years, the Budget, the Parliament Bill, and National Insurance dominated public attention.

However, in 1912 it was clear that action on a Welsh Disestablishment Bill could no longer reasonably be delayed. The government had already committed itself to introducing a third Irish Home Rule Bill. The passage of the Parliament Act now meant that, within two years, the Lords' veto could be overridden and the separation of Church and State in Wales be safely accomplished. For the next two years, then, without much enthusiasm outside Wales and amidst some muttering of discontent amongst rank-and-file Liberals in

[14] *Wales*, March 1914, pp. 202–4.

England (supported by C. P. Scott in the *Manchester Guardian*)[15] about the severity of the terms of disendowment imposed on the Welsh Church, the government ploughed on with a disestablishment measure. McKenna introduced the first version in April 1912. It was twice passed by the House of Commons and twice rejected by the Lords. Finally, on 19 May 1914, the Welsh Church Bill received its third reading in the Commons for the third successive parliamentary session. There was now no constitutional obstacle to the passage into law of the Welsh Bill, nor indeed to the Irish Home Rule Bill, since that had also made its laborious progress through the Commons for the three requisite sessions.

This last phase of the battle for disestablishment was indeed monotonous. Lloyd George caused some initial excitement in May 1912, by accusing the aristocratic defenders of the Welsh Church of being themselves beneficiaries of the plunder of secularized church property in the reign of Henry VIII. Their hands, he declared, 'were dripping with the fat of sacrilege'. Lloyd George's views, colourfully expressed, were endorsed by the Liberal historian, A. F. Pollard, a biographer of Henry VIII; they were also echoed in memorable satirical verse by G. K. Chesterton with the refrain, 'Chuck it, Smith!'[16] Otherwise, Lloyd George seemed as bored as everybody else. The debates were often learned. The authorities of Stubbs, Maitland, Freeman, even of Giraldus Cambrensis were bandied across the floor of the House. There was much delving into medieval and dark-age Welsh history, into the title to glebe and the origins of tithe. But there was a general impression of a lack of passion. Even in Wales, rallies in support of the bill lacked the old fervour. In the world of the Tonypandy riots and the Curragh mutiny, the Welsh Church somehow seemed a less compelling priority. For all that, on the eve of war in 1914—and without the threat of violence that was looming in Ireland—Welsh Liberalism stood on the threshold of achieving its historic objective, sought for three generations past. Church commissioners to administer the secularized tithe, glebe and other endowments had already been appointed, and were shortly to begin work. The Welsh MPs sang their national anthem in triumph in the lobby of the House of Commons. For what it was worth, Welsh Liberalism had battled through to a historic victory.

There was only one real challenge to the Liberal ascendancy in this period, and this was without doubt a desperately serious one. The labour movement in Wales, as it had done with increasing intensity since 1898, menaced the traditional ascendancy of middle-class Liberalism, and the social and cultural assumptions of class collaboration and of national pride that went with it.

In political terms, the challenge came from the Labour Party, as the LRC had been christened just after the January 1906 general election. Labour had, after all, won a seat at the polls, Hardie hanging on to his seat at Merthyr Tydfil and defeating an unofficial Liberal in the process. He was then elected the first chairman of the parliamentary Labour Party, and provided an angry voice on behalf of rupturing the Liberal alliance and casting Labour on the high seas of independence. The threat from the Labour Party, and from the socialist ILP in particular, much preoccupied Welsh Liberals after 1906. Lloyd George, in a major speech to the Welsh National Liberal Federation at Cardiff in October of that year, devoted much attention to explaining that the Liberals, with their zeal for temperance, education, and land reform, were truly the party of the working man. Two years later, in October 1908, Lloyd George, again addressing the Welsh Liberal Federation, had moved on much further. Only a bold social reform policy—pensions, labour exchanges, health and unemployment insurance, housing reforms, anti-poverty programmes, and national development through public projects and afforestation—would ward off the challenge of socialism, and prevent British Liberalism from falling down the steep slope of decline that had been the fate of so many continental Liberal parties.

Meanwhile, the Labour Party continued to grow in Wales. The ILP claimed 95 branches in south Wales and nine in the north by 1910. It had penetrated the slate-quarrying districts of Caernarvonshire and Merioneth, where the poet Silyn Roberts was an ardent propagandist for the Labour cause. It had made headway in Wrexham and Flintshire in the north-east. The quarrymen now had a thriving Labour journal, *Y Dinesydd*. Labour found supporters even in the theological colleges of Bala and Aberystwyth, and won the allegiance of the Welsh Methodist divine, the Revd J. Cynddylan Jones. In south Wales, there were ILP strongholds from Llanelli to Newport, with particularly strong branches in Briton Ferry and Aberdare. However, it was the increased militancy and political commitment of the South Wales Miners' Federation that was now the main spur to the Labour Party, especially in the coalfield. Newer miners' agents, men like Charles Stanton in Aberdare, David Watts Morgan in Rhondda, Vernon Hartshorn in Maesteg, were strongly committed to working within the Labour Party. In 1908, when the Miners' Federation of Great Britain voted in favour of affiliation to the Labour Party, the Welsh miners voted overwhelmingly with the majority, and indeed determined the outcome of the vote. The old Lib-Labism of pre-1898 days was dying. As a result, the four Welsh 'Lib-Lab' MPs were projected on to the Labour benches, Mabon himself most unwillingly, John Williams (Gower), William Brace (South Glamorgan) and Tom Richards (West Monmouthshire) with scarcely more enthusiasm. As the temper of labour unrest mounted in the valleys, it became more and more difficult for the old progressive alliance between Labour and Liberalism to be maintained. Labour candidates were threatened in south Wales seats from East

Carmarthenshire to Breconshire. In the election of January 1910, the Labour challenge was, in fact, contained without much trouble. Ben Tillett, the dockers' leader, was swamped at Swansea Town by the influence and largesse of Sir Alfred Mond. Keir Hardie again came only second in the poll at Merthyr Tydfil, well behind the Liberal, Edgar Jones, a Baptist schoolteacher.

But the clash between Labour and Liberalism continued to mount. There was a fierce contest at a by-election in Mid-Glamorgan in March 1910 when a tinplate owner of no political talent or background narrowly defeated the local Labour miners' agent, Vernon Hartshorn. This was a particularly bitter by-election since the Liberal chief whip had tried in vain to persuade Mid-Glamorgan Liberals to give Labour a free run. It was followed by several more difficult contests at the general election of December 1910. In East Glamorgan, Clement Edwards (Liberal), once a radical journalist on the *Labour World* but now distinctly right wing, held off the challenge of Charles Butt Stanton, the Aberdare miners' agent, considered to be a near-revolutionary at this period. In Mid-Glamorgan, Hartshorn was again defeated, this time by J. Hugh Edwards, standing on behalf of Welsh national-ism and Liberal nonconformity in opposition to the stateless, allegedly atheistic socialism. In Gower (West Glamorgan), the Labour member, John Williams, beat off the threat of a last-minute unofficial Liberal of strongly anti-socialist outlook. After 1910, relations between Liberals and Labour in south Wales continued to deteriorate. Labour spokesmen continued to attack the Liberals as the mouthpieces of capitalism. It was the former Liberal MP, D. A. Thomas, who owned the Cambrian Combine and the mines at Tony-pandy, and another, Judge Bryn Roberts, who had given hostile decisions against the miners in the courts and had been denounced for his pains as a 'boss union smasher'.[17]

Liberals, for their part, were far from passive. They often took the offensive in an anti-socialist crusade, in which Clement Edwards and W. F. Phillips, an ex-minister and ex-member of the ILP who had stood unsuccessfully in Gower, took a leading part. A new journal, *Y Gwerinwr*: the *Monthly Democrat*, published in 1912, attacked socialism with great vigour. It tried to tar all Labour men with the same Marxist brush. There was a real threat of contests between Liberals and Labour all over south Wales. An ILP man stood against Towyn Jones in the East Carmarthenshire by-election in August 1912, but came bottom of the poll. The Merthyr Liberals were emboldened to challenge Keir Hardie in this two-member seat by putting up a second candidate. A Liberal, nonconformist barrister, T. Artemus Jones KC, very much a product of the national movement of recent years who had acted as counsel in the Penrhyn quarry cases, was selected in 1913. He would stand against Hardie at the next general election, whenever it was held. The Merthyr ILP itself viewed these developments with much alarm. Hardie him-

[17] *South Wales Daily News*, 30 July 1908; *Merthyr Express*, 21 August 1909.

self asked Labour Head Office to send down an organizer to 'lick his party into shape again'.[18] On the eve of war, in south Wales the Liberals faced an increasingly hostile Labour Party. The alliance which had endured since 1903 seemed in jeopardy.

But in 1914 that alliance was still not yet ruptured. For the most part, the community of outlook between Liberals and most Labour spokesmen was retained. They shared the same Welsh values, the same class enemies, the same commitment to free trade and civil equality. Men like Brace or even Hartshorn were enthusiastic for Welsh objectives such as a national educational council or church disestablishment. Even Keir Hardie, for all his hostility towards the Liberals with whom he was nominally allied, received their votes at Merthyr without demur, and supported disestablishment and other Welsh causes loyally enough in the House of Commons. The Lib-Lab ethos still permeated much of the Labour Party. In any case, even had it wished to mount a full-scale challenge to the Liberals, the Labour party was in no position to do so. In every case in 1910 and later, where there was a direct, head-on clash between Liberals and Labour at the polls, Labour came off second best. In some ways, the industrial militancy and disturbances of the 1910–14 period hurt the Labour Party even more than the Liberals, since it was Labour which had to make the case to angry colliers and railwaymen for constitutional, gradualist action. The local grass-roots machine of the Labour Party, even in Hardie's base at Merthyr, was still surprisingly weak. The ILP's national organizer reported in November 1910 that many ILP branches in south Wales were 'in a very weak condition and semi-stagnant'.[19] More, the appeal of Lib-Labism, nonconformity, and Welshness, that 'little Bethel' mentality which Hardie's *Merthyr Pioneer* despised, was still powerful, especially in the mining community. The old traditions of thought and of social action were too strong to be shaken. The Labour Party had undoubtedly established a formidable base for future expansion. It had a vigorous local press, such as *Llais Llafur* in Ystalyfera and the *Pioneer* in Merthyr. But as an independent, nationwide party, it was still in its infancy. It was still the sprawling pressure-group, the loosely-constructed 'labour alliance' it had always been. The centralizing work of Arthur Henderson had yet to percolate through the constituencies. Political labour did not yet menace the Liberal ascendancy in Wales to any decisive extent.

The growing industrial militancy, especially among the miners, was a very different matter. It is here, from 1908 onwards, that the threat to the Liberal ascendancy in Edwardian Wales really lay. As has been seen, the miners had

---

[18] *Merthyr Express*, 21 July 1913; Hardie to A. Peters, 'Sunday' (October 1913) (Labour Party Archives, LP/CAM/13/1/245).

[19] Independent Labour Party, NAC minutes, 23 November 1910 (British Library of Political and Economic Science).

already rejected the Liberal past by voting in 1908 to affiliate to the Labour Party. This was confirmed in 1913 when the political levy by trade unions to support the Labour Party was endorsed in a nationwide ballot. Even more, the Welsh miners seemed to be reacting against the very fabric of industrial free-enterprise capitalism. There was pressure for a minimum wage, with the issue of shift payments in 'abnormal places' such as the Naval Collieries at Tonypandy especially contentious. There were appalling human tragedies such as the mining disaster at Senghennydd in 1913 which cost the lives of 439 men and further inflamed an already embittered mining community. There was also the brute insensitivity of coalowners who built up such combines as D. A. Thomas's Cambrian Combine with its £2 million of share capital, and who were intransigent on wage advances and heedless of minimum safety regulations. All these factors were bringing south Wales close to social revolution and making it the cockpit of class war.

In addition, there were structural factors inherent in the south Wales mining industry. There were high labour costs, a low rate of productivity, technical inefficiency in terms of introducing mechanization, the general sensitivity of south Wales as an exporting region to fluctuations in the world export trade in coal. There was also a steady rise in the cost of living after the turn of the century which fostered still further the miners' sense of grievance. A new factor was that the implementation of the Mines Eight Hours Bill in 1909 brought much tension to south Wales, especially over the miners' demand for a minimum wage, including for miners working underground in 'abnormal places' where the extraction of coal was unusually difficult because of geological factors. The negotiations of new wage rates and shift payments in 1909–10, indeed the very definition of what 'an eight-hour day' in the deep Welsh mines might comprise, were conducted against a highly-charged atmosphere which made some kind of social explosion almost inevitable. The growing class gulf between employers and miners—remote, impersonal oligopolistic combines headed by tycoons such as D. A. Thomas and Sir William T. Lewis on the one hand, the growing strength and solidarity of the Miners' Federation driven on by grass-roots militancy in local lodges on the other—these made the situation deteriorate with alarming speed.

There was a series of major industrial disputes in the coal industry, from that involving the Powell-Duffryn pits in Aberdare in 1908 onwards. But by far the worst episode came in the Rhondda and concerned Thomas's Cambrian collieries in 1910. There was a bitter and unsolved dispute over the price list to be attached to the Upper Five Foot Seam at the Naval Colliery, Penygraig. The men refused to accept the price list of 1s. 9d. per ton, plus 1d. per ton of hard stone. This, they claimed with much reason, would not enable tonnage rates to be high enough to permit a permanent living wage. On 1 September 1910, eight hundred men at the Ely pit were locked out. The miners then formed a Cambrian Combine Committee under the chairmanship of Will John and the socialist Tom Hopla. On 1 November, with further negotiations at a standstill, all the 12,000 miners in the Cambrian collieries at Penygraig, Llwynypia, Clydach Vale and Gilfach Goch came out on strike; a desperately tense atmosphere soon built up throughout the Rhondda. By the start of November, there were thirty thousand men on strike throughout the coalfield, with the miners of the Aberdare valley joining their fellow 'slaves of the lamp'[20] in the Rhondda. Violence soon followed. On 7–8 November there were wild scenes of rioting in Tonypandy around the Cambrian pits, with attempts to stop blacklegs from entering the pits and efforts to break into the colliery power-houses and boiler-houses. There was hand-to-hand fighting between striking miners and local police (some of them former unemployed workers). Keir Hardie called in vain for a government inquiry to investigate the physical injuries sustained by the miners. One man, Samuel Rays of Tonypandy, died from a fractured skull, a martyr for the Welsh working class as much as Dic Penderyn had been in 1831, though far less well recalled. Winston Churchill, the Home Secretary, at first acted with restraint, while Haldane, the Secretary for War, was even more cautious and held back a detachment of troops at Swindon. But later that day, 8 November, Churchill sent a further telegram to General Sir Nevil Macready of Southern Command that cavalry could be moved into 'the disturbed district', and 'without delay', in effect countermanding Haldane, the Secretary for War.[21] After further direction from the Home Office, infantry from the Lancashire Fusiliers, the Royal Munster Fusiliers, and the West Riding Regiment were dispatched to the coalfield from 9 November, and detachments of cavalry, the 18th Hussars, were stationed at Pontypridd. For several weeks they patrolled the Rhondda under the direct command of Macready. On 22 November it was reported to the Home Office that infantry with fixed bayonets had been used at Penygraig, after police had been stoned by the local population. Not until January did the authorities deem it safe for Macready to be returned to War Office duties in London.

For Churchill, initially attacked by the right-wing press for weakness, the reputation he gained, accurately enough, as the man who had sent troops to Tonypandy made his name reviled amongst the British working class. 'Tonypandy' joined Peterloo, Tolpuddle, and Featherstone in the people's martyrology. Churchill was unpopular in the Welsh valleys for decades to come, even as late as the general election of 1951. Almost sixty years later, on 30 November 1978, the Prime Minister, James Callaghan could provoke uproar in the House of Commons by referring to the 'family vendetta' of the Churchills against the miners in Wales and elsewhere. Since Churchill's

[20] See Martin Barclay, '"The Slaves of the Lamp": the Aberdare Miners' Strike, 1910', *Llafur*, vol. 2, No. 3 (Summer 1978), pp. 24–42.

[21] Robin Page Arnot, *South Wales Miners 1898–1914* (London, 1967), pp. 189–90, quoting HO Papers.

reaction, when challenged in the House in 1910, was to congratulate police and troops for maintaining law and order, while 'a savage war' was going on in the Rhondda',[22] and to refuse any further inquiry, he and his defenders could not complain.

There was trouble in other valleys, too. In Aberdare, the aggressive miners' agent, Charles Stanton, threatened the owners with 'fighting brigades' of miners in retaliation for the violence by the coalowners and the police. Tension continued to be high in the coalfield for months to come. In his memoirs, Macready, the commander of the troops in the area, commented on the truculent and autocratic attitude of Leonard Llewelyn, the main coal-owner involved, and of his general manager, E. L. Hann. The Cambrian strike dragged on until August 1911, with none of the major issues resolved. The major change that had occurred, indeed, was that an increasingly belligerent South Wales Miners' Federation was now resolved to campaign for a minimum wage for all miners instead of concentrating simply on payments for work in 'abnormal places'. It urged the MFGB to call a nationwide stoppage. In April 1912, a national strike took place on behalf of a minimum wage. It was a cry to which the Asquith government had to respond, as Lloyd George and other ministers urged. Nowhere was there greater class solidarity than in south Wales. All over the coalfield, the peaceful, productive thriving life of the valleys seemed to be fatally disrupted by violence and class war. In Ebbw Vale and Tredegar, Jewish landlords and shopkeepers were a popular target for working-class anger in August 1911.[23] In Tonypandy, the legacy of destruction took months to clear up. Worst of all, during a national railwaymen's strike in the summer of 1911, troops shot down and killed two railway workers during the strike at Llanelli. Deaths totalled six in all. More than any other sector of the industrial world, south Wales seemed about to fall apart into class violence as Marx had long ago predicted. After serving until 1898 as the very model of class harmony and the moral imperatives of the Lib-Lab spirit, Wales was now the prototype of the crisis of capitalism in its violent death agonies.

The roots of this extraordinary mood of unrest and conflict in the valleys between 1908 and 1914 were many and profound. As has been noted, there were long-term causes inherent in the physical environment, the structure of ownership, the pattern of collective bargaining and the market circumstances of the Welsh coal industry. Much attention then and later has rightly focused on one additional factor—the element of generational change. It has been seen that after the turn of the century, many young immigrant miners, mostly from England, rebellious against the constraints of Lib-Labism, Mabonism, the chapels, and Welsh community life, entered the coalfield, with powerful

---

[22] *Parl. Deb.*, 5th ser. xx, p. 420 (24 November 1910).
[23] Cf. Geoffrey Alderman, 'The Anti-Jewish Riots of August 1911 in South Wales', *Welsh History Review*, vol. 6, No. 2 (December 1972), pp. 190–200.

effect. There were also rebels from rural Wales, like the bearded young miner-poet Huw Menai from Anglesey, who campaigned for the Marxist Social Democratic Federation and wrote a regular column in the SDF journal, *Justice*. These younger men increasingly captured positions of authority in local lodges, then on the executive committee of the SWMF itself. In a few short years, they destroyed the pacific ideology of which Mabon, himself the ageing, helpless witness of these years of violence, had been so long the symbol and the voice.

One new ideological factor emerged in 1909—ironically enough from the privileged pastures of Oxford University, itself a source of such powerful change in the peaceable world of linguistic and literary studies, through the Dafydd ap Gwilym society and men such as Owen M. Edwards. The 'Oxford man' so revered in Wales now made a decisive impact upon the ideas of the coalfield. In March–April 1909, students at Ruskin College, the working-men's college founded at Oxford in 1899 to which several Welsh miners had already gone, went on strike; they were associated with the principal, Dennis Hird, who had just been dismissed by the college.[24] The strikers urged that Ruskin was merely propping up the existing capitalist social and economic system, instead of challenging and overthrowing it on Marxist lines. Welsh miners at the college, like Noah Ablett from Porth and Ted Gill from Abertillery, argued that workers' education was as essential a part of the class struggle as was industrial or political action. Shortly after, a new Labour college was set up by the rebels in the north Oxford suburbs. Later it moved to Regent's Park in London under the name of the Central Labour College, with the support of the Western Valleys miners in south Wales amongst others. They agreed to send young Frank Hodges, soon to be elected agent for Garw valley, to the new Labour college.

The impact of the Central Labour College movement on the Welsh coalfield was immense. Indeed, it was soon being supported by funds from the South Wales Miners' Federation, as well as by the railwaymen. In the social consciousness of Welsh workers, it played something of the role that Aberystwyth and *Cymru Fydd* had done for the national consciousness of the middle-class Liberals twenty years earlier. It inspired a new growth of rank-and-file militancy, somewhat on the lines of the 'syndicalist' model of workers' control current in the French union, the CGT, and in the writings of Sorel. Many Welsh miners were active amongst the Ruskin rebels and in the Central Labour College movement. There were Frank Hodges, Noah Rees, Will Mainwaring, and Ted Gill. Above all, there was Noah Ablett, the tenth child of a large mining family at Porth, Rhondda Fawr, born in 1883. His early thoughts turned towards the nonconformist pulpit, and then the civil service, but a serious pit accident frustrated this idea. After his student period at

Ruskin, he became a formidable Marxist dialectician, with a growing sympathy for syndicalism and workers' control. He wrote two important pamphlets, 'The burning question of working-class Education' and 'A minimum wage for Miners and how to get it'. He debated passionately throughout the coalfield with T. I. Mardy Jones, a defender of the official authorities at Ruskin. Ablett was to become the inspiration for a new generation of left-wing socialists in south Wales, the most important ideologue produced by Wales generally in the Edwardian period. As a propagandist, as an educator and organizer, above all as a public speaker with a rare, Lenin-like charisma, he served his class and his generation with the same kind of stimulus that Tom Ellis had provided for his own after 1886. Ablett and others formed in January 1909, just before the Ruskin strike, the so-called Plebs League, centred on the Rhondda. It was committed to class war, direct action and industrial, as opposed to political, tactics in overthrowing the capitalist tyranny.

When the news of the Ruskin strike came through in April, a powerful new impetus was given to the Plebs League to expand throughout the Rhondda valleys. The Plebs club at Tonypandy became from now on the nerve-centre of revolutionary syndicalism in the valleys, where learned young Marxists like Ablett or Mainwaring could harangue rapt audiences of colliers. Among them was A. J. Cook, a youthful lodge official in the Rhondda No. 1 District. They started up a new journal, *Plebs*, and in August 1909 the Plebs League was strong enough to hold its own first 'annual meeting'. It continued to grow during the tension and violence of the Cambrian strike. Ablett and his colleagues delivered a series of private manifestoes to the rank and file. The *Rhondda Socialist*, ominously sub-titled 'The BOMB of the Rhondda workers', first appeared on 19 August 1911. The ideas of de Leon's variant of industrial unionism, Sorel's call for workers' syndicates and the liberating effect of a general strike, the militant cries of Tom Mann back from Australia and of Big Bill Haywood of the Western Federation of Miners in America (who visited south Wales in 1910) swept through the Rhondda and neighbouring valleys with the torrid passion of a religious revival—which, in some ways, was what it was. The Liberal newspaper, the *Rhondda Leader*, deplored in April 1912 that the Rhondda had become 'the happy hunting ground for the foreign evangelists of socialism'.[25] In 1913, the *Rhondda Socialist* was re-christened the *South Wales Worker*, a sign of a wider outlook. It claimed a circulation of over 6,000 and, indeed, a readership higher than that of all other local newspapers.

The growth of the Plebs League was intimately associated with the growth of the Central Labour College movement in south Wales. Tutorial classes were conducted, by Ablett, Will Mainwaring, Will Hay and others, in Marxist theory, sociology and industrial economics. A whole new network of

[25] *Rhondda Leader*, 6 April 1912.

working-class self-education and activism was being created, radiating outwards from Tonypandy and the Rhondda Fawr, to enlist the hearts and minds of angry young miners for the class struggle. The young Arthur Horner, a Merthyr boy born in 1894, originally destined also for a career as a theological student, was merely one of the better-known enthusiasts for the Central Labour College and its socialist classes. Like others, he was impelled towards syndicalism rather than towards state socialism and nationalization. Noah Ablett argued that the latter meant bureaucracy rather than industrial democracy. Frank Hodges, another strong advocate of syndicalism at this time, pointed out that, in France and elsewhere, employees in publicly-owned industries had been used to crush the rights of other workers.[26] Another, even younger man (born in 1897) and destined to make an even greater impact on Wales and the world than Arthur Horner or Frank Hodges was also deeply stirred by Ablett and the socialist crusade of the Plebs League and the Central Labour College. This was Aneurin Bevan of Tredegar.

The impact of this new impetus towards industrial action upon the somewhat stately activities of the SWMF was considerable, particularly during the excitements of the Cambrian stoppage. At one critical moment, three of the older members of the executive were killed in a train crash. Will John, Tom Hopla, and Noah Rees, all Rhondda militants, were elected in their stead; Noah Ablett also joined the SWMF ruling body. These Rhondda men formed a powerful radical group on the executive henceforth. Despite the attempts by the MFGB to settle the Cambrian strike in April–May 1911, the Rhondda representatives, Ablett, Hopla, Rees, and Tom Smith left the negotiations, and dissociated themselves from their own leaders and the Lib-Lab conciliation that they associated with Mabon and Brace. There were other militants on the SWMF executive, too, men with un-Welsh names such as Vernon Hartshorn in the Ogmore valley, and George Barker of Abertillery, to be followed shortly by the brilliant young Englishman, still in his twenties, Frank Hodges of the Garw valley.

More ominous still than these developments were tendencies to form a rank-and-file movement distinct in organization and outlook from the formally elected leadership of the Federation. Again, Plebs League members in the Rhondda were in the vanguard. In March 1911, the existence of an Unofficial Reform Committee, based on Tonypandy, was revealed; when exactly it was begun is hard to determine, though a Reform Committee appears to have been founded as early as May 1910, before the Cambrian strike erupted. It called for a radical restructuring of the Miners' Federation, with considerable decentralization. From the summer of 1911, the Unofficial Reform Committee began to draw up a reform programme distinct from that of the SWMF. Prominent socialists from the Rhondda, Ablett, Mainwaring,

---

[26] Cf. Kenneth O. Morgan, 'Socialism and Syndicalism: the Welsh Miners' Debate, 1912', Soc. for the Study of Labour History, *Bulletin* No. 30 (Spring 1975), pp. 22–36.

W. F. Hay, Noah Rees, Tom Smith, C. L. Gibbons, and George Dolling, were deputed to draft a new programme for the unofficial rank-and-file movement. A high proportion of those engaged in the meetings of the Unofficial Committee had been students at either Ruskin or the Central Labour College; almost all were active in the Plebs League. The outcome was the *Miner's Next Step*, published in early 1912, probably the most famous document of industrial revolt ever produced in the Welsh or any other coalfield. It laid down a series of immediate demands for a minimum wage of 8s. a day plus a seven-hour working day. It pointed out that no benefit had accrued to the miners despite the rise in the selling price of coal since 1900. Indeed, it claimed that real wages had fallen by 10 per cent in that time. Most striking of all, it rejected the official policy of state ownership of the mines and called instead for workers' control to be secured by a militant industrial policy of escalating demands upon the coalowners, irritation strikes and simultaneous stoppages of work. The workers of south Wales should be amalgamated into 'one national and international union'.[27] But it was clear that power should rest with the rank and file. Miners' agents should be delegates of the men; union 'leaders' should be overthrown; a new commonwealth based on industrial democracy and communal ownership for the benefit of the workers and their families should be created.

This powerfully argued document had immense messianic appeal. It caused ripples of fear throughout the political and industrial world. It had some sympathizers on the executive of the SWMF, apart from the Rhondda men, notably James Winstone and Ted Gill. However, the end of the minimum wage strike in May 1912 does see something of recession in this tide of industrial militancy. The Plebs League, the Central Labour College movement, the Unofficial Reform Committee itself, did not seem to expand. Indeed, some of the younger miners' agents, notably George Barker and Vernon Hartshorn, argued forcefully against the quasi-anarchy of workers' control or syndicalism and instead advocated class solidarity, state control, and nationalization.[28] The appeal of political action remained powerful, too, as the strong vote in 1913 by the Welsh miners for the political levy and for continued affiliation to the Labour Party indicated. By the end of 1913, the Plebs League's publications were collapsing. A series of bodies, the Rhondda Socialist Society, the Industrial Democracy League, and the like, all tended to peter out. Ablett himself was now somewhat at odds with other Marxists like Hay and Gibbons as to whether it was best to work within the SWMF for radical change, or else strike out separately for workers' independence. The SWMF managed to reassert itself and a new breed of moderates such

[27] *Miners' Next Step* (Tonypandy, 1912), p. 19.
[28] *South Wales Daily News*, 13 September 1912 for Hartshorn's views; cf. Morgan, loc, cit., pp. 26–8, for Barker's.

as David Watts Morgan, Alfred Onions, and T. I. Mardy Jones, socialists but very far from revolutionary syndicalists, undoubtedly gradualist and moderate in outlook, began to emerge.

One interesting test was the coalfield election in the late summer of 1912 for the three south Wales representatives on the executive of the MFGB. The old Lib-Lab, William Brace, with 40,991 votes, came easily at the top of the poll, with the anti-syndicalist, Hartshorn, second and George Barker third, displacing the erratic Stanton, who had been a leading advocate of violence during the Cambrian strike. It was clear by 1914 that the Plebs League and other organs of extreme views, had little impact beyond the Rhondda, and perhaps the Aberdare valleys. The valleys of Monmouthshire, with their ties with miners in England, the anthracite men from Ammanford to Neath with their close attachment to Welsh values, all regarded the Plebs League and its doctrines of industrial unionism with suspicion. Here, Noah Ablett's writ did not run. When war broke out in August 1914, the Plebs League was in marked decline, and Ablett himself a somewhat isolated and disillusioned figure. The era of industrial militancy in south Wales seemed for the moment to have passed by. Physical confrontations between the police and striking miners were replaced by orthodox, if tough, collective bargaining between the miners' executives and the representatives of the owners, with an increasingly active role being played by Board of Trade conciliators such as G. R. Askwith. Riotous Tonypandy was not much more than a memory by August 1914, even if one charged with bitterness and an urge for class revenge. The *Miners' Next Step* was widely circulated and widely read, but it was more an exemplary text for the Labour College tutorial classes than an immediately useful blueprint for revolutionary action.

The extent to which the industrial revolt which surged up in the valleys of the south-east of Wales after 1908 posed a fundamental challenge to the dominant philosophy of Welshness and Liberal reformism is still highly debatable. Without doubt, the ideology of Ablett and his friends was totally distinct from the kind of philosophy that animated most radical Welshmen in rural and industrial areas alike in the early twentieth century. It was economic not social in emphasis; it spoke the language of class war and revolt; it dismissed Welshness in the call for the international solidarity of the workers of all countries. On the other hand, even the Plebs League and its ancillary bodies were in many ways testaments to Welsh consciousness, too. The classes of the Labour College owed much to the Sunday school and to the educational progress in Wales since the eighties. They owed more still to the warm communal consciousness of industrial villages in the coalfield. Men like Horner, Mainwaring, even Ablett, retained a close awareness of the distinctiveness of their region and their nation. The *Miners' Next Step* ended in the apocalyptic imagery of populist nonconformity—'Then mankind shall at last have leisure and inclination to live as men and not as the beasts which perish'.[29] Will John, imprisoned during the Cambrian strike, was a staunch Baptist and advocate of temperance. Indeed, the very emphasis on local rather than national ownership of the mines, in the Welsh valleys as in Clyde-side in Scotland, was partial evidence of the sense of separate identity in these Celtic societies. It was a lesson absorbed by the Communist Party after 1920: it based itself to a great extent on pre-war pockets of support in the strong-holds of the Plebs League and the Unofficial Reform Committee, and cited Lenin to support a programme of Welsh and Scottish home rule. From the start, the Communists pledged themselves to a respect for national minorities as Lenin decreed (and as the Georgian Stalin overruled). But this argument cannot be pressed too far. Obviously in realistic terms a society envisaged by Noah Ablett or Will Hay would be totally different in structure and aspiration from that fashioned by the Liberal creators of contemporary Wales and their Lib-Lab allies, even if a kind of Welshness would survive the socialist revolution. They and Owen M. Edwards or Lloyd George were worlds apart.

A stronger line of argument is that the impact of the new militancy and the unofficial movements among the miners, while ideologically compelling and in the long term highly important, had only a comparatively limited impact even in the valley communities themselves before 1914. Until the war, Lib-Labism and orthodox forms of working-class organization still held sway, finally perhaps even in the cauldron of the Rhondda itself. Most Welsh miners still adhered either to the constitutional orthodoxies of the Labour Party or to the older Liberalism. They preferred the known imperatives of the non-conformist gospel to the earthly millenarianism of Ablett and the apostles of the new secular religion. These imperatives were, after all, not only testimony to the resilience and vitality of Welshness and Welsh culture. Through the enterprise and industrial expansion in the valleys, they were the key to economic progress also. The beguiling appeal of the Liberal past and the solidarities and sanctions of Welsh life still bound middle-class and working-class people together with a common sense of tradition and destiny. It had its varieties of folk symbols and focuses, from the chapels to the national rugby team, where the classes could come together peacefully in celebration of common values.

To break away from this pattern was hard indeed, especially in view of the overwhelming sense of achievement prevalent throughout Wales in the Edwardian era. Peace and prosperity seemed to reinforce at every turn the main developments in society since the early eighties. A sudden cataclysm, a world war, a lurch into economic stagnation and mass unemployment, and the picture of modern Wales would look very different. But at the start of July 1914, these calamities seemed extremely remote, almost unthinkable. Lloyd George told an audience at the Mansion House that, internationally, the sky had never looked more relatively blue. There were hopes that such

[29] *Miners' Next Step*, p. 30.

hazards as Anglo-German naval rivalry would soon diminish and the beneficent, healing effects of commerce and enterprise once more restore peace among the nations. For Lloyd George, as for the great mass of his countrymen in July 1914, blue skies and serene horizons alone seemed to lie ahead.

PART II

THE ORDEAL
1914–1945

CHAPTER 6

THE CRISIS OF WAR

'I am moving through a nightmare world these days', wrote Lloyd George to his wife on 3 August 1914. All his prejudices were engaged against war with Germany, as they had been against war with the Boers in 1899. But, he concluded, if little Belgium were to be invaded, he would have no option but to endorse the Cabinet's decision, resulting from Grey's policy, to go to war. 'I must bear my share of the ghastly burden though it scorches my flesh to do so.'[1] After 4 August, Lloyd George moved rapidly into a new mood of almost blithe adventure in meeting the challenges of total war. He flung himself into salvaging the national finances, and safeguarding the currency and credit system. 'It might be good fun to be the advance guard of an expedition to the coast of France', he wrote to the Master of Elibank.[2]

As with Lloyd George, so with the vast majority of his fellow-countrymen. The overwhelming mass of the Welsh people cast aside their political and industrial divisions, and threw themselves into the war with gusto. Liberal intellectuals, most active in cultural pursuits during the years of peace, were now most ardent in support for the war. In the *Beirniad*, academics from Sir John Morris-Jones downwards were strongly pro-war. In that journal in 1915, Morris-Jones, so seldom moved to political pronouncement, attacked in bellicose terms 'Germany's New Religion', that nationalistic creed of Nietzsche, Treitschke, and Bernhardi which, he claimed, underlay Germany's aggressive foreign policy as the root cause of war. In the same periodical, Llewelyn Williams, a Liberal MP and a humane, civilized man, denounced German atrocities as reported by the British press, including the (physical) destruction of the library at the University of Louvain.[3] Nonconformist ministers whipped up their congregations and urged them to enlist in what seemed a holy crusade on behalf of liberal values. 'It is but a short step from the morality of Nietzsche to the massacre of Louvain', wrote the Revd D. Miall Edwards with breathtaking lack of logic.[4] Preachers like the Revd John Williams, Brynsiencyn, academics like Professor Henry Jones and Principal

---

[1] Lloyd George to his wife, 3 August 1914 (*Family Letters*, p. 167).
[2] Lloyd George to the Master of Elibank, 4 August 1914, quoted in Cameron Hazlehurst, *Politicians at War, July 1914 to May 1915* (London, 1971), p. 117.
[3] W. Llewelyn Williams, 'Y Rhyfel', *Y Beirniad*, October 1914.
[4] D. Miall Edwards, *Y Geninen*, January 1915.

Harry Reichel, even miners' agents like Charles Stanton and Ted Gill (both distinctly on the far left in pre-war days) addressed recruiting meetings and urged able-bodied young Welshmen of military age and sound physique to flock to the colours. They had immense success. By the end of 1914, *Welsh Outlook* could record with pride that the task of raising 50,000 men for the Welsh Army Corps was making dramatic progress. In all, 280,000 Welshmen were to serve in the army, navy, and air force. Welshmen, indeed, enlisted in such vast numbers that the proportion of the male population engaged in the armed forces (13.82 per cent) eventually outstripped that for either England or Scotland. Soon periodicals and pamphlets were booming 'what Wales has done in the war'.

The reason why a land with long traditions of radicalism and anti-militarism should respond to the patriotic call with such fervour is not in doubt. Of course, it throws immense suspicion on the depth of the radicalism that animated Liberals and Lib-Labs before 1914, as well as on the alleged revolutionary fervour of Welsh workers. But the decisive factor was that most Welsh men and women felt that, in a sense, it was their war, a crusade to defend their basic values. 'Gallant little Belgium', 'Gallant little Serbia', tiny but no doubt equally gallant Montenegro, were small, defenceless nations, like Wales itself. The sympathy enlisted for the Boers in some parts of Wales in 1899 was now operating in reverse. This was, so Lloyd George proclaimed to a massed audience of London Welshmen at the Queen's Hall on 19 September 1914, a war fought on behalf of the 'little five-foot-five nations', in defiance of the bullying Hun, 'the road hog of Europe'.[5] The cause of the Belgians, many of whom were accommodated in homes in Wales, particularly strengthened the sense of identification with the causes for which the war was ostensibly being fought. Serbia, too, played its emotional part. David Davies MP, Lord Kenyon, and others inaugurated a fund to aid homeless Serbian refugees. Lloyd George lavished praise on the Serbs with much reference to the fourteenth-century battle of Kossovo. The Serbs, no doubt like the men of Harlech, could sing defiantly of their defeats.

Welsh national sentiment was enlisted in more practical fashion. Lloyd George had visions of raising 'a Welsh Army'. After a brisk passage of arms between him and Lord Kitchener, the Secretary of State for War, in full Cabinet, a new Welsh Division was created in November 1914, under the command of General Sir Ivor Philipps, a Liberal MP and a scion of the famous Pembrokeshire family of Picton Castle. Recruits in North Wales were raised by Brigadier-General Sir Owen Thomas, an Anglesey man, a strange combination of agrarian radical and military patriot. He had commanded the Prince of Wales Light Horse in the South African War; he was later to become a Labour MP. Recruiting drives for this division, for the Royal Welsh Fusiliers

[5] *The Times*, 21 September 1914.

and for the Welch Regiment stepped up sharply. Another development to stir patriotic emotion was the new brigade of Welsh Guards, formed in early 1915 under Colonel Sir Murray Threipland. The 38th (Welsh) Division was to gain especial renown during the war, in the carnage on the Somme in July 1916, and in the engagement at Mametz Wood, and the capture of Pilckheim Ridge in 1917. Wyn Griffith's *Up at Mametz* is a moving evocation of these terrible engagements. In addition, there was a Labour battalion under the command of David Watts Morgan, former miners' agent in the stormy Rhondda No. 2 District, now promoted to the rank of major and awarded the DSO for his part in the battle of Cambrai where the Welsh Labour battalion held up the German advance at a crucial time. Other Welsh troops gained acclaim in the course of Allenby's sweep through Palestine in the autumn of 1917, in the various battles for Gaza and the battle of Megiddo. Welsh troops wrote home to say how the biblical names of sombre childhood days in the chapel or the Sunday school, had come alive for them at last. Organizations such as the London Welsh Committee and the Honourable Society of Cymmrodorion, headed by such national eminences as Sir Vincent Evans of eisteddfodic fame, were heavily preoccupied with recruitment campaigns. Chapels and colleges donated funds for war purposes. There was heavy enlistment in the Welsh university colleges amongst students, and Officer Training Corps flourished there. Welsh poets such as W. J. Gruffydd, R. Williams Parry, 'Cynan', and I. D. Hooson served, no doubt with reluctance, in the fighting services. The *eisteddfod* itself was taken over for the cause of jingoism. At the Bangor *eisteddfod* in 1915, Lloyd George, now Minister of Munitions, delivered a warlike address and lavished praise on the Welsh military tradition throughout the ages, from the bowmen at Crécy to the current heroes now achieving immortality (quite literally) in the mass slaughter in the trenches on the western front. A new breed of military hero was being created, a Christian warrior perhaps, a man like Brigadier-General Sir Owen Thomas, with the full benediction of most nonconformist ministers and all the Welsh and denominational press—this in a nation which had once idolized Henry Richard, the gentle apostle of peace.

Perhaps emotion reached its fullest flood at the national *eisteddfod* held at Birkenhead in 1917. Here the chair was awarded posthumously to the Merioneth shepherd, E. H. Evans of Trawsfynydd, writing under the pseudonym 'Hedd Wyn'. His poem, appropriately, was written on the subject of *Yr Arwr* (the Hero). In fact, Hedd Wyn had been killed in battle shortly before the *eisteddfod* took place and the chair was draped in black in his honour. Henceforth, Hedd Wyn was always revered as a kind of Welsh Rupert Brooke or Wilfred Owen, a youthful sacrifice for what was claimed to be a war fought for Welsh national libertarian values.

Patriotic fervour reached heights of hysteria in Wales rarely matched in other parts of the United Kingdom. Much of this was the work of Lloyd

George. From late 1914 onwards, he became identified with an ever more belligerent approach to the war, with 'a knock out blow', a 'fight to a finish' and 'the unconditional surrender' of the central powers. When he became Minister of Munitions in May 1915 and then Secretary for War in succession to Kitchener in July 1916, he was all the more securely placed to press on with this belligerent policy. He was urged on by his venerable Uncle Lloyd in Caernarvonshire, surprisingly jingoistic in his last years. The preface to Lloyd George's war speeches published in September 1915, *Through Terror to Triumph*, contained barely-veiled support for universal male conscription in place of voluntary recruitment. From the autumn of that year he was aligned with leading Unionists like Curzon, Carson, and Milner in endorsing the conscription policy that was so reluctantly accepted by most of his fellow Liberals. The 'ginger group' of Liberals who supported him in this, the 'Liberal War Committee' founded in January 1916, included some prominent Welsh figures, including Ellis Griffith, another pillar of nonconformist radicalism, Sir Ivor Herbert and, less surprisingly, Sir Alfred Mond. Their example permeated the nation.

Jingo fever led to some distasteful episodes far removed from the liberal, humane standards which Welsh national spokesmen claimed to uphold. There was persecution by his congregation in Pwllheli of the anti-war radical, the blind Methodist minister, Puleston Jones. Principal Thomas Rees of Bala-Bangor Independent College was expelled from the Bangor golf club on one celebrated occasion. Perhaps the most unhappy episode of all concerned the eminent linguist, Professor Hermann Ethé of Aberystwyth. He was now in his seventies, a member of staff there for many years and with a high international reputation. He had no known political views, though he had uttered words of sympathy for the humane German traditions of Goethe, Kant, and Schiller while abominating Prussianism. But he was, nevertheless, a German by birth and blood. When he returned to Aberystwyth shortly after the outbreak of war in 1914, he was confronted by an angry rabble of local citizens. Harangued by a local solicitor and doctor, they demanded the expulsion of Ethé from the college. Some even proposed that he be shot. Sympathizers with Ethé were physically attacked, while another professor was driven out of the town because his wife was German. The elderly Ethé had to take flight from the town almost immediately after his arrival. The following year, despite some mild remonstration on the grounds of humanity by the college principal, T. F. Roberts, Ethé was deprived of his chair by the Aberystwyth college council, in return for a small pension. He died in Reading in 1917 unable to return to 'the college by the sea' he had served with such distinction. This kind of senseless act of persecution made some wonder what had happened to the civilized values of *Cymru Fydd*. Nonconformist ministers appeared to be preaching the creed of 'praise the Lord and kill the Germans'. It was hard to reconcile the spectacle of the Revd John Williams of

Brynsiencyn,[6] 'Lloyd George's chaplain' as he was called, preaching in the pulpit in full military uniform, with the gentle message of the Prince of Peace.

But there were always important minorities of dissenters who did not succumb to this wanton war hysteria. In Liberal and nationalist circles, there was dividing of hearts and consciences. Almost all the Welsh-language newspapers, the *Cymro*, *Herald Cymraeg*, *Genedl*, and so forth, were strongly pro-war. Many peddled a crude anti-Teutonic racism. The few who dissented at first did so privately and in the safety and privacy of their own homes. Some, like D. R. Daniel, once Lloyd George's colleague and admirer, went out of public life entirely. Others found solace in membership of the anti-war radical movement, the Union of Democractic Control. Certainly, when Bertrand Russell conducted a propaganda tour on behalf of the No Conscription Fellowship in June–July 1916, and demanded the immediate opening of peace negotiations, he won warm support in south Wales in such socialist towns as Briton Ferry. There he addressed 'a really wonderful meeting—the hall was packed, they were all in highest point of enthusiasm. They inspired me and I spoke as I have never spoken before.'[7] Russell's meetings at Merthyr Tydfil and Cardiff were also highly successful, and indicated a depth of growing popular revulsion against the slaughter.

Welsh critics were also finding their voice, and showing immense courage. On 30 September 1914 Principal Thomas Rees had written an open letter to the Independent newspaper, *Y Tyst*, whose editor, the Revd H. M. Hughes, Cardiff, was passionately pro-war. In this, Rees condemned crude anti-Germanism and lies about alleged German atrocities, and appealed to the pacifist tradition in Wales.[8] By 1915, there were clear signs that some of the cultural intelligentsia who had lent such distinction and grace to Edwardian Wales in the years of peace were rebelling against a war that flouted all their values. W. J. Gruffydd, whose mind was especially tortured, translated into Welsh an anti-war sermon by the pacifist Maude Royden. The most important outlet for these men was the Welsh monthly, *Y Wawr*, published at the University College of Wales, Aberystwyth. It was edited by Ambrose Bebb, later a founder-member of Plaid Cymru. Here, sometimes in cautious and indirect fashion, T. Gwynn Jones and others spoke of their sense of moral outrage at the brutality of war. They were joined by the gifted young poet, Thomas Parry-Williams. He had visited Germany before the war and had been repelled by German student life with its duelling and celebration of the martial virtues. But he drew the conclusion that Britain should offer a higher scale of values and adhere all the more firmly to the imperatives of civilization and peace. Parry-Williams's poetry henceforth contained an

---

[6] Cf. R. R. Hughes, *John Williams, Brynsiencyn* (Caernarfon, 1929), pp. 226 ff.

[7] Bertrand Russell to Lady Ottoline Morrell, 4 July 1916 (Lady Ottoline Morrell Papers, McMaster University, Ontario, by courtesy of Ms. J. Newberry).

[8] Principal Thomas Rees, letter on 'The War and the Churches', *Y Tyst*, 30 September 1914.

element of despair which contrasted markedly with the idyllic serenity of much of his pre-war writing. *Y Wawr* remained a powerful antidote to the war fever until censorship by the college authorities at Aberystwyth in 1918 led to its ceasing publication.

In October 1916 there appeared another distinguished anti-war journal, *Y Deyrnas*. This was much more openly political and was edited by the formidable Principal Thomas Rees. He took an uncompromisingly Christian-pacifist stand. Here, and in other journals like *Y Dysgedydd*, he deplored the failure of European Christianity to withstand the floodtide of war. T. Gwynn Jones lent him strong support, as did another distinguished poet, E. Tegla Davies. There was much discussion of the pacifist crusades of men like Henry Richard and S.R. in the past. But the influence of the *Deyrnas* was broadened in 1917–18 by the support of those who had originally accepted the necessity of war in 1914 but who now reacted strongly against the attacks on civil liberties and the illiberal treatment of dissenters that the war brought in its train. It acted as the voice of the Fellowship of Reconciliation which held a conference at Llandrindod in September 1917 to protest against the imprisonment of so many blameless citizens simply for reasons of conscience.[9] Messages of comfort were given to conscientious objectors in Pentonville and other prisons. Morgan Humphreys took the same line in *Y Goleuad*.

In fact, the treatment of conscientious objectors from 1916 onwards gave rise to countless instances of injustice. Some, like the pacifist minister, George Maitland Lloyd Davies, a leading figure in the Fellowship of Reconciliation, found themselves becoming, for all their self-effacement, symbols of hope for the dissenting minority. Davies himself went to Wormwood Scrubs and was sentenced to hard labour. This did not prevent him writing for *Y Deyrnas, Y Dinesydd* and other anti-war periodicals. Interestingly, the lieutenant-colonel at Chester who sentenced him to prison observed, 'God knows, I am condemning a far better man than myself'.[10] Tribunals which considered the cases of conscientious objectors in Aberystwyth, Tregaron, and other places were obviously loaded in favour of privilege and position, with not a labourer or working man in sight on the bench. Prosperous farmers and solicitors, and former high sheriffs in Cardiganshire, acted rigorously to suppress or imprison those who adopted an anti-war stand on grounds of conscience. On the other hand, the butlers of landowners like Waddingham of Hafod were rapidly exempted from military service.[11]

Military conscription in general caused much heart-searching among Welsh Liberals. Three Liberal MPs voted against the first reading of the Conscription Bill on 6 January 1916, Llewelyn Williams, E. T. John, and G.

---

[9] *Y Deyrnas*, September 1917: open letter to Lloyd George by Dr Thomas Rees and the Revd D. Wyre Lewis. Cf. article by Rees in *Y Dysgedydd*, July 1915, p. 299.
[10] E. H. Griffiths, *Heddychwr Mawr Cymru* (Caernarfon, 1967), vol. i, p. 85.
[11] Papers on Cardiganshire Military Appeals Tribunals, 1916–18 (National Library of Wales).

Caradog Rees, recently elected for Arfon. Five others (John Hinds, Haydn Jones, Ellis W. Davies, J. Towyn Jones, and J. Hugh Edwards) abstained, though these five were to vote tamely with the government in the end. The most powerful dissentient, apart from E. T. John who migrated to the Labour Party, was Llewelyn Williams. He had been a strong supporter of the war in 1914–15 and a close ally of Lloyd George since the days of the Cymru Fydd League in the nineties. He now joined with Sir John Simon, who had resigned from the Home Office, in severing all ties with Lloyd George and his friends. He regarded conscription as the very negation of the libertarian values to which Liberals had always subscribed. He became the bitterest of enemies of Lloyd George whom he frequently accused of demagoguery and dictatorship. Their estrangement lasted until Williams's premature death in 1922. By the last year of the war, in fact, it was clear that the monolithic endorsement of the government common in Liberal circles in 1914 was fast being undermined. Leading nonconformist figures like Herbert Morgan and James Nicholas, the successive ministers of Lloyd George's own Baptist chapel at Castle Street, were now outspokenly attacking the war. The militaristic Revd John Williams of Brynsiencyn was having less enthusiastic receptions. The social and cultural consequences of the war and its attacks on civil liberties were causing more and more disillusion among Liberal intellectuals, almost as much as the loss of life at the front. By 1918 it was clear that Welsh Liberalism was undergoing a massive crisis of conscience. The moral certainties of the pre-war years prevalent amongst the Liberal middle-class élite had evaporated for ever.

Labour dissentients were also few in number at first. The great majority of miners' agents seemed to endorse the patriotic call. Mabon himself lent his name to recruiting posters, and joined Victor Fisher's British Workers' League with its national socialist overtones. Keir Hardie was savagely attacked for his opposition to the war. On 6 August 1914, a howling mob shouted him down in his own constituency of Aberdare and broke up his meeting. At their head was Charles Butt Stanton, whose erratic mind turned easily from bellicose syndicalism to bloodthirsty jingoism. Hardie said in despair to a Merthyr friend, the famous socialist barber, Llew Francis, that he now understood the sufferings of Christ at Gethsemane.[12] By the end of 1914, he was himself broken in spirit and undergoing a form of public crucifixion. He was even compelled to give a kind of despairing endorsement to recruitment drives, in the pages of the Merthyr *Pioneer*.[13] He faded away in 1915 and died in September, a sad, disillusioned, old, old man of fifty-nine. Meanwhile the remnants of the heady days of the Plebs League and the Unofficial Reform Committee, men like Ablett and Horner, kept their heads down in 1914–15 and tried to keep out of harm's way. Horner migrated for a

[12] Kenneth O. Morgan, *Keir Hardie: Radical and Socialist* (London, 1975), pp. 265–6.
[13] *Merthyr Pioneer*, 15 August, 28 November 1914.

time to Ireland to enlist in Jim Connolly's Citizen Army. Some former Plebs League members like Ted Gill of Abertillery became, in their turn, recruiting agents. Socialist pacifists in the ILP met with short shrift from the authorities. The Revd T. E. Nicholas, minister of Seion chapel, Glais, and the Welsh editor of the Merthyr *Pioneer*, often fell foul of the establishment for his Marxist and anti-war views. The Chief Constable of Glamorgan, Captain Lindsay, made frequent attempts to have him prosecuted. With more sense, the Home Office ignored Lindsay's missives of complaint, and his further attacks on Ablett, Arthur Cook and others.[14]

Other ILP men were not so fortunate. One notable victim in 1917 was Morgan Jones, a miner's son from Bargoed, a graduate of Reading University, and an active member of the No Conscription Fellowship. His imprisonment for anti-war propaganda became something of a *cause célèbre*, especially as it had been preceded by his dismissal from the school in which he taught. By this time, the ILP was becoming bolder in its criticisms of the war. It was given new impetus by the revolution in Russia in February 1917 which released, according to Ramsay MacDonald, a 'springtide of joy' all over Europe. Nevertheless these were still minority voices. To make more headway, socialist and other critics needed mass working-class backing from the trade unions. But in fact, the workers seemed to be benefiting from the higher wages and collective controls that total war brought with it. The depressed iron-works of Monmouthshire, even the almost-defunct lead mines of north Cardiganshire were given new life. It would need the additional strains imposed on organized labour by universal male conscription for labour dissenters who opposed the war to make a decisive impact.

In the main, then, Welshmen lent whole-hearted support to the war until at least the summer of 1917. A major factor in this was, of course, the advance to the pinnacle of power by Lloyd George, in whom so much of the nation's moral and emotional capital was invested. His identification with the Welsh spirit seemed closer than ever in the war years. It reached a climax in his speech to the Aberystwyth national *eisteddfod* when he compared the singing of the Welsh people to the nightingale that sang at the darkest hour of the night—'Let the people sing'. Between August 1914 and December 1916 Lloyd George advanced relentlessly towards a new nationally-based authority. He had become the central figure in all political calculations. When he moved, after some hesitation, from the Treasury to the new Ministry of Munitions in May 1915 it became clear that he had acquired an even more powerful base for extending his political and industrial domination. Nor did his Welsh associates and family fail to back him now. Uncle Lloyd, as has been seen, was a strong supporter of the war down to his death in February 1917. So was his loyal brother, William, minding the solicitor's business in Criccieth,

[14] Deian Hopkin, 'Patriots and Pacifists in Wales, 1914–18', *Llafur,* vol. 1, No. 3 (May 1974), pp. 27–41.

and so also was his wife, whose unhappiness stemmed more from her husband's liaison with Frances Stevenson than from the advent of war.

Finally, after an anxious and complicated series of manoeuvres in the first week of December 1916, Lloyd George became Prime Minister on 6 December. The final moments of this crisis owed much to the activities of various Welsh associates of Lloyd George. There was David Davies, member for Montgomeryshire and heir to the wealth of Llandinam, who helped drum up potentially pro-Lloyd George support amongst the Liberal backbenchers, in partnership with Dr Christopher Addison and F. G. Kellaway. There was Thomas Jones, who helped line up support for his countryman amongst labour leaders like Jimmy Thomas of the Railwaymen. Lloyd George's premiership saw the emergence of a veritable Welsh Mafia in the councils of central government. His new Cabinet secretariat included as its deputy-secretary under Hankey the formidable Thomas Jones, the self-styled 'microbe' whose influence over the course of policy in war and in peace was to be profound under Lloyd George (and, indeed, under Bonar Law and Baldwin after him). The Prime Minister's personal secretariat or 'garden suburb' also had a strong Welsh contingent. The five founder-members included David Davies (who shortly quarrelled with his leader) and Joseph Davies, a commercial statistician and shipping expert from Newport. In Lloyd George's personal entourage there were figures such as John Rowlands, his personal secretary, to be joined later by other Welshmen such as Clement Jones, Evan R. Davies, and Ernest Evans. Sir J. T. Davies served as principal private secretary, along with the ever-present Miss Stevenson. The Welsh character of the premiership, in fact, was more pronounced than the Irish character of the American presidency under John F. Kennedy in 1961. The Prime Minister's home at 10 Downing Street looked like a typical Welsh home, frugal, even austere, Welsh in speech, occasionally stirred by the singing of Welsh hymns around the hearth. If this was only one facet of the extraordinary Lloyd George *ménage* during the 1914–18 war, it was a facet with which the vast majority of Welsh people readily identified.

Elsewhere in the administration, there were numerous other Welshmen of importance. Almost all the Welsh Liberals supported him in opposition to Asquith in December 1916. Indeed, the Welsh National Liberal Council was the one regional body solid in his support. Only a handful of Liberal members notably Llewelyn Williams, Reginald McKenna, E. T. John, and Ellis Davies, were hostile to the government. For their loyalty, the Welsh Liberals were rewarded with patronage in abundance. Sir Herbert Lewis at the Board of Education, Sir Alfred Mond at the Office of Works, even, barely credibly, the Revd Josiah Towyn Jones as a junior whip—these were some of the fruits of guessing right in December 1916. Lord Rhondda, formerly D. A. Thomas and bitterly estranged from Lloyd George since 1896, was brought out of exile to become first President of the Local Government Board and then Food

Controller, where he proved an immense success. More widely, a regime of powerful figures emerged under the aegis of the centralization and collectivization that war brought. Sir Henry Jones, the Hegelian philosopher and professor at Glasgow, was employed by the War Office as a propagandist for recruitment drives. Amongst the new regime of wartime businessmen who profited from the war, and whose names cluster in *Who's Who in Wales* in 1921 like so many limpets, one name alone may suffice. Sir Evan Jones, an engineer from Fishguard, became organizer of civilian labour for the defence of London, Controller of Dyes, petrol controller and chairman of the Road Transport Board. In due course he became involved with the National Library of Wales and the university; almost inevitably he was elected a Liberal MP (for Pembrokeshire) in 1918. Here were the new conquerors of wartime Wales, self-made, pragmatic, almost apolitical, yet associated in their way with the populist traditions of the Welsh democracy. They were heirs and legatees of the Lloyd George revolution of 1916.

Beneath this political and constitutional transformation, the governmental and eventually the social structure of Wales underwent profound changes. Indeed, the consequences of total war in these respects proved permanent, long after the hysteria and the emotion of the immediate wartime period were forgotten. The state impinged upon the daily life of people in Wales as never before. There were control boards for shipping, engineering, shipbuilding, and agriculture. The Ministry of Munitions became a pioneer in introducing powerful new physical controls upon production and supply, prices and profits. The mines and the railways were put under public control for the duration of the war. The railways experienced an integration that was to lead eventually in 1923 to the amalgamation of most Welsh lines under the Great Western Railway, with the exception of the mid-Wales line to Shrewsbury which fell to the London, Midland & Scottish Company. There was also a vast expansion of social provision. Warfare and welfare so clearly went hand in hand. The state now began to intervene to build subsidized houses and to peg urban rents for working-class tenants. For example, the Burry Port Garden Suburb Company was registered to build homes for workers at the Pembrey ordnance factory. Public education was radically reformed in the Fisher Act of 1918 (though this failed to include a Welsh Educational Council). Health and hospital provisions were improved, with benefit in such areas as infant mortality and maternity services. Food and other vital commodities were rationed and there were widespread price controls. The working class and their unions now became clients of a new corporate order. Wages went up for industrial and agricultural workers, the eight-hour day was widely extended, there was a considerable expansion of unemployment insurance to take account of the new mobility of labour during the war. As a result, living standards for working people rose steadily during the war years. In consequence, trade unions, protected in their status in relation to collective bargaining under the Treasury Agreement of March 1915 (though suspending the right to strike, in return) dramatically increased their membership.

A new leviathan of government, a massive extension of collectivism and of centralized government transformed the nation's social and economic life, and wrenched it into radically new directions. Some of these changes brought particular satisfaction in Wales. For instance, Lord Rhondda's notable success in implementing a flexible but efficient system of food rationing and of maximum prices for basic foodstuffs won widespread national acclaim. His more important pressure in the councils of central government, for instance his imaginative plans for abolishing the old poor law and for recasting the social services and structure of local government generally, remained unknown to the public at large. The daily life of Wales became galvanized by new instruments of central direction. For example, the Welsh National Insurance Commission, under Sir Thomas J. Hughes, became an exceptionally powerful body, with the dramatic extension of the unemployment scheme and the changes in the labour market. Men like the secretary of the commission (until December 1916), Thomas Jones and his assistant Percy Watkins became bureaucrats of authority and influence. They were clearly destined for rapid promotion in the ranks of government in London as well as Cardiff.

As a result of all this, the Welsh economy showed a picture of prosperity and success even more striking than before 1914. The mines and docks throbbed with yet more life, and tried to cope somehow with the insatiable demand for Welsh coal in British and French industry and in naval vessels. Welsh steel-making picked up. New blast furnaces were opened at the long-stagnant works at Blaenavon and Ebbw Vale, and the steel-making capacity of the latter was much increased. The John Summer works in Shotton on Deeside opened up more blast furnaces, while the rayon factory at Flint (acquired by Courtaulds in 1917) began a new era of textiles manufacture. Working people in the coalfield, and to some degree in the rural areas as well, basked in still greater affluence. Even the depressed slate industry of Gwynedd found renewed life with new demands for Welsh slate for house and other building. On the other hand, the Welsh slate industry was firmly declared in 1917 to be 'non-essential' and not, therefore, to be a recipient of government largesse in relation to labour and raw materials. On the whole, however, Wales like the rest of Britain found that war socialism brought with it affluence and renewed economic growth on the home front.

The effect of these changes, together with some of the financial and commercial by-products of the war years, was to lead to a great divide in Welsh society. Throughout the latter part of the nineteenth century, indeed up to 1914, there is an essential continuity in the social pattern in Wales, rural and industrial. After 1914–18, this was no longer the case. Total war brought about a massive watershed in Welsh social history. The character of the social structure, and indirectly of cultural and religious life, could never be quite the same again.

In the Welsh countryside, the war brought massive changes. In addition it provided a powerful accelerator to changes already in the making in rural society before 1914. In some respects, it brought renewed prosperity to the upland farms of north, mid- and west Wales. The demand for Welsh milk, livestock, and corn soared ever upwards; more money circulated in the farming community than ever before; rural banks did immense business. The Welsh Council of Agriculture through Professor Bryner Jones was active in providing technical advice and assistance. In association with the research work of R. D. Stapledon, a brilliant agricultural botanist of world renown on the staff of the University College at Aberystwyth (soon to become the head of the new Plant Breeding Station in 1920), dramatic improvements were made in the efficient production of food. A new development was the spread of the Agricultural Organization Society, a body originally founded at Bangor for north Wales in 1911 and in Brecon for the south in 1914. It encouraged farmers to enter trading societies on a co-operative basis. By 1917 there were seventy such societies in south Wales with nearly 12,000 members, and sixty branches with 6,000 members in the north. Another wartime development was the creation of Allotment Societies in rural areas, to give further assistance to small-scale production. The farmer by 1918 was undoubtedly more prosperous, more anxious to purchase the holding which brought him his livelihood. He benefited directly from state assistance, especially from the high guaranteed prices offered for the production of oats and wheat (a rare crop in Wales) under the government's Corn Production Act of 1917.

Prosperity was now filtering through to the farm labourer also. He had been the forgotten man of Welsh agrarian debate over the past hundred years, and usually left in the end to seek his own salvation in the mines and factories of the south instead of on impoverished upland smallholdings. Now farm labourers became much more valuable, as a vital agent in increased food production. They were generally given exemption from conscription under the provisions laid down by military tribunals. The Corn Production Act gave agricultural labourers a new deal, too, a guaranteed minimum wage and a fairly consistent standard of living for the first time. The abortive campaigns waged by 'ap Ffarmwr' on behalf of north Wales agricultural labourers in the nineties received retrospective sanction. The labourer had never known so much recognition and esteem.

But the most dramatic change in the countryside concerned neither the tenant farmer nor the labourer, but the landlord. The war years added to the problems of the landowner and added to his sense of fighting a rearguard action against political democracy and punitive taxation, a sense already highly developed before 1914. During the war, of course, agricultural prices rose steeply, perhaps by as much as 300 per cent. On the other hand, net rents fell, and on most estates income fell by up to half even though the value of the land itself might increase steadily. Almost any kind of investment seemed better than land. Thus it was that the tendency to sell up portions or even the whole of estates, already well advanced in 1910–14, continued apace after the outbreak of war. Many major estates in Wales sold up heavily, usually to their land-hungry tenants. This was true of the Beaufort estates in Breconshire, the Abergavenny estates in Monmouthshire, the estates of Bodelwyddan in Denbighshire, of Aberhafesp in Montgomeryshire, even ironically the Hawarden estate of the Gladstones in Flintshire, all claiming to be the victims of Lloyd George's land taxes.[15] Industrial estates, the property of landowners who had profited hugely in the past from leases, rents, and mineral royalties, also began to be sold up in large quantities. Lord Tredegar sold up much of his industrial land in Monmouthshire in 1916, to be followed by much of the Talbot estate of Margam, Glamorgan, in 1917, and the Hanbury estate of Pontypool Park in 1918. This process was to continue with increased impetus after 1918. Wales, truly, was changing hands during the war. The owner-occupation of holdings was becoming more and more the rule rather than the exception. A 'green revolution' was in the making, as in rural Ireland. Thomas Gee, S.R., and other Victorian champions of the insecure, permanently-dependent tenant farmer class would not have known what to make of it all. In this and other respects, indeed, the standing of Welsh landlords was in rapid decline. Their finances were collapsing; their social pretensions were out of date. It was known, for instance, that domestic servants were much harder to come by in rural Wales than in rural England. In Cardiganshire, every major figure, the Powells of Nanteos, the Pryses of Gogerddan, the Lisburne family of Trawscoed cut a somewhat pathetic figure, financially impoverished despite such surface ostentations as the 'Gogerddan hunt'.

The landlords no longer gained from their association with the Church. Disendowment was already under way, as the church commissioners were already undertaking their work in preparation for post-war change even though the operation of the Disestablishment Act had been suspended, along with Irish Home Rule, in September 1914. The value of lay patronage for the Welsh gentry was, therefore, no longer obvious. The Welsh Church, led by the dexterous political figure of Bishop A. G. Edwards of St. Asaph, obviously regarded disestablishment as a foregone conclusion. The Welsh Liberal members in a rare display of effective protest, had forced Asquith to withdraw a Welsh Church Postponement Bill in July 1915. This was designed to postpone the operation of disestablishment until six months after the end of the war, but Liberals pointed out that that was time enough to have the bill repealed by a future Unionist majority. By 1917, Welsh churchmen had obviously come to terms with the fact that disestablishment and disendow-

[15] John Davies, 'The End of the Great Estates and the Rise of Freehold Farming in Wales', *Welsh History Review*, vol. 7, No. 2 (December 1974), pp. 191–2.

ment were inevitable. In October 1917, a convention at Cardiff set up a new representative and governing body for the Welsh Church; judges such as Sir John Sankey and Lord Atkin were enlisted to help draw up a constitution for the new, independent Church of Wales after disestablishment. The main concern of the Church was certainly not for the profits of gentry, but for maintaining its own finances in good order. Thus in R. E. Prothero's Tithe Act in November 1918 it was laid down that although Welsh tithe fetched only £109 in the open market, the Welsh councils would have to pay over £120 for purposes of commutation when the tithe was secularized. This kind of move did not increase the affection between rate-paying landlords and the Church. In this and other respects, the war was bringing the Welsh countryside to the effective end of centuries of history. The social ascendancy of the landlord over the rural community was in every respect now a phenomenon of the past. In terms of local authority, the landed gentry had already been overthrown by democratically-elected county councils. In terms of finance, they faced high wartime taxation side by side with falling returns from rent rolls. There was also the loss of life of so many heirs of landed families in fighting at the front. For centuries since the Union with England, indeed for long before that, Wales had manifested the almost complete control of the landowner over the social and political life of the rural community. Henceforth, the countryside was to become the domain of the freeholding farmer. The *werin* were at last entering upon their inheritance, though it took a world war to speed them on their way.

In industrial Wales, too, especially in the coalfields in the south, the war years brought mighty changes, not least in the temper of industrial relations. As has been noted already, the initial response of most Welsh workers' leaders in the mining and other industries was to give an overwhelming favourable endorsement of the 'patriotic' call. When men like Charles Stanton, miners' agent of Aberdare and a leading militant during the Cambrian stoppage, turned into recruiting agents, something fundamental was taking place in the mentality of the mining community. Ted Gill, formerly of the Plebs League, was another strong supporter of the war and a pillar of recruitment campaigns. Noah Rees, part-author of the *Miners' Next Step* and of the constitution devised for the new industrial commonwealth, took a line similar to that of Gill. The ILP and other organs of dissent went into the shadows. Men like Ablett were seldom heard. Keir Hardie's friends in Merthyr socialist circles, men like Llew Francis, Edmond Stonelake, and the Revd Thomas Nicholas, faced harsh pressures. The *Pioneer* fell on hard times. The other ILP newspaper, *Llais Llafur* of Ystalyfera, underwent an editorial revolution a few months after war was declared. Instead of being ferociously socialist and hostile to militarism and capitalism, it now became a voice for 'patriotic labour'. Symbolically, it changed its name and its main language for news coverage. *Llais Llafur* became the *Labour Voice*. Eventually it was to turn into just another slightly sensationalist parochial newspaper.

The temper of the mining community was dramatically confirmed in a famous by-election at Merthyr Boroughs in November 1915. It followed the death of Keir Hardie, whose anti-war views had led to much criticism, and became a litmus test of how far the voters of Merthyr sympathized with the attitude of their late member. There was a suggestion of Hardie's Scottish ally, Bob Smillie, president of the MFGB, being nominated as Labour candidate. But in the end the ILP and the local Labour Representation Committee put up James Winstone, the president of the South Wales Miners. Winstone was no pacifist; he had addressed recruiting meetings and had a son serving at the front. But he was a member of the ILP and called upon men like Ramsay MacDonald and Fred Jowett to address meetings at the Merthyr Olympia skating-rink on his behalf. Inevitably then Winstone was tarred with the anti-war brush. In opposition to him there stood the pugnacious Stanton, still the miners' agent for Aberdare, as a pro-war Labour candidate. He ran with Liberal and Conservative support and also received, technically, the official backing of the Labour Party national executive. Stanton fought an uninhibitedly pro-war campaign. He denounced 'the brutish butchers of Berlin' and freely attacked Winstone as unpatriotic and seditious.[16] In addition, Stanton clearly benefited from the fact that the ILP organization in Merthyr had never been as powerful as the presence of Hardie as member might suggest. His 'patriotic' campaign easily carried the day. He defeated Winstone by 4,206 votes on a low poll. Stanton gleefully declared that the boys in the trenches would rejoice at his victory. Lord Milner and his 'social imperialist' friends regarded the Merthyr by-election as a historical turning-point in the history of British labour and set out to found a British Workers' League to which Mabon lent his name. Even in Hardie's own mining stronghold, the seat of Henry Richard and the shrine of Dic Penderyn, the appeal of patriotic jingoism and of establishment attitudes was overwhelming.

Nevertheless, it soon became clear that the war was producing massive changes in the coalfield, and that the minds of the miners were turning to social and economic demands quite as revolutionary as those heard in 1910–14. The temper of industrial relations deteriorated sharply in 1915, Lloyd George's Treasury agreement with the unions notwithstanding. There was a major strike in July 1915, indeed an official strike declared by the SWMF executive against the terms of the Treasury Agreement, on behalf of a new and higher standard wage rate. The terms agreed by the SWMF executive with the Board of Trade negotiator and with Walter Runciman, acting on behalf of the government, were turned down at a delegate conference on 12 July by 1,894 votes to 1,037. This was, in effect, the equivalent of nearly a 43,000 majority of the entire workforce. That a national stoppage by the miners should take place at all during the crisis of wartime when the existence

---

[16] See Stanton's maiden speech, *Parl. Deb.*, 5th ser., lxxvii, pp. 225–8.

of the country was believed to be at stake aroused scandalized concern in the London press. 'Germany's Allies in Wales' was the *Standard*'s verdict on the Welsh miners. But the solidarity of the workers was proof against these verbal onslaughts. On 20 July, after Lloyd George himself had intervened, the miners and owners' representatives met at the Park Hotel, Cardiff, in the presence of Lloyd George, Runciman, and Arthur Henderson. The appearance of three leading members of the coalition government shows the seriousness with which the government viewed the crisis. In the end, after a ten days' stoppage, the miners won all their main points, in particular a standard wage for underground miners of 3s. 4d. a day, plus 50 per cent. Wartime pressures had enabled the unions to make advances that far outstripped those of peacetime years.

After this, tension and industrial bitterness in the mining valleys continued to mount. Indeed, Stanton's victory in the Merthyr by-election in November 1915 was really at variance with the underlying mood of social protest, allied to mounting political objections to the war itself. Miners enlisted in the ILP in increasing numbers as one surviving voice of anti-war feeling. In 1916, some of the old echoes of the Unofficial Reform Committee began to be heard once again. The classes of the Central Labour College were again started in the Rhondda and Aberdare valleys, with Wil John Edwards as an organizer and Will Mainwaring as the ideological inspiration. By the end of 1917, there were thirty-one classes active in the Rhondda, with younger men like Horner and Cook rising to prominence within them. There were also fringe movements such as Sylvia Pankhurst's Workers' Socialist Federation, strongly syndicalist at first as expressed through its journal *Workers' Dreadnought*, later a strong partisan of the Bolshevik revolution in Russia. By the end of 1917, it was clear that the Unofficial Reform Committee, with Ablett back at the helm, was in existence again, spreading its Marxist/syndicalist gospel of workers' control and direct industrial action.

But the most spectacular developments concerned the growing radicalization of the South Wales Miners' Executive itself. Now truly Lib-Labism and Mabonism were in their death agonies. Younger miners' agents emerged like Frank Hodges in Garw, Noah Ablett and Will Mainwaring in the Rhondda, S. O. Davies (a former ministerial student at Aberystwyth) who was elected agent for Merthyr in 1918. Arthur Cook held no official position at this time, but his reputation rose rapidly during the war, especially in 1918 when he was imprisoned for three months for anti-war propagandist activities. So did that of Arthur Horner who suffered six months of hard labour in Wormwood Scrubs. The Miners' Federation was now strongly committed to the nationalization of the mines and a socialist programme for the public ownership of the commanding heights of the economy. Commentators were struck by the growing mood of social militancy in south Wales, as in Clydeside in Scotland, with 'advanced' socialist ideas making headway. The men listed several specific grievances. The adoption of new technology led to growing charges that the owners were careless of the health and safety of their workers. The terrible toll of accidents in south Wales gave further substance to these demands. It was noted, too, that more sophisticated costing methods tended to force wages down, despite the huge profits made by the coal companies. Bad labour relations played their part, with managers and other officials remote from the workforce and all too prone to discipline or victimize militant union officials or other 'agitators'. Relations between the cost-conscious owners and the representatives of the miners reached new heights of class bitterness.

A powerful new impetus to working-class militancy came with the intro-duction of military conscription to all adult males between the ages of eighteen and forty-five, in May 1916. Apart from being a threat to trade-union privileges and to civil liberties generally, that was thought to be the precursor of industrial conscription and other forms of the direction of free labour. The Welsh miners in February 1916 declared their fervent opposition to military conscription, and only narrowly failed to persuade the MFGB as a whole to oppose it, and by strike action. There was growing tension over proposed increases in wage rates, and the curtailing of miners' holidays. The old Welsh sentiment no longer applied in the valleys. When Lloyd George again tried to address the Welsh miners, with General Smuts and Mabon to help him, he failed to get a hearing, in a way reminiscent of his being howled down by the Scottish engineers in Glasgow in December 1915. In 1917 the valleys were seething again with class bitterness. A massive new encouragement came in Russia with the February revolution followed by that in October. It aroused immense enthusiasm amongst Welsh miners, railwaymen, and steelworkers. Soldiers' and Workers' Councils appeared in the Rhondda on the model of Petrograd. Maerdy was renamed 'little Moscow'; the red flag flew at pitheads. The most powerful voice of Maerdy socialism, operating under an assumed name because of his anti-war activities in Wales and Ireland, was Arthur Horner, who was finally arrested and imprisoned for sedition. Here and in other respects, south Wales seemed the very cockpit of class war, a centre of neo-Bolshevist extremism, an 'El Dorado' for every species of revolutionary socialist ideology.

In the summer of 1917, alarmed at the deteriorating pattern of labour relations throughout Britain, the Lloyd George government appointed a Commission of Industrial Unrest. That reporting on 'No. 7 Division', south Wales, painted an alarming picture of deteriorating conditions.[17] Its members were Thomas Evans, a coal manager; the miners' agent Vernon Hartshorn (now a pro-war Labour moderate); the socialist Edgar Chappell as secretary; and the benevolent Daniel Lleufer Thomas as chairman. Witnesses before it

[17] *Report of Commission of Inquiry into Industrial Unrest: No. 7 Division* (Cd. 8668), pp. 5–39.

included Ablett and Hodges on behalf of the SWMF. It was, by its very composition, a body friendly to the men rather than to the coalowners, and it painted a frightening picture of mounting social tension. It drew attention especially to long-term sociological and economic factors peculiar to south Wales—the flood of newer, young immigrants, especially from England; the bleak pattern of slum housing and environmental decay in valleys with teeming populations; above all, the fears aroused by the growth of vast oligopolistic combines. The three groups associated with Lord Rhondda, United National, and Thomas Beynon expanded so much in 1915-16 that they produced 40 per cent (over 14 million tons) of the entire output of the coalfield as a whole. This impersonal system, with the divorce of management from ownership and far more remote relations between masters and men, was held to be the root cause of much of the tension. The outcome was seen in the messianic impact of 'direct action' or syndicalist theories, surging throughout trades councils, shop stewards (in the engineering trades), pithead lodges and Labour College classes, with the further impact of revolutionary Bolshevism. The commission was well-meaning and benevolent, but helpless. Its proposals for extending the machinery of the conciliation boards, introducing the Whitley Council scheme for joint management or workers' consultation in the mining industry, standardizing price lists for coal and the equalization of wage rates throughout the coalfield, made scant impact. Its comments about extending adult education seemed irrelevant. The benevolent social planners, the moral imperatives to which Lib-Labs like Lleufer Thomas had always subscribed since the days of *Cymru Fydd*, the ideals of the School of Social Service or the Housing and Development Association, both of which claimed Lleufer Thomas as their chairman, were being swamped by the class bitterness and potential violence of industrial or post-industrial capitalism.

In 1918, fuelled by practical grievances such as high rents and food shortages, the mood of the miners became more belligerent still. The unofficial movement now went into eclipse again simply because the official leadership of the SWMF, headed by men like James Winstone, was now so radical, with ideologues like Noah Ablett powerful on the executive itself. The Welsh members of the MFGB executive began to press hard for a 30 per cent wage increase, secure in the enormously enhanced membership and augmented strike funds of the South Wales Federation during the war. The importance of the Welsh in the national union was seen when at the age of thirty-one, Frank Hodges, the brilliant (and at this stage firmly Marxist) agent of the Garw miners, was elected secretary of the MFGB itself, to become a key figure, along with Bob Smillie of Scotland and Herbert Smith of Yorkshire, in wage bargaining with the government. The Welsh miners and trades councils in south Wales ardently endorsed the new Labour Party constitution of June 1918, with its commitment to socialist control of the means of production and distribution. Constituency Labour Parties sprang up throughout the coalfield, and in other areas like Wrexham, the port of Holyhead in Anglesey, and the quarrying areas of Caernarvonshire as well. Some Labour activists like Silyn Roberts and David Thomas were concerned that Labour's head office in London, and Arthur Henderson in particular, looked with disfavour on proposals to create an autonomous Welsh Council of Labour. To men like Henderson and the trade-union leaders whose views he reflected, this would be a concession to Welsh nationalism which would weaken the centralized strength of the Labour Party's official machinery. It was a view vehemently shared by Egerton Wake, the party's organizing secretary in Scotland and Wales who deplored the excesses of the 'Celtic temperament'.[18] Even so, as the world war seemed in September and October 1918 to be manifestly reaching its end at last, the Labour Party in south Wales emerged as powerful and coherent. Full-time agents were appointed in Swansea and elsewhere. Behind this political front, the massed, militant ranks of the mining proletariat were poised for a major transformation of the economic and social structure of their nation.

A general overview of developments in Wales during the First World War leads to only one possible conclusion. In theory, the initial Welsh fervour for the war, the new dominance of Lloyd George meant that the war marked the culmination of thirty years of Liberal, nationally-conscious aspiration and progress. In fact, it is clear that the war marked an immense break with the past, in social and ultimately in political terms. In no part of the British Isles was the contrast between pre- and post-war conditions more pronounced.

In most of Wales, those largely farming upland areas which formed the great mass of the geographical extent of the land, the war marked the virtual end of an old social order. The rule of the gentry, and associated with them their Anglican allies, was manifestly over. With the sale of so many great estates, the changes in property-holding merely confirmed the effect of changes in local government and social authority. The gentry lost any sense of predominance. Equally, with the Welsh Church on the eve of disestablishment and facing the prospect of being thrown on to its own financial resources with some cheerfulness, the authority of the bishop and his clergy over a wider society was becoming moribund also. That class hierarchy which had fuelled the campaigns and the rhetoric of nonconformist radicals for a hundred years was being dismantled visibly year by year. In the coalfield, the authority of the coalowner and the shipowner, the Lib-Lab ethos that so often underpinned their position, were also clearly under strain. The South Wales Miners' Federation, together with the various militant and unofficial movements that it had spawned, betokened an immense change in social and industrial relationships. The unions, above all the miners, would become increasingly assertive and class-conscious. The last remnants of Lib-Lab class collabora-

[18] Ross McKibbin, *The Evolution of the Labour Party, 1910–1924* (Oxford, 1975), pp. 168–9.

tion were disappearing, or would disappear once the immediate euphoria of the return of peace died away. At least, the coal mines and Welsh industry generally were still flourishing, with booming demand throughout the war years. If the general pattern of economic progress suddenly changed and mass depression followed, then the capacity of south Wales to avoid a social revolution of cataclysmic proportions would indeed be in doubt.

The Liberal élite of Wales took comfort from the apparent triumph of their generations of effort in the rural areas, with the demise of the landlord. On the other hand, the rise of class-conscious socialism in the valleys was a dangerous sign of fundamental decay. In the most economically dynamic areas of the land, Liberalism was stagnant and Welshness of little account. The old Welsh objectives aroused little interest during the war. Temperance reformers welcomed the Central Control Board to regulate the liquor trade, but plans for a regional settlement of the drink issue in Wales, made by the omnipresent Lleufer Thomas amongst others, aroused little general concern. Pressures for Welsh home rule, a cause staunchly upheld by *Welsh Outlook*, tended to founder on the earnest plodding personality of E. T. John, now on the point of joining the Labour Party after the introduction of conscription. A conference met, inevitably, at Llandrindod Wells in June 1918, called by David Davies, and E. T. John amongst others to promote devolution in Wales and with the avowed support of south Wales Conservatives like L. Forestier-Walker and Labour leaders such as MacDonald and Lansbury. But it fell flat.[19] In any case, it was dominated by the quiescent old guard of Liberal nonconformity and, as such, automatically suspect to working-class bodies such as the South Wales Miners' Federation.

In the educational field, pressures to secure a Board of Education for Wales alone made little headway. The Fisher Act of 1918 was silent on the point. The royal commission under the chairmanship of Haldane which investigated the University of Wales in 1916–18 was more encouraging. It confirmed the federal, national structure of the university, while granting more autonomy to the individual colleges. As it happened, the university was granted a member of parliament, along with other British universities, in the 1918 Representation of the People Act. Separatist sentiment emanating from the University College, Cardiff, found no favour. The general organs of the university, its court, council, and senate in each college were endorsed. An important new development in 1920 was to be the opening of a fourth university college in Swansea, set in Singleton Park, once the home of the Liberal MP, Sir Hussey Vivian. An interesting innovation, one supported strongly by H. A. L. Fisher at the Board of Education and by Lloyd George himself, was for the levying of a penny rate by the local authorities. In Haldane's view, this would bind them more closely to their national university. In return, the local authorities were given a majority of one on the University Court. In effect, the middle-class

[19] *Welsh Outlook*, July 1918: 'Notes of the Month'.

élite who had supplied so much of the momentum and the money for the movement for higher education had their authority confirmed. Haldane himself also had the satisfaction of seeing that more emphasis was placed on extension or extra-mural education. In particular, that department to be headed at Aberystwyth by the Revd Herbert Morgan, a socialist minister formerly in charge of Castle Street Baptist chapel in London, was to have an especially powerful impact on the cultural and intellectual life of mid-Wales. The national culture generally was confirmed by decisions taken to set up a University of Wales Press and a Board of Celtic Studies, both inaugurated in 1922. Yet, on the whole, the Haldane Committee, despite itself, probably strengthened the forces for anglicization within the University of Wales. The old academic senate, one of the very few unifying forces in the university, was abolished. The reconstituted court of the university quite failed to act as the kind of itinerant 'educational parliament' that Haldane himself fondly hoped would minister and respond to the 'enlightened democracy' of Wales.[20] Professionally more expert, more specialized in its disciplines, more disparate in its collegiate institutions, the University of Wales, too, was beginning to turn its back on *Cymru Fydd*.

The effect of the war, then, was far from establishing the Liberal élite of nonconformist Welsh Wales in new authority and power. Rather it was to riddle it with new doubts, even in its own cherished field of education. The battle against the old enemies, 'the unholy Trinity' of the bishop, the brewer and, above all, the squire, somehow seemed less important now that it was being won. Amidst the conformist pressures of total war, the old values lost something of their validity, the old self-confidence was draining away. After the golden glow of hope that characterized so much of its activities in the years up to 1914, Liberal Wales entered upon its silver age.

[20] See Eric Ashby and Mary Anderson, *Portrait of Haldane at Work on Education* (London, 1974), pp. 123–30.

CHAPTER 7

THE POST-WAR MOOD

With the declaration of an armistice on 11 November 1918 Wales entered a prolonged period of reflection, soon turning to disillusion, cynicism, and even at times to despair. The mood of the post-war period, as in Britain generally but with distinct national emphasis on Wales, soon turned sour. Yet the advent of peace was briefly marked by the continuation of that patriotic frenzy which characterized so much of the war years. Lloyd George called a snap 'khaki' election for December 1918, even before the troops had begun to demobilize, to endorse his Coalition government of Unionists, Liberals, and a handful of 'patriotic Labour' men. Its 'couponed' candidates stood as the spokesmen of national unity and the representatives of 'the man who won the war'. In Wales particularly, the elections were fought amidst an atmosphere of national euphoria without parallel in modern times, not even during the Boer War. Anti-government Liberals who had failed to receive the 'coupon', men such as Llewelyn Williams in Carmarthen Boroughs, Reginald McKenna in North Monmouthshire and Ellis W. Davies in Caernarvonshire, were reviled as unpatriotic and sectional for their attacks on the Welsh Prime Minister during the war years. Pacifists among the Labour Party candidates, especially those representing the ILP, had an even harder time. The Revd T. E. Nicholas, fighting as an ILP man at Aberdare, was physically assaulted, especially by women electors, voting for the first time and now swept along in the national lust for vengeance. Anti-German demands for hanging the Kaiser and for massive reparations from the 'Hun' to pay for war damage reverberated throughout the land, not only from pro-government candidates. Lloyd George himself, who delivered a few major speeches in English urban centres such as Bristol, Leeds, and London, did not deign to speak at all in Wales which he believed to be impregnable. He held aloof, in presidential detachment and splendour, from the 'party ding-dong'[1] of electoral conflict.

The results confirmed all his hopes. Even though the Welsh electorate had been expanded by over 50 per cent to 1,170,974, with the implementation of universal male suffrage and the enfranchisement of women of thirty and over in the 1918 Reform Act, the results in Wales gave the Coalition a huge endorsement. In the thirty-six Welsh constituencies, which had now been

[1] Philip Kerr to Lloyd George, 20 November 1918 (House of Lords Record Office, Lloyd George Papers, F/89/1/13).

redistributed by boundary commissioners, 'couponed' supporters of the Coalition were returned in twenty-five, mostly by vast majorities. Twenty of these were Coalition Liberals (including the new University of Wales seat which returned Sir Herbert Lewis with a 61 per cent majority over Labour), four were Unionist, and one (C. B. Stanton at Aberdare) represented the patriotic Labour 'National Democratic Party'. Only one Asquithian Liberal was returned, Haydn Jones, elected unopposed for Merioneth. Anti-war Liberals like Llewelyn Williams and Ellis Davies were massacred at the polls. Everywhere there was an immense emphasis on patriotism, retribution, and support for the Prime Minister whose own majority at Caernarfon Boroughs soared to over 85 per cent of the poll. The one Coalition Liberal defeat (Sir Ellis Griffith who lost Anglesey after twenty-three years as its member) was also in its way a tribute to wartime emotion since the victor here was even more 'patriotic' than the pro-war Griffith himself.[2] This was Brigadier Sir Owen Thomas, a friend of Lloyd George and recruiting officer for the Welsh Division, running as an erratic and temporary member of the Labour Party with the aid of dockers' and railwaymen's votes in Holyhead. The Labour Party captured ten seats in Wales and 30.8 per cent (163,000) of the votes cast, a notable advance. Welsh miners in particular loomed large in the parliamentary Labour Party's membership of only fifty-seven. But it was noticeable that the Labour men actually elected were moderates like John Williams at Gower, William Brace at Abertillery, Vernon Hartshorn at Ogmore, Tom Richards at Ebbw Vale, Alfred Onions at Caerphilly, and the aged 'Mabon' at Rhondda West. Mention should also be made of Dai Watts Morgan, returned unopposed from Rhondda East, or rather Major David Watts Morgan CBE, DSO, the hero of Cambrai, and soon to be nicknamed 'Dai Alphabet' for his pretensions. Even the Labour representation, then, confirmed the wartime mood of jingoism and the endorsement of Church, king, and nation.

In fact, it very soon became apparent that the frenzy of the 'coupon election' was a wholly misleading index of the mood of post-war Wales. Indeed, its racialism and extreme nationalism died away almost as soon as the polls were declared, shortly after Christmas Day. There were a few echoes in the immediate aftermath of peace, especially in cases of vindictive hostility towards those who had been conscientious objectors during the war (and who, indeed, had been deprived of their vote in the 1918 Reform Act). A particularly unpleasant case of this kind occurred at the University College of Wales, Aberystwyth, which had seen the expulsion of Professor Hermann Ethé during the war. In 1919 it was decided to appoint a new Professor of Welsh in succession to Professor Edward Anwyl, the distinguished philologist who had resigned in 1913 to become principal of Caerleon Training College (and who had died soon afterwards). After some debate on the college

---

[2] Cf. E. W. Rowlands, 'Yr Etholiad Cyffredinol ym Môn, 1918', *Transactions of the Anglesey Antiquarian Society and Field Club*, 1976–77, pp. 57–79.

council, the poet Thomas Gwynn Jones was appointed Professor of Welsh Literature, the chair being endowed by the Llandinam family. Gwynn Jones's radical, indeed socialist, political views were not held against him. However, great trouble arose when it was proposed to elect another eminent poet, Thomas Parry-Williams, to a second chair, that of Welsh Language. Parry-Williams was known to have been a pacifist and conscientious objector during the war, and a contributor (invariably on literary themes, it is true) to *Y Wawr*. Ex-servicemen's organizations protested strongly, not least because Parry-Williams's main rival for the chair was Timothy Lewis, an ex-serviceman himself, though far less distinguished as a scholar and writer than Parry-Williams. There was a year's delay before in 1920 Parry-Williams was indeed appointed to the new chair of Welsh, with Lewis being given a readership as a consolation prize.[3] The whole affair caused much bad blood in academic circles.

But this kind of legacy of wartime patriotism soon evaporated. Welsh scholars and writers now increasingly viewed the war with disgust as a symbol of uncivilized mass brutality. Indeed, it is notable that the war was largely ignored in literature of the post-war period, almost as if there was a collective national shame at this aberrant support for barbarism. There were no significant 'war poets' of the type of Wilfred Owen and Siegfried Sassoon in England;[4] Hedd Wyn was recalled as an example of meaningless sacrifice not of national heroism. One exception, perhaps, was the poem by 'Cynan' entitled *Mab y Bwthyn* (the son of the cottage) which won the crown in the Caernarfon *eisteddfod* in 1921 as a ballad by an authentic soldier-poet. But its main characteristic was its evocation of the pastoral sentiment of the lyric poetry dominant in Wales prior to 1914; it was not strictly speaking a 'war poem' at all. If anything, Cynan emphasized the shame, rather than the glory, of war. Nor did prose writing on the war find much favour in Wales. The famous story of wartime escape from German and Turkish prisons, *The Road to Endor*, written by E. H. Jones, the son of Sir Henry Jones and briefly the editor of *Welsh Outlook*, had little impact in his native land.

As the war became more distant, those who had opposed it became more honoured in their own country. Puleston Jones, the blind preacher, again became a respected figure in the Methodist pulpit. Principal Thomas Rees now gained the acclaim of troubled Liberal intellectuals like W. J. Gruffydd. One wartime martyr who aroused especial sympathy was the saintly, Gandhi-like George Maitland Lloyd Davies of the Fellowship of Reconciliation who had suffered imprisonment and generally harsh treatment for his pacifist views during the war. He now became a symbol of public redemption and

³ E. L. Ellis, *The University College of Wales, Aberystwyth, 1872–1972* (Cardiff, 1972), pp. 204–5.
⁴ D. Tecwyn Lloyd, 'Welsh Public Opinion and the First World War', *Planet*, February–March 1972, p. 27.

atonement, cleansed from the bogus religiosity with which the government invested the Cenotaph and the tomb of the Unknown Soldier. Davies's parliamentary candidature for the University of Wales in the general election of 1923, in which he stood as a Christian Pacifist with a general sympathy for Labour, aroused strong support in radical and nonconformist circles. The university had been predictably Liberal since 1918 as befitted its ties with *Cymru Fydd* and the national campaigns of pre-1914. Davies now won the seat by the margin of just ten votes. This caused a sensation. It was a public rejection of war and military values by the graduate electors of Wales, as startling in its own way as the Oxford Union 'King and Country' debate ten years later. It showed how the Welsh intelligentsia was moving away from the unthinking commitment to official Liberalism and to Lloyd George's leadership, and was turning to a new, post-war radicalism of a far more committed kind.

Post-war Wales, in fact, soon emerged as a very different kind of society, different from the emotion of the war years, almost light years away from the kind of stratified society that had made up so much of the principality before 1914.

One vital component in the old society was the old hierarchy, the social ascendancy of the Established Church and the landed gentry, whose downfall had been clearly foreshadowed during the war. Now it perished utterly. One crucial landmark came on 1 June 1920. On that day, eighty years of sectarian warfare were brought to an end and the Welsh Church, comprising the four dioceses of Llandaff, St. David's, Bangor, and St. Asaph, was disestablished. Bishop A. G. Edwards of St. Asaph was formally invested as the first Archbishop of Wales. At the armistice, the situation had still been fluid with regard to disestablishment and even more disendowment. The passage of the Welsh Disestablishment Bill in September 1914 had been accompanied by a suspensory measure to postpone its operation until after the war. No-one knew quite what would happen then, especially since the financial aspects of disendowment had been so dramatically affected by such wartime factors as the inflation in the price of land and of tithe. Bishop Edwards had been quietly lobbying Bonar Law and the Unionists to obtain more favourable financial terms, during the last weeks of the war. Bonar Law told Lloyd George that the Bishop was 'very moderate. All he wishes is the Glebe = £10,000 a year & a lump sum of two millions. He would be satisfied for the election with a statement by you that the long continuance of the War has created problems which were not foreseen which make it right that some details of the financial arrangements should be reconsidered by the new Parliament.' The Prime Minister, however, refused to commit himself at this stage other than to confirm that disestablishment would be put into effect. Earlier Lord Salisbury had written to Selborne of his fear that the fact that many Unionists were declaring for imperial federation boded ill for church endowments. 'I am afraid that even the fact that many Unionists have declared for Federation is a grievous blow to the Welsh Church because the fact that Federation is pending will be used as strong argument against touching the subject until a Welsh Parliament is established.'[5] His family relative, Lord Robert Cecil, resigned from the government on the typically quixotic issue of the Welsh Church. Otherwise, nothing much happened until Lloyd George returned from Paris in July 1919 after the signature of the treaty of Versailles.

Then developments were rapid. Lloyd George conducted brisk negotiations with the Welsh bishops, to whom he promised a Treasury grant to cover the loss of ancient endowments. Bishop Owen of St. David's put pressure on Davidson, the Archbishop of Canterbury, to reach a quick settlement and pursue 'the path of forgiveness'.[6] The Free Church Council and the Welsh members of parliament were also won over to a speedy settlement. On 6 August, Shortt, the Home Secretary, introduced a hurriedly concocted Welsh Church Temporalities Bill, the contents of which appeared to be largely unfamiliar to him.[7] It included the astonishing reversal of view that there had been no lapsed vested interests at all during the war because the bill only gave the Church what was rightfully its own under the Act of 1914. The bill had produced some debate amongst ministers in the Cabinet Home Affairs Committee on 5 August. The President of the Board of Education, H. A. L. Fisher, had commented wryly on the obstructive attitude of the Cecil brothers, together with some other backbench Tory churchmen like Samuel Hoare and Ormsby-Gore. 'It was rather curious', he observed, 'that the Government having introduced a Bill designed to meet the view of extreme High Churchmen, the latter should oppose it.'[8] Shortt's speech in the Commons concentrated on the difficulties that the Welsh county councils would face in the adjustment of the disendowment arrangements as the Church had benefited so greatly from the wartime inflation in the price of tithe. There was also the pressing difficulty that the Welsh Church Commissioners would face in finding the money they would have to pay to the representative body of the disestablished Welsh Church—almost £3½ million in all. Loans and a remittance of rates would cover most of this, while the balance of one million pounds would be made up by a direct grant from the Treasury. Disendowment would thus become a gradual process. The Welsh county councils would acquire the secularized endowments of the Church on a long-term basis. From £48,000 in 1920 they would find their income rising to £212,000 by 1950.

Almost everyone welcomed these arrangements, whether they understood

---

[5] Bonar Law to Lloyd George, 22 October 1918 (Lloyd George Papers, F/30/2/51); Lord Salisbury to Lord Selborne, 12 June 1918 (Bodleian, Selborne Papers, I:7, ff. 30–1).

[6] Eluned Owen, *The Later Life of Bishop Owen* (Llandysul, 1961), pp. 410–11.

[7] T. Huws Davies to Sir Henry Primrose, 3 August 1919, Primrose to Huws Davies, 11 August 1919 (NLW, Huws Davies Papers, MS 16,354C).

[8] Minutes of Home Affairs Committee, 5 August 1919 (PRO, CAB 26/1).

them or not. There were a few voices of dissent on either side. Three Welsh Liberals, Haydn Jones, Sidney Robinson, and David Davies (who was soon to become an Independent Liberal) all voted against the Temporalities Bill which amounted, they claimed, to *ailwaddoliad* (a 're-endowment') of the disestablished Church by the British taxpayer. They were joined by various nonconformist spokesmen in Wales, and by Asquithian Liberals such as Llewelyn Williams. He was an admirer of Roman Catholicism who was in fact to be ministered to by a Catholic priest on his death-bed, but he welcomed another stick with which to trounce his *bête noire*, the Prime Minister. There were also Anglican critics. In the House of Commons, Lord Hugh Cecil denounced the settlement as 'robbery of God', and his brother Lord Robert backed him up.[9] There were also Unionist critics in the Lords, particularly over the acquisition of churchyards by the local authorities and over the finality of the severance of the Welsh dioceses from the Convocation of Canterbury. Lloyd George brushed aside these protests when the bill returned to the Commons: by 19 August it had become law. Clearly, most MPs and most church leaders in Wales welcomed the end of the old sectarian bitterness. There was much agreement with the views of the Labour member, the steelworker Tom Griffiths of Pontypool, a Sunday school teacher in a Methodist chapel in Neath. He declared that Church and nonconformist boys had fought and died together in the trenches and it was wrong to revive the old animosities now.[10] The Church was formally disestablished on 31 March 1920. At the ceremony of investiture of its first Archbishop at St. Asaph, those present included religious leaders from various denominations, including the Roman Catholic, and also the Prime Minister.

The disputes that attended the final passage of disestablishment and disendowment were soon forgotten. The disestablished Church proved to be far more vigorous and thriving than in the days of the establishment. It soon made good the initial loss of endowments, partly through the financial dexterity of Sir Owen Philipps, Lord Kilsant (a shipowner who was later to be imprisoned for fraud). By the thirties, the Welsh Church was financially thriving, with the acquisition of land and desirable urban property in London. Later it was to acquire Bush House in the Aldwych. The new organizational freedom of the Church was impressively shown in the creation of two new dioceses in south Wales, Swansea and Brecon, which was carved out of St. David's diocese, and Monmouth which was formed out of Llandaff diocese. The Church also became markedly more in tune with Welsh national feeling and much more sympathetic to the Welsh language than in the pre-1914 period. Indeed, in the 1960s, Welsh churchmen were to show a surprising sympathy for the cause of Welsh nationalism, cultural and political. By 1935, the second Archbishop of Wales, C. A. H. Green, formerly Bishop of

[9] *Parl. Deb.*, 5th ser., cxix, p. 470.
[10] Ibid., p. 493.

Bangor, openly admitted that the coming of disestablishment had been a boon to the Church as a religious and social institution.[11] On the other hand, the coming of disestablishment also clearly marked the end of any claim to social primacy that the Church could make, especially in urban Wales. It was now but another denomination, struggling against the secularism and the socialism of the twentieth century. In terms of its influence upon the social and political life of Wales it was now of secondary importance at best.

Just as the Church was disestablished after 1918, so, too, were the landed gentry. The process of the sale of estates, accelerated during the war, became a flood between 1918 and 1922 when landlords took advantage of the inflation of land prices to sell up most of their holdings. By 1926, the Welsh rural freeholder, the legatee of his nation's 'green revolution', was the dominant feature of rural society, in sole legal possession of his family farm, at the cost of often severe mortgages and of the high interest rates imposed by the banks. Lloyd George's new land policy for the Liberals, *The Land and the Nation* published in 1925, caused heart-searching in Wales. Sir Alfred Mond, then Liberal member for Carmarthen, resigned from the party in protest. He was to be succeeded in a by-election in Carmarthen in 1928 by Colonel W. N. Jones, a Liberal who rejected the Lloyd George 'green book', while a pro-Lloyd George Liberal, Captain R. T. Evans, was turned down as candidate. With freeholding owner-occupiers so numerous in Wales proposals like the 'cultivating tenure', through which Lloyd George seemed to be threatening a kind of undercover nationalization of freehold cultivable land, were inevitably not popular.

The years between 1918 and 1922 had seen the most dramatic phase of a process of land transfer which formed the background to all this. In this period, more than a quarter of the land of Wales changed hands: after all, most Welsh landlords had even more powerful financial and social pressures leading them to sell up their estates than had their English counterparts. Some famous estates passed into oblivion, and estate agents found business booming in rural and industrial Wales alike. Immense sums were raised by landlords—£227,000 for the Cefn Mably estates by the Kemeys-Tyntes in three days in September 1920; £120,000 for the Glynllifon land in Caernarvonshire; £200,000 for Baron Hill property in Anglesey; £124,000 for the Bute land in Glamorgan, were only some of the more spectacular examples.[12] And in the vast majority of cases it was tenant farmers who were the purchasers. Few Welsh landowners sold all their estates, although those of Lords Glanusk, Newborough, and Penrhyn (a hated name from the recent past) were largely parcelled out. There was a further surge in the land market in

[11] C. A. H. Green, *Disestablishment and Disendowment: the Experience of the Church in Wales* (London, 1935).
[12] John Davies, 'The End of the Great Estates', pp. 192–3.

1924—5, when further parts of the Penrhyn estate in Caernarvonshire, the Nash and Bute estates in Glamorgan, the Pontypool Park estate in Monmouthshire and others were sold up. Thereafter, the land market became more sluggish and depressed. Fewer successful auctions were to be recorded by the end of the twenties, because of the sharp deflation and dear money of the middle and later part of that decade.

The tenant farmers who bought up their holdings during this social revolution were not necessarily fortunate. The value of capital invested in agriculture by owner-occupiers declined sharply, by over 20 per cent between 1925 and 1931. Mortgage indebtedness became severe and debt charges more difficult to sustain. Some mortgagors took over their holdings; estate agents and solicitors found themselves by the early thirties becoming alternative landlords in their turn. Clearly, the 'green revolution' did not meet all the hopes of Liberal nonconformists in the past, any more than the coming of 'religious equality' had done in 1920. For all that, there is obviously an immense shift in social relations and in perceptions of the social structure to be detected henceforth. The gentry subsided as if they had never been. Great houses eventually turned into public or private institutions—Gogerddan became the plant-breeding station for Aberystwyth University College in 1953, Trawscoed a centre for the Forestry Commission, Golden Grove an agricultural college, Wynnstay a boarding school. Most ironically of all, some of the Penrhyn estate property near Bethesda became a nursing home for quarrymen suffering from silicosis and other forms of industrial disease, a kind of posthumous atonement by the gentry. The political influence of the gentry was now in total eclipse. Welshpool, once a stronghold of Anglican Toryism under the influence of Powis Castle, now became a bastion of Montgomeryshire Liberalism. When the Pryses of Gogerddan intervened in the Cardiganshire by-election of February 1921 it was generally treated as an irrelevance.[13] Only a few great houses remained as beleaguered remnants of an ordered, if stagnant society. Notable landowners still appeared as lords lieutenant, high sheriffs, or justices of the peace. They supplied presidents for the National Museum. They patronized local historical and antiquarian bodies: the chairmen of the Cardiganshire Antiquarians from their foundation in 1909 down to the late 1970s were all squires. But their regime in real terms was dead. Landlordism, no less than the thousands of young servicemen who sacrificed their lives between 1914 and 1918, was a casualty of total war.

The passing of the old social order, notably in the rural areas, led to the passing of an old political order also. After the declaration at the polls in December 1918, the general ascendancy of Liberalism still appeared to be confirmed, even if more shakily than in the past. Twenty-one out of the thirty-six Welsh MPs were still Liberals, all save one supporters of the Coalition government

[13] *Welsh Gazette*, 3 February 1921.

—at least in name. Lloyd George's writ still ran here. The Welsh National Liberal Federation was the only regional body in the Liberal Party not in Asquithian hands. It was presided over by Lord St. David's, a wealthy businessman and, as J. Wynford Philipps, a former associate of Lloyd George in the Welsh Party up to 1908.

But this Liberal façade was insubstantial and could not last long. There were two kinds of difficulty, one internal, the other external, that confronted Welsh Liberals after 1918. They ensured that, in time, Liberalism in Wales underwent the same kind of erosion and decline as in England and Scotland. There were, firstly, the growing signs of disintegration from within the party's ranks. The growing mood of disenchantment and disillusion with the aftermath of war had a profound impact upon Liberal morale. Wartime journals such as the *Deyrnas* kept going after the war to hand on the message of the Union of Democratic Control and of wartime dissent generally to a younger generation. Throughout the summer of 1919, Principal Thomas Rees and other contributors in the *Deyrnas* wrote passionately in criticism of the punitive character of the peace terms being drafted in Paris, on Lloyd George's failure to support a League of Nations and on the abandonment of President Woodrow Wilson's Fourteen Points.[14] There was also much condemnation of the persecution of conscientious objectors after the war, and of the economic harvest of shortages, inflation, and high food prices that the war had brought. When the *Deyrnas* went out of publication in November 1919, a victim of falling revenue from advertising and high costs, in many ways its once heterodox views were fast becoming the conventional wisdom. They had especial impact upon the young, amongst ex-servicemen, many of whom returned home to find no employment, and amongst post-war students in the University of Wales for whom George Maitland Lloyd Davies and other pacifists were now honoured figures.

The history of the Coalition government was also a cause of much anxiety to many Liberals. After all, an alliance with the Tory enemy was a total aberration when viewed against the staunch radicalism of Wales since 1865. At first, Lloyd George's claims that the coalition was truly the repository of Liberal values had some credence. There was a major programme of social reform in 1919–20, in particular the housing drive launched by Dr Addison which had considerable impact in towns like Cardiff and Swansea. Under the 1919 Housing and Town Planning Act, a further 119 houses were built in Rhiwbina Garden Village, and a further 52 in Barry Garden Suburb, where the GWR were to help build another 108 in 1925. But this programme soon went into reverse and was finally crushed by the Geddes Axe. It was a notable Welsh MP, Sir Alfred Mond, appointed Minister of Health in April 1921, who presided over the ruination of Addison's housing programme and the ending of support for slum clearance.

[14] *Y Deyrnas*, May–July 1919, *passim*.

There were other causes of Liberal anxiety, too, notably the belligerent policy of 'retaliation' employed by the Coalition government against Sinn Fein in Ireland. The enlisting of the Black and Tans and the Auxis, the use of coercive methods to crush Irish nationalism, all seemed a mockery of the ethic to which Welsh Liberals subscribed. Winifred Coombe Tennant, a noted eisteddfodic figure (*Mam o Nedd*) and a leading organizer for the Coalition Liberals in Wales, told Lloyd George a bleak tale of growing Liberal disaffection—the growth of opposition to the government in the Liberal Associations of Wales, the growing hostility of the nonconformist ministry, the attacks from university staff and students. 'The staffs of the Welsh Colleges almost to a man were opposed to you and at least 80% of the students.' There was also government policy—'*Ireland* is being run for all it is worth against you.'[15] In due course, the government changed its policy in Ireland. The passage of the treaty with the Sinn Fein leaders in December 1921 was a total reversal by the British government. It owed much to the Celtic sympathy shown by Thomas Jones in persuading his fellow-countrymen, and also Irish leaders such as Arthur Griffith and Michael Collins, to show flexibility in negotiation. But by then the damage had already been done in Welsh Liberal circles. There were also more local causes of disaffection, such as the government's failure to press on with a Welsh council for education or to show any real sympathy with the cause of devolution. Lloyd George urged his fellow-Liberals to press for home rule rather than for a Secretary of State for Wales—'Go for the big thing'[16]—but it was obviously a very minor issue in his list of priorities. The Prime Minister himself, usually seen in Churt with Frances Stevenson rather than in domestic felicity in Criccieth, seemed more and more remote from his native land.

Some Liberal critics took refuge in supporting the cause of Asquithian Liberalism. They formed a Welsh Liberal Federation in January 1921 with such prominent anti-government Liberals as Llewelyn Williams, Ellis Davies, Judge Bryn Roberts, and Rhys Hopkin Morris active within it. The *Genedl Gymreig*, edited by that man of letters, E. Morgan Humphreys, strongly supported them. Their manifesto attacked the government for failing to promote Welsh causes in relation to temperance, land reform, and devolution, and for betraying the nonconformist position on disendowment.[17] In February 1921 there was a bitter contest between Lloyd Georgian and Asquithian supporters in a by-election in Cardiganshire. The two rival Liberals were nicely chosen. The Lloyd Georgian candidate was Captain Ernest Evans, an Aberystwyth-born barrister, a Methodist and also a member of Lloyd George's private secretariat. The Asquithian candidate,

[15] Winifred Coombe Tennant to Lloyd George, 31 March 1921 (Lloyd George Papers, F/96/1/15).

[16] *Welsh Outlook*, September 1920, 'Notes of the Month'.

[17] *South Wales News*, 10 January 1921.

and indeed the official selection of the Cardiganshire Liberal Association, was the near-veteran W. Llewelyn Williams, the Prime Minister's bitter opponent. In springlike weather, the Liberals of the county fought out a bitter civil war. There was fierce argument over Ireland and on Welsh issues; there was above all violent conflict over the personality and reputation of Lloyd George himself. The main government campaigner, in fact, was Dame Margaret Lloyd George who made over sixty speeches in the constituency. There were ugly scenes, with Sir John Simon and the blind preacher Puleston Jones howled down at Borth, and the Revd R. J. Rees was eventually forced out of his pastorate at Tabernacl Chapel, Aberystwyth, after pressure from 'Wee Free' members of his congregation. On the whole, there was something of a religious and sociological division in the county. Methodists generally supported the government; Independents, Baptists, and Unitarians were opposed. Coastal towns, Aberystwyth, Borth, Newquay, and Cardigan were pro-Coalition; the upland farming areas and inland towns such as Tregaron were Asquithian.[18] In the end, Evans won by the reasonably convincing margin of over 3,000. But the damage had been done. Indeed, Cardiganshire Liberals fought a running civil war in the elections of 1922 and 1923; there were two rival Liberal clubs in being in Aberystwyth. In the end, the anti-Lloyd George candidate, Hopkin Morris, defeated Ernest Evans in the 1923 election, fighting on behalf of Independent Liberalism and the old values.

Despite the Coalition victory in Cardiganshire in 1921, the government encountered a growing erosion of support. All over Wales, from Caernarfon to Cardiff, there were stories of Liberal Associations defecting to Independent Liberalism, and of growing criticism of Lloyd George himself. By August 1922, Sir Alfred Mond could tell Lloyd George that many south Wales Wee Frees were openly supporting Labour, and that Coalition Liberal party organization all over the coalfield was in a state of collapse.[19] This process of internal disintegration told severely against the Welsh Liberal Party. Intensified by the civil war between supporters and opponents of Lloyd George, local Liberal Associations withered away. More than in any other part of Britain, they were ill-equipped to meet the new challenge of Labour. At the level of local government, Liberal representation in the boroughs and county councils of south Wales fell away sharply. By 1923, Liberal councillors were commonly found in alliance with the Conservatives in 'ratepayers' movements designed to frustrate Labour with anti-socialist pacts. Indeed, the downfall of the Lloyd George Coalition government owed something to this Liberal erosion in Wales. The famous by-election in Newport on 18 October 1922 saw the Coalition supposedly represented by a local solicitor who described himself as

---

[18] See Kenneth O. Morgan, 'Cardiganshire Politics: the Liberal Ascendancy, 1885-1923', *Ceredigion* v, No. 4 (1967), pp. 332-5.

[19] Sir Alfred Mond to Lloyd George, 10 August 1922 (Lloyd George Papers, F/37/3/17).

an Independent Liberal 'without prefix or suffix'. He came bottom of the poll, below the Labour candidate whom many (including Austen Chamberlain) had expected to win, and far below the victorious Conservative, the Swansea businessman Reginald Clarry. The last-named had made much play with the government's extension of the Welsh Sunday Closing Act to Monmouthshire in 1921 and had gained the support of local licensed victuallers. The next day, 19 October, the Unionist MPs at the Carlton Club, having heard the glad tidings from Newport, voted out the Coalition government. Lloyd George promptly submitted his resignation to the King. So Wales, in a way, played a key part at a crucial time in severing Liberal ties with the Tory enemy and in terminating the quasi-presidential regime of Lloyd George.

Even more serious than internal decay was the external challenge of Labour. From 1919 onwards, the Labour Party was obviously poised to challenge the Liberals in every industrial seat in Wales. The militancy in the coalfield associated with the mining disputes of 1919–21 merely added passion to the Labour cause. In the summer of 1919 there was a desperately close contest in the Swansea East by-election, with the Liberal majority falling sharply and a 5 per cent swing to Labour. Indeed, Labour might well have won the seat but for a pre-election increase in the domestic selling price of coal. Thereafter, every south Wales constituency was at risk. In December 1920, Labour in the person of George Barker retained Abertillery with a much-increased majority. In August 1921, Labour also easily held on to Caerphilly. Its candidate was Morgan Jones of the ILP, a former member of the No Conscription Fellowship who had been imprisoned during the war for refusal to be conscripted and again after it for desertion. He was the first conscientious objector to be returned to parliament. In two elections in July 1922, there were two more Labour victories within one week, at Gower where David Grenfell, the miner's agent for the Western District, defeated a Liberal schoolmaster and at Pontypridd where another ILP man, T. I. Mardy Jones, the parliamentary agent for the SWMF, swamped a Liberal opponent to register a Labour 'gain'.

In the general election of November 1922, Liberals, especially 'National Liberals' associated with Lloyd George, faced disaster at the polls in the face of Labour's onslaught. In the coalfield, six seats were captured from the Liberals by Labour—Llanelli, Aberavon, Swansea East, Neath, Aberdare, and Merthyr. These included some interesting newcomers. R. C. Wallhead, the chairman of the ILP and an old colleague of Keir Hardie who had also been imprisoned during the war, gained Merthyr Tydfil, while Ramsay MacDonald himself was elected for Aberavon, where his campaign had aroused almost revivalist fervour amongst the miners of the Afan valley. George Hall, an official of the Miners' Federation, crushed Stanton at Aberdare. Remarkably enough, there were also two Labour gains in north Wales. In Wrexham, Labour's victorious candidate was the economic historian and extra-mural lecturer, Robert Richards; more astonishingly, Caernarvonshire saw the victory of the secretary of the Quarrymen's Union, R. T. Jones, a member of the ILP, it is true, but also an advocate of temperance, home rule, and the cause of the Welsh language. A Labour victory here in this, admittedly idiosyncratic, constituency showed the depth of the shift in the mood in the quarrying community since the days of the Penrhyn strike. In all, Wales returned eighteen Labour members, six Conservatives (all in the coastal arc between Barry and Newport), one Independent (in Anglesey) and eleven Liberals of various shades. Only one of these eleven, Swansea West which Sir Alfred Mond narrowly retained, could be described as an urban, industrial constituency. Liberal Wales was being hemmed into the rural fastness like the Men of Harlech in the past.

The general elections of 1923 and 1924 saw the general pattern of growing Labour dominance confirmed. In the election of December 1923, Liberal candidates made some headway with the defence of free trade after Baldwin's call for tariff protection. This may have won them the mercantile shipping seat of Cardiff East through Sir Harry Webb. Goronwy Owen, an indirect relation of the Lloyd George family, recaptured Caernarvonshire. On the other hand, as has been seen, there was the remarkable episode of the loss of the University of Wales seat to a Christian Pacifist. Labour's growing challenge in the industrial south was shown when Walter Samuel, an ex-miner who eventually became a judge, defeated Mond in Swansea West. Labour now claimed twenty seats in Wales, with the possible addition of the university seat since G. M. Ll. Davies took the Labour whip in the House, to the delight of some of his younger admirers.[20]

The general election of 1924 was less successful for the Labour Party. It followed the somewhat ignominious end of the first Labour government, with first the débâcle of the Campbell case and then the publication of the so-called 'Zinoviev letter' during the campaign. MacDonald himself saw his majority at Aberavon fall by over 1,000. The main beneficiaries, however, were the Welsh Conservatives who now captured nine seats, their best tally in Wales since 1895, and surpassed by 1874 alone in recent times. They again won all three Cardiff seats, and also captured Brecon and Radnor, Pembrokeshire, and Flintshire, all former Liberal seats. The Liberals did win back Swansea West, where Walter Runciman narrowly defeated Samuel; they took Wrexham from Labour and regained the University seat, which was to remain Liberal for the rest of its existence until it was abolished in 1950. Ironically, the victor over G. M. Ll. Davies in the University was Ernest Evans, the champion of coalitionism in Cardiganshire in 1921–2, and now restored to greater favour among the Liberal intelligentsia. In all, Wales returned sixteen Labour members, eleven Liberals and nine Conservatives.

[20] Principal Thomas Rees to George M. Ll. Davies, 17 December 1923 (NLW, Lloyd Davies Papers, MS 2153).

Despite these shifts in individual constituencies, it was clear that Wales had undergone a massive political change since 1918. Liberalism was obviously more the party of a past era, strongest in Welsh-speaking rural areas which adhered to nonconformist and Welsh traditions. This might make an impact in Anglesey or Cardiganshire, but conveyed less and less to an urban, industrial electorate. By 1924 there was no Liberal seat in Glamorgan or Monmouth, apart from Swansea West. The premises upon which Liberalism based itself had been undermined by the war and by the changes that followed it. Lloyd George's rise and fall had emphasized features of these changes, and added colour to them, but they were really a symptom, not a root cause of Liberal decay. So far as the old values did have political resilience, it was the Labour Party which was taking them over. The Daily Herald's *Book of Labour Members* in 1923 illustrated graphically how large a proportion of the twenty Labour MPs returned in that year were Welsh-speaking and active nonconformists. An analysis of such Labour members as Evan Davies, Charles Edwards, David Grenfell, Tom Griffiths, Vernon Hartshorn, William Jenkins, Will John, R. T. Jones, Robert Richards, and David Watts Morgan reveals a high proportion of chapel deacons, lay preachers, Sunday-school teachers and advocates of temperance. By contrast, David Williams, the member for Swansea East, was a choirmaster in an Anglican church. Political nonconformity was now far more obviously an asset to the Labour Party than to the Liberals which it had supplanted, at least as far as its elected representatives were concerned. Above all, the Liberals seemed to have lost touch with the miners and other electors in the industrial areas. Liberal candidates did not seem even to understand the mind of the working man any longer. 'The mind of the miner was impervious to any national question. The only subject that interested him was More pay, Shorter Hours of Work, no Income Tax for Wage Earners; more facilities for drinking,' wrote a disconsolate Liberal candidate for Abertillery in 1920. A prominent Swansea Liberal noted the difficulty in keeping the allegiance of chapel congregations and their ministers since the passage of disestablishment. 'Marx's Capital has ejected the Bible from the minds of thousands of young Welshmen, while the Liberal Party has indulged in a Rip van Winkle sleep.'[21] The evidence of 1922−4 suggested that these slumbers were likely to continue undisturbed for a long while to come.

Beneath and beyond these political and electoral changes was the much more aggressive and class-conscious stance of the Labour movement after the war. In no other aspect of Welsh society were the new values introduced into the post-war scene more noticeable. The secret report prepared for the government in September 1919 on the extent of 'direct action' movements and their

[21] G. Hay Morgan, cited in F. E. Guest to Lloyd George, 6 January 1921 (Lloyd George Papers, F/22/3/2); Mond to Lloyd George, 10 August 1922 (loc. cit.), quoting W. C. Jenkins.

effect in slowing down industrial production paid particular attention to south Wales. Clydach, the centre of Sir Alfred Mond's nickel works, was said to be 'a hotbed of theoretical Bolshevism'. The Rhondda was a centre of extreme syndicalism. *Western Mail* reporters offered to collaborate with Scotland Yard by sending them reports of subversive speeches made at meetings of workers.[22]

The miners, in particular, were under increasingly militant leadership—far more so than their parliamentary spokesmen such as Brace, Hartshorn, and Watts Morgan could indicate. A rising star was S. O. Davies, elected agent for the Merthyr miners in 1918 and a committed Marxist. More important was Arthur Cook, a member of the South Wales Socialist Society and a founder-member of the Communist Party who described himself as 'a humble follower of Lenin'. In November 1919 he was elected agent for the Rhondda No. 1 District in preference to Noah Rees. Cook left the Communist Party in 1921 but soon emerged, nevertheless, as a powerful, even tempestuous, orator and ideological influence, both on the executive of the SWMF and on various revived versions of the unofficial movement. Closely associated with Cook was the young Arthur Horner, checkweighman at Maerdy in the Rhondda No. 1 District, another (and lasting) adherent of the British Communist Party with a record of imprisonment and a major strategist for a new class-based policy to overthrow capitalism in the valleys. Not surprisingly, with such new leaders as these, the Welsh miners took the most 'advanced' line in all the major confrontations that shook the coal-mining industry between 1919 and 1921. Indeed, it was a Welsh representative, Frank Hodges, who served as secretary of the Miners' Federation of Great Britain during this period. No coalfield reacted with more bitterness to the failure in 1919 to secure an immediate 30 per cent wage increase. This was followed by the alleged 'betrayal' of Lloyd George and Bonar Law in failing to implement a majority recommendation by the Sankey Commission to take the mines into public ownership. Even the moderate Vernon Hartshorn said that the Welsh miners felt 'deceived, betrayed, duped' by the government's decision on Sankey. In 1920 the South Wales District more than once voted for a national strike and voted against a return to work when a strike took place. In September 1920, the majority in south Wales for a miners' strike was 141,721 to 40,047. There was immense solidarity in south Wales when a national stoppage did take place in March–July 1921, after the de-control of the mines and the ending of the government subsidy. The realization that the affluent times were over and that, from the end of 1920, there was a huge loss of trade and mass unemployment in south Wales for the first time added a new dimension of bitterness.

The national miners' strike of 1921 was a kind of dress rehearsal for 1926, with the same solidarity and courage in the face of hopeless odds. Safety-men at Maerdy and Tylorstown were brought out on strike, along with face-

[22] Reports in Milner Papers (Bodleian, MS Eng. Hist. c. 702).

workers. In the end the miners had to return to work, crushed and humiliated, on the owners' terms. Even Ablett and Cook finally supported the ending of a strike that was manifestly pointless. There were massive wage cuts in the months and years to follow. The good times were over for the Welsh miner, and indeed for industry as a whole. Conversely, there was intense anger in the mining community at what was regarded as the 'betrayal' of the men by their secretary, Frank Hodges, who suggested to a meeting of MPs on the evening of 14 April 1921 that a temporary wage settlement might be agreed to before the wider questions of a national pool for wages or the nationalization of the mines. This led to the collapse of the Triple Alliance the next day, 'Black Friday' (15 April), since neither the railwaymen nor the transport workers would now support the miners in a general strike. The bitterness of this episode was later captured in Idris Davies's passionate poem, *The Angry Summer*:

> The telephones are ringing
> And treachery's in the air
>
> . . . .
>
> And this Friday goes down in history
> Yellow, and edged with Black

The role of Hodges was much reviled thereafter, and it was with much relish in 1924 that the south Wales men saw another of their number, Arthur Cook, replace him as secretary of the Miners' Federation of Great Britain.

One feature of the post-war period was a further revival of the 'unofficial' movements of pre-1914. These had enjoyed a temporary renewal of life during the latter stages of the war. The militants now showed their teeth. Will Mainwaring challenged Brace in the election of the SWMF president, while Cook stood against James Winstone for vice-president, though neither polled well at this stage. Under pressure from the newly-formed Communist Party, there was new pressure for a 'minority' movement within the framework of the SWMF, endorsed by S. O. Davies and Horner amongst others, though it was not until 1924 that this reached institutional form and the so-called MMM, the Minority Movement, was born.

Equally significant as a pointer to the long-term future was the renewed activity of the Central Labour College movement in the Welsh coalfield. By the end of 1920 it had greatly expanded its tutorial classes in the Rhondda, Aberdare, and Neath valleys. The organizer and lecturer in the Rhondda No. 1 District, which included Maerdy, 'little Moscow', was Will Hay, with new stature as one of the relatively few miners' leaders who had opposed war in 1914 and whose judgement had been triumphantly vindicated. The Central Labour College Movement was now thriving, endowed with funds from the south Wales miners as well as from the National Union of Railwaymen. The result was a growing connection between the Central Labour College proper in Regent's Park, London, and a generation of militant young Welsh miners. A remarkable new breed of them now studied at the college in London. Among their tutors was Will Mainwaring on Marxist economic theory.[23] Their influence was to be writ large on the British working-class movement for decades to come. Their impact was also profound on Wales. Indeed, the young miners, steelworkers, and railwaymen who studied at the Labour College between 1919 and its closure in 1928 formed in their way a new élite of leadership, just as significant for the Wales of their generation as the Liberal nationalists of *Cymru Fydd* were for theirs.

Some of these young men from the first gravitated to the far left and to the Communist Party. There were militants like Jack Jones of the Cambrian Lodge, Rhondda, who was to fight in Spain with the International Brigade in 1937. There was Idris Cox, later an editor of the *Daily Worker* in 1935–7. There was also Lewis Jones from the Cambrian Lodge, best known later as author of the novels on mining life, *Cwmardy* and *We Live*. But the usual impact on these young workers was to impel them into the mainstream labour movement, into trade unionism and into the Labour Party. Ness Edwards was a student at the Labour College from 1919 to 1921. He was to become an activist in the coalfield Labour College classes, an historian of the Miners' Federation, and finally Labour MP for Caerphilly and a member of the Attlee government after 1945. James Griffiths, a young miner and ILP activist in Ammanford in the anthracite coalfield, was a Labour College student at the same time. Less doctrinaire than some of his comrades, more Welsh in commitment and speech, he was to become a miners' agent, the president of the SWMF, Labour member for Llanelli from 1936 and a leading figure in the Attlee government of 1945 and the Wilson administration of 1964, as Minister of National Insurance, Colonial Secretary, and finally the first Secretary of State for Wales. As an architect of the social insurance scheme of 1946, he was to be a major pioneer of the welfare state, as well as a warm-hearted and courageous patriot.[24] Morgan Phillips, a student at the college in 1926–8, was to go into the Labour Party machine. He served as general secretary of the party from 1944 to 1962; the supreme *apparatchik*, he exercised considerable influence upon Labour policy as well as upon its organizational structure.

The most brilliant of them all was a young Tredegar miner, born in 1897, who also studied at the college from 1919 to 1921. This was Aneurin Bevan, the 'sensual puritan' in Michael Foot's vivid description, the most creative and dynamic personality in the socialist movement of his generation. The precise influence of the Labour College upon Bevan's always restless personality is hard to determine. He seems to have been a wayward student, who found it difficult to observe an organized routine or to follow rules such as rising early

[23] W. W. Craik, *The Central Labour College* (London, 1964), p. 117.
[24] James Griffiths, *Pages from Memory* (London, 1969).

for breakfast.[25] Yet even then, Bevan proved himself a wide reader and a superbly effective talker and orator upon socialist themes. Soon he was to show more constructive gifts as an organizer, an ideologue and a Labour MP. He first ascended the ladder to power in April 1922 when he was elected (fourth in the poll) to the Tredegar Urban District Council. Bevan's Welshness was never in dispute, since he came from a home steeped in Welsh values and Welsh names. He himself bore the name of a celebrated sixth-century bard. But he added to a sense of close identification with the life of the west Monmouthshire valleys an eclectic, cosmopolitan outlook that took him into a sophisticated version of libertarian Marxism, far removed from the Lib-Lab creed of his Welsh-speaking Baptist father. It was his experience of the struggle and suffering in the valleys of south Wales that was decisive in the intellectual and political odyssey of the young Aneurin Bevan in the early 1920s, rather than the formal discipline of the Central Labour College. But he associated himself too, not only with local intimates in the Query Club at Tredegar, but also with a new generation of working-class leaders who were to make the valleys, scarred with poverty and squalor, alive with new ideas and new inspiration.

The young Marxists of the coalfield, then, were testimony to the extra-ordinary transformation in the mood of south Wales, contrasted with the years before 1914, or perhaps before 1910. Their influence and energy were proof of the new doctrines sweeping through much of post-war Wales. Conversely, established creeds and institutions were facing challenge and stress as never before. If the war brought a vast new increment of strength to the secular gospel of socialism, in its most aggressive, Marxist forms, it brought a marked recession for the nonconformist chapels, through which the native genius had expressed itself so powerfully in so many areas for the past four generations. Those structural factors which had weakened the chapels before the war—the burden of debt; the over-expansion in thinly-populated rural areas; the difficulty in making contact with the non-Welsh-speaking population; above all the inability of the chapels to retain their hold over the industrial and urban masses in the south—all these were intensified after the war. It became clear, in the aftermath of the armistice, that the chapels were no longer the social or spiritual forces that they had been in Victorian or even in Edwardian Wales. Such influence as they retained—and there were still powerful and distinguished ministers in the land such as Elfed Lewis or Philip Jones—was largely in the Welsh-speaking hinterland of north and central Wales. One major difficulty for the chapels, therefore, was the clear evidence brought out in the population census of 1921 that a declining proportion of the Welsh people spoke their native tongue—indeed, only

[25] Michael Foot, *Aneurin Bevan*, vol. i (London, 1962), pp. 37–40.

929,000 or 37.2 per cent. The numbers showed for the first time an absolute drop since the previous census—50,000 less since 1911.

The chapels were manifestly struggling. In part this was the result of factors common to religion in other parts of Britain. The secular appeal of socialism or trade-union activity tended to erode the impact of chapels among working men. Labour Party meetings, unlike Liberal, were frequently held on a Sunday. Younger workers, even if they subscribed to the ideas and the rhetoric of the pulpit, forsook the chapels. They found in the miners' lodge or library, the WEA, the working-man's club or pub a centre of social activity, fellowship, and consolation which the chapels, usually dominated by middle-class deacons and ministers unfamiliar with the working-class world, failed any longer to supply. In south Wales, too, leisure-time activity made powerful inroads into the claims of the chapel and the Sunday school, particularly at week-ends. Rugby, association football, and other sports retained their appeal. So, too, did the public house, the music hall, and the new attractions of the cinema. The boom in wages during and just after the end of the war gave the miners and their families money to spend and new opportunities to enjoy. The Select Committee on Betting was told of the vast sums spent by Welsh working men on betting on horse-racing, greyhounds, and other pastimes: this intelligence was greeted with scandalized dismay by one member of the Committee, the mining MP and respectable Rechabite, David Grenfell. When he was told by a superintendent of the Glamorgan county police that the Welsh were enthusiastic gamblers, the exchanges went as follows:

Grenfell: It is strange. I do not know my own country?

Rees: Well, you know, of course, down in Swansea where you are, it is a different type from where I come from [Neath]. They gamble there very freely.

Grenfell: Is it not generally well known that it is the inferior races of the world who gamble and not the superior races? . . . Are not the Chinese the greatest gamblers known? . . .

Chairman: I think we are getting rather wide.[26]

Apart from the delights of gambling, there was also the more relaxing prospect of travelling further afield, out of the grime and squalor of one's own village or valley, to Sunday excursions in Barry Island or Swansea, or further still on cheap rail-tickets to Aberystwyth or Rhyl. The advent of the motor car also made a powerful impact on the mobility of local communities; in rural areas even more than in industrial the geographical and cultural isolation of the past was now much less marked, and many rural railway lines began to show a serious loss of custom. Meanwhile the advent of radio brought another social revolution. Broadcasting began in Wales with the opening of the Cardiff station, 5WA, on 13 February 1923, and another was launched at Swansea the following year. Soon efforts were to be made to harness the new broadcasting medium for the promotion of the Welsh language and Sabbata-

---

[26] *Select Committee on the Betting Duty*, Parl. Papers 1923, I, questions 5448–50. (I owe this reference to Dr Ross McKibbin.)

rian values, but the appearance of the 'wireless' in people's homes meant also that the first heady intimation of wider forms of entertainment, including the attractions of the 'continental Sunday', could penetrate the privacy of Welsh households.

In all these ways, the new world was bringing new challenges, intellectual and cultural, to which the chapels were finding difficulty in responding. Puritanism, Sabbatarianism, the full rigours of a hell-fire fundamentalist creed barely reconstructed from the days of Daniel Rowland and George Whitefield, conveyed less and less to twentieth-century society. It jarred particularly on the generation of young Welshmen back from the trenches in France, or from service in the Dardanelles or Palestine. A powerful cultural divide was in the making.

One should not exaggerate this decline in the vitality of the chapels. Down to the Second World War, they retained a large membership: it was numbered at well over 400,000 throughout the twenties. The chapels still contributed mightily to the *eisteddfod*, to popular music-making and to cultural life in all its varied aspects. The decline of the chapels was a gradual one. Even as late as 1961, in fighting against the proposed repeal of the Welsh Sunday Closing Act of 1881, the chapels still showed that they could exert considerable influence upon social values and behaviour, even if this largely took the form of prohibitive edicts against forbidden fruit, however rare or refreshing. But the symptoms of decline were manifestly there in the twenties, and freely admitted in the denominational press, with evidence in falling annual figures of membership and a wider sense of bewilderment and decay in the post-war era.

The chapels found it more and more difficult to adapt their ideas and outlooks to the intellectual and cultural standards of the post-war generation. They had never been intellectually adventurous or innovative. New ideas in theology, in science, in social criticism, in meeting the challenge of 'modernism' or of Darwinism had seldom flourished in the pages of nonconformist publications, let alone in the pulpit.

The very naïveté of the chapels' approach led the Calvinist Methodists in particular into a great crisis from 1927 onwards. This involved the powerful personality of 'Tom Nefyn', the Revd Tom Nefyn Williams, minister of a Methodist church at Tumble, near Llanelli. He put forward a series of decidedly heterodox views. He published a tract which rejected out of hand the Methodist *Cyffes Ffydd* (Confession of Faith). This opposed the Trinity, the story of the Virgin Birth and of the Resurrection of Christ, and urged a more rationalist view of the Bible. He also sharply attacked the Methodist Church for moral hypocrisy. The adulterer, the blasphemer and drunkard were condemned, the miser and the shoddy businessman were left alone or even honoured—Tom Nefyn was a man of strong social conscience.[27]

[27] *Carnarvon and Denbigh Herald*, 13 April 1928.

Inevitably, he fell foul of the official *sasiwn* (association) of the Methodist Church, despite the warm support he received from younger ministers and laymen in the connection. Eventually, at the Nantgaredig *sasiwn* in Carmarthenshire in 1928, he was expelled for heresy, a martyr for conscience in his way like his sixteenth-century predecessors, even if he was faced with a gentler form of Inquisition. It was natural, of course, that the elders of the Church should wish to guard their fundamentalist doctrines without which their connection would have little meaning. In the *Llenor*, Welsh intellectuals like R. T. Jenkins and W. J. Gruffydd, rationalists and admirers of the eighteenth-century *philosophes* in France, condemned the Methodist elders for intolerance and upheld Tom Nefyn's right to dissent.[28] This is not a very convincing line of argument. The Calvinist Methodists were as entitled as any other body to have their own articles of belief and to declare that particular views of an extreme kind were incompatible with them. Indeed, in 1930 Tom Nefyn actually recanted his opinions. Declaring that he now found himself to be an adherent of the same beliefs he had held at the time of his conversion back in 1917, he again entered the official Methodist fold. As *Welsh Outlook* observed, he had followed the same path of recantation taken by so many heretics throughout the centuries.[29] The authorities in the Methodist Church had in many ways acted not ungenerously toward him. The real problem was rather that Tom Nefyn's heresy had exposed the total inadequacy of Welsh nonconformity to meet the challenge of modern thought and knowledge. The crude fundamentalism, pre-Darwinian attitudes towards science, the plain, honest incomprehension of the Methodist elders towards a theological rebel made their church appear hidebound and antiquated. It all strengthened the view, advanced by a nonconformist minister like Rhondda Williams, that the chapels were strong on oratorical bombast from the pulpit and in cruelly long-drawn-out funerals, but weak in self-criticism, intellectual vitality, and, perhaps, in a sense of Christian humility.

The declining image of the chapels and of religious life generally in post-war Wales had been much influenced by the shock effect of the short stories and plays of Caradoc Evans. A native of rural Carmarthenshire, once a draper's assistant in Carmarthen and then in London, Evans had a powerful impact on the literary consciousness and ideas of post-war generation. His place in the evolution of an 'Anglo-Welsh' tradition of literature will be considered later, in Chapter 9. Here it needs to be emphasized that his volumes of short stories, *My People* (1915), *Capel Sion* (1916) and *My Neighbours* (1919) were highly influential in their savage, satirical picture of Welsh rural life in Cardiganshire and Carmarthenshire, and also of the avaricious ways of the London–Welsh business fraternity. The hypocrisy, the philistinism, the social tensions and sexual guilt that underlay the Welsh community, as Evans viewed it, were outlined with devastating effect. His account of peasant vice, dishonesty, and avarice shocked a generation used to pious, almost uncritical celebration of the God-given purity and naturalness of the *werin* in the rural areas from which so many of the leaders of modern Wales, from Lloyd George and Owen M. Edwards downwards had sprung. Of course, Evans's views were highly coloured and highly prejudiced. They caused legitimate offence: his play 'Taffy' was booed by a London audience in 1923.[30] There were many creative, constructive, even noble features of the face-to-face Welsh rural community which he chose to ignore. But Evans did at least show that there was an alternative view, and he delivered it with devastating wit, colour, and linguistic flair. It all chimed in with a growing market in England for the satires of T. H. W. Crosland in depicting mercilessly the less flattering features of the 'unspeakable Celt', shown most recently in 'Taffy was a Welshman'. Not the least of Evans's targets were the chapels, those citadels of the self-important and the parochial. He ridiculed mercilessly the pretensions and snobberies of the *sêt fawr*. He satirized, too, the hypocrisies of strict Sabbatarianism, for example the guilt feeling aroused by the buying of Sunday newspapers. Caradoc Evans exposed a world in which the sanctions of chapel puritanism no longer held good.

His point was reinforced by the extraordinary violence that attended attempts to play Sunday golf on the Aberdyfi links in October 1927. Players were physically threatened for such ungodly activity, and there were attempts to turn horses and cattle loose on the greens unless Sunday golf was banned. This kind of lawlessness, condemned amongst others by Lord Justice Atkin, a resident of Aberdyfi,[31] contrasted markedly with the peaceable nature of Welsh nonconformists in the past, with the proud traditions of Wales being 'the land of the white gloves' (*gwlad y menyg gwynion*) through the absence of criminal activity. It made the chapels appear hypocritical, intolerant and somewhat absurd. It lent fuel to charges against which the religious bodies, already undermined by the war and riven by self-doubt, were quite unable to defend themselves.

Socialism, as voiced amongst the miners and other workers; secularism, as symbolized by critics of the chapels—these suggested some of the new values which characterized the post-war mood. In addition, there was something even more fundamental to be detected in Wales at this time—a growing questioning of the national movement itself from which so much of the vitality of the nation had flowed since the 1880s. The older style of cultural leader, as shown by men like Morris-Jones and O. M. Edwards, was becoming dated in its turn. Morris-Jones, who was to die in 1929, was slightly tarnished now after his vigorous defence of the First World War. Edwards, still at the height of his

[30] Trevor L. Williams, *Caradoc Evans* (Cardiff, 1970), p. 89.
[31] *South Wales News*, 24 October 1927; *Cambrian News*, October 1927, *passim*.

intellectual powers, with his periodical *Cymru Coch* still appearing regularly, died tragically early in 1920. The younger style of author, for example W. J. Gruffydd, shortly to found a new *Llenor* to replace Owen M. Edwards's earlier version, rationalist and astringent, was far more critical and mordant in his observations on the cultural and religious scene in Wales. When the national *eisteddfod* eventually returned to Wrexham in 1933, it was noted ironically that the previous time it had been held there in 1888 it it had been marked, not only by Gladstone's famous address, but by a crown-winning prize *pryddest* by 'Elfed' on the subject of the 'Sabbath in Wales'. The brilliant young poet Thomas Parry-Williams, once full of the optimism and moral certainties of the romanticists of pre-1914, now turned away from poetry to the writing of serious-minded analytical literary essays. Poetry, he felt (and no doubt his feelings were heightened by his own personal crisis during and just after the First World War) were about hypocrisies, disloyalties, and lies, rather than a simple affirmation of nobility, truth, and beauty.

This change of mood had consequences beyond the purely literary. It penetrated to all levels of Welsh intellectual and social life. Indirectly, it led to the confident national spirit current in Wales before 1914 being increasingly questioned. Indeed, some young Welshmen did not consider the faith of their fathers to be truly nationalism at all. 'Official Liberalism', 'the hobby of corpulent and successful men', through which wealthy and self-important barristers, drapers, or shipowners rose to effortless prominence via the formal dinners of the Society of Cymmrodorion or at denominational assemblies, or through an *eisteddfod* shorn of contact with a living popular culture, was a jaded thing.[32] The pristine, pure ideals of *Cymru Fydd*, of Tom Ellis in his glorious prime, seemed forgotten.

The effect was a marked reaction against the style of national self-awareness omnipresent in Welsh life before 1914. It was a reaction that took many and varied forms. Some young idealists took refuge in a wider concept of internationalism, which would include the best of the old sense of nationhood of pre-1914 days and yet soar above it. One of the pioneers of this approach was David Davies of Llandinam, later Lord Davies, once a warm supporter of Lloyd George and an apostle of 'a fight to the finish', now a passionate enthusiast for Woodrow Wilson, for a League of Nations, and a world view of political and moral problems. In 1919 he founded a new chair of International Politics, the first of its kind anywhere in Britain. The first holder was that eminent political scientist, the Philhellene and intimate of Gilbert Murray, Sir Alfred Zimmern. This appeared to be a splendid appointment. Zimmern threw himself into the national life of Wales and wrote warmly in the *Welsh Outlook* and elsewhere on the virtues of Welsh self-government. Unfortunately, Zimmern became romantically involved with the French wife of one of his colleagues. The hopes of the Greek Commonwealth perished,

[32] See comments by Saunders Lewis, *Welsh Nationalist*, January 1932, p. 1.

and Zimmern had to leave the Calvinist pastures of Aberystwyth, an un-repentant sinner. It was an unhappy affair for David Davies in particular, since Zimmern's French friend, Madame Barbier, had already quarrelled with the Llandinam family over musical matters during the war. The eviction of Zimmern might be regarded as another victory for the nonconformists who had dominated the land for so long—and Aberystwyth University College since its foundation.

They had gained another moral victory a year earlier when the majority of the Aberystwyth university council rejected the advice and influence of David Davies and the personal endorsement of Lloyd George. H. A. L. Fisher, Hankey, and other eminences, in rejecting Thomas Jones's application for the principalship of the college by the sea. Instead, they chose the more pedestrian J. H. Davies, a local man, a Methodist, and the college registrar. It was a bitter blow to Thomas Jones who remembered his rebuff all his life, even when he was later to become president of the college. In particular, he resented the kind of religious interrogation he had undergone at Aberystwyth and in an earlier inquisition at Cardiff, which had exposed his own rationalist, or perhaps deist, view of orthodox religion. 'Why isn't the fool religious?' asked one puzzled councillor at Cardiff.[33] This kind of episode might suggest that parochialism, not the international spirit, governed the commanding heights of Welsh national life. Still, the chair of International Politics survived all these personal difficulties, and the distinguished historian, Charles Webster, occupied it with great distinction for the next ten years. In 1936, after an interval, he was to be succeeded by the eminent specialist on international relations, particularly on the affairs of Soviet Russia, E. H. Carr. A similar outlet for post-war internationalism was the prominence of many Welshmen, notably nonconformist idealists like the Revd Gwilym Davies and Major Wynn Wheldon, in the League of Nations Union. A separate Welsh branch was formed at Shrewsbury in early 1922, under the inspiration (and with the financial support) of David Davies.[34] This was a most thriving body in Wales. It served as a forum for disillusioned or displaced Liberal nonconformists and others anxious to play their constructive part in harnessing the moral force of opinion in the direction of world peace, in enforcing international law and collective security without endorsing pacifism.

Other Welsh men and women turned away from internationalism to a new and heightened nationalism. Some young writers, men like D. Gwenallt Jones for instance, found a sharp contrast between the care lavished on subject nationalities in the Treaty of Versailles, after a war supposedly fought on behalf of small nations, and the total ignoring of Wales. The failure of Lloyd George to exert his influence on behalf of Welsh home rule caused

[33] Lord Pontypridd, quoted in E. L. Ellis, op. cit., p. 208 n.
[34] Goronwy J. Jones, *Wales and the Quest for Peace* (Cardiff, 1970), pp. 97 ff.

much disillusionment. There was some intellectual interest in Welsh and Scottish home rule immediately after the war. The cause was fanned by *Welsh Outlook* and by the continuing activities of E. T. John. A Speaker's Conference on the government of Scotland and Wales reported in May 1920: its members included four Welshmen, Lord Aberdare, John Hugh Edwards MP (Liberal), Charles Edwards MP (Labour), and L. Forestier-Walker MP (Conservative). But it was hardly calculated to set public opinion aflame. Forestier-Walker signed Murray MacDonald's scheme for local parliaments with devolved powers, while the other three somewhat unwisely signed both the MacDonald scheme and the Speaker's own plan for regional grand councils. MacDonald's scheme alone, they averred, 'could satisfy the national aspirations of both Scotland and Wales'.[35] But the reports, like other schemes for devolution in the future, were obviously dead letters. Lord Birkenhead, the Lord Chancellor, observed loftily that 'we had muddled along tolerably well for ten centuries'.[36] This seemed to sum up the tone of much of English—and, indeed, of Scottish and Welsh—reaction. Welsh self-government was urged with much enthusiasm still in *Welsh Outlook*, under the editorship from 1921 to 1925 of a warm-hearted patriot, T. Huws Davies, the secretary of the Welsh Church Temporalities Commission. E. T. John, now an unorthodox member of the Labour Party, continued his campaigns on behalf of local home rule, and also launched a new Celtic Congress on a pan-Celtic basis, Goedelic as well as Brythonic. Little came of these moves, nor was Welsh opinion much stirred one way or the other. A series of conferences in Llandrindod Wells, Shrewsbury, and other familiar venues in 1919–22, all designed to consider measures to promote Welsh self-government, yielded nothing. Lloyd George offered sympathy but nothing more.

A Government of Wales Bill, introduced by Sir Robert Thomas (Liberal, Wrexham) on 28 April 1922 was talked out on first reading by that enthusiastic veteran obstructionist, Sir Frederick Banbury. It was, wrote Beriah Gwynfe Evans to E. T. John, a 'fiasco'.[37] John and Evans now nominated themselves as the 'de Valeras' of Welsh home rule within the Labour Party.[38] They had support from some Welsh Labour members, notably Will John (Rhondda West) and Dai Grenfell (Gower). E. T. John stood for parliament for Brecon and Radnor (1922), Anglesey (1923), and Brecon and Radnor again (1924) as Labour and Welsh nationalist candidate. Each time he was soundly defeated. In his final venture in 1924 he came bottom of the poll, and gradually faded out of public life until his death in 1931. Welsh home rule, it seemed, was moribund, if not dead. The Welsh

---

[35] *Conference on Devolution, 1920: a Letter from Mr. Speaker to the Prime Minister* (Cmd. 692), Parl. Papers, 1920, xiii, p. 12.
[36] *Parl. Deb.*, House of Lords, xxxiii, pp. 521–30 for Birkenhead's speech.
[37] Beriah G. Evans to E. T. John, 2 May 1922 (NLW, E. T. John Papers).
[38] Beriah G. Evans to E. T. John, 5 May 1922 (ibid.).

local authorities who assembled at Shrewsbury in March 1922 were more anxious at the prospect of domination by Cardiff and the south (echoes of 1892) than fired by the heady appeal of nationalism.

The situation with regard to administrative devolution was also disappointing. By 1925 journalists could list a whole series of failures since the end of the war.[39] The Ministry of Health Act in 1919 had transferred the powers vested in the Welsh Insurance Commissioners since 1912 to a new Welsh Board of Health, under the secretaryship of Sir Percy Watkins. In the same year, a Welsh department was set up at the Ministry of Agriculture and Fisheries. The Welsh Board of Health, however, aroused little enthusiasm. At first it was to have so slight a measure of authority that it could not even appoint charwomen without the approval of Whitehall. Meanwhile, the Poor Law and other authorities had been transferred from mid-Wales to Staffordshire for local government purposes. The national arrangements made for Wales under the Ministry of Pensions had been abolished. Probate work for north Wales was by 1925 being administered from Chester, not from Bangor as previously. For purposes of factory inspection, Wales had been divided into two divisions, worked from Liverpool for north Wales and from Bristol for the south. Most important of all, in education, since the death of Sir Owen M. Edwards, Wales had been divided up for purposes of school inspection into north and south divisions. The Central Welsh Board, after years of conflict with the Welsh department of the Board of Education, had meekly surrendered many of its powers to Whitehall. Previously, the departmental committee inquiring into Welsh secondary education under the chairmanship of the Hon. W. N. Bruce in 1920, had made some depressing criticisms of the much-honoured Intermediate Education Act of 1889 and had proposed that it be repealed owing to the disorganization prevalent in the Welsh secondary education system. Even this symbol of nationhood seemed at risk.

This was not a complete picture. The Welsh Board of Health, for instance, did manage to expand its powers and in 1931 was to assume the general functions of the Ministry in co-ordinating and supervising public health services in Wales. In May 1940, just before the fall of the Chamberlain government, Walter Elliot, the Minister of Health, was to extend much further the Welsh Board's powers and administrative machinery.[40] The *Medical Officer* was soon complaining that, under pressure from the Cardiff Cymmrodorion and others, the Welsh Board of Health was giving undue preference to Welsh speakers in making medical appointments.[41] But the overall picture was a depressing one for nationalists—an institutionalizing of the division between north and south Wales, and a failure to achieve either autonomy or the recognition of separate identity in the organs of government.

[39] *South Wales News*, 1 August 1925.
[40] *British Medical Journal*, 2 May 1931; *Local Government Journal*, June 1940.
[41] *Medical Officer*, 1 May 1926.

Even so, there were forces within Wales pressing for a more active view of nationalism. This was much inspired by contemporary examples in Ireland and the eventual success of Sinn Fein in forcing the British imperial government to the conference table. The impact of men like Arthur Griffith, the success of the southern Irish in achieving a free state with wider powers of national statehood, the very brutality and incomprehension with which the London government had handled the problem of Irish nationalism between 1919 and 1921, had a powerful influence upon some elements in Welsh radical and nonconformist circles. Students in the University of Wales reacted with particular warmth. Not only was there the example of Ireland to admire, and the 'fourteen points' of President Woodrow Wilson to recall. There was also the wanton lack of interest shown by a declining Liberal Party, a union-minded Conservative Party and a centralized Labour Party to pay heed to Welsh national sentiment, and to formulate a proper programme for the government of Wales.

The outcome was the formation of *Plaid Genedlaethol Cymru* (later Plaid Cymru), the first nationalist political party in the history of modern Wales, and much the most enduring. Its existence is also to be classified as in some sense one of the consequences of the First World War. It was formed in very obscure circumstances at a meeting in a temperance hotel during the Pwllheli *eisteddfod* in August 1925. It was the result of the merger of two small groups, *Byddin Ymreolwyr Cymru* (the Welsh Home Rule Army), founded at Caernarfon in 1924, and *Y Mudiad Cymreig* (the Welsh move-ment), a militant pressure-group on behalf of the Welsh language based on a few academics in the university. Its six founder-members were constituted as the executive of the new nationalist party. They comprised the Revd Lewis Valentine, Moses Gruffydd, and H. R. Jones of *Byddin Ymreolwyr*, and Fred Jones, D. J. Williams, and Saunders Lewis of *Y Mudiad Cymreig*. Outstand-ing among them was the distinguished writer, Saunders Lewis, a Liverpool Welshman who had been a war casualty: he delivered a powerful inspirational address to the first Plaid Cymru summer school held at Machynlleth in 1926, symbolically on the alleged site of Owain Glyndŵr's 'Welsh parliament' in 1404. The preponderant element of the early Plaid Cymru were nonconfor-mist radicals of the old school, many of them pacifist during the war. Typical of these was Iorwerth Peate, a young academic, steeped in the Independent traditions of 'S.R.' of Llanbrynmair. The first party president was a Baptist minister, the Revd Lewis Valentine. But there were also important figures including Saunders Lewis and Ambrose Bebb, cosmopolitan men who saw life in a European context, and were deeply attracted to French Roman Catholicism. They saw the new party as embodying the organic unity of Wales and of medieval European Christendom as it had existed long ago, before the sectarian divisiveness introduced by the statist nationalism and the Protes-tantism of the sixteenth century had fragmented Welsh culture. Ambrose

Bebb was a lecturer in the University of Rennes and the Sorbonne between 1920 and 1925 and contributed a Welsh-language column to *Breiz Atao*, the journal of the Breton nationalist movement. He and Lewis tried to emphasize the links between Wales and the Latin, Catholic culture of the Mediterranean countries. Both were much influenced by right-wing French Catholic nationalist writers such as Maurice Barrès and Charles Maurras of *Action Française* —much to the dismay of nonconformist democrats (also Francophiles) such as W. J. Gruffydd and R. T. Jenkins. Lewis and Bebb urged that Wales should adopt Maurras's slogan, *Politique d'abord*!, with the need for vigorous political action to sustain national and social culture. Lewis entered the Roman Catholic Church himself in 1932, though the fact was not publicly revealed for some considerable time.

At first, Plaid Cymru was not formally committed to self-government for Wales.[42] Its three main objectives all concerned the protection of the Welsh language, including the making of Welsh the only official language, recognizing it as an obligatory medium in official business and government administration, and using it as a medium of instruction in education at every level from primary schools to the university. The party's main concerns were intellectual, cultural, and moral. It was more of a pressure-group on behalf of the language than an organized political party. Its membership by 1930 stood at just 500. The Welsh culture and the Christian message were the twin poles of the new party's ideology. In political, social, and economic terms, Plaid Cymru was in many ways conservative, perhaps a response to the Catholicism of so many of its key members. It endorsed co-operative methods and small-scale forms of production in place of centralized planning and state ownership. It was not sympathetic to mass trade unionism. At first, its economic ideas were rudimentary, though the gap was soon to be filled by its leading economic expert, Dr D. J. Davies, who spelt out 'the economics of self-government' in considerable detail.[43] He was, appropriately enough, a warm admirer of the self-sufficient co-operative methods adopted by farmers in Ireland and Denmark, and had gained a doctorate at Aberystwyth in agricultural economics. He married an Irish girl whom he had met during a visit to Jutland. Gradually, Plaid Cymru became more organized. A fresh departure for the new party in 1926 was the founding of its own newspaper, *Y Ddraig Goch*, originally the journal of the Welsh colony in Patagonia. After some controversy as to whether the party should try to extend its appeal to non-Welsh speakers, an English-language newspaper, the *Welsh Nationalist,* appeared some time later, in January 1932. The outstanding impact of the party was a personal one. Saunders Lewis replaced Valentine as president of Plaid Cymru in 1926, and retained this office until 1939. He was already the editor of the party newspaper, where he had succeeded Ambrose Bebb, and its leading

[42] See Saunders Lewis, *Egwyddorion Cenedlaetholdeb* (1926).
[43] D. J. Davies, *The Economics of Welsh Self-Government* (Caernarfon, 1931).

ideologue. Lewis was to be for the next twenty years—perhaps for the rest of the century—the dominant inspiration and cultural stimulus in making Welsh nationalism a force in Welsh and British life.

But at first this tiny movement aroused little support. It aroused fierce opposition from Lloyd George downwards: he prophesied that the new party would wither in a night like Jonah's gourd. Plaid Cymru's immediate significance lay rather in the future, a portent of how the pressures of the post-war years, and the emotional and ideological upheaval that had taken place within the enclosed world of Liberal nonconformity had released a new, potentially dynamic and challenging movement to capture the hearts, minds and souls of nationally-conscious Welshmen.

Wales by the mid-twenties, then, looked and sounded a very different kind of society from that relatively placid, self-confident, and successful nation that had gone to Armageddon with such cheerful expectation in 1914. An older social order had passed away with the disestablishment of the Church and the decline of the landed gentry. But fulfilment of their traditional objectives had brought little joy to the nationally-conscious Liberal élite who had dominated Welsh life and directed its quest for social and religious equality and for a more democratic order since the eighties. Indeed, the post-war world brought merely anxieties and strains more exhausting than the relatively mild domination of the clergy and the squire had ever brought in the previous century. The political fabric of the Liberal Party was now in total disarray. Its machinery and organization was collapsing at both the local and parliamentary levels in the coalfield, with only the appeal to tradition and to conservative values to sustain the remnants of the older radical heritage in the rural areas. Lloyd George himself was more and more a suspect and even discredited figure, one who no longer commanded the instinctive admiration and trust of his own people. His premiership had brought few dividends for his native land, and he could no longer take its support for granted. Shattered in organization, undermined in morale in much of the country, Welsh Liberalism was quite unable to counter the vigorous challenge of Labour in south Wales, either in its political or its industrial aspects. The revival of the 'unofficial' movements of pre-war years and the emergence of a new young generation of Marxist or *Marxisant* leaders like Aneurin Bevan suggested a sharp reversal of secular beliefs. Meanwhile the spiritual basis of Liberal Wales seemed less and less relevant to a post-war generation. The chapels were less central to the society which had produced them. The nonconformity of pre-1914 seemed a dated movement, founded on sentiment, intellectual stagnation, and outmoded rhetoric. So, increasingly, did the nationalism, such as it was, of pre-war. Welsh nationalists after 1919, apprehensive for the future of their culture and the survival of their language in a manner scarcely conceivable in the optimistic years of the Edwardian renaissance, sought new channels for expressing the old national sentiment. Even though at first only a tiny party, the rise of Plaid Cymru is, therefore, of much significance, a powerful indication of the revulsion against pre-war definitions of nationality and a demand by literary and cultural spokesmen for a more coherent and aggressive faith.

In Wales, more than most parts of Britain or of Europe, the post-war mood, with its swirling eddies of change and its uprooting of historic, cherished landmarks, brought a revolution in assumptions and priorities. It was a slow, perhaps undramatic revolution. It was very different from the experience of Ireland, with its 'troubles' and civil war. Welsh nationalism, even in its Plaid Cymru version, was a pacific movement, one which sought transformation by moral suasion and by all-conquering force of a free conscience. But even though the new battles to assert and define the Welsh identity might take place in literary periodicals, on eisteddfodic platforms, and in the hearts of idealistic young Welshmen and women, rather than through force of arms, they were real enough. They were to inaugurate a phase of self-examination and self-doubt, spurred on by a sense of cultural cleavage and failing nationalist momentum in Wales, a phase of internal tension and torment which survived the passing of the Second World War, and had many positive, as well as purely destructive, consequences. It was a phase, which, even in the 1980s, was still very far from over.

CHAPTER 8

WALES'S LOCUST YEARS

The erosion of the political and cultural traditions of post-war Wales was damaging but far from fatal to the wellbeing of the nation. Infinitely more serious and sweeping in its impact on the life of Wales was the prolonged economic depression of the inter-war period. From the start of the 1920s and emphatically so after 1923, right down to the latter years of the 1930s, when the rearmament programme began to have some impact on economic activity as in other regions of Britain, Wales, especially the coalfield, was paralysed by a collapse in its industrial, manufacturing, and commercial life. It experienced mass unemployment and poverty without parallel in the British Isles. After the seemingly limitless industrial progress of the half-century up to 1914, an advance that continued in its major features during the wartime years, south Wales plunged unprepared into a depression and despair which crushed its society for almost twenty years and left ineradicable scars upon its conscious-ness. Thirty years and more after the end of the Second World War, the legacy of the decades of depression still formed a grim folk memory for households and families in Wales. As British capitalism lurched into a massive crisis in the years after 1922, the Welsh valleys were foremost amongst its helpless victims.

For a brief heady period until the start of 1921 the cheerful prosperity of the pre-war and wartime years continued. There were even new pits opened up, like Llay Main colliery near Wrexham in 1923. The militancy of the miners and other south Wales workers during and after the inquiries of the Sankey Commission on the coal mines in 1919 built up against a background of wage advances and a reduction in working hours achieved during the war. There were also tragically deceptive omens of a resumption of economic growth and social advance after the armistice. The very confidence of the south Wales miners' claim for a 30 per cent wage advance in March 1919 was evidence of the optimism of the time. The collieries were booming throughout that year, with coal exports from Welsh ports rising from 2,092,289 tons in December 1918 to 2,993,850 tons twelve months later. Further, the value of each ton rose steeply, from £1 13s. 2d. in December 1918 to £3 4s. 2d. in December 1919. Despite the reduction in the price of coal sold in the home market, coalowners could still show immense profits of over £70 million for the year. At the start of 1920, a record number of 272,000 men were employed in the collieries of Wales in all grades of work. There was a background, too, of confidence in the stock exchange, with a vast market in new shares, the floating of innumerable new companies, and great confidence being voiced in the chambers of commerce of Cardiff and Swansea, despite the lengthy industrial disputes of 1919–21.

But the warning signs very soon came. In April 1920 the government was forced to push up the bank rate to 7 per cent to counter the speculative, inflationary boom of post-war. In May, domestic prices suddenly collapsed as the government, the Federation of British Industries and the chambers of commerce recognized the start of a period of industrial depression without parallel in recent history. By the end of 1920, this had imposed its grip on coal mining as on every other industry, as foreign and domestic demand fell sharply away. It was the start of a slump in the staple industries of Britain, coal, steel-making, and shipbuilding, which was to drag on for another fifteen terrible years.

South Wales suffered probably more acutely than any other industrial region from this prolonged stagnation of trade and industry. It had a uniquely high proportion of its working population engaged in extractive industry, mining, metal manufacture, quarrying, and the like. It suffered from being an area of primary production rather than of manufacture of finished products, and it remained so until after 1945. Other parts of Britain, the east Midlands for instance, were to show clear signs of economic recovery in the later twenties, as domestic demand for consumer durables and the products of new light industries picked up. The motor-car industry was especially thriving. There was a further revival in such areas in the mid-thirties, after the disastrous, shattering slump of 1929–33, with a further recovery of consumer demand fuelled by cheap money, and a boom in house building. There was even some expansion in parts of Wales, notably in the coastal towns of north Wales, Rhyl, Prestatyn, Llandudno, Bangor, and Caernarfon, in the thirties, as small industries were brought in and domestic building picked up. Tourism brought money in to seaside resorts. In the north-east, Flintshire was relatively prosperous in the thirties, owing to the expansion of steel-smelting and building, and the manufacture of rayon by the thriving Courtaulds factories. In south Wales, by contrast, depression and unemployment, especially in the inland valleys, were endemic and unrelieved. Dependent more than any other industrial region on a vigorous export trade, it was more completely the victim of structural depression and stagnant trade than anywhere else in Britain, especially among miners and steelworkers. Unemployment rose from 13.4 per cent in Wales in December 1925 to 23.3 per cent in December 1927. By July 1930, the figure was 27.2 per cent of the insured population—a proportion, of course, which left out of account categories of workers who did not come within the purview of the national insurance acts. At this same period in July 1930, the respective proportions of the insured population that were unemployed stood at only 15.8 per cent for England and 17.9 per cent for Scotland. While there were pockets of severe unemployment elsewhere that were as alarming as those in Wales, notably the north-east of England and Clydeside in Scotland, Wales, especially the mining valleys, did appear to be experiencing a total ordeal all its own.

The *Industrial Survey of South Wales* commissioned by the Board of Trade and directed by Hilary Marquand, the Professor of Industrial Relations at Cardiff, was published in 1932; a further, up-dated survey appeared in 1937. These provided a bleak statistical commentary on this industrial cataclysm. The Pontypridd—Mountain Ash—Rhondda urban districts showed in December 1930 a proportion of 30 per cent of the insured population as unemployed. In the Rhymney—Tredegar area to the east, an area equally devoted to coal mining, the proportion stood at 27.4 per cent.[1] In the Newport area, with its dependence on a steel industry now in a state of near collapse, the proportion of unemployed was as high as 34.7 per cent. After the financial crisis of 1931, things became worse still. Unemployment in south Wales in June 1932 stood at nearly 150,000. This was especially severe in towns at the heads of the central and eastern valleys of the coalfield, in Merthyr Tydfil above all. In June 1935, the percentage of the wholly unemployed in the Merthyr area was given as 47.5 per cent, the worst figure to date. In effect, over half the working population of Merthyr was on the dole. Only the coastal ports escaped some of the worst rigours of the depression. Cardiff, with its range of commercial and distributive trades, managed for much of the time to sustain a reasonable level of activity. Swansea and district, too, as will be seen, were reasonably thriving owing to the greater variety in their industrial base and the relative health of the tinplate industry until the early thirties. For most of the rest of industrial south Wales, the depression was total and unrelieved.

The root causes of this depression are familiar enough. The massive contraction of international trade from 1921 onwards was accompanied by a vast loss of overseas markets. This had especially serious effects on the coal and steel industries, and eventually on tinplate. Exports of British coal generally fell right away in value from £137 m. in July 1920 to only £43 m. a year later; they continued to languish thereafter. There was a deceptive recovery in 1923 when exports of coal from south Wales and elsewhere suddenly rose sharply again as a result of a coal strike in the United States and the French occupation of the Ruhr. As soon as the American and German mining industries began to expand again, the slump in Britain resumed the more drastically. The steam and bituminous coal of the Welsh valleys, and to a lesser extent their anthracite coal, were the main victims. By 1929 south Wales, which had once supplied almost a third of the world's output of coal, now produced less than 3 per cent. Other nations, notably the Poles, were developing their own, more modernized coal industries, and this cut away

[1] *Industrial Survey of South Wales* (Cardiff, 1932), chapter I.

many traditional outlets. The Italian market, as David Davies bitterly complained in *Welsh Outlook*, was lost to Welsh mines largely because of the demand for German 'reparations' that would be paid in coal imposed by the victorious allies from 1920 onwards.[2] Italian industrial production rose sharply after the war, but it was Germany that supplied it with raw materials. The two and a half million tons exported from south Wales ports to Italy in 1913 had been lost for ever. The French and Belgian markets were also lost after a hopeful period in the twenties. This was partly because of the competition from the thriving German coal industry, partly because of restrictive measures by the French government in the thirties which introduced a quota system for coal imports. Meanwhile, the American coal industry was dominating the markets of north America, including Canada; it was supplying the transport and industry of central and south America as well. As it happened, the American mineworkers were led by a Welsh-American, John Llewellyn Lewis. Welsh coal was being displaced all over the world, and was increasingly dependent on flagging domestic demand.

In fact, the south Wales coal industry was particularly ill-equipped to withstand these foreign challenges. Largely because of geological and physical factors, the cost of production in the valleys was notoriously high. Productivity per man was known to be low, and wage costs excessive in strictly economic terms. A government white paper in 1921 pointed out that the net cost per ton of coal mined in south Wales and Monmouthshire was 60s. 9d., compared with a United Kingdom average of 38s. 11d. and a figure of barely 31s. in Yorkshire.[3] The struggling Welsh coal industry, then, was simply not able to compete with aggressive competitors overseas. It was further burdened by ill-conceived fiscal policy by the British government. In particular, there was the decision taken by Winston Churchill, while Chancellor of the Exchequer in 1925, to return to the gold standard at the pre-war parity against the dollar. This meant, in effect, a 10 per cent appreciation in the external value of sterling. It was a decision that was defended by all the apostles of economic orthodoxy in the city, by Montague Norman, the governor of the Bank of England, by Treasury advisers such as Otto Niemeyer, and even by Philip Snowden speaking on behalf of the Labour Party. It was thought to lead the way back to stable currencies and business confidence from which all thriving international commerce would grow, and had been recommended by the Cunliffe Committee back in 1918. But the outcome was a disaster for British coal exports which were now seriously over-valued in relation to foreign currency, and was directly responsible for increasing unemployment and further decline in the Welsh mining industry. It further accelerated the loss of overseas markets. In addition, the sluggish performance of British industry depressed home demand for coal, while the growth of motorized

[2] David Davies, 'The Coal Position in South Wales', *Welsh Outlook,* October 1929, pp. 38 ff.
[3] *South Wales News,* 29 April 1921.

transport reduced the demand for coal from the railways.

Welsh steam coal exports also suffered acutely from another factor, crucial to the heady economic progress of pre-1914, namely the declining use of coal in the world's mercantile marine. Even before the war, prescient observers such as the late Lord Rhondda and Professor Jevons had seen the potential threat of oil, as the internal combustion engine was increasingly used in ocean-going naval vessels. By the mid-twenties, the use of oil had far outstripped that of coal. The new fuel was cheaper in consumption, easier and swifter in bunkering, cleaner to handle. It required far less labour when being taken aboard. To a limited degree, south Wales benefited from the change-over to oil, as will be seen, with the establishment of the Anglo-Iranian Company's new oil refinery at Skewen near Neath in 1921 and the use of the Queen's Dock in Swansea for the berthing of tankers. But, in general, the decision of the British and other navies to change from coal to oil, though justifiable on economic and technological grounds, was harmful to Wales. It meant that south Wales coal lost yet another major customer.

By the end of the twenties, then, it was manifest that the decline in the trade in coal and the linked decline in the export of steel and in the activity of Welsh ports were deep-seated and permanent in their effects. It was impossible to argue now that it was merely a temporary phenomenon, the product of the exceptional dislocation of markets and the fluctuation in international currencies after the war, while British industry adjusted itself to new market conditions. It was clearly indicative of a fundamental decay in the entire fabric of the economic life of the coalfield, and in those communities that depended on it for their livelihood. South Wales, in the dismal jargon of the day, was truly a 'depressed area'. The further shattering effect of the slump from the end of 1929 onwards, following the crash of the Wall Street stock market and the terrifying collapse of the American economy, merely confirmed an already well-established and appalling pattern.

The coal industry is clearly the most conspicuous example of this continuous decline and decay. After the brief flurry of recovery in 1923 with the French invasion of the Ruhr, the coalfield seemed to be sunk in hopeless stagnation. Until well into the thirties, there was no sign of any recovery. Each January, official statistics documented in the bleakest fashion the previous year's picture of decline. By 1934 the situation was desperate, with the collapse of demand in the major markets of Europe and north America being accompanied by measures of economic nationalism such as the restrictions imposed by the French government whose quotas favoured American coal but were disadvantageous to that mined in Wales. With markets such as the French now lost, capital investment in the coal industry stagnant, and the labour force contracting through unemployment or emigration to the Midlands and southern England, the output of coal steadily diminished, with prices and profits falling away. South Wales, which had produced a quarter of all the coal mined in Britain before the war, saw its share fall to 19.1 per cent in 1924 and to 18.3 per cent in 1925. Thereafter, recession was continuous. As an index of this, the number of miners employed in south Wales pits fell steadily from 218,000 in 1924 to 126,000 ten years later.

It was, above all, the steam and bituminous coal of central and eastern Glamorgan and Monmouthshire (and, indeed, of Flintshire and the Wrexham area in north-east Wales) which saw the most serious decline in production. The anthracite coalfield in western Glamorgan and eastern Carmarthenshire was far less disturbed for many years. The output and export of anthracite from Welsh pits remained higher than pre-war throughout the twenties and the early thirties. In 1935, when the percentage of unemployment stood at over 51 per cent in Merthyr Vale and well over 40 per cent in the Rhondda and Aberdare valleys, it stood at no more than 13.8 per cent in the Amman valley in east Glamorgan.[4] The port of Swansea remained relatively thriving from the anthracite coal export trade, quite apart from the buoyancy of the tinplate industry and the growing business to be gained in handling oil shipments for the refinery at Skewen. On the other hand, in 1934 unemployment in the Llanelli—Swansea district still stood at 19 per cent, a grim enough total. But things were much worse to the east of Swansea. In 1931—3, when unemployment in south Wales was registered at totals nine times higher than in 1925, it was in steam-coal valleys such as the Rhondda, Merthyr Vale, Aberdare, and Rhymney that unemployment was most acute. In the Rhondda, the percentage of insured miners out of work stood in June 1932 at 52.9 per cent. Three years later, it had improved only marginally to 45.9 per cent. The number of miners employed in the collieries of the Rhondda fell by almost half between 1927 and 1936, from 39,177 to 19,873.[5] This was at a period when the anthracite valleys between the Vale of Neath and the Gwendraeth were steadily increasing their share of the total working population of the Welsh coalfield. It was, then, the steam-coal trade that was most disastrously affected by the loss of European markets and by the use of oil in place of coal in land and sea-going transportation.

With the coalfield in crisis, especially in relation to bituminous and steam coal, the number of collieries in south Wales steadily diminished. Not surprisingly, those that remained became increasingly cost-conscious. A leading coalowner such as Sir Evan Williams, of Powell Duffryn, Cardiff Collieries and many other enterprises, the chairman of the Coalowners' Association of Great Britain at the time of 'Black Friday' in 1921, became a leading advocate and practitioner of wage reductions. He played a major part, in association with Scottish coalowners such as Sir Adam Nimmo, in making the owners that degree more intransigent in meeting the miners' demands in the years that led up to the general strike in 1926. Inevitably, the pre-war and wartime trend for

---

[4] *Second Industrial Survey of South Wales* (Cardiff, 1937), vol. i, p. 71.

[5] E. D. Lewis, *The Rhondda Valleys*, p. 254.

the amalgamation or merger of major colliery concerns became more and more pronounced. By the end of the twenties, all the pits in the Rhondda, for example, were owned by just three giant concerns—the Welsh Associated Collieries, Powell Duffryn, and the Ocean Coal Company. These were the re-christened heirs of the giants of pre-war years, namely D. A. Thomas's Cambrian combine, Sir William Lewis's 'Lewis Merthyr Consolidated', and David Davies's Ocean group respectively. In 1935, the Welsh Associated and the Powell Duffryn group finally amalgamated to form Powell Duffryn Associated Collieries, on paper the largest producer of coal in the British Isles. Its new managing director, presiding over the contraction of this empire of coal, was E. M. Hann, once the defender of the Aberdare collieries at the time of the disturbances in 1910. Fewer companies in practice meant fewer jobs, a perpetuation of the same system of ownership without any improvements in efficiency, in introducing new methods of mechanization or in moderating the climate of labour relations. Here was a new species of bastard capitalism, to parallel the bastard feudalism of centuries earlier, large agglomerations of ownership thinly concealing a contracting productive base.

This, then, was the general bleak picture of the Welsh coal industry in the inter-war years. Not until after 1936 was there any sign of recovery. Even the earlier phase of industrial revival, so marked in some regions of Britain from 1933, was not evident in south Wales, with its heavy dependence on the coal industry. Only after 1936, through the expansion of some heavy industries and engineering trades with the impact of rearmament and the emergence of somewhat more hopeful conditions of international trading, did south Wales make some episodic return to fuller levels of economic activity. After 1936, indeed, in view of the immensity of the crisis over the past fifteen years, it was not surprising that south Wales showed, for a moment, a more rapid rate of recovery than other areas of Britain. But coal had only a modest share even in this marginal improvement.

Steel production was no less depressed and stagnant than was the export of coal. The backward technology of Welsh steel plants, especially those at the heads of the valleys, had been apparent before the war. The Dowlais works, for instance, had been struggling since the eighties. Now the incapacity of the Welsh steel industry to face up to stern competition from the United States and Germany became starkly apparent. Steel manufacture largely closed down in the valley towns away from the coast. The old Cyfarthfa works near Merthyr were finally closed in 1921. In 1930 the major part of the Dowlais works was finally closed also, with 3,000 men thrown out of work. A smaller section of the Dowlais works continued to operate with up to 800 men still finding employment there. In 1936, this closed, too. Dowlais, more than almost anywhere in Wales, had been virtually a one-industry company town, with its iron and steel manufacture. With the works shut down, an entire community found its social and economic existence destroyed. In the inland

valleys of Monmouthshire, the works at Blaenavon closed down in 1922 and
the blast-furnace section, two years later. So, too, did that of Tredegar, while
in 1929 steel-making ceased, apparently for ever, at Ebbw Vale as well. The
general tendency was for steel-making now to be concentrated wholly on the
coast, from Newport in the east to Llanelli in the west. The most encouraging
aspect of Welsh steel-making was in west Wales, where there was a ring of
fifteen steel-works in an arc from Llanelli to Margam. Thirteen of them were
engaged in the production of steel bars for domestic industry. Here the
position was slightly less bleak, while the introduction of tariffs after 1932
assisted west Wales steel exports. But there was still, even here, a persistent
pattern of reductions in output of steel between 1923 and 1935, with heavy
unemployment amongst steelworkers. Again, a major component of the
south Wales economy was quite ill-equipped to cope with the pressures of
changing markets, new competitors, and low investment.

Not surprisingly, the same picture of combinations in ownership began to
show in steel as in the coal industry. Guest, Keen & Nettlefolds had built up its
steel empire long before the war, notably when it bought up the Dowlais
works and created the new works at East Moors in Cardiff. Now in 1920, the
same company bought a controlling shareholding interest in John Lysaghts of
Newport, another of the steel giants. In the past, this kind of development,
like the spread of the Richard Thomas concern amongst the steel and tinplate
mills of west Wales, might have been justified on grounds of technological
efficiency as a rationalization of methods of production. The mines, the coke-
producing plant, the water supplies, the blast-furnaces, rolling mills, and
transport facilities of Guest, Keen would all now be operated under a joint
system with consequent economies of scale. But the combinations that
followed in the steel industry from the early twenties onwards were obviously
the product of weakness not of vitality. The smallest were going to the wall,
the few giants trying to salvage what coastal steel plants remained.

Welsh tinplate also suffered in common with other metal-based industries
during the depression. Demand was generally buoyant for much of the
twenties; such firms as Briton Ferry Steel, Baldwins, and Richard Thomas
were thriving between 1919 and 1926. The demand for tinplate for the canning
of food continued to be a strong one. There was a fall in exports in the late
twenties as world trade contracted and as the Americans in particular built up
their own industry. But there was still enough strength in the Welsh tinplate
industry in 1928 for Welsh manufacturers to reach an agreement with their
American counterparts to ensure that Welsh producers were allocated 70 per
cent of the combined exports of both countries. But the onset of more acute
depression after 1929 showed up more clearly deep-seated problems of
antiquated plant and excess capacity. Exports began to fall away sharply in
1930, and by 1931 were down by 75,000 tons compared with the previous year.
In the eastern coalfield, tinplate exports from Newport, Cardiff, and Barry

fell away from 79,000 tons in 1929 to 53,000 two years later. An additional factor that applied in the tinplate industry was the belated adoption by tinplate makers such as Richard Thomas of new technical processes following the vertical integration of different tinplate firms. This often threw many workers out of employment. So, too, did the use of quotas of production which often resulted in the tinplate being produced in other parts of Britain instead. By the mid-thirties, the good years were plainly over for the Welsh tinplate industry. Unemployment was heavy and the unions were forced to accept work-sharing schemes that involved six-hour shifts and shorter working weeks as ways of distributing what work there was amongst all tinplate workers.

With this contraction in trade and production, it followed that the docks of south Wales entered upon hard times also. Swansea, it is true, remained comparatively thriving until the early thirties. The town in which Dylan Thomas lived in the twenties, that 'lovely, ugly town' which gave him such inspiration, seems to have been a bustling and active one.[6] There was much new building, as in the Townhill estate built up on the heights above the town. There were civic monuments of which the new Guildhall, designed by Percy Thomas and completed in 1934, took pride of place, with those celebrated panels by Frank Brangwyn which the House of Lords had turned down. There was also a most thriving newspaper press, with a morning and evening daily, and three weeklies, all much livelier than their later equivalents. Anthracite and steel production remained fairly prosperous in the west Wales area. The nickel works at Clydach benefited from the demand for nickel steel from the growing automobile industry. There was also the import of oil for the new oil refinery near Skewen, brought in from Persia, Iraq, and Kuwait, with the model village of 'Llandarcy' built near the refinery to accommodate the staff of the Anglo-Persian company. The Queen's Dock was busy in handling ocean-going tankers, and Swansea as a port never knew the full rigours of depression experienced elsewhere in south Wales. But, for the trade of Barry and Cardiff, so dependent on the export of Welsh steam coal from the Rhondda and elsewhere, the slump was a disaster. The main docks in both these towns virtually closed down for prolonged periods. Even in 1935 nearly 25 per cent of the working male population of the Cardiff/Barry district was registered as wholly unemployed. Cardiff shipping, one of the wonders of the British economy down to 1914, entered a period of near-collapse. The number of those employed in shipbuilding and repairing, ship servicing, and dockyard labour generally fell sharply in the later twenties, showing a fall of 36.5 per cent for Cardiff alone in 1930, by comparison with 1923. Here again a pivot of the south Wales economy was on short time, if not at total shut-down.

Throughout the coalfield, south Wales in the depression years of the

    [6] See Peter Stead, 'The Swansea of Dylan Thomas', *Dylan Thomas Remembered* (Swansea, 1978), pp. 8–24.

twenties and thirties offered a widespread picture of stagnation, of idle pits and steel-works, and of growing dereliction. A growing mood of hopelessness coloured public debate on the economic condition of south Wales after the mass unemployment of the 1929–32 period, which rose at one point to over 203,000. Thomas Jones, normally slow to be stirred to public wrath, proposed, with biting sarcasm, in July 1935 that the planners might well turn the coalfield into a kind of open-air museum of industrial archaeology, a new Avebury or Stonehenge, a monument to the early industrialization and to the forgotten technical processes of a bygone age. South Wales could be scheduled as 'a grand national ruin', its population exported to Hounslow or Dagenham, spurred on by the cry, 'First stop, Paddington'.[7] Thomas Jones was writing angry satire. But in 1939 PEP was to propose, apparently in all seriousness, that Merthyr Tydfil be written off as a town and its population transferred *en bloc* and rehoused on the coast in the Usk valley in Monmouthshire.[8] It was no longer economically valid, so PEP claimed, to locate industry in the heads of the valleys around Merthyr, so far from the trade outlets on the coast. It was unfair to ask the British taxpayer to subsidize so unproductive a wasteland. It was inhuman to the people of Merthyr and neighbouring communities to keep them in such an insanitary and forbidding terrain. As for Merthyr, so for Ebbw Vale, Abertillery, Blaenavon, Bargoed, Mountain Ash, and a score of other places. South Wales seemed to have little economic rationale and its antiquated industry little future.

The depression in industry, it should be noted, was paralleled by depression in agriculture. After the partial recovery after the turn of the century and the temporary affluence of the war years, Welsh upland farmers again found the going hard. Circumstances varied considerably according to the type of agriculture pursued. In general, Professor Ashby found that highland farmers had done tolerably well in the twenties.[9] Sheep husbandry had been especially profitable: in the period 1925–8, breeders and fatteners of sheep had earned profits that approached those of pre-war. Cattle breeds were changing from the Welsh Black to the Shorthorn, and later the Friesian. Milk production had increased, but this called for relatively little labour and tended to reduce still further the working population on the land. In other respects, Welsh farmers faced mounting difficulties that became far worse after 1929. The 'great betrayal' of the Coalition government in 1921 by repealing the Agriculture Act and ending state subsidies to provide guaranteed prices for wheat and oats had some effect in Wales where oats were much grown. The production of cereals generally fell away sharply, and much land dropped out of arable

[7] Thomas Jones, 'What's Wrong with South Wales', printed in *Leeks and Daffodils* (Newtown, 1942), pp. 89 ff.

[8] J. W. England, 'The Merthyr of the Twentieth Century', in Glanmor Williams (ed.), *Merthyr Politics: the Making of a Working-Class Tradition* (Cardiff, 1966), p. 82.

[9] A. W. Ashby, 'The Agricultural Depression in Wales', *Welsh Outlook,* November 1929, pp. 335–8.

cultivation. Prices fell, too, for pigs and other livestock, while there was a lack of high quality in beef cattle and lambs. Generally, Welsh farming was marked by a relatively low level of mechanization, poor qualities of the produce for market requirements, and a lack of technical organization in the industry, especially on the marketing side.

By 1930, it was clear that the agriculture of most nations was sunk in deep crisis. American farmers in the mid-West were faced with a slump in prices and a collapse of world markets. British farmers were hardly in more prosperous condition. In Wales, the hill farmers, with their relatively scanty capital, their financial problems in acquiring more modernized equipment and machinery, and often high rates imposed on small productive areas, suffered along with everyone else. As has been seen, Welsh freeholders were burdened with severe mortgages and heavy bank charges after purchasing their holdings in the years just after the war. In addition, there were the basic physical problems of the barren, highly-marginal character of much land in north and west Wales, and frequent difficulties of harvesting caused by drought or else unduly heavy rainfall. By the early thirties, agriculturists in most parts of Wales were struggling. The average income of families drawing their livelihood from the cultivation of the land was, according to Professor Ashby, barely in excess of £100 p.a.[10] The depopulation of rural communities continued apace, often with shattering effects on that native culture which the country areas had so largely kept alive. In this and other respects, the quality of life in rural, no less than in industrial, Wales, remained meagre.

The only real sign of long-term recovery, in fact, came with government action from 1933 onwards. This arose from the marketing board principle, introducing guaranteed prices for basic farm produce. This idea was originally introduced by Dr Christopher Addison during the second Labour government in 1931 and was developed further by Walter Elliot, Minister of Agriculture in the National government, from 1933. The establishment of the Milk Marketing Board in 1933 had a powerful effect in rural Wales: one writer has even seen it as marking the 'turn of the tide' for Welsh agriculture.[11] The number of milk producers in Wales rose from 10,510 in 1934 to 20,223 in 1939. The Board paid farmers a 'pool price' for milk, in return for a levy from the producer, and acted as distributive intermediary between the farmer and the milk companies and retailers. Milk production increased and the price rose, with the aid of government subsidies, though the market in the depressed, impoverished industrial areas remained a limited one. On the other hand, the profit for Welsh milk producers was distinctly modest, while as has been noted above, the amount of additional labour that was attracted was negligible.

[10] *Welsh Housing and Development Yearbook*, 1935, p. 53.
[11] Brinley Thomas (ed.), *The Welsh Economy* (Cardiff, 1962), p. 82.

Against this background of near-collapse in industry and stagnation in agriculture, the reaction of successive governments and planners throughout the inter-war period was persistently negative and ineffective. There were useful proposals from local agencies such as the Welsh Agricultural Council which offered a series of suggestions on methods of increasing efficiency in food production. Professor Stapledon in Aberystwyth conducted pioneering research into improvements in crop yields and in strains of grasses. But bodies like this, located in Wales, were advisory only. It required vigorous and intelligent action in London to try to turn back the tide of economic depression, and it was precisely this that was lacking.

From early 1920, as has been seen, governments, largely Conservative in complexion, relied on high bank rate, a contraction of the note issue and controls on the money supply, with a maintenance of orthodox methods of budget balancing and the rigid control of government expenditure. This deflationary policy was continued with equal zeal by Philip Snowden during the first Labour governments of 1924 and 1929–31. It was only altered from 1932 onwards when Neville Chamberlain at the Treasury deliberately pursued a policy of cheap money, while modestly raising direct subsidies to industry from £20 million in 1933 to £28 million in 1935. Prior to this, the policy of restriction and deflation offered no hope at all to the special problems of the Welsh coalfield. One crucial government decision, Churchill's policy of the return to gold at the pre-war parity in 1925, was disastrous in its impact on the staple industries of south Wales, especially coalmining, as has been seen. There were voices that called for a more rigorous approach. John Maynard Keynes was a persistent critic of the retrenchment and negativism of governments in the twenties and early thirties, with their appalling social consequences for older industrial regions like Scotland, the north-east and south Wales. He joined his old adversary, David Lloyd George, in producing a series of dynamic new schemes for 'pump-priming' of the economy, for encouraging new methods of capital investment, for general counter-cyclical activity by the central government, and for public works programmes such as road building and house construction to encourage employment. Keynes inspired a series of tracts, published under the auspices of the Liberal Party, in the late twenties. Notable among them were the 'yellow book', *Britain's Industrial Future* in 1928, the 'orange book', *We Can Conquer Unemployment* in 1929, and *Can Lloyd George Do It?* which recommended a public works programme to the extent of £100 millions spread over three years to combat unemployment.

These aroused much interest in Wales, and widespread sympathy from Welsh industrialists. But discussion was inevitably coloured by the controversial past and present role of Lloyd George in British politics. Labour leaders in Wales were generally suspicious of the public works proposals, which they regarded as an extension of traditional methods of 'outdoor relief' for the poor. Indeed, the Keynesian schemes were canvassed with a good deal of over-optimism as to the rapidity with which economic activity could be stimulated throughout the whole of the economy owing to the 'multiplier' effects on employment. There was much suspicion in Labour circles as to the practicability or desirability of transferring unemployed miners to build roads in other parts of the country. The Conservative reaction was bleakly summarized by Neville Chamberlain in March 1928.[12] He decided that up to 200,000 miners in south Wales were unlikely to find permanent employment in the mining industry ever again: for instance, six of the seven collieries at Blaina would never reopen. The only solution was a mass transfer of population to other parts of Britain where work would be available. One of the main problems, Chamberlain added, was that miners were ignorant of skills applicable to any other industry. The practical questions of where these miners would be dispatched, what alternative employment would be provided for them, and how the mechanics of what was, in effect, a mass direction of labour would be arranged, Chamberlain did not explain. Meanwhile, the Treasury kept up an attitude of blank negation towards public-works schemes emanating from Keynes or anyone else. They would be inherently inflationary and lead to a deficit in the budget (which Keynes argued was a positive virtue). More, a boost in public investment to promote expansion would lead to the diminution of funds available for private investment—a highly dubious argument, as economists have later pointed out. Above all, 'business confidence', that totem of Treasury thinking up to the Second World War, would be gravely undermined by a statist public-works programme that would appear as the harbinger of red revolution.

After some unconstructive years at the hands of the Baldwin government from 1924 to 1929 (years which included the débâcle of the general strike as will be discussed in Chapter 10), south Wales did no better when the second Labour government took office under MacDonald (now member for a Durham constituency) in 1929. Unemployment sharply deteriorated from the end of that year, with the world collapse of trade following the crash in Wall Street in October. The government, or at least Philip Snowden at the Treasury, took a sternly Gladstonian view of public works policies, and no structural change in the industrial base of the coalfield took place at all. The Coal Mines Act of 1930 was strongly attacked by Welsh miners' leaders, and in any case was never fully implemented. South Wales was allocated an output of 11,859,000 tons under the Mines Act (18.9 per cent of the British total) for the year 1931, but actual production fell consistently below the target figure from quarter to quarter. There appeared to be no economic strategy at all for reviving the staple industries of Wales.

All that existed until 1934 were well-meaning local experiments, on a voluntary and co-operative basis, to deal with the sociological problems of

[12] *South Wales News*, 27 March 1928.

particular communities. One such was the educational settlement founded in 1926 at Maes-yr-Haf at Trealaw in the Rhondda, inspired by the Quakers and under the guidance of A. D. Lindsay, the Master of Balliol. In addition to helping with industrial re-training for out-of-work miners, and setting up workshops for furniture-making and the like, it also assisted with material relief for those on the dole, and their dependants. But Maes-yr-Haf, like another settlement later founded at Pontypool, was largely an institution of educationalists and social workers, rather than an instrument of economic change. More directly related to the economic difficulties of the valleys was another Quaker enterprise, the Community Study Council, founded at Brynmawr which provided some notable social surveys and provided practical help from unemployed miners and steelworkers. George Maitland Lloyd Davies was amongst those directing it. It was paralleled by other Quaker settlements at Merthyr and Aberdare, and by the more general activities of the Society of Friends Coalfields Distress Committee. There were also local co-operative societies and other ventures, all the work of dedicated and idealistic people passionately moved by the plight of the unemployed and the poor. From 1933, the National Council of Social Service, presided over by the omnipresent Sir Percy Watkins, served to co-ordinate the operations of the unemployed workers' clubs and bodies of educationalists.

Yet these worthy organizations could, inevitably, provide help that was only piecemeal and could grapple with but a fraction of the manifold problems of south Wales. The basic structural economic weaknesses remained untouched. Even after the appearance of some genuine signs of sustained economic recovery in other parts of Britain from 1933 onwards, under the National government, south Wales showed no sign of a revival. Unemployment in 1935 was almost as high as it had been in 1932; indeed, in the Aberdare valley the rate of unemployment amongst miners (44.6 per cent) was actually worse in 1935 than it had been three years earlier. What south Wales needed, in Hilary Marquand's famous tract of the period,[13] was a 'plan' for its overall regional development and a powerful stimulus to its very economic existence if it was to survive at all.

Some suggestions were offered by Professor Marquand in his *Economic Survey* in 1932. He called here for a more adventurous policy, above all for the introduction of new light industries to diversify the industrial structure of south Wales, based to such an undue extent on declining staple industries. The *Survey* did add that there appeared to be a widespread prejudice in south Wales towards occupations other than those engaged in primary production or in extractive industry, and noted the difficulty in persuading manual workers to acquire new technical skills. The 'arts and crafts' aspects of the Brynmawr settlement run by the benevolent Quakers had attracted some derision in this respect. Marquand's 'plan' as advocated by him in 1936, went

[13] Hilary A. Marquand, *South Wales Needs a Plan* (London, 1936).

much further. He produced two alternative blueprints. The 'blue plan', which a Conservative government might favour, included a minimum programme of public-works programmes including perhaps a Severn Bridge, the setting up of subsistence production communities and the encouragement of tourism to such places as Barry Island, Porthcawl, and the Gower peninsula. His 'pink plan', the programme of a future Labour government which Marquand himself obviously preferred, involved much more extensive state intervention to direct the location of new industry, to provide authorities for regional planning throughout Wales, and for harnessing local schemes with Labour's proposed Board for national investment. This last was being advocated by the quasi-Keynesian 'XYZ' group including Nicholas Davenport, Hugh Dalton, and three young economists, Hugh Gaitskell, Evan Durbin, and Douglas Jay. Clearly, something fundamental needed to be done, to recast the industrial framework of south Wales as it had endured for over a hundred years. There should be much more purposeful activity and regional intervention by the National government, including incentives and financial assistance for new firms and manufacturers to move into older industrial communities and risk their capital.

This degree of governmental involvement, and the application of central funds to this purpose, the National government was quite unable to give. Its policy of tariffs and imperial preference assisted the Midlands and the south rather than the exporting industries of Wales. Very little was done for south Wales at all in the thirties. There were some modest, small-scale efforts at industrial training, to try to equip unemployed men and women with new skills, but this was all very limited. The Committee on Women's Training and Employment, for instance, set up courses at Aberdare, Abertillery, Bargoed, and Cardiff among other places, but the main consequence was to train adults and juveniles for the unskilled work of domestic service, in any case a calling that would take them out of south Wales. By 1932, 50 per cent of the adult women and 72 per cent of the juvenile girls trained in this way found employment outside Wales.[14] This was no kind of answer to deep-seated problems of the coalfield.

There was, at long last, something of a new departure in government policy in 1934. A committee of inquiry was held into industrial conditions in certain 'depressed' areas in 1933–4.[15] It painted the anticipated bleak picture of conditions in south Wales. In the eastern part of the coalfield, in particular, from the Rhondda to Pontypool, unemployment was especially severe, running to 44.5 per cent compared with 28.6 per cent in the western anthracite region. The proportion of insured coalminers that was wholly unemployed or temporarily out of work ran to 45.5 per cent. For iron- and steelworkers, the

---

[14] *Industrial Survey*, chapter VIII.

[15] *Report on the Investigation into Industrial Conditions in Certain Depressed Areas* (Cmd. 4728), Parl. Papers, 1933–4, xiii.

proportion was 40 per cent. The whole of the region from Merthyr Tydfil to Brynmawr was in particularly serious straits. No less than 36.8 per cent of the working population of Brynmawr had been without regular work for over five years. However, the general drift of the report, reminiscent of so many discussions of the economic problems of rural Ireland in the nineteenth century, was that the problems of Wales should be exported. Able-bodied workers, especially the young, and eventually their families also, should be ferried across the British Isles to the Midlands and the south-east of England. Still, the committee did recognize that such a pyrrhic solution, involving the deliberate destruction of long-established industrial communities, was at best a long-term programme. In any case, its practicability in sociological, and indeed in human, terms was in grave doubt.

Something much more immediate needed to be done to assist south Wales at once. To this end, with unwonted initiative, the government passed in 1934 a Special Areas (Development and Improvement) Act, under which a commissioner was appointed for each of four 'special' or distressed areas. This was followed up in 1936 by the Special Areas Reconstruction (Agreement) Act under which a Reconstruction Association was set up with a nominal capital of £1 million to provide financial assistance to employers or firms wishing to set up industries in the unattractive 'special' areas. Later on, more inducements were added, including the letting of factories and the offer of rent, rate, and tax relief to any firms willing to take the plunge into the 'depressed' regions of Britain. Among the four 'special areas', western Monmouthshire and most of Glamorgan, excluding the Cardiff–Barry areas and the district around Swansea, was designated as one. Sir Malcolm Stewart was appointed as Special Commissioner for Wales. He was MacDonald's nominee and not known to the Conservative members of the Cabinet. In 1935, the South Wales Industrial Development Council, that had been set up three years earlier, proposed the setting up of trading estates, among other novelties. However, as Lord Portal pointed out, the council included no major industrialists and illustrated the way in which south Wales had been by-passed by more recent phases of industrial development in Britain.

For the next few years, the special commission conducted its operations in Wales, until brought to an abrupt halt by the Second World War in 1939. Its annual reports from 1935 onwards were a tale of modest improvement. In 1935 it published an account of the investment grants made to south Wales, a small proportion of the £2 million allocated by parliament to assist in the economic rehabilitation of the 'special areas'. In 1936, the commission detected some signs of economic improvement in the coal and steel industries, and a fall in the number of the unemployed amongst the insured working population from 156,000 in December 1934 to 142,000 in December 1935. Grants of £9,500, a paltry enough sum in all conscience, had been offered to the Industrial Development Council of South Wales and Monmouthshire for 'research work'. Otherwise there was the usual story of the patchwork provision of amenities for the unemployed—social settlements in Trealaw, Merthyr Tydfil, Bargoed, Risca, and elsewhere; school camps in a variety of locations on the coast, from Pembrey to Barry; a sports club at Abertillery, a recreation club in Blaenavon and so on. Measured by the desperate seriousness of the industrial situation in south Wales the optimism and complacency of the commission seem hard to endorse.

In 1937, there were few more tangible signs of progress.[16] No new factories were recorded as having been founded in the Welsh 'special areas' since the previous year, while the tally of unemployed had hardly fallen at all. More seriously, the Welsh coalfield had failed to match other coalfields in keeping abreast of an expanding home demand from industry; unemployment amongst miners had not greatly diminished. There had been growing economic expansion in parts of south Wales, but almost entirely in coastal towns such as Swansea and Barry which were outside the scope of the Special Areas Act. The commissioners spoke cautiously (but apparently in all seriousness) of the possibilities of encouraging tourism in the mining valleys. The new open-air swimming pool and public park in Caerphilly, hard by the ramparts of the Norman castle, were cited. But it seemed improbable that the valley communities, with the slag heaps and other environmental scars of the industrial revolution all around them, would be able to improve their economic prospects by encouraging tourists in significant numbers.

In 1938, there was at last significant progress to record, notably the new powers given to the government to buy up industrial sites to offer inducements to new industries. These had been implemented in many areas and new factories were to be set up in Dowlais, Merthyr, Porth, Llantarnam, and Cwmbran. There was also one very important new concept—the first government-assisted trading estate at Treforest, just north of Cardiff. The first factory was occupied there in 1938. By the end of 1939, there were sixty to seventy firms in production at Treforest, some of them run by Austrian and Czech refugees fleeing from totalitarian regimes on the continent. In all, 2,500 workers were employed at Treforest by September 1939, and new opportunities were opening up for male and for female workers.[17] The trading estate scheme was to be much more actively developed after 1945, and the Treforest estate much expanded. On balance, it was much the most hopeful and constructive new idea to emerge from the years of the special commissioners' operations. In 1939 further progress was reported, even in such depressed communities as Dowlais and the Rhondda. A quite impressive series of public-utility projects undertaken by various local authorities in Glamorgan and Monmouthshire was listed. Two new factories were set up in

[16] *Third Report of the Commissioners for the Special Areas* (Cmd. 5303), Parl. Papers, 1936–7, xii.

[17] J. F. Rees in *The Cardiff Region: a Survey* (Cardiff, 1960), p. 109.

the Rhondda in 1939, the larger being Polikoffs who specialized in clothing manufacture: this was partly financed by a loan from the Nuffield Trust.

By the coming of war, then, there was some progress to record, notably at Treforest. But the efforts of the special commissioners were generally meagre. Their powers were limited and the capital placed at their disposal absurdly small. Malcolm Stewart, the hard-working head of the commission, complained how his efforts were obstructed by bureaucratic restrictions imposed by the Ministry of Labour. Further, grants could be made to local authorities only for public projects 'for which no specific grant is payable by any Government Department',[18] a serious limitation. A few small schemes such as sewage works were nowhere near sufficient. While unemployment began to fall in south Wales from 1936 onwards, this was attributable to the indirect effects of the new boost to the British economy generally given by increased rearmament. Relative to some other, more thriving parts of Britain, the Welsh coalfield actually fell back. In any case, with its continuing high unemployment in the coal, steel, and tinplate industries, it showed far fewer signs of recovery than did, for instance, the mid-industrial belt of Scotland with its far more diversified industrial base. On the whole, the special areas development was an ill-conceived, half-hearted palliative devised by Neville Chamberlain and other financially-orthodox ministers. Its record between 1934 and 1939 amply confirmed the criticisms made by left-wing socialists such as Aneurin Bevan and by radical young Conservatives like Harold Macmillan of the 'Next Five Years' group, when it was first launched by the National government.

Something approaching a recovery from depression in Wales required much more direct intervention from the government. But this ran entirely counter to the economic policy that prevailed in the thirties. There is, indeed, only one example of partial intervention of a direct kind by the National government in these years, though one that later became symbolic with the introduction of the more vigorous 'location of industries' policy after 1945. The old Ebbw Vale steelworks had been closed down in 1929, putting 10,000 steelworkers out of employment. There was a prolonged effort by the local authority and by the local MP, Aneurin Bevan, to try to put pressure on the government and the special areas commissioners to get the works reopened. Finally in 1935 there was loud protest in south Wales when Sir William Firth of Richard Thomas & Co. announced that a new strip-mill would be located at Redbourn in Lincolnshire, rather than in Wales. It was claimed that this would enable the firm to concentrate all the processing of steel and tinplate production on the one site, and make their processes continuous, thus enormously increasing industrial efficiency. However, there were other factors at work. Firth, regarded as something of a rogue elephant amongst

---

[18] Marquand, *South Wales Needs a Plan*, p. 92.

British steelmakers, was personally friendly with Aneurin Bevan.[19] In addition, there was a massive campaign in Monmouthshire where it was argued that the works at Ebbw Vale should be reopened to house the new strip-mill. It was argued that it was not inefficiency which had led to the closure of Ebbw Vale, but rather tariffs which had affected tinplate manufacturers who could no longer get cheap steel bars from abroad. Ebbw Vale, it was claimed, had good coking coal, limestone, and water supplies, added to readily available blast-furnaces. There was also, of course, appalling local unemployment.

The Welsh Labour MPs mobilized and sent a deputation to Baldwin, the Prime Minister, in 1935. They were reinforced by the authority of Lloyd George who pleaded the cause of the economic revival of his nation. Baldwin appears to have put some pressure on Richard Thomas to alter their plans and it was then announced that the new plant was to be established at the reopened Ebbw Vale works instead. In September 1938 the strip-mill began production at Ebbw Vale. A highly modern iron, steel, and tinplate complex was thus set up there, the most technologically advanced of its kind, with two blast furnaces, three open-hearth furnaces, a fifty-six-inch strip-mill, and a cold reduction plant. In the perspective of the inter-war years, the decision of Richard Thomas to site the new plant at Ebbw Vale was a unique example of co-operation between private industry, the local authority, members of parliament, and the central government. It was by no means free from criticism, then or later. Many experts argued that it was uneconomic to reverse the long-established trend of moving industry away from the rim of the coalfield and to set up a major plant in the inland heart of the valleys where costs would inevitably be high. Siting the new works at Lincolnshire, or indeed west Wales would, on strictly economic grounds, have been more appropriate. There was, in fact, some opposition to the Ebbw Vale decision in west Wales where industrialists now feared for the future of the local steel plant at Swansea and Llanelli. Further new development in steel might now take place at Newport or elsewhere in Monmouthshire, rather than in west Wales. There was a good deal of new investment in the Ebbw Vale plant in the 1940s and 1950s, especially in the setting up of new electrolytic processes. But, in the end, Ebbw Vale proved to be a casualty of high costs as the markets for steel contracted in the later 1960s. In 1975–6 the steel-making plant established after so much controversy in 1938 was closed down for ever, with thousands of steelworkers made redundant. On the other hand, it was clearly right that sociological rather than narrowly economic considerations should move the authorities in the thirties, with the enormous structural unemployment in Monmouthshire and elsewhere in south Wales. Otherwise, the story of government intervention to try to alleviate the economic decay and social hardship of south Wales in the inter-war period was a relatively blank one.

[19] Michael Foot, *Aneurin Bevan*, vol. i, pp. 216–17.

The main consequence of these traumatic changes in the Welsh economy, with which governments were unable effectively to grapple, was really felt elsewhere. It was to be seen not so much in the formal indices of economic decline, measured in statistical terms, but in the cataclysmic effect upon the social and cultural life of whole communities, until very recently thriving and prosperous. Even at a distance of over forty years, the experience of south Wales and its people between 1923 and 1939 bears all the hallmarks of a major tragedy. The most obvious aspect of this is to be seen in the immense impact of mass unemployment. As has been seen, it stood at over 50 per cent of the insured population in places such as Merthyr Tydfil, Dowlais, Blaina, and Brynmawr in the early thirties. At its worst in December 1933, the Ministry of Labour recorded the number of unemployed in Wales as a whole, north and south, as 208,000, which amounted to 32.3 per cent of the insured adult population. Compared with the situation in London and the south-east of England at this time, the position in south Wales was three to four times worse. Even in 1939, unemployment in south Wales alone stood at well over 100,000. In the Rhondda valleys in 1934, with their total dependence on the steam-coal industry, 60.8 per cent of the men registered at the unemployment office at Pontypridd, and 63.7 per cent of those registered at the Ferndale office were recorded as unemployed, according to special areas commissioners. In Merthyr, the proportion was 69.1 per cent, and in Dowlais, where the steel-works was closed, a staggering 73.4 per cent. The commissioners blandly recorded that 2,030 men in Dowlais, out of an insured male population of 4,392, were 'surplus to the normal needs of existing industries and services'.[20] The western valleys of Monmouthshire, from Brynmawr to Blaina, the Aberdare, and the Maesteg district in central Glamorgan (especially the Pontycymmer region) showed an equally disturbing picture.

The impact of all this on whole towns and villages was calamitous, with able-bodied young-old men hanging around street corners, 'on the dole', for years at a time. Local shops, services, and entertainment went into decline. With so little to retain its active working population, community life in all its aspects steadily shrank. Chapel congregations diminished, kept going in many places by the elderly or by miners who had left work early through industrial disease or injury. In addition, congregations often found it financially impossible to support their ministers. In Cwmavon in 1930 it was reported that all nine chapels there were without a minister. Marriages had to take place at the registry office at Neath, ten miles away.[21] Merthyr, Dowlais, and the Rhondda valleys also showed marked decline in the nonconformist pastorate. Many famous choirs disappeared from the musical life of Wales as tenors or baritones became harder to find. Local rugby teams found it difficult to retain vigorous young men. A particular factor operating here during the

---

[20] *Report on the Investigation*, loc. cit.
[21] *Welsh Outlook*, March 1930, p. 60.

depression was the inducements offered by Rugby League clubs in the north of England to unemployed rugby players in the Welsh valleys to turn professional. Many star players 'went north' into permanent exile; in one year, virtually the entire Pontypool pack departed from the Welsh rugby scene. Entire communities seemed to be dissolving.

Not surprisingly, much of the publicity gained by Welsh workers in the thirties came from their involvement in marches by the unemployed to London to try to put pressure on public opinion. One of the stock images of that period, too, is of cloth-capped Welsh miners, like Dai and Shinkin depicted on the kerb of the Charing Cross Road in Idris Davies's bitter poem, 'Do You Remember 1926?', singing hymns before London theatre queues in the hope of winning a few coppers from the affluent citizens. Some historians of late have tended to paint a more cheerful picture of the thirties than once used to be prevalent. No doubt, amongst the owner-occupiers of London, the home counties, and the east Midlands, with their cars, their housing estates, their thriving new light industries based on consumer durables, hire purchase and the newer technology, the thirties were not such a bad time in which to live. But in south Wales, this verdict cannot possibly be accepted. The thirties there were a time when a whole society was crucified by mass unemployment and near-starvation. Much of it made only an indirect impact on the public consciousness. Emphasis was laid then, and later, on Edward VIII's visible, and no doubt genuinely-held, sense of shock at the poverty he beheld in Dowlais in November 1936. 'Something must be done', the King observed, and he became something of a public martyr in south Wales at the time of the abdication a few weeks later. More relevant, perhaps, was an open letter that circulated in the streets of Pontypool at the time of his visit. 'Today you will be visiting the towns and villages of our valleys, and a valley blighted by the dead hand of poverty. We regret that your tour has been planned in such a way that the terrible effects of this poverty will not be seen.'[22] As Haig's chief of staff was told in 1917 as he surveyed the muddy shambles and carnage after the battle of Passchendaele, 'it was worse further on up'.

The most drastic human effect of this prolonged and mass unemployment was to be seen in the vast emigration from south Wales. Even though the school population rose steadily, and the proportion of pupils over sixteen increased from 16 per cent in 1930–1 to 19.2 per cent in 1933–4, the prospects for school-leavers of employment in their own communities were extremely bleak. There was a steady drift of younger Welshmen and their families to the newer industries of the south-east of England and to the Midlands. There was a more planned migration, too, orchestrated by Neville Chamberlain after 1931 and assisted by the Ministry of Labour, in the transfer of tens of thousands of Welsh working people to the London suburbs of Hounslow or Dagenham, to the engineering works at Coventry, the light industries of

[22] *Western Mail,* 19 November 1936.

Watford and Slough, and the Morris motor-car works at Cowley, Oxford. The Welshness of this university citadel now extended beyond the academic portals of Jesus College. The Oxford Welsh Glee Singers flourished, for instance. In Oxford and elsewhere, Welsh migrants played something of the same kind of role as political activists and industrial militants, active in the Labour Party and trade-union branches, that Irish migrants had done a generation earlier.

The net effect was that 430,000 Welsh people left their country between 1921 and 1940. Curiously enough, the population of Wales remained fairly constant at this time, due to the high rate of natural increase amongst the population that remained. But without doubt, there was a vast displacement of people from the valleys. The population of the Rhondda fell 13 per cent in the twenties and probably by a higher proportion still in the thirties: this is impossible to quantify as no census of population was taken in 1941 owing to the war. In all, its population declined from 162,000 to 111,000 in 1951, with a disproportionately high ratio of elderly men and women left behind. Probably no other part of Europe showed such an extraordinary loss of population over this period. Merthyr showed an equally alarming loss of people. A total of 16,900 people left the town between 1921 and 1931: a further 9,668 were assessed as having left by 1939.[23] Throughout the mining valleys, most acutely in those of eastern Glamorgan and western Monmouthshire, indeed over virtually the whole of south Wales outside the ports of Swansea and Cardiff, thousands of young people were leaving their native land every year, leaving their closely-knit village communities to work in more impersonal but at least operational English factories, and to live in anonymous suburban housing estates instead of back-to-back valley terraces with their warm neighbourliness. Almost as acutely as for the migrants who crossed the Atlantic to the United States in the previous century, it was a violent uprooting and cultural shock. But it was invariably and necessarily a permanent one, since, as Thomas Jones observed in a famous lecture, the exiled natives (*yr alltudion* of Welsh folklore) never returned.[24]

For the population that remained in the valleys to battle out the depression, the quality of life cannot have been anything other than meagre. Life on the dole was desperate indeed for an unemployed worker in south Wales, indeed a struggle for bare existence. At the end of the twenties, an unemployed man received 23s. a week for himself and his family, plus 2s. per child. From this, perhaps 6s. to 7s. had to be paid out as rent for what accommodation he was able to obtain. From what money remained, all food, clothing, and other necessities had somehow to be found. In any case, the financial strain of maintaining the unemployed was increasingly beyond the means of impoverished local authorities in south Wales: there was much talk of a breakdown of

[23] J. W. England, op. cit., p. 91.
[24] Thomas Jones, *The Native never Returns* (a lecture to the Cymmrodorion Society, 1942).

local government in Wales during the thirties. The rate income of local authorities had largely disappeared with the closure of mines and steel-works, while pushing up the rates for what industry survived merely led to still higher unemployment. There were, in the thirties, six out of thirteen county councils where a penny rate produced less than £1,000; in half of the thirty county boroughs, it produced less than £100, and the same appalling story was told in twenty-four of the fifty-nine district councils. In these circumstances, help had to be obtained from outside. Rates in Merthyr per head in 1935–6 amounted to 28s. 5d., of which public assistance amounted to nearly 15s. In 1938, so PEP recorded, the amount of unemployment assistance to the unemployed of Merthyr equalled over twice the entire rateable value of the town. It was said that the average British taxpayer had to pay over £1 a week simply to keep the average family in Merthyr alive. Meanwhile, the Unemployment Assistance Board set up in 1934 created enormous resentment in south Wales as in other industrial areas, for its bureaucratic and seemingly inhuman approach. The full indignities of the 'genuinely seeking work' provision, often accompanied by financial and even moral inquisitions of the unemployed man, the rigours of the means test which entailed minute investigation of the savings, kinship structure, marital status, and other aspects of a working man's existence provoked frequent explosions of anger. Being kept alive on these terms was scarcely worth while.

It was clear that the social provision afforded by these impoverished local and central authorities was quite incapable of tackling the problems thrown up by the depression years. Working-class housing in south Wales, already far below standards in much of England, went further into decay, as the Welsh Housing and Development Association Yearbooks and the Inquiry into the Anti-Tuberculosis Service in 1939 sombrely recorded. Wales had already taken less advantage of the public housing acts of 1919, 1923, and 1924 than had other parts of Britain: in all, they yielded only 55,750 completed houses down to the end of the twenties. Nor was much use made of Arthur Greenwood's Slum Clearance Act of 1930. With the contraction of funds and heavy unemployment in the building industry, the number of new houses built in Wales either by local authorities or through private enterprise fell steadily from 10,851 completed in 1926 to only 1,410 in 1931.[25] Only after 1933 was there much improvement: 8,257 houses were erected in 1935. Much of the housing in south Wales was notoriously sub-standard and deteriorated throughout the period. Allen Hutt reported in 1933 that 35 per cent of the working-class houses in Swansea were fifty to a hundred years old.[26] In Cardiff, the percentage of houses containing more than one family increased from 28.3 per cent in 1925 to 57.8 per cent in 1927. Yet these two towns were administered by local authorities whose energy and public spirit in building

---

[25] Welsh Housing and Development Yearbook, 1927–32, passim.
[26] Allen Hutt, The Condition of the Working Class in Britain (London, 1933), pp. 10–11.

assisted houses won high praise from the Clement Davies Committee in 1939. The problem was simply beyond the powers even of the most public-spirited councils.

Medical officers of health gave alarming accounts of the extent of slum housing. They reported that in 1930 there were 2,025 houses in Cardiff unfit for human habitation; the total for Swansea was 946 and for Merthyr Tydfil 891. Further, in Merthyr there were 118 basement or cellar dwellings of extreme squalor, and no less than 400 basement tenements in the Rhondda. Little could be done to improve, let alone eradicate, unventilated or damp houses that were infected with tuberculosis and other diseases. Indeed, slum housing and lung disease in Wales were intimately connected. Working people had to live in insanitary terrace houses in a grave state of disrepair, frequently menaced by pit flooding, or by landslips resulting from the intensity of coal mining in the area. Every now and then there would be an alarming movement of coal tips, though no tragedy comparable with that of Aberfan in 1966. Schools which had once been proud symbols of the rise of elementary and secondary education in the later Victorian era now became increasingly derelict and unhygienic, with inadequate sanitation or heating and few facilities for drying the clothes of rain-sodden children who had made their way to school in bad weather.

It followed that one feature of social life in the valleys in the inter-war period which was consistently alarming was the state of public health. Authorities invariably commented on the shortage and high cost of hospital facilities, the lack of adequate preventive medicine, and the paucity of medical and nursing services (although one of the very few bright aspects of the depression was that the ranks of St. John's ambulancemen swelled considerably in the thirties owing to the large number of unemployed men available). Public hygiene in areas like the Rhondda or Dowlais, for instance in the condition of the sewage system, was a by-word for squalor. The standards of health inevitably fell sharply. The figures for mortality and for malnutrition were markedly more grim for Wales, north and south, than for other parts of Britain. The Ministry of Health's annual reports on maternity services in the thirties and the special *Report on Maternal Mortality in Wales* (Cmd. 5423) showed that illness among mothers and death in childbirth were significantly higher than for England or Scotland. In 1937, the overall death rate for England and Wales was 9.3 per cent per 1,000 persons. By contrast in the Rhondda valleys, it stood at 13.4 per cent. Medical Officers of Health attributed this grim fact simply to the undernourished, ill-housed, ill-clad condition of the population during these years of poverty and unemployment. The statistics for child illness were equally dismal. In 1935, 14.6 per cent of all the children in the Rhondda were declared to be undernourished. They were lacking in good, nutritious food, and in adequate supplies of fresh milk, this last being particularly extraordinary in view of the flourishing (and subsidized) state of the liquid milk industry in Wales at the time. Children were frequently underclothed and not unusually went barefoot to school. Money collected towards the royal Silver Jubilee celebrations in 1935 went towards the purchase of boots at a Rhondda school. As elsewhere, young children were particularly the victims of their valleys' status as 'a depressed area'.

South Wales in the thirties, then, showed all the symptoms of a sub-standard society in terms of housing, health, and a decent environment. The statistics for industrial accidents, for industrial diseases such as silicosis and pneumoconiosis were generally more gloomy for south Wales than for any region of Britain. So they were for serious infections such as diphtheria. One scourge, however, appeared to be almost a peculiarly Welsh phenomenon. This was tuberculosis, popularly known as TB, or *y dicái* in Welsh. The *Medical Officer* noted how all the Celtic races had been pushed towards the west where they faced the warm wet winds of the Atlantic. Hence their vulnerability to TB.[27] There had been a fierce campaign against this illness in Wales since David Davies, Thomas Jones, and others had launched the Welsh National Memorial Association back in 1910. The Association had formed voluntary agreements with local authorities to attack TB in various localities, and until the late twenties the statistics were encouraging. Seventeen sanatoriums had been built or adapted for the purpose, among them Madame Patti's old home at Craig-y-Nos in the upper Swansea valley. The *Lancet* noted that between 1905 and 1925 the death-rate from TB in Wales was considerably diminished. The *Welsh Outlook* showed that the rate had fallen from 1,468 per million in 1911 to 896 in 1932.[28] Even so, making further progress was virtually beyond impoverished and harassed local authorities in Wales. In any case, insanitary environmental conditions and malnutrition during the depression years in south Wales had led to the progress made earlier in combating TB being suspended. The death-rate now remained stationary in Wales: it was not to fall again until after 1940.

After much public outcry, a powerful departmental committee was set up under Clement Davies, the Liberal MP for Montgomeryshire. After some controversy as to the scope of its findings, it presented its report in March 1939. It was a terrible indictment of social conditions in Wales, rural and industrial, of insanitary and slum housing, of long-condemned school build-ings still in active use for educating younger children, of out-of-date processes still being used to deal with sewage and with industrial waste, of polluted water supplies, of failures to provide clean, fresh milk and adequate midday meals for schoolchildren, and other social horrors. These were endemic in the industrial regions of south Wales with their mass unemployment. But the account of the incidence of TB in rural Wales made it appear that progress there too had only been piecemeal since the foundation of the National

[27] *The Medical Officer*, 18 March 1933.
[28] *The Lancet*, 18 March 1939; Dr D. A. Powell, 'Health', *Welsh Outlook*, December 1933.

Memorial Association in 1911. In all, Wales supplied the seven counties that headed the list in England and Wales for deaths from tuberculosis. While for England and Wales, as a whole, mortality was 724 per million of the population, in Caernarvonshire, Merioneth, Anglesey, and Cardiganshire the figures were over one thousand and in many areas were getting worse.[29] The committee made some sweeping recommendations, many of which were destined to be shelved during the war years, for creating new units of administration to cope with TB on a more effective basis, and for a wider network of medical officers of health and sanitary inspectors on a full-time basis, to cover the whole of the principality. The report was warmly applauded by professional journals concerned with public health. 'It is at once a scientific dissertation on tuberculosis, a text book of public health and sociology, a manual of housing and a post-graduate course in the administration of local government services. As to the last-named, after the publication of this report, let PEP look to its laurels.'[30] The entire effect was markedly to shock the public conscience and galvanize it into supporting urgent action on this aspect of the social pollution in Wales that the depression years only made worse. A new anti-tuberculosis association, designed to draw in community action to assist with governmental agencies, was founded, although by 1942 this, too, was being attacked for inadequacy in dealing with the 'white scourge'.

One striking fact, however, that emerged from the findings of Clement Davies's inquiry into tuberculosis was the marked divergence between rural and industrial Wales. It revealed not only the failures of the system to cope with TB in Wales, but also the inability of many district and county councils to undertake their own preventive work. The voluntary system created by the Memorial Association was simply not enough. On the other hand, this situation was much more pronounced in rural areas. It was here that middle-class, cost-conscious local councillors and officials showed up so badly before the inquiry. Time and again, fear of adding to the burden of rates led to the neglect of vital work in preventing the spread of a disease acknowledged to be a unique and appalling scourge. In addition, there was indolence in amalgamating small local authorities, while sometimes nepotism intruded in appointing unqualified sanitary inspectors or not appointing full-time medical officers. By contrast, the local authorities of industrial south Wales, even in such places as the Rhondda, Merthyr, and Brynmawr, which were suffering from serious financial problems and a contraction of income owing to the fall in rateable values during the depression, were zealous in fighting TB and other lung diseases. Here, social duty came before concern for the financial protection of ratepayers. Labour-led local authorities in south

[29] Ministry of Health: Report of the Committee of Inquiry into the Anti-Tuberculosis Services in Wales and Monmouthshire, 1939, p. 24.
[30] *Medical Officer*, 8 April 1939.

Wales maintained a high level of expenditure upon health, housing, education, and other necessities. The local authority in Merthyr in 1933 contrived to ensure that over 90 per cent of the town's secondary school pupils had free places, while those in Newport and Swansea fought hard against the Board of Education's means test and sought to make the fees chargeable in intermediate and secondary schools largely nominal. Indeed, the local councils sometimes went beyond the levels of spending permitted. The Bedwellty Board of Guardians in the Rhymney valley in 1927 had fallen foul of Neville Chamberlain, then the Minister of Health, by spending money on poor relief beyond the precepts allowed by central government. In particular, there was a massive granting of relief on loans. The authorities here were merely superseded, not actually imprisoned for defiance of the law, as has been the fate of the Poplar Board of Guardians in the East End of London a few years earlier. The replacement Guardians of Bedwellty discontinued the large-scale issue of clothing, books, and coal to recipients of out-relief, and also the practice of giving relief to men living in lodging houses and single men without dependants who were not householders. The total out-relief paid out by the Bedwellty Poor Law Union was cut from £528,777 in the year to March 1927 to only £38,322 for the half-year ending 30 September 1927.[31] The total paid out in 1927–8 amounted to only £31,453, and no further borrowing had proved necessary.[32] The advocates of strict economy, whatever the social cost, had won the day.

However, the Bedwellty case did spur on the Ministry to a more centralized approach to the local services. In 1929 Chamberlain organized the replacement of the old poor law authorities by new public assistance committees, run by the local authorities and far more closely supervised in their activities. For all that, during the thirties local authorities in south Wales generally spent up to the limit of their legal capacity in trying to cope with the social consequences of unemployment and depression. The tuberculosis inquiry bore all this out. It showed that, despite all the hardship and poverty of the thirties, the social conscience and communal feeling in the valleys, as expressed through their elected representatives, shone through undimmed. Even in the worst rigours of the depressed years, through formal activity by the local authorities, through a mass of informal voluntary acts of neighbourliness by private organizations and by ordinary citizens, through small donations from the Carnegie Trust and of course by indirect subventions from the taxpayer notably through public assistance, the Welsh coalfield somehow managed to survive a social and psychological crisis that would have left many communities prostrate and helpless.

[31] *Report of the Guardians of the Bedwellty Union*, 1927. (Cmd. 2976), Parl. Papers, 1927, xi; Siân Rhiannon Williams, 'The Bedwellty Board of Guardians and the Default Act of 1927', *Llafur* (Spring 1979), pp. 65–77
[32] *Report* of the Guardians, 1928 (Cmd. 3141), Parl. Papers, 1928, xii, p. 5.

The quality of social life in industrial Wales during these terrible years is hard to assess or to understand for a later generation that did not live through it. The creation of the welfare state after 1945 erected a massive barrier of incomprehension between those who had endured the trials of the thirties and the more fortunate who came after. Of couse, despite mass unemployment and mass emigration, life went on during the depression. South Wales remained in some respects a lively, bustling place in spite of it all, especially perhaps in towns like Swansea and Cardiff somewhat removed from the endemic decay of the inland mining and steel communities. The *South Wales Daily Post* in Swansea (which became the *Evening Post* in 1932), for which the young Dylan Thomas worked as a reporter, conveyed the impression of a vital, self-confident town, despite the impact of the slump. Religious and musical life continued to exist. It was still a land of song: in 1937 Sir Malcolm Sargent conducted the Three Valleys choral festival at Mountain Ash. Miners still managed the occasional solace of the Sunday-school outing so deliriously described by Gwyn Thomas in *A Welsh Eye*.

There was always the anodyne of sporting activity, now more varied than ever. There had been since 1921 a Glamorgan cricket team in the county championship, though it aroused somewhat limited interest at first beyond the coastal ports of Swansea and Cardiff, and in any case usually finished at the bottom of the championship table. There was more interest in association football, in Swansea, Cardiff, Newport, and Wrexham. In 1927 Cardiff City won the FA cup by beating Arsenal at Wembley Stadium. But soccer was not really a Welsh institution; appropriately, the (fortuitous) winning goal was scored for Cardiff by a Scotsman called Ferguson. It resulted from an error by the Arsenal goalkeeper, a Welshman, Dan Lewis. Rugby continued to capture far more support amongst the sporting population of south Wales, even though the Welsh international team was much depleted by migrations to the paid ranks of the rugby league in the north of England and fared badly in international matches throughout the twenties and early thirties. There was recovery from 1933, when England were beaten at Twickenham for the first time in twenty years, and a further historic victory over the New Zealanders at Cardiff in 1935. Ironically this owed less to local products of the valleys than to young public-school men coached at Llandovery or Rydal and then at Oxford or (more usually) Cambridge. In 1935, the entire Welsh back division against the New Zealand 'all blacks' was university-trained, a kind of social revolution in its modest way. Boxing was another opium for the Welsh masses, especially the heavy-weights. Tommy Farr, an unemployed ex-fairground fighter from the historic town of Tonypandy, aroused much fervour in 1937 when he almost defeated the American world heavy-weight champion, Joe Louis, in New York. But this was all transient escapism from the no less brutal realities of a jobless, hopeless future.

The social atmosphere of south Wales is perhaps best approached through the new literature of poverty that it threw up. There were many Welsh examples of George Orwell's account of the road that led to Wigan Pier, or Walter Greenwood's pathetic saga of 'Love on the Dole'. Much of the literature in Wales was, inevitably, highly partisan and often intensely ideological. Perhaps for that reason, it captured imperishably the heroism, compassion, and comradeship of the working people of Wales during these years of suffering and privation.

Lewis Jones, a leading figure in the Communist Party, an active member of the unemployed marches in the thirties, and a fiery crusader on behalf of Republican Spain, wrote two remarkable novels which combined insight into character and the tender aspects of human relationships with vivid accounts of the social and industrial struggles at the time. *Cwmardy* in 1937 covered the period from the turn of the century down to the end of the First World War. *We Live,* published posthumously in 1939, was a further extraordinary saga, mostly autobiographical, of the experiences of the miners from Black Friday in 1921 down to the later thirties. Lewis Jones died, tragically and unexpectedly, at the age of forty-one in January 1939: his death was an immense loss to imaginative social literature. Bert Coombes, a Wolverhampton man by origin, who worked forty-two years underground in the anthracite pits of the Swansea valley and elsewhere, produced a remarkable series of works, an autobiography, short stories, documentaries, and film scripts, from the late thirties onwards. He first attracted the attention of John Lehmann, the editor of *New Writing*, with his short stories. They etched the work experience of the Welsh miners, the hardship and the physical dangers in unforgettable detail. His autobiography, *These Poor Hands*, set mainly in the twenties and published by the Left Book Club in 1939, sold 60,000 copies in three months and earned high praise from J. B. Priestley amongst other reviewers. Later there followed *Those Clouded Hills* (1944) and *Miners' Day* (1945). Coombes's writings were, perhaps, all the more effective for their precise, unemotional tone and for avoiding the kind of Marxist polemics that intruded in the novels of Lewis Jones. Idris Davies, a Monmouthshire miner, who suffered serious injury in a pit accident, became a notable poet of protest, most obviously in his celebrated epics, *Gwalia Deserta* and *Angry Summer*. In simple and compelling language, which earned the admiration of T. S. Eliot (who greatly helped Idris Davies in having his poems published) they recaptured the passion and courage of those years. The general strike was evoked with especial feeling, 'that summer of soups and speeches, the sunlight on the idle wheels and the deserted crossings'. Other literature of the period was less class-conscious, more suffused with Christian mercy and forbearance, even resignation. Kitchener Davies's Welsh-language poem, 'The Wind that is Blowing' (1952) is a most impressive example here. Taken together, this vein of literature recreated more effectively than any other source the essence of the impact of the depression on social life in south Wales:

it managed to avoid the well-meant sentimentality of the film, *Proud Valley*, made in 1939 and starring (improbably) Paul Robeson.

Some of this literature may be generalized or idealized in tone. A pedantic historian's assessment could suggest that the depression varied in intensity from valley to valley: as has been seen, the coastal ports and the anthracite coalfield in the western valleys fared relatively well during much of this harsh period. There were more fundamental causes of the depression than the brutality and inhumanity of the coalowners and the authorities generally, real enough though these factors were. But, in terms of the way that the depression years shaped popular sensibilities and folk memories, it is perhaps through the literary medium, through the art of the novelist, the poet, or the folk remembrancer, that the reality of desperate suffering is best experienced.

What emerges very clearly is that this south Wales world during the era of depression and mass unemployment remained an intensely local one. It was local institutions that loomed largest in recollections of the period. It was the miners' club or welfare hall that provided intellectual stimulus and human comradeship—and, often, political inspiration as well. The miners' libraries accumulated from that period, and mercifully retained in archive form by a later generation after 1970,[33] are a remarkable testimony to the variety of political, economic, philosophical, and imaginative literature that refreshed the minds of the Welsh workers. In the mid-thirties, it was calculated that there were 109 workmen's or welfare institutes in south Wales, containing about 750,000 books. Thomas Jones feared in 1934 that these institutes were losing their appeal: 'the cinema and billiards were going strong and education was going weak'.[34] But by contrast with the world of post-1945, this was a remarkably cultured, inquiring generation in the thirties, for all the pressures of mass poverty which encouraged cheap forms of light relief. It was often the workers' educational association or the miners' institute in the village that kept alive the educational and cultural aspirations of the movement for adult education and improvement. Equally, it was often the local 'Co-op' which loomed largest as a source of food and other supplies, and even more as a provider of ready credit on easy or virtually non-existent rates of interest. Without the 'Co-ops', indeed, it is difficult to see how many miners' and steelworkers' families could have remained alive in the depression years. The Co-ops also helped keep the industrial struggles in being in 1921 and 1926, and during the 'stay-down' stoppages directed against company unionism which will be described in Chapter 10. With all these local centres of activity, the close-knit loyalties of the valley communities became even more solid and intense.

In some respects, of course, the pressures of the depression brought working men and women in south Wales closer together to their comrades in

[33] In the South Wales Miners' Library, Maes-yr-Haf, Swansea.
[34] Thomas Jones, *Leeks and Daffodils*, p. 137.

other depressed industrial areas. The marches of the unemployed, the protests against the means test, in which men like Lewis Jones and Will Paynter were active in south Wales, were directed against common class enemies. They knew no regional or national frontiers. The crisis of British capitalism was nation-, indeed worldwide. On the other hand, the very intensity of suffering in south Wales, the very dependence of these mining villages upon their own resources, financial and moral, their continuing sense of a shared historical heritage, made them all the more cohesive and self-reliant. In that sense, an economic depression which bade fair to emasculate the Welshness of the south Wales valleys by destroying them as communities and as economic units actually intensified that emotion in some ways. Loyalty to purely local institutions, notably the old 'Fed' as the South Wales Miners' Federation had come affectionately to be called, became the more profound. A Welsh-speaking president of the union like James Griffiths of Ammanford, elected in 1934, was admirably equipped to mobilize it. The industrial struggles that were fought under the banner of the 'Fed'—the fight against 'company unionism', the 'stay-down' strikes of 1935-6, and the campaign against the Schiller award on wages—were peculiarly Welsh developments. They drew attention to the specific geographical, social, and even cultural problems of the miners in Wales. They were expounded at pithead or miners' lodge level by miners' agents and other officials, often Communists like Arthur Horner, Will Paynter, or Will Whitehead, more directly in touch with the purely local grievances of the miner than was the necessarily more remote executive of the Federation. A sense of the isolation and detachment of the valley communities was reborn during these dreadful years and in some sense continued to flourish in later decades. Perhaps the later electoral success of Plaid Cymru in the valleys, in appealing to the local sentiment of electors in places like Merthyr, Aberdare, Caerphilly, and the Rhymney valley between 1967 and 1976 must be related to this longer-term tradition.

Thus, as the valleys somehow survived through the inter-war period, and even found some renewal of life during the years of the Second World War, their sense of a Welsh identity to some degree survived also. The unemployed of the coalfield were not merely stateless workers of the world, indistinguishable from a generalized mass proletariat. Nationality bound them together to some degree, as surely as did fraternity. Through the fires and torment of suffering in the twenties and thirties, they emerged with a somewhat more powerful sense of belonging to a community and a nation with a heritage and shared values all its own.

CHAPTER 9

WELSH AND ANGLO-WELSH

The onset of economic depression brought obvious and visible strains to the fabric of Welsh society and culture. More insidious and less apparent, but equally worrying for a growing number of contemporaries, was the emergence of more formidable cultural barriers than had hitherto existed between those who did and those who did not speak the Welsh language. The changing balance between these two communities added to the tension of life in the inter-war period.

The divisions between the Welsh and the 'Anglo-Welsh' were already familiar before the war. The fierce conflict in 1895–6 which saw the collapse of the Cymru Fydd League and of the first Welsh home rule movement was a clear portent of this change. The speeches at Newport in January 1896 of English-speaking businessmen such as Robert Bird of Cardiff, and indeed the role of D. A. Thomas himself, were testimony to the growing fears of the mercantile and industrial community of the coastal ports of south Wales, especially in the south-eastern strip ranging from Barry to Newport, of domination by an increasingly distinct Welsh-speaking population in the north and west of the country. In the years up to 1914, and even more in the war years, the cultural and linguistic divisions became more pronounced between the industrialized coalfield, especially eastern Glamorgan and Monmouthshire, and the mainly agricultural hinterland. Thus developed a yawning cultural gulf, widened by the flood of new immigrants from England, by the new capital investment in the south and the conformist, centralizing pressures eventually brought in by industry and commerce. It was a gulf between that 'Welsh Wales' of the natives and that 'American Wales' of the new immigrants in the south detected by Sir Alfred Zimmern in 1921.[1]

This new division was far more damaging than longer-standing linguistic differences between those extensions of the old marcher lordships along the eastern fringes of Wales—parts of Flintshire, the hundred of Maelor, eastern Montgomeryshire, Radnorshire, much of Breconshire, most of Monmouthshire east of the Usk. There were also a few English, or Anglo-Norman, enclaves further west, like the Gower peninsula in Glamorgan and the southern part of Pembrokeshire, to the south of Milford Haven. These cultural divides were long-established, almost a heritage of the Middle Ages

[1] Sir A. Zimmern, *My Impressions of Wales* (London, 1927), p. 37.

and the Edwardian conquest. The *mores* of the people, say between Welsh-speaking Llanidloes and English-speaking Welshpool in Montgomeryshire, or between Fishguard and Tenby in the different halves of Pembrokeshire were long happily adjusted to these worlds of dual cultures and dual identities. These divisions often had political implications: for instance, Liberalism in Montgomeryshire and in Pembrokeshire before 1914 roughly flourished with the Welsh-speaking regions west of Newtown or north of Haverfordwest. So, too, did the most powerful area of Montgomeryshire nonconformity, as 'S.R.' of Llanbrynmair had known well. But these facts were well known and caused little friction between the different communities. In any case, the self-confidence and buoyancy of Welsh national spokesmen in the period before 1914 about the future of their language and the fate of their culture generally meant that the increasing tendency for the majority of the people to be non-Welsh-speaking and for Welsh monoglots to dwindle to a small minority was held to pose no threat. Wales between 1896 and 1914 was a culturally divided land, but one happily resigned to peaceful co-existence.

The position after 1919 was very different. The decisive change, of course, was that the decline in the speaking of Welsh became very much more apparent. A new note of alarm about the future of the language, fears that it might disappear during the course of the century, entered public debate. So, too, did concern by the English-speaking community that the Welsh-speaking minority was being given undue priority in appointment to public positions. The censuses of 1901 and 1911 had already shown that the proportion of the population that spoke Welsh was falling, and that Welsh speakers, the bilingual and a fast diminishing number of monoglots, were in a numerical minority. But the statistical evidence up to 1911 still showed that the absolute number of those speaking Welsh was rising. If Welshmen living in England were included, it seemed probable that over a million British citizens spoke the Welsh language on the eve of the First World War, most of them as their first language for day-to-day communication and conversation. In addition, there were substantial communities in the United States and other overseas countries.

The 1921 census brought a rude awakening. When the returns were published in 1924 they revealed that only 929,183 of the population in Wales spoke Welsh, compared with 977,000 in 1911. The proportion of the population over three years old that this total represented had fallen from 43.5 per cent in 1911 to just 39 per cent ten years later. Some quite legitimate complaint could be made by Welsh newspapers such as the *Baner* about factors which might have led to an underestimate of the total of Welsh speakers in the census returns.[2] Over 100,000 Welsh people did not provide any information at all, while the inclusion in the figures of some English tourists, temporarily staying at seaside resorts as visitors, added further distortions. Certainly, the mechan-

[2] *Baner ac Amserau Cymru*, 1 May 1924.

ism of the census still had many built-in imperfections. For all that, the general picture was beyond dispute, and it was a melancholy one for Welsh patriots. The native language remained exceedingly strong in the predominantly rural counties of north, central, and west Wales. In Anglesey, over 87 per cent of the population spoke Welsh; a proportion of over 80 per cent was recorded in Merioneth, Cardiganshire, and Carmarthenshire as well. Yet, even here, there were disturbing trends. The heaviest fall, proportionately, in any county, as far as Welsh speakers were concerned, took place in Caernarvonshire. This was undoubtedly the result of the influx of English people, many of them elderly, to such coastal resorts as Llandudno and Conway. The steady anglicization of counties along the English border went on. Radnorshire hardly seemed to be a Welsh county at all by now. It was almost as English as Hereford or Shropshire. Flintshire was becoming increasingly English with the influx of holiday-makers to places such as Rhyl, the growth of industry along Deeside which brought in many workers from Lancashire, Cheshire, and Shropshire, and its role as a dormitory residential area for the wealthy middle class of Merseyside and the Wirral. In the industrial coalfield, the situation was the most serious of all. Two-thirds of the population of Glamorgan (66.9 per cent) were recorded as speaking only English. In Monmouthshire, the figure was well over 90 per cent (93.4 per cent) with only the Rhymney valley in the western fringe as a surviving Welsh enclave.

The decline in the speaking of Welsh went on steadily during the twenties. It was hastened by the steady erosion of so many Welsh-speaking rural communities through the depression of agriculture, which led to the migration of many young men and women, and by the shattering effect of mass unemployment and emigration on Welsh mining and tinplate towns and villages in south Wales. In the 1931 census, it was found that the proportion of Welsh speakers had fallen still further, to 37.2 per cent. There were still, extraordinarily enough, 97,932 recorded as monoglot Welsh—but in 1921 the figure had stood at 156,995. Those registered as bilingual were given as 811,329, compared with 772,188 ten years earlier. The total, therefore, of those able to speak Welsh was 909,000 out of a population of nearly two and a half million (2,472,378). Much the same pattern emerged as in the previous census. The great bastion of the Welsh language remained the western fringe of north, mid, and west Wales, furthest away from England and sealed off by the mountains. In the six counties of north Wales, Anglesey recorded a percentage of 87.4 of Welsh speakers, followed by Merioneth with 86 per cent, and Caernarvonshire with 79.7 per cent. These figures were identical with, if not higher than, those of 1921.[3] They remained a massive stronghold where the native language held overwhelming sway. The only exception in this region was the coastal strip of north Wales, from Prestatyn west as far as

[3] D. Trevor Williams, 'Linguistic Divides in North Wales: a Study in Historical Geography', *Archaeologia Cambrensis*, xci (1936), 194 ff.

Penmaenmawr, including Rhyl, Abergele, Rhos-on-Sea, Colwyn Bay, Llan-dudno, and Conway. In the fashionable resort of Llandudno, with such attractions as its pier and promenade and the scenic beauties of the Orme's Head, 67.5 per cent of the population were recorded as monoglot English. Conversely in the more industrialized counties of north Wales, adjacent to the English border and the industrial belt of Cheshire and south Lancashire, anglicization was very marked. Denbighshire, the home of such national heroes as Thomas Gee and Thomas Gwynn Jones in the recent past, showed less than 50 per cent (48.5) of its population able to speak Welsh. The industrial town of Wrexham was overwhelmingly anglicized, even though the mining districts of Llay and Rhosllannerchrugog nearby remained largely Welsh, with the Rhos male-voice choir celebrated at the *eisteddfod*. Through-out north Wales, the distribution of Welsh monoglots was overwhelmingly concentrated on elderly people of sixty-five and older, or else on young children up to the age of nine. In other words, inability to speak English was stronger among those by-passed by the cultural pressures of an industrialized, urbanized society, or else those still too young to have experienced them. The great bulk of working people and their spouses, aged between ten and sixty-four, lived in a bilingual world where English was becoming more and more dominant.

In south Wales, rural Cardiganshire was overwhelmingly Welsh in speech as it had always been, and so too was Carmarthenshire. Here the native language was as thriving in closely-knit industrial villages such as Amman-ford, Brynamman, and Llandybïe as it was in rural towns such as Llandeilo and Newcastle Emlyn. The steel town of Llanelli was perhaps the community with the largest Welsh-speaking population anywhere outside Glamorgan. In Glamorgan itself, in the mining valleys of the central and eastern parts of the county, in the coastal ports of Barry and Cardiff, the speaking of Welsh was confined to a small minority. This was true, also, of southern Pembrokeshire, below the 'lansker'. In Monmouthshire, beyond Rhymney, the language had virtually disappeared. Overall, the picture was that Welsh, spoken by over half the population in 1901 was now spoken by three-eighths only.

There were still excellent grounds for not being over-despondent about these language statistics. In many areas of the land, the Welsh language was overwhelmingly predominant. Indeed, its resilience in the face of the cultural and economic pressures of the post-war world was remarkable. Compared with Gaelic in the crofting districts of the north-west of Scotland, Welsh was still lively enough. It was much more vigorous than Erse in Ireland, for all the efforts of de Valera and Sinn Fein. Welsh was still widely used in industrial communities in west Glamorgan, Carmarthenshire, and eastern Denbigh-shire. But it was obviously fighting a rearguard action against overwhelming odds. No census was taken in 1941 because of the war, but it would surely have shown a further decline in the numbers of Welsh men and women able to converse in their own language. Those who could read Welsh, and, particularly, those able to write it with grammatical accuracy were fewer still. What was especially disturbing was that the proportion was lowest among young people. Whereas, in 1931, persons aged forty-five and over showed a proportion of 456 per thousand able to speak Welsh, children under fourteen revealed a proportion of only 276 per thousand. The coming generation, it seemed, was already considerably bereft of its cultural inheritance and traditions.

To some extent, the factors that promoted the anglicization of Wales in the twenties and thirties were much the same as they always had been. English was still the language of business and commerce, of learning and the arts, or most of them. Welshmen who wished to 'get on' naturally adopted the predominant language. This had the more force with the onset of unemployment and depression, and the need for working people to cling with the more tenacity to what jobs were to be had, on more or less any terms. Again, the torrent of English or quasi-American culture, through newspapers, books, and, increasingly, the radio (and television after 1936 though this did not reach Wales until 1952), necessarily swamped the local output of Welsh material from native sources. In 1931, it was noted that 10,174 new books were published in England, including pamphlets, while the number of new Welsh books was but 109.[4] There were few Welsh publishing houses, just a handful of pioneers like Hughes & Sons at Wrexham and the Brython Press in Liverpool; for scholarly publication, there was an increasingly thriving University of Wales Press, first launched in 1922. But, in facing the English big battalions, the meagre ranks of the Welsh book trade were completely out-gunned. At less rarefied levels, leisure activities such as popular sport, the music hall, the impact of English radio introduced into remote Welsh households, and the advent of the cinema, had a profound effect upon isolated Welsh communities. Wild West films, Charlie Chaplin and Al Jolson, jazz and popular dance music became staples of the cultural world of the young and the youthful in Wales. They offered excitements with which the *cymanfa ganu*, the local choir and the Sunday-school outing could hardly compete.

Movements of population—the increase of tourism to north and mid-Wales, the migration of English and Irish workers into the coalfield even during the depression years, together with the growing standardization of economic and commercial life that linked the industry of south Wales with Avonside and the Midlands, and of north Wales with Merseyside—all these were accentuated during the inter-war years, too. But in addition, the economic pressures of that period told severely against the Welsh language. The depression in farm prices, the declining demand for agricultural labour as mechanization slowly set in and the extent of arable land contracted, meant a steady drain of population from the uplands and the small villages of the

---

[4] 'Welsh Books', *Welsh Outlook* (May 1933), pp. 29 ff.

hinterland. The mass migration of so many young Welsh people, often Welsh-speaking, from the industrial valleys of the south during the depression years also contributed to a serious process of uprooting and dislocation. As villages lost their younger generation, as chapels and choral festivals went into decline during the twenties and thirties, so that social culture with which Welsh was uniquely associated suffered heavily also. A process of desperate defence against the cultural, social, economic, and political factors which promoted anglicization (and, indeed, americanization through the cinema and other agents of transatlantic mass culture) preoccupied Welsh patriots from the twenties onwards, and continued to do so thereafter.

The Welsh-language world in the inter-war period, then, was operating against a background of a growing sense of difficulty and perhaps of decline. And yet one profoundly encouraging sign was that the culture through which that language most fully expressed itself and through which the genius of the Welsh was modulated, was never more healthy. In the literary world, in the writing of poetry, essays, short stories, literary criticism, *belles lettres* of all forms, Welsh culture, especially in the twenties, was vigorous and creative. Indeed the immediate post-war years were an even more brilliant era, perhaps, for Welsh literature than was the Edwardian high noon before 1914. Some of the giants of that earlier age had passed away. Owen M. Edwards died prematurely in 1920. His literary magazine, the red-covered *Cymru,* did not long survive him. John Morris-Jones remained active in university and eisteddfodic circles but he, too, died relatively young in 1929. His journal, *Y Beirniad*, did not survive the war which it had so forcefully supported. But the most brilliant of the pre-war generation were still very active and productive. T. Gwynn Jones (now installed in a chair at Aberystwyth) and W. J. Gruffydd (now a professor at Cardiff) were still in vigorously creative vein. As late as 1944, Gwynn Jones was to publish *Y Dwymyn* (the fever), an experimental volume which sought to combine the old *cynghanedd* with modern *vers libre* Thomas Parry-Williams, recovering his morale after the trauma of his conscientious objection during the war, was still an important figure. His new style of verse, however, which he called *rhigymau* (rhymings or jottings) were more casual, deceptively informal comments by a sensitive man whose conscience had been wrenched apart by four years of mass slaughter and by personal harassment thereafter. On the other hand, Parry-Williams could also produce the extraordinarily complex, almost painful, self-dissection of psychological experience in *Cerddi* in 1931. There were formidable younger poets, too, the young 'Gwenallt' (D. Gwenallt Jones), born in 1899 and imprisoned as a conscientious objector during the First World War. He was soon to emerge as a writer of great stature. His first published volume of poems, *Ysgubau'r Awen* (Sheaves of Poetry), which came out in 1939, was highly committed, even doctrinaire, in outlook, drawing a sharp contrast between the glory of Wales in its golden past, and its squalor at the present time. It was a contrast between the princess and the harlot. And there was also that exponent of the anti-democratic Catholic ethos J. Saunders Lewis, a Liverpool Welshman born in 1893 and a veteran of service on the western front. Deeply intellectual, fastidious in his professionalism as a writer, Lewis was to prove himself a poet, essayist, novelist, and dramatist of almost limitless talent. Culturally and politically, his presence was to loom massively over Welsh-speaking Wales for the next two generations.

These brilliant writers, and many others who came behind them, found a superb new platform in 1922 with the publication of the monthly, *Y Llenor*, edited with characteristic determination by that powerful critic, W. J. Gruffydd. For over thirty years, this provided a unique outlet for the creative writers of Wales with always the hallmark of Gruffydd's somewhat acerbic but ultimately highly idealistic personality. It was founded, self-consciously, to fill a massive gap in the literary life of Wales, and to provide literature of the highest cultural and artistic quality for the enjoyment of ordinary people. Gruffydd himself was a mordant critic of the difficulties encountered in applying the highest standards to Welsh literature. He was especially critical of the *eisteddfod* which he regarded as an amateur peasant festival incompetently run, with often inadequately equipped adjudicators of the main literary competitions. It was much afflicted by puritan morality: Gwenallt's magnificent *awdl*, *Y Sant*, was turned down for the chair at the Treorchy *eisteddfod* in 1928 for emphasizing unduly the saint as sinner. One judge dismissed it as 'a heap of impurity'. Gruffydd's view was echoed by G. J. Williams, another distinguished university teacher, in the *Llenor*.[5] The leaders of the Gorsedd were neither bards nor poets. They had turned the *eisteddfod*, in Williams's severe phrase, into 'the refuge of quackery', reminiscent of the low literary standards of the second half of the previous century. In addition to this sometimes destructive and unduly harsh criticism, one senses in Gruffydd's comments as editor of the journal a profound sense of a shift of mood after the war, new challenges to the puritanism and the somewhat unthinking optimism of the Liberal-national values of pre-1914, and the necessity for finding new cultural parameters within which Welsh literature could flourish and evolve as a living art form.

The *Llenor* was faithful to its own exacting standards. For the remainder of the twenties and thirties, it was a remarkable vehicle for the poetry of Williams Parry and Parry-Williams, the literary criticism of Saunders Lewis, G. J. Williams, and Ambrose Bebb, the literary and historical essays of R. T. Jenkins, and the short stories of Kate Roberts. Stimulated in large measure by authors connected with the national university, largely supplanting the self-trained, self-educated peasant lyricists of the previous century, the *Llenor* marked a new golden period of creative imaginative writing in Wales. It contrasts sharply with the demographic problems illustrated by the statistics

[5] G. J. Williams, 'Yr Eisteddfod a'r Orsedd', *Y Llenor* (Summer 1922), pp. 131–8.

of the language censuses. There were new currents of thought in abundance, a more aggressive, self-confident socialism and pacifism; a new sympathy with medieval Catholicism and the ideology of French conservative Catholic essayists; a fiercer commitment to Welsh political nationalism. These different strands of thought were widely apparent in the columns of the *Llenor* and other, more established, periodicals such as the *Traethodydd* and the *Geninen*. One author expressed them all. 'Gwenallt' moved rapidly from left-wing socialism (and pacifism during the First World War when he was imprisoned) to a sympathy for the Roman Catholic Church, and then an attachment to Saunders Lewis and the more committed partisans of the young Plaid Cymru. By contrast, W. J. Gruffydd himself, a more urbane and cosmopolitan figure, strove to offer new variations on the Liberal themes of pre-1914. Other writers oscillated between these two positions, with much public exposure of conscience. Beyond doubt, it made the literary world of Welsh-speaking Wales in the twenties exceptionally lively.

In the thirties, there was apparent a somewhat different note in the poetry of the time. Naturally, the appalling pressures of that decade, the mass unemployment and poverty, the challenge of totalitarianism in Europe and its suppression of civil and political liberty, left its imprint on poets in Wales as everywhere else. Much of the almost carefree romanticism of the earlier period disappeared. A new, more anxious tone could be detected. Saunders Lewis's writing reflected a general despair with liberal democracy itself. Often a note of extreme conservatism crept into his writing as into his political utterances. He derived partial inspiration from Charles Maurras, the leader of *Action Française*. But Lewis was undoubtedly an inspiring and creative figure. Again, there were younger poets, men like Waldo Williams and Euros Bowen, both born in the twentieth century, who heralded a new, freer type of self-expression, liberated from the stricter metres of the past. But like almost all Welsh poets, like Iorwerth Peate, Caradog Pritchard, and others later in the decade, they responded closely to shifts in the mood and rhythms of Welsh society rather than take refuge in introspective and purely personal forms of literary examination.

Equally interesting in many ways was the growth of new forms of creative prose writing in Welsh. William Rees (who became Professor of Welsh History at Cardiff in 1930) gave a powerful impetus to the study of medieval Wales after 1282, where J. E. Lloyd had left it. The writing of modern history owed much to the literary grace and charm of R. T. Jenkins. His works on Welsh history during the eighteenth and early nineteenth century certainly had their limitations. They were *belle-lettriste* as much as scholarly. They laid heavy stress on the rural community and on the nonconformist outlook. His friend, the Bangor University librarian Tom Richards, wryly commented that Jenkins's history of eighteeenth-century Wales should be entitled 'a history of the Methodist revival with some incidental comments on the woollen industry'.[6] The iron-works and coal mines of south Wales were a faraway country of which Jenkins, brought up in Bala in Merioneth, knew little. Even so, he produced the first major surveys of modern Welsh society to be written in the Welsh language. Instead of being left stranded in 1282, Welsh history in more recent centuries was now recognized as having a validity and importance of its own. Elsewhere in the university with the aid of the Board of Celtic Studies, scholars like Griffith John Williams, Ifor Williams and Henry Lewis were exploring the literature of the past from a historical perspective. G. J. Williams's work on the literary and ideological world of late eighteenth-century 'Jacobin' Glamorgan was especially valuable, not least for his complete exposé of the bardic frauds perpetrated by Iolo Morganwg and continued by the *gorsedd* at the *eisteddfod* annually ever since. Ifor Williams's editing and interpreting of the celebratory verse of Aneirin and Taliesin, and the *englyn* poetry associated with Llywarch Hen, also illustrated the new standards of scholarship promoted by the national university.

The Welsh short story was another art form given new life. Kate Roberts, born the daughter of a Caernarvonshire quarryman in 1891, and another contributor to the columns of the *Llenor*, was the most remarkable author here. Beginning with *O Gors y Bryniau* in 1925, and *Rhigolau Bywyd* in 1929, her searching accounts of the struggles against poverty and despair in the north Wales quarrying community and (to a lesser extent) in south Wales mining villages have been compared to the stories of Katherine Mansfield or Chekhov. Like a Russian author, Kate Roberts was able to find idealism, heroism, tragedy, psychological tension of all kinds in the seemingly hum-drum lives of Welsh peasants, rural and industrial. Like other local authors, she provided an imaginative commentary on the subtly changing everyday world of the small towns and rural communities of her native Gwynedd. She wrote with especial perception and poignancy about children and about the trials of old age.

The Welsh novel also made its tentative appearance during the later thirties and the wartime years. Kate Roberts herself had written in the *Llenor* (as had the English-language writer, Geraint Goodwin in *Welsh Outlook*) of the difficulty in finding stimulation for the art of the novelist in Wales.[7] Readers wanted accounts based on the familiar realities of daily local life, which made the short story the more appropriate medium. Wales, in any event, lacked the kind of sophisticated urban bourgeoisie which had enabled the novel to flourish in England or France. Most Welsh people were concerned with scraping a living together in a harsh physical environment, instead of enjoying the cultural leisure in which the novel could thrive. No one had done for rural or industrial Wales what Arnold Bennett had done for the five towns of the

---

[6] A. Llywelyn-Williams, *R. T. Jenkins* (Cardiff, 1977), p. 22.

[7] Kate Roberts, 'Y Nofel Gymraeg', *Y Llenor* (Winter 1928), pp. 211–16; Geraint Goodwin, 'Thoughts on the Welsh Novel', *Welsh Outlook* (March 1930), pp. 72 ff.

Potteries or Thomas Hardy for Wessex. To a degree, this remained true. Even Saunders Lewis's romantic novel, *Monica*, published in 1930, was not a complete success. But at least one considerable novelist made his appearance during the Second World War. He was T. Rowland Hughes, yet another product of the slate-quarrying community in Caernarvonshire who moved on to lecture at Coleg Harlech and then became a BBC producer. He began as a poet but then turned to writing novels. Starting with *O Law i Law* (1943), a study of a bachelor quarryman, Hughes provided the first significant novels to appear in Wales since the works of Daniel Owen at the end of the last century. He based his work mainly on insights into the *mores* of the closely-knit world of the Caernarvonshire quarrymen and their families. *Y Chwalfa* (1946) was a powerful portrayal of the impact of the Bethesda quarry strike of 1900 on family and community life. Hughes undoubtedly generated a new interest and excitement about the potential of the novel and the short story, in contrast to fixed-metre and free verse, as a means of using the Welsh language for artistic expression. No generation was neglected in this renaissance. Tegla Davies's boys' stories, *Hunangofiant Tomi* and *Nedw*, were classics of their kind, appreciated by readers of all ages.

The general state of Welsh literary culture, then, was distinctly healthy during the inter-war years, even if it tended to be appreciated by a relatively small class of educated middle-class *literati* and nonconformist ministers who hovered around the university. There were other heartening signs, also. The teaching of Welsh language and literature in elementary, and, to a growing extent, in secondary education made steady progress. It was spurred on by the evidence from the census returns that Welsh schoolchildren were losing touch with their native language, even more rapidly than were their elders. A report by the Welsh Department of the Board of Education in 1927 was hailed as a landmark in many circles for the encouragement it gave to the teaching of Welsh at all levels of education from entry into the primary school right up to the university. It was noticeable, however, that its recommendations entailed no radically new departure, since the powers of the Ministry of Education would be permissive and depend on the goodwill and energy of local authorities in interpreting the mandate of the ratepayers, and the wishes of parents, according to their own lights. Welsh remained simply 'a subject' rather than a dynamic form of communication throughout the whole educational system. Nevertheless, the progress of Welsh as a subject for instruction and examination in schools, increasingly the battle-ground for the future of the language, was a steady one during the thirties. A new development was the growth of small privately-run nursery schools, maintained at their own expense by patriotic Welsh parents. One corollary of this was the opening at Aberystwyth in 1939, under the auspices of *Urdd Gobaith Cymru*, of Lluest independent primary school with the instruction conducted wholly in the Welsh language, under the inspired headship of Norah Isaac. Its pupils numbered 43 in 1943 and 90 in 1947. Soon afterwards appeared a powerful pressure-group for the Welsh language, *Undeb Cymru Fydd*, headed by T. I. Ellis, the son of the apostle of Cymru Fydd in the eighties. On the whole, Welsh-language enthusiasts had much to show for their efforts during these years.

The growth of sound broadcasting was another source of concern. The BBC began transmitting programmes to Welsh and other households from the early twenties. A station, 5WA, was founded at Cardiff in February 1923, while others followed at Swansea in 1924 and Bangor in 1934. Religious services in Welsh were programmed through the transmitter at Daventry. There was much anxiety, especially in educational and university circles, at the relatively meagre attention paid to Welsh by the Corporation, and that Wales, unlike Scotland and Northern Ireland, was not at first granted a broadcasting service of its own. The Central Council for School Broadcasting, under the chairmanship of H. A. L. Fisher, had no organization in Wales represented among its twenty members or its fifteen nominated members, save for one NUT representative who happened to be of Welsh origin. There was much anxiety that broadcasting was overwhelmingly in the English language, emanating from London.

A more encouraging departure in 1935, in response to growing demands for a better broadcasting service in Wales, was the establishment of an additional transmitter near Plymouth to provide for the west of England, so that the existing west regional transmitter at Washford Cross could be devoted exclusively to a Welsh service. A relay station at Bangor would carry its programmes to the mountainous regions of the north. The University of Wales Advisory Committee on broadcasting (which included Saunders Lewis) pressed hard for a separate Welsh region of the BBC. Finally on 4 July 1937 separation was achieved and a Welsh home service came into existence, with a full output of programmes from Cardiff, Swansea, and Bangor studios. The Welsh programmes of the BBC were sometimes criticized for their undue emphasis on the more sombre and traditional aspects of Welsh culture—with chapel services at length and seemingly interminable hymn singing. But there were also talks, documentaries, and plays about Wales in both languages, and specially commissioned works by Welsh authors, including soon Dylan Thomas. There were lively light entertainment programmes produced by Sam Jones, and excellent programmes on sport. There was also the important development of a BBC Welsh Orchestra, originally founded in 1928 and re-founded in 1935. By the Second World War, the influence of sound broadcasting as a medium for injecting new life into the Welsh-language world was being more widely recognized. Pressure continued to mount for a growing output of Welsh programmes, more appointments of Welsh-speaking drama producers and production assistants, and for improved transmitting facilities to the mountainous areas where Welsh was most widely spoken. The responsiveness to this pressure of the BBC, and its regional director, the past and future Liberal MP, Rhys Hopkin Morris, was another relatively hopeful sign for the future of the language.

Another was the foundation in 1922 of a new organization to minister to the Welsh-speaking young. This was *Urdd Gobaith Cymru*, more popularly *Yr Urdd*, the Welsh League of Youth. It was founded by Ifan ab Owen Edwards, the son of the great national leader of pre-war days and himself an extra-mural lecturer at the University College Aberystwyth. The purpose of the new movement was to infuse among the young people a love of the native language and culture. Throughout there was a strong association with Christian morality, and also with Greek ideals of cultural and physical beauty. The basic emphasis was on non-political national consciousness, and on assisting the language during its crisis of survival. The movement grew rapidly. *Urdd* branches were attached to schools and chapels. There were summer camps, appropriately near Llanuwchllyn by the shores of Bala Lake, the home of 'O.M.'; there followed regional and then national *eisteddfodau* for the *Urdd*. Another novelty, somewhat redolent of the youth movement in Europe in the twenties, were the games or *mabolgampau*, much influenced by the amateur, Olympic tradition. The *Urdd*'s publications also expanded fast. *Cymru'r Plant* was taken over, and *Yr Aelwyd* was added to it in 1940. By 1927, the *Urdd* had 5,000 members; by 1934, it claimed 50,000.[8] It was a powerful pressure-group on many fronts. It pushed hard to promote the sale and publication of Welsh-language books and magazines, especially for the young: the number of Welsh books sold rose from 1,025 in 1937 to 54,043 in 1944. It urged the more extensive use of Welsh in schools broadcasting. It was most active in pressing for nursery and elementary schools to be conducted solely through the medium of Welsh. As has been seen above, the first private Welsh-language school was founded at Aberystwyth by the *Urdd* in 1939 with the young Owen Edwards, the son of Ifan ab Owen Edwards and the grandson of 'O.M.', among the first seven pupils.

But the main impact of the *Urdd* was in capturing the imagination of the young, in stimulating a positive, non-nationalistic love of country and of its literary and artistic heritage, in providing the youth of Wales with the kind of educational, cultural, and moral inspiration so much needed in the swirling tides of post-war Britain and the years of the depression. Much attention was paid to making this an outward-looking patriotism, one that would reinforce the bonds of Welsh schoolchildren with the young in other lands. Cruises were organized to Norway, Brittany, and other smaller societies that seemed to be in tune with the aspirations of the *Urdd*. All in all, the *Urdd* was one of the most heartening innovations in Wales after the war. It was unquestionably a movement that enriched the lives of a new generation of schoolchildren and

⁸ Cf Gwennant Davies, *The Story of the Urdd* (Aberystwyth, 1973); R. E. Griffith, *Urdd Gobaith Cymru* (Aberystwyth, 3 vols., 1971–3).

infused them with a warm-hearted, non-exclusive, benevolent sense of patriotism. Its dramatic success showed the need of young people in different parts of the principality for some organization to provide them with cultural and leisure activities, with the opportunity to make young friends in a healthy, open-air setting, and to comprehend it all within a framework of Welshness. Ifan ab Owen Edwards created a movement as appropriate and necessary for his own generation as were the crusading literary enterprises of his father twenty years earlier. The *Urdd* gave the Welsh language a fresh chance. It left realistic ground for hope that the younger generation would less readily neglect their native culture and inheritance than their parents and grand-parents had so wantonly done.

Movements like this, together with the general vitality of the *eisteddfod* (despite the attacks of the *Llenor*), and of Welsh literary and musical circles in the twenties and thirties, provided ground for optimism about turning back the tide of conformism and anglicization. There was also the activity of the Welsh Folk Song Society and the department of folk culture of the National Museum, founded in 1936; they did for Welsh airs and folk-tunes what Cecil Sharp had done for English. Yet to a growing number of Welsh intellectuals this optimism, when measured against the statistical facts, was almost absurdly misplaced. The declining use of Welsh, the contraction of Welsh-language publishing, the diminishing impact of the chapels seemed to a growing number of patriots to call for more decisive action than the benevolent but strictly non-political activities of the *Urdd*, or attempts to put pressure on the BBC or the Ministry of Education from the outside. A growing sense of alarm, even despair, at the erosion, perhaps ultimately the disappearance, of a centuries-old culture was increasingly in evidence in the discussions of Welsh observers and commentators in the thirties. Only one possible solution seemed to them to present itself—full self-government for Wales, on the same basis as that achieved by the Irish Free State in 1922. Only thus could a Welsh government, responsible solely to its own people, take the necessary measures to protect and revive the native language. So a growing number of literary and intellectual figures turned, reluctantly and often without much sophistication in terms of party political experience, to pursue the path of politics. It was in order to support the cause of the embryonic Plaid Cymru that several Welsh literary figures—Kate Roberts, Waldo Williams, Iorwerth Peate, and many others—and a growing number of academics, university professors, college lecturers, and schoolteachers, turned their efforts and energies.

Plaid Cymru, as was seen in Chapter 7, began in very humble circumstances in 1925, with its foundation at the time of Pwllheli *eisteddfod*. From 1932 the party was committed to achieving Welsh self-government on a dominion basis like Canada or Australia, and to gain representation for Wales at the League of Nations. It was also laying more emphasis on economic and social issues.

But central always was the preservation of the lanugage, which was throughout the period up to 1945 the crucial objective in the party's growth and propaganda. At first, the party was a small one indeed. It claimed a membership of 500 in 1930. By 1939 this had risen, according to official sources, to 2,000.[9] Sales of *Y Ddraig Goch* and (to a lesser extent) of the *Welsh Nationalist* also climbed steadily upwards. In the columns of the *Llenor* and other Welsh-language publications, the extent to which Plaid Cymru attracted the allegiance of the intellectual élite of the land was highly impressive. But in terms of mass support, Plaid Cymru as a party found the going extremely hard. Very reluctantly, Saunders Lewis, its unchallenged leader, modified his initial determination to sever all links with Whitehall and Westminster. It was decided to broaden the party's support by fighting parliamentary elections. There seemed to be no other non-violent, democratic way of winning national freedom for Wales. But there was scant success to show. In the 1929 general election, Plaid Cymru fought an election for the first time, when the Revd. Lewis Valentine contested Caernarvonshire. He polled just 609 votes, just over 1 per cent of the total, an almost humiliating result. In the 1931 general election, two seats were fought. In Caernarvonshire, again, Professor J. E. Daniel of Bala-Bangor college, an eminent Congregationalist theologian, polled somewhat better than Valentine had done, but still gained only 2.2 per cent of the vote. More encouraging was Saunders Lewis's own candidature for the University of Wales seat. Here he polled 17.9 per cent, gaining 914 votes from this small electorate, though Lewis's own distinction as a poet and *littérateur* may have swollen his total amongst university graduates. In 1935, Caernarvonshire was fought a third time, now with somewhat greater success. Daniel gained 2,534 votes (5.7 per cent of the total). But he finished far behind the Liberal, Goronwy Owen, and once again lost his deposit.

Clearly Plaid Cymru, though occasionally given publicity when it was belaboured by Lloyd George and other leading Welsh figures, was still a small and relatively insignificant group at this period. It gained a solitary local election victory in Merioneth in 1934. Then in September 1936 it sprang into dramatic prominence, when three leading members of the party, Saunders Lewis himself, the Revd. Lewis Valentine, and the schoolmaster-author D. J. Williams, took part in the burning of an RAF bombing school at Pen-y-Berth near Penrhos aerodrome in the Llŷn peninsula in Caernarvonshire, and then informed the authorities of their responsibility. There had been much local protest at the proposal to build this school, with the physical and cultural damage that would result to a traditional Welsh farming community. There was much more protest when the Baldwin government decided to transfer the case from a local Welsh court to the Old Bailey, on the specious grounds that a

---

[9] Alan Butt-Philip, *The Welsh Question* (Cardiff, 1975), p. 17. J. E. Jones, *Tros Gymru* (Swansea, 1970) gives 3,750 as the figure for 1939.

Welsh jury would probably show undue bias. This decision caused immense uproar in Wales from men and women of all parties. Lloyd George, no friend of Plaid Cymru, wrote angrily from Jamaica of how the craven, appeasing Baldwin government would cringe before Mussolini in Abyssinia but would wantonly bully gallant little Wales. 'This is the first Government that has tried Wales at the Old Bailey. . . . They might at any rate have had a second trial, or removed it to some other part of Wales, but to take it out of Wales altogether and, above all, to the Old Bailey, is an outrage that makes my blood boil.'[10]

In the event, the 'three' were imprisoned in Wormwood Scrubs for nine months after refusing to give evidence before the Old Bailey judge in English; later they returned to Wales amidst much acclaim. Welsh nationalism had acquired its first martyrs, which every popular protest movement requires. Saunders Lewis remained a controversial and, in some ways, a persecuted figure thereafter. A play originally requested by the BBC Welsh region, on the instructions of the regional director, Hopkin Morris, did indeed go ahead and was broadcast on St. David's Day, 1937, under the title *Buchedd Garmon*. Lewis and his two colleagues heard it on a radio in the prisoners' recreation room in Wormwood Scrubs. On the other hand, Lewis was removed from his lectureship in Welsh at the University College of Swansea during his trial—and before his conviction. Later he retired from public life to conduct his studies in first, a Roman Catholic seminary, then a school, in remote parts of Cardiganshire and Carmarthenshire. He also resigned his presidency of Plaid Cymru in 1939 after serving almost since the foundation of the party. D. J. Williams resumed his post at Fishguard county school in Pembrokeshire, after acting as adjudicator for the Machynlleth *eisteddfod* in 1937 while serving out his term in prison. Most of his writing for the remainder of his long life was a commentary on the threats posed to the culture and way of life of peasant communities in Wales. In a sense, he remained rooted in Pen-y-Berth for the rest of his literary career.

The martyrdoms of Saunders Lewis, Valentine, and D. J. Williams provided an immense, if short-lived, boost to the appeal—and to the membership—of Plaid Cymru. There was a mass public subscription to pay the defence costs after the trial. The circulation of *Y Ddraig Goch*, the party newspaper, rose by 2,000. For writers and intellectuals, the imprisonment of 'the three' for an idealistic gesture committed on behalf of nationalist and pacific values had a profound impact. The memory of Pen-y-Berth was to form an essential strand in the moral and national consciousness of a generation of Welsh-speaking intellectuals. The novelist Kate Roberts now turned increasingly to political themes, such as the way in which the British educational system helped destroy the heritage of Welsh schoolchildren. She became a powerful critic of contemporary political and literary movements in

---

[10] Lloyd George to Megan Lloyd George, 1 December 1936 (*Lloyd George: Family Letters*, pp. 212–13).

the columns of the Welsh press. The poet R. Williams Parry, hitherto without any particular commitment to political affairs, almost a mystic in outlook and temperamentally drawn to the lonely and the oppressed, suddenly began to infuse his poetry with political protest. This was seen in the sonnets 'J.S.L.' and the pugnacious verse of 'Cymru' in 1937. The appeal of Plaid Cymru was broadened to attract advocates of non-violence more generally, especially Christian pacifists sprung from the nonconformist chapels. One of them, an intelligent young Aberystwyth and Oxford graduate, Gwynfor Evans, successfully moved a resolution in favour of non-violent direct action in specific cases at the annual Plaid Cymru conference in 1938. For the rest of his career, which included a presidency of Plaid Cymru lasting over thirty years and two periods in parliament, Gwynfor Evans was to serve as the apostle of 'non-violent nationalism'.[11]

But, despite the moral impact of the imprisonment of the 'three' in 1937, Plaid Cymru and its leading figures remained too controversial to sway the hearts and minds of many Welsh people, even Welsh speakers, in the thirties. As has been seen, it was most strongly rooted in intellectual and cultural groups in the university, in the literary circles connected with the *Llenor* and, to some degree, in the BBC in Wales. Amongst the mass of the working population, whatever their language, Plaid Cymru appeared as a small esoteric group of Utopian fanatics. Home rule for Wales seemed to be the chimera of a few eccentrics. The idea had never made any headway since 1896, nor did it appear likely to do so now. Plaid Cymru's dominant personality, Saunders Lewis, a dignified but intransigent figure, aroused strong feelings, hostile as well as admiring. His advocacy of methods of direct action caused much debate. His ardent Roman Catholicism caused more, especially as it tended to be tinged with anti-democratic and anti-liberal sentiments. There were Welshmen who accused Plaid Cymru of the same kind of racialism and exclusivist nationalism associated with the Nazi and Fascist parties in Germany or Italy. In 1942, in a speech at the Honourable Society of Cymmrodorion later printed under the title, *The Native never Returns*, Thomas Jones included a blistering attack on Plaid Cymru and its leaders. Sentiments expressed in favour of the corporate state of Fascist Italy were widely quoted. 'It is a Mussolini that Wales needs!' Ambrose Bebb had once written.[12] A left-wing patriotic group, the *Gwerin* movement, started at Bangor University College in 1935 by the young Goronwy Roberts, made much of the 'national socialism' of Plaid Cymru and its sympathy with the 'distributist' economics of fascist Italy.

These accusations were hotly disputed by members of the party at the time and are hard to endorse now. The worst that could be said was that Plaid Cymru veered towards the social conservatism and anti-statism of Vichy

---

[11] Gwynfor Evans, *Non-Violent Nationalism* (Alex Wood Memorial Lecture, London, 1973).
[12] Ambrose Bebb, 'Achub y Gymraeg: Achub Cymru', *Y Geninen*, May 1923.

France; as a party it was neither fascist nor anti-Semitic. Ambrose Bebb's sympathy for France in the face of Hitler's aggression was emphatic. On the other hand, the authoritarian, anti-liberal pronouncements of Catholic traditionalists within the party such as Saunders Lewis left it vulnerable to such charges at a time when extreme nationalism was in disrepute. Furthermore, Plaid Cymru's detachment from 'England's imperialist war' between 1939 and 1945 also alienated some possible sympathizers and made it appear equivocal on the main moral issues of the day. In August 1940, Professor Daniel, now the president of Plaid Cymru, explained that 'this is a clash of rival imperialisms from which Wales, like the other small nations of Europe, has nothing to gain but everything to lose. . . . It does not accept the popular English view that this war is a crusade of light against darkness. It does not admit the right of England to conscript Welshmen into her army or regard it as the duty of Wales to help London to beat Berlin.' Saunders Lewis cut short a debate on the 'second front' at the party's annual conference at Lampeter in December 1942 on the grounds that strategic questions such as this were of no concern to a party that simply opposed the war.[13] The German *Abwehr* contemplated making contact with individual unnamed Welsh nationalists as possible supporters on the line of Quisling in Norway or the Breton separatists in France. Lloyd George (incredibly enough) was sometimes visualized as a Welsh Pétain or a *Gauleiter* for Wales.

The controversy that surrounded Plaid Cymru and its leading figures, and its capacity to divide Welsh-speaking men and women from each other, were emphasized in January 1943 when a by-election took place in the University of Wales, Ernest Evans having moved to a judgeship. Saunders Lewis was nominated as the Plaid Cymru candidate, and received the backing of a distinguished array of literary and religious figures. To fight him, the Liberals nominated no less a personage than Professor W. J. Gruffydd; he had actually been a prominent member of Plaid Cymru in the thirties and had even been nominated as the party's vice-president. On the other hand, he had often attacked Saunders Lewis's style of anti-liberal nationalism in his editorial notes in the *Llenor*. Although of no known attachment to the Liberal Party, his record made him not an inappropriate defender of the old order within the national university. The entire episode showed the fierce divisions that political nationalism had opened up in literary circles. The *Llenor* was fiercely riven by the by-election, which caused a permanent breach between the rival supporters of Lewis and Gruffydd. The journal was never quite the same again. In the end, Gruffydd won easily at the expense of a clutch of four opponents. He polled over 52 per cent of the vote, though it is worth noting that Saunders Lewis, with 1,330 votes (22.5 per cent) obtained easily Plaid Cymru's best poll to date. Believing himself to be victimized for his Catholic faith, Lewis then left party politics for good. Not until a much later phase in his

[13] *Western Mail*, 5 August 1940, 8 December 1942.

life, in 1962, and then fortuitously and indirectly, was he to emerge again as a charismatic figure in Welsh life.

In general, this University of Wales by-election—and the controversy that surrounded the philosophy and tactics of Plaid Cymru in the thirties—showed that, concerned though they were about the decline of the language, most Welsh-speaking people were hesitant about turning to political nationalism or the cause of separatism. On balance, involvement with a wider British world, politically, economically, and culturally, seemed to offer the healthiest way forward. Here Welsh people were merely echoing the conclusion, voiced in their different fashions, by Tom Ellis and the young David Lloyd George after the *Cymru Fydd* débâcle in 1895–6. In this sense a book, *Wales Drops the Pilots*, published by W. Hughes Jones in 1937 which viewed Ellis and Lloyd George as the two 'lost leaders' of the Welsh national movement, was misconceived in its basic historical argument. Most Welsh people still differed profoundly in their priorities from their Celtic counterparts across the Irish Sea. They rejected an inward-looking exclusiveness and sought rather to make Wales a recognized, dignified partner within a wider world. On the other hand, the general refusal to turn to political nationalism left the defenders of the language somewhat bereft of effective weapons. They were left with peaceful pressure, moral suasion, an appeal to the minds and the consciences of the English master race. These methods had produced a number of impressive victories over the past fifty years: they inspired the ideals of *Urdd Gobaith Cymru* during its rapid expansion in the 1930s. There were hopes, as will be seen in Chapter 10, that the Labour Party, through its Welsh representatives at Westminster, might look with more sympathy on modified forms of devolution for Wales, and might at least question the persistent centralization of the Webb tradition since 1918. In particular, Labour might embrace the idea of a Secretary of State for Wales, an intermittent theme in politics since 1892. But these were vague expectations. The reality was a Welsh language in decline, however distinguished the literary uses to which it was still put, and a series of sociological and psychological tensions which cut at the very heart of Welsh nationhood.

While these developments were agitating the consciences of Welsh speakers, that clear majority of the population who spoke only English were trying in their own way to come to terms with the problems of identity and of communication. They were trying to make sense of their existence as English-speaking Welshmen. In the thirties this took a much more distinct form. The fact increasingly dawned that an inability to speak Welsh did not mean that a man or woman had lost his or her sense of Welsh nationality, or an involvement with the cultural and national problems of their people. Thus it was that the concept of 'Anglo-Welsh' culture, a highly necessary one in view of the growing anglicization, began to crystallize and acquire more coherent form.

The exact content of this 'Anglo-Welsh' tradition had always been very hard to decide. As Glyn Jones noted, the idea had none of the class or 'ascendancy' overtones associated with the 'Anglo-Irish' school of Yeats or Moore.[14] Of course, there had been many poets in the past who were of Welsh blood but who wrote mainly or exclusively in the English language. George Herbert in the seventeenth century, Gerard Manley Hopkins in the nineteenth were often associated with this tradition. But attempts to link them with a continuous Anglo-Welsh culture were necessarily vague, if not absurd. What emerged, during and after the First World War, was something more precise. A growing range of authors emerged, Welsh by birth and nationality but speaking only English, who wrote to some degree about their native land. However, what links them together is not so much that Welsh places and episodes provided them with their subject-matter. Rather, they responded to a kind of Welsh consciousness, and to concern about the Welsh identity. Their art was shaped by the predicaments and experiences of the Welsh people. A clearly definable Anglo-Welsh literature began to emerge. Soon it gushed forth, especially from south Wales, in a roaring torrent, and established itself as a major element in British twentieth-century literature.

Tracing the starting-point of the literary movement is always a peculiarly elusive and frustrating task. But most critics seem to agree that the short stories of Caradoc Evans, written during and just after the First World War, mark the start of a new departure. Caradoc Evans was disturbing and unfamiliar. In Professor Gwyn Jones's words, 'He was like a bad smell coming in through the window.'[15] As had been seen, Caradoc Evans's books of short stories, *My People, Capel Sion,* and the rest, administered a powerful shock to the moral sensibilities of the nonconformist middle class, especially through their satirical portrayal of small-town Welsh rural life. Evans continued to be a controversial figure, reviled by most of his countrymen, for the rest of his life until he died just after the end of the Second World War. He had a well-publicized divorce in 1932 and married the novelist Countess Barczynska. He eventually moved to live in Aberystwyth, much to the distaste of the faithful at the local Sions, Salems, and Silohs. An invitation from the BBC in 1937 to lecture on Welsh nonconformity, surely a rash move, was withdrawn when the full impact of the text was appreciated by the authorities. For all that, although a Welsh speaker himself, Caradoc Evans had a powerful, positive and long-term effect on Welsh authors whose first or only language, for purposes of creative writing, was English. To quote Gwyn Jones again, 'the war horn was blown, the gauntlet thrown down, the gates of the temple were shattered'.[16] It was partly a matter of the superb literary effect. Evans

---

[14] Glyn Jones, *The Dragon has Two Tongues* (London, 1968), p. 47.

[15] Gwyn Jones, 'The First Forty Years: Some Notes on Anglo-Welsh Literature', *Triskel One* (Llandybïe, 1971), p. 79.

[16] Ibid., p. 77.

had a remarkable feel for language and for linguistic manipulation which had been compared with that of James Joyce. He created almost a private language, not least in his use or invention of a curious form of Welsh slang, all his own.

In addition, Evans broke free from several barriers, perhaps myths or illusions, which had long shackled creative writing in Wales. He destroyed, cataclysmically and without pity for the sensibilities of his opponents, the influence of puritanism and Sabbatarianism upon Welsh literary craftsmanship. He broke free, with no less effort, from the illusory attachment to Welsh rural life as a kind of pastoral, latter-day Utopia, a Garden of Eden entered by courtesy of the Great Western Railway. This powerful rural nostalgia had permeated much of Welsh literature, especially that written in the Welsh language: the historical works of R. T. Jenkins, the folk studies of Iorwerth Peate, the novels of Kate Roberts, the verse of almost every major Welsh poet were testimony to this idealization of the *werin* still current in the thirties. In the hands of Caradoc Evans, the *werin* suddenly became a breed of No-good Boyos. His achievement had serious limitations. He was an embittered author, writing out of a spirit of revenge. His lack of compassion diminished his literary stature. And yet, for all his emphasis on liberation and on revolt against social and religious convention, Evans remained deeply rooted in the Wales he satirized. He was profoundly influenced by the patterns of its society, the language of its poetry, the eternal majesty of its landscape. He was trying to provide his own, mordant commentary on a land he loved, nonconformist warts and all—but he was endeavouring to do it, and with astonishing effect, in English. Therein lay the novelty.

By the early thirties, there was a new generation of authors prepared to follow along some, at least, of the paths that Evans had blazed, though with a far more compassionate and much less exaggerated view of Welsh society. There were now significant Anglo-Welsh novelists in existence. For the first time, Welsh authors were providing the kind of insights into their world that Hardy or Arnold Bennett had done for their regions of England. Novelists emerged with new things to say about the Welsh and their experience. Sometimes they wrote on almost forgotten communities, as in the case of Geraint Goodwin from Newtown, who died young in 1941. He chronicled the *mores* of country life in the border counties of Montgomeryshire, Radnorshire, and Breconshire. How far they subscribed to a Welsh, or even an Anglo-Welsh tradition was something about which these writers could differ considerably. Rhys Davies was the son of a grocer from Clydach Vale, whose first novel, *The Withered Root* (1927), a study of an evangelist during the Welsh religious revival of 1904, made a considerable impact on critical opinion. But he could, in the opinion of Keidrych Rhys's *Wales*, 'only write about Wales when peacefully away from the country'.[17] When Rhys Davies

[17] *Wales*, No. 3 (Autumn 1937).

was asked in *Wales* (June 1946) 'Are you an Anglo-Welsh writer?', he replied simply, I am only a writer'. His most intimate friend was D. H. Lawrence, that other emigré from a mining community. Descriptions such as that he was serving as a kind of Welsh Chekhov meant little to Davies: 'Down with Passports to Art!' he declared. On the other hand, Glyn Jones, another distinguished Anglo-Welsh author of the thirties and a Merthyr man who chose to write in English even though he knew a good deal of Welsh, declared proudly, 'I have never written a word about any country other than Wales nor any people other than Welsh people.'[18] The involvement of many of these new authors with the cultural, social, and political tensions of their native land in the twenties and thirties was beyond question. It was significant that, inevitably, many of them were of working-class origin, the sons of miners or steelworkers or railwaymen. Many of them had worked down the pit before turning to literature. And some, such as that adopted Welshman Bert Coombes of Wolverhampton, remained working men even after this metamorphosis.

Some of the new strains were exemplified in the personality of Jack Jones, born at Porth, Rhondda, in 1884 and, in turns, collier, pugilist, soldier, trade-union militant, parliamentary candidate (Lloyd George Liberal), door salesman, navvy, and much else, before becoming a best-selling novelist.[19] His first novel, *Rhondda Roundabout*, was written in between visits to the Rhondda labour exchange twice a week. In this book and in later works like *Black Parade* and *Unfinished Journey*, he provided a new voice in the somewhat over-respectable atmosphere of Welsh literature in the 1930s. With passion, sometimes with sentimentality, he provided a direct cry from the proletariat of the valleys, celebrating the warmth, heroism and nobility of the common people of the south Wales mining community. He was always deeply involved in the history and folk memories of his own region. *Off to Philadelphia in the Morning* was a moving account of the life of the composer, Joseph Parry, who had worked in the pits as a boy in Merthyr in the 1850s, before emigrating to find fame in the United States, receiving academic distinctions from Cambridge and other universities and serving, briefly, as Professor of Music at Aberystwyth. Joseph Parry's odyssey is that of the Welsh themselves, climbing out of poverty and despair to find new qualities of cultural and intellectual creativity. It is in many respects an oblique comment on the life of Jack Jones himself. In later life, Jack Jones became something of an institution, always a danger to a creative writer. He even served as president of the Anglo-Welsh section of the Welsh Academy in the 1960s. Television gave him a new, more popular audience; perhaps the old poacher was joining the establishment at last, if not exactly turning gamekeeper. How enduring Jack Jones will prove remains to be seen. Without doubt, in the

[18] Glyn Jones, op. cit., p. 38.

[19] See Gwyn Jones, 'Jack Jones', *Planet* 1 (August–September 1970), pp. 32–7.

literary context of the thirties, he provided a powerful example to authors, usually of working-class background, anxious to comment upon aspects of their social and national consiousness through the alien tongue of English.

Even more striking in the thirties was the rise of a new generation of poets, largely from south Wales, who were labelled with lasting effect, as the 'Anglo-Welsh'. Some of them were deeply involved with the social and political crises of their own industrial community, as in the socialist poetry of Idris Davies. His 'I was born in Rhymney', a simple autobiographical ballad, was as committed and ideological as his better known 'Do you remember 1926?'. Davies's message in his early poetry was unmistakable.

> I went to church and chapel
> Ere I could understand
> That Apollo rules the heaven
> And Mammon rules the land.

His poetry, simple and direct, often reached considerable levels of sophistication. Notable examples of it were the thirty-six sombre poems included in the volume, *Gwalia Deserta* in 1938, and *The Angry Summer* (1943), a recollection of the general strike. As has been seen, T. S. Eliot, a man of very different political outlook, was one of the surprising variety of critics who praised Idris Davies's poetry. But most of the new Anglo-Welsh poets were more indirect in their Welshness and usually less political, save in the sense that they were deeply aware of their background of economic and ideological upheaval in south Wales. Glyn Jones of Merthyr, Alun Lewis of Aberdare (who was to die in India during the war), and Vernon Watkins of Swansea were amongst those who caught the attention of literary critics in the early and mid-thirties. Glyn Jones, himself almost bilingual, became a man of letters of extraordinary fertility and invention.

But rather than provide a somewhat meaningless catalogue of names, it is perhaps more helpful to discuss a poet who transcended them all, one of Wales's few acknowledged geniuses. This was Dylan Thomas of Swansea, a writer who moved to the little port of Laugharne in eastern Carmarthenshire in his most creative period in the forties and early fifties. He knew adventurous times in London, Oxford, and (fatally) New York, but remained deeply committed to west Wales and the Swansea area for the whole of his brief life.

Born in 1914, Dylan Thomas was already well established by the late 1930s as a younger poet of rare quality, with a genius for language and for sophistication and subtlety in the expression of complex ideas and emotions. He published in the *New Age*, in *New Verse*, and the *Criterion*, he won literary prizes, he got to know Edith Sitwell, he gave poetry readings and talks on the

BBC, he was already becoming (with destructive results) a familiar figure in the pubs and cafés of the bohemian underworld of Soho and Chelsea. Clearly his reputation was one that transcended national or ethnic boundaries. In the United States, his poetry was also to bring him fame, if not yet fortune sufficient to keep up with a chaotic pattern of living and spending. Clearly, attempting to isolate the 'Welshness' or even the 'Anglo-Welshness' of Dylan Thomas as revealed in his poetry, to detect echoes of the *cynghanedd* or other techniques from Welsh *cerdd dafod* in his use of the English language is a difficult enterprise, perhaps one of doubtful utility. When Glyn Jones met Dylan Thomas again, after some years of absence, after 1945, Thomas expressed his regret that his friend did not sufficiently reject 'Welsh nationalism and a sort of hill farm morality'.[20]

And yet the extent to which an awareness of some kind of Welshness was interwoven with the very essence of Thomas's personality, as a poet and as a man, is surely beyond question. It makes him, therefore, an authentic and powerful figure in the emergence of the Anglo-Welsh *genre* in poetry. Dylan Thomas came from a Welsh-speaking family in Swansea, though he himself knew the language not at all. He enjoyed a warm, understanding relationship with his old, endlessly patient Welsh parents, perhaps a more stable, reassuring element in his career than his Irish wife. Thomas was no less aware of memories of his great-uncle, a celebrated eisteddfodic bard from southern Cardiganshire, Gwilym Marles or Marlais, who gave Dylan Marlais Thomas his middle name. Swansea in the twenties and thirties, then as later, was at best a half-Welsh world, washed by the 'two-tongued sea' in Swansea Bay. Away from such closely-knit Welsh-speaking communities as Morriston and Llansamlet in the older parts of industrial Swansea, east of the Tawe, the commercial and residential part of this growing, thriving town, spreading west along the curve of the bay towards Mumbles Head and the Gower beyond, was undoubtedly English in speech and outlook. The young poets and painters and musicians in whose company Dylan grew up, Daniel Jones, Fred Janes, Mervyn Levy, Vernon Watkins, later intimates like 'Ralph the Books', were cosmopolitan and sophisticated in outlook, endlessly questioning, experimental, rebellious.

Yet Thomas was always deeply aware of the layers of Welshness in Swansea, too, its complex relationship to its hinterland as a kind of frontier town, hard against the Welsh-speaking country areas of Carmarthenshire and 'the good, bad boys of the lonely farms'. The two-tongued sea brought in alternating tides of Welshness and world-consciousness, to enrich the life of the town with equal measure. Thomas was, at least in his earlier years, deeply involved with his own traditions and his own family. His poem, 'After the Funeral' (written to mark the death of 'an aged peasant aunt', Ann Jones) was a deeply-felt evocation of the simple values of the chapel-going people of the

[20] Glyn Jones, op. cit., p. 198.

bleak hills. His poetry was often, though certainly not always, shot through with the ambivalences and tensions of a Wales he knew and undoubtedly loved—rural and urban, chapel-going and profane, Welsh and English, unforgiving and deeply compassionate. As one of his many biographers has truly remarked, 'No major English poet has ever been as Welsh as Dylan'.[21] He always remained, even in the headiest days of international adulation which ultimately were to kill him off in alcoholic stupor at the age of thirty-nine, the Swansea adolescent who never wholly grew up, 'the artist as a young dog' eternally larking about on the sand-dunes of Swansea Bay, wasting time happily in the Kardomah (later in the Three Lamps) or playing out the vivid, exhilarating fantasies of childhood among the old men sitting in the sunshine in Cwmdonkin Park.

Dylan Thomas, never any kind of nationalist, virtually apolitical in outlook, had a profound love of his native land. He could satirize it without the vindictive cruelty with which Caradoc Evans shocked his countrymen. It is the more ironic that Thomas, with his drunkenness and irresponsibility and yet with his strong loyalties and sense of cultural identity, should be reviled in parts of Wales twenty-five years after his death, or that 'Under Milk Wood' should be so misunderstood. For it is in the short stories and the broadcast talks that the affection for Wales and the deep understanding of its peculiarities and prejudices that moved Dylan Thomas to the core of his being, came out most clearly. His short stories on his boyhood in Swansea are marvels of their kind, an extraordinary mixture of humour, pathos, and compassion, with a special insight into part of south Wales as it emerged after the First World War. 'Under Milk Wood', broadcast by the BBC in 1952, was really based on a broadcast talk delivered early in the war under the title 'Quite Early One Morning'. It is based not on Laugharne, an English village, an enclave in Welsh west Wales that survived from the Norman invasions of centuries earlier, but on the little seaport of Newquay in Cardiganshire. It affords a marvellous panorama of the gentle tensions of small-town, parochial, chapel-going Welsh life, with its admixture of hypocrisy and spirituality, with its rich tapestry of personal kinships, relationships, and ambiguities expressed through the simple people of his native land. Dylan Thomas is, obviously, the major Welsh poet of the century (with R. S. Thomas perhaps his only conceivable rival), a giant-like figure in the crystallization of that Anglo-Welsh literary tradition which can be discerned in the latter part of the inter-war period. But he is also, in his gentle portrayal of such local titans as the Reverend Eli Jenkins, Mrs Ogmore Pritchard, Polly Garter, and the rest, a folk chronicler without compare of an eternal society, given a nobility and a stature that will endure as long as English literature is read. Dylan Thomas, so often derided as a kind of latter-day Caradoc Evans, a drunken, lecherous, roaring no-good Boyo, lurching free from the chains of

[21] Constantine FitzGibbon, *Dylan Thomas* (London, 1965), p. 19.

Welsh puritanism, is, among other things, the devoted folk remembrancer of a dignified, proud, secure little world which he drew in the round, in all its puny majesty. He gave it a universal meaning as the great artist alone can do. He wrote, as he said himself,[22] in praise of man and in praise of God—and perhaps in praise of Wales also. He would have been 'a damn fool' if he hadn't.

These young Welsh poets and essayists found more and more recognition in the thirties. They often knew each other well. For instance, Dylan Thomas, Vernon Watkins, and Glyn Jones were very close in the later thirties, and helped each other to gain wider audiences. They often met in congenial surroundings such as 'Griff's' Welsh bookshop at Cecil Court, just off the Charing Cross Road in London. They helped sharpen each other's sense of Welshness. Undoubtedly, they made the English-speaking majority of their land increasingly aware of its national distinctiveness. They now had local journals to publicize their work. Keidrych Rhys's literary quarterly, Wales, first published in the summer of 1937, was a landmark in the dawning of Anglo-Welsh literature, just as the Llenor was for Welsh-language writing. Many of the best of the young novelists, essayists, and above all poets of their generation wrote in it. Keidrich Rhys himself described it as 'a sort of forum where the "Anglo-Welsh" have their say, as poets, story writers and critics chiefly'.[23] Its first issue was remarkable enough, with a lively tale by Dylan Thomas, 'Prologue to an Adventure' that displayed many verbal pyrotechnics, poetry by Glyn Jones, Idris Davies, Vernon Watkins, and others, and indeed seventeen poems in all, most of them very good. Dylan Thomas was a frequent contributor to its columns: in the third issue of Wales in autumn 1937 he published one of his important poems from this period, 'We Lying by Seasand', as well as a short story. In August 1939, Wales widened its horizons to offer an 'eisteddfod number': it included a Welsh-language poem by the socialist minister-bard T. E. Nicholas, with, to balance it, a story by Caradoc Evans and some acid comments by Keidrich Rhys himself in the editorial. Meanwhile, in 1938 there had appeared in London, under the editorship of Robert Herring, Life and Letters Today, which came to be regarded for a while as an additional Anglo-Welsh magazine, and featured poems by Dylan Thomas, Vernon Watkins, Gwyn Jones, and many others.

Another native publication appeared in March 1939, the Welsh Review, edited by Gwyn Jones, the son of a Blackwood miner who was to rise to become Professor of English at the University College, Aberystwyth, and was himself a distinguished writer and a warm patron of Anglo-Welsh authors. This was a more widely-ranging publication than Keidrich Rhys's Wales, with much coverage of political and social questions as well as affording a further platform for young Welsh writers. Both Wales and the Welsh Review had

[22] Foreword to Collected Poems 1934–1952 (London, 1952).
[23] Wales, No. 2 (August 1937), p. 35 (editorial).

much effect and offered immense encouragement to new authors. Professor Gwyn Jones later wrote, 'I wanted all my writers and readers to feel that, despite the barrier of language, they belonged with and to Wales'.[24] In the end, the war suspended publication of both *Wales* and the *Welsh Review*. The *Review* continued to appear between 1944 and 1948 before it was killed off by crippling financial burdens. *Wales* had a second lease of life in 1943–9 and a third (still under the editorship of Keidrich Rhys) in 1958–9. *Life and Letters Today* ceased publication in 1950. But the vital spark had been lit, as far as Anglo-Welsh writers were concerned. Keidrich Rhys's own edition of *Modern Welsh Poetry* in 1944 showed the extraordinary vein of literary creativity that had been discovered since the first appearance of his magazine seven years earlier. After the war, there were Anglo-Welsh periodicals such as *Dock Leaves*, edited by Raymond Garlick which first appeared in 1949 and turned into the more enduring form of the *Anglo-Welsh Review* in 1957, eventually edited by Roland Mathias. Later on, as will be noted in Chapter 12, there were to be *Poetry Wales* and *Planet* for the English-language writer in Wales. The full implications of all this were far from being fully clear at the advent of the Second World War in 1939. But beyond doubt a major new tradition in the cultural life of the nation had been launched, in a way that bade fair to build new bridges between the increasingly divided, 'two-tongued' linguistic communities.

In other areas, too, 'Anglo-Welshness' became a powerful element in cultural life. In many of the arts, there was still relatively little to report. Welsh drama, such as Emlyn Williams's 'The Corn is Green', flourished only on the London stage. Welsh architecture, too, was still embryonic. In part this was a result of the primitive character of town planning in much of the land, of which Edgar Chappell eloquently complained in the yearbooks of the Welsh Housing and Development Association.[25] There were a few notable landmarks in architecture. There was Percy Thomas's monumental, neo-classical Guildhall for Swansea (1934) and his Temple of Peace in Cardiff (1938); there was also the Italianate civic centre in Newport (1939), set on a hill above the town. A more original and colourful approach came from Clough Williams-Ellis, a benevolent socialist and friend of Bertrand Russell who ran the Council for the Preservation of Rural Wales. He began work (as a conservationist gesture) on an Italianate resort at Port Meirion on the border of south Caernarvonshire and Merioneth.

Painting in Wales was still a somewhat feeble plant. Augustus John, portrait painter and international Bohemian celebrity, kept up his Welsh associations. But his impact in creating a native Welsh school of art was non-existent. There were distinguished younger painters emerging, some of

---

[24] Gwyn Jones, 'The First Forty Years', loc. cit., p. 92.
[25] *Welsh Housing and Development Year Book*, 1933, p. 29. Edgar Chappell was at the time the chairman of the Glamorgan Housing and Town Planning Committee.

them products of the Swansea School of Art. The most powerful of them was Ceri Richards who left Swansea for the Royal College of Art in London in 1924. While his work in the thirties was heavily influenced by Picasso, Matisse, and Max Ernst, he also benefited from more native inspiration. He claimed to draw heavily on the influence of Dylan Thomas for his 'visual metaphors'. Following a commission to provide a visual treatment of Thomas's 'The Force that through the green fuse', he built up a close relationship with the poet. In addition, Richards often turned to traditional Welsh rural or industrial scenes for his themes. During the Second World War; he worked as a 'war artist' for a time and returned to the tinplate mill in Gowerton where his father had worked all his life. His sketches here of the roller-men and furnace-men of the pack mill provided a powerful comment on the dominant, all-encompassing power of the industrial machine and the helplessness of the worker in the face of it. Later he turned to religious themes: his 'Deposition', a treatment of the dismemberment of the body of Christ after the crucifixion, hangs in St. Mary's Church, Swansea. But Richards was a rare spirit, while his works after his death in 1970 were given far more prominence in the Tate Gallery and elsewhere than in his native land. In general, Welsh art was hardly a meaningful concept, nor one that related with any precision to either Welshness or Anglo-Welshness.

Music in Wales was a somewhat different matter. Here, some new themes emerged which served to unify the cultural sensibilities of people in each of the linguistic communities. The *eisteddfod* remained a powerful element in national life, but it was concerned almost entirely with choral singing, or with such traditional arts as *penillion* singing by children. The male-voice choirs, pulverized by the economic depression and mass emigration, were not as flourishing as before 1914, though there were still superb choirs such as the Morriston Orpheus, directed by Ivor Sims and splendid choral festivals such as the Three Valleys at Mountain Ash. Elsewhere, the musical side of the *eisteddfod* offered little in terms of novelty or artistic experiment. A creative young Welsh composer like Daniel Jones kept his distance from it. Composers and instrumentalists in Wales were in the main few in number and unsophisticated in quality. Only through the export of leading Welsh singers to the opera houses of Covent Garden or La Scala—tenors like Parry Jones, Evan Williams, or Tudor Davies, for instance—and through the frothy light-musical concoctions of Ivor Novello of Cardiff (the son of Dame Clara Novello Davies, the founder of the Welsh Ladies Choir) did Welsh music make any wider impact. The Welsh National Orchestra, backed by the BBC, at first survived for only three penurious years between 1928 and 1931, though after 1935 it was to have a happy and enduring reincarnation.

Something of a change, however, did take place in the inter-war years and this owed almost everying to the strenuous personal efforts of Sir Walford Davies. He was Welsh only to a very minor extent by blood; until 1918, he had achieved fame in England, largely as organist and choral director at the Temple Congregational chapel in London. Then he became both Professor of Music at the University College, Aberystwyth, and also, in effect, a kind of director of the Council of Music set up to promote musical education in Wales. Walford Davies was a distinguished, if not outstanding, composer. After he had left Aberystwyth in 1926, worn out by his evangelizing on behalf of classical music, he was to become Master of the King's Musick in succession to Sir Edward Elgar. He was also a deeply religious man, for whom devotion to music and homage to God were almost inseparable. Walford Davies had a powerful influence on the appreciation of serious music in Wales. In his eight years at Aberystwyth he became a crusader of extraordinary single-mindedness. He spread the gospel of music vigorously in Aberystwyth itself—its music festival brought composers like Elgar, Vaughan Williams, German, and Holst, conductors like Sir Henry Wood and Adrian Boult, to the little seaside town. He also worked tirelessly in promoting musical education and music festivals among the schools and villages up and down the land. As director of the Council of Music in Wales, a post he retained after he had left Aberystwyth, he helped generate a concern for orchestral and instrumental music comparable with the passion for choral singing in the past. He was also imaginative enough to see the potentiality of broadcasting for the spread of musical education in schools and colleges. Walford Davies was in the best sense a popularizer, a man who built on a native love of choral singing and made musical appreciation more professional and more profound. After his efforts, there were indeed many new respects in which the Welsh could be claimed as a musical nation.

But he operated, too, at a more rarefied level, culturally and socially. Walford Davies had come to Aberystwyth largely through the persuasive efforts of that many-sided philanthropist David Davies of Llandinam, and his two remarkable sisters, Gwendoline and Margaret. Throughout the period from 1920 to 1940, Walford Davies and the Davies sisters organized a remarkable series of musical performances, orchestral concerts, chamber concerts, solo recitals by pianists, violinists, cellists, and singers of international distinction. Most impressive of all, there were great choral concerts. All these activities were conducted in Gregynog Hall, newly purchased by the Davies family in 1918 in the remote countryside north of Newtown in Montgomeryshire. The music room (formerly the billiard room) was initially the main salon used. Later, a large concert hall was added to the back of the house. The range of the Gregynog festivals widened: from 1933 to 1938 major festivals of music and poetry were held there as well. Clearly, this gave new horizons to the cultural life and social pretensions of the Welsh intellectual and academic bourgeoisie who flocked to these remarkable performances. Their impact on Welsh musical life more generally may, however, be questioned. While international celebrities by the score performed there, and complex works by Holst, Vaughan Williams and other composers often figured on the programme, Walford Davies and the Davies sisters considered Welsh composers to be mostly inferior and not worth much attention. So, beyond string quartets based on Welsh folk songs, composed by such as E. T. Davies, the director of music at the University College of North Wales, Bangor, and a particular enthusiast for organ music, native music had scant outlet at Gregynog. For all that, it was undoubtedly a powerhouse of artistic inspiration for at least a segment of Welsh society in the twenties and thirties, an institution unique in its time.

Gregynog encouraged other arts in Wales, too. The monthly periodical, *Welsh Outlook*, was published there until it was wound up at the end of 1933. Its founder, Thomas Jones, was always deeply enmeshed in the Davies world. The Gregynog Press provided rare examples of specialist printing and book-production, and produced some remarkable instances of the art of the printer, down to the Second World War. Some eight of the Gregynog books were in the Welsh language, printings of sixteenth-century poetry and the like.[26] On the whole, however, Gregynog may be safely lodged in the world of the Anglo-Welsh. None of the Davies family spoke Welsh, nor did any of the production staff at the Gregynog Press. The atmosphere of this country house was testimony to that growing attempt to link the Welsh world with wider cultural and aesthetic inspiration. In practice, that meant that it was conceived in the English language, and in terms of the artistic and commercial canons of England and the English class system.

In all these respects, Wales was a culturally thriving and lively country in the thirties. Yet it was equally clearly a divided one. The Anglo-Welsh authors and patrons of music were undoubtedly sincere in their attachment to Welshness. Glyn Jones later wrote 'The only thing English about an Anglo-Welsh writer ought to be his language'.[27] He himself tried valiantly to bridge the linguistic divide, and actually served as adjudicator of Welsh literary competitions at the national *eisteddfod*. Emyr Humphreys was later to write with facility and distinction novels in Welsh and in English. Yet the very existence of the Anglo-Welsh school merely served to heighten popular awareness of the cultural divide between the two linguistic communities. It was exemplified by the social contrasts between the cosmopolitan life of the coalfield in the south, and the relatively unchanged world of the pastoral uplands. The rapid success gained by Dylan Thomas and other Anglo-Welsh authors was evidence of growing anglicization and americanization of culture and society.

During the Second World War, this cultural divide became more pronounced. It is impossible to document with precision the changes that took

---

[26] G. Tegai Hughes and others (eds), *Gregynog* (Cardiff, 1977), p. 116.
[27] Glyn Jones, op. cit., p. 208.

place between 1939 and 1945 because no language or other census was held in 1941. But the pressures upon the culture and language of a contracting, mainly rural society became all the more powerful. Between 1939 and 1945, the retreat of the Welsh language must have continued apace. It did not much avail that the authorities showed somewhat more sensitivity and flexibility towards its use. For instance, the passage of the all-party Welsh Courts Act introduced by Herbert Morrison in 1942 gave legal validity to the use of Welsh in court proceedings—a kind of posthumous victory for Saunders Lewis and his nationalist colleagues in the bombing trial in 1937. It also reflected the fact that 23 out of 36 Welsh MPs spoke their native tongue. On most other levels, the challenges to Welshness were infinitely more shattering even than in 1914–18. Through newspapers, film newsreels, and above all through the radio, the impact of total war, the speeches of politicians and generals and admirals, delivered in English or translated into it, made their impact insidiously on more and more households and families. Native institutions such as the *eisteddfod* went into temporary eclipse. When Lloyd George died in March 1945, in somewhat pathetic circumstances in the family home at Criccieth, at the age of eighty-two, it was almost symbolic of the passing of an era, the final curtain on the human tragi-comedy of Welsh-speaking, noncon-formist, Liberal Wales which Lloyd George's own career had so directly embodied. But that career had also diverged the more markedly from it—witness the home at Churt in Surrey, and the second marriage to Frances Stevenson in 1943. Adopting a title to become Earl Lloyd-George of Dwyfor in January 1945, an ironic fact for Wales's great commoner and the hammer of the peers in 1909, was a sign of shifting values. Somehow, one cannot imagine Thomas Gee or Henry Richard accepting a peerage.

During the war, Englishness seeped into Wales through all kinds of channels. There were thousands of evacuees, children fleeing from the blitz and Nazi bombing in England. Lancastrians and Midlanders ended up in Anglesey, Caernarfon, Merioneth, and Cardiganshire; Londoners landed up in Glamorgan, even, ironically enough, amongst depressed families in the Rhondda who now had yet another burden to sustain. They often absorbed a good deal of Welshness when they landed there. Polish migrants to the Vale of Aeron in Cardiganshire or to the coalfield around Wrexham soon became happily trilingual and absorbed into the local community without any diffi-culty of adjustment. But, without doubt, Welsh schoolchildren were much affected in their turn in speech and in thought-patterns by these strangers from England or beyond, perhaps youthful prophets of a more exciting world. In part, this underlay the founding of the Urdd school at Aberystwyth in 1939. The impact of English and other non-Welsh soldiers, billeted upon Welsh communities along the Cardigan Bay coast in the years up to the D-Day landings in Normandy in 1944 was also profound. Not infrequently they married local Welsh girls, and they usually returned after the war (if they survived it) to cities and towns in England, their families with them. Inter-marriage between the nations meant, usually, that Welsh went to the wall, and that the children of such families forgot, or were never told, what it was to be Welsh. The government showed intermittent recognition of Welsh sentiment, as has been seen. There was a 'Welsh day' inaugurated in the House of Commons on 17 October 1944; the first such debate was launched, appropriately enough, by Lloyd George's daughter, Lady Megan, now Liberal member for Anglesey. Wales was recognized as a unit for planning purposes and in terms of the consideration of post-war reconstruction, as will be seen in the next chapter. The Welsh Advisory Panel of the Ministry of Reconstruction made a powerful plea in 1944 for Wales to be treated as a distinct unit for industrial and commercial planning after the war. But this could be no more than a façade. The pressures of wartime, impinging on local societies even more directly than after 1914, along with the growth of more powerful and persuasive instruments of mass communication, merely added to the doubts and fears of patriots for the future of the country and its culture. Whatever 'the Welsh way of life' comprised, it was clearly being swamped by the collectivist, centralizing forces entailed in another total war. The worlds of the Welsh and of the Anglo-Welsh, for all the patriotism and the occasional nationalism of the apostles of the latter, continued to diverge. The heightened cultural sensibilities of the twenties and thirties, then, did not bind Wales more closely together. In some ways, they helped perpetuate its divisions. The more hopeful national movements of the thirties were swamped in a new holocaust of violence through which the distinctiveness and the personality of small nations would be the more decisively undermined.

CHAPTER 10

THE LABOUR ASCENDANCY

The economic depression and the cultural divisions of the inter-war period and the Second World War coincided with a totally new phase of political and social leadership in Wales. By 1922 it was clear that the classes and organizations that had dominated public life since the later Victorian era were in full retreat. From the early twenties until the end of the Second World War—indeed for at least three decades after 1945—a period of Labour ascendancy over the political and industrial life of Wales was inaugurated even more overwhelming in extent than had been the Liberal ascendancy of the years from 1880 to 1914. In the general election of 1922, Labour put up 28 candidates in the 36 Welsh seats and they polled 40.8 per cent of the total vote in Wales, an increase of 10 per cent in Labour's share of the vote since the 'coupon election' of 1918. This proportion of the votes showed an overall tendency to rise during the mass unemployment and industrial conflict of the twenties. In the 1923 general election, Labour's share of the Welsh vote rose to 42.0 per cent. After slipping back slightly in the election of 1924, with the confusion that surrounded the fall of the first Labour government accompanied by some tendency for Conservatives and Liberals to fight on a joint anti-Labour or 'anti-socialist' platform, Labour's vote then rose again. In the general election of June 1929, which heralded the return of the second minority Labour government, Labour polled 577,554 votes in Wales. Its thirty-three candidates gained 43.9 per cent of the vote.

Clearly, then, since the war a political revolution had taken place. In no part of the British Isles was Labour more firmly entrenched than in the south Wales valleys. Virtually every industrial seat in Glamorgan and Monmouthshire, excluding eastern Monmouthshire, Newport, Cardiff, the Vale of Glamorgan (Llandaff and Barry), and Swansea West was a seemingly impregnable Labour stronghold, with Labour candidates of almost any complexion and drawn from any wing of the party assured of the almost automatic loyalty of a large and growing majority of the electors, male and female. Llanelli in eastern Carmarthenshire was another safe Labour seat by this time, while Carmarthen, with its mining areas in the Amman and Gwendraeth valleys, and Wrexham in the north-east, which included collieries and steel-works, were other constituencies where Labour was showing a steady increase in strength. At a more local level, the almost unbroken ascendancy of Labour on the county councils of Glamorganshire and Monmouthshire after 1919, and on bodies such as urban district councils in industrial areas was a further confirmation of a seemingly irreversible tendency. Wales, a citadel of traditional Liberalism in the recent past, had turned rapidly into a stronghold of the far left, with a growing army of MPs and local councillors as their spearhead and a mass army of trade unionists and their families behind them. The entire structure of authority in Wales had been revolutionized.

As has been seen, the foundations of this change had been laid in the period between 1918 and 1924. Labour then emerged clearly as the voice of protest and of radical change in opposition to the Coalition government after the armistice, and the Conservative governments that followed it. The high passion aroused in the coalfield during the period of the Sankey Commission on the mines and the 'betrayal' of workers' solidarity on 'Black Friday' between 1919 and 1921 saw marked increase in class consciousness and in industrial solidarity. The Labour Party was the inevitable political legatee. Profound sociological and economic transformations in the coalfield led to an almost automatic transformation in party politics, the more emphatic in view of the massive expansion of the electorate under the new Represenation of the People Act in 1918. In more direct terms, the advance of Labour meant a growing influence of the representatives of the trade unions, the miners above all. Of the sixteen Welsh Labour MPs returned at the general election in October 1924, thirteen were, or had been, prominent trade-union officials. Twelve of them were miners, the sole exception being the steelworker, Tom Griffiths who sat for Pontypool. Long-established miners' agents such as Vernon Hartshorn (Ogmore) or David Watts Morgan (Rhondda East) were again returned, along with newer personalities such as George Hall (Aberdare), Morgan Jones (Caerphilly), T. I. Mardy Jones (Pontypridd), and David Grenfell (Gower). Most of these trade-union spokesmen did not cut a dominating figure either in parliament or on the hustings. Most of them were destined to enjoy years of relative obscurity on the backbenches with only George Hall, Dai Grenfell, and Vernon Hartshorn due to attain ministerial office later in their careers. But parliamentary or rhetorical distinction was not why they were selected by constituency or divisional Labour parties. They were chosen for their record of devotion, industry and efficiency in the world of the trade union, for their activity as miners' agents, councillors, and local public leaders, above all as symbols of a class, the almost anonymous spokesmen of the proletariat of the coalfield, now for the first time within sight of the commanding heights of political, if not of economic power.

The three Welsh Labour MPs in 1924 who were not trade unionists are also worthy of note. Llanelli was now represented by a medical doctor, Dr J. H. Williams of Burry Port, Labour's candidate before the war and finally victorious in 1922. This was a reward for long and loyal service to the socialist cause, not least for confronting the coalowners in cases involving disabled miners injured in pit accidents. Merthyr, as has been noted in Chapter 7, returned R. C. Wallhead, the former president of the ILP and a disciple of the socialist and pacifist traditions of Keir Hardie. And for Aberavon Ramsay MacDonald was returned again; it was a natural seat for him in view of its powerful ILP branch at Briton Ferry and its largely working-class electorate of miners and steel- and tinplate workers. MacDonald's first post-war venture in by-elections had been a disastrous episode at Woolwich in 1921 where he was reviled as a pacifist and a traitor by the right-wing press; he had been defeated by a candidate holding the Victoria Cross who stood as a supporter of the Coalition. In south Wales, MacDonald found a safe haven. He now had fresh prestige after his period as Labour's first Prime Minister—and also as Foreign Secretary, where he had achieved marked success especially in connection with disarmament. MacDonald, like that previous chairman of the parliamentary Labour Party, Keir Hardie, now bade fair to use south Wales as the springboard for a limitless political ascent, on and on and on, up and up and up, to adopt his own characteristic style of rhetoric.

The main political interest in the mid- and later twenties lay in whether the growing success of Labour (marginally checked in 1924) could be frustrated by some kind of revival of traditional Liberalism. The Liberal heritage was still a powerful one in Wales; ten Liberal candidates were returned there in 1924, a quarter of the parliamentary Liberal Party. The old causes could certainly not be discounted, especially after the reunion of the Lloyd Georgian and Asquithian wings in November 1923, and the return of Lloyd George as the voice and the inspiration of almost all Liberals. The renewed challenge of Liberalism in the years 1925–9 was very much associated with Lloyd George personally. The great majority of Liberal Associations in Wales had remained faithful to him even in the difficult years of coalition between 1918 and 1922. The majority of the Asquithian dissidents returned to support their old hero after 1923. One exception was in Cardiganshire where the barrister, Rhys Hopkin Morris, took on the mantle of Llewelyn Williams (who had died) and defeated the incumbent Lloyd George Liberal, Ernest Evans, with some ease in 1923. This was after a Conservative intervened to take 6,000 votes away from Evans and doom him to defeat. Cardiganshire, apart from Camborne in Cornwall, was the only seat in 1923 where Liberals of rival persuasions remained unreconciled and fought one another. Hopkin Morris remained hostile to Lloyd George and refused to accept his titular leadership in the general election of 1929.

But Lloyd George's dramatic new programmes, the 'green book' on the land in 1925, the 'yellow book' on industrial recovery in 1928, the 'orange book' on conquering unemployment in 1929, aroused much excitement amongst most other Welsh Liberals. After being encumbered for years with the remnants of the old Liberalism of pre-1914, disestablishment, temperance, church schools and the like, they now had an up-to-date dynamic programme, thoroughly relevant to the needs of a new century, and conceived by Keynes, Henderson, Layton, Rowntree, and others drawn from the finest economic intelligence of their generation. Lloyd George's schemes, however, did not command universal approval in Wales. In particular, as has been seen, *The Land and the Nation* (1925) aroused some anxiety for its proposals to create a system of 'cultivating tenure', a kind of quasi-nationalization of the land, under which the state would resume the ownership of cultivable land and then let it to tenants at favourable rents. After the 'green revolution' of 1918—25 which had seen so many freeholders freshly installed on their holdings in rural Wales, these prospects for apparently undermining the new system of free proprietorship caused much dismay. Sir Alfred Mond left the Liberal Party on this account and crossed the floor to sit as a Conservative, in protest against the 'green book'. 'He had gone to his own place', observed Lloyd George. However, Mond was perhaps no loss since he was unpopular in Wales as a capitalist, an industrialist and, not least, a Jew. He sat for Carmarthen as he had done since a by-election in 1924. When he resigned his seat in 1928 to sit in the House of Lords as Lord Melchett, the resulting by-election in Carmarthen caused some disarray among local Liberals. They had deposed as their prospective candidate, Captain R. T. Evans, a Lloyd George supporter and a warm advocate of the doctrines of the 'green book'. Instead, they nominated Colonel W. N. Jones, a landowner who opposed the 'green book' proposals and was also, apparently, a kind of protectionist. With some diffidence, Lloyd George spoke in his support in the by-election. But morale was not good amongst Carmarthen Liberals and the majority fell from nearly 10,000 to only 47 in the face of a vigorous Labour challenge.

Despite these local difficulties, Lloyd George continued to inject new life into Welsh Liberalism as a general election approached in 1928—9. Never had Liberalism in the principality (outside Cardiganshire) been more totally under his sway. Indeed, it was becoming dynastic in character. His son, Gwilym, had already sat for Pembrokeshire in 1922—4 and seemed likely to be returned again next time. His far more radical younger daughter, Megan, had been nominated in Anglesey in 1928 (after some local machinations in which Dame Margaret was much implicated)[1] and seemed certain to retain this established Liberal seat. Goronwy Owen, a family relative, was already installed in Caernarvonshire. The former Prime Minister's private secretary, Ernest Evans, now represented the University of Wales, to make a kind of family entourage of five. Beyond the confines of the family circle, Lloyd George's influence permeated Liberalism widely as the general election approached in 1929. The 'orange book', *We Can Conquer Unemployment*, was held up as a kind of all-purpose panacea for ending the slump and

[1] Lloyd George to his wife, 30 March, 26 April, and to Megan Lloyd George, 22 May 1928 (*Family Letters*), pp. 207—9.

unemployment by Liberal candidates who made it the centre-piece of their programme. Even Hopkin Morris in Cardiganshire endorsed the main arguments of the 'orange book', while measuring his distance from Lloyd George personally. Liberal candidates in rural constituencies claimed that public-works schemes as outlined by Lloyd George and Keynes might save money on the rates. In industrial constituencies, J. Jenkins (candidate for Merthyr) and D. L. Powell (Ogmore) urged that road building, house construction, and other publicly-financed schemes would end the decay endemic in the coalfield since 1923. Many Welsh industrialists signed petitions in support of the pump-priming schemes of *We Can Conquer Unemployment*. They represented banking, construction, chemicals, electricity, engineering, insurance, oil, and textiles, the second industrial revolution much more than the first. They claimed that Lloyd George's proposals were 'economically and financially sound'.[2] Never, it seemed, had Liberalism confronted Labour with a more radical, challenging, and relevant programme.

Lloyd George had most of the glamour and captured most of the headlines in 1929. But it was Labour that won most of the votes. Indeed, the effect of the election was to confirm that Wales was even more strongly Labour territory now than it had been in the early years of the decade. Of course, the angry reaction that followed the general strike in 1926 powerfully spurred on Labour's progress. The Liberals, it is true, did increase their poll in Wales, though less impressively than in some other parts of Britain. Their proportion of the Welsh poll rose from 30 per cent in 1924 to 33.5 per cent now. Given a system of proportional representation their claim of dominance in Welsh politics might still have seemed impressive. Lloyd George complained that his party had been 'tripped up by the triangle' in three-cornered seats. But the effect was to see the tally of Welsh Liberal seats fall slightly, from eleven to ten. Pembrokeshire and Flintshire were captured from the Conservatives. But three seats in mainly industrial or urban areas were lost to Labour. In Swansea West, from where Runciman had beaten a judicious retreat to Cornwall, Walter Samuel recaptured the seat for Labour by a narrow majority. In Carmarthen, not surprisingly after the recent by-election, the barrister, Daniel Hopkin won this mixed agricultural/industrial seat for Labour with a 1.6 per cent margin. And in the north-east, at Wrexham, on a 13 per cent swing, Robert Richards regained the seat for Labour with a majority of over 6,500. The Liberal challenge had been rebuffed decisively. Never again was there to be any prospect of the old custodians of the radical conscience regaining their former standing in Wales. Indeed, the future was to reveal only a steady retreat from the ten seats gained in 1929 until the election of 1970 when only Montgomeryshire was left in Liberal hands.

For Labour, by contrast, the future was never more glowing. In all, it now

[2] *Western Mail*, 29 May 1929.

held 25 of the 36 Welsh seats. In addition to gaining Swansea West, Carmarthen, and Wrexham from the Liberals, a further six were won from the Conservatives, whose tally of Welsh constituencies fell to only one (Monmouth), their worst-ever showing, apart from the débâcle of 1906, worse even than 1945 was to prove. Labour took most satisfaction from the winning of all three Conservative-held seats in Cardiff. With its multiplicity of trades, Cardiff had never been as hopeful territory for Labour as had been the more homogeneous and sociologically closer-knit valley seats—a pattern reproduced by Labour's weakness in much of London, Birmingham, Liverpool, Bristol, and other urban areas in the twenties. All the Cardiff seats were finely balanced: in each, the Liberals continued to poll about a quarter of the votes while there was some cross-voting among anti-socialist voters. But the new impact and organizational strength of Labour in Cardiff were impressive. The most notable of the three new Labour MPs in Cardiff, perhaps, was Arthur Henderson's son, returned for Cardiff South, a seat he had held before in 1923−4. The other gains from the Conservatives were Newport (a seat Labour had long threatened to capture), Llandaff and Barry (where the working-class vote of the latter just about outweighed the clericalism and conservatism of the former), and a freak gain in Brecon and Radnor, largely attributable to Labour's strength in the industrial fringe on the south of Breconshire, from Ystradgynlais and Abercrave in the south-west to Brynmawr in the south-east. Two of the new Labour MPs are worthy of note. W. G. Cove, a formidable left-wing spokesman for the National Union of Teachers, succeeded MacDonald at Aberavon, as the new Prime Minister found a new haven in Seaham Harbour in Durham. Cove was to remain member for Aberavon for the next thirty years and a vigorous advocate of a comprehensive, universal system of state education. And Aneurin Bevan pursued his hunt for the elusive talisman of political power behind the Tredegar UDC, and was returned for Ebbw Vale. 'Where does power lie in this particular state and how can it be attained by the workers?'[3] For Bevan, the most brilliant of all the Labour recruits in 1929, the quest for power was to prove a baffling one—'you always saw its coat-tails disappearing round the corner'.

The next general election, that of October 1931, was a very different affair. It followed the disastrous collapse of the economy, with all the mass unemployment that resulted, the run on the pound in July−August 1931, followed by the collapse and resignation of the second Labour government after hopeless divisions over cuts in the social services. MacDonald now re-emerged as the head of a so-called 'National government' which almost all his party totally rejected. The new government promptly left the gold standard in September and then called a general election. The 'doctor's mandate' election of that October was marked by a good deal of hysteria, with much personal bitterness between MacDonald, Snowden, and J. H. Thomas,

[3] A. Bevan, *In Place of Fear* (London, 1976 reprint), p. 21.

who all joined the 'National government', and their old Labour followers. Labour's fortunes collapsed everywhere amidst the pressure exerted by political and financial circles to show that a victory for Labour would mean socialist ruin and a collapse in the nation's financial and commercial system. In all, only 46 Labour and five ILP members were to be returned, in place of the 289 elected in 1929. They confronted a massed army of some 554 supporters of the government, Conservative, Liberal, and 'National Labour'. It was one of the most devastating electoral landslides that Britain had ever known.

Naturally, these developments left their imprint in Wales. Labour lost eight seats here, while in Cardiff Central Sir Ernest Bennett retained his seat as one of the miniscule group of 'National Labour' supporters of MacDonald. Five seats were lost to the Conservatives, at Brecon and Radnor, Llandaff and Barry, Cardiff East, Cardiff South, and Newport (to Reginald Clarry, the hero of 1922). Labour seats also fell to 'National Liberals' (who supported the Simonite faction of the party) at Carmarthen and Swansea West, and to a loyalist Liberal supporter of Herbert Samuel at Wrexham. On the other hand, it is noticeable that the collapse of Labour's vote was much less pronounced in Wales than elsewhere. Indeed, with 16 members out of a parliamentary Labour Party of 46 (Wallhead, the ILP member for Merthyr, also rejoined the Labour Party in 1932 despite the disaffiliation of his party), the Welsh element, almost all miners, loomed large in the strength of the new, much-truncated parliamentary opposition. Further, while in Britain as a whole Labour's share of the poll had slumped to only 30.8 per cent (compared with 37 per cent in 1929), in Wales the reverse was true. Labour's share of the vote, extraordinarily enough, actually rose from 43.9 per cent in 1929 to 44.1 per cent in the 'doctor's mandate' election of 1931. These figures are misleading, of course, as there were some unopposed returns in 1931. Even so, it is clear that, amidst financial cataclysm and a mood of wild panic in 1931, south Wales beyond the coastal ports of the southern fringe remained secure for Labour. Most of the Labour majorities in the valleys were quite unaffected by the pressures surrounding the election. Some even increased in size. The general mood was one of intense class bitterness, both at the supposed 'bankers' ramp' that had led to the downfall of the second Labour government and at the 'betrayal' by MacDonald of his former allies and admirers in the working-class movement of south Wales.

Certainly, no real alternative to Labour's dominance presented itself. The swollen vote of candidates supporting the National government was as obviously unreal as had been the vote of 'couponed' supporters of the Coalition of Lloyd George in 1918. The Liberals were in even more disarray than before, with their ranks divided, like Gaul, into three parts. Four 'National Liberals' were returned, followers of Simon who were virtually indistinguishable from the Conservatives in their voting allegiance. They included such former pillars of rural Liberalism as R. T. Evans, formerly an enthusiast for Lloyd George's 'green book', now member for Carmarthen; and Dr Henry Morris-Jones, a nonconformist physician, now representing Denbigh. A rather more surprising recruit to National Liberalism was Clement Davies, a progressively-minded barrister who had succeeded David Davies as member for Montgomeryshire in 1929. He was to remain a supporter of the National government, though a highly independent-minded one, down to 1940. There were also four 'official Liberals' who followed Herbert Samuel into support for the National government in October 1931 and who followed him out of it in 1932 when the government adopted tariffs and imperial preference. There remained only Lloyd George's family group of four, himself, Megan, Gwilym, and Goronwy Owen. They were indeed, the only Liberals in the House formally lined up in opposition to the government and in general sympathy with Labour, even though Gwilym, always the most conservative of the family, had briefly served in the government as a junior minister prior to the election.

Lloyd George's personal charisma in Wales was now manifestly in decline. He was almost seventy and had been laid low by a serious operation at the time of the formation of the government in August. He spent much of his time now in seclusion at Churt, writing his war memoirs, with only occasional appearances in his native land such as the annual Thursday speeches to the national *eisteddfod*. Liberalism in Wales was largely leaderless now. Local organization was moribund. The Liberal press was also in decline. The old Cardiff daily, the *South Wales News* went out of circulation in 1928 and was absorbed by its more lively rival, the Conservative *Western Mail*. The Swansea *Cambria Daily Leader* had also disappeared while a weekly like the Aberystwyth *Cambrian News* (once a formidable mouthpiece of Gibson) was increasingly local and unpolitical in emphasis. Many adherents of Liberalism went out of politics for good. They found fulfilment above all in the Welsh branch of the League of Nations Union, presided over by Lord Davies of Llandinam, where the traditional commitment to peace and disarmament could be safely expressed in a non-partisan setting.

Of course, Lloyd George remained a potentially influential figure, old though he now was. In January 1935 he returned with powerful effect to make a speech to his Bangor constituents which called for a British 'New Deal' and a national attack on unemployment and industrial stagnation. This programme would feature public-works programmes and counter-cyclical policies much on the lines that he and Keynes had advocated in 1929. Later in the year, Lloyd George widened his attack and launched his 'Council of Action for Peace and Reconstruction' in which policies designed to attack unemployment would be combined with a more vigorous peace policy and support for the League of Nations. He made much use of the chapels in promoting this new popular crusade.[4] He still believed that in Wales and elsewhere they formed the

[4] S. Koss, *Nonconformity in Modern British Politics* (London, 1975), pp. 216 ff.

spearhead of radicalism. The support was gained of several leading Welsh nonconformist ministers including the Revd. Elfed Lewis and the Revd J. D. Jones, Bournemouth. Lloyd George used biblical imagery to press home his arguments: the public-works proposals were linked with the parable of the vineyard. But it was clear that the day had passed long since for this kind of one-man crusade to have much effect. Lloyd George was now a figure from the past, associated with a society and a culture that were fast disappearing. He seldom caught the imagination of the young now. In the words of Gwyn Jones in the *Welsh Review*, he represented 'the sarcophagus not the symbol of Welsh radicalism'. He added that 'for men and women of the reviewer's age [Professor Jones was born in 1907], Mr. Lloyd George has counted for next to nothing in public life',[5] Even if this is exaggerated, it cannot be disputed that Liberalism, either in its Lloyd Georgian or other manifestations, was much in decay and in no condition to withstand the aggressive upsurge of Labour.

After 1931, the Labour Party inevitably became the dominant voice of protest in Wales at the National government's domestic, and then foreign policies. Aneurin Bevan in particular became a most formidable spokesman for the working class in attacking the 'special areas' policy, in condemning the operations of the Assistance Boards for the unemployed, and in denouncing the means test. Later in the decade, notably during the civil war in Spain after July 1936, Bevan was to emerge in a wider context as a devastating critic of the inconsistencies and evasions of the so-called policy of non-intervention endorsed by Britain's National government. It was natural that in the next election of October 1935, Labour should regain some of the ground lost in 1931. Wrexham and Carmarthen were won back, and Labour now claimed 18 seats once again, half the Welsh total. Its share of the poll in Wales rose to over 45 per cent. Only in Cardiff, where Labour had distinguished candidates in each of the three seats (John Dugdale, Fenner Brockway, and H. L. Nathan—none, however, Welsh) was there a disappointing performance. Otherwise, Labour showed that it had clearly more than retained its strength and morale. In addition to maintaining its old strength in the mining valleys, it could put up a good fight in most of rural Wales as well. In Merioneth, Thomas Jones, representative of the Ffestiniog slate quarrymen, polled over a third of the vote and cut the Liberal majority in this traditional stronghold, Liberal since 1868, to just over 1,000. Even in the rural heartland (there were good Labour polls in Anglesey, Caernarvonshire, and Cardiganshire as well) the tide of Liberalism continued to ebb. The returns as a whole showed that eighteen Labour and seven Independent Liberals were returned, as against eleven variegated supporters of the National government.

The Welsh Labour Party in the House was more impressive now than in 1929. Aneurin Bevan was reaching new heights as an orator and critic of the deficiencies of the capitalist system. Merthyr returned, at a by-election in

[5] *Welsh Review,* i, No. 3 (April 1939).

1934, S. O. Davies, a sombre-clad representative of the ILP who had been a Marxist miners' agent after 1918 and much involved with the Minority Movement of the mid-twenties. For a time he had been a member of the Communist Party. For over thirty years, 'S.O.' was a somewhat eccentric but much-revered figure in Labour circles. He was much less revered by the party whips who expelled him from the parliamentary Labour Party on three occasions on a variety of issues. With his strongly left-wing stance on foreign policy and defence issues, and also his strong commitment to Welsh home rule (he was a Welsh speaker) Davies was a highly distinctive figure who built up a powerful personal following in Merthyr. This was to be seen in 1970 when attempts by the official machine to force him out on the grounds of age (Davies was now over 80) were triumphantly rebuffed.

Another powerful, and ultimately highly influential recruit to the Welsh Parliamentary Labour Party, as it was now organized, came in 1936 when James Griffiths, the president of the South Wales Miners' Federation, a former product of the Central Labour College, as has been seen, was returned for Llanelli in a by-election, swamping his National Liberal opponent by over 16,000 votes. Griffiths, the product of a militant, bitter generation, a veteran of the problems of the anthracite coalfield, the general strike in 1926, and the fight against company unionism in the thirties, was, in reality, a moderate figure of genuinely creative gifts. He campaigned strongly for anti-tuberculosis measures after the report of the Clement Davies Committee. Issues such as national insurance he made very much his own, and this was recognized by the award of high office in the Attlee government after 1945. He was to serve in Labour cabinets in 1950–1 and 1964–6, and to act for a time as deputy-leader of the party under Gaitskell, the most influential Welshman ever to rise to prominence in the party hierarchy. Jim Griffiths had a rare gift as a reconciler, an ability to appeal to all wings of the party. He was the only non-Bevanite to retain his seat as a constituency representative on Labour's national executive after 1951. He combined a deep-rooted attachment to his own mining community in west Wales with a profound and subtle sense of the arts of the possible. He was also a fluent Welsh speaker and a devoted supporter of Welsh national causes, including devolution. Appropriately, he was to serve as the first Secretary of State for Wales in 1964. He illustrated that process by which a class-conscious working-class movement could broaden its appeal, and strike firm roots amongst wider ranges of society and among men and women of patriotism and goodwill in all parties in Wales.

By the later thirties, then, the pattern of Labour's parliamentary ascendancy was clear beyond dispute. It was in total control of all the valley seats from Llanelli to Pontypool. It was making new inroads into seats in other areas of Wales, too, from Carmarthen to Anglesey, from Pembrokeshire to Wrexham. It faced a Conservative Party, which, along with its National

Liberal satellites, was vigorous only in the coastal strip from Swansea to Newport, in the old marcher territories of eastern Monmouthshire and Breconshire, and amongst elderly or retired voters in north Wales coastal resorts. The Liberal Party, as has been seen, was a decaying party throughout most of this period. In the valleys and in most of the urban and industrialized areas of Wales, it was defunct. Plaid Cymru until 1945 was scarcely a political party at all, and in no position to challenge for any parliamentary seat.

At the political level, in fact, Labour faced only one conceivable opponent for the long-term future. This was the Communist Party which had made some headway in south Wales since its foundation in 1920, notably in areas such as the Rhonda valleys where traditions of 'unofficial' rank-and-file movements, and of the Minority Movement of 1924–6 were powerful. There were some picturesque spokesmen for Communism in Wales. One impressive example was the Revd Thomas Nicholas, Glais, formerly Keir Hardie's Welsh editor of the *Merthyr Pioneer*, and a distinguished poet. He was finally expelled by his congregation for his left-wing activities, and in the Second World War was imprisoned for sedition after some remarkably free-wheeling invasions of civil liberty by the Cardiganshire police. He finally set up business in Aberystwyth as an unlicensed dentist, where dental therapy and left-wing ideology served almost as parts of the same highly distinctive treatment. Nicholas until his death in 1971 was a eccentric and much-loved symbol of the nonconformist radicalism of pre-1914 diverted into more revolutionary channels. Another Aberystwyth man, David Irvon Jones, an active Unitarian and member of the International Socialist League became the first (indeed probably the only) Welshman to be given a state funeral in the USSR (in 1924).[6] Meanwhile in south Wales, there were such talented literary Communists as Lewis Jones, the author of *Cwmardy*.

But the most important Welsh Communist was Arthur Horner, A. J. Cook's lieutenant in the Rhondda No. 1 District in the early twenties and a founder member of the party. Horner's political activities were much less significant than his industrial ones, but he did spearhead the one direct conflict between Labour and Communism in Welsh politics. He stood for Rhondda East against the distinctly right-wing figure of David Watts Morgan in 1931 and polled over 30 per cent of the vote. In March 1933, on Watts Morgan's death, there took place an exceptionally tense by-election between Horner (Communist) and William Mainwaring (Labour). Mainwaring, part-author of the *Miners' Next Step* and an old Central Labour College Marxist, was now very much an establishment right-wing social democrat. There was also a Liberal in the field, but he did not count. This was a historical battle for the allegiance of the unemployed miners of Rhondda and their families, fought out with much personal bitterness between Mainwaring and

[6] See Islwyn ap Nicholas, *Heretic at Large* (Llandysul, 1978).

Horner.[7] In the end, Mainwaring triumphed with a majority of 2,899 over Horner. It was a victory he repeated in 1935 with his majority rising to over 8,000 over Harry Pollitt. The Communist Party, and Horner in particular, retained much strength in the Rhondda over the years and probably increased it during the Second World War. In 1945, Harry Pollitt, editor of the *Daily Worker*, was to stand against Mainwaring this time and to cut his majority to less than a thousand. For all that, Mainwaring's narrow electoral majorities in 1933–5 were of much significance. They confirmed the strength of official Labour, just as the *Cymru Fydd* débâcle of 1896 confirmed the strength of official Liberalism. They showed that, in the political and industrial maelstrom of the thirties, south Wales still remained attached to the wider working-class movement of the British Labour Party and the Trade Union Congress, rather than take refuge in a purely local or particularist protest, conceived in terms of industrial rather than political action. The challenge of the sectarian far left had been rebuffed as effectively as had that of the orthodox, traditionalist right.

These political triumphs for Labour were but the political or parliamentary façade for a growing radicalization of south Wales during the depression years. Every major development in the industrial and economic history of the region from 1921 onwards underlined the fierce loyalty of most working people in the coalfield to their class and to its formal union representatives. As has been seen in Chapter 8, after the onset of depression and the collapse of the miners' strike in April–July 1921, there followed a bleak period. Under the dictates of the coalowners, swingeing wage cuts were implemented, as the only method they understood of making the Welsh coal industry internationally competitive. In some areas, wage cuts were imposed of as much as 75 per cent, the highest in any British coalfield. It was inevitable, then, given the wider background of mass unemployment, that the class struggles in south Wales should take on an even more bitter form.

The miners were shattered and broken financially after the collapse of the national coal strike in 1921, and no major industrial dispute followed for the next four years. There was, however, a remarkable explosion of industrial conflict in 1925 in the west Wales anthracite coalfield.[8] This area had remained relatively thriving since the war and its peaceable Welsh-speaking miners—men very much in the mould of Jim Griffiths—seemed more tranquil than their comrades in the eastern valleys with their high rate of immigration from England. The localized anthracite pits were very much village enterprises which had sprung up since the end of the last century. Most of the

---

[7] Materials in W. H. Mainwaring Papers, consulted by kind permission of Mrs J. Tudge.

[8] Hywel Francis, 'The Anthracite Strike and the Disturbances of 1925', *Llafur*, vol. 1, No. 2 (May 1973), pp. 15–28.

leaders of the anthracite men, however, save for James Griffiths, were from eastern regions of the coalfield. One of them was S. O. Davies himself. The strike erupted after a series of attacks by two new combines, the Amalgamated Anthracite and United Anthracite, both formed as recently as 1924, on the traditional working customs down the anthracite pits. From the start of July 1925, all the miners from Ammanford as far up the valleys as Abercrave went out on strike after the dismissal of two miners who refused to be moved from their traditional work places. There was much violence, usually caused by the import of blackleg labour, mostly in and around the small town of Ammanford. Almost two hundred miners were eventually prosecuted for their part in the riots that followed; fifty-eight were sentenced to terms in prison. These sentences were confirmed with scarcely-veiled satisfaction by the Home Secretary, Joynson-Hicks. There followed the mass victimization of miners who had been on strike and a renewed campaign by the coalowners on such hallowed working practices as the 'seniority rule' for employment. The entire episode, which ended in a reluctant return to work at the end of August, left memories of seething resentment and class bitterness throughout the hitherto peaceful anthracite coalfield. It confirmed that, even in this Welsh-speaking, chapel-going, rugby-playing community, industrial upheaval and economic pressure were pushing the miners on towards open class war.

In May 1926 that class war seemed to have arrived at last. The temper of the Welsh miners was now exceptionally bitter. The Minority Movement in south Wales, between 1924 and 1926, had been a further explosion of that rank-and-file militancy recurrent since 1910. It was stimulated in part by the employers' mindless pressure for further wage cuts, in part by the demand for district wage agreements. A Minority Movement representative, S. O. Davies, had been elected vice-president of the South Wales Miners' Federation in 1925 by a large majority over the right-wing Arthur Jenkins. More generally, the executive of the SWMF was increasingly firmly committed to a stern defence of its members' living standards. It no longer included Noah Ablett, whose health and prestige were now being undermined by drink; but it did contain other militants such as S. O. Davies and Mainwaring. At pithead level, there were effective advocates of direct industrial action like Arthur Horner at Maerdy. Overshadowing them all at this time was the towering figure of Arthur Cook, since 1924 the general secretary of the Miners' Federation of Great Britain, a militant Marxist and the most compelling socialist orator in south Wales. Cook's influence was later to wane dramatically. In 1931 he even appeared briefly as a supporter of Sir Oswald Mosley's 'New Party'. In time, his role became a hopeless one. As E. P. Harries later explained, it was impossible for Cook to play the revolutionary firebrand on platforms at week-ends, and also the conciliatory negotiator during the week, prepared to haggle in wage bargaining and even accept the need for wage cuts.[9] But in May 1926 Cook's prestige and inspirational influence were at their height.

When the General Strike took place on 3 May 1926, the Welsh miners, inevitably, were deeply involved. Indeed, the General Strike originated with a national miners' strike, the result of the refusal of the government to continue the subsidy to the coal industry, and the implementation of further wage reductions, after the report of the Samuel Commission. For the nine exciting days of May, therefore, the Welsh miners—and most of the workers in Wales generally—were 'solid', as they were to be for several months after May 1926 until the miners who remained out on strike were eventually forced back to work by sheer starvation. Pits were idle, factories were empty, trains and buses ceased to run. In mining areas, whole communities were mobilized to ensure that work came to a standstill, but that food and other essential supplies were brought in. Councils of Action were formed in mining villages to co-ordinate and run local transport services from chapels to workmen's halls. This almost spontaneous expression of class and community solidarity made an immense impact on the young men and women who took part in it. Will Paynter, for instance, always avowed that 1926 was Year One as far as he was concerned.[10]

Many testimonies have survived from the impact of that traumatic year. A study of Pontypridd has shown the immense effectiveness of the strike through the operations of the local strike committee and other voluntary and *ad hoc* organizations.[11] The strike committee negotiated the arrival of Co-op lorries with food supplies; it put pressure on bus and tramway drivers to join the stoppage; it negotiated with electricity power workers to ensure that what were deemed to be essential services were fully maintained. It even arranged for the musical and sporting entertainment of local people while the strike continued. Of course, even in south Wales, the strike was never 100 per cent 'solid'. By 11 May there were reports in the newspapers that the docking of vessels in Cardiff was being resumed, that tramway men were again at work in Cardiff, and there was a slow trickle of strikers returning to their jobs.[12] But on the whole it is the extraordinary loyalty and solidarity of the strikers that forms the abiding impression. South Wales was a 'Class One' region, according to the TUC's categories. Indeed, the evidence tends to suggest that the strike could have become even more total had the TUC given more trenchant instructions to its members in the localities and allowed categories of workers who were considered 'second line' to join the strike, as many of them were demanding. It was in London, not in areas like south Wales, that

---

[9] Quoted in Peter Stead, 'Working-Class Leadership in South Wales, 1900–20', *Welsh History Review*, vol. 6, No. 3 (June 1973), p. 352.

[10] *Llafur*, vol. 2, No. 2 (Spring 1977), p. 25.

[11] E. Watts-Edwards, 'The Pontypridd Area' in Margaret Morris (ed.), *The General Strike* (London, 1976), pp. 411–25.

[12] *South Wales News*, 11 May 1926.

the weakening of resolve came. It is worth pointing out that workers in other parts of Wales also took part in the General Strike with remarkable fervour. In north-east Wales, services and strike organizations were largely run by the Transport Workers Union. In north-west Wales, the railwaymen bore the brunt. A thousand men stopped work in Holyhead, the port in Anglesey which served as the gateway to Ireland, and paralysed its activities. In Bangor and Caernarfon no newspaper appeared, as the printers displayed their fellow-feeling with miners and stopped work. Meanwhile in south Wales, it was calculated that at least 90 per cent of the workers requested to stop work by the TUC had joined the stoppage. Furthermore, this extraordinary social demonstration had been totally peaceful, with police and strikers observing a calm co-existence, and towns and villages tranquil enough.

The decision by the general council of the TUC to call off the General Strike on 12 May caused an enormous revulsion in south Wales, comparable to 'Black Friday' in 1921. There was much tension amongst railwaymen in Cardiff and elsewhere over whether to obey their union's instruction and to return to work. But by 18 May most categories of workers had returned to their jobs. The miners were left to fight on, and to suffer, alone. A terrible war of attrition now followed, with a lock-out by the coalowners and mass victim-ization of those considered to have been activist during the General Strike. The poverty and suffering in the valleys now became more intense, even if the glorious summer weather of 1926 made conditions more bearable. It was in this dreadful final phase that the General Strike and its aftermath made their full impact upon the consciousness of the coalfield. As autumn set in, con-ditions were even more grim. Edward Greening of Aberdare, sixteen at the time, was one later witness.

Gone were the golden summer days of swimming in the river Cynon, the cheerful crowds of men and boys digging on the tips and coal patches of the Aberdare area . . . gone were the fun and the glamour of the jazz bands, the swimming gala and the flower shows; the delights of the Go-as-you-Please competitions; the cold autumn rains of late October had now come. Our families after five months of desperate poverty now faced the prospect of a grim winter.[13]

Inevitably, the miners had to surrender. On 1 December there was an orderly return to work throughout the Welsh coalfield.

It had been a period accompanied by intense debates and conflicts between Arthur Cook and other miners' leaders as to the correct strategy to adopt; Cook himself, so long the apocalyptic messiah of his men, was now attacked for defeatism. A post-mortem was begun on the value and the realities of the struggle. Some miners' leaders, for instance Oliver Harris, the treasurer of the SWMF from 1926 to 1931, came to believe that the very notion of a general strike needed to be looked at afresh, without ideological preconceptions.[14]

[13] *Llafur*, vol. 2, No. 2 (Spring 1977), p. 36.
[14] Ibid., p. 29.

Certainly, he considered the prolongation of the strike for six months after May to have been an immense blunder. Cook himself was much chastened at the collapse of that general strike for which he had orated and preached since 1910. As has been noted, he finished up a sympathizer with Sir Oswald Mosley's New Party. His impact upon the mining community and the British working class was never to be the same again.

Arthur Horner remained close to Cook, but now he became the voice of that continuing minority who advocated direct industrial action. However, instead of the quasi-syndicalism of his youth, Horner in middle age advocated something like the 'one big union' of the American de Leonists. He now supported the abolition of the Welsh Miners' Federation in favour of one nationwide miners' union—for which, in practical terms, there was everything to be said. Horner went back to Maerdy, bitter and crushed in spirit. 'If the whole coalfield had stood as firmly as Maerdy we could have won,' he concluded.[15] But what precisely 'won' meant in this context, when neither the miners nor anyone else were committed to taking over the fabric of government and the operations of the state itself, was not made clear. On balance, the suffering of the General Strike and its aftermath did bring one positive consequence in its train. It marked the effective end of the compelling myth of industrial action as a means of overthrowing gradualism and moderation, and enforcing total change. The pendulum eventually swung back towards men like James Griffiths, Enoch Morrell, Arthur Jenkins, and Oliver Harris, joined now by former militants like Will Mainwaring who saw that only through peaceful, non-revolutionary, democratic socialism would a real revolution in the life of the valleys be brought about. Nineteen twenty-six would never be forgotten in the Welsh valleys—but neither would it ever be repeated.

The General Strike left a legacy of bewilderment and despair amongst the miners and other workers in Wales. All the suffering seemed to have been in vain. This was underlined after 1929 with the onset of a phase of still more appalling economic disaster which saw mass unemployment rise to new heights. In these circumstances, it was not surprising that trade-union solidarity showed signs of weakening. Union funds ran down to a mere £9,000 credit balance, and so did affiliated payments to the Labour Party. The latter was partly the result of the Baldwin government's Trade Disputes Act of 1927 which had substituted contracting-in for contracting-out as far as the political levy to the Labour Party was concerned. By 1932, the SWMF which had claimed 136,000 members in the mid-twenties, now saw its membership run down to only 60,000. Poverty, emigration, the disillusion that followed the General Strike all took their toll. So, too, as will shortly be seen, did the growth of company unionism and the prevalence of blacklegs. When James Griffiths became president of the SWMF in 1934 he found that, out of 140,000

[15] A. Horner, *Incorrigible Rebel* (London, 1960), p. 91.

miners in the coalfield, only 76,000 were actually members of the union. The first task for the union was to encourage miners to join, and to resist the downward drift of wages that had continued since 1923. This wage situation was accentuated in 1931 when an obscure lawyer, F. P. Schiller KC, had awarded a new system of differential wages to distinguish between married, single, and childless miners. It was a system that seemed to the Miners' Federation to set the level of wages scandalously low. For a married man at the worst period of the depression, for example, Schiller awarded just 7s. 6d. a day, on the basis of his assessment of the profits and general economic viability of the mining industry.[16]

In 1934, the miners felt sufficiently emboldened to try to secure a modest general increase in these starvation wages, and to launch a campaign for an increase of 2s. a day for miners of all grades. The miners' 'two bob' could become as evocative a cry as the 'dockers' tanner' had been long ago. Some progress was made when Ernest Brown, the Minister of Labour, sent the matter to arbitration which raised the Schiller award by a modest amount. There was at this time much awareness of the destitution and hardship widespread in the mining community. The middle-class conscience in the suburbs was beginning, faintly, to be stirred. This awareness was tragically reinforced in the autumn of 1934 by the impact of the appalling colliery explosion in the mining village of Gresford, near Wrexham, when over 260 miners and three rescue workers lost their lives in a pit explosion. Their bodies were left in an underground charnel house while the pit was closed down. After Gresford, some action on behalf of the miners had to come, and in early 1935 there was a small breakthrough. The daily subsistence wage was raised to 8s. 1d. It was pathetically small, and went nowhere towards restoring the miners' loss of purchasing power since 1923. But it was at least the first pay increase for over ten years. The miners, perhaps, were starting on the road back at last.

There was another challenge to be met by industrial labour in these years, one as fundamental as the decline in wages and in living standards. This was a threat to the very existence of trade unionism itself. Non-unionism had hardly been a problem in south Wales before 1926—merely a matter of a few recalcitrant or forgetful individuals. But after the devastating effect of 1926, with the tension aroused from July onwards as a few men began to drift back to work, new independent unions came into being. They were associated with the so-called 'Spencer Unions', centred on the coalfields in the English Midlands. At Point of Ayr colliery in Flintshire, company unionism first appeared in the north Wales coalfield. A new Industrial Union appeared in this large and relatively thriving colliery, as a rival to the official North Wales Miners' Union: it was claimed that by 1936 wages in Point of Ayr were 23 per cent higher than in the north Wales coalfield as a whole.

[16] Hywel Francis and David Smith, *The Fed* (London, 1980), pp. 176–7.

In south Wales, a miner named Gregory became the secretary of the new 'Industrial Union'.[17] It was clearly intended to undermine the SWMF, the old 'Fed', and to form a new company union. Impetus was given to the movement by the opening of a new modern pit at Trelewis early in 1926. The Taff-Merthyr Steam Coal Company who opened it insisted that no miners employed there should or could be members of the 'Fed'. It was claimed that by the end of 1927 no less than 50,000 Welsh miners were members of this 'anti-political' breakaway movement. Many who had been blacklegs in 1926 naturally turned to it as their new spiritual home. This threat roused SWMF leaders of all political shades, from Vernon Hartshorn to Arthur Horner, but the SWMF executive, shattered in finances and in morale after the General Strike, was largely helpless. When James Griffiths became president of the SWMF in 1934, he launched a vigorous recruiting drive in the coalfield. More important, the structure of the Federation, largely unreformed since pre-war days in spite of the demands of the syndicalists, was radically altered, with direct representatives of the rank and file now placed on the executive and a reduced status for miners' agents. But it was at the local level that the main protest against company unionism was expressed—in places like Trelewis which had been company towns since 1926 and in places like Bedwas and Bedlinog where anger against traitors to the union coming from miners and their wives often spilled over into physical violence.

The most dramatic, spontaneous episode of all came at Nine Mile Point colliery near Bedwas, Monmouthshire, in October 1935. Here the local miners decided to adopt the tactic of the 'stay-down stoppage', previously used with success by Hungarian miners, to drive out of the pit those few miners who were not members of the Federation. The Welsh miners thus anticipated by well over a year 'stay-in' strikes in American car plants at Flint, Michigan, and elsewhere. After a remarkably heroic resistance by hundreds of miners who stayed down the pit for over a fortnight, despite the cost to their health, the battle was won. The company union there disappeared. So, too, was it won, more peacefully, at Bedwas colliery, another centre of non-unionism, where the coalowners were persuaded to recognize only the SWMF for purposes of wage negotiations. By the end of 1935, as a result of skilful action by the executive of the Miners' Federation and heroic efforts at local pits such as Nine Mile Point, company unionism in the coalfield was virtually extinct. Another saga in the history of the coalfield, comparable in courage with that of Merthyr in 1831, had ended with total victory for the union, for class solidarity, and the shared values of a whole community.

After such episodes as these, it is not surprising that the industrial society of south Wales was throughout the thirties largely consumed by class bitterness. There was the perennial background of unemployment and of mass emigra-

[17] D. Smith, 'The Struggle against Company Unionism in the South Wales Coalfield, 1926–1939', *Welsh History Review*, vol. 6, No. 3 (June 1973), pp. 354 ff.

tion. There were the recurrent indignities of the dole and the means test. There was the constant participation of Welsh miners in demonstrations of the unemployed and in hunger marches on the Jarrow pattern. The symbol of this steady shift to a more militant mood, side by side with the election of new leaders in the union, came in May 1936 when Arthur Horner was elected the first Communist president of the SWMF after James Griffiths had been nominated as parliamentary candidate for Llanelli. Horner's arrival was accompanied by much ominous muttering in the daily press. In fact, he was to prove a remarkably resilient, effective and pragmatic president of the Welsh miners. As befitted a sound Marxist, he was prepared to bide his time and to accept the system much as it was, for purposes of immediate collective bargaining, pending the advent of a socialist revolution. He worked well with his moderate general secretary, Oliver Harris. One of his important early achievements was the 1937 Daywage Agreement, negotiated with Sir Evan Williams himself, with whom Horner struck up a remarkably good relationship. This reduced many anomalies in wage rates and reduced the number of grades of miners from 150 to only six. It was a marked advance towards the principle of 'equal pay for equal work'. On the other hand, Horner insisted that the miners observe their side of the agreement in an ordered, disciplined fashion, and that unofficial stoppages, stay-down strikes, and the like, be avoided. There was some talk amongst the miners of the poacher having turned gamekeeper. Even so, the emergence of Horner as president did surely herald a growing radicalism in the coalfield as younger agents and other miners' representatives, many of them members of the Communist Party, came to the fore. There were other active Communists in the union, like Idris Cox, Will Paynter, Will Whitehead, and others, giving a sharper edge to the class consciousness of the period. Dai Dan Evans of Abercrave, who was to succeed Horner as agent for the anthracite district in 1939, was to declare that the three books that had most powerfully influenced his outlook were the Communist Manifesto, *Wage, Labour and Capital* and *Money, Price and Profit*, all by Marx. He was active in disseminating Marxist economic ideas through Labour College classes in the Dulais and Swansea valleys. Another talented Communist, Lewis Jones, as has been seen, became the folk chronicler of this society in two remarkable novels.

There were political radicalism as well as industrial. In all, 174 volunteers from south Wales fought in Spain with the International Brigade in 1936–9. Of these, 122 were miners, most of them active in the Miners' Federation. They were, in part, Communists like Will Paynter, responding to the Comintern's new and more flexible strategy announced in its support for Popular Front governments in Spain and France. In part, they were socialists or radicals responding, as men had done in 1789, to the cause of oppressed liberty overseas, in this case in the face of insurgent and increasingly well-armed Fascism. The Spanish Civil War was a major landmark, not only for poets, but also for the maturing political and industrial consciousness of the coalfield.[18] The existence of the two famous Welsh sea-captains, 'Potato' Jones and 'Ham and Egg' Jones who ran the Nationalist blockade to bring food in to Basque towns gave the Republican cause much sentimental appeal throughout Wales. Politicians of all shades applauded the efforts of the Republicans in Spain. Lloyd George declared that the outcome of the war in Spain would decide whether Europe was to be governed by democracy or by dictatorship. But it was the Welsh miners and others who fought in the International Brigade, and in some cases who died there, who brought the international aspect of class and political struggle most directly home to their people.

Throughout these troubled years, the Labour ascendancy in the valleys and throughout the great bulk of industrial south Wales became more and more complete. Local government in Monmouthshire, Glamorgan, and eastern Carmarthenshire was where this ascendancy showed itself most emphatically, with Labour now in almost total control of the local authorities there (outside Cardiff), from the early twenties. But there was really a series of intersecting Labour-run worlds, that of the county or urban district councils, with their various ancillary committees, that of the constituency or divisional Labour Party, that of the Workers' Education and adult or extra-mural education movement, above all, that of the trade union, the lodge or pithead or shop-floor union branch where the new Labour conquerors exerted an almost instinctive, automatic control over local society and culture. If the Liberal élite of lawyers, professors, ministers and businessmen before 1914 may be observed in conspicuous display promenading amidst the hotels and parks of Llandrindod Wells, or in the leafy suburbs of north Cardiff, the Labour élite of the years after 1922 is far less ostentatious or easily detectable, almost anonymous, buried in innumerable urban district councils and pithead lodges, in grimy committee rooms with damp, peeling walls. Unlike the Liberal élite, the Labour ascendancy, and its representatives, generally lived deeply entrenched in the community from which it had sprung. Some more affluent or socially privileged miners' agents lived in more fashionable detached houses somewhat removed from the faceless terraces in which most working-class families lived—Arthur Jenkins in Abersychan, a Labour MP and the father of a future Chancellor of the Exchequer, is one example. But the great majority of Labour leaders necessarily retained their intimate, almost indissoluble identity with their class which they had served for most of their adult lives and which had propelled them to local power and patronage. In time, the monolithic control that these new Labour authorities achieved in the coalfield bred its own temptations. The corruptions usually associated with absolute power (at least in Lord Acton's dictum) sometimes emerged; by

[18] See the final chapter of Lewis Jones, *We Live* (1939).

the 1960s accusations of misgovernment or of abuse of patronage were widespread, even in the writings of so good a socialist as Glyn Jones.[19] It may be noted that similar patronage by Liberal bosses over the decades, such as that exercised by Alderman Gwarnant Williams in Cardiganshire, attracted far less publicity in the newspaper press. The writ of the middle class and the Methodists in rural Wales remained comparatively unchallenged and untainted.

In the context of south Wales in the inter-war years, at its time of greatest economic and social need, it seemed clear that these local councillors and aldermen, usually Labour, fulfilled an immensely valuable and crucially important public service. In this at least, they recall some of the more positive aspects of the ward bosses and precinct controllers in the Democratic urban politics of the United States. As was noted in Chapter 8, the dedication, public spirit, and social awareness of the local councillors in the valleys was warmly praised by the Clement Davies Committee of Inquiry into the anti-tuberculosis service in Wales reporting in 1939. They commended the local authorities of Swansea, Cardiff, and Glamorgan for their zeal in providing publicly-assisted housing despite the economic difficulties with which they were crippled; by contrast, the local authorities of Merioneth and Montgomeryshire were severely censured for 'grave dereliction of duty' over health and housing, and those of Anglesey for 'apathy'.[20] In south Wales, the councils had done their best to remove insanitary slum housing and the root causes of TB. It was also noted by the committee, that, throughout the depression, the local authorities for Carmarthenshire, Llanelli, Barry, Mountain Ash, Rhondda, Cardiff, Merthyr Tydfil, Swansea, Abertillery, Ebbw Vale, and Newport (to which should be added Wrexham in north Wales) contrived to maintain free midday meals for schoolchildren. Free school milk was also general in south Wales, though exceptional in the north (for example only seventeen departments out of 109 in Caernarvonshire provided it).

These men and women on local authorities, then, provided the essential fabric of social and welfare services far beyond what impoverished, low-rated authorities, often serving areas with falling populations, could be reasonably expected to maintain. In addition, they kept whole communities alive during industrial crises such as that of 1926 by mobilizing transport, organizing food distribution, and arranging for subsistence distribution. They displayed much enterprise in approaching such bodies as the Nuffield Trust and the Carnegie Foundation in attracting light industry or else new cultural or educational services for their villages or valleys. As they always related the desperate priority of maintaining subsistence and employment to those wider cultural and intellectual objectives to which the Welsh working class had traditionally aspired. Fierce opposition was put up by Labour councillors in Merthyr,

---

[19] In *The Learning Lark* (1960).
[20] *Report* of the Committee of Inquiry, pp. 148, 168, 174, 179, 184, 188.

Swansea, Newport, and elsewhere to the Board of Education's notorious circular 1421 in September 1932 (accompanied by circular 170 in Wales) which tried to cut down the number of free places in secondary schools and to impose a new means test for fee payments. Spending was kept up by local councils on libraries and public parks and swimming pools. The great majority of this Labour élite stayed obscure and unpublicized to the end of their years of public service—and often suffered ridicule or abuse when their stint of office had passed by. They invariably remained relatively poor, still occupying the same drab houses in the same drab neighbourhoods. They were in many respects the unsung heroes and heroines of south Wales in the depression years, a vulnerable vanguard in the struggles of the workers of the valleys for improvement and for survival.

Most of these aspects of government at the local level related to issues of direct economic subsistence, to employment and social welfare, to pressure for new industries or (more commonly) to save old ones, to political pressure and moral exhortation to keep the valley communities alive and to rekindle their dignity and pride. But, as has been noted, there were always broader visions entertained, even during the blackest years of 1929–33. Nowhere was this more impressively demonstrated than in the attachment of this Labour élite to the support of workers' education. The Workers' Education Association, organized by such idealists as John Davies, once a farm boy in rural Cardiganshire, became a major cultural institution and a powerful social and political base in south Wales in the thirties. It provided alternative stimulation to political and industrial protest and escapist sport. It survived in full measure despite repeated onslaughts from the Tory *Western Mail* on the alleged Bolshevism and other subversive doctrines inculcated in WEA classes. The tutorial groups and day schools flourished just the same: by 1933, there were over two hundred WEA classes with over 4,000 students. Again, there was the National Council of Social Service which dispensed money from the Carnegie foundation to assist adult education. The WEA was the main beneficiary of its largesse.

But the most impressive example of the attempt to keep these wider horizons in view originated from far outside the coalfield—and, indeed, in large measure from those associated with the Liberal élite before 1914. This was Coleg Harlech, a residential working-men's college founded at Harlech, on the northern Merioneth coast, in 1927.[21] Its main inspiration was Thomas Jones, whose years as the original 'fluid person' in Whitehall and as deputy secretary to the Cabinet had not dulled his concern for the social and educational well-being of his native land. Indeed, through the monthly that he founded, *Welsh Outlook*, he had throughout the twenties been proclaiming the need for a new institutional advance in the social and cultural fields in Wales. Through his friendship with the philanthropic coalowner, David

[21] Peter Stead, *Coleg Harlech: the First Fifty Years* (Cardiff, 1977) is definitive.

Davies MP of Llandinam, and his new links with the Davies family through the Gregynog connection, and also through the flow of information about Welsh affairs that seeped into the Cabinet office. 'TJ' was ideally placed to turn some of these aspirations into reality. In particular, he was deeply concerned at the rootlessness and cultural deprivation of the coalfield in the twenties. He saw a progressive movement on behalf of adult education for the benefit of the workers as a social solvent, an antidote to Bolshevism and class war. His main collaborators were Silyn Roberts the poet, like Thomas Jones himself a sympathizer with the labour movement, who was now secretary of the University of Wales Appointments Board, and that other celebrated progressive bureaucrat, Percy Watkins, secretary of the Welsh Board of Health. All three sought an instrument for reconciling capital and labour in the mining communities and for finding peaceful avenues towards industrial reform. Such episodes as the violence that marked the anthracite strike around Ammanford in 1925 reinforced the determination of Thomas Jones and his colleagues to map out a new approach.

Jones's vision was of a residential college that would educate working men for citizenship and industrial leadership, and imbue them with a more constructive social outlook. The opportunity was provided by his contact with George Davison, a wealthy anarchist who had bought an imposing house, Wern Fawr, at Harlech, overlooking Cardigan Bay. After much subtle persuasion, Jones persuaded Davison to sell this house. Money to pay the running costs and the salaries of the staff of a new college were raised from the Carnegie Trust, as well as from such unlikely capitalist sources as Sir Alfred Mond, Lord Astor, and Sir David Llewellyn, the coalowner. Jones's wide contacts also enlisted the practical help and encouragement of Lord Haldane, that passionate enthusiast for adult education. With the assistance of the WEA and of the adult education or extra-mural branches of the university colleges, the new college for working men opened in the autumn in 1927. Its first warden was a Rhondda man, himself of nationalist rather than of socialist persuasion, Ben Bowen Thomas. Ten students came into residence in the course of the first academic session, but numbers then increased steadily. Coleg Harlech faced a variety of problems. It faced for a time some ill-informed assaults in the press which saw it as a kind of Ruskin College in north Wales to indoctrinate the workers with extremist ideologies. In fact, the purpose of Coleg Harlech was the precise opposite. Finance was also inevitably a serious difficulty for any institution set up during the depression years. Much depended on TJ's unique skills in tapping the consciences and the wallets of wealthy donors. At first many of the students, miners, railwaymen, and steelworkers left Harlech merely to return to the dole queue, their years of high-quality instruction in the arts and social sciences seemingly wasted.

For all that, by the later thirties, Coleg Harlech had become a thriving, expanding, and increasingly sophisticated institution, a creative and novel response to the hopelessness and unemployment of the depressed years. By 1937, it was estimated that 220 students had passed through the college; 209 of these were Welsh, and 91 of them miners. Many of them had moved back into their own communities, without difficulties of cultural adjustment, to become leaders in trade unionism, local politics, or adult education. Further, new links had been built up with the organized labour movement. James Griffiths, while president of the South Wales Miners' Federation in 1934–6, had succeeded in obtaining an agreement from the Federation's executive to provide financial assistance for Coleg Harlech, on the same basis as that provided for Ruskin. On balance, Coleg Harlech represents another face of the Welsh labour movement in these years, one less involved with immediate difficulties of class conflict and unemployment, more a reflection of wider horizons of self-education and citizenship. It acted as a force for unity and hope in a divided, despairing nation. It committed the Welsh workers, or some of them, not only to the cruel present, but to a promising future.

The cohesion and strength of the Labour ascendancy in Wales were further strengthened by the course of social and economic change during the Second World War. This was a war which, unlike that of 1914, the vast bulk of Welsh workers strongly supported for the whole of its duration. Especially since Spain and Munich, there was a passionate commitment to the belief that this was a people's, indeed, a workers', war, far more so than that of 1914. It was being waged against totalitarian dictators who had crushed workers' organizations and political liberties in their own lands and who threatened their extinction everywhere in Europe. It was noted that enlistment as unpaid Civil Defence workers was exceptionally heavy in Wales. Even Communists found it almost impossible to resist the patriotic call, despite the Ribbentrop–Molotov pact to divide up Poland. Arthur Horner defied the might of the Comintern in endorsing the war effort in 1939–40. When the Soviet Union entered the war, Welsh Communists could, of course, commit themselves to the struggle without embarrassment, and could now lead the call for a second front in western Europe to assist the heroic efforts of the Red Army. Pacifists in Wales seem to have been very few in number. Invariably they were men who held religious objections to violence; sometimes they were also Welsh nationalists like the young Gwynfor Evans. Civil liberties were more faithfully respected than in 1914–18, although even here there were some remarkable abuses such as the imprisonment without trial of the veteran socialist, the Revd Thomas Nicholas, for alleged sedition. His *Prison Sonnets* (written by 'No. 2740') provided a powerful riposte from this unquenchably resilient spirit. 'Stay Put', a parody on a Home Office circular read out by the Swansea prison chaplain, is an especially poignant form of poetic protest. Conscientious objectors were sometimes harassed for scant reason; the vindictive dismissal of Iorwerth Peate from the Folk Studies department of the National Museum aroused some controversy. A few political nationalists were imprisoned for refusing to be conscripted, including A. O. H. Jarman, editor of Plaid Cymru's journal *Y Ddraig Goch*. Otherwise, enthusiasm for the war was as marked in Wales now as when Lloyd George had led the nation in that earlier war. The downfall of Neville Chamberlain in May 1940, partly as a result of backbench manoeuvres of some Welsh MPs, of whom the most important were Clement Davies and Megan Lloyd George, two Liberal members, raised enthusiasm to new heights. Welsh opinion was encouraged by the presence of leading members of the Labour Party in the new Churchill government. Churchill himself, long a suspect figure in the valleys, became more popular. The troops sent to Tonypandy in 1910 were temporarily forgiven if not forgotten.

It has become a familiar enough theme with historians that the Second World War had the general effect of forcing British public opinion further to the left, along the progressive 'road to 1945'.[22] Two factors are usually stressed here—the new enthusiasm for social 'planners' like Beveridge and Keynes, and the egalitarianism induced by wartime controls and by the experience of serving in the armed forces. Precisely how these two elements are related, if at all, historians have been less successful in explaining. However, the general movement of opinion to the left, shown in by-elections and in the success of the Common Wealth Party in particular, is clear enough, especially after 1941. This movement probably had less significance in south Wales which was so strongly left-wing in sympathy anyhow, but in other parts of the nation, in the north and mid-Wales, opinion was perhaps also somewhat radicalized by these wartime experiences.

Certainly there was the social solvent of communal suffering and sacrifice. South Wales suffered acutely from German air-raids. There were 985 civilian killed here during the course of 1941 alone. Worst hit was Swansea, whose town centre was largely wiped out in fire-bomb raids on 19–21 February 1941. In all, 282 houses were demolished and 11,084 more damaged; 387 Swansea citizens were killed and a further 412 seriously injured. Much of Dylan Thomas's 'lovely ugly town' had ceased to exist. Cardiff was also heavily attacked. The death toll after Luftwaffe bomber raids on 2 January 1941 rose to 165. By the end of October 1941, 600 houses in Cardiff had been destroyed and a further 29,998 damaged.[23] Llandaff Cathedral and Cardiff Castle were among the historic buildings to suffer from the bombing. The dockyard areas of Pembrokeshire were also severely hit. Clearly, a new classless, communal effort would be required to raise these ravaged cities from the ashes. The impatience with pre-war shibboleths at a time of such crises became increasingly discernible.

Welsh figures were closely involved in every new surge of reform during the

---

[22] Cf. Paul Addison, *The Road to 1945* (London, 1975), a superb book.
[23] *Western Mail,* 21 October 1941.

war to transform it from a nationalistic struggle against the Axis powers into a longer-term crusade for social and economic reconstruction, for truly providing that land fit for heroes believed to have been promised in 1918, for taking revenge on the years of the means test and the hunger marches. It was a Welsh Labour member, James Griffiths, who voiced the criticism from the parliamentary Labour Party in February 1943 when the Churchill government refused to commit itself to an early implementation of the Beveridge report on social insurance. Those who voted against the government that day included Lloyd George, casting his last vote in the Commons; appropriately it was on behalf of those social reforms which had been the abiding passion of his youth and middle age. Another Welsh Labour member, Aneurin Bevan, the foremost wartime critic of the government, voiced the demand for an alternative domestic policy. His *Why Not Trust the Tories?* published under the pseudonym 'Celticus' in 1944, was a fierce onslaught on government attitudes towards social questions. It was a plea for post-war socialist strategy, including much public ownership; at the same time, Bevan linked his proposals with an earlier libertarian tradition that went back to the Levellers and Tom Paine. Welsh Labour men like James Griffiths were also very active in the Welsh advisory panel of the Ministry of Reconstruction which issued an important report in 1944. It called for a massive post-war attack on the social and economic stagnation endemic in Wales for the past twenty years, and for the nation to become a unified planning unit for this purpose.

On social and economic themes, the voice of the Welsh Labour Party was ringing and unambiguous. But it was noticeably more coy over whether to press for a commitment to some form of political or administrative devolution in Wales, for which it was criticized by the Liberals and by Plaid Cymru. In fact, the Labour Party had been most reluctant throughout the inter-war period to endorse anything that might remotely resemble separatism. Old E. T. John had died in 1931, full of disillusion with the Labour Party's Webb-like dedication to the centralization of government. Since the First World War, the Labour Party had looked askance at any recognition of the individual status of Wales, even within its own party structure. Not until 1937 were the combined Labour parties in the coalfield recognized as representing south Wales as a region. A 'South Wales Regional Council of Labour' then came into being (partly to counteract Communist influence in the valleys) and spoke on behalf of a united south Wales at annual conferences of the Labour Party. A unified 'Regional Council of Labour' representing Wales as a whole was not to be formed until 26 April 1947, under the secretaryship of Cliff Prothero.[24] Nor had the Welsh Labour MPs been particularly active in pressing for any deviation from the traditional socialist centralism which provided the basic framework for any integrated economic planning for

[24] *Reports of the Thirty-Seventh Annual Conference of the Labour Party,* Bournemouth, 1937, p. 36; *Report of the Forty-Seventh Annual Conference,* Scarborough, 1948, p. 137.

Britain as a whole. On the other hand, there were certainly some south Wales Labour MPs anxious for at least a token extension of devolution: James Griffiths and David Grenfell were prominent among them. On 30 June 1938 a deputation of Welsh MPs had seen Neville Chamberlain and had pressed the case for a separate secretaryship for Wales, on the lines of that conceded to Scotland as long ago as 1885. Chamberlain's reply included an admission of the reality of national sentiment in Wales, but it yielded nothing of substance.[25] Chamberlain cited the distinct system of law and administration in Scotland as a reason for the impossibility of conceding a secretaryship of state to Wales—an argument that was to be heard many times again, over the next forty years. The Munich crisis then obliterated these considerations from political debate. A new approach was made to the Churchill government on 7 July 1943, this time by the 'Welsh Parliamentary Party' as a whole, whose chairman was a Conservative who sat for Cardiff and whose vice-chairmen were Megan Lloyd George and Aneurin Bevan. Here again, though, the demand for a Welsh Office led nowhere. Nor did the Board of Education permit any devolution to Wales under the terms of the Butler Education Act of 1944.

However, these moves did indicate that even the labour movement in Wales retained some sense of a separate identity, and that sympathy with a more decentralized, devolved approach to economic and social planning was still alive. On 17 October 1944, the first 'Welsh day' debate was held in the House of Commons, led off by Megan Lloyd George. Historians, following Sir Reginald Coupland,[26] have laid most emphasis here on a brief speech delivered by Aneurin Bevan, which ridiculed the very idea that there were distinct social and economic problems peculiar to Wales and separable from those of Britain generally. How, Bevan asked, did Welsh sheep differ from those which grazed in Westmorland or Gloucestershire? But Bevan, with his strongly Marxist aversion to any divergence from centralized planning, and his ingrained suspicion of the Welsh-speaking population of the rural areas, was not a typical figure in the Labour Party in this context. He moved more and more in the London world of journalists and politicians, as Lloyd George had done before him; his new contact with the Beaverbrook press was a symbol of this. He seldom joined the other Welsh Labour MPs, most of whom appared to be slow-witted trade unionists without intellectual sophistication, at the 'Welsh table' in the House of Commons dining room. There were more representative speeches in this 'Welsh day' debate, otherwise a forgettable occasion, from James Griffiths, S. O. Davies, Robert Richards, and other Labour members more sympathetic to administrative, and even economic, devolution for Wales. Indeed, Bevan was alone in adopting a carping tone during the debate.

[25] Chamberlain to J. Griffiths, 27 July 1938 (James Griffiths Papers, NLW, C2/1).
[26] R. Coupland, *Welsh and Scottish Nationalism* (London, 1954), pp. 369–70.

This concern for a post-war programme, which would combine socialist measures for indicative planning with a sympathy for Wales and its special needs, loomed large in the discussions on the Welsh advisory panel on post-war reconstruction in 1942–4. James Griffiths, one of its leading members, called for a Welsh Planning Authority to work out the industrial needs and priorities of Wales as a distinct region or nation, to 'broaden the base' of local industry and to supersede the 'special area' authorities of pre-war days with all their known inadequacies.[27] This kind of view increasingly coloured the tone of public debate in 1944–5 as it became increasingly clear that the war was being won and that the framework of post-war planning needed to be filled out with practical detail to turn it from the drawing-board stage into immediate reality. Reconstruction needed to be far less vague than it had been in November 1918, and the needs of Wales must be intimately involved with it.

The main outlines of a possible post-war programme were now becoming much clearer. There was the strong advocacy in the Beveridge report (which Labour largely appropriated as its own) of a comprehensive fabric of social security 'from the cradle to the grave', and of a national health service. Nowhere was this last more urgently needed than in Wales as innumerable pre-war health surveys, medical officers' reports, and government statistics had shown. There was also new pressure, voiced by Aneurin Bevan in particular, for a national drive for new houses. He poured scorn on the Churchill government's schemes for 'half a million steel boxes'. Over 200,000 houses had been needed even before the war and the destruction it brought; none had been built since 1939.[28] At the macro-economic level, there were the new techniques pioneered by Keynes and the economic section of the War Cabinet for a planned approach towards production and investment, for the measurement of aggregate demand and for the stimulating of public expenditure.

There was much wartime experience of collectivism at work. The Essential Work Order of 1941 had directed work to industries working on war contracts, such as the Royal Ordnance Factories at Bridgend, Hirwaun, Glascoed (near Pontypool), and Pembrey in south Wales, and Marchwiel in the north-east. The Bridgend factory alone employed 37,000, mainly women, by the end of 1941, while the activities of the Treforest trading estate were much expanded. In Flintshire, a large aircraft factory was set up at Broughton. The Barlow Report of 1942, on the geographical distribution of industry was of especial interest to Wales with its advocacy of new policies to provide for the redistribution and relocation of industry in Britain, with a national planning board to promote within each region a diversified and well-balanced industrial substructure. The ideas of the Barlow Report were already being

[27] *Wales*, July 1943, pp. 7–10.
[28] 'Celticus' [A. Bevan], *Why Not Trust the Tories?* (London, 1944), pp. 65–78.

developed in practice by the Board of Trade, notably through its Factories and Warehouses department under Sir Cecil Weir and such Welsh civil servants as Emrys Pride.[29] Its policy for allocating factory and warehouse space in the older industrial regions and setting up new regional offices of civil servants and businessmen in such places as Cardiff and Ruthin anticipated a complete break with the 'distressed areas' policy of the thirties. New methods of operational research were adopted. Under Hugh Dalton, the Board of Trade began an active policy of forcefully steering new light industry to the Welsh valleys, such as the new watch factory established at Ystradgynlais at the head of the Swansea valley, an old mining town. The passage of the Distribution of Industry Act in 1945, the outcome of the 'development areas' plans worked out in the Board of Trade over the past two years, and designed to give the Board of Trade powers to direct firms to the older industrial regions, was a great breakthrough. It suggested a complete contrast with the passive policies which had led to endemic unemployment and industrial stagnation for so many dreadful years.

There was also much more direct control of private industry by the state, especially in the case of the coal mines. The Minister of Fuel and Power, Major Gwilym Lloyd George, implemented some wide-ranging changes in October 1943 when he persuaded a reluctant Churchill that the government should secure operational control over the coal mines and become the direct employer of the various private managements for the duration of the war. A National Coal Board was set up with wide powers over production targets and the conduct of collective bargaining. Churchill and other Conservative ministers vetoed any complete nationalization.[30] But clearly policies such as these heralded a massive post-war shift towards the national direction of the mining industry, and a clear statement that an inefficient privately-owned industry could not minister to the national needs. The dramatic increase in the supply of coal and other fuels that resulted from this new method of operation was a further pointer to a new post-war policy for the mines, and a resolution that the doctrinaire 'de-control' methods adopted in 1919—21 could not be tolerated a second time.

Finally, the trade-union movement in Wales and elsewhere had flourished during the Second World War as it had done during the First, with the immense wartime demand for labour. In place of the 'treasury agreement' of 1915 with the later accusation of bad faith when the government failed to prevent wartime profiteering in return for the unions' agreement to waive the right to strike, there was now the markedly sympathetic policy of Ernest Bevin at the Ministry of Labour, which saw wages rise markedly for miners, steelworkers, railwaymen, dockers, and others. Union membership rose

---

[29] E. Pride, 'The Economic Province of Wales', *Trans. Hon. Soc. Cymm.*, 1969, part I, pp. 78–80; First Interim Report of Welsh Advisory Council (1943), pp. 111 ff.

[30] See G. Lloyd George's memorandum to the War Cabinet on 7 October 1943 (WP 446).

consistently for the first time since 1921. One famous landmark that disappeared was the old 'Fed', the South Wales Miners' Federation, since the new system of nationwide wage bargaining made it expedient for the miners to form the National Union of Mineworkers in January 1945 in place of the former district-based organizations. The NUM at once called for a national day-wage system and the abolition of piecework methods of payment, as part of a new, egalitarian Miners' Charter. Their solidarity thus reinforced, the miners' commitment to sweeping policies of social and economic change became all the more powerful. Pressure built up for a post-war programme based on widespread public ownership of major industries, state intervention on behalf of indicative planning, full employment policies, comprehensive social welfare, and a closer relationship between central government and the trade union movement. This became the matrix of Labour's post-war election appeal in 1945.

   In May 1945, the Labour and Liberal ministers resigned from the Churchill government on the ending of the war in Europe. After a brief interlude of 'caretaker' Conservative government, Churchill called a general election. On 26 July the results were declared, after the counting of servicemen's ballots. As is well known, the outcome was an enormous Labour landslide, one of those seismic shifts in opinion comparable with 1931 or 1906. Labour had 393 members returned, together with six others representing ILP, Common Wealth, and Communists. Confronting them were only 210 Conservatives and allies, while the Liberal tally added up to a mere twelve. These last included the very dubious case of Gwilym Lloyd George who soon declared himself to be a 'National Liberal'. By all accounts, the Labour leadership, with the exception of that astute machine politician, Herbert Morrison, was astounded that Labour had even won at all in the face of Churchill's charismatic appeal, let alone that the victory had been so overwhelming and complete. But, whatever surprise there might have been in England and Scotland, the results in Wales were wholly predictable. Labour's share of the poll in the 35 Welsh seats (excluding the university seat with its method of proportional representation), rose to 58.5 per cent, compared with 48 per cent for the United Kingdom as a whole. Labour captured 25 seats in Wales, including seven gains. There was one loss recorded, rather surprisingly, in Carmarthen, when Hopkin Morris, the former Liberal member for Cardiganshire and ex-regional director of the BBC, defeated Moelwyn Hughes (Labour). Everywhere else, there were sweeping Labour advances. All three Cardiff seats swung decisively to Labour. The victors here were all interesting personalities. George Thomas in Cardiff Central was a schoolteacher from the Rhondda, a Methodist, a teetotaller, a future Cabinet minister and Speaker of the House. Professor Hilary Marquand, returned in Cardiff East, was the Professor of Industrial Relations in Cardiff University College and the author of the famous industrial surveys of the thirties. He was to join the government immediately on entering the House of Commons. And in Cardiff South, a mixed, sprawling constituency which took in the old decaying dockside community of Bute Town and Tiger Bay as well as the fashionable suburbs of Penarth, there was elected a young left-wing naval officer with a background of white-collar trade unionism, James Callaghan, who was destined to rise higher than any of his new colleagues.

There were other Labour gains in Caernarvonshire (where Goronwy Roberts, the founder of the *Gwerin* movement at Bangor in the mid-thirties, swamped the old Liberal member, Sir Goronwy Owen), and at Llandaff and Barry, a victory for another Labour lawyer, Sir Lynn Ungoed-Thomas. There were almost several other Labour gains as well, since strong polls were recorded at Anglesey, Merioneth (where the Liberal majority fell to 112), and Pembrokeshire (where Gwilym Lloyd George clung on by 178). Majorities of over 20,000 were recorded in Caerphilly, Neath, Ogmore, Pontypridd, Abertillery, Bedwellty, Ebbw Vale, and Aberdare, while James Griffiths's majority of 34,000 in Llanelli was the largest in the British Isles. In Rhondda West, Labour was unopposed. The valleys were totally impregnable Labour territory—with the interesting exception of Rhondda East where Will Mainwaring held off the Communist, Harry Pollitt, by 972 votes, and no Conservative dared stand at all. The Labour ascendancy in Wales was in 1945 more total and all-embracing than ever.

The opposition parties fared predictably badly. Plaid Cymru put up eight candidates, but all lost their deposits, save for Miss Gwenan Jones in the university seat. The Liberals retained seven seats, all well removed from industrial areas, except for Carmarthen and Pembrokeshire. As has been seen, the credentials of Gwilym Lloyd George to be included in the Liberal ranks were highly debatable. Even the rural fastnesses were being challenged by Labour. The high polls of its candidates, Cledwyn Hughes in Anglesey and Huw Morris-Jones in Merioneth, were both distinctly ominous. A fateful and symbolic loss for Liberalism, though one that party workers had anticipated, was the victory of the Conservative, for the first time since 1886, in Lloyd George's old constituency of Caernarfon Boroughs. This seat had greatly changed during the war years, with the influx of English civil servants and academics. Fear for its retention had been a compelling factor in inducing Lloyd George to take an earldom at the end of 1944. His successor, a Liverpool academic, Professor Seaborne Davies, lacked the Lloyd George magic, although had not Plaid Cymru taken 1,500 votes away from him, he might well have retained the seat he had held for just three months. But all over the principality the message was clear. The 'strange death' of the once-great Liberal Party was perilously near. It had now become a party of the past and of the elderly, in Arthur Schlesinger's phrase a party of memory not one of hope.

The Conservatives and their National Liberal allies retained just four seats from the shambles—Caernarfon District, Denbigh (with its many elderly coastal residents), and the anglicized border constituencies of Flintshire and Monmouth, these last retained by two promising younger Conservatives and future ministers, Nigel Birch and (from October 1945) Peter Thorneycroft. Elsewhere there was little save a deluge of forfeited deposits.

The general election of 1945 provides a suitable final comment on the ordeal of Wales during the twenties and thirties. The campaign was charged with folk memories and communal bitterness, which Churchill's talk of a Labour 'gestapo' reinforced. It confirmed the arrival of a powerful, socially cohesive Labour élite, still Welsh in many of its instincts and aspirations, but far less committed to the native language and to political separatism than the old Liberal ascendancy had been. It emerged out of struggle and protest in the thirties to full authority, a symbol of revenge on a cruel past of depression and unemployment, and a beacon of hope for a more bearable and fulfilling world.

PART III

THE RENEWAL
1945–1980

CHAPTER 11

RESTRUCTURING THE ECONOMY

Like the rest of Britain, Wales faced a variety of formidable and unfamiliar problems in the post-war world. By far the most pressing was the need for a recasting of its economic structure, to end the industrial stagnation and mass unemployment that had crippled the nation for almost the whole of the inter-war years. The deliberations of the Welsh Advisory Council of the Ministry of Reconstruction in 1944 were shot through with a fierce determination that the land should not be allowed to sink into the economic decay that had paralysed it for so long. In particular, the industrial base should be broadened, so that the undue dependence of the working population on a few staple heavy industries and on a narrow range of industrial occupations based on coal, steel, tinplate, and quarrying, should be transformed. The Welsh economy needed to be revitalized. In the conventional wisdom of the time, which went largely unchallenged for the first two decades of the post-war period, this meant that it needed to be diversified.

The decline of south Wales had not been arrested by the economic expansion that the wartime years had brought with it. Despite the stimulus to industrial production provided between 1939 and 1945, major Welsh industries had continued to decline. In the tinplate industry, for instance, the production of tin, terne, and blackplate fell from 976,000 tons in 1940 to only 511,800 in 1945. There were now only 10,000 workers in the industry, compared with 26,000 in 1939, as a result of the loss of so many men to the armed forces and to munitions work. In coal mining, the number of miners employed in the south Wales pits had fallen from 136,000 in 1938 to 112,000 in 1944. This policy of thinning out the labour force had been directly contrary to the advice of the wartime Minister of Mines, the Welsh Labour MP, David Grenfell. Output of coal in that period had fallen from 35.3 million tons to only 22.4 millions, while of course coal exports had virtually disappeared. South Wales was left with a legacy of inefficient, high-cost coal mines, some of which had been worked for over a hundred years, of steel-works and tinplate pack mills that still lagged behind the technologically more advanced plant of north America. There was also a labour force still in many ways embittered and disillusioned, despite the improvements in wages and conditions of work achieved during the wartime years. The high rate of absenteeism and relatively low increase in productivity in the Welsh mines was a portent here.

The South Wales Coalfield regional survey in April 1946 painted a hopeful prospect, with coal output projected at 47 million tons in 1954, and an increasing adoption of newer methods of mechanization to stimulate production and productivity. A former Liberal MP, J. Emlyn Jones, in the midst of a general plea against state control which flew in the face of all the wartime experience, called for an aggressive search for exports to the old markets, and for south Wales to claim once again its share of 20 per cent of the total coal output in Britain.[1] A generally optimistic view was taken about possible competition from European countries such as Germany and Poland, in view of the toll of physical devastation and general dislocation that they had suffered during the war.

Even so, there were many ominous signs that the pre-war determinants of physical and geographical difficulties, a narrow industrial base, and a tense atmosphere for labour relations might again plunge south Wales into further depression once the immediate euphoria of victory and demobilization had spent itself. Some observers noted that the only method of securing a more viable coal and steel industry in the valleys was through rationalizing production, concentrating effort on fewer units of operation and diverting some of the work force to other trades not traditionally associated with south Wales. This might mean some temporary unemployment.[2] Certainly, it would mean a more flexible attitude towards employment possibilities and working conditions, a breaking-down of old prejudices that would be difficult to achieve. In addition to these factors affecting industry, Welsh agriculture, still largely based on small-scale upland farms run on a family basis, was still relatively under-capitalized and under-mechanized. The drift from the land seemed likely to continue—indeed, a thriving national agricultural policy would seem to demand it, in spite of the endemic rural decay that would result. The future of the Welsh economy after 1945, then, seemed problematical, if not without hope.

In fact, the immediate post-war years, particularly the period up to 1952, saw a remarkably swift return to the prosperity and growth last known in pre-1914 days. Despite some gloomy prophecies, the war years after 1939 had actually brought many new elements highly favourable to the prospects for economic life in Wales. They had created the core of a potentially strong manufacturing sector, on a much broader base than before. They had created new growth points, such as the area in mid-Glamorgan based on the vast ordnance factory at Bridgend that was shortly to be turned into a huge trading estate. They had provided new employment opportunities, not least for women workers. Above all, they had created a new pool of skilled labour, much more adaptable to newer technology, much more familiar with the

---

[1] J. E. Emlyn Jones, 'Welsh Industrial Reconstruction', *Wales* (Summer 1945), pp. 35–8.

[2] A. Beacham, 'The Future of the South Wales Coalfield', *Welsh Review*, June 1946, pp. 138–44.

handling of modern machinery and well suited for employment in engineering and light manufacturing. With favourable conditions in the British economy generally, as post-war restocking got under way, south Wales industry immediately began to expand in dramatic fashion. There was once again full employment. The mines, steelworks, tinplate mills, and docks were again busily at work. Vast numbers of new factories were built, usually with government assistance. There was a sustained high rate of capital formation and of investment. By the start of 1950, the *South Wales Industrial Review* could even talk of a second industrial revolution which had totally transformed the economic and employment pattern in south Wales.[3]

Of course, the years immediately after 1945 undoubtedly did bring almost intractable problems for the British economy generally. There were the associated problems of a massive post-war external debt, of repeated crises for sterling resulting in the Cripps devaluation of 1949, of dollar shortages, and desperate crises in raw materials. When the economy finally seemed to be regaining its equilibrium in 1950, there came the Korean War which saw a vast rise in the prices of imported raw materials, a massive increase in Britain's adverse trading balance and a depletion of the gold and currency reserves. At home, these unpalatable economic facts, quite beyond governmental control, showed themselves in years of austerity, rationing, and controls for the ordinary consumer. They did not add to the popularity of the post-1945 Labour government. They led to the crises surrounding the pace of rearmament and the proposed cuts in spending on the National Health Service which saw Aneurin Bevan resign from the Labour Cabinet, along with Harold Wilson, in April 1951.

Still, for the working population of Wales, these were far less awesome crosses to bear than the endless unemployment and industrial collapse of the inter-war years. Indeed, for the vast bulk of the people, the period from 1945 to 1951 was a time of great hope and progress, with rapidly rising living standards. Production in the coal, steel, and other industries rose sharply. In early 1948, the South-West Division of the Coal Board registered with pride a record weekly production of 592,400 tons, with a labour force that was 9,000 less than in 1943 when the previous weekly record was set. Hugh Gaitskell, the Minister of Fuel and Power, spoke of Welsh coal again being available for export from 1948 onwards.[4] Steel production records were broken at the same time by Guest, Keen and by Richard Thomas and Baldwins. New light industries, government-backed advance factories and trading estates flourished. The six south Wales ports, Swansea and Barry above all, were buoyant, with export shipments in 1948 up by 37 per cent compared with a year previously.[5] A growing mood of optimism could be discerned amongst

---

[3] *South Wales Industrial Review*, vol. 2, No. 3 (January 1950), p. 1.
[4] Ibid., vol. 2, No. 1 (February 1948), p. 1.
[5] *South Wales Ports Handbook*, 1948.

leaders of the industrial, manufacturing, and commercial community, and amongst the unions. The old problems had not wholly disappeared. It was noted that at times of economic difficulty, unemployment in Wales tended to be higher than the British average. In November 1947, at a rate of 5.2 per cent of the adult working population, it was the highest of any region in Britain. However, the total of 44,000 recorded was inflated by including disabled workers, and these, too, were being catered for in new 'Remploy' factories at Treforest and elsewhere. Unemployment fell steadily after that, until by July 1955 it stood at a mere 13,400. In effect, unemployment, for so long the scourge of this so-called 'depressed area' had virtually disappeared. A new generation was growing up with no experience of the misery and starvation that had dogged the lives of their parents and grandparents. These were years of full employment—and of full order books, especially in a period when potential overseas competitors such as the West Germans and the Japanese had yet to rebuild their war-ravaged economies. As the fifties broadened into more continued affluence, with domestic industry rejuvenated and able to participate in a more sustained upturn of world trade, it seemed that at last most of Wales, outside the more remote rural areas such as Anglesey and the Llŷn peninsula, was climbing confidently out of the trough of economic depression into which it had been thrust for so long. At last, the Welsh people were putting the bad times firmly behind them.

The causes of this new surge of prosperity were much debated. It was difficult to know whether to link it with the nationalization of basic industries that was carried out by the Attlee government between 1946 and 1950. When gas was taken into public ownership, a new Wales Gas Board was created. In time it was to lead to heavy investment in Wales, and to the development of a petro-chemicals industry around Swansea Bay, amongst other by-products. On the other hand, the Attlee Cabinet decided, in December 1946, to confirm a decision to divide the nationalized electricity industry in the principality into two.[6] This was in spite of the protests of James Griffiths, as will be seen in Chapter 13. The South Wales Electricity Board would cover the industrial areas of the coalfield, while the remainder of Wales would be linked, much to the irritation of nationalists, with the Liverpool area in the Merseyside and North Wales Electricity Board. However here, too, public enterprise continued to thrive. There was also the nationalization of the railways, with the old GWR being virtually transformed into the Western Region of British Railways, and of road haulage, with Wales being absorbed into the western division of the British Transport Authority, both in 1947. Civil aviation was also taken into public ownership; this resulted in a mild expansion of the airports at Hawarden and Swansea, and a considerable development of Rhoose airport near Cardiff, with impressive growth both in passenger and freight traffic, internationally as well as on inland routes.

[6] Cabinet Paper, December 1946 (CAB/129/15).

But the most traumatic of these measures of nationalization was undoubtedly that relating to the coal mines. When the mines entered into public ownership on 1 January 1947, there was immense rejoicing in the valleys, notwithstanding the unlucky fact that nationalization coincided with an unprecedentedly severe winter and massive shortages in fuel supplies that led to a five-day week and economies in power distribution. For the Welsh miners and their families, nationalization meant the fulfilment of a fifty-year dream, the reward for all the suffering endured from Black Friday onwards. No tears were shed for the old private coalowners. With their record in regard to managerial efficiency, production levels, pit safety, and above all relations with their workers, they had few friends. Perhaps they did not deserve any. They then proceeded to deny historians public access to their records deposited at public expense in the National Library of Wales. But the new National Coal Board, with south Wales included as part of the 'South-West Division' did not herald any sustained improvement in the fortunes of what was still basically a declining industry. There was considerable new investment in the period from 1948 to 1953; nearly £32 million was invested in pits in the Cardiff region alone. The Maerdy pits were reconstructed. The Hafod-yr-ynys pit in Monmouthshire was modernized substantially. No less than £4,500,000 was invested in the new mining project at Nantgarw, with which a new model village for the colliers was associated. Later still, there were show-case pits such as the new anthracite colliery at Cynheidre, near Llanelli, opened in 1960, and Abernant in the Swansea valley. There was, in addition to this progress in efficiency of production, a clear improvement in the climate of labour relations with the ending of private ownership. No major strike occurred in the pits until 1972.

On the other hand, the new official structure of the public corporation that the National Coal Board represented proved to be almost as remote from the rank-and-file miner as the old capitalist owner and his agents had been. Industrial democracy was set aside in favour of the Morrisonian vision of the technocratic, managerial corporation. The *Miners' Next Step* might never have been written. By the mid-fifties, absenteeism (17 per cent in Wales, well above the British average), conflict over production norms, and talk of possible pit-closures marked the publicly-owned coal industry. Even the huge investment at Nantgarw colliery, with its new techniques of horizontal mining, yielded scant returns. Output there was less than 100,000 tons a year, and the new seams were abandoned. For all that, the taking of basic industries into public ownership—and this applied to the nationalization of iron and steel as well when the Steel Board was constituted in 1951—did coincide with, and helped promote, a more thriving and harmonious atmosphere in the Welsh industrial scene.

A different aspect of government policy after 1945 which undoubtedly was vital in helping on economic recovery in Wales was the new strategy adopted to diversify, stimulate, and modernize the industrial structure. As many agencies had long urged, culminating in the 1942 Barlow Report, central government intervened with powerful effect to introduce new manufacturing, to diversify employment and to provide alternatives to the older staple industries. The whole of south Wales was scheduled as a development area and its administration was taken over by an increasingly interventionist Board of Trade. After 1964, these powers gradually passed to the Welsh Office. There were several aspects of this new policy by central government. One of the most striking was the coercive powers used by the Board of Trade to restrict the growth of further manufacturing industry in London, the south-east and the Midlands and to encourage it in older industrial areas such as south Wales. These operated partly through loans, tax and other concessions to industrialists to persuade them to venture into the older areas, partly through the use of Industrial Development Certificates as laid down under the 1947 Town and Country Planning Act. In addition, there was a wider panoply of powers under the 1945 Distribution of Industry Act, to which was added another measure by the Attlee government in 1950, and also a vigorous use of building licences and other physical controls. The results were spectacular indeed. By 1949, 179 new factories had been opened in various parts of south Wales, of which 112 were government-sponsored. The demand for building space and surplus factory sites in south Wales from industrialists and manufacturers was almost overwhelming until the early fifties. Long-depressed communities were rejuvenated. In the Rhondda, for instance, twenty-five government-assisted factories had been set up by 1955, devoted to the manufacture of clothing, children's toys, bicycles, and many other consumer products. The entire employment structure of the Rhondda, historically dependent almost uniquely on the mining of coal, had been totally revolutionized. The same held true of Merthyr, Dowlais, Blaenavon, and many other places designated by governments as irredeemably 'depressed' in the thirties.

Central government intervened in other ways also. There was the conversion of the old wartime ordnance factories for peacetime industrial purposes. The factory at Bridgend, for instance, became the basis of a giant new trading estate, employing over 30,000 workers; the same held true of the ordnance factory at Hirwaun on the northern rim of the coalfield. In addition, the government sponsored, through the Board of Trade, a vast programme of building advance factories, plant built with Treasury finance, ahead of demand from industrialists. This brought in such major firms as Imperial Metals to Gowerton, Girlings' car components to Cwmbran, Northern Aluminium to Rogerstone, and Lines (children's toys) to Merthyr. Engineering firms also developed rapidly, notably South Wales Switchgear and Aberdare Cables. Never had government intervened so directly in the locating and prior support of new industry. By the start of 1951, as a result, the

Board of Trade's controller for Wales, Captain Oram, could report that jobs for 64,000 workers had been created since 1945 and that unemployment was largely confined to a few small pockets in eastern Glamorgan and western Monmouthshire, between Merthyr and Blaenavon.[7]

The trading estate idea, conceived in the late thirties, was also given new encouragement by the government. The old Treforest estate now employed 20,000 workers. It expanded its operations so greatly that it was able to divert factories into Merthyr and other localities to employ a further 15,000.[8] As has been noted, trading estates also flourished in Bridgend and Hirwaun, after the conversion of the old munitions plant. Another trading estate to take root was at Fforestfach on the north of Swansea, where twelve initial factories were built to the particular specifications of the tenants. Instead of mining and tinplate, it was children's clothing, mechanical toys, electrical accessories, and even potato crisps which now provided the base of employment in this part of the Swansea region. In the north-east, the huge Royal Ordnance plant at Marchwiel, near Wrexham, was also turned into a large trading estate in 1946, as part of a government-created Welsh Industrial Estate Corporation. British Celanese and Firestone Tyres were amongst the larger firms attracted here, to give new opportunities to a workforce too long dependent on declining coal mines, steel, and brick-making.

Under government sponsorship, too, Wales now began to attract some of the largest names in private industry—names that the special areas commissioners in the thirties had noted as being conspicuously lacking in the roster of firms in south Wales. Among these were a vast steel-erecting plant at Treorchy, a plastics works at Barry, and a massive rubber factory at Brynmawr (of striking architectural design), due to employ at least 1,000 men and women. A larger Hoover factory outside Merthyr, which employed over four thousand workers, largely transformed the economic fortunes of this historic town, which had suffered so long from depression and despair. Another, highly significant, development was the huge new plant created at Pontypool by British Nylon Spinners in 1948. This was notable for being able to produce, in a very short period, a high standard of yarn manufacture from workers with no previous experience of textile production.[9] Here again, the workforce of south Wales, not least its women, was becoming more adaptable and acquiring new skills in, perhaps, more congenial industrial surroundings than in the past. Another reason emerged for the virtual elimination of so many pre-war pockets of structural unemployment, and for the total of unemployed in south Wales falling by the mid-fifties to the lowest levels recorded in peacetime.

The introduction of new, especially light, industries was one essential arm

[7] *South Wales Industrial Review,* vol. 2, No. 4 (February 1951), p. 1.
[8] J. F. Rees in *The Cardiff Region: a Survey* (Cardiff, 1960), pp. 109 ff.
[9] *Industrial Directory of Wales,* 1952, p. 48.

of government policy in Wales in these boom years after 1945. The other was the dramatic modernization of older industries, to give them a more secure long-term future and greater capacity to resist competitive pressure from overseas. In no industry was this modernization more impressive than in steel and tinplate The two large combines of Richard Thomas & Co. and Baldwins Ltd had amalgamated in January 1945, with government encouragement. Now 340 out of the 500 pack mills in south Wales would be under the control of this one large enterprise. It was also announced that a major new steel-works and hot strip-mill would be built at Port Talbot. Hugh Dalton, then the President of the Board of Trade in the Churchill government, warmly supported this development, while the new Attlee government made it clear that they would support the siting of a new steel plant in west Wales and nowhere else. The giant Steel Company of Wales came into being in 1947, formed from a merger of Richard Thomas and Baldwins, Guest Keen, John Lysaghts, and the Llanelli Associated Tinplate Company. Its main enterprise was the foundation of the new steel-works, the mammoth Abbey Works built on the sand flats to the east of Port Talbot. With government backing and encouragement, the new Abbey Works came into production in November 1951. With its four blast-furnaces, twenty-one open-hearth furnaces, new coke-ovens and other ancillary features, all supplying an eighty-inch strip-mill, it was the largest steel works in the British Isles. Its production capacity rose from an initial one million to nearly three million tons a year. It provided employment for over 17,000 men by 1963, The Afan valley suddenly became a boom area of staggering proportions, with south Wales foremost among the steel-making regions of Britain once again, and one of the technological giants of the industrial world.

Associated with the new Abbey Works, to relieve the decay of the old, technologically obsolescent pack mills of the tinplate industry, three new cold-reduction plants were set up, one at Margam itself, another at Trostre near Llanelli, the third at Velindre north of Swansea. The last two clearly were sited with local employment needs in mind. The cold-reduction plant of Trostre alone received 7,000 tons of steel a week from the Abbey Works. With the Ebbw Vale works also booming, as a result of the new electrolytic process introduced during the war, and the John Summers works at Shotton steadily increasing its steel-making capacity, this rejuvenated steel and tinplate industry provided another fundamental reason for the extraordinary and heartening economic upsurge that the post-war years brought to Wales. Indeed, its economic performance outstripped any other sector of Britain after 1945. Output in Wales rose by 23 per cent between 1948 and 1954, compared with only 18 per cent for Britain as a whole.

This period of economic growth reached a plateau by the early fifties. From about 1954 the growth in the economic performance of south Wales was at best comparable with that of the rest of the United Kingdom. Then in 1957–8 there came a recession and a return of unemployment, although on a far less severe basis than that experienced before the war. The Conservative government under Macmillan, now in office, responded with another boost to the development area policy, to illustrate that statist interventionism to a considerable extent was now a bipartisan policy. Industrial Development Certificates again steered industry to Wales. The 1960 Local Employment Act was used to encourage private industry again to venture into south Wales and other older industrial regions, through tax and rate concessions. There was a further surge in introducing new, technologically advanced industries such as engineering, chemicals, and artificial fabrics. With government aid, a £2 million Prestcold refrigerator factory was leased near Swansea. More important, south Wales now became a major centre of the motor-car industry for the first time. In 1959–60 were set up large new plants of the Rover car company at Cardiff and the Fisher/Ludlow car-body press works at Llanelli. Indeed, the car industry was to provide a new base for employment and economic activity in many parts of south Wales for years to come.

The most impressive physical landmark of this second wave of economic advance in the early sixties, however, was again connected with the modernization of the old steel industry. After much competition from the Ravenscraig site in Scotland and elsewhere, a vast new sixty-eight-inch strip-mill was established on a green-field site at Llanwern near Newport, the RTB/Spencer works. Beginning production in 1962, it became the third largest steel plant in Wales, behind the Abbey Works and John Summers. By the end of 1963, it claimed a productive rate of 1,400,000 tons of crude steel per annum, with potential of nearly two million tons.[10] There was thus an arc of major steel-works along the entire length of the Welsh coalfield, from Llanwern in the east, to Llanelli in the west. In addition, much investment at this time took place in other major steel-works. The Richard Thomas & Baldwin plant at Ebbw Vale with its two electrolytic tinning lines, and the Summers works at Shotton on Deeside in the north-east, both continued to thrive. The new blast-furnace at Shotton was the largest in Britain and raised the potential production of this steel-works to over two million tons a year.

In a totally different region of Wales, there was also modernization and progress to record in the early sixties. Oil now became almost as central to the Welsh economy as coal and steel had been in the past. The old Anglo-Iranian refinery at Llandarcy, near Skewen, now owned by BP, had continued to expand. In 1961 BP built an oil terminal on Milford Haven in Pembrokeshire to connect across the eighty miles of south Wales with its refinery. The Llandarcy refinery was now able to process eight million tons of crude oil a year. In fact, the economic picture in Pembrokeshire became transformed, as it was realized that the deep waters of Milford Haven had the capacity to berth ocean-going oil tankers from the Middle East at all states of the tide. In

[10] *Development in the Iron and Steel Industry: Special Report* (HMSO, 1964), p. 133.

addition, there were readily available railway facilities and power supplies. The first new development came in 1960 when Esso opened a large new refinery to deal with crude oil imported on the company's super-tankers. The BP refinery in 1961 was followed by a Texaco refinery in 1964; a Gulf Oil refinery, with an associated petrochemical plant and deep-water marine terminal in 1968; an Amoco refinery in 1973; and, also in 1973, a huge new power station to burn heavy fuel oil from the Gulf and Texaco refineries, and the BP ocean terminal, one of the largest in Europe. By the seventies, giant tankers of 250,000 tons were being accommodated. In 1979–80 came two giant catalytic 'crackers' to boost the output of petrol. This transformation of the beautiful coastline of Milford Haven and central Pembrokeshire generally caused much heart-searching. The creation of massive refinery storage tanks, electric pylons, and the rest, brought severe environmental problems which the planners seemed unable to solve. There was also the point that the boost to employment by the new refineries was largely temporary, lasting just as long as the refineries were actually being built. Relatively few people were needed actually to run these giant installations—only 1,849 people were directly employed in oil installations in Pembrokeshire in 1974.[11] Controversial though it might be, however, the growth of the oil-refining industry in Milford Haven was a token of the further modernization and transformation of the Welsh economy. Milford Haven soon became the leading oil port in Britain, with 30 million tons shipped each year. By the early 1970s, it was the second most active port in Britain in terms of the cargo shipped. Had it not been for the interruption of oil supplies after the Arab–Israeli war in 1973, Milford Haven might even have overtaken London itself as Britain's busiest port.

A third and final surge of economic activity in south Wales came in the later 1960s. This followed the advent of the new Labour government under Harold Wilson in 1964 and its concern to employ new planning techniques to combat renewed economic difficulties. In 1966 the whole of south Wales, except for the south-east region between Cardiff and Newport, was given development area status. In 1969 this was extended to cover the whole of the region apart from Chepstow. Again, the now traditional range of government incentives was used, including the building of advance factories so far as economies in government expenditure permitted. There was also an emphasis on the more efficient use of labour, including the selective use of Regional Employment Premiums to subsidize manpower (a scheme worked out in the Welsh Office under Cledwyn Hughes) to assist the development areas. The most visible sign of this policy was the introduction of new companies into south Wales, with the car industry again leading the way. The Ford company took over the old Prestcold plant to the east of Swansea in 1965 and gave employment to 2,000 men, making axles and gear-boxes. The Borg-Warner automatic transmission company set up at Kenfig Hill in mid-Glamorgan, while Girlings set

[11] Brian John, *Pembrokeshire* (Newton Abbot, 1976), pp. 210 ff.

up a major car component firm at Cwmbran new town in Monmouthshire. The car industry, in fact, continued to expand in south Wales, despite the temporary depression of the domestic car market following the large rise in oil and petroleum prices in 1973. It was announced in 1977 that the Ford company would set up a huge £180 m., 2,500-job engine factory, this time at Waterton, Bridgend, near to the existing trading estate. Another development was the £70 million invested in the Baglan petrochemical complex by the Wales Gas Board in 1968—71, due to employ 5,000 men.

It was, however, service employment as much as new industry which seemed to many observers to provide the salvation for the renewed economic difficulties of Wales in the later 1960s. To this end, a new passport office was set up at Newport, an investment grants office at Cardiff, a much-criticized Ministry of Transport car registration and licensing centre in Swansea, and, most spectacular, the transfer of the Royal Mint from London to Llantrisant, 'the hole with the mint' in the argot of some unkind critics. Indeed, it was noticeable by now that the service sector was now the most rapidly growing element in the Welsh employment pattern. With over 345,000 people employed in service occupations, office jobs of a white-collar kind, and the like, the total by 1968 had virtually doubled since the end of the war.[12] However disturbing some academic economists might find the drift from industrial and manufacturing jobs in south Wales and other areas, the new emphasis on clerical and other white-collar occupations contributed further to that broadening of the base of employment discernible since 1945. It helped to make the Welsh economy that much the more resilient in withstanding the new challenges that the mid-seventies were to bring.

Long before this period, indeed by the mid-1950s, it had become clear that a revolutionary change had taken place in the economic structure of south and north-east Wales. The industrial character of the nation bore little resemblance to that of pre-1939. This had a number of important economic and sociological consequences of which perhaps two above all stand out.

The first, apparent in the fifties, overwhelmingly dramatic in the sixties, was the deliberate and consistent rundown of the Welsh coal industry. No sector of the British mining industry underwent a more remarkable contraction after 1945. Even in 1960 there were still 106,000 employed in the pits of Wales. By 1970, there had been a dramatic fall to only 60,000. By 1979, the total was not many more than 30,000. An entire way of life in south Wales seemed to be coming to an end. From the start of nationalization in 1947, there had been a gradual process of the closure of smaller, uneconomic pits, and the overhauling of older ones. Even in the boom years after 1945 there were difficulties. The South-West Division of the Coal Board had to report a loss of £10 million in 1947 and a further loss of £5 million in 1948. Almost half the 300

[12] Graham Humphrys, *South Wales* (Newton Abbot, 1972), p. 78.

mines the NCB acquired employed less than 250 men. But it was the end of the fifties that saw the National Coal Board, under the regime of Lord Robens, embark upon a major policy of pit closures. Between 1957 and 1959, twenty-three collieries ceased production. The major reason undoubtedly was the continuing encroachment of oil upon the domain of coal, for naval vessels and other forms of transport, for industrial use in factories and in power stations, and in domestic heating. South Wales, where costs of production were notoriously high and where the technical problems of raising coal were most acute, stood to feel most severely the impact of the closures that now resulted. The effects were dramatic. In the Rhondda as late as 1958, there were still twelve major pits working, with an output of over 2,380,000 tons. By 1969, there was but one (the famous Maerdy) still working in this old citadel of King Coal. By the mid-sixties the Rhondda West constituency, still represented by the miners' nominee, contained less than 4,000 working miners of all grades, where in 1920 it had included more than 20,000. The Labour party and other local institutions were increasingly dominated by representatives of the AEU, the Engineers' Union, and the Tailors and Garment Workers, not the miners. Historic names, associated with the industrial greatness of Rhondda as well as with social conflict, the collieries of Lewis Merthyr, the Cambrian, Parc and Dare, Gelli, and the rest, passed into history.

All over south Wales, communities once dependent on their pits saw the industrial centre around which their lives revolved disappear. An average of ten pits a year closed down in the sixties. This applied even in the anthracite coalfield of west Wales which had escaped some of the worst rigours of the depression in the past. There were only 21 anthracite collieries in Wales in 1963, compared with 39 in 1948. The process continued relentlessly: in the Swansea region, of the anthracite collieries inherited by the Coal Board in 1947, only three were still working in 1970, and two of these (Gwendraeth and Ammanford) were shortly to close down also.[13] As this closure of so much of the coalfield gained momentum, it is remarkable how little protest was aroused. There was an outcry over one closure, the anthracite pit at Cwmllynfell at the head of the Swansea valley in 1959, where an isolated little community faced economic ruin. But here again a combination of redundancy payments to the miners made unemployed, plus new employment in the region (even if it meant much longer journeys to work with perhaps a forty-mile round trip to Swansea as the price of keeping off the dole), managed to placate all discontent. Miners often seemed all too willing to move to more agreeable and healthier work in factories: the old pull of the comradeship of the pit, founded too often on struggle and physical danger, was losing its force. The south Wales miners, traditionally militant and in the van of industrial protest, accepted these closures with remarkable docility and

[13] W. G. V. Balchin (ed.), *Swansea and its Region* (Swansea, 1971), p. 233.

resignation.[14] The secretaries of the National Union of Miners at this period were two Welsh Communists, first Arthur Horner until 1959 and then Will Paynter. The south Wales miners also had Communist leaders, men like Will Whitehead and Dai Francis and Dai Dan Evans. Yet even these committed Marxists faced the erosion of the coal industry without undue demur. Perhaps they regarded it as part of the inevitable disintegration of the British capitalist system as long ago foretold by the prophet Marx. More likely, they accepted, as intelligent men and economic realists, what appeared to be the conventional wisdom of the time.

Until the seventies, the gentle winding-up of much of the Welsh coal industry appeared to be an inevitable process, a clearing of the legacy from the first industrial revolution. Between nationalization in 1947 and the oil crisis in 1974, 150 collieries in south Wales were wiped out; 75,000 jobs disappeared with them. The age of coal appeared to have passed, as endless floods of cheap imports of oil from the Middle East seemed destined to provide the basis of the nation's energy supplies in the future. There was proof now of massive British oil reserves in the North Sea, and perhaps in the 'Celtic Sea' between Wales and Ireland as well. South Wales was partly benefiting from this revolution in energy supplies, as has been seen, with the importance of oil refining in Milford Haven and Llandarcy. (It was less beneficial to the port of Swansea, which saw the quantity of oil handled there fall from 4,532,000 tons in 1952 to 3,231,000 in 1958.) In addition, there were now nuclear-based power stations sited in north Wales, at Wylfa Head in Anglesey and at Trawsfynydd, although not without some local protest as will be seen. Hydro-electric schemes were also thriving in mid-Wales and in Merioneth. Faced with this inexorable economic logic, the miners seemed to be acquiescing in their own decline, the minority who remained at work in the pits basking in steady employment and reasonable wages. They at least seemed no longer to remember 1926. In place of the old class militancy, that fierce industrial culture associated with the miners' clubs, welfare halls, and the WEA, there was a shallow proletarian capitalism based on drinking clubs, bingo halls, and cheap holidays abroad. Spain was the most popular venue for these last, the Franco regime notwithstanding. Even the memories of the Spanish Civil War, so it seemed, meant little to the relatively affluent descendants of the heroes of the thirties and of the International Brigade.

Of course, the pattern changed dramatically, or appeared to, with the immense, threefold increase in the price of oil early in 1974 following the Arab–Israeli war and the consequent oil embargo imposed by Saudi Arabia and other major oil-producing states in the Middle East. Suddenly coal became important again. In the confrontations between the National Union of Mineworkers and the Heath government that resulted in national miners'

---

[14] Cf. Arthur Horner, op. cit., pp. 222 ff.

strikes in February 1972 and February 1974—the first since 1926, incidentally—the Welsh miners were zealous in the struggle. Henceforth, they were
lined up with miners from Yorkshire and Scotland in adopting the most
militant postures on the wage claims of up to 60 per cent, together with other
fringe benefits. The Welsh were also the only miners in Britain originally to
vote against the National Coal Board's subsequent productivity scheme,
relating higher wages to higher production norms, a scheme originally
approved by the NUM national executive. There were sound historical
reasons for the Welsh miners' hostility to such a plan. With memories of
bloody disputes over 'abnormal places' in the past, and a deep awareness of
the physical difficulties of extracting coal in south Wales, however hard the
miner worked, there was an understandable resentment of 'setting miner
against miner' and 'pit against pit' in the chase for higher production. It might
well cost lives in the coalfield where the tragedies of industrial injuries and
accidents had been commonplace for over a century and a half. Even so, the
Welsh miners, too, had eventually to knuckle under at a time of incomes
control, and to accept the new productivity scheme.

   In the mid 1970s, the Welsh coal industry looked for a while in a somewhat
more hopeful condition. Baleful prophecies such as that made by Lord
Robens in 1967 that only six pits and 9,000 jobs might remain in the south
Wales coal industry by the 1980s were seen to be ludicrously wrong. Indeed,
there was now a desperate shortage of labour in the mines. There were
increased investments in the coal industry now, with the 'linked pits'
programme of north Gwent and the creation of highly modern pits like that at
Betws near Ammanford where a £400,000 computer network could provide
instant information on pumping, air flows, and hazards of methane gas, and
other vital matters. Anthracite seemed to be particularly thriving now, and so
did the demand for coking-coal, notably for the Steel Corporation's plans for
expanding the Abbey Works at Port Talbot. A massive new coking mine near
to Margam was under consideration in 1976.[15] More generally, the British
coal industry now acquired a new value in terms of energy resources and
savings on the huge bill for oil imports. Nevertheless, the overall picture from
1947 to the end of the seventies was unmistakably one of a Welsh coal industry
in contraction. The Welsh coalfield continued to make losses (£46 m. on deep
mine operations in 1979–80), production targets were frequently not met,
absenteeism continued to be a problem, more and more miners aged fifty-five
and over were given early retirement as machinery increasingly took over the
cutting of coal and the transportation of it to the surface. In early 1979 the
National Coal Board called for the closure of ten further Welsh pits, including
the once ultra-modern Abernant pit in the Swansea valley, and Maerdy, the
last remaining coal mine operating in the Rhondda. There was an unavailing
struggle to preserve Deep Duffryn in Mountain Ash. In the latter decades of

[15] *Western Mail*, 3 November 1976.

the twentieth century, it became clear that coal could no longer dominate the industrial life of Wales as it had done so conclusively from the 1850s to the 1950s.

Steel was another staple heavy industry and major source of employment which declined in similar fashion. At first, this seemed most unlikely with the massive investment of the Steel Company of Wales in the Abbey Works at Port Talbot and the growth of the strip-mill at Llanwern. In the north-east, the Brymbo and John Summers works were also booming until the early sixties. With the expansion of the economy in the fifties and the sixties, and the insatiable demand for steel for cars and other purposes, the future for the Welsh steel industry (which produced almost a quarter of all steel ingots produced in Britain) seemed glowing indeed. The annual reports of the Iron and Steel Board were a hymn of praise to progress and growth. But here, too, the legacy of low productivity, managerial inefficiency, and a falling rate of capital investment began to take its toll. This was, no doubt, in part assisted by the political gyrations that afflicted the industry, with nationalization in 1951, denationalization in 1953, and renationalization in 1965. By the end of the sixties, it was obvious that the worldwide demand for steel was falling sharply, and that in any case Welsh steel was being priced out of many markets by more efficient and productive steel industries in West Germany, the United States and Japan.

The seventies brought the same process of contraction for Welsh steel-making that the sixties had brought for Welsh coal mining. After much delay (partly occasioned by the fact that East Flint was a Labour-held marginal constituency) it was announced that the Brymbo steel-works at Wrexham might be cut back as part of the nationwide rationalization programme, while the massive John Summers works at Shotton, now losing £33 million per year, was also operating under a threat of closure, even though given a reprieve beyond the 1979 general election. The Steel Corporation sought to close it by 1981. The history of steel-making on Deeside (now given development area status like the mining valleys of south Wales) suddenly appeared close to its end. So did vital elements of the south Wales steel industry. This now consisted of four plants, three on the coast, the giant Abbey Works at Margam, the RTB Spencer mill at Llanwern, and the ancient Guest, Keen works at East Moors in Cardiff, the heir to the old Dowlais factory. The fourth was the Ebbw Vale plant so dramatically rescued in 1938. For some years after 1945, the Ebbw Vale works, under Richard Thomas & Baldwins flourished mightily, with new investment in electrolytic tinning methods. But it was clear that the facts of economic life were against Ebbw Vale. It was sited far from sea outlets, it had no room to expand (hence the decision to set up a new works at Llanwern), it was becoming technologically dated. One of its three blast-furnaces closed down in 1962. After years of debate, steel-making at the main Ebbw Vale works was closed down in 1975—6 and its large workforce made redundant. This brought embarrassment to the MP for Ebbw Vale, Michael Foot, now a leading figure in the Labour government, but years of financial loss seemed to leave the government and the Steel Corporation with no real choice. Shortly, after much speculation, it was confirmed that the East Moors works in Cardiff, many of whose workers lived in the constituency of the then Prime Minister, James Callaghan, would also be closed down. East Moors finally went out of production in early 1978. It, too, was antiquated by comparative standards.

The Port Talbot and Llanwern works continued to thrive, despite frequent stoppages in production caused by industrial disputes. In 1977, the government approved an £835 m. expansion programme at Port Talbot. However, major questions continued to be posed about their alleged excess of labour and criticisms of over-manning were frequent. Reports suggested that the Abbey Works, with over 15,000 men employed there, could flourish more efficiently with barely half that number. Certainly the Welsh steel industry, apparently the pivot, along with oil, of the new model Welsh economy of the sixties, seemed likely to follow King Coal into contraction if not oblivion. That crude steel and foreign coking coal should be imported into south Wales, was indeed a portent of the times.

The other dominant feature of the changing industrial structure of Wales, especially of south Wales, from the late 1940s onwards was the growing concentration of economic activity and of employment opportunities in a narrower and narrower segment of south Wales. It was the coastal strip of southern Glamorgan, particularly of the south-east in the area from Barry to Llanwern, comprehending Cardiff and Newport, which absorbed much of the new industry of the south. In the north-east, it was an area on Deeside in eastern Flintshire, extending downwards in the direction of Wrexham, which was the major growth-point of economic life. As a result, there was a steady flight of the working population from the heartland of Wales to the periphery on the north-east and south-east, adjacent to England. The censuses of 1951, 1961, and 1971 told of a steady drift of population from the mining valleys. Places like the Rhondda, Aberdare, Merthyr, Bargoed, and Abertillery all lost population, despite the relative success of the government's advance factory and development programme. This process was confirmed by the Beeching cuts of rail services in the early sixties which deprived towns like Aberdare, Dowlais, and Abertillery of any rail link at all. Those workers who still lived in the valleys often became commuters, travelling long distances to the coast to find their employment. In the early seventies, there was a net outflow of 9,370 workers from the Rhondda daily, mainly to Pontypridd and Cardiff to the south.[16]

An enormous redistribution was taking place, with the county boroughs of

[16] Humphrys, op. cit., p. 94.

Cardiff and Newport increasing their population by 40 per cent in the fifties and sixties at a time when industrial south Wales generally was increasing by only 5 per cent, and most of the rest of Wales actually losing population. Cardiff and Newport were not only growing fast, absorbing much of the surplus labour of the valleys and offering new service employment in place of the hard manual work of past years. They were increasingly tied in with the industrial growth of the Bristol Channel and Avonside region generally, with the development of industry straddling both sides of the water. The pull to the south-east became more and more acute, with employment, cultural opportunities and population increasingly located on the southern fringe of coastal Glamorgan and Monmouth. The Julian Hodge empire greatly expanded Cardiff's role as a centre of finance and insurance. In this sense, the closure of the Ebbw Vale steel-works in the mid-seventies was symbolic, the tolling of a muted knell for at least a part of the economic and social life of the mining and steel valleys.

Of course, this picture should not be exaggerated. As has been seen, government intervention and industrial diversification limited the extent to which the valleys lost their population. There were other growth areas in Wales apart from the Cardiff region. There was, for example, the development of a large conurbation along the northern rim of the Vale of Glamorgan in the sixties and seventies, with Bridgend as the centre of an incipient linear city extending from Aberkenfig in the west to Llantrisant in the east. The Bridgend Industrial Estate was the heart of this. It was extended in later years by the growth of service employment based on Bridgend, with hospitals, police, fire service, and other organizations located there. The huge Ford car-engine factory, announced in 1977, spurred on a large new housing estate at Brackla.

West Wales, too, survived this pressure from Cardiff to some degree. The new tinplate works at Velindre and Trostre, the growth of new industries in east Swansea and towards Neath and Llandarcy, the thriving trading estate at Fforestfach, the remarkable buoyancy of the port of Swansea from the late forties onwards with the prosperity accruing from the shipments of oil from the Middle East—all these gave Swansea a flourishing air in the post-war years. Swansea also became a major centre of commerce, business and investment. In the later sixties, there was talk of 'Swansea Bay City' extending from the Gower peninsula as far as the mammoth steel-works at Port Talbot. But there was much local fear that west Wales and Swansea would also suffer in the long term from the drift to the south-east. Much anxiety was expressed at the completion of the Severn Bridge in the later sixties, linking south Wales with Bristol and Avonmouth. It was feared that this would add still further to the drift of industry to the Newport – Cardiff – Barry region, or perhaps take it out of Wales altogether, to the detriment of Swansea, Neath, and Port Talbot. One pointer was that the Swansea airport, at Fairwood Common, virtually went out of business in the sixties, in the face of the superior competition of the Cardiff airport at Rhoose. In the latter, the runway had been extended to accommodate 1/11 aircraft and Trident jets, suggesting an international aspect to Cardiff's air services that Swansea could never match.

Other fears were also voiced at this drift to the south-east. There was the environmental problem of urban sprawl with so immense a concentration of people in one narrow segment of land. The road traffic of Cardiff by the seventies was a formidable hazard. There was also the burning cultural problem associated with expanding the anglicized south-east at the expense of Welsh-speaking areas in west Wales. Institutions such as the BBC or the national university became little oases of Welshness in a vast cosmopolitan territory. Other developments during the 1960s and early seventies, the completion of the 'Heads of the Valleys' roads along the rim of the coalfield, the extension of the M4 motorway from London as far as the eastern suburbs of Cardiff all added to fears that prosperity and economic growth would be unfairly concentrated in a small part of Wales, with much of the rest by-passed. The remainder of south Wales was comparatively static. Even Swansea showed little new industrial growth in the sixties, save for the side-effects of the petro-chemical development in Baglan Bay at the mouth of the Neath river. The one idiosyncratic example of growth was Milford Haven in Pembrokeshire, and, as has been seen, once the refineries were completed, unemployment and industrial stagnation tended to be the pattern even here. For all its prosperity, much of south Wales west of Cardiff still seemed in danger of becoming that monument to wasted opportunities that Thomas Jones had satirized in the thirties.

In north Wales, it was Flintshire, mainly the anglicized eastern part of the county close to Cheshire, that was growing. Here again, people were on the move—and relentlessly towards England. As in south Wales, the coalfield steadily contracted; with it disappeared some of the most vigorous strongholds of industrial Welsh culture. In the early sixties, the north Wales coalfield still maintained six collieries, Bersham, Gresford, Hafod, Ifton, Llay Main, and Point of Ayr, the last the only one in Flintshire; they employed 6,000 men and produced two million tons a year. By the later 1970s, these had been cut down to just two. Gresford, with its memories of industrial disaster, closed down for ever in 1974. By contrast, light industries in the valley of the Dee from Wrexham-Marchwiel to Connah's Quay and Queensferry were flourishing. The Marchwiel trading estate expanded with the arrival of such disparate commercial giants as Firestone tyres and Kellogg's cornflakes. Broughton had its large de Havilland aircraft factory, sited there since 1939. There were also major textile industries, notably the Courtauld rayon plants that had grown steadily since the twenties, to replace the older industrial structure based on coal, steel, chemicals, and brick-making. Wrexham even exported lager to Germany. Flintshire, like Glamorgan and Monmouthshire, showed a steady rise in its population throughout the period from 1945 to 1980. Cultural institutions sprang up such as the new arts and theatrical complex at Mold. This was the product of a continuous growth in diversified light industry. But it was a development that tied Flintshire all the more closely to industrial Cheshire, south Lancashire, and Merseyside, rather than to the Welsh hinterland. In north and south Wales alike, the same process of geographical redistribution towards the periphery and the steady denuding of the central areas went on remorselessly.

For all that, these years in south Wales and the north-east, years which saw the closure of much of the coal and steel industries and the resettlement of much of the working population, brought with them economic progress and affluence. The industrial base of the nation was by the end of the seventies far broader and far more modernized. Some outside observers (usually middle-class) might bemoan the new 'confetti culture' or 'admass' popular entertainment that took over from the WEA, the miners' lodge and, perhaps, the Sunday school. Some might regret that the old social cohesion and neighbourly loyalties, bred amidst the hardship and the terrors of the pit, might disappear in the rootless, almost trivial atmosphere of factories that made vacuum cleaners, zip fasteners, roller skates, television sets, potato crisps, and other attributes of modern society. But the spread of greater material wealth, and of healthier, more agreeable conditions of work brought widespread satisfaction, as will be discussed again in the following chapter. It ill behoved middle-class critics to disparage the quality of life of working-class people enjoying the amenities of a more secure existence for the first time and revelling in its comforts. To none did this apply more forcefully than to working-class women. In place of the old prejudice against female employment, it was noted that after 1945 women supplied almost 40 per cent of the total labour force. Gwyn Thomas was a Rhondda boy who witnessed at first hand the poverty in his home village of Porth in the twenties and thirties, the barefoot children, the soup kitchens, the means test, and other scourges. He wrote later of the 'psychoses of poverty and dread' that had scarred his childhood in the depression.[17] The old pressures had disappeared, with lessened social friction, heartening statistics for adult health, child malnutrition, and industrial disease. There was a mood of optimism that south Wales had not known since 1914. For most of south Wales and some of the north-east, too, the passing of an older industrial order was only to be welcomed, along with the greater serenity and security that resulted. In addition, the continuing strength of the WEA and adult education, and of the Open University in Wales after 1969, showed that many of the old cultural and intellectual values survived or took new forms even in this unfamiliar new world. Indeed the adult education movement became progressively engaged in vocational and compensatory education, with extra-mural departments, technical colleges,

[17] Gwyn Thomas, *A Welsh Eye* (London, 1964), p. 24.

and the WEA running industrial day-release courses for junior managers and trade unionists.

If industrial Wales exhibited many of the signs of modernization and success in the post-1945 period, a very different story was to be told of the rural hinterland, west of Swansea, north of the Brecon Beacons, extending across the entire geographical heart of Wales as far as Anglesey and the north Wales coast. Side by side with the growth in the south of the country, north and mid-Wales experienced a steady drift and decline. Their depopulation became a phenomenon with which successive governments tried to grapple. The main causes of this decline were well established long before 1939, even before 1914. Agriculture in fact maintained the advance established during the Second World War, and boosted by the guaranteed prices created under the 1947 Agriculture Act of the Labour government. The upland farmers now found new affluence and confidence resulting from increased production, steadier price levels, and expanding markets. At least four-fifths now took part in co-operative schemes for storing, grading, and marketing produce. Farm holdings became larger—those of under twenty acres gradually disappeared. Sales of milk (boosted by the operations of the Milk Marketing Board) and of breeding sheep showed in 1968 a total volume that was double that of 1947. On the other hand, increased mechanization meant inevitably a further decline in the demand for agricultural labour and this added to the flow of depopulation from rural areas. There was also a marked decline in the number of rural craftsmen as the 'golden age of the horse' passed away: blacksmiths and saddlers became far less numerous and those who remained had to turn their skills to other tasks and become all-purpose farm mechanics. The overall total of those employed in agriculture fell from 91,000 in 1931 to 77,000 in 1951. Full-time male workers on Welsh farms fell from 31,301 in 1951 to 14,237 in 1968, and the total continued to drop thereafter.[18] In any case, farms in Wales continued to be relatively precarious enterprises and small in scale compared with those of England or Scotland. One result was the formation of the Farmers' Union of Wales in December 1955 (*Undeb Amaethwyr Cymru*), the result of complaints by farmers, especially in south-west Wales, that the National Farmers' Union was unduly dominated by large farmers in England and failed to pay sufficient heed to the needs of Welsh farming in marketing organizations and at an annual price review.

In addition to this fall in the population engaged in work on the land, there was also a steady decay of such industry as there existed in rural Wales. The slate-quarrying community of Gwynedd, for instance, entered upon a period of prolonged decline from the end of the Second World War. While much of the native culture of the quarrying villages survived, and reached wider audiences (for instance through the activities of the remarkable amateur

[18] *A Strategy for Rural Wales:* Report by the Welsh Council, March 1971.

antiquarian, Bob Owen of Croesor in the far north of Merioneth) slate quarrying as an economic enterprise steadily folded up. Major quarries such as the Oakley in Blaenau Ffestiniog, the Dinorwic in Llanberis, and the Dorothea in Dyffryn Nantlle all closed down, the inevitable result of competition from cheaper imported roofing materials, and also of the decline of the domestic construction industry. By 1972 there were only five quarries still at work in north Wales—Penrhyn in Bethesda, of such fateful memories, which employed 350 men, one in Nantlle, two in Ffestiniog, and a small one at Aberllefenni, near Corris, in southern Merioneth.[19] Indeed, these last four employed a mere handful of men. Slate quarrying impinged on the public conscience now largely through the existence of a generation of elderly ex-quarrymen, acute sufferers from silicosis and other lung diseases that were an occupational hazard. There was something of a recovery in the slate industry in the later 1970s, with some revival in more specialized aspects of the housing market and some demand from the tourist trade for slate clocks, ornaments, and the like. By 1978, it was reported that there were now 550 quarrymen employed in Gwynedd. The purchase of the old Penrhyn quarry, which still employed 250 men, by Marchwiel Holdings (a firm of building contractors who used slate waste as filling material) was a pointer to a more hopeful future.[20] But, in general, slate quarrying, like other small-scale enterprises, the woollen industry, clothing manufacture, scattered throughout rural Wales from Anglesey to Carmarthenshire, was far too small in scale and local in aspect to provide major sources of employment to arrest the drift of young people from the Welsh countryside.

A much more substantial development was the opening-up of the Rio Tinto Zinc Corporation's aluminium reduction plant, at a capital cost of £80 millions, near Holyhead in Anglesey in 1970. This was much needed. Anglesey's employment problems had been severe for years. With unemployment rising to 13 per cent, it had been described in 1962 as 'the new depressed area of Wales'. Rio Tinto (by 1979 owned by Anglesey Aluminium, a subsidiary of the Kaiser Corporation) employed in the first instance almost a thousand men. It provided some salvation for unemployed men over a wide region, taking in quarrymen from the Nantlle valley in Caernarvonshire on the mainland, and even from Merseyside. Even so, the work provided by Rio Tinto was necessarily mainly for the benefit of Anglesey people; the rest of rural Wales continued to decay. Other possible mining enterprises in rural areas, for example copper mining in the Mawddach estuary in central Merioneth in the hinterland of Barmouth, were halted owing to the environmental damage they would cause to a particularly scenic area which benefited greatly from tourism. Elsewhere in the north-west, some employment was provided by the Wylfa Head power station in Anglesey and later by the

[19] Tim Maby, *Planet* 10 (February/March 1972), pp. 67–74.
[20] *Financial Times*, 23 August 1978.

construction of another nuclear power station at Trawsfynydd in Merioneth. The Buchanan Inquiry in 1958 supported the controversial decision of the planners to build a power station here, over the objection of ecologists and also of many nationalists who deplored the drowning of yet another small village to provide water supplies for the new power station.[21] Trade unionists in the area were enthusiastic at the prospect of new work. For a time, while the power station was actually being built, Trawsfynydd, so long a bleak and isolated community, suddenly bore the air of a boom town, reminiscent of the American west. But much of the labour was immigrant, some of it Irish, since local labour was in such short supply. In any case, after the power station had actually been completed and was in operation, few men were needed, much as in the case of the oil refineries of Pembrokeshire. Meanwhile, an impressive sweep of the Merioneth landscape, the home of Hedd Wyn himself, had been permanently disfigured.

Clearly, much more needed to be done to build up other sources of rural employment. Forestry employed a few workers. The Forestry Commission was acquiring land at the rate of 10,000 acres per year in the fifties, and by 1969 owned about 385,000 in all.[22] The commission's acquisition of Trawscoed, a country house near to Aberystwyth, symbolized the dislodgement of the squires in favour of the planners. The regimented, severe plantations of conifers on the hillsides neither provided much work nor added to the beauty of the rural scene. They had serious effects on ecology, including insect and bird life. The Forestry Commission's operations were fiercely attacked in the writings of the nationalist D. J. Williams, notably in *Hen Dŷ Ffarm*. There was also some rural employment to be had from the construction of other capital projects such as the reservoirs at Clywedog in Montgomeryshire and Tryweryn in Merioneth (both much contested by nationalists as will be seen in Chapter 13), and from hydro-electric schemes such as those at Tan-y-grisiau in northern Merioneth and Nant-y-Moch in northern Cardiganshire in the Rheidol valley. Defence expenditure (for instance at RAF Valley) provided some civilian jobs in Anglesey. The army camp at Tonfannau in Merioneth was kept open for years to provide local employment even though it had little value in purely military terms.

But everything pointed to rural Wales, especially mid-Wales, becoming a decaying, run-down area, thriving on tourism for a few months in the summer, but otherwise with little to retain its able-bodied younger population. The population of rural Wales did rise slightly in the 1960s—by 15,000 (2.4 per cent). But this was almost entirely due to the influx of elderly residents seeking a peaceful haven for their retirement; in financial terms they added further burdens on local social, welfare, and community services in such

---

[21] 'Report on the Proposals to Construct a Nuclear Power Station at Trawsfynydd' (non-parliamentary, Ministry of Power, 1958).

[22] *Cymru: Wales, 1969* (Cmnd. 4293), Parl. Papers, 1969–70, xxviii, p. 72.

places as Llandudno. They also had some impact on the political affiliations of Gwynedd and Powys, as the 1979 general election was to show.

The tendency to regard rural Wales as a kind of wasteland, and to speed on the process of its decline, was hastened by key decisions affecting public transportation. The Beeching Report on the railways in March 1963 made some drastic suggestions about the closure of railways in rural areas.[23] In all, railway mileage would be reduced from 637 miles to only 363, despite the impact on local employment and the fact that this would make nonsense of serious attempts to bring industry to many rural areas. Much of this disastrous report was implemented, with the blessing of both Conservative and Labour governments. Many railways in rural Wales, that from Swansea to Aberystwyth through the heart of Carmarthenshire and Cardiganshire, that from Barmouth to Ruabon, along the Mawddach and Dee valleys, that cutting across the Llŷn peninsula, from Bangor to Pwllheli, together with a myriad of local lines down the south Wales valleys, were closed down. There was desperate pressure to keep alive the Cambrian coast line from Machynlleth to Pwllheli along the northern Cardigan Bay coast, and also the mid-Wales line from Shrewsbury through Llandrindod Wells towards the outskirts of Swansea. The first was saved mainly because of a large Butlin's holiday camp at Pwllheli. The second was preserved partly because George Thomas, then the Secretary of State for Wales, pointed out to the Wilson government in 1968 that it ran through six marginal constituencies. Beeching's more drastic projections even visualized the winding-up of the main mid-Wales link from Shrewsbury westwards to Aberystwyth. In a few years, it seemed, rural Wales would retain only two major railways, along the coastline of north Wales as far as Holyhead and the gateway to Dublin, and from Cardiff westwards to Fishguard in the south, with sea links to Rosslare and Cork. Both were designed to link Wales to England and to Ireland rather than to provide an integrated public transport system for the principality itself. It was no longer possible to travel from the north of Wales to the south by train, save via Shrewsbury or even London—'for Wales, see England', indeed.

Some of the more extreme Beeching proposals (reminiscent of the Geddes Axe of earlier businessmen) were staved off. By the seventies it became clear again that rural communities, with skeletal local bus services and many elderly citizens who could not afford cars or perhaps drive them because of infirmity, needed a basic rail structure. In any case, the roads of a mountainous, rugged land such as Wales could not cope with the transport needs of the age, especially the freight of food and other supplies. In the seventies, the railways became more fashionable, especially as tourism to all parts of Wales boomed. But the impact of Beeching was a very serious one. It left many small towns and villages stranded, their schools under threat of closure, their industries moribund, their young people with nothing to do, their older

[23] *Western Mail*, 28 March 1963.

citizens with nowhere to go. Much attention, therefore, was devoted by governments and by governmental agencies from the sixties onwards to try to prevent rural Wales from becoming a kind of vast Indian reservation, beautiful but barren, depopulated and dying.

The most effective policy seemed to be to try to build local centres of small-scale industry. From the early fifties to the late seventies, such towns as Caernarfon, Ffestiniog, Bala, Welshpool, Aberystwyth, Llandrindod Wells, and Llandovery had small and localized industrial developments, with some positive results. A little town like Rhayader in Radnorshire was doubled in size (a decision that some town and country planners considered to be a mistake). Advance factories, notoriously difficult to attract to remoter country areas, were encouraged; some larger firms also moved such as the Ferrodo brake linings factory set up in Caernarfon. Much use was made after 1964 of the Regional Employment Premium scheme to write off the tax charges for those industrialists willing to invest their capital in such 'risk areas' as mid-Wales. More sustained efforts were made to try to create a base of urban amenities and services at a few select growth-points which would serve as a centre for a wider area. Support was also given to country bus services. A fuel rebate was given to the operators of bus passenger services such as Crosville Ltd from 1964 onwards, and local authorities were empowered to give assistance by way of grants or loans to the operators of rural bus services under section 34 of the 1968 Transport Act.

But these measures had a limited and localized effect. A few scattered factories, sprinkled through upland Wales like the autumn leaves at Vallombrosa, with scant relationship to each other or the wider economic growth of the community, were at best a palliative. There was, evidently, no simple answer to the problem. The pattern of depopulation, of an ageing society and an economically stagnant area suitable largely for development as a kind of national park was hard to alter. By the mid-1970s, a booming tourism, with the growth of caravan parks and chalets and other features of the twentieth-century leisure industry, was the most dependable source of annual income for many of these tourist areas. Pony-trekking in Radnorshire and Brecon revived the folk appeal of the horse, the Welsh cobs of the Llanarth stud gained in renown, while the old narrow-gauge slate railways of Welshpool in Montgomeryshire, Tal-y-Llyn in Merioneth, and Ffestiniog in the north of the same county, became major tourist attractions.

But tourism did not always bring in as much revenue as might have been anticipated to holiday resorts. The days when visitors stayed for two weeks or more on end in one single hotel or boarding house were past. Instead, cars meant that tourists could move from town to town each day with much ease, while the advent of caravanning meant that longer-term residents tended to stay, on a self-catering basis, on parks outside town perimeters and did not greatly patronize local shops, stores, or cafés. In any case, the unappealing fare of many of these last did not particularly attract the custom of alien gourmets. The hotel trade was in some decline now. Of the ten seafront hotels in Aberystwyth in 1945, only one had survived by 1960. The remainder had been turned into student hostels or local government offices. Llandrindod Wells, the fashionable spa of pre-1914 and the twenties, once a sort of Welsh Wiesbaden, became something of a ghost town, its massive Edwardian hotels no longer in such regular demand, its communications whittled down, although Llandrindod's popularity as a conference centre and its proximity to the English Midlands as well as south Wales still gave it life.

The most imaginative proposal for arresting the decline of the population of mid-Wales and the rural areas generally especially in counties like Montgomeryshire and Radnorshire where the exodus of young people was most serious of all, was that offered by James Griffiths, the first Secretary of State for Wales. In 1965 he proposed the idea of a new town in mid-Wales, something on the lines of that established at Cwmbran in Monmouthshire near to Newport in 1952, a town which had now risen in population to 34,500 by 1964. Griffiths proposed a new community of 60,000 people somewhere in the nearly-deserted Severn valley close to Caersws in Montgomeryshire.[24] This plan was not, however, greeted with immense local acclaim. Farmers were hostile. Welsh nationalists and others feared that the population of this new town might be drawn largely from English overspill from the west Midlands, and that it would have to compete with Telford new town in Shropshire. Others suggested, with racist foreboding, that these migrants might be black, brown, or yellow in hue. In the end, economic pressures, added to a good deal of hostile opinion in Labour's ranks, led to Cledwyn Hughes, the new Secretary of State, turning down the idea of a new town in mid-Wales in February 1967 (probably rightly, in view of its probable effects on other small towns near by). The concept did not re-emerge until Raymond Williams's novel, *The Fight for Manod*, in 1979. Instead, it was proposed to double the size of neightbouring Newtown, the birthplace of the pioneer socialist Robert Owen, as it happened. A new Mid-Wales Development Corporation would be set up to promote economic activity in the area, and to provide financial support. These moves had some effect, and Newtown certainly exanded, although slowly. Its population was expected to reach 11,000 by the early eighties. But, as report followed report, and debate followed debate, the problems of rural Wales remained as intractable as ever. The few industries these regions tended to attract tended to be secondary plant, the first factories to feel the impact of trade recession and to lay off their workers, male or female. The growing affluence of industrial and urban Wales in the post-1945 period was accompanied by a continuing decline in the rural uplands, even if the countryside was freed from the desperate poverty of pre-war years by the ministrations of the welfare state, and a general sustained

[24] James Griffiths, op. cit., pp. 177–80.

growth in consumer-led, if government-sponsored, capitalism.

The governmental infrastructure designed to shape this new economy took many and varying forms. The Labour government after 1945 was relatively unsympathetic towards Welsh and Scottish devolution. But it did recognize the need for new instruments of economic planning that were more sensitively attuned to the wishes of the local people than were a nexus of centrally-directed bureaucracies. The main initiative from 1945 to 1964 for planning the Welsh economy lay with the Board of Trade. It was, however, a notable weakness of central government that the key decisions for Welsh economic life were dispersed through a range of government departments, Transport, Agriculture, Health, Labour, and many more, with always the controlling hand of the Treasury. The Ministry for Welsh Affairs launched by the Churchill government in 1951 when the Conservatives returned to power provided some co-ordination at the centre, but little more. It had no decision-making powers of its own and was unable to transfer any to Wales. Essentially it was a minor arm of the Home Office, later of the Ministry of Housing and Local Government.

The main novelty of the post-war economic governmental fabric was the creation of a council for Wales and Monmouthshire in 1948. As will be seen later, this was devised by Herbert Morrison, as an alternative to the kind of devolution preferred by James Griffiths and other Welsh Labour spokesmen (though emphatically not by Aneurin Bevan).[25] It was intended to provide information to assist the government in London to conduct its policies in the economic province of Wales. But it was otherwise powerless and intended to be so. It lived on fitfully until 1966, with increasing disillusion or boredom surrounding its efforts. At first, however, it did seem to be making some impact. It consisted of twenty-seven members, including twelve from the local authorities, and eight from industry (management and unions) under the chairmanship of the north Wales trade-union leader, Huw T. Edwards. It set up panels to deal with rural depopulation, unemployment, and marginal land; the recommendations of the last two panels were generally imple-mented. There was, however, a growing sense of strain with the Conservative governments from 1951 onwards, especially with Henry Brooke when he assumed the Ministry for Welsh Affairs in 1957 (along with the Ministry of Housing). A proposal from the Council for Wales that £60 millions be allocated to a Welsh Rural Development Agency was criticized by Brooke and rejected by the Macmillan government. There was further tension on political issues, notably the Welsh Council's proposal for a Secretary of State for Wales in 1957, which Macmillan turned down in the December of that year. In the end, a series of clashes with the government over the Council's proposals for south Wales ports, rural depopulation, and the fishing industry,

[25] Cabinet Minutes, 23 January 1946 (CAB 129/6). See below, p. 378.

together with such cultural matters as Welsh publishing and political disputes over the governmental structure led to Huw T. Edwards's resigning the chairmanship in 1958. Later, he reinforced his protest by leaving the Labour Party for Plaid Cymru. Apart from the issues of substance between himself and the Conservative government—notably appointing D. P. Lewis, 'an obscure Brecon county councillor',[26] as Minister of State under the soubriquet of Lord Brecon—Edwards's protest was really a gesture of despair at the powerlessness of the Welsh Council in influencing the decisions of central government in England on economic policy. 'Whitehallism had not the slightest prospect of ever understanding Welsh aspirations', Edwards declared. [27]

Without Edwards at its head, the Welsh Council was a less vocal and aggressive body. It continued to do useful work under its new chairman, R. I. Aaron, a philosophy professor, but mainly on cultural and linguistic questions rather than economic. The Labour government in 1964, in addition to setting up the Welsh Office, set up a Welsh Economic Planning Board and an advisory Economic Council for Wales. This clearly undermined what little authority the Council for Wales ever had. It expired, almost forgotten, on 11 June 1966, and was never resurrected.

It was replaced by the new Welsh Economic Council in 1966. After the early resignation of one of its main figures, the economist Professor Nevin, the Secretary of State for Wales, Cledwyn Hughes, himself took over the chairmanship of the council for a time. In 1968 a new all-Wales advisory council was set up under the chairmanship of another economist, Professor Brinley Thomas from Cardiff. Richard Crossman scathingly commented that it 'would do nothing but supervise tourism'.[28] At the same time, a new Development Corporation for Mid-Wales, with somewhat stronger powers, was created under the chairmanship of Emrys Roberts, a former Liberal MP prominent in Wales. It was turned into a new Development Board for Rural Wales in April 1977 under the same chairman, with a budget of £4 million a year. Its main function was clearly to promote the development of new industries in mid-Wales and to develop further growth points such as Newtown.

More generally, there was founded in January 1976 a powerful new Welsh Development Agency with finance amounting to £100 million. This was substantially increased in November 1978, partly perhaps as a result of the government's wish to preserve Plaid Cymru support in the Commons in voting for the Queen's Speech, more as a result of larger financial allocations for the National Enterprise Board. The Welsh Development Agency, in

---

[26] *The Economist*, 21 December 1957.

[27] Huw T. Edwards, 'Why I Resigned', *Wales*, November 1958.

[28] Richard Crossman, *The Diaries of a Cabinet Minister*, vol. 2 (London, 1976), p. 377 (12 June 1967).

association with the incentives offered by the Department of Industry, could offer much more assistance to industrialists interested in venturing into Wales; the situation in 1978 was a distinct advance even on the Board of Trade's powers after 1945. Virtually the whole of Wales was now a development area, with the Glamorgan mining valleys and Anglesey and Caernarvonshire marked off as special development areas. Among the incentives for expansion offered for Wales and other development areas, there were regional grants for capital expenditure on new buildings and machinery (22 per cent grants in special development areas, 20 per cent elsewhere); financial assistance, particularly for employment-creating projects where loans at concessionary rates and interest relief grants were available; government factories either built in advance of demand or else custom-built, all managed by the Welsh Development Agency; training services for skilled workers; and grants and allowances for workers transferred from other areas. The old Industrial Development Certificates were now no longer required either for development or special development areas.

This formidable battery of powers was reinforced by the growing executive force of the Welsh Office from 1964 onwards, in taking over, in the course of years, the functions of the Board of Trade, the Ministries of Agriculture and Transport, and other departments and co-ordinating their activities. But the general premise of all these bodies, from the Council for Wales to the Welsh Development Agency, was that they existed to advise, to encourage, and to warn. They had no fundamental power of executive decision-making, no effective global budget of their own, no real capacity to plan the economic development of Wales as a coherent and balanced whole. Nor, of course, was any of these bodies popularly elected; nomination and co-option remained the rule. In the later 1970s, with a decision about an elected assembly still awaited, and its relation to the Welsh Office and to the existing infrastructure of governmental planning in Wales still in flux, the machinery of economic development, much improved though it was, still had a somewhat piecemeal air. No coherent 'economic plan' for Wales had been drafted, since the expiry of George Brown's ambitious Department of Economic Affairs in the mid-sixties. Nor, perhaps, could such a plan emerge while economic policy for Britain remained so uncertain, constantly interrupted by shifts in government policy over the money supply, public expenditure, and the allocation of resources, and eternally disturbed by external fluctuations in money markets and world trade.

More interest in practice attached to the agencies concerned with specific resources than to these necessarily somewhat grey co-ordinating bodies. One resource above all captured the public imagination—water. Far more than coal, steel, or even oil, it animated much public controversy. The economic, ecological, and political aspects of harnessing the abundant water supplies of Wales led to fierce public outcry, often with nationalist implications. There

was passionate controversy, as will be seen in Chapter 13, over the construction of Tryweryn reservoir in northern Merioneth in the late fifties and early
sixties, and some demonstrations of passive resistance by supporters of Plaid
Cymru. The Tryweryn problem had many cultural aspects. There was also the
extraordinary fact that there was no local or other authority in Wales which
could influence the decision of the Liverpool corporation at all: Liverpool
could even choose to resell the water it imported from Wales. No one in
Wales, it seemed, had any control over this precious commodity, so vital for
industry as well as for domestic use, which meant so much to the impoverished
rural heartland. There was further conflict in 1965 over the construction of
another reservoir at Clywedog in Montgomeryshire, again for the benefit of
an English city, Birmingham. Here again, nationalist passions could be
aroused, and mysterious bomb explosions followed. But it was really more an
urban—rural conflict than one involving the Welsh in opposition to the
English: further controversy, though not so passionate, surrounded the
creation of a new reservoir in south-west Breconshire for the benefit of the
large conurbation of Swansea some thirty to forty miles away. In 1971 the
Welsh Council's special report called for a Water Development Authority for
Wales to provide a comprehensive overview of the use of water resources, and
to safeguard specifically Welsh interests. It should have powers to control
flooding, build new reservoirs and more generally to try to balance out the
various interests of different communities, agricultural and industrial. The
Heath government in 1971, acting through the then Secretary of State for
Wales, Peter Thomas, announced the creation of such a Welsh authority,
which would include the Wye basin (though significantly not the Severn)
within its aegis. Since then, some of the passion associated with the water issue
in rural Wales seemed to disappear (despite large increases in water-rate
charges); though it was still noticeable (and decidedly odd) that Wales, with
its exceptionally heavy rainfall especially in mountainous areas, should be
amongst the first regions to suffer water scarcity at the first signs of drought.
Similar agencies, to take a similar overview of other natural resources,
including minerals, land utilization, and conceivably oil, had still to be created
as the seventies came to their close.

Assessments of the performance of the Welsh economy since 1945 invariably
occasioned fierce and partisan debate. Inevitably, the growth of political
nationalism seriously affected the argument, since Plaid Cymru and others
argued vehemently that only central planning bodies, directly elected by the
Welsh people and responsible to them alone, located in Wales and catering
primarily if not exclusively for Welsh needs, would lead to a more sustained
economic advance. Otherwise, it was argued, Wales would continue to show a
stuttering kind of performance, with brief periods of growth alternating with
an instantaneous response to any worldwide slump in trade, the more rapid as

the peripheral and precarious nature of industry in Wales made itself felt. The political aspects of this will be considered later, but undoubtedly they loomed large in the public mind in the seventies. A British economy near to total collapse did not augur happily for the continued association of Wales with the economic structure of its larger neighbour. There was some temporary credence, as in Scotland, in the cheerful prospects of an independent, economically self-governing Wales, with the possibilities of oil from the so-called 'Celtic Sea' out in St. George's Channel. 'Rich Wales or Poor Britain' was Plaid Cymru's somewhat implausible slogan in the 1974 general elections. But since 1974, as the prospects of Celtic oil receded fast, this theme disappeared. Oil played only a marginal part in public debate in Wales, by contrast with Scotland where North Sea oil was now a physical and impressive reality and a vital contribution to British energy supplies. The nationalist argument, however, did generate much useful debate on how much progress Wales had really achieved since 1945, and how firmly based such progress as had been made really was.

In many ways, Wales retained even at the end of the 1970s some of the air of a 'special area', as its 'development status' under the Department of Industry indicated. Even after years of diversification, an undue proportion of workers was employed in heavy industry of the old type; there was an undue proportion, too, in service employment, with relatively few in newer technologically advanced industries. The computer, new developments in electronics, let alone the silicon chip, had yet to be fully assimilated to the Welsh scene. Employment in Wales tended to flow to industries more concerned with finishing products made elsewhere than in forming the base of manufacturing *de novo*. It was something of 'a branch factory economy'. In addition, much new industry was capital-intensive (oil, chemicals, power stations) not labour-intensive, and absorbed all too few displaced miners, steelworkers, and quarrymen. Unemployment was still a problem for Wales in the late seventies. The total rose to over 100,000, not as severe as for the north-east of England or parts of Scotland, but still higher than the British average. Even in a thriving town like Wrexham, with a vigorous council active in attracting new industry from America and elsewhere and using sophisticated techniques of industrial promotion, unemployment in mid-1978 stood at 14.1 per cent, though it later improved. In Gwynedd and parts of rural Wales, as has been seen, the problem was endemic, and long-lasting. The early months of 1979, immediately before and just after the referendum on devolution, brought further gloomy news for some of the traditional industries. There were proposals for more pit closures; in the steel industry, the British Steel Corporation announced 1,600 redundancies in the Abbey Works at Port Talbot and in the tinplate and galvanizing works that remained at Ebbw Vale, while the prospect of a further 6,000 redundancies on Deeside with the closure announced of the John Summers works at Shotton remained a very real one. Clearly, the staple heavy industries of Wales were still ailing giants.

More disturbing was the inability of successive governments and governmental agencies to create more new jobs in Wales. No less than 60,000 jobs disappeared between 1964 and 1970 alone, and perhaps 100,000 or more in the entire period 1964 to 1976. The Welsh population still rose, but slowly, and by less than the national average. The major increase took place, as has been seen, in Glamorgan, Monmouth, and Flintshire, along the English border. Even here, the growth was at 5 per cent between 1951 and 1971, less than half the British average. In the ten years 1961–71, Gwent (Monmouthshire) increased its population by 4.1 per cent, compared with 3.3 per cent for Wales generally and 5.3 per cent for the United Kingdom. Too high a proportion of the population was in the less skilled categories of workers. Certainly, too high a proportion of it was elderly and unable to contribute directly to the creation of new wealth. The migration of the able-bodied and of many school-leavers to south-east Wales, or to Merseyside, the Midlands or Avonside in England, continued, though at a far less drastic rate than before 1939. Much of the worst impact of the slowing-down of the British economy was moderated as far as Wales and other regions were concerned by the direct intervention of the central government in bringing in new factories and such regional development policies as selective investment grants. The economic survival of the principality relied heavily on direct sponsorship and a long-term programme of productive and social investment by the Westminster government. With a change of emphasis heralded by the Conservative election victory in 1979, the future of these was doubtful. Economists were frequently prone to criticize those measures that governments had taken between 1945 and 1979 for being too piecemeal, for concentrating the larger subsidies on places where they were least productive, for encouraging the growth of capital intensive industries in areas such as Pembrokeshire where labour was in short supply.[29] The very value of 'diversification' of the economy was questioned in a precarious, competitive world where large units predominated and the rest might go to the wall. The 'Welsh economy', even supposing such a concept to be precisely definable, was at best at a point of transition by the late 1970s, not at a point of take-off.

If the comparison is with the south-east of England or the Midlands, still more if it is with the other countries of the European Economic Community, then the economic growth of Wales after 1945 may be seen to be sluggish and its restructuring only a partial success. If, however, the contrast is made with Wales in the pre-1939 era, and with the sociological and resource realities of the British economy in the twentieth century, then it is clear that the conclusion must be a more optimistic one. Undoubtedly, even in the worst

[29] e.g. Edward Nevin, 'The Economic Future of South Wales', *Planet* 3 (December 1970–January 1971).

years of the mid-1970s, levels of individual purchasing power and savings, levels of employment, rates of capital formation, the general quality of life for the working population had shown an immense surge forward in the period between 1945 and 1980. The impoverished, shattered nation of the thirties was unrecognizable now, even in the poorest of rural areas. There was a pervasive sense of confidence and optimism.

This showed itself in the willingness of most Welsh people to endorse entry into the Common Market in 1975. When the membership of the EEC originally came up for debate in 1973, there was much opposition in Wales. Many of all persuasions felt that, within the framework of the EEC, with its central areas of growth in France, western Germany, and northern Italy, there was no viable regional policy to assist geographically peripheral areas such as southern Italy, Brittany—or Wales. The Welsh Labour members voted against the Common Market by twenty to five. The Welsh Liberals, led by Emlyn Hooson, declared themselves to be against the Common Market, despite the policy of the national party. Plaid Cymru was inevitably hostile to a further diminution of Welsh sovereignty. But by 1975, partly perhaps because it was felt that a Labour government had obtained a more favourable deal in its efforts to 're-negotiate' the Treaty of Rome, and had even modified the hated Common Agricultural Policy, Welsh opinion had changed markedly. Despite criticism from the Labour left, from Plaid Cymru, and some Liberals, Wales voted by 66 per cent in favour of entry into the Common Market. Gwynedd voted as resoundingly as did Glamorgan and Gwent. This may have betokened a general sense of optimism that Wales, with its varied industry, improved agriculture, a versatile labour force, and abundant supplies of energy (coal, water, hydro-electric and nuclear power) could seize new opportunities within a larger economic community, rather than retreat into a siege mentality suspicious of larger groupings and foreign competition. There may also have been a belief that Wales would benefit from involvement in the European Economic Community as it had from membership of the British, especially since 1945. On the other hand, by the time of the European elections in 1979, discontent with the agricultural and budgetary policies of the EEC was again very widespread.

Government figures released in September 1971 gave credence to the view that Wales as a whole benefited from its integration into the British economy (a view shared by the voters in the 1979 devolution referendum). There was a general picture of the Welsh budget in deficit, by anything between £114 m. and £182 m. when capital accounts were added. This applied even in 1968–9 when the British national budget showed a large surplus of £273 millions as a result of the operations of Roy Jenkins, then Chancellor of the Exchequer.[30] In terms of its contributions to defence, to debt charges and to external

[30] Graham Rees, 'The Welsh Economy' in Brinley Jones (ed.), *Anatomy of Wales* (Cardiff, 1972), p. 78.

relations, Wales paid out relatively little. In return, it received considerable inflows in terms of welfare payments, government subsidies, rate-support grants, new influx of capital, and the like. Economists mostly argued that Wales flourished by the import of resources from the rest of the United Kingdom, though the relationship of this to the question of how well Wales would fare if its economy became entirely separate from that of England was obscure. The issue rested on so many imponderable and unquantifiable factors, such as the interest charges on the national debt that should be attributed to Wales. After all, much of this debt accumulated during two world wars which had no direct bearing on normal current government transactions. Plaid Cymru and others also questioned the method of calculating the share of expenditure on defence and foreign relations.

With certainty in these matters impossible to attain, the future of the Welsh economy in the 1980s and beyond becomes the province of the macro-economic and the scientific soothsayers, the new folk remembrancers of the age. One may wish them well since so many economic prophecies have been falsified and overturned in the years after 1945. The historian, concerned largely with secular change in a definable sequence of years, and attempting to measure the indices of change in relation to past experience, can look back on the period from 1945 to the late seventies as one of transformation, growth and some promise, with, at least in parts of Wales such as the south-east, a mood of vitality and buoyancy much at variance with the sombre tone of the inter-war years. At the dawn of the eighties, the future remained uncertain. Some frightening developments came in December 1979 with the British Steel Corporation announcing plans for a massive cut of more than 11,000 jobs in Port Talbot and Llanwern works by the end of the following summer. In effect, steel-making there was to be halved. With the consequent effects of this on coal-mining and other industries, and on once-thriving towns like Port Talbot, unemployment in south Wales threatened to rise yet again to alarming levels. A national steel strike, the first since 1926, underlined the problems of the industry. The Welsh TUC talked of calling a general strike. Yet, even with these bleak auguries, it might reasonably be hoped that a tragedy on the scale of the thirties could still be averted. A new economy had risen from the ashes of the old since 1945. So much progress ought not to be wantonly discarded; an intelligent regional policy could be salvaged. Despite the predictable troubles of the economy in the early 1980s, the remaining years of the century might yet be a more settled and fruitful time for the working men and women of Wales.

CHAPTER 12

THE NEW SOCIETY

At the start of the Second World War in 1939, Wales appeared in major respects to be much the same kind of society that it had been ever since the industrial expansion of the later nineteenth century. Its economic structure was dominated by the same staple industries. There was the same kind of balance between its urban and rural communities. There was the same dominant ethos striving to assert itself, based on the nonconformist, radical values of pre-1914. Wales in the thirties, even the labour movement in the mining valleys, was largely dominated by men whose outlook had been shaped by those exciting years at the turn of the century, and who saw an essential continuity between the land of their fathers and the harsher world in which they themselves had to make their way in middle age. But in the thirty-five years after 1945, Wales, in common with other European countries, underwent sweeping social transformation. Many of the features of this were shared with the rest of the developed world. Some, though, especially in their cultural and moral aspects, had a special relevance and impact for the principality itself.

The tempo of change became especially rapid with the long era of relative affluence which Britain experienced from the end of the Korean War in 1953 to the Middle East oil crisis of 1973. All parts of Wales, the small towns and hamlets of the remoter countryside, the sprawling conurbations of Deeside, Swansea Bay, the new town at Cwmbran, the coastal strip from Cardiff to Newport, the dockside areas around Milford Haven in Pembrokeshire, most dramatically of all the inland mining villages of south Wales, underwent profound changes in their mode of life which amounted to little less than a social revolution.

One major aspect of Welsh life, though, remained superficially much the same as pre-war, though with latent structural changes apparent to close and careful observation. Presiding over this new society was the old Labour ascendancy built up in the valleys and towns of the coalfield during the twenties and thirties. Indeed, the domination of the Labour Party and of the trade-union movement over the social and political leadership élites of the land became even more overwhelming and seemingly impregnable between 1945 and 1966 than it had been before the war. The demise of the Liberal élite that had governed the public life of Wales before 1914 and had cast its shadow over many social and cultural institutions since (witness the influence of that formidable Liberal, Rhys Hopkin Morris, over the BBC in Wales while its regional director between 1936 and 1945) was speeded up. Truly, Liberal Wales became increasingly moribund in the fifties and sixties. It became more closely yoked even than before to the old, rural nonconformist attitudes and values. While there were in England and Scotland frequent symptoms of Liberal 'revivals' during parts of this period—the success of Liberal candidates in the west country in Torrington in 1957 and North Devon in 1959; the appeal of Liberals to 'Orpington man' in the commuter suburbs of London and elsewhere in the early sixties; the success of David Steel in winning Roxburgh and Selkirk in the Scottish lowlands in 1965—in Wales, Liberals underwent a process of slow and depressing retreat. Here Orpington man seemed hardly to exist. Certainly, there appeared to be neither the sociological base, nor the will, for a recovery of the grand old cause.

In the February 1950 general election, held after the boundaries of the thirty-six Welsh seats had been redistributed, an election which saw the Labour government's majority fall from nearly two hundred to only six, the Liberals retained only five seats in Wales. All five were largely rural—Anglesey, Merioneth, Cardiganshire, Montgomeryshire, and Carmarthen. Pembrokeshire was now lost to Labour, while the Liberal-held university seat had been abolished along with all other forms of double voting. Anglesey and Merioneth were now held by the most slender of margins. In the October 1951 general election, when the Attlee government finally fell from power, these two rural seats were lost also. In Anglesey, Lady Megan Lloyd George, who had held the seat as a Liberal since 1929, was defeated by a Holyhead solicitor, Cledwyn Hughes, a Welsh-speaking radical and an admirer of the Lloyd George tradition, but one who drew much strength from working-class voters in the Holyhead district. In Merioneth, the workers of Blaenau Ffestiniog and Trawsfynydd were sufficiently numerous to return T. W. Jones, a senior trade unionist from Wrexham/Maelor, at the expense of Emrys Roberts. This was a generally depressing election for the Liberals, and especially for Clement Davies, still the MP for Montgomeryshire and Archibald Sinclair's successor as leader of the party nationally. In 1951, the Liberals put up only nine candidates in Wales; the industrial constituencies were more or less written off. In the next general election of May 1955, the Liberals hung on to their three remaining seats, but another was lost in February 1957 when Hopkin Morris, the sitting member for Carmarthen, died. In a fiercely-contested election, much coloured by the emotion aroused by the Suez invasion, Lady Megan Lloyd George won the seat as a Labour candidate with a 3,000 majority; she defeated a Liberal farmer who, curiously enough, supported the Eden policy in Suez. It was a significant comment on the Lloyd George tradition that the child of Lloyd George who most conformed to her father's radical iconoclasm should confirm the leftward drift of Liberal Wales, and settle contentedly in the Labour Party for the rest of her days.

The general election of October 1959 brought further signs of Liberal decay. Only eight candidates were put up, and only Montgomeryshire and Cardiganshire were won. Significantly, in both seats the Conservatives gave the Liberals a free run against Labour. Only 5.3 per cent of the Welsh electorate voted Liberal in 1959. The next few years saw scant revival in the principality, in contrast to the marginal recovery of the party nationally under the new leadership of Jo Grimond. In 1962 Clement Davies died, and the resultant by-election in Montgomeryshire was won by a substantial margin by Emlyn Hooson, a Welsh-speaking barrister and a product of the University College, Aberystwyth. But this was the sole consolation the Welsh Liberals could point to at this time. In 1964, the party retained its two remaining seats in mid-Wales, but in the March 1966 general election one of these two surviving bastions, Cardiganshire, that had been represented by Roderic Bowen since 1945 and had been continuously Liberal since 1880, was captured by Labour for the first time. The fact that Conservatism in Cardiganshire in 1966 attracted almost a fifth of the vote cost the Liberals dear; but it was obvious that the old appeal to an instinctive commitment to the traditional values and memories was no longer enough. The victorious Labour candidate, Elystan Morgan, another Welsh-speaking barrister from UCW, Aberystwyth, who had recently been a candidate for Plaid Cymru, was precisely the kind of articulate, progressive young professional man who would have been a natural Liberal less than a generation earlier.

By the early seventies, then, Liberals in Wales had seen their tally of seats fall from seven in 1945 to just one (Montgomeryshire). The Liberal position in local government had collapsed totally. Well-known Liberals, active in county councils in Cardiganshire and elsewhere, stood as Independents in the sixties. The Welsh Liberals had now formed their own organizational structure, separate from the national party, under the presidency of their one MP, Emlyn Hooson, and took their own line on many issues. For instance, the Welsh Liberals were hostile to entry into the Common Market. But this was the isolation of weakness. With its Welsh patriotic elements tending to defect to Plaid Cymru, younger radicals moving to Labour, and some of the remainder elderly and gradually departing from the scene, Welsh Liberalism was in an advanced state of decay.

Conversely, these were thriving years for the Labour Party. For the party nationally, this was a somewhat difficult period. The government's majority fell to only six in 1950, and it was finally turned out of office in the autumn of 1951. There followed thirteen years of internecine party quarrelling and of the frustration of being in opposition. Labour's share of the poll fell consistently in general elections in Britain until 1964. There were fierce internal arguments about economic and defence policy, with the powerful leftist forces of Aneurin Bevan and his 'Tribunite' supporters involved in several bitter disputes. After the 1959 general election, Labour seemed in total disarray, with the followers of Hugh Gaitskell ranged against a broad-based coalition committed to 'Clause Four' and to unilateral nuclear disarmament. But in Wales Labour's position was as strong as ever. In 1950, the party captured twenty-seven of the redistributed Welsh seats, and 58 per cent of the vote, almost exactly the same proportion as in the halcyon year of 1945. Morale amongst party workers was high after the active social, economic, and colonial policies of the Attlee government. Voting was heavy everywhere, often well over 80 per cent. One of the new members was Mrs Eirene White, the daughter of Thomas Jones, that old Fabian, in East Flintshire. The same story was told in 1951 when voting in Wales and elsewhere was even more intense than in 1945 and the Labour Party obtained its highest-ever poll, amounting to nearly 14 million votes. Labour again held on to 27 Welsh seats; Anglesey and Merioneth were won from the Liberals as has been seen, while two other constituencies, Barry in the south and Conway in the north, were lost to the Conservatives, making that party's total six. Both these last two constituencies, significantly enough, were highly anglicized: Barry included the rural Vale of Glamorgan and some of the more affluent Cardiff suburbs; Conway contained the elderly and generally conservative residents of Llandudno and Conway itself.

In the 1955 general election, Labour's share of the poll remained much the same at 57.6 per cent, and all twenty-seven seats were retained. As has been seen, Carmarthen was soon to be added to the list. Once again, a move to the right in England and Scotland was not paralleled in Wales. But there was something of a swing against Labour in the 1959 election, with a slight fall in its share of the Welsh vote to 56.5 per cent, and the loss of Swansea West to the Conservatives. This last was always a finely-balanced constituency with an older, industrial working-class core in the centre of the town, in the Victoria, Brynmelin, and Townhill wards, balanced by an affluent suburban fringe in Sketty, West Cross, and along the bay towards Mumbles. In 1964, however, an election which saw Labour return to office once more, Swansea West was recaptured for Labour by Alan Williams, a polytechnic lecturer in economics. All the other Labour seats were impregnable, from Anglesey to Newport. One notable addition to the Welsh Labour ranks by now was Michael Foot, elected in 1960 as the parliamentary heir of his close friend, Aneurin Bevan, for Ebbw Vale and the voice of that socialist radicalism with which Bevan (until, perhaps, his last three years) had always been associated. Foot, a west-countryman of Liberal background, was in time to prove far more sympathetic to Welsh national aspirations than his mentor from Tredegar had ever been.

In the general election of March 1966, Labour's triumphs in Wales were the most sweeping yet. Thirty-two out of thirty-six Welsh seats were captured. As emphatically as the Liberals before 1914, Labour had become the party and the conscience of Wales. Four more seats were won in 1966, Cardiganshire from the Liberals, and Conway, Cardiff North, and Monmouth from the Conservatives. All four new Labour MPs, Elystan Morgan, Ednyfed Davies, Edward Rowlands, and Donald Anderson, were professional men—solicitors and college or university lecturers. The general election of 1966, then, seemed to set the seal on a relentless half-century of progress by Labour, a process that completed that political ascendancy built up ever since the end of the First World War.

At all levels, the evolution of Welsh society and the ascendancy of the Labour Party seemed inseparably intertwined after 1945. In Labour governments, Welshmen or Welsh MPs were well to the fore. When the Attlee government resigned in 1951, its members included James Griffiths as Colonial Secretary and Ness Edwards as Postmaster-General, as well as (until April 1951) Aneurin Bevan. Later on, Griffiths and Bevan both served as deputy-leaders of the party under Gaitskell in the fifties. When Harold Wilson formed his new Labour government in October 1964, James Callaghan (Cardiff South East) became Chancellor of the Exchequer, and later Home Secretary in 1967; John Morris (Aberavon) served at the Ministry of Power, Cledwyn Hughes (Anglesey) at the Commonwealth Office, and James Griffiths (Llanelli), the veteran miners' leader, became the first Secretary of State for Wales, with Goronwy Roberts (Caernarfon) as his Minister of State. There were other Welshmen, sitting for English constituencies, also prominent in the government, with Ray Gunter, a Monmouthshire trade unionist, as Minister of Labour, and Roy Jenkins, originating from Abersychan before translation to Balliol, who was destined to rise to the Treasury by 1967. If Wales was identified with Labour at the pinnacle of power, there was also a blanket domination of the county councils of Glamorgan, Monmouthshire, and (less overwhelmingly) of Carmarthenshire, of the corporation of Swansea, and of the local authority of Wrexham in the north-east. A new regime which entrenched Labour dominance in many of the educational, commercial, and cultural institutions of the south and much of the rest of Wales had been firmly established. This resulted, in the main, in honest, well-intentioned government, although the monolithic quality of Labour rule led to disturbing allegations of corruption and some court cases in Swansea and elsewhere in the 1970s.

Underpinning this Labour ascendancy, of course, was the position of the trade unions, deeply enmeshed with the dominant institutions and leadership élites of all aspects of Welsh life. There arose trade-union patrons of immense influence such as Llewelyn, later Lord Heycock, a former engine-driver from the Dyffryn Yard loco sheds, Port Talbot, who became a personality of transcendent authority on the Glamorgan county council. His special interests were by no means wholly materialistic, since they included education at all levels (including the university), the schools museum service, the Welsh

National Theatre and the promotion of the Welsh language in primary and secondary schools. In 1963 the national *eisteddfod* made him a druid. Heycock's position graphically illustrated the rise of new working-class groups to local leadership and their intellectual and cultural impact. At the same time, the prominence of apparently traditional trade-union bosses of this type concealed the changing pattern of support that Labour was now claiming; indeed, the nomination of the Cardiganshire-born barrister, John Morris, instead of Heycock, as Labour candidate for Aberavon in 1959 showed that there were limits to the power of even the most influential and enlightened industrial figure. Increasingly, it was middle-class figures such as university lecturers, lawyers, schoolteachers, civil servants, and journalists that formed the core of Labour activists in many places. In the valleys, the miners were rapidly losing power, and had been supplanted by other groups such as steel white-collar workers in BISAKTA, engineers in the AEU, supervisory staff in ASTMS, and unions representing industries such as garment manufacturing. By 1970, only two Labour MPs were direct nominees of the National Union of Mineworkers, Rhondda East, and Merthyr, though other seats were held by trade unionists. Elsewhere, Llanelli was now held by a London barrister, Rhondda West by a former schoolmaster, Caerphilly by an ex-headmaster, Abertillery by another barrister. The Welsh Labour movement, the very stronghold of proletarian solidarity for so many years, was now becoming bourgeoisified in its turn, like the German SPD before it. In Cardiff and south-east Glamorgan circles, Labour leaders such as James Callaghan and George Thomas, while most loyal constituency members, were also friendly with the millionaire financier and insurance director, Julian Hodge, and became directors of his new Bank of Wales. If this was a Labour ascendancy, the fulfilment of a Marxist dream, its social components were very different from those of the thirties. Many old-time activists lamented loudly the decline in socialist zeal and working-class identification that, in their view, resulted.

In superficial respects, the fabric of Welsh society seemed after 1945 to retain its threads of continuity with the pre-war era. In most other ways, though, it was being transformed. Throughout the land in the fifties and sixties, as post-war austerity gave way to growing and more sustained consumer-led affluence, styles of life changed most dramatically. The quality of life seemed notably transformed. There was more money to spend, more protection against the misadventure of life. South Wales, like other older industrial areas, benefited considerably from such redistribution of wealth as occurred after 1945, and through the social security framework provided by the welfare state. The National Health Service, the creation of a distinguished son of the valleys, Aneurin Bevan, was especially popular here. It was popular, so it appeared, even amongst Welsh doctors, with perhaps a stronger involvement in the local community than some of their English counterparts. The *Lancet* noted that a higher proportion of general practitioners in Wales (37 per cent) than in England agreed to operate under the Health Service in 1947 without waiting for the approval of the executive of the British Medical Association.[1] There was a steady improvement in standards of health amongst the old, in child and maternity welfare and the general quality of physical wellbeing. In particular, the dreaded 'white scourge' of tuberculosis had by the seventies virtually disappeared.

There was also a steady improvement in the condition of housing and of schools and hospitals. In the years after 1945, there was a considerable programme of subsidized 'council' house-building by the local authorities to start the much-delayed process of clearing that old, semi-slum property in Wales so frequently criticized by the Housing and Development Association in the thirties. In Swansea, recovering from the ravages of the wartime blitz, there was a massive programme of public housing (6,000 in all) between 1946 and 1952. In Cardiff, the older, picaresque communities of Butetown and Tiger Bay around the docks were largely demolished. Merthyr's equally famous 'China' also disappeared, and so in 1972 did the birthplace of Aneurin Bevan in Charles Street, Tredegar. In addition to thousands of council houses and 'prefabricated' dwellings built after the war, substantial discretionary grants were paid to occupiers in urban and rural areas to modernize or improve older property. In the fifties, there was a boom in private house-building and in the activities of housing associations and co-operatives. People moved out to agreeable suburbs, to Sketty or Killay, for instance, in Swansea, where an older residential area like Walter Road became a domain of offices and surgeries. Building societies, lending money to prospective home-owners on relatively easy terms, sprouted in most of the towns and cities of the principality. Their glossy offices dominated much of the central area of Swansea, Newport, and Cardiff. The figures for owner-occupation, traditionally low in much of Wales with its large proportion of working-class residents, rose sharply. The year 1965 was a record one for house-building, with 19,524 houses built in the course of it.[2] On the other hand, it should be pointed out that this was but a small dent in the 175,000 new dwellings that the Welsh Office itself admitted were needed in the decade 1961–71. One beneficial move here came as a result of a long campaign by George Thomas, the Labour member for Cardiff West. This was the Leasehold Enfranchisement Bill (1967) which enabled house-occupiers of leasehold property to buy their property outright in the case of houses having a rateable value of over £40 per annum. This was a matter which caused especial concern in Newport, Cardiff, Swansea, Merthyr, and other towns in south Wales, where so much urban land had been bought up by landed dynasties such as the Beauforts and the

[1] The *Lancet*, 5 June 1948.
[2] *Wales 1965* (Cmnd. 2918), Parl. Papers, 1965–6, vii, p. 99.

Butes a century earlier. It was also of importance elsewhere in such places as Aberystwyth, Llandudno, and Caernarfon.

Better housing and wider distribution of home ownership were part of a new and materially more comfortable society. There were also more, and more interesting, things for people to do than in the introspective days of depression when a Sunday-school trip to the coast or a sunny day on the beach had seemed to be the limit of leisure-time recreation. There was now a sharp rise in the private ownership of cars (so important for rural communities, especially with the Beeching axe of rail services after 1963), in the sale of consumer durables such as washing machines, in the spread of television to Welsh homes from the mid-fifties (though people were not always able to receive the programmes beamed from BBC or later HTV transmitters because of geographical difficulties resulting from the mountainous terrain). Mass entertainment impinged on popular styles of life, even on the sacred day of Sunday. In the mining villages of south Wales, drinking clubs and the euphoria of bingo halls cashed in on the new affluence. By contrast, many lamented the relative decline of the WEA, of the cultural excitement of the world of adult education, and the political vitality of working-men's clubs and welfare halls. Affluence, in the view of some critics, brought with it a dulling of the sensibilities and of the intellect of such a traditionally active and creative community. The valley towns, in particular, showed a more tranquil, anodyne appearance, as clubs and other entertainments claimed their patrons during the evenings, and as adult males commuted long distances to work in trading estates or in factories in Swansea, Port Talbot, Cardiff, or Llanwern during the day. The valleys, once throbbing with life, appeared almost a new Sinai by day, and a new Samaria (though scarcely a new Sodom) when dusk fell. Everywhere, life seemed more conformist, more impersonal. The neighbourliness of old communities gave way to the alien impersonality of housing estates or commuter suburbs. Much of the vital culture of the Welsh heartland disappeared with them.

As always, mass sport retained its public appeal, notably in south Wales. Here again, the consumer faced a new and bewildering range of choice. Cricket became ever more popular as a summer pastime, especially when the Glamorgan cricket team, consisting almost wholly of local players under the captaincy of Wilfred Wooller, a famous pre-war rugby international, won the county championship in 1948. In Swansea at St. Helen's and at Sophia Gardens in Cardiff, some of the enthusiasm traditionally linked with rugby was now associated with 'the Welsh cricket team', even though it was later afforced by Pakistanis and West Indians of great skill. The England cricket captain of the day, Ted Dexter, was even put up as a Conservative to fight James Callaghan in Cardiff South East in the 1964 election, though with distastrous consequences for the Tory cause. Association football was another popular pastime, though mainly in rural Wales and the coastal ports.

None of the four major clubs, Cardiff, Swansea, Newport, and Wrexham, was sufficiently successful to arouse massive support. Another club, Lovells Athletic, representing a confectionery factory near Newport, disappeared as a result of changes in consumer demand. Boxing still attracted some leading Welsh performers from heavy-weight to fly-weight. But by the sixties it was clear that it was fading in appeal as the depression years, with the encouragement they offered to hungry young men to make a little money by beating each other senseless, passed away.

Always, there was rugby, more emphatically a national passion than ever. By the seventies, there was a spectacular new national stadium by the banks of the Taff in Cardiff, with international tickets given as inducement to purchasers of debentures. The national rugby team and the major Welsh clubs showed a steady revival in the post-war period. From the mid-sixties, indeed, Welsh rugby reached a peak of excellence to equal that of the golden age of the century. The English were routed with embarrassing and monotonous regularity, even at Twickenham. Triple Crowns and Grand Slams were repeatedly won and all other countries (except New Zealand) defeated. These triumphs were gained through the traditional Welsh style of brilliant back play, by skill and speed rather than by brute force. Two half-backs became idolized as never before: Barry John, the outstanding stand-off half of his day between 1967 and 1973, and Gareth Edwards, a durable and determined scrum-half who played for his country fifty times between 1967 and 1978 when he retired. These two conformed to an older pattern. Both were Welsh-speaking, reared in the chapel, both the sons of miners, in Cefneithin in eastern Carmarthenshire and Gwaencaegurwen in the Swansea valley respectively. But there the resemblance with past traditions ended. Both were taken up by the mass communications media and by promotional enterprise which showed that the amateur traditions of Welsh rugby (which had resulted in migrants to rugby league being exiled for life) were skin-deep only. But it was natural that men like John and Edwards should exploit their supreme skill for legitimate reward. They retained their modesty and their loyalty to the valleys which had bred them. Both were splendid ambassadors for their native land.

What was more debatable was whether the heady excitement of international days at Cardiff Arms Park, with its emotional cascades of hymn-singing, did not blunt the passion for a more solid and political form of national self-expression. Beating the English through skill with an oval leather ball appeared to be satisfaction enough. It was noticeable, too, that Welsh rugby did not embrace all the values dear to south Wales in the past. All the leading Welsh players save one (J. Taylor of London Welsh who was then dropped by the selectors despite showing no obvious loss of form) repeatedly played against South African teams, despite protests by churches, trade unions, and other bodies against the evils of *apartheid* in sport. Peaceful student demonstrators against a visit of the South African team to play at Swansea were manhandled as violently as had been suffragettes in the past. A sport-mad nation seemed to obliterate more profound areas of its moral consciousness in blind pursuit of this latest opium of the people.

In most ways it was a more agreeable world in material and financial terms in which Welsh working people now lived. Certainly, the floods of summer tourists that penetrated the rural fastnesses from Pembrokeshire to Anglesey seemed anxious to share it with them, despite such hazards as the road signs demolished or defaced by the Welsh Language Society. Pockets of poverty remained until the late seventies, especially in rural areas where the amenities of life were less accessible and the population an ageing one dependent on pensions or other fixed incomes. But many blemishes had gone for ever. The new post-war Swansea was unattractive in design but commercially booming. The old slums of the Cardiff dockland, of much of east Swansea or the poorer areas of Wrexham had been demolished with enormous social benefit. In the mining valleys the environment was much enhanced by the closing of older collieries and other industrial plants, by the clearing of waste land and the plantation of coal tips with coniferous trees. The Rhondda was returning to the green, natural landscape it had been until the 1860s when industry scarred the land. Merthyr was less of an urban wasteland and, indeed, after the completion of the 'heads of the valleys' roads in 1964 became, like Brynmawr, a service centre for the northern rim of the coalfield. In the lower Swansea valley (an area of appalling industrial pollution), a notable project for collaboration between the local authority, the central government, the university college and voluntary agencies managed to rehabilitate the ugly, poisoned earth of the old copper tips.

There was, in November 1966, one appalling reminder of the grimmer aspects of pre-war social deprivations when a huge coal tip towering above the mining village of Aberfan suddenly subsided and a mass of mud, slurry, and coal waste swallowed up over a hundred schoolchildren. This desperate tragedy had a powerful impact upon the national conscience, and led to a successful campaign for the Welsh Office to spend large sums to remove some larger coal tips and render others more secure by levelling them off. Aberfan was a unique, terrible reminder of the old dangers, tragedies, and industrial hazards that had befallen south Wales repeatedly in the past. It was, mercifully, a solitary episode in what was otherwise a story of increased improvement and enjoyment.

By the seventies, much of the old character of Welsh community life was disappearing in much of the country. Smaller towns in the countryside, places like Llangefni or Dolgellau or Tregaron, might remain much the same in outward appearance but elsewhere there was rapid change. Some country towns became growth centres for light industry, as was the case with Rhayader. Seaside resorts were transformed in the wake of the demands of tourism and the influx of elderly residents mainly from England. The close-knit character of mining and tinplate villages was disappearing as their industrial base changed. More and more of the people were on the move, working further and further from their homes; former miners in the Rhondda commuted to Cardiff or the Treforest trading estate each day, while the steel-works and car factories at Llanelli, Swansea, Port Talbot, and Llanwern acted as magnets for other workers from the inland valleys. Sometimes families moved entirely, being sucked into the new urban sprawl of the south-east, or into the linear urban development between Bridgend and Llantrisant. The old, warm back-to-back comradeship was being replaced by the more anonymous life style of housing estates, where every Welshman's home was his castle and the neighbours dropped in much less frequently, if indeed they were known at all.

As the old society passed away, much of the old certainty of moral values, or what remained of it, also did so. The extent to which Wales became a more 'permissive' society, to adopt the term current in the 1960s, is hard to assess and impossible to quantify. Undoubtedly the land shared in the consumer boom of the time, in the mood of self-liberation and self-expression, and the world of pop culture that swept through Britain in that deceptive era. On a more permanent basis, young people in Wales simply through the erosion of many older communities appeared to become more rootless, certainly much less enmeshed in a familiar small-scale world of the local pit or pub or chapel. Youth culture in its various forms flourished in Wales in the sixties: the *Urdd* received a new lease of life. It was noticeable that the Welsh Language Society and Plaid Cymru made an especial appeal as protest movements to the young, to schoolchildren, and to university students above all, even when they did not speak Welsh. After all, the preservation of a local folk culture was very much the kind of idealistic, emotional cause which appealed to the hearts and the generosity of a new generation for whom the older causes, including that of socialism, now appeared increasingly stereotyped. Welsh-language pop culture, folk singers such as Dafydd Iwan (an architecture student and prominent Plaid Cymru candidate) became symbolic of peaceful protest for the young. This protest often had marked political overtones, such as in the satirical 'Carlo', an ironic comment on the investiture of Charles as Prince of Wales at Caernarfon in 1969.

How far the young became sexually or emotionally emancipated at the same time is impossible to assess precisely. A certain *frisson* was caused in 1966 when 'Youth is my Sin', a novel by the youthful John Rowlands, was alternatively commended or deplored for providing the most explicit description of the sexual act yet written in Welsh. But the evidence from nineteenth-century novels, or indeed from the early and later life of Lloyd George, suggests that permissiveness was always there in rural communities, flavoured, then as later, by the exquisite, aphrodisiac taste of forbidden fruit. A sociological study of a north Wales village in the early sixties (actually Croesor in northern Merioneth) noted the high rate of illegitimacy in rural Wales, and the relative absence of the moral stigma attached to the unmarried mother.[3] Children brought up by a grandmother were, in effect, relegitimized in the eyes of the community. Certainly, the public moral code of the chapel and the private codes of individual citizens often showed a wide disparity. Whether Welsh attitudes were equally enlightened towards male or female homosexuality it is impossible to say. Traditionally, the virile rugby-playing Welsh were not sympathetic to 'effeminate' arts such as the ballet. On the other hand, it was a Welsh MP, Leo Abse (Pontypool) who pioneered the removal of legal restrictions on male homosexual acts conducted in private between consenting adults, and his career did not seem to suffer. By contrast, his reform of the laws on abortion fell foul of Roman Catholic and other religious lobbies. In general, it may be surmised that moral permissiveness in Wales was deep-rooted and even instinctive. It was there before Caradoc Evans depicted it, before Freudian psychology was invented to explain it away, before Kingsley Amis wrote on the racy experiences of 'Chaucer Road, Aberdarcy', or 'Brynbwrla'. It will no doubt survive, whatever the prevailing climate of opinion.

Women in Wales undoubtedly benefited from a new sense of personal and occupational freedom in the post-1945 period. Traditionally, the Welsh woman's place was the home, taken up with menial daily toil and the upbringing of large families of noisy children—with chapel on Sunday. Welsh working-class life, as depicted in *How Green was my Valley* by Richard Llewellyn and countless other works, emphasized the role of the male wage-earner as head of the household in every major sense. Middle-class chapel-going routine laid stress on the obedience and dutifulness of the wife as cook, cleaner, mother, and moral support for her husband and his professional career. The 'chapel walk', when young men might be approached, was a rare traditional excitement for an unmarried girl. It was an unusual wife like Margaret Lloyd George who refused her husband's command to come and live wherever his career dictated—in David Lloyd George's case, London where the parliament to which he was elected was located. Women were not very successful in obtaining much professional advancement in Wales before 1939, other than in the favoured profession of school-teaching. There were a few women Welsh-language authors such as the novelist, Kate Roberts, and the poetess, Dilys Cadwaladr; there was the woman composer Grace Williams, and the woman painter Margaret Lindsay-Williams. But these were rare exceptions. Working-class women were not encouraged to find employment, even in the worst depression years.

After 1945, this changed dramatically. Much more decisively than in the

[3] Isabel Emmett, *A North Wales Village* (London, 1965), pp. 101–18.

First World War, that of 1939–45 encouraged women to find work in new factories and in industrial occupations. This was carried on in the newer industries and trading estates created after 1945, which provided employment for women workers in large numbers. In Merthyr Tydfil by 1965 women composed one-third of the entire labour force in the town. In factories and other workplaces, they found new opportunities for securing an independent income and enjoying an independent life outside the home, often continued in clubs and dance halls in the evenings and in week-ends. The statutory dominance of Welsh males over household decision-making went on (assisted by the Inland Revenue which continued to classify a wife as the dependant of the male income-earner), but it was a more equal sexual relationship than in the past. Middle-class girls stayed on at school in much greater numbers. They entered a wider range of occupations than hitherto, even though school-teaching retained its appeal for the special pedagogic talents of the Welsh, and primary schools in London, Birmingham and elsewhere were heavily staffed by recruits from the principality. The BBC, ITV, and the university all employed women in key posts, as to some degree did the Welsh Office. It was a gradual process of emancipation, mainly of benefit for the middle class. There is scant evidence that the more aggressive or misanthropic forms of 'Women's Lib' made much impact in a friendly country like Wales. But at least the prospect of a more rewarding, outgoing style of life for one half of the Welsh population was made possible. Another possible gain to women, perhaps, arose from the changing pattern of birth-rate, with a population 'bulge' in the sixties followed by a declining rate of increase. Families now became smaller, while males, less compelled to migrate out of Wales to find employment, now outnumbered females in the population structure.

The young, and the female young in particular, manifested growing signs of freedom from the old sanctions and taboos. But there was mounting evidence that these sanctions were in any case losing what moral or emotional force they still retained. Wales was traditionally a puritanical, Sabbatarian land, its ethos created by chapels of sepulchral austerity and by flamboyant pulpit oratory which preached hell and eternal damnation. After 1945, the impact of the chapels on social life continued to diminish, reinforced by the steady decline of the Welsh language through which most chapel services were conducted. The largest nonconformist denomination, the Methodists now christened the 'Presbyterian Church of Wales', claimed 152,000 members in 1955, 137,000 in 1962–3, and 133,000 in 1967–8. Even these figures were probably inflated. In rural areas, in country towns such as Caernarfon or Tregaron, or older industrial communities such as Brynamman or Morriston, chapel-going would be strong, especially among the other age-groups. But in much of urban and industrial Wales in particular, and amongst younger people of all social classes, the chapels were failing to retain their hold. There were key areas of national life where the role of the chapels was still important. The national *eisteddfod* had still room for the preacher-poet, men like the archdruids Crwys or Trefin. There were still great nonconformist orators like the venerable Elfed Lewis, who died full of years and honour in his ninety-fourth year in 1954, his voice clear and bell-like almost to the last. The chapels lent their considerable authority to campaigns for the preservation of the Welsh language and to the Parliament for Wales movement in 1950–6. So, it can be added, did many nationally-minded clergymen of an increasingly cymricized Church in Wales, like G. O. Williams, Bishop of Bangor and Glyn Simon, Bishop of Llandaff. It may be, in addition, that the moral disapproval of the chapel and its stern deacons inhibited people for some time after 1945 from reading Sunday newspapers, from playing golf or other pastimes, or even from publicly washing on the sabbath the cars that were intended to take their owners to chapel.

But the chapels depended above all on the sanctions that controlled everyday social behaviour, like the spiritual power exercised by Roman Catholic priests in rural Ireland or Italy. In a much less puritanical age, these were simply disappearing, or else becoming butts for irreverent humour in radio and television comedy programmes. The Reverend Eli Jenkins in *Under Milk Wood* still preserved his dignity, pride, and sense of cultural tradition. Many of his real-life equivalents felt that they were losing theirs. Their stipends were alarmingly small. An inquiry reported to the North Wales Association of the Calvinist Methodists in September 1956 that, of 561 ministers who had replied to a questionnaire, 338 were receiving less than £400 per year, and only 43 more than £500.[4] In many cases, ministers' wives had to supplement the family income by taking on part-time work; often they were schoolteachers whose weekly salary was notably larger than that of their husbands. These impoverished men faced dwindling chapel congregations in small rural communities or indifference in large towns. The theological colleges which had often trained them, Bala-Bangor, Aberystwyth, Brecon, or Swansea Memorial College, had far fewer students and scantier resources than of yore. All in all, the profession of the nonconformist minister was a contracting one to which few young Welsh men (and, by biblical definition, no young Welsh women) sought to aspire.

The defeats that the chapels sustained were mostly local and privately inflicted. A few were more public and, therefore, more painful. In particular, the erosion of the 'Welsh Sunday' and the emergence of the so-called 'continental Sunday' with its nameless horrors or enticements was a new battleground for the age-old conflict between the pulpits and the forces of secularism and material comfort. The big battalions were no longer ranged on the side of the Almighty. Well might men speculate on how many divisions the *sasiwn* could summon up by comparison with the secularist Stalins, those publicans and sinners, who confronted it. In the early fifties, the Sunday

[4] *Carnarvon and Denbigh Herald*, 21 September 1956.

opening of cinemas was contested in many south Wales towns. In Swansea in 1950 there was a majority of only 2,909 in that large town on behalf of opening Sunday cinemas. In Cardiff, two years later, the vote was 55,935 in favour of Sunday cinemas, and 21,542 against, a decisive defeat for the forces of organized religion.[5] At least there was the consolation that Sunday cinema-goers might not be chapel-goers and that congregations might not be too drastically affected. The battle went on in town after town in south Wales; gradually, with the opening of various forms of mass entertainment, puritanism beat a reluctant retreat. North and mid-Wales remained more wedded to Sabbatarianism, though even here the urgent financial need to appeal to Sunday trippers and other tourists led to substantial erosion of the traditional Welsh Sunday. By the seventies, the merry refrain of electronic popular music rang forth on the promenade of Aberystwyth, though it was suppressed before hymn-singing by 'Côr y Castell' in the evening.

The vital symbolic battle concerned the Sunday opening of public houses. Under the Licensing Act of 1960, strongly opposed by George Thomas and other Welsh MPs, it was laid down that local polls would be conducted in the counties and county boroughs of Wales to decide whether opinion was or was not in favour of Sunday opening. A local option poll, on a county basis, would be fairer, it was felt, than allowing Cardiff and the populous south to swamp the views of rural areas. In the autumn of 1961, these polls were held. They aroused somewhat languid interest from many of those in favour of Sunday opening. Even many publicans and licensed victuallers were reluctant to disturb their day of rest. In any case, it was well understood that Wales, north and south, teemed with private drinking clubs which were open on Sunday. This applied to sixty-eight of the seventy available in the Rhondda valleys, for instance. Ostensibly designed to serve the social needs of ex-servicemen, the British Legion, rugby players, golfers, and the like, they were clearly able to provide drink on a day when public houses were closed and refreshment denied to all save the long-distance 'bona fide traveller' in hotels. The immense number of Conservative clubs in the Welsh valleys obviously had alcohol, rather than political indoctrination, as their purpose in so socialist an area.

On the other hand, opponents of Sunday opening and the champions of the sabbath day felt most passionately. After all, apart from safeguarding the Welsh Sunday, nonconformists and others believed that drinking, unlike cinema-going, was evil in itself, bad for public health, bad for road accidents, bad for the moral tone of daily life and the well-being of the family. Nonconformist ministers were active in the crusade to defend the old way of life. They aroused sympathy from wider circles. Many members of Plaid Cymru were chapel-goers or else resented on political grounds attempts to divide Wales through local option polls. In any case, the 1881 Sunday Closing Act

[5] *Western Mail*, 27 September 1952.

was a grand memorial to Welsh legislative independence, one that Gladstone himself had supported at the time. The idea of Sunday as a day of rest that had especial significance for Welsh people appealed to many not normally counted within the ranks of chapel members. In debates on the 1960 Licensing Bill in the House standing committee, Labour members like the teetotaller George Thomas, James Griffiths, and T. W. Jones warmly upheld the Welsh Sunday as rooted in popular culture and folk tradition. Churchmen were, significantly, much less committed to the cause. The Archbishop of Wales, Dr A. E. Morris, wrote on 'The Christian Use of Alcoholic Beverages', a modest protest against the idea of total abstinence.[6] He even defended Sunday opening, although he maintained that four hours' opening time would be enough for any man, however thirsty.

The polls showed how powerful these varied religious, national, and moral sentiments still were. They revealed a marked cultural fissure in the land. Industrial, anglicized south and east Wales voted 'wet' on somewhat low polls—Glamorgan, Monmouthshire, the county boroughs of Cardiff and Swansea, Breconshire, Radnorshire, together with Flintshire in the north-east. Conversely, the eight authorities in the mainly Welsh-speaking northern and western areas, Anglesey, Caernarvonshire, Denbighshire, Merioneth, Cardiganshire, Pembrokeshire, Montgomeryshire, and Carmarthenshire, voted strongly to preserve the dry Welsh Sunday. In Merioneth, the majority was 65 per cent of those voting; in Cardiganshire it was 61 per cent. Clearly, the old emotions could still be aroused. In Carmarthenshire and Pembroke-shire, the steelworkers of Llanelli and the dockers of Milford Haven were not sufficient to turn the tide. But the inroads that were made provided much lamentation. A leading Independent minister in Morriston complained that 'Swansea had bowed the knee to Bacchus'.

As public houses opened at once in the seven 'wet' areas, there was a steady Sunday pilgrimage from the drinking fraternity of the 'dry' counties to hostelries on the nearest county borders. The poll was due to be held every seven years. That taken in 1968 showed that the power of the old values had diminished since 1961. Only four of the 'dry' counties, Anglesey, Caernarvonshire, Merioneth, and Cardiganshire—all Welsh-speaking rural counties where Plaid Cymru was relatively strong—confirmed their previous vote. Pembrokeshire, Montgomeryshire, and Denbighshire now voted for Sunday opening. It was a somewhat pathetic commentary on the waning authority of organized religion. Like the Liberal Party with which they were so closely identified, the chapels and their ethos were retreating to the rural fastnesses, setting their face against secularism and materialism which flew against all their deepest and most cherished convictions—but convictions which the young, the industrial workers, and their wives, and perhaps the languid middle class as well, no longer took very seriously. Even though no

[6] Ibid., 13 September 1961.

nationwide poll was taken in 1975, another permanent nail was laid in the coffin of Welsh puritanism and those social and institutional symbols which served to perpetuate it.

In this secular, unsentimental world, there was more tension than before between the generations. It was gently indicated in the Welsh plays of John Gwilym Jones in the fifties. Welsh children, like their mothers, were traditionally ruled by the moral code of the household and the social hierarchy outside. They should be diligent and dutiful, work hard in school and pray hard on Sundays, 'get on' and, if at all possible, make some money. The casualness, even anarchy of the long-haired young, their frequent contempt for the Welsh language and the native culture, their liking for pubs, snackbars, amusement arcades, and dance-halls or for just hanging around street corners shocked their elders more than in most parts of Britain.

On the other hand, it was reassuring that much of the zest of the young still went into the traditionally rewarding channel of education. There was a considerable expansion of education at all levels in the aftermath of the 1944 Education Act. In the fifties, the proportion of pupils attending grammar schools in Wales varied between 36 and 50 per cent, compared with 18–25 per cent for England. More and more secondary schoolchildren stayed on into the sixth form. Indeed, in such rural counties as Cardiganshire, the figures for those proceeding to higher forms of education rose to over 60 per cent of the school population, the highest in the British Isles. The grammar schools flourished as they had seldom done since the first wave of the creation of 'county schools' in the nineties. It was not surprising that the disappearance of these schools as a result of the creation of comprehensive secondary schools created much local controversy. The abolition of such famous schools as Cardiff High School for Boys and for Girls, the Bishop Gore School in Swansea, Lewis School in Pengam, and Grove Park School for Girls in Wrexham caused much heart-searching, especially as their social intake had been much broader-based than in many English grammar schools. For all that, the end of the dreaded 'eleven plus' was warmly applauded by teachers' organizations and others, and the comprehensive system rapidly took root in rural and urban areas alike. Indeed, Anglesey as far back as 1951 was the first county authority to turn its schools into a complete comprehensive system. The proportions of sixth formers gaining qualification for university entry did not at first seem to decline, although at the end of the 1970s, statistics of educational attainment were somewhat discouraging. The much-vaunted Welsh superiority in the sphere of education could no longer be automatically assumed.

One consequence of the 1944 Education Act was that primary and secondary schools were merged even more completely with the English educational system. The old Central Welsh Board, which had survived endless battles with the Welsh Department and the central government since the early years of the century, now gradually faded from the scene. Its examining functions were taken over by the Welsh Joint Education Committee in 1948, and in April 1949 the CWB finally disappeared. So vanished the last vestige of institutional distinctiveness in Welsh state-maintained education, and the last major link with the glorious educational upsurge of the late-nineteenth century.

The University of Wales entered upon a great period of expansion in the late fifties and the early sixties, especially after the publication of the Robbins Report in 1964. This outlined the alleged need for a much larger university student population, especially in the applied and pure sciences. To those who pointed out that the proportion of those experiencing higher education in Britain was extraordinarily low by comparative standards, Kingsley Amis, until 1963 a lecturer at the University College of Swansea, replied that 'more means worse'. In fact, the University of Wales expanded throughout the sixties and early seventies. The Kelsall Report showed that 40 per cent of its pupils were children of working-class parents, the highest proportion in Britain. By the academic year 1978–9, the number of students in the university receiving full-time instruction had risen to 19,553, of which post-graduates numbered 3,307.[7] There were now seven institutions affiliated to the university. In addition to Cardiff, Bangor, and Aberystwyth, all constituent colleges since the beginning in 1893, and the School of Medicine at Cardiff affiliated since 1921, there was also the University College of Swansea. Although it dated from 1920, its early years were stunted by the depression. Its real expansion occurred in the 1960s, when a series of tall concrete and glass structures, some of them halls of residence, some buildings for applied science, rose in the grounds of Singleton Park overlooking Swansea Bay. With 3,851 students in 1978, second only to Cardiff, Swansea had been the most rapidly-growing college in the land since the war.

Since so many geographically dispersed institutions were concerned, a lively controversy blew up in 1963–4 over whether the university should not be defederalized and split up into a number of local or civic institutions. There was also an important cultural or quasi-political aspect, namely that the university was an all-Wales institution, the product of a national campaign in the past century, and that to break it up now would further fragment and divide Wales. Indeed, the initial motion brought before the university court to defederate the university came from the Caerphilly local authority which claimed to detect nationalist influences at work in the nation's colleges. The campaign to defend the federal university was most ably marshalled by Alwyn D. Rees, a social geographer, cultural nationalist, and head of the extra-mural department at Aberystwyth.[8] Through the monthly *Barn*, and also

[7] *Annual Report of the University of Wales*, Session 1978–9.
[8] See the appreciations of him in the special number of *Barn*, January–February 1975.

through a *University of Wales Review* edited by him in the spring of 1964, Alwyn Rees kept up a vigorous flood of argument and satire to demolish the pretensions of the defederalists. Many of the latter came from Cardiff, as they had always done. They were supported by leading figures in the capital city such as James Callaghan and George Thomas. The university court, however, heavily drawn from the local authorities, strongly resisted a motion to split the university up, even though it was supported explicitly by three college principals of Cardiff, Swansea, and Bangor (all three being of Cambridge or Oxford background), and implicitly by the fourth, Dr Thomas Parry, a distinguished Welsh scholar now principal of Aberystwyth.[9] Llewelyn Heycock, the trade-union leader, berated his Labour colleagues who sought to split up the 'people's university'. The new Labour government, through Anthony Crosland when Secretary of State for Education, upheld the decision of the university court, and the university remained thenceforth national and intact. Indeed, no clear case on educational grounds had ever been made for splitting it up. It could hardly be claimed that its federal structure was holding the university back, with its rapid rate of expansion and (in the sixties, though perhaps not later) a favourable share of grants from the University Grants Committee. The factor of geographical remoteness between the constituent colleges was greatly exaggerated; after all, even Wales possessed the telephone.

The threat of defederation reared its head again briefly in 1966 when the College of Advanced Technology, situated on the opposite side of Cathays Park from the university college, bid for its own independent university status. This was the thin end of the defederal wedge. In the end, the Labour government decided that it must settle for membership of the university as a sixth constituent college. It became the University of Wales Institute of Science and Technology (UWIST) and in February 1972 had to shelve over-optimistic plans for expansion that would have taken it out of Cathays Park. Yet another institution was brought under the umbrella of the university in 1972. An old theological argument ended when St. David's College, Lampeter, entered the university as basically a liberal arts college; in 1978 it had 672 students, the smallest total in Wales. Lampeter had faced difficulties for many decades, perhaps inherent in its refusal originally to join the university in the nineties. It was still widely represented as a college for training Anglican clergymen; the Bishop of St. David's presided over its council. Its admission into the university with a resultant eligibility for UGC grants, was a portent of its expansion as an academic institution—and of the ending of its special sectarian character as a preponderantly Anglican college in a nonconformist countryside.

Thus by the seventies, the University of Wales comprehended seven institutions of higher education. Its prestige had risen steadily; it increasingly

⁹ Cf. Alwyn D. Rees (ed.), *University of Wales Review,* Summer 1964.

attracted a wide range of students. One feature of this growth, one attacked by Alwyn Rees in *Barn* for instance, was that over half of the university's students now came from England. The special relationship of the Welsh colleges with their own localities was being eroded fast. Rees called in vain for a checking of the expansion of the growth of the Welsh colleges and the formation of a new college (perhaps on the site of Bangor Normal, due to be closed down) where instruction would be conducted solely in the Welsh language. This theme provoked demonstrations and 'sit-ins' by students in Bangor University College, especially by partisans of the *Adfer* movement described below, in 1978–9.

But to most observers, until the heady optimism of the Robbins Report was exploded by the problems of the later seventies, expansion meant progress, and the university was never more thriving. Its colleges were vigorous, distinct institutions yet involved in some sense in a common national framework. One novelty was that the old mansion of the Davies family of Llandinam, Plas Gregynog, north of Newtown, was bequeathed to the university, and used for inter-collegiate seminars and colloquia with great success from 1964 onwards. In Cardiff, the University of Wales Press produced a steady stream of monographs, texts, and musical works of high quality, despite a small staff. The Board of Celtic Studies fostered research work of much importance in history and law, language and literature, archaeology, and, most recently, social studies. Welsh graduates increased in number and sought a wider range of employment than hitherto. It was noticed, however, that young Welsh men and women were reluctant to enter industrial or commercial life and preferred the status of the less remunerated professions of school-teaching or lecturing. Applications for applied science places in the national university did not increase markedly, despite the optimistic projections of the Robbins Committee. On balance, the University of Wales was very much of a success story in these years. It confirmed the wisdom of successive governments in maintaining it as a nationwide, integrated, federal system to minister for Wales as a whole.

It was not the educational but the linguistic aspects of education, however, that most agitated the new society. More than any other feature of Welsh life, education became the battleground for those locked in conflict over the survival of the Welsh language. The censuses of 1951, 1961, and 1971 told an inexorable and predictable story—that, in the face of outside pressures from an increasingly anglicizing world beyond, the proportion of those speaking Welsh was declining steadily. It fell to 28 per cent in 1951, 25 per cent in 1961 and to barely 20 per cent in 1971. These 20 per cent were now largely concentrated in areas of north, mid- and west Wales where unemployment was highest and opportunities for young people most meagre. There was particular alarm that young people in particular seemed to be either forgetting their native language, or never speaking it. The Welsh Joint Education Committee reported in April 1961 that, out of 389,558 children in Welsh schools aged between five and fifteen, only 68,585 (17.6 per cent) could speak or understand Welsh. The number of children between seven and seventeen for whom Welsh was the first language was only 37,608. It was taught as a second language to 181,109 others. The situation was not entirely without hope. In industrial Flintshire and urban Cardiff, the proportion actually went up during the fifties, while falling in other parts of Wales. A new Welsh-speaking intellectual middle class was mushrooming in the Cardiff suburbs, as a result of the growth of the BBC, HTV, the university, the Welsh Office, and other institutions in the capital city. But the overall message of the statistics was clear enough. The proportion of the coming generation able to communicate in Welsh at all was small and still declining. The eventual extinction of the language within two or three generations was very probable. It was inevitable, then, that dispute and debate about the place of the language should take place at all levels of Welsh education—about Welsh nursery schools, about the instruction in primary schools, about all-Welsh secondary schools, about all-Welsh university and student hostels, and the appointment of university and college lecturers to instruct pupils through the medium of Welsh. A powerful report by the Council for Wales on the condition of the Welsh language in schools in 1961 fuelled the debate still further.

By the sixties, Welsh was widely taught as a basic school subject in primary schools and some secondary schools in every Welsh local authority; the only exceptions were that three secondary schools in Monmouthshire, one in Radnorshire, and none at all in Newport taught Welsh.[10] But it was clear that more positive action was needed for the language to survive at all. In 1967 the Central Advisory Council for Education (Wales), under the chairmanship of Professor Charles Gittins, a non-Welsh-speaking Professor of Education, issued its report. It is noticeable that the report for England submitted at the same time dwelt on teaching methods and on school facilities and other technical matters. The Gittins Report, by contrast, concentrated almost entirely on protecting the Welsh language and using it to express the cultural, social, and spiritual values of the society which gave it birth. A cautionary note was struck in a reservation by Professor David Marsh, a Welsh-speaking sociologist from Nottingham University, which disputed the need to give Welsh so prominent a place in primary education. With Gittins behind it, however, the place of Welsh as a school subject was much more secure. More still was needed, in the view of some patriots, however. Rather than simply have Welsh as one of many school subjects, perhaps an optional subject that would be rejected in favour of another language such as French or German, and rather than have it simply used for a few hours of formal instruction and

---

[10] *Council for Wales and Monmouthshire: Report on the Welsh Language Today*, 1963 (Cmnd. 2198), p. 123.

then neglected for the rest of the day and at weekends, all-Welsh schools to create the right kind of cultural environment should be created.

Gittins gave new stimulus to the Welsh Schools movement. It had originally been stimulated by *Urdd Gobaith Cymru*, since the late thirties, with schools at Aberystwyth and elsewhere. It was also strongly backed up by *Undeb Cymru Fydd*. This was a pressure group founded during the Colwyn Bay *eisteddfod* in 1941 under the secretaryship of T. I. Ellis, son of the old Merioneth apostle of *Cymru Fydd*, and the chairmanship for a time of Cassie Davies, a schools inspector of decidedly nationalistic outlook.[11] Now, particularly in Glamorgan, parental pressure built up for all-Welsh primary schools. These parents tended to be articulate, determined members of a new middle class for whom speaking Welsh meant high social status and acceptability. By 1970, these schools numbered forty-one, with over 5,000 pupils. In addition, there were eight Welsh-medium comprehensive schools, beginning with Rhydfelen School, Pontypridd, in 1962. It began with 80 pupils; by 1975, it had 1,000. Two other Welsh-medium schools were founded in Glamorgan, at Barry and Ystalyfera; three in north-east Wales at Wrexham, Rhyl, and Mold; one in Carmarthenshire at Llanelli; and one in Cardiganshire at Aberystwyth. By 1974 there were an estimated 4,000 pupils at the Welsh-language comprehensive schools.

Much depended for their progress, however, on an adequate flow of Welsh-speaking pupils from primary schools, and here there was much difficulty and sometimes conflict. While in general the Welsh-medium schools were accepted benevolently by English-speaking parents, and given amiable patronage by Llewelyn Heycock and the Glamorgan Education Committee, in some towns (even in Aberystwyth, because of its largely English university teaching and administrative staff) there were loud protests by parents at so Welsh-oriented a programme of instruction. In addition, there were accusations that the teachers at these schools were frequently members or supporters of Plaid Cymru and that they engaged in the indoctrination of the impressionable young children under their charge. These were necessarily almost impossible to prove or disprove, but they added to the heat engendered. The whole controversy over *Ysgolion Cymraeg* was a complex one, involving the clash of widely distinct educational, social, and national issues. But by the late seventies, the place of the Welsh language in the elementary and secondary schools was undoubtedly much more zealously guarded than had been the case in the forties or fifties.

At the university level, things were much more difficult. There seemed no prospect of money being found to establish an all-Welsh college, or for sufficient staff to run it. Nine 'appointments through the medium of Welsh' were made in the various university colleges in the quinquennium 1960–9 to teach history, philosophy, theology, and education, but, necessarily, not

[11] R. Gerallt Jones, *A Bid for Unity: the Story of Undeb Cymru Fydd* (Aberystwyth, 1971).

many students were able to benefit from the instruction thereby provided. By the 1970s, less than 40 per cent of the student population of the national university came from Wales at all, and only a small fraction of these, perhaps 5 per cent of the total, were Welsh-speaking. Inevitably, with the national university part and parcel of the British system of university admissions, qualified students from England or overseas could enter without difficulty— hence the attacks on expansion voiced in *Barn* and elsewhere. The Welsh language represented a rearguard action of patriotically-inclined students in the colleges, and became a favourite theme for demonstrations in Bangor especially.

What did survive in the university, and indeed flourished mightily in the sixties and seventies, was a sense of Welshness and a serious concern with Welsh issues. It was noticeable that the history of Wales, for example, attracted a wide range of undergraduate, graduate, and lay interest, and that departments teaching it flourished everywhere. Broadcast talks on Welsh history proved very popular. It was noticeable, too, that, whereas university lecturers in language and literature usually tended to be nationalists, those teaching the history of Wales, even the medievalists, tended to be Labour. More and more attention was focused upon the history of Wales, social, political, and economic, in the nineteenth and twentieth centuries. This emphasis was apparent in the academic work of David Williams, Professor of Welsh History at Aberystwyth from 1945 to 1967, whose *Rebecca Riots* in 1955 was a marvellously lucid and dispassionate study of these rural disturbances in west Wales in the 1840s. It was very different in tone from that somewhat sentimental idealization of the rural *werin* that had characterized the writings of earlier authors on modern Wales. In 1960, a new academic journal was founded, the *Welsh History Review*, edited at first by Professor Glanmor Williams of Swansea. Soon it was to appear twice a year and flourish mightily. Another new development, also based on Swansea, was the creation of a new research project, financed by the SSRC, in 1971, to rescue the industrial and political records of the Welsh labour movement and of the coalfield generally. Oral testimony through tape-recordings was another source conserved here. One by-product of this was the establishment of a journal, *Llafur*, in 1972 devoted to Welsh labour history; another was the creation of a library in Swansea to house the books and other records relating to the miners. The trade unions were also closely involved with this development, along with archivists and academics.

In this and other respects, a growing and intelligent interest in Welsh history, both for its own sake and as a living and continuous part of daily social experience, was built up. No longer was it simply the domain of the anthropologist and the antiquarian. No longer either was it regarded as coming to an end with the Act of Union under Henry VIII (though work of exceptional quality continued to be done on medieval Welsh history). A more traditional, but deeply interesting, aspect of the conservation of social culture was the founding of the open-air folk museum at St. Fagan's in Lord Plymouth's former home outside Cardiff, in 1946. This flourished under the direction of that devoted custodian of the rural values, Iorwerth Peate from Llanbrynmair. Here, a profound study of rural crafts and traditions, folk songs, vernacular poetry, and the like added up to an impressive assembly of the components of the Welsh cultural heritage, equal in quality to the folk museums of Scandinavia on which St. Fagan's was, to some extent, based. In this and other ways, academics and others confirmed their attachment to aspects of Welshness. They remained devoted to the Welsh past, anxious to relate it to the Welsh present, with passion but also with realism.

More and more it became clear that a central theme, perhaps the ultimate abiding theme of post-war Welsh society was the preservation and definition of its Welshness and its traditional culture. The dialogue and even debate between the Welsh and the Anglo-Welsh assumed a sharper tone. Their co-existence became that degree less peaceful.

In terms of inspiration and literary creativity, Welsh-language culture was still very thriving for most of this period. Some of the newer creative forms that had emerged in the great years of the twenties and thirties continued to attract distinguished work. The Welsh novel, for instance, became an increasingly effective and mature art form, even if one inevitably geared to a high degree to the life of rural communities. T. Rowland Hughes continued his series of impressive novels on the Caernarvonshire quarrying community. *Chwalfa* (1946) brilliantly evoked the atmosphere of the Penrhyn quarry strike in the nineties. His premature death in 1949 was a major loss to Welsh letters. Kate Roberts, on the other hand, produced a steady stream of remarkable novels, or perhaps 'long short stories', her energies undimmed by the passing years. Her acute observations of patterns of life and human relationships, based mainly on the Denbighshire neighbourhood where she lived, continued to be appealing, often exciting. She showed remarkable insight, too, into male—female relationships, as in her study of the decay of young love in *Y Golled*. She was followed by a series of remarkable young novelists, many of them also female. An especially gifted young male writer was Islwyn Ffowc Elis, whose first novel, *Cysgod y Cryman*, appeared in 1953 when he was still in his twenties. It was notable for its contemporary outlook, its freedom from nostalgia for a past society. The historical novel also flourished, in the hands of such authors as Rhiannon Davies Jones and Geraint Dyfnallt Owen, the latter himself a professional historian employed by the Historical Manuscripts Commission.

The short story, however, still proved to be the classic medium for creative prose writing in Wales. No single author perhaps, made such an impact on his readers here as did the Pembrokeshire-based D. J. Williams, ex-miner, ex-schoolmaster, ex-martyr since he was one of Saunders Lewis's comrades-in-arms in the bombing incident in Llŷn in 1936, for which Williams like his friends served nine months in Wormwood Scrubs. As increasingly was the case in the Welsh short story of the fifties and sixties, D. J. Williams (who died in 1970) introduced an aggressively nationalist, anti-English note into his writings. He cheerfully accepted that art was, and should be, propaganda for great causes. His most influential work was *Hen Dŷ Ffarm*, a kind of rambling fictional autobiography, suffused with passionate love for the Carmarthenshire farming community in which he grew up and brimming over with anger and bitterness at English governments and English-inspired bodies like the Stalinists of the Forestry Commission who laid it waste with regimented plantations of fir-trees, destroying an age-old society and its way of life, along with the deep-rooted culture that went with it. D. J. Williams became something of a cult figure to nationalists of Plaid Cymru and the Welsh Language Society, second only to that Welsh version of Russell and Marcuse, Saunders Lewis himself.[12] There were Welsh dramatic works being produced, too, notably through Lewis in particular, often with strongly religious or political overtones. The verse drama *Blodeuwedd* (1957), which took its theme from the Mabinogion, was especially striking and original. On the other hand, there had never been a strong dramatic tradition in Wales, no urban élite, no Abbey Theatre or audiences attuned to sophisticated dramatic expression. Such theatres as existed in Wales, the New Theatre and later the Arts Theatre in Cardiff, the Grand Theatre in Swansea, performed overwhelmingly in the English language, though the handsome *Theatr y Werin*, established on the university campus on the hillside above Aberystwyth in 1973, and the attractive Clwyd Arts Centre set up in Mold, did try to redress the balance with a flow of productions in both languages.

Poetry continued to prove the most characteristic form of creative writing to appeal to local writers. The old giants gradually passed from the scene. T. Gwynn Jones died in Aberystwyth in 1949. Williams Parry produced an important volume of 'winter poems' (*Cerddi'r Gaeaf*) in 1952 after years of silence, but died soon afterwards. Thomas Parry-Williams, however, remained active and creative in Aberystwyth until the 1970s and produced a series of acute, highly complex, and intensely introspective poems. He also continued to make a powerful personal impact on the cultural life of his country through his role as a key *eisteddfod* adjudicator for 'crown' and 'chair' until the later 1960s. With such men as Parry-Williams still alive and intellectually active, the Welsh-reading public was kept in intimate touch with that glorious wave of lyrical romanticism that had swept through the land and its literature before and after the First World War. There was still an audience for Welsh poetry. The poetry page of 'Dewi Emrys' (D. Emrys James who died in 1952) in the weekly *Cymro* was widely read and eagerly discussed. It

[12] Ned Thomas, *The Welsh Extremist: a Culture in Crisis* (London, 1971), pp. 72-8.

provided a platform for the controversial poems of Harri Gwynn, for instance, which the *eisteddfod* rejected partly, it would appear, on moral grounds. Dewi Emrys's page became a kind of public seminar or teach-in for young poets, a forum of communication between older and newer writers, almost unique in the cultural life of Britain. A steady stream of effective and influential poetry was produced in the late forties and early fifties, notably the somewhat morbid writings of Caradog Pritchard, a successful journalist; the verse of Iorwerth Peate, full of nostalgia for lost rural idylls and the world of Samuel Roberts of Llanbrynmair; Alun Llywelyn-Williams, thoughtful, intellectual, almost academic in approach; and Dilys Cadwaladr who became in 1953 the first woman to win the Crown at the *eisteddfod* with a poem, 'The Veil'. There was still powerful, highly nationalistic poetry being written by Gwenallt Jones and again by Saunders Lewis. Some of the latter's work, however, aroused controversy for its anti-democratic and satirical tone. His *Byd a Betws* in 1941 was thought by some to convey overtones of anti-Semitism in its rejection of the need for war with Nazi Germany. (Conversely, his later work the play *Esther* (1958) was a powerful treatment of the pressures undergone by the Jews as a subject race.)

There were other important poets emerging in the late fifties and early sixties, often more cosmopolitan in outlook than their predecessors. Among them were Gwyn Thomas, with his resigned condemnation of the brutalities and cruelties of everyday life; T. Glynne Davies, with his cynical, self-deprecating outlook; R. Gerallt Jones, who wrote some effective narrative poetry for radio broadcasting; and Dafydd Rowlands the young crowned bard at the 1969 national *eisteddfod*. A different note was struck by the 'Cadwgan' group of poets, of whom Rhydwen Williams and Pennar Davies were the most prolific. Scholarly, even pedantic in outlook, they led a kind of revolt against the lyric romanticism of the past. Perhaps the most interesting of all the newer school of poets to reach distinction in the post-1945 era were three men very different from one another. There was Waldo Williams, whose *Dail Pren* (1956), based on poetry written over the past thirty years, offered rich insights into the tortured passions of one who was both a Quaker and a committed nationalist. His work was infused throughout with deep humanity and compassion, and with a pervading sense of universal mystery. Euros Bowen, an Anglican clergyman who began publishing poetry only in 1947 when he was in his forties, produced five major volumes of poems between 1957 and 1973. He was more of a literary craftsman, concerned with technique and structure, more in the tradition of T. Gwynn Jones. Order and control pervaded and shaped his writing. Bowen termed himself a 'sacramental poet',[13] but critics have also linked his poetry with the French Symbolist tradition, as an example of the poetic experimentalism of Rimbaud, Mallarmé, and other continental poets of an earlier generation, now influencing the somewhat enclosed world

[13] Dafydd Glyn Jones, 'Welsh Poetry since 1945', *Triskel One* (Swansea, 1971), p. 60.

of Welsh lyric poetry. Finally, there was Bobi Jones, a university lecturer at Aberystwyth and a Renaissance man amongst Welsh authors, whose poetry displayed dramatic, almost reckless experiments in language and the use of metaphor. His work was often said to embody the strengths and perhaps some of the limitations of one who was not a Welsh speaker during his childhood in Cardiff. Certainly, it reflected an evangelical, fundamentalist Calvinism of rare intensity. In all these respects, however, the extraordinary fertility of Welsh poetry was impressive. Young poets continued to make their impact throughout the seventies, from Derec Llwyd Morgan whose *Pryderi* appeared in 1970, to Alan Llwyd who won both chair and crown at the 1977 national *eisteddfod* at Wrexham. The cultural and political predicament of Welsh-speaking Wales gave momentum and passion to the writing of the new generation, in their response to an encroaching, suffocating world. The world of Welsh poetry, then, was thriving—and was now institutionalized. There was founded in 1960, in somewhat self-conscious imitation of the French 'Immortals', the Welsh Academy. Its annual periodical *Taliesin* (edited at first by Gwenallt Jones) attracted most of the best poets and prose writers working through the medium of Welsh.

In purely literary terms these were years when the native culture was still very much alive. Verse such as that written by Euros Bowen and Bobi Jones still found readers, even if not on so impressive a scale as that by Gwyn Jones and the giants of the past. The *eisteddfod*, an all-Welsh-language body since the implementation of the new 'rule' in 1951, still served as a kind of focus for the arts and crafts in Wales. From the sixties, it began to offer encouragement, with the aid of the Arts Council, to painters, sculptors, and designers. The televising of the *eisteddfod* undoubtedly gave it new impact as a national event of popular significance. But the tragedy was that the Welsh-speaking population was now in irreversible decline, and most people were increasingly oblivious to the creative work that talented authors were producing in their midst. The competitors for strict-metre verse at the *eisteddfod* no longer excited mass attention; they were a televised spectacle like a football match, soon forgotten once the result was known. Poetry no longer attracted a wide readership. Welsh newspaper publishing was in serious decline, as major newspapers like the *Genedl Gymreig* wound up. After 1950, only two Welsh-language weeklies survived at all. *Y Cymro*, the more 'popular' of the two in style, continued to attract a readership of several thousand from its offices at Oswestry across the English border. The *Baner*, once the great paper of Thomas Gee of Denbigh, limped on through the sixties, in the face of falling circulation and mounting costs. Advertising was harder to obtain, much of the readership elderly. The *Baner* achieved new vigour through its championing of the nationalist causes, but by the later 1970s it was fighting for survival. In addition, there were purely denominational weeklies, such as the *Goleuad* (Methodist), the *Tyst* (Independent), *Seren Cymru* (Baptist), the *Llan* (Church of Wales) and the *Ymofynydd* (Unitarian), all with apparently small circulations. By far the most thriving of the Welsh-language periodicals or newspapers, significantly enough, was wholly political, *Y Ddraig Goch*, the organ of Plaid Cymru. There was also the monthly *Barn*, launched in 1962 by the Liberal lawyer, Alun Talfan Davies, which flourished with the campaign to defend the federal structure of the national university. Under the brilliant editorship of Alwyn Rees, it maintained for many years a readership of over 4,000. But the total readership of all the newspapers and periodicals in Welsh by the later seventies was less than 30,000 and still falling.

The facts of inexorable decline were mounting as far as the language was concerned. As has been seen, it spurred on the campaign for Welsh schools, and for the implementation of the 1967 Gittins Report. The 1951 census, the first since 1931, showed a frightening decline since the previous census twenty years earlier. Only 714,686 (28.9 per cent) were recorded as speaking Welsh, of whom but 345,000 were under forty-four years of age. The native language, it seemed, was more and more the preserve of the elderly and of depopulated rural areas. The most rapidly expanding parts of the country—Monmouthshire, eastern Glamorgan, and Flintshire—were among the most extensively anglicized, with the exception of the new middle-class intelligentsia installed in the north Cardiff suburbs. The same story was underlined in the 1961 census which saw the total of those speaking Welsh now recorded as 656,002, or 26 per cent, compared with a tally of over half the population at the start of the century. Welsh monoglots had largely disappeared, though apparently 362 people in Cardiff, and even 129 in Newport (mainly young children perhaps), claimed no knowledge of English whatsoever. As was noted above, there was especial concern over the decline of Welsh speaking amongst children. In 1961, only 14.7 per cent of children aged between five and nine could speak the language, compared with 15.9 per cent ten years earlier.

The 1971 language census showed a further decline, with Welsh speakers now 542,400, just 20.8 per cent of the population. But there were now some hopeful signs for enthusiasts for the language. The rate of decline in 1961–71 had been slower than in the previous decade in many areas, while bilingualism amongst schoolchildren up to the age of fourteen had been maintained and was even on the increase—obviously a product of the educational policy pursued since 1961. There was much more goodwill amongst local authorities, less prejudice amongst English-speaking parents, more sensitivity shown by government departments. By 1972, there were over seven hours of television broadcasting put out weekly by the BBC in the Welsh language, and a similar quantity broadcast by the commercial company, Harlech Television. After years of pressure by a variety of public bodies, the government white paper on broadcasting in July 1978 gave its blessing to a fourth television channel devoted solely to Welsh-language broadcasting. Its services were scheduled to begin in late 1982. In any case, the presence of Owen Edwards, the grandson of 'O.M.' and son of the founder of the *Urdd*, as Welsh controller, was a happy omen for those concerned with the future of the language in the broadcasting media.

But the facts of decline remained, and seemed impervious to these new developments. The endless flow of immigrants and tourists from England, the anglicized force of London-based mass communications and other central institutions, the tendency for parents of linguistically mixed marriages to prefer English as the basic language for their children, the pervasive prejudice (especially pronounced in south-east Wales) that the native language was a kind of antiquarian survival out of place in contemporary society—all these factors combined to emasculate still further a language so recently buoyant and self-confident. The emotional background against which these poets and literary draftsmen of the 1945–80 period operated, was one of desperation, even of despair at the disappearance of that precious heritage and tradition which gave their craft its inspiration and their very existence its sense of purpose. The Welsh Language Society, *Cymdeithas yr Iaith Gymraeg*, founded in 1962, was one important consequence, as will be discussed at length in the next chapter.

The new society after 1945, then, was not only an increasingly secular one but increasingly anglicized as well. The trend was for anglicized or even for bilingual Welsh men and women to merge into a wider English 'admass' culture, with foreign overtones. They read London-based newspapers, even though the *Western Mail* retained its Welsh coverage under its new owners, the Thomson organization, and kept up a circulation of about 100,000. The radio, television, theatre, cinema, mass entertainment that shaped the cultural world of the new generation was overwhelmingly English in its provenance, with influences from the United States and to some degree Europe (witness the growth of continental restaurants or delicatessens in a land notable for its gastronomic conservatism, where broth and Welsh cakes had often seemed the limit of culinary endeavour in the past).

The Anglo-Welsh literary tradition remained a very lively one, and gained new vitality from the support of the Welsh Arts Council after 1945. Anglo-Welsh poetry remained very vigorous, long after the tragic and unnecessary death of Dylan Thomas in New York in 1953. Poets like Glyn Jones, John Tripp, Roland Mathias, and Raymond Garlick considered themselves to be writing primarily for a local readership in terms of local themes and traditions. Glyn Jones also turned to writing some effective novels, in particular *The Learning Lark* (1960), a gentle exposé of the secondary education system and local government. In his book *The Dragon has Two Tongues* (1968) he remained the idealistic champion of the Welshness of the Anglo-Welsh writer, and his cultural identity. Amongst other novelists Gwyn Thomas produced a torrent of comic and richly inventive creations, novels and radio plays. The very comedy of his portrayal of the economic deprivations of the Rhondda in the thirties infused his work with a kind of optimism. Rhys Davies continued to provide mordant commentaries on the ethos of puritanical nonconformity, though much less bitterly so than Caradoc Evans, whom he closely resembled. A writer far more sympathetic to that ethos. Emyr Humphreys, showed that the Anglo-Welsh novelist could write work of some distinction in both languages. By contrast there were the trilogy of socialist novels by the Cambridge don, Raymond Williams of Abergavenny, from *Border Counrty* in 1960 to *The Fight for Manod* in 1979, all marked by a deep insight into the compassion for the rural communities of the Welsh borderland.

There were still outlets for the Anglo-Welsh poet or prose writer, despite the demise of the *Welsh Review* and the eventual disappearance of Keidrich Rhys's revived *Wales* in 1959. A most refreshing literary quarterly was *Dock Leaves*, published at Pembroke Dock from late 1949 onwards and the work of Raymond Garlick and a group of writers living 'in the southern part of Pembrokeshire', which provided a platform for authors who chose to write in English. It maintained a most lively existence for several years before transforming itself into the *Anglo-Welsh Review* in 1958, a more handsome publication liberally supported by the Arts Council, and edited from 1961 by Roland Mathias. In 1965 there appeared the first issue of *Poetry Wales*, published in Merthyr and edited by Meic Stephens. This offered new opportunity to talented young Anglo-Welsh poets. It was followed in August 1970 by *Planet*, also supported by the Welsh Arts Council, and edited by Ned Thomas, a folk nationalist cum libertarian socialist, based on Tregaron. Until 1980, this provided another critical forum for Anglo-Welsh authors and poets, and for the discussion of cultural, political, and social themes relevant to the Welsh experience. By 1977 the Welsh Arts Council could note with justified pride the enhanced status of the writer in Wales, with about 1,200 authors resident there, and about four hundred Welsh- and English-language titles published each year. Their literary horizons were wider than ever before, even if patronage was sometimes lavished on work of limited merit. On the other hand, much of the financial support for these writers necessarily found its way to publishers and booksellers rather than to the authors themselves who remained relatively impoverished.

Many of the pioneers of the Anglo-Welsh movement in the thirties had disappeared by the fifties. Anglo-Welsh writers remained extremely heterogeneous: Raymond Garlick (himself an Englishman) was careful to disavow the existence of any 'school'.[14] But Vernon Watkins, 'a Welsh poet writing in English' as he described himself,[15] continued to produce highly original poetry from 'The Ballad of the Mari Lwyd' onwards. Often his work was

---

[14] *Dock Leaves*, vol. 2, No. 6 (Michaelmas 1951), p. 1.
[15] Gwen Watkins and Ruth Pryor (eds.), *I That was Born in Wales* (Cardiff, 1976), p. 15.

related to Welsh themes, to the landscape of his beloved Gower peninsula, or his friendship with Dylan Thomas. Watkins's death in Seattle in 1967 was a profound loss to Welsh letters. Conversely, there emerged at least one new Anglo-Welsh poet of outstanding quality, R. S. Thomas, a Church of Wales parish priest born in Cardiff but based first on Manafon in rural Montgomery-shire, then on Eglwysfach in northern Cardiganshire, later still on Aberdaron in Llŷn. Thomas rapidly proved himself to be a poet of rare humility, compassion, and sensitivity, as such volumes as *Stones of the Field* (1946), *Poetry for Supper* (1958), and *Tares* (1961) indicated. A Christian deeply devoted to the countryside, he was in both senses a pastoral poet. He was deeply attached to the mysteries of the 'Welsh Hill Country':

> I will sing
> The land's praises, making articulate
> Your strong feelings, your thoughts of no date,
> Your secret learning, innocent of books.

But he wrote of nature with insight and subtlety, totally free from Words-worthian sentimentality. 'Cynddylan on a Tractor' was a protest against the social consequences of the mechanization of farming and the break-up of rural hill communities that resulted. Thomas often introduced a markedly nationalist note into his writing, and indeed he himself strongly endorsed Plaid Cymru. Some of his poetry from the forties onwards included a commentary on the varied experiences and responses of Iago Prytherch, an introspective hill farmer first depicted in 'The Peasant' (1946), the custodian and celebrant of a rural Welsh way of life threatened with endemic decay and the incursions of an alien culture.

Yet, despite the clear element of cultural nationalism in R. S. Thomas's poetry, it became clear that the Anglo-Welsh tradition owed less and less to the direct inspiration of a native culture, despite the anxiety of writers like Roland Mathias and Meic Stephens to relate the two cultures of Wales to each other and to forge a united tradition. It was not so easy to distinguish from the 'regional' varieties of English literature such as the Geordies of the north-east. The Anglo-Welsh writer, however patriotic, sometimes provoked broadsides from his more nationalistic Welsh-language fellow-countrymen. Bobi Jones in 1953 derided him for 'importing and adapting [his] culture from an uninteresting and impoverished England'. Pennar Davies attacked Dylan Thomas for his ignorance of the native language and for his 'lack of moral substance' compared with Kitchener Davies, a far superior poet in Pennar Davies's opinion.[16] The Anglo-Welsh tried to rebut these criticisms with passion, sometimes with wit. Wynford Vaughan Thomas, an eminent broad-

[16] *Dock Leaves*, vol. 3, No. 8 (Spring 1953), pp. 23–8; ibid., vol. 5, No. 15 (Winter 1954), pp. 14–17.

caster and the son of a famous Swansea composer, wrote cheerfully of the Anglo-Welsh exile experiencing 'Hiraeth in N.W.3'.

> Glorious welcome that's waiting for me
> Hymns on the harmonium, Welsh-cakes for tea,
> A lecture on Marx, his importance today,
> All the raptures of love from a Bangor B.A.!

But many of those who experienced such emotions (though not Vaughan-Thomas himself) stayed contentedly in their exile in Hampstead or elsewhere in suburbia, and seldom returned home.

More generally, there did not seem to be the same degree of intense commitment to Anglo-Welsh cultural life as to the native culture in its indigenous state. The periodical press offered evidence here. *Barn* flourished throughout the later sixties and early seventies, bearing a strongly nationalistic message. But *Welsh Outlook,* an Anglo-Welsh variant founded at Swansea in 1965 by a group of lawyers, academics, and broadcasters in partial imitation of its predecessor founded by Thomas Jones fifty years earlier, survived for only three months.[17] There were five Welsh-language literary periodicals (*Llên Cymru, Traethodydd, Genhinen, Lleufer,* and *Taliesin*) as against only one in English. The cultural experience of the English-speaking Welshman, however patriotic, was diverging more and more from that of the native 'speaker'. Indeed, when so many allegedly Welsh-speaking men and women spoke a kind of anglicized *patois* and were unable to write or read the language which they professed to speak, when they complained of 'university Welsh' or 'BBC Welsh' which they were unable fully to comprehend, it was hard to know how seriously the English-speaking majority should take the claims or the statistics of the partisans of Welsh-language culture.

Other art forms in Wales also owed much to the dominant English or European culture. In the visual arts, the Welsh landscape still attracted several artists of major repute. The most remarkable of them, perhaps, was Josef Herman, a Pole who settled in the mining town of Ystradgynlais in the upper Swansea valley from 1943 onwards. He became passionately absorbed by the relation of working people to their landscape. His vivid studies of the miners, painted in the bold expressionist realism of Millet or Courbet, formed a powerful visual hymn to the dignity of labour. Significant native painters emerged such as Brenda Chamberlain, David Tinker, and Kyffin Williams, while the '56 Group Wales', led by Arthur Giardelli, acted as champions of the *avant-garde*. Mention should also be made of that extraordinary London Welshman, the writer-painter-visionary, David Jones, with his deep intellectual involvement with the Mabinogion and with Arthurian Legend. Meanwhile, popular interest in the visual arts was greatly stimulated by the

[17] The leading article of *Welsh Outlook*, No. 1 (April 1965) was written by the present author.

crusading work of David Bell, assistant director of the Welsh Arts Council after 1945 and the curator of the Glynn Vivian art gallery in Swansea. But no native style of art seemed to result. One informed writer could record in 1972 that the visual arts were 'a minor activity, hardly impinging upon the consciousness of the nation'.[18] Thereafter came something of a resurgence, partly through the efforts of the Welsh Arts Council in supporting artists, craftsmen, and designers. The Council's own gallery, 'Oriel', in Cardiff, opened in 1974, became a lively centre for exhibitions of contemporary and other arts. New art centres were established at Wrexham, Mold, Aberystwyth, Builth Wells, Newport, and elsewhere, while there were new developments such as the centre for the visual arts at Llandudno, based on the old Mostyn Gallery. Art in Wales may not have been Welsh art in any precise sense, but it was more widely appreciated and understood than ever before.

Music flourished much more—but again mainly in a cosmopolitan context. The Welsh National Opera Company, based on Cardiff and set up in 1946, rapidly became a major company with a high international reputation, and a superb array of soloists including Sir Geraint Evans and the sopranos Gwyneth Jones and Margaret Price. It also encouraged orchestral music and helped promote the founding of the Welsh Philharmonia in 1973. But the Welsh National's performances were inevitably of German or Italian opera, with perhaps some Janáček or Britten thrown in. Apart from a rare offering from Arwel Hughes or Grace Williams, its Welshness was largely in name only. By the late seventies, even many of its leading soloists came from beyond Offa's Dyke.

In addition, with the existence of a growing public educated in orchestral as well as in choral music, with flourishing festivals such as those at Swansea and Fishguard, and with greater standards of professionalism in musicianship, there were now for the first time distinguished modern Welsh composers. Grace Williams, Arwel Hughes, and David Wynne, all born in the early years of the century, were well established before 1945. Alun Hoddinot, William Mathias, and David Harries came from a younger generation, born in the inter-war years. Their Welshness was not in doubt. They turned for inspiration (often in their lighter compositions admittedly) to native Welsh folk tunes, traditional airs and ballads, hymns, even nursery rhymes, much as Vaughan Williams had done in England. Some of Grace Williams's most ambitious compositions, notably her *Missa Cambrensis* written for the 1971 Llandaff festival, drew on the rhythms and cadences of traditional Welsh poetry and oratory. Alun Hoddinot's orchestral work *Landscapes* was an evocation of Snowdonia that was inspired by T. H. Parry-Williams's poem, *Eryri*. Composers like Hoddinot and Mathias insisted that a Welsh consciousness and a sense of cultural identity permeated their work more profoundly

[18] J. R. Webster, '"For Wales—see England": the Artist in Wales', in R. Brinley Jones (ed.), *Anatomy of Wales*, p. 243.

than in the mere use of folk tunes or *penillion*. For all that, their audiences clearly knew no barriers of race or language, and their musical idioms were universal. The relationship of this modern Welsh music to vernacular native culture was a peculiarly elusive one at best. Even so, the musical scene in Wales in the later seventies was a most heartening one. One critic had complained in 1953 that experimental works by composers like Daniel Jones of Swansea were usually performed outside their native land.[19] Twenty-five years later, this no longer held true as difficult works for orchestra, chamber ensembles, and solo instrumentalists, full of chromatic and tonal complexities, frequently received their premières in Wales. In any case, the Welsh were surely not alone in preferring Mozart and Beethoven to the discordances and atonalities of Hindemith, Berg, or Schoenberg. More generally, there was the marked encouragement for music shown by local authorities in Dyfed and elsewhere; there was the superb quality of the Welsh National Youth Orchestra (through which Hoddinot, for example, graduated); there were the rising standards of the BBC Welsh Symphony Orchestra (now sixty-six strong and supported by a £134,000 grant from the Welsh Arts Council in 1978—9) and the vigorous crusading work of the music departments of the university colleges of Bangor, Aberystwyth and Cardiff. There was also scheduled for completion in 1981 a new national concert hall in Cardiff, which would give the principality a major purpose-built centre for the performance of orchestral and other music for the first time. In these and other respects, the Welsh might feel that now they were truly a musical nation, more significantly so than ever in the past.

A more novel sign of musical advance came with the involvement of Welsh folk music with the newly-launched International *eisteddfod* at the attractive town of Llangollen on the river Dee in 1947.[20] It was held annually as a kind of forum for native music, dancing, and other traditional art forms for visitors of many countries. This festival was under the musical direction of W. S. Gwynn Williams, a distinguished musician and a leading authority on Welsh folk song. It enabled traditional folk airs, some of them long buried in remote rural communities, to flourish as part of a wider resurgence of folk art. Competitions for children's and youth choirs were added in 1953; subsequently international choirs attended, originating from as far afield as Los Angeles and Kiev. Here at Llangollen, at least, Welsh culture and a wider international movement in fostering the arts appeared to be happily reconciled for mutual enrichment.

Despite the tension and the passion aroused by the decline in the Welsh language and the increasingly English tone of the Anglo-Welsh milieu, the

---

[19] John Stuart Williams, 'Music and the Composer in Wales', *The Welsh Anvil: Yr Einion*, V (July 1953), pp. 42—7.

[20] See article by Dr Sydney Northcote, *Carnarvon and Denbigh Herald*, 5 July 1957.

existence of an institution like the International *eisteddfod* showed that these matters need not be taken too tragically. On the whole, passionate concern with the Welsh language in this period retained a sense of proportion. It remained constructive and non-violent. Instead of taking refuge in a kind of Welsh fortress, a form of cultural apartheid, most Welsh writers and artists felt anxious to participate in the wider world of artistic experiment and experience that linked the British, European, and north Atlantic communities. For all their legitimate anxiety about the language, Welsh artists shed much of their introspection, and their art benefited accordingly; thus, authors such as Euros Bowen turned to European traditions such as those of the French symbolists instead of drawing exclusively from the familiar values and forms of rural Welsh life.

There were organizations which strove to create a kind of Welsh Gaeltacht like that in the west of Ireland, in which a closed society would conduct every aspect of its life through the Welsh language. Stronger efforts would be made to ensure that homes that came up on the market were bought by Welsh-speaking families instead of being bought up by wealthier immigrants, often from the Midlands, sometimes interested largely in property speculation or the status prestige of maintaining a 'second home' in some Welsh wilderness. The effort of the *Adfer* society, based on Bangor, to preserve the Welshness of local communities by legislation on house purchase, or else by direct community action, aroused the sympathy of many who were not nationalists; but the general attempt to create a kind of Welsh-speaking Bantustan, based on the separate but equal development of the Welsh race, seemed to most to be a kind of illusion or chimera. More hopeful would be attempts to relate a continuing, living Welsh culture to a framework of experience that was inescapably nation- and continent-wide, in which the Welsh were subjected to the same kind of cultural exposure and stimulation undergone by other small, rural-based communities. The Gaeltacht, after all, had not saved the Irish language; its fortunes were at a much lower ebb than those of Welsh. It was not clear how the policies of *Adfer* would protect the Welsh language from the twentieth century either.

A different kind of approach thus seemed to be required—and this meant applying a political approach to the cultural problems of the language and its literature. Underlying, and increasingly dominating this new, more affluent, more secular, more realistic but also more anglicized society was a growing argument about the political and governmental destiny of Wales. The argument picked up momentum in the mid-sixties; it was still exceptionally vigorous in the late seventies. The apparently dead cause of Welsh self-government rose, like Lazarus, from its entombment. Whether a living Welsh community could survive, whether its way of life would have any meaningful existence without the creation of a Welsh state (or at least without some drastic modification of the framework of the United Kingdom) preoccupied more and more thoughtful people in this period. It chimed in with a wider concern to protect local cultures, small communities, and a sense of the intimate and the known against the threat of the 'curse of bigness'. In part at least, the threat to Wales appeared to consist of the challenges posed by the sheer fact of size in the modern world. Thus it was that this new society, and these cultural forces, inspired a new concern with Welsh political nationalism and with radical forms of devolution in government and decision-making. It led on to a new and exciting debate on the meaning and future of the Welsh identity.

CHAPTER 13

NATIONALISM AND DEVOLUTION

In 1945, and for several years afterwards, Welsh nationalism seemed to be as dead as the druids. Self-government in any form aroused little more than derision among most of the public. There appeared to be little in Wales to parallel the powerful force of insular nationalism in Eire, with its new pressure for republican status (fulfilled in 1949) and for an ending of the partition of Ulster so that a united, self-governing Ireland could be created. There was, in short, no Welsh de Valera and no Welsh Sinn Fein. Nor did Welsh nationalism even show the vitality of the Scottish National Party north of the border, which at least had returned Dr R. D. McIntyre at a by-election in 1945 at Motherwell. At the general election in 1945, eight Plaid Cymru candidates stood, mainly academics or intellectuals who enjoyed a somewhat ethereal relationship to the hard realities of party politics. They included scholarly figures like Professor Daniel and Ambrose Bebb. Seven of these lost their deposits, most of them in humiliating circumstances. Only in the university did Plaid Cymru manage a respectable proportion of the vote; even here, Professor Gruffydd, the sitting Liberal, gained 74 per cent of the votes cast. At no level in Welsh life, other than in the non-political realms of creative literature, did Plaid Cymru seem to make much impact. Its major figure, Saunders Lewis, was now in disillusioned, even embittered seclusion. The president of the party, elected in 1945, was an articulate young Aberystwyth and Oxford graduate, Gwynfor Evans, a pacifist, and leading Welsh Independent. The candidate for Merioneth, he had yet to make his name. Political nationalism seemed an inevitable, almost predestined, victim of a process of integration through which the economic and political pressures of wartime, allied to the euphoria of victory over the Axis powers, brough the nations that made up the United Kingdom even closer together and re-inforced their common patriotism and loyalty to Crown and parliament.

Wales, like Britain generally after 1945, was governed by a Labour Party which laid massive emphasis on centralization in economic and social planning, and which regarded the maximum degree of integration of the British Isles as vital for balanced industrial growth and regional development. The trade unions ignored national or linguistic boundaries in the cause of workers' solidarity. The dominant figure of the Labour movement in Wales, Aneurin Bevan, the new Minister of Health, was passionate in his hostility to any form of devolution that might look like a surrender to nationalism. He was also fiercely aware that the English-speaking population of the coalfield formed by far the largest section of the nation, and was determined to fight off any suggestion of domination by a small Welsh-speaking middle-class élite drawn mainly from the rural hinterland. On the other hand, James Griffiths, Minister of National Insurance, due to enter the Cabinet as Colonial Secretary in 1950, was a staunch advocate of Welsh devolution and pressed the cause of a Secretary of State. The Labour government of 1945–51, however, made few gestures of concession to national sentiment in Wales. There was, as has been seen, some recognition of Wales as a distinct entity in the nationalized industries such as the formation of the Wales Gas Board. Conversely, no such approach was adopted in the publicly-owned electricity industry, which was divided up into two boards, one covering south Wales, the other spanning the north and Merseyside. James Griffiths circulated a note to the Cabinet on 17 December 1946 protesting about these decisions. 'The proposals to divide Wales in the Electricity Bill will be criticised both on grounds of National sentiment and on the grounds that they provide an arbitrary division of areas which, for other administrative purposes, are treated as a single unit.'[1] But his plea that Wales and Monmouthshire be constituted under a single Area Board went unheeded by the Cabinet.

On a wider front, demands from the Welsh Labour members, represented by D. R. Grenfell and W. H. Mainwaring, that a Secretary of State be created so that Wales might have a ministerial voice in the Cabinet, were brushed aside. Attlee declared that a Welsh Office would be an 'unnecessary duplication' of administration. A Cabinet paper drafted by Herbert Morrison in January 1946 argued comprehensively against a Welsh Secretary of State on the lines of the Scottish.[2] He cited, as Neville Chamberlain had done in 1938, the separate legal and administrative tradition in Scotland. He also argued that administration in Wales would deteriorate in quality if a new Welsh Office were created. 'Wales could not carry a cadre of officials of the highest calibre and the services of high English officials would no longer be available.' In any case, the Secretary of State would have no responsibility for economic affairs. 'The proper remedy for Wales, as for Scotland, is to ensure that they both form part of a single economic plan for the whole country and are not thrown back on their own sectional resources.' He rejected even the modest proposal for a permanent Advisory Council for Wales and Monmouthshire. 'It is difficult to devise a plan by which such a Council would not become either a dead letter or a dilatory nuisance.' In the *New Statesman,* Kingsley Martin commented sharply on the government's negative approach to Welsh national demands. An official Labour publication at the time of the

[1] Note on the Electricity Bill, 17 December 1946, CP (46) 462 (CAB 129/15)
[2] 'The Administration of Wales and Monmouthshire', 27 January 1946, CP (46) 21 (CAB 129/6).

general election in 1945, had listed five main promises—a Secretary of State, a separate Welsh Broadcasting Corporation, an end to the forced transference of labour from Wales to England, a new north–south Wales trunk road, and a central body to plan and develop the Welsh economy. 'All five have now been turned down in Westminster.'[3]

But demands continued to grow from the Welsh Labour group of MPs and the Welsh Regional Council of Labour, voiced in parliament by such new members as Goronwy Roberts from Caernarfon and George Thomas from Cardiff, and in the party machine by the general secretary, Cliff Prothero, for a wider recognition of the needs of Wales in central government. The Attlee Cabinet was forced to pay heed to them, especially after the Conservatives had pledged themselves to set up a Minister for Welsh Affairs. The question of a Welsh Secretary of State, or of further devolution in some form, was considered in 1948 by the Cabinet's Home Services Committee, of which the three dominant members were Morrison, Bevan, and Griffiths.[4] In the end, despite Bevan's opposition, the committee, in liaison with the Machinery of Government Committee, proposed an advisory council drawn from the local authorities and both sides of industry. It was much the kind of idea that Morrison himself had dismissed in 1946. The precedent of the Scottish Economic Committee was cited, and it was agreed that the new council should deal with cultural as well as with economic questions. On Griffiths's suggestion, the powerful north Wales trade-union leader, Huw T. Edwards, was appointed chairman. On the other hand, the role of the new Council for Wales was a distinctly minor one. Morrison and Bevan vetoed Griffiths's suggestion that the Council be presided over by a minister of Cabinet rank. Morrison described such an appointment as a 'buffer minister' whose presence would not be conducive to efficient government. His Cabinet Paper of October 1948 argued that a ministerial chairman would find himself in 'an embarrassing position' and that 'the difficulties which would arise between the chairman and other Cabinet ministers would strengthen the demand for a Secretary of State for Wales'.[5] The most that would be permitted would be for individual ministers of Cabinet rank to attend meetings of the Council on occasions. For the rest, Griffiths was forced to commend to the House a council whose feeble powers went counter to the main thrust of his argument in the Cabinet committees. The Welsh Council for the next eighteen years proved to be largely 'the dead letter' that Morrison had visualized. Labour's leaders were quite unwilling to go any further. When in 1950 Goronwy Roberts, a younger man of more nationalist outlook, urged the secretary of

[3] New Statesman and Nation, 24 August 1946.

[4] James Griffiths and his Times (Welsh Labour Party, 1978), pp. 41–2.

[5] Memorandum on 'The Administration of Wales and Monmouthshire', CP (48) 228 (CAB 129/30); Conclusions of Cabinet, 15 October, 18 November 1948 (CAB 128/13); correspondence of Morrison and Griffiths, October 1948 (NLW, James Griffiths Papers, C/2/6–11); Morrison's speech to inaugural meeting of Council for Wales, 17 May 1949 (ibid., C/2/31).

the Labour Party, Morgan Phillips, that Labour show more sympathy with the Parliament for Wales movement, he received short shrift.[6]

The Conservative Party was equally committed to a unionist view of Wales, as befitted its traditional stance in the north of Ireland. It was historically an anglicized party; its candidates seldom spoke Welsh, were frequently Anglicans, and viewed Welsh nationalism with a hostile eye. The hopelessness of the Conservative cause in most of the principality after 1945 was shown by the dispatch of young English-speaking products of Eton, Oxford, or the Guards, like so many Foreign Legionaries, to lose their deposits in Welsh constituencies. There was, however, an important change when the Conservatives returned to office in October 1951. Churchill now set up a Ministry of Welsh Affairs, to be held conjointly with the Home Secretaryship. This followed a somewhat vague promise by R. A. Butler in the 'Welsh Day' debate in the Commons on 26 January 1948 that the Conservatives would appoint a minister to act as 'a watchdog' or 'ambassador' on behalf of Welsh interests, a promise he confirmed that October during the Conservatives' annual party conference, held at Llandudno. It was interpreted as part of a Conservative effort to erode what remained of the Liberal vote in north Wales constituencies. But the new Ministry aroused little enthusiasm from a nation so overwhelmingly anti-Conservative in its politics. The first Minister of Welsh Affairs, the Scottish lawyer, Sir David Maxwell-Fyfe, who sat for a Liverpool constituency, was treated with affectionate derision as 'Dai bananas'. More enthusiasm was kindled by his successor in 1954, Gwilym Lloyd George, an authentic Welsh speaker even if his 'National Liberal' credentials had taken him out of his native land to Tyneside. When he was succeeded in January 1957 by Henry Brooke, the Minister of Housing and Local Government, tension between the Ministry and the Welsh nation knew no bounds. It was Brooke who approved the acquisition of the water of the Tryweryn valley in Merioneth by Liverpool and did not intervene to prevent the flooding of this small community despite the passionate hostility aroused in Wales. Every Welsh Labour MP voted against the Tryweryn bill, even anti-nationalists like Ness Edwards. There were constant disputes, too, about the refusal of the Ministry, under Brooke's direction, to endorse proposals from the Council for Wales for the economic development of the country or for the reorganizaing of its governmental system. As has been noted in Chapter 11, Huw T. Edwards resigned as chairman of the council on this account. A suggestion in 1957 that there should be a Secretaryship of State met with short shrift from the Macmillan government. Instead, the little-known Breconshire councillor, D. P. Lewis, was made Minister of State under the title of Lord Brecon. In 1961, the unpopular Brooke was replaced as Minister for Welsh Affairs by Sir Keith Joseph.

[6] Goronwy Roberts to Morgan Phillips, 5 August 1950 (Transport House: Morgan Phillips papers). I owe this reference to Dr Henry Pelling.

On the whole, the thirteen years of Conservative rule from 1951 to 1964, like the Labour years of 1945–51, saw no significant concession to demands in Wales for greater powers of self-government; they served merely to highlight the weaknesses of the existing system in the principality. There was slightly more progress, though not much, in responding to pleas for assistance to the Welsh language. More money was provided for publishing Welsh books; the Welsh Arts Council was set up with increased funds for this purpose and also for such activities as the forming of the Welsh Theatre Company in 1962. A private member's bill, carried by Peter Thomas (Conservative, Conway) in 1959 with all-party support, enabled local authorites to support the national *eisteddfod* from the rates. After pressure from the Welsh Parliamentary Party, a committee was set up by Sir Keith Joseph, under the chairmanship of the eminent lawyer, Sir David Hughes-Parry, to examine the status of the Welsh language in law and government. But this was a modest return, especially in view of the growing decline of the language as revealed in successive censuses.

Yet there were many signs during these years that demands for greater powers of self-government had far from disappeared. Indeed, in the post-war period they increased in momentum. The most important of these was the 'Parliament for Wales' campaign, a body devoted to the modified home rule on the model of the Scottish Covenant movement.[7] It was founded on an all-party basis in 1949 under the auspices of *Undeb Cymru Fydd*, the language pressure-group whose secretary was T. I. Ellis. The president of the movement was Lady Megan Lloyd George, then a Liberal, and it rapidly enlisted the support of many Labour and Liberal spokesmen. Plaid Cymru, also, took a decision to back the campaign and participate in its propaganda— a decision which reflected the political awareness of Gwynfor Evans in contrast to the last-ditch intransigence of the almost apolitical Saunders Lewis. A leading member of Plaid Cymru, Elwyn Roberts, acted as secretary to the movement. Conservatives and even Communists also lent their support. Between 1950 and 1956, the Parliament for Wales campaign made considerable impact on Welsh opinion. In 1955, S. O. Davies (Labour, Merthyr) introduced a private member's bill on behalf of Welsh home rule, though its support in parliament proved derisory. In 1956, Goronwy Roberts (Labour, Caernarfon) presented a petition to parliament which contained 250,000 signatures, many from industrial areas like the Rhondda as well as from rural districts. It enlisted the support of at least five Welsh Labour MPs, Goronwy Roberts, T. W. Jones, and Cledwyn Hughes from Gwynedd, Tudor Watkins (Brecon and Radnor), and the Marxist individualist, S. O. Davies from Merthyr. They aroused the anger of the Labour whips and party officials, and there were threats of party disciplining. Aneurin Bevan (himself

[7] Alan Butt Philip, *The Welsh Question* (Cardiff, 1975), pp. 257–61. See Cledwyn Hughes, 'Westminster should shed its load', *News Chronicle*, 8 February 1956.

a frequent rebel) intervened to prevent a 'witch-hunt'. But the Parliament for Wales movement was too shapeless, broad-based and ill-organized to make permanent headway. Nor did it arouse much interest in the most urban and industrial areas. Members for urban constituencies like George Thomas and James Callaghan in Cardiff, not to mention Aneurin Bevan in Ebbw Vale, were strongly opposed to a quasi-nationalist splinter movement of this kind. Even James Griffiths was opposed to a Welsh parliament, at this stage. By 1956, the Parliament for Wales campaign was struggling, financially deep in the red, and the movement disintegrated.

Nor did Plaid Cymru present a very dangerous challenge to the existing parties. There was some hope from a vigorous campaign fought for the first time in industrial south Wales; in a by-election at Aberdare in December 1946, the Plaid Cymru candidate, Wynne Samuel, a barrister, polled 7,090 votes, 20 per cent of the poll. But there were no further by-elections to keep up this momentum before the next general election was called. In 1950, Plaid Cymru put up only seven candidates; all lost their deposits and they polled only 17,000 votes altogether. In 1951, the party put forward only four candidates (at Aberdare, Llanelli, Rhondda West, and Wrexham), and all did very badly. Clearly the party's thunder, if any, was being stolen at this period by the 'Parliament for Wales' campaign. In 1955, there was certainly some advance, with eleven candidates now fielded and 45,119 votes obtained. In Rhondda West and Llanelli in the south, in Merioneth and Wrexham in the north, the party made some progress, though it was nowhere able to come close to victory. The later fifties saw more headway, fanned by the demands from a Council for Wales for a Welsh Office and by the resignation of Huw T. Edwards, not only from the council but also from the Labour Party, in order to join Plaid Cymru. In October 1959, the party put up twenty candidates. They polled now 77,000 votes, while the average share of the poll gained by each candidate rose also. Deposits were saved at Caernarfon, Merioneth, Anglesey, and Llanelli.

But the party remained a small, largely rural-orientated movement, based on a declining constituency of Welsh speakers. Its social base was particularly limited, if intellectually distinguished. Sixteen of its twenty candidates in 1959 were university graduates, twelve of them from the University of Wales. Ten of them were lecturers or schoolmasters. Among the broad mass of the Welsh people, especially amongst trade unionists and the working-class electorate generally, Plaid Cymru made little impact. Its organization was rudimentary, indeed virtually non-existent in most of English-speaking, urbanized Wales. It remained very much a party of amateurs, seemingly out of place in the real world of the machine politicians and the organization men.

However, a number of issues arose, in themselves somewhat tangential to party politics, and provided Plaid Cymru with added momentum. The first of these was the Tryweryn affair in the late fifties. The decision to submerge the homes of a small community and to hand over the valuable commodity of water to the mighty English corporation of Liverpool, with the Welsh local authorities powerless to affect the decision, aroused much anger in Wales, from those in all parties and in none. But Plaid Cymru derived especial benefit for a time, since the emotive appeal of preserving rural Welsh communities, and also of conserving 'Welsh water' for local benefit rather than have it transferred free of charge to English cities, had clear nationalistic implications. Members of Plaid Cymru were prominent in passive resistance and in demonstrations against the building of the reservoir at Tryweryn. On the other hand, such strength as this brought the party was transient. Its share of the poll in Merioneth in 1959 where Gwynfor Evans was again the candidate was, at 22 per cent, virtually identical with that of 1955. The big battalions won their inevitable victory over local sentiment. The reservoir at Tryweryn was built, just the same.

More productive for the party was the growing concern for the future of the Welsh language, given new edge by the publication of the findings of the 1961 language census. Members of Plaid Cymru, especially in the school-teaching profession, were very active in the movement for the promotion of *Ysgolion Cymraeg* in English-speaking regions such as Glamorgan and Flintshire. There was much protest by party members at the closing of small village schools in rural communities such as the Llŷn peninsula in western Caernarvonshire, which could only add further to the difficulties of the language. A more general theme was the role of the Welsh language in radio and television programmes put out by the BBC. Although there were popular Welsh programmes, notably the daily magazine programme *Heddiw* introduced for some years by Owen Edwards, they formed only a very small proportion of the total output of programmes received in Welsh households. Pressure built up for a separate television service. BBC (Wales) first began to transmit programmes in February 1964, amidst complaint from English speakers that Welsh-speaking producers and broadcasters loomed too large, and from Welsh speakers that they were unable to receive the programmes owing to technical transmission problems. Plaid Cymru was now prominent in advancing demands that Welsh-language programmes (seven hours a week in the first instance) be given a much larger share of broadcasting time and that, when technically feasible, a separate channel be devoted to Welsh-language programmes only. Much controversy dogged the broadcasting media (the BBC and the short-lived commercial WWN) for some time to come.

A far more powerful stimulus than these disparate campaigns was the re-emergence in 1962 of the veteran nationalist, Saunders Lewis, who had been in retirement for some years. In a powerful lecture on BBC radio, *Tynged yr Iaith* (The Fate of the Language), delivered on 13 February 1962, Lewis made a vigorous plea for more assertive methods in upholding the language.[8]

---

[8] Translated in Gerald Morgan, *The Dragon's Tongue* (Cardiff, 1966).

'Success is only possible through revolutionary methods', he declared. The future of the language was more important than self-government. The language alone should form the basis of any viable form of politics or nationalist ideology in Wales. This appeal for a more militant, committed approach to the defence of the language and its use for governmental and official purposes with a status equal or superior to that of English made an immense impact, especially upon students and others of the younger generation. The spectacle of one of the legendary martyrs of 1936 re-emerging from the past to spearhead, or at least to associate himself with, the contemporary struggle for cultural national assertiveness was an inspiring one. The consequence was the formation of a new society during the Plaid Cymru summer school at Pontardulais in 1962. This was the Welsh Language Society, *Cymdeithas yr Iaith Gymraeg*. It soon enlisted the support of hundreds of young members of, or sympathizers with, Plaid Cymru. Later, Saunders Lewis himself agreed to come out of retirement, at least to the extent of acting as its president. It launched its own newspaper, *Tafod y Ddraig*. A totally new chapter in the history of the movement to ensure the survival of the language was now to begin. Relentless, if usually non-violent, pressure was to be exerted on governmental agencies from the Post Office upwards, to ensure that they would be made unworkable unless they gave full recognition to the use of Welsh.[9] There would be powerful consequences for the political and social development of later twentieth-century Wales.

From about 1963 onwards, an entirely new tone was detectable in the forces of Welsh nationalism, cultural and political. The persuasive Fabian tactics of an older pressure-group like *Undeb Cymru Fydd* were by-passed. The new Welsh Language Society achieved dramatic results in enlisting the energies and the idealism of the young, especially among the university student population. Its methods for fighting for the language went far beyond previous tactics of petition and peaceful persuasion. There were frequent mass demonstrations, and the technique of the 'sit-in' was adopted. Beginning with a blockade of traffic in Aberystwyth in February 1963, in protest at the refusal of the Post Office there to use Welsh-language notices and official forms, a series of more militant demonstrations were held in government offices, central and local, throughout Wales. Local taxation officers, borough treasurers, libraries, and universities found the peaceful tenor of their lives disrupted from 1963 onwards by groups of angry, noisy, and determined Welsh-speaking students, demanding equal status for their native language and prepared to use all methods short of overt violence to force their point home, whatever the consequences in terms of fines or imprisonment.

The tactics of the society were not always so peaceful or non-violent. Its leading members frequently appeared in the courts (often before magistrates

[9] Colin H. Williams, 'Non-Violence and the Development of the Welsh Language Society, 1962–c.1974', *Welsh History Review*, vol. 8, No. 5 (December 1977), pp. 426–55.

highly sympathetic to their cause and prepared to show the maximum of leniency compatible with their duties), charged with sabotage or damage to property. They climbed up television masts, they defaced public buildings, they placarded and sometimes invaded the studios of the BBC and commercial television, they disrupted the academic activities of the university colleges. Most familiar of all, they assaulted road signs with their paint brushes, white or tarred, to obliterate English names such as Newtown or Lampeter; sometimes, far less creditably, signs relating to road safety were similarly abused. By 1968, the Welsh language had become political dynamite in a manner inconceivable six years earlier at the time of Saunders Lewis's historic lecture. Hitherto non-political, peaceful branches of *Urdd Gobaith Cymru* were now taken over by angry militants zealous in the cause of their language. There was even a breakaway movement from the Women's Institute movement, *Merched y Wawr*. The apolitical national *eisteddfod* became an annual forum where members of the Welsh-language movement would vent their fury on English institutions and English-based politicians. The amiable figure of George Thomas, appointed Secretary of State for Wales in 1968 very much as the representative of English-speaking south-east Wales in contrast to his predecessor Cledwyn Hughes, became the special target of what came popularly to be called 'the Welsh extremist'.[10] This extremism usually took the form of angry words or the dexterous use of whitewash. But there was an uglier side, with the small fanatical fringe of the 'Free Wales Army' who conducted parades and manoeuvres and paid homage to the militant exploits of the Irish Republican Army and the Provisional Sinn Fein. The life of Cledwyn Hughes was threatened at the Aberavon *eisteddfod* in 1966. There were alarming bomb explosions in government and other public buildings in Wales, and it seemed only a matter of time before deaths took place. One small child had his hands blown off by such a bomb. In the end, the Free Wales Army, from which Plaid Cymru and the Welsh Language Society strongly dissociated themselves, lost momentum when two of its leading saboteurs were imprisoned.

By 1968, the Welsh-language movement was at its zenith. It could claim partial credit for triumphs such as the Welsh Language Act of 1967 giving Welsh equal validity with English, and a far more sensitive response from government departments than had been achieved by the peaceful petitioning of pre-1962. Cledwyn Hughes's warm reaction to the Hughes-Parry Report was symbolic. Welsh youth was now caught up emotionally in the heady rebellion of student youth all over Europe and north America. With the riotous students of Berkeley and Columbia, the Sorbonne and Nanterre, with the terrors of the mass bombings on north Vietnam and the heady spring days of freedom in Czechoslovakia, there was no shortage of idealistic causes to fire the imagination of students and schoolchildren in Wales. In truth, the

[10] Cf. Ned Thomas, 'The George Thomas Era', *Planet* 1 (August–September 1970), pp. 4–8.

Welsh-language movement had virtually nothing in common with any of these overseas movements; but in so far as it inspired the young and seemed to appeal to a traditional folk culture in contrast to the shoddiness and false glamour of commercialized capitalism, it helped speed on militancy. By the late sixties, there was a thriving Welsh pop culture, with a booming sale in Welsh records and a new adulation for folk singers such as Dafydd Iwan whose songs were overtly political and strongly anti-English. It was less clear now that exposure to a wider world would extinguish the Welsh language. On the contrary, the example of student demonstrations and riots in other lands might make its defenders the more aggressive, more aware of their kinship to student protesters everywhere. When it was announced that Prince Charles would be invested as *soi-disant* Prince of Wales at Caernarfon Castle in July 1969, much as the former Edward VIII had been in 1911, the derision of nationalists knew no bounds. The new Prince had no connection whatever with Wales. He was then a student at Cambridge, although a somewhat artificial term of 'study' at Aberystwyth was fitted into the summer term of 1969 and he had to undergo a crash course in the Welsh tongue. On the other hand, it should be said that the Prince attracted much public sympathy by the dignity with which he confronted a difficult political situation imposed on him, while a fluent speech in Welsh that he delivered at the Urdd *eisteddfod* redounded very much to his credit.

The impact of all this excitement on Plaid Cymru was somewhat indirect. At first they had been suspicious of Saunders Lewis's message and openly critical of his view that the language was fundamentally more important than self-government. After all, the party had made some inroads into English-speaking areas such as Aberdare and Rhondda West; a growing element in the party activists were working-class representatives of these communities, very different in cultural and social background from Gwynfor Evans and other long-standing leaders. In the general elections of October 1964 and March 1966, Plaid Cymru somewhat kept its distance from the Welsh-language movement. The years since 1959 had not been happy ones for Plaid Cymru, with its inability to make significant party capital out of the Tryweryn affair, and a growing fragmentation in its membership. In the October 1964 election, the party actually put up no less than 23 candidates, three more than in 1959. But they did badly in general. Only 69,000 votes were polled and the share of the poll secured by each candidate fell from 10 per cent in 1959 to 8 per cent five years later. With the Labour Party regaining its strength and returning to power with a programme highly attractive to Welsh electors, including the setting up of a Secretaryship of State, Plaid Cymru was left in somewhat frustrated impotence. The only notable improvement in the party's fortunes took place in Carmarthen, although even here Gwynfor Evans still lost his deposit.

In March 1966, Plaid Cymru, still counting the cost of the poor results of

1964, was faced with another election which strained its resources to the utmost. In the circumstances, it did well to field as many as twenty candidates, and maintain more or less the same share of the poll. In all, 61,000 votes were gained, 4.3 per cent of the Welsh total. Gwynfor Evans again improved his position in Carmarthen, winning 7,000 votes, 16 per cent of the poll. There was also some encouragement to be found in Aberdare, Caerphilly, and Rhondda West in the coalfield. But on the whole, the 1966 election again left the impression that Plaid Cymru was still a small, fringe movement of extremists, with no real prospect of winning a parliamentary seat. It seemed almost a political irrelevance. The upsurge of the Welsh-language movement had, if anything, confused the party, and in particular blunted its appeal to anglicized south Wales.

The situation was totally transformed in July 1966 when a by-election took place in Carmarthen shortly after the general election. Here, if anywhere, was a chance of a real breakthrough. Plaid Cymru had its strongest possible candidate available, Gwynfor Evans himself. He was resident in the constituency as a self-employed market-gardener at Llangadog, he was an alderman on the county council, he was very much at the height of his intellectual and charismatic powers. The Labour Party in Carmarthen was in some disarray, after the death from cancer of Lady Megan Lloyd George and a feeling that perhaps she ought not to have been a candidate in the election three months earlier. Overall, as Sir Harold Wilson recorded in his memoirs, the climate was unpromising for Labour, with acute economic difficulties, strikes and a sterling crisis so soon after a triumphant election.[11] For disillusioned voters in Carmarthen, angry with the economic failures of the Labour government, with the effects of the new Select Employment Tax on rural service industry, and with the attitude of the Labour-dominated county council towards rural schools, Plaid Cymru offered an attractive, non-Conservative alternative. Pit closures in the Gwendraeth and Amman valleys in the east of the constituency were another factor. Even so, when all these elements are taken into account, the electoral victory by Gwynfor Evans, by over 1,500 votes, with a poll of 16,179 votes (39 per cent) over a strongly nationalistic Labour candidate, Gwilym Prys Davies, was too sweeping to be explained solely by reference to purely local or fortuitous factors. The swelling tide of national consciousness since the early sixties had needed a political outlet. The return of Gwynfor Evans to Westminster as Plaid Cymru's first-ever MP provided it. Henceforth, Plaid Cymru became credible, an appealing alternative to an apparently ageing, timorous, and entrenched Labour Party, which showed all the symptoms of too long a monopoly of power. Gwynfor Evans himself, once he had been allowed by an indulgent Speaker to take his oath in Welsh, proved to be an effective spokesman for Wales, dignified, courteous, but with a shrewd eye for the prospects

[11] Harold Wilson, *The Labour Government, 1964–70* (Pelican Books ed., 1974), p. 328.

of ventilating the manifold grievances of his nation.

After the Carmarthen by-election, Labour viewed the challenge of Plaid Cymru with great apprehension. It was paralleled by the rise of the Scottish National Party (SNP) in Scotland, notably the return of Mrs Winifred Ewing in the Hamilton by-election in November 1967, and the capture of many local authorities by the Scottish Nationalists. It was noted that the SNP were as powerful in Cumbernauld new town and industrial areas such as Strathclyde as in remote rural communities in the highlands. Plaid Cymru benefited from this nationalist advance in Scotland—and added to it, mightily. Two by-elections took place in Wales over the next two years. In each case, Labour found itself vulnerable in its own working-class valley strongholds as it had never been at any stage in the past fifty years. In March 1967, in a by-election in Rhondda West (where in the general election, twelve months earlier, Labour had polled nearly 80 per cent of the vote, and all other candidates had ignominiously lost their deposits) Plaid Cymru cut Labour's majority from 17,000 to only 2,306, a huge swing of nearly 30 per cent. The potential of Plaid Cymru for appealing to working-class resentment of a stagnant economy, the closure of most of the local collieries, mounting unemployment, and the slow progress of the government's advance factory programme was clearly shown. Neither Welsh self-government nor the status of the language seems to have played much part in the campaign.

At Caerphilly in July 1968 there was another sensation. Here Plaid Cymru's candidate, unlike the trade unionist selected by Rhondda West, an academic, Dr Philip Williams, born in the constituency but now a highly qualified university physicist at Aberystwyth, fought a campaign of resource and quality. By contrast, Labour offered a stale programme, an uninspired candidate, and a run-down party machine. The Labour majority again came tumbling down, from 21,000 in 1966 to only 1,874 now, a swing to Plaid Cymru of nearly 40 per cent. Once again, unemployment and local economic grievances, such as the closure of a major pit at Bargoed, formed the core of Plaid Cymru's campaign. Welsh self-government figured only modestly, while the activities of the Welsh Language Society were largely suppressed in so anglicized an area. Obviously now any Labour seat in Wales, however huge the previous majority, was at risk. Plaid Cymru seemed to offer something new, youthful and dynamic in contrast to the disillusion of the Harold Wilson era. It was believed that the veteran James Griffiths was persuaded to stay on as member for Llanelli until the 1970 election to avoid another difficult by-election in which Carwyn James, a celebrated stand-off half for the local rugby team and a master at Llandovery College, would be the Plaid candidate. Even a 26,000 majority at Llanelli, it seemed, could no longer be taken on trust. One unduly apprehensive miners' official told Griffiths, 'You had better realize that all your seats are marginal now'. [12]

[12] J. Griffiths to R. H. S. Crossman, 2 December 1967 (Griffiths Papers, C/3/16).

In the face of these extraordinary events, the established political parties were somewhat at a loss. The Conservatives adhered faithfully to their traditional unionism. Indeed, their spokesman in the House on Welsh affairs from 1964 to 1970 was David Gibson-Watt, who sat for the English constituency of Hereford although he was admittedly descended from an old Radnorshire landowning family. The Liberals kept up their traditional commitment to Welsh and Scottish home rule; but Plaid Cymru was stealing their thunder and (as in Carmarthen) their votes. But it was the response of the Labour Party and the government that would be most crucial. Labour had, of course, set up the new Secretaryship of State for Wales in October 1964, with the much-respected veteran James Griffiths as first occupant or 'charter secretary' in Harold Wilson's words. He was backed up by Goronwy Roberts as Minister of State, a long-established sympathizer with self-government since his involvement in the *Gwerin* movement in the thirties. There were expectations that a real extension of governmental devolution might follow. In particular, there was known to be an extensive reform of the local government system in England and Wales—the Redcliffe-Maud Committee was shortly to be set up in this connection—and it was believed that a major shake-up of the governmental structure, including perhaps an elective Welsh assembly to crown the edifice, might result.

But by the time of the Carmarthen by-election in July 1966, it was clear that the expectations built up by the Welsh Office had not been fulfilled. Indeed, it had caused surprise when Labour had originally announced its support for a Secretaryship of State back in 1959. This was a marked change of policy compared with Attlee's time, which owed much to the presence of James Griffiths as deputy-leader of the party at that period. Griffiths had chaired the policy-making committee which had included a Welsh Secretary of State in the 1959 manifesto *Forward with Labour*. This proposal owed much to the effective case for a Welsh Office previously argued by the Council for Wales under Huw T. Edwards's chairmanship. In addition, the Welsh Labour Group, headed by Cledwyn Hughes, had held key meetings with Gaitskell, while James Callaghan became a convert when he saw how a Scottish Secretary of State, sitting in the Cabinet, could gain priority for the Forth Bridge instead of one crossing the Severn. Aneurin Bevan, who had resisted the proposal for a Welsh secretaryship, took his defeat with good grace. The Welsh Office began life in 1964 with a fair range of powers. It took over housing and local government, road transport, and aspects of local planning. In 1969 it was to embrace health and agriculture as well, with education shortly to follow. The department's 'oversight powers' meant that other departments had to consult it on the application of their functions and on appointments to public bodies in Wales. In its early years, the Welsh Office was given temporary accommodation in Whitehall; in 1971 its growing status was confirmed when it largely moved to Cardiff. The enhanced stature of the

Welsh Office was illustrated in 1967 when the relocation of the Royal Mint was decided in favour of Llantrisant in Glamorgan, rather than Scotland (as argued by William Ross, the Scottish Secretary) or Washington New Town in Durham (as demanded by Anthony Greenwood, the Minister of Housing and Local Government). The issue was finally thrashed out in full Cabinet, after a Cabinet committee had reported in favour of Llantrisant and James Callaghan (then the Chancellor, and a Cardiff MP) had indicated his support. The episode strengthened Cledwyn Hughes's position in the Wilson Cabinet, as Welsh Secretary of State.

Even so, the new Welsh Office could not be a powerful department. Its administrative cadres of civil servants had to be recruited from a wide area. In 1967 the new department simply did not have the staff equipped to produce the new economic plan for Wales, and the aid of outsiders had to be enlisted. It was much restricted in trying to evolve new or independent functions, inevitably so perhaps since the affairs of England and Wales remained so intimately interwoven. The Welsh Office was more modest in its activities than was its long-established Scottish counterpart. It had no global budget, little executive force. It had no power over key decisions of economic planning which were still made by ministers and civil servants in Whitehall. The work of its economic advisory council was slowed down by toothcombing Treasury officials. It was really a co-ordinating department in Wales for policies conceived elsewhere. For all the good intentions of its founders, the Welsh Office managed to fan the flames of nationalist discontent, though admittedly the latter was probably beyond reconciliation by this time.

On a wide range of issues, the Labour government succeeded only in adding to discontent in Wales between 1966 and 1968, at the time when Plaid Cymru was most buoyant and aggressive.[13] There was, it is true, some concession to nationalist feeling on the language, an area where Labour had to be careful not to offend its supporters in industrial and anglicized districts. The Hughes-Parry Report on the status of the Welsh language won general endorsement for the principle that the language should enjoy 'equal validity' with English for official, governmental, and legal purposes. The 1967 Welsh Language Act carried this through on to the statute book. On the other hand, the committee's proposals that Welsh be given a special status in appointments to posts in central and local government, and that priority be given to Welsh speakers in this connection, foundered on the protests of the English-speaking majority. Beyond this, there was little that the Welsh Office, hamstrung by centralist pressures in government, could show. The plan for a new town for mid-Wales near Caersws, originally sponsored by James Griffiths, proved controversial as was noted in Chapter 11, and was finally dropped in 1967 in favour of the expansion of Newtown in Montgomeryshire and other mid-Wales towns. The new Welsh Economic Council set up in 1967

[13] Cf. 'Inaction for Wales', *Socialist Commentary* (June 1967), and *Western Mail*, 23 June 1967.

was again an advisory body whose views were at the mercy of the Treasury and the London government. The much-criticized Council for Wales had been replaced merely by another nominated, non-elected body. The deterioration in the economy that set in from mid-1966 had especial impact in Wales where the subsidiary industries that the land tended to attract were the first to be cut back in the aftermath of trade recession and 'squeezes' on credit. Unemployment in the mining valleys as well as in some rural areas, soared to over 10 per cent. This was a central theme in the Plaid Cymru campaigns in Rhondda West and Caerphilly in 1967–8. In addition, the general policy of deflation pursued by the Treasury, especially under the regime of Roy Jenkins from 1968 to 1970, while having a most positive effect on the balance of payments and the external strength of sterling (both 'blown off course' in July 1966), had also somewhat handicapped the establishment of new industry in Wales as in other geographically peripheral areas.

The main problems of the government, however, concerned the fabric of government and were partly of their own making. Cledwyn Hughes, appointed Secretary of State in 1966, was a nationally-minded Welsh-speaking Welshman from Anglesey, and a good democrat concerned about the lack of adequate public discussion of Welsh affairs. He was anxious to meet the nationalist challenge with a positive extension of self-government to Wales. Even before the Carmarthen by-election, the Welsh Council of Labour had approved in May 1966, a demand for an elected council for Wales, and prominent Labour figures like Gwilym Prys Davies were pressing the idea. In the original draft of his white paper on local government (December 1966), Cledwyn Hughes had proposed an ambitious scheme for a Welsh regional council. In addition to rationalizing the new larger Welsh counties that were eventually to be created, he sought to set up an elected council as the apex of a new system, and to legislate, independently of England and Scotland. This produced a fierce clash in Cabinet with Richard Crossman who wanted to bring Wales within the terms of the Redcliffe-Maud Committee on local government: Cledwyn Hughes won this encounter. Crossman thereafter gave him staunch support, and urged that a Welsh 'Council or Parliament' be set up, as part of a wider scheme for decentralization and an extension of popular self-government, including new 'city regions'.

But there was much resistance from major figures in the Cabinet. The Scottish members were deeply hostile. In the end, Cledwyn Hughes was allowed only to put forward a form of co-opted council, the Economic Council for Wales, yet another advisory body as has been seen. Crossman and Barbara Castle were critical of this decision, but they had the fairness to recognize that the blame lay not with Cledwyn Hughes but rather with William Ross and other colleagues in the Cabinet and with south Wales Labour MPs like Ness Edwards who resisted to the death any form of devolution.[14] The Cabinet's

---

[14] G. Prys Davies, memorandum on 'The Political Situation in Wales', November 1967

Devolution Committee, which Crossman had managed to have set up, yielded nothing. The government's decision to retain the sternly centralist Willie Ross at the Scottish Office and to replace Cledwyn Hughes at the Welsh Office in early 1968 with George Thomas, a relentless opponent of nationalism, confirmed the position that Labour and its Prime Minister were adopting. With hindsight, the failure of the Cabinet to endorse Cledwyn Hughes's entirely practical scheme for an elected council in 1967 seemed to have been a lost opportunity, perhaps a fatal one. A real form of governmental devolution could have been introduced, relatively uncontroversially, as part of a wider scheme for reorganizing local government. When Labour did present a scheme for devolution to the Welsh people twelve years later, a remodelling of the county councils had already taken place. Devolution in 1979, unlike that visualized in 1967, seemed to the electors merely the creation of another expensive and superfluous tier of local government, rather than the natural outgrowth of the extension of local decision-making and of democratic accountability.

But the party had to produce something more positive after Carmarthen, Rhondda West, and Caerphilly. It is true that support for Plaid Cymru seemed to wane in 1969–70 as signs of economic improvement occurred.[15] The balance of payments went back into surplus and the more rigorous measures of deflation could be reversed. As was noted in Chapter 11, regional industrial policies were given a new impetus in the late sixties, including a new emphasis on service employment. In 1969–70 regional development policies reached new heights of activity. In that year, £38,600,000 were paid out to industry in the form of investment grants, £11,700,000 in the promotion of local employment, and a further £16,600,000 in the form of Regional Employment Premiums and additional payments under Selective Employment Tax. The sixty-two government advance factories set up since 1964 were now beginning to be occupied and to start work. In addition to this partial recovery of the economy, the mass emotion aroused by the investiture of the Prince of Wales at Caernarfon Castle was a useful weapon for the Labour government in deflating Plaid Cymru. After all, most of the Welsh were royalists, too. Prince Charles's appearance as a student at Aberystwyth attracted the usual enthusiasm from flag-waving citizens, mostly female. Unionist sentiment was markedly reinforced.

But more had to be done on the governmental side to meet adequately the challenge posed by the nationalists. The decision in 1967 to set up yet another nominated council had provoked general dissatisfaction. Pressure was exerted by younger Welsh members of the government, John Morris and

---

(Griffiths Papers, C/3/14); Richard Crossman, *The Diaries of a Cabinet Minister, Volume Two* (London, 1976), p. 377 (12 June 1967). Here and elsewhere, I am indebted to Lord Cledwyn of Penrhos for valuable information.

[15] Gwynoro Jones, *The Record Put Straight* (Carmarthen, 1973).

Elystan Morgan, junior ministers at the Defence and Home Offices, in particular, for something more ambitious. They appear to have been joined in 1968 by James Callaghan, formerly a strong opponent of devolution but now, as Home Secretary, interested in reorganizing local government, not least with the implications for regional government likely to accrue from Britain's future membership of the European Common Market.[16] There was the forth-coming Redcliffe-Maud Report in May 1969 with proposals for a radical overhaul of the local government system as it had endured since 1888. Most powerful of all, it appears that the government, from Harold Wilson downwards, were truly shaken by the near-disaster for Labour at the Caer-philly by-election: George Thomas, the Secretary of State, was, accord-ing to Crossman, terrified, not least by the spectacle of the Welsh regional organiser Emrys Jones sitting alone in the deserted Caerphilly committee rooms on the very eve of the poll.[17] In fact, Emrys Jones himself was a keen devolutionist and was striving to extend the less centralist emphasis of the Welsh Regional Council of Labour under Cliff Prothero from 1947 to 1966. Unlike Prothero, he wanted the Regional Council to concern itself with policy as well as with organization.

These various factors resulted in the appointment in the early autumn of 1969 of a royal commission on the constitution, under the chairmanship of the economic journalist, Geoffrey (later Lord) Crowther. It had wide and exceptionally vague terms of reference, which could include the role of the Ombudsman and almost every conceivable aspect of the working of central and local government. But clearly its main brief was to consider the prospects for governmental devolution in Scotland and Wales. Its members included two Welshmen, Sir Ben Bowen Thomas and Alun Talfan Davies, both Welsh-speaking with strong associations with Aberystwyth University College, and both known to be highly sympathetic to Welsh self-government. There seemed for the first time a theoretical prospect of home rule becoming a major issue for the first time since *Cymru Fydd* in the 1890s. But it was highly theoretical at this stage. The Labour Party went through much internal controversy in producing its evidence before the Crowther Commission. There was intense division within the Welsh Council of Labour, and some criticism of the way in which Transport House in London was alleged to be trying to influence the evidence to be given by Labour's local spokesmen in Cardiff. In the end, the Welsh Council of Labour declared itself in favour of an elected rather than a nominated assembly, with modest executive and no legislative powers, an assembly that would provide a mild concession to nationalism without impairing the integrity of the United Kingdom. The Welsh Conservatives cut an even more curious figure. Although Edward

---

[16] Personal information, Sir Harold Wilson.

[17] Richard Crossman, *The Diaries of a Cabinet Minister*, vol. iii (London, 1977), p. 145 (18 July 1968).

NATIONALISM AND DEVOLUTION

Heath had declared himself in favour of regional self-government for Scotland at Perth, and Sir Alec Douglas-Home had chaired a Conservative committee which drew up limited plans for a Scottish assembly, the Conservatives in Wales refused to give evidence to the Crowther Commission at all. The party in the principality seemed as un-Welsh as ever.

It was difficult to know at this stage how seriously to take the Crowther Commission. Its findings were slow, its procedures cumbersome. Many observers surmised that the Wilson government viewed it, like so many royal commissions, as a means of smothering discussion of a potentially embarrassing political issue until the report could come out years later when the public was apathetic. At any rate, the government's strategy seemed to work. In 1970, Plaid Cymru suddenly became aware of a loss of momentum. When the general election came in June, although Labour did not do well and the Wilson government unexpectedly fell from power, Plaid Cymru's performance was a grave disappointment compared with the by-elections. This was predictable, perhaps. Apart from the euphoria of by-elections, when the media could focus attention on minority parties and all party organizers and workers could be thrown into one grand campaign effort, Plaid Cymru had not struck firm roots. In local government, the party had done much less well to date than had the SNP in Scotland. Its most ambitious effort had been in the county council elections of April 1970 when fifty-six officially-endorsed candidates had been put up, eighteen of them in Glamorgan. But, in all, only seven were returned in the country as a whole (although it should be noted that in rural areas such as Cardiganshire and Caernarvonshire, many Plaid candidates ran as 'independents' and were elected, sometimes unopposed). Plaid Cymru lost one of the two seats it held on the Glamorgan county council, and one of its three seats in Carmarthenshire. There were a few isolated pockets of strength in the coalfield where powerful ward branches existed, such as Llanfabon ward in Caerphilly and the Gadlys ward of Aberdare. But, in general, Plaid Cymru had plenty of enthusiasm and youthful idealism, but not much to show in terms of organization or votes. In the June 1970 general election, the party fought all thirty-six seats for the first time, following a pre-election pledge by Gwynfor Evans. It did by no means badly. Plaid Cymru candidates polled in all 175,016 votes, 11.5 per cent of the Welsh total. They gained over 30 per cent of the vote in Aberdare, Carmarthen, and Caernarfon, and over 25 per cent in four others. This was far from unimpressive, and a system of proportional representation would have reflected the fact. Yet the party finished up, under the 'first past the post' system, with no seats, twenty-five lost deposits, and the shattering defeat of Gwynfor Evans at Carmarthen. Another blow was that J. E. Jones, a senior party organizer, died in a car crash during the campaign. For Plaid Cymru, 1970 was a turning-point at which Welsh politics obstinately refused to turn. It seemed to be the same fringe party of amateurs, outgunned by the big battalions.

Labour did lose ground in Wales in 1970, but not to Plaid Cymru. Four seats were lost to the Conservatives, all by narrow margins. Of these, Cardiff North, Conway, and Monmouth had been won from the Conservatives only as recently as 1966. Pembrokeshire also went Conservative, due to a split in the local party where Desmond Donnelly, once a Bevanite and now very right wing, had resigned from the party and formed his own New Democratic movement. In Merthyr, there was another shock, when to the stupefaction of the pundits, the eighty-two-year-old veteran, S. O. Davies, refused to resign on grounds of age and defeated the official candidate, Tal Lloyd of the Engineers, by a large majority of over 7,000. The individuality of Merthyr politics persisted.[18] Even so, the pattern of politics in Wales, if not in Britain, was generally confirmed in June 1970. Labour ended up with twenty-seven seats out of thirty-six, with the Conservatives holding seven and the Liberals one. Labour was still overwhelmingly in the ascendancy in the politics of Wales.

There were observers who speculated on the coming death of Welsh nationalism after 1970. It seemed as if Labour would resume its traditional role in Wales as the party of protest and reform, now that the Conservatives under Edward Heath were back again in office. There were promising issues for Labour spokesmen such as local unemployment (the Welsh rate rose from 3.4 per cent in June 1970 to 5.8 per cent in January 1972), and the higher cost of school milk. In the local government elections of May 1971, Labour had extraordinary gains in borough seats, even in such unlikely areas as the affluent middle-class suburb of Whitchurch in Cardiff. Eleven seats were gained in Cardiff, nine in Newport (giving Labour control) and four in Barry. The old solidarity with the trade unions was reinforced by Labour's support for the national miners' strike which began in January 1972 and its much more formidable sequel, the miners' strike of February 1974 which led to a three-day week and saw the downfall of the Conservative government under Edward Heath. There was much derision at the Conservative Secretary of State of Wales, Peter Thomas, sitting as a member for the London constituency of Hendon South. Meanwhile the Crowther Commission (renamed Kilbrandon when Crowther died and was replaced by this Scottish peer) pursued its slow and deliberate path betwen 1970 and 1973, with only vague hopes that a new step forward towards self-government might result.

But Welsh nationalism, cultural and political, was far from dead. Pressure continued to mount on behalf of new recognition for the Welsh language, especially in education in the light of the recommendations of the 1967 Gittins Report. There were growing signs of nationalist fervour amongst university students, for instance in demands for hostels reserved for Welsh speakers, to which the authorities at Aberystwyth and Bangor finally acceded. The quantity and quality of Welsh-language programmes put out by the BBC and

18 See Alun Morgan's article in *Morgannwg* xxii (1978), 61–81, on this election.

HTV continued to attract fierce controversy; demands grew for the new fourth channel to be given over to the Welsh language alone, a proposal which many television producers viewed with much misgiving. Politically, Plaid Cymru was far from moribund, as was seen in another by-election, at Merthyr Tydfil in April 1972 after the death of S. O. Davies. Here, Ted Rowlands retained the seat for Labour (or perhaps won it back), but with a majority of only 3,710. Emrys Roberts, for Plaid Cymru, polled 37 per cent of the vote and his poll was 11,852 in all. Evidently, the power of Plaid Cymru to appeal to radical, working-class sentiment amongst the socialist voters of the valleys was undiminished.

Above all, when the Kilbrandon Report was issued in October 1973, it proved to be very far from the irrelevant document that some had visualized (or hoped) when the commission was appointed four years earlier.[19] On the contrary, devolution for Wales and Scotland became, for the first time since the 1890s perhaps, serious and major political issues. The Kilbrandon Commission itself was divided in mind, as was not unusual with such bodies. Confusingly, four possible schemes of local self-government were offered. Eleven of the thirteen commissioners recommended a legislative assembly for Scotland, rather like the old Stormont in Northern Ireland, and also an elected assembly for Wales but with far more modest, basically executive, powers. They did acknowledge fears expressed in Wales and Scotland (and, indeed, in outlying regions of England such as the north-east) about the growth of centralized power and remoteness of government. They accepted, too, some of the views expressed on the inability of the Scottish and Welsh Offices to meet adequately local or national demands in those nations. However, six of the eleven, including both the Welsh representatives, Bowen Thomas and Talfan Davies, went further and called for a full legislative assembly (or 'Senate') for Wales also, a virtual parliament with its own budget, its own tax-raising powers, and authority over a wide range of subjects, including local government, housing, road and other transport, agriculture and education. Westminster would retain its ultimate control, but its overriding powers would be invoked only 'in exceptional circumstances'. At the same time, all thirteen commissioners rejected 'separatism' and insisted on the maintenance of the unity of the United Kingdom. A rigid federal structure was also firmly rejected. The variety and complexity of the commission's many reports attracted derisive comments from Conservatives, and from south Wales Labour members too. The whole Kilbrandon exercise was dismissed as 'a dead duck' by Leo Abse (Pontypool), a dedicated opponent of Welsh nationalism.[20] But what lodged in the public mind—and created major tactical problems for both Labour and Conservative parties— was the majority call for an elected assembly for Wales, of perhaps one

[19] Report of the Commission on the Constitution, 1973 (Cmnd. 5460).
[20] *Western Mail*, 1 November 1973.

hundred members, with developed executive and perhaps legislative powers. No public inquiry, not even the Speaker's Conference in 1920, had ever gone so far. The apparatus of non-elected, purely advisory, powerless bodies that had served the principality since 1946 might be rudely swept away.

How seriously the Labour Party intended to proceed with the multifarious recommendations offered by Kilbrandon was not clear at first sight. But the general election which followed in February 1974 left the party with no option but to make some kind of imaginative response to the demands of Welsh political nationalism. The Welsh constituencies had been somewhat altered by redistribution since 1970. For instance, Cardiff was now carved up into four constituencies instead of three, whereas the Rhondda, with its declining population, now consisted of only one constituency, instead of two as had been the case since 1918. Interestingly, in that one it was the schoolmaster Alec Jones, not the miners' representative, who was selected as Labour's candidate. The polls in February 1974 did show some real signs that Labour's hold over Wales, so impregnable since 1945 or even 1922, might now be weakening—not in favour of any one party, but to be replaced by a more fragmented pattern. Like the Congress Party in India, or the Social Democrats in Sweden, the Labour Party was suffering from some of the strains and problems of years of monolithic rule. Therefore, while the party emerged as nationally the largest party with 301 seats and was eventually able to form a minority government under the premiership again of Harold Wilson, there were setbacks in Wales.

Labour's share of the poll in Wales fell to under 50 per cent for the first time since the war—to 46.8 per cent of the vote as compared with 51.6 per cent in 1970. Labour now held only twenty-four seats, while the Conservatives' tally rose to eight. Two suburban Cardiff seats were held by the Conservatives, while, rather surprisingly, Pembrokeshire was retained by Nicholas Edwards, now the party's spokesman on Welsh affairs and a descendant of the first Archbishop of Wales. Labour lost three further seats at this election. One, Cardiganshire, had long been marginal. The able barrister Elystan Morgan who had held it for Labour since 1966, faced vigorous opposition from both the Liberals and from Plaid Cymru who much resented his defection from their ranks to join Labour back in 1964. There was a good deal of tactical cross-voting and the result was that Morgan was defeated by the Liberal, Geraint Howells, a farmer. A partial recovery for the Liberals in mid-Wales, one not anticipated by a survey of local opinion carried out at Aberystwyth University College in 1970–1,[21] therefore resulted, although overall the Liberals, with just two seats and only 16 per cent of the vote, were still in feeble condition in Wales.

The real shock lay in Labour's two defeats by Plaid Cymru. Both were in mainly rural Welsh-speaking areas of declining population and high un-

[21] Peter Madgwick and others, *The Politics of Rural Wales* (London, 1972).

employment. In Caernarfon, Goronwy Roberts, the member since 1945, was defeated by Dafydd Wigley, a cost accountant, very much typical of the newer type of technocratic leader of Plaid Cymru, in contrast to the cultural commitment of Saunders Lewis or the nonconformist populism of Gwynfor Evans. In Merioneth, the sitting Labour member was also defeated, by Dafydd Elis Thomas, a college lecturer at Bangor. It was noticeable that Wigley, and even more Elis Thomas, appealed strongly to Welsh radical, even socialist traditions, and placed heavy emphasis on social and economic issues as well as cultural and linguistic. Plaid Cymru, then, was again restored as a credible political force. It claimed two MPs, and almost managed a third when Gwynfor Evans failed by only three votes to recapture Carmarthen. Overall, the party's performance was less impressive. Its progress in the mining valleys had been checked; it had lost ground in Aberdare, Caerphilly, Rhondda, and Merthyr. It had dwindled in urban Wales almost to the point of extinction. Only in four or five mainly rural Welsh-speaking areas did it show strength. But it was seats that mattered. With two parliamentary spokesmen, both soon to show themselves highly capable performers in the House, the party's stature was restored.

With Labour now in a minority and dependent on the goodwill of such minor parties as the Ulster Unionists, the SNP, and Plaid Cymru, it was not surprising that the Labour government now began to take devolution more seriously, and to launch inquiries into ways of implementing some of the proposals offered by the Kilbrandon Commission. A consultative document, *Devolution within the United Kingdom: some Alternatives for Discussion,* was published in June. At the general election in October 1974, every Labour candidate in Wales was clearly committed to some kind of elected council, as an alternative to separatism.[22] It was a policy that reflected a change of heart on the part of such Labour leaders as James Callaghan and Roy Jenkins, as well as the growing influence of devolutionists such as John Morris, Gwilym Prys Davies, and the Welsh regional secretary, J. Emrys Jones. In October 1974, in fact, Labour suffered further shocks. The Conservatives held on to their eight seats with some ease. The Liberals retained Cardiganshire with an almost identical majority of 2,400. Labour's tally of seats fell to twenty-three. In fact, the party's overall share of the Welsh poll improved markedly, rising to 49.5 per cent, with its share of half the Welsh votes almost restored. Majorities in the industrial constituencies of the south were as enormous as ever, while the challenge of Plaid Cymru here had clearly been turned back. In the Rhondda, once fearful of the menace of the nationalists, Labour's majority was over 34,000, back to the astronomic levels of the fifties. In fact, Plaid Cymru mounted a serious challenge in only three of the thirty-six seats—and it won them all. In Caernarfon, Wigley retained the seat with a solid majority of 2,894; Merioneth was held with a majority of 2,592, an increase of 2,000 on

[22] Denzil Davies MP to James Griffiths, 25 September 1974 (Griffiths Papers, C/3/26).

the preceding February. Eventually the strength of Plaid Cymru in these rural areas was firmly based now. Most important for party morale, Gwynfor Evans recaptured Carmarthen by a majority of over 3,300, a handsome revenge for two previous defeats. Still the party's president and inspiration, Gwynfor Evans was well placed to lead a final transition from the years of struggle and isolation in the forties and fifties to a position of influence and credibility in the seventies.

The precise intentions of the Labour government with regard to Scottish and Welsh devolution after the October 1974 general election were uncertain. However, the broad views of the government had already been set out in a white paper, *Democracy and Devolution*, published in September 1974 just before the election. This laid down that there would be directly-elected assemblies for Wales and Scotland, with the Welsh one having only executive powers instead of the legislative role granted the Scottish assembly. These assemblies would be financed mainly through a block grant allocated by Parliament. There would be no reduction in the number of Scottish or Welsh MPs at Westminster, and the Secretaries of State for the two nations would remain in the British Cabinet. The provision about the number of MPs was particularly significant: if the number of Welsh members was reduced from thirty-six to thirty-one and Scottish representation similarly reduced, it would be hard for Labour, perhaps even impossible, for it ever to form a government again. There was much debate and dispute within the party over the broad principles of devolution. The Cabinet had now come reluctantly to support devolution as an essential antidote to national pressure for separatism, a half-way house which would nullify the threat of independence while offering a genuine advance towards local self-government and participatory democracy. This was spelt out again in a series of white papers, culminating in *The English Dimension* in December 1976, a paper designed to reassure regional opinion in England about the impact of devolution for Scotland and Wales.

Some Cabinet ministers were now strongly in favour of devolution. Notable among them was Michael Foot, deputy-leader of the government. The new Secretary of State for Wales, John Morris, a Welsh-speaking native of Cardiganshire, was a staunch supporter of devolution. Amongst the Welsh Labour members, men like Cledwyn Hughes (chairman of the parliamentary Labour Party, 1974–9, whose exclusion from the Cabinet was surprising) and Tom Ellis, the member for Wrexham, were committed devolutionists, as were the majority of their colleagues, even such men as Roy Hughes who represented the highly anglicized constituency of Newport. On the other hand, some south Wales Labour MPs were strongly hostile, or had become so since 1974. Echoes of the *Cymru Fydd* divisions of the 1890s were heard as Leo Abse (Pontypool), Neil Kinnock (Bedwellty), Donald Anderson (Swansea East), Fred Evans (Caerphilly), and Ioan Evans (Aberdare) declared their implacable opposition. More surprisingly, they were joined by

Ifor Davies, the Welsh-speaking member for Gower. Devolution, they argued, would inevitably lead to separatism, to the negation of that central-ized planning for which, they contended, socialism always had stood. Wales might lose its allocation of finance from the Consolidated Fund. Devolution might lead, also, to the domination of the land by a small Welsh-speaking minority, mostly crypto-nationalists. There was support from many English MPs, from both the left and the right of the Labour Party, fearful that devolution for the Celtic nations might lessen the prospects of governmental assistance for their own areas. Members from the north-east were particularly anxious on this point. There were also Scottish Labour men, notably Tam Dalyell (West Lothian), who argued that it was unfair that Welsh and Scottish MPs could vote on English issues after devolution, while English members would be denied the reverse privilege. The precedent of the Stormont parliament in Northern Ireland was not an appealing one.

But in general most Labour opinion, especially in Wales, argued that to do nothing would be suicidal for the party in the face of the challenge of Welsh and Scottish nationalism, fired anew by the glowing prospects of revenues from North (and perhaps 'Celtic') Sea oil. The Welsh TUC, a body formed in January 1973 on the Scottish model after years of pressure from local trade-union leaders and much resistance from Congress House in London, was strongly pro-devolutionist. Like its Scottish counterpart, it believed that corporate economic planning in Wales would be much assisted by a local assembly. Its main complaint was that the Welsh assembly would have so much weaker powers than the Scottish version. In any event, Welsh and Scottish national feeling was a political fact, ranging far beyond the confines of Plaid Cymru and the SNP. It was respectable and constitutional, and politicians would have to adjust their minds to its existence. After all, in its early years, Labour, especially through such ILP figures as Keir Hardie and Ramsay MacDonald, had been staunchly committed to Welsh and Scottish home rule on the same lines as the Irish. It could be argued that Labour was returning to its roots, to a more libertarian, less centralist version of socialism.[23]

On 13 December 1976 James Callaghan, now Prime Minister, moved the second reading of the government's Devolution Bill designed to set up separate elected assemblies in Scotland and Wales.[24] A somewhat derelict Coal Exchange in the dockside area of Cardiff was earmarked for use for the new eighty-strong Welsh assembly, in place of the Temple of Peace in Cathays Park originally selected. There would be a block grant of £850 million for the new assembly to spend on agreed purposes, and a further £300 million from the rates plus capital borrowing. The passage of the Devolution Bill was troubled from the start. Many English Labour MPs were openly unhappy, as

[23] Cf. John Osmond, *Creative Conflict: the Politics of Welsh Devolution* (London, 1978).
[24] *Parl. Deb.*, 5th ser., vol. 922, pp. 975 ff. (13 December 1976).

was the 'cave' of five or six Labour members in Wales. There were those who argued that the bill would play into the hands of the nationalists by proving to be only a stopping-place to complete separatism. On the other hand, there were those who criticized it for not going far enough and not granting the Welsh assembly parity of powers and status with the Scottish. There was much criticism of many anomalous or ambiguous features of the bill, including the relationship of the new assemblies to the Westminster parliament in the case of disagreement between them, and also the powers still vested in the Secretaries of State. Clashes of statute law might occur between England on the one hand and the Celtic nations on the other.

While these arguments and counter-arguments were waged, mainly in Labour circles, the Conservatives were also divided. Edward Heath, together with such as Alick Buchanan-Smith, a former shadow Secretary of State for Scotland, was a strong supporter of devolution, partly on grounds of legislative efficiency, partly as an aid to the fabric of regional government within the Common Market. On the other hand, Mrs Thatcher and most of her front-bench spokesmen, including the spokesman on devolution, Francis Pym, were clearly hostile. There were clear signs of boredom or irritation that a bill of this kind should be introduced at a time of 30 per cent inflation, rising unemployment, and the crisis in Rhodesia, among other more apparently pressing matters. On 16 December, the bill passed its second reading by 292 votes to 247, with a good deal of cross-voting revealed. Ten Labour MPs voted against it, while thirty more abstained; five Conservatives (including Edward Heath) voted with the government, and twenty-eight abstained. A significant concession had been made by the government just before the vote, when it agreed to hold referendums in Scotland and Wales after the passage of the bill through parliament but before it received the formal royal assent. The government had previously resisted this on the grounds that it had a clear mandate from the electors since devolution was contained in the October 1974 election manifesto. The new idea of the referendum was embodied in the bill in committee on 10 February 1977, as a new clause 40, amidst much procedural confusion. It was noted that these referendums would be mandatory unlike the consultative referendum attached to Britain's joining the European Common Market. Subsequently, on 15 February, Michael Foot announced that the Welsh and Scottish referendums would be consultative, too; in the end, the government could do what it liked.[25] Opinion in Wales, as shown in public opinion polls, seemed generally favourable to the bill, and markedly hostile to any separation from the United Kingdom. Even a majority of those who voted for Plaid Cymru were, significantly enough, hostile to complete independence for Wales. But the degree of enthusiasm for devolution in Wales seemed markedly less than in Scotland. This was evidenced by the fact that the SNP had won eleven seats in Scotland in

[25] Ibid., vol. 926, p. 275 (15 February 1977).

October 1974, and come second in many more, whereas Plaid Cymru had won but three and had poor prospects in most other places.

Even so, there was every sign that nationalism in Wales was still a considerable threat. In the borough elections of 1976, Plaid Cymru made some headway in south Wales. Most dramatically of all, it actually gained control of the borough council at Merthyr Tydfil where there was much local resentment at the conduct of a long-entrenched Labour majority. Labour's representation on a 33-member council fell from 25 to merely eight. The Rhymney district council in Monmouthshire, or Gwent as it was now re-christened, also had a Plaid Cymru majority. There was continuing dissatisfaction with the fabric of government in the land. Since 1973 the old county councils had disappeared, and new larger, local or regional authorities had been set up instead—Gwynedd, Clwyd, Powys, Dyfed, Gwent, adapting historic names from the Middle Ages, together with East, Mid, and South Glamorgan. These new authorities proved cumbersome and expensive to run, and were much criticized for being out of touch with local feeling. Powys was a huge sprawling authority extending from the borders of Denbighshire to the rim of the mining valleys of Glamorgan, Gwynedd extended from Holyhead to the Dyfi estuary. In Dyfed, the councillor for Borth in the northern end of Cardiganshire had a round trip of a hundred miles to take him to council meetings at Carmarthen. There was much talk of having a new look at the structure of local government set up in 1973, and perhaps a rehabilitation of the district councils, which in some cases were virtually the old county councils with which most citizens appeared to identify. Certainly some kind of rationalization would have to be undertaken unless Wales, with county, district, and parish councils, together with additional elections for Westminister and for the European parliament at Strasbourg (let alone its own assembly) were not to become the most governed country on earth, with innumerable and highly expensive series of elections.

In fact, the government's portmanteau Devolution Bill soon came to grief early in 1977. It experienced immense difficulty through its lack of an overall majority in the House, together with the harassing tactics of Conservative and Labour opponents of devolution, assisted by Enoch Powell, now an Ulster Unionist. On 22 February, when only a few clauses of the bill had been passed, the government's guillotine motion was defeated by 312 votes to 283. Twenty-two Labour MPs (two being Welsh) voted against the guillotine, and a further twenty-three abstained, of whom three came from Wales. The government now offered all-party talks, an idea that inevitably foundered. Scottish and (to a lesser degree) Welsh devolution loomed large in the talks on a Liberal–Labour pact held between James Callaghan and David Steel in March.[26] The Liberals failed to gain any satisfaction on one of their

---

[26] Alastair Michie and Simon Hoggart, The Pact (London, paperback, 1978), pp. 115–28. Cledwyn Hughes acted as mediator between the two party leaders.

demands—that the assemblies should be elected on proportional representation—but their wish that the assemblies should have greater revenue-raising powers, independent of the Treasury, did win some concession from the government. Devolution was certainly a central element in the pact announced in May. After much uncertainty, the government announced on 26 July that it would now reintroduce devolution but in the form of two separate bills for Scotland and for Wales: the Welsh Liberals, in fact, were hostile to this decision. Nevertheless, the Scottish Bill and the Wales Bill were introduced as separate measures in November. The Welsh Bill passed its second reading by 295 votes to 264 on 15 November 1977, and the government promptly introduced the guillotine procedure to ensure its passage.

This time it was clear that devolution was going to reach the statute book in some form, partly because of the Lib–Lab pact, partly because many Labour dissidents were coming to heel on a matter the government now treated as an issue of confidence. The Scotland and Wales Bills ground their way laboriously through the committee stage between February and April 1978. The most important change in the bill resulted from an amendment to the Scotland Bill moved by a Scottish expatriate Labour member, George Cunningham, who sat for an Islington constituency in north London. This specified that a repeal order would be laid if less than 40 per cent of the electorate were 'deemed' to have voted 'Yes' in the referendum. In addition, if a general election were held before the referendum took place, the latter would be postponed for at least three months. This provision, which clearly made the achievement of devolution very much more difficult and demanded an inordinately high poll, was later added to the Wales Bill also. Even in this somewhat mutilated form, however, devolution remained a priority for the government. Labour rebels were less numerous now, with the party whip being fiercely cracked. With the safeguard of a referendum to come, even anti-devolutionists could vote for bills that would at least provide for this test of local opinion. On 9 May 1978, a day that brought little recognition in England but a significant one in the annals of Welsh politics, the Welsh Bill passed its third reading by 292 votes to 264. Lords amendments to include proportional representation were rejected by the government. The Scotland and Wales Bills both received the royal assent on 31 July 1978.

There was now a prospect of some kind of self-governing Welsh assembly, being created with responsibilities in the first instance for housing, education, health, planning, and the environment. The Welsh Development Agency was also to be devolved. The powers of the new assembly laid down in the bill were undeniably modest and fell far short of the legislative powers granted to the Scottish assembly. Only in such small areas as the power to appoint to nominated bodies such as the Welsh Health Authority or Tourist Board did the Welsh assembly approach any legislative authority. The usual argument adopted here was the legal and administrative distinctiveness of Scotland in the past as compared to Wales, though the point was never made very clear by the government. What the Wales bill did create was a form of 'horizontal devolution' unique in the United Kingdom constitution, under which a distinction would be made between 'primary' and 'secondary' legislation at Westminster, somewhat on the lines of the relationship between the *Länder* and the Federal government in West Germany.[27] Political experts spent much time mulling over the precise implications of the Welsh style of devolution for central and local government in Britain generally.

What seemed probable, given the very nature of political life, was that a Welsh assembly, if it came into existence, would provide a powerful focus of nationhood. It was also likely, given human nature and the tendency for any organization to maximize its own role, that the assembly would, in the course of time, acquire more powers and a wider range of social and economic responsibilities. The publicity it would inevitably attract would also be an important factor in enhancing its status. In the latter months of 1978, therefore, much attention was paid to the forthcoming referendums in Wales and Scotland. As in the past, the divisive factor of the Welsh language was much cited by opponents of devolution; they were helped by further militancy by the Welsh Language Society, and much-publicized appearances in the courts that autumn. How vigorous Plaid Cymru now was seemed debatable: there had been no by-elections since the last general election to test opinion. On the other hand, a minority government had to pay attention even to a party whose representation at Westminster numbered no more than three. In the Queen's speech on 1 November, several concessions were offered to Welsh opinion, including more funds for the Development Agency, the announcement of a Welsh-language television channel to begin its operations in 1982, and substantial compensation for victims of silicosis (a major element in the constituencies of Dafydd Wigley and Dafydd Elis Thomas). This ensured that Plaid Cymru MPs, unlike the Scottish Nationalists, voted with the government. Most important of all, the referendums on Welsh and Scottish devolution were timed for 1 March, St. David's Day, 1979. The outcome seemed hard to predict. Officially, the Labour Party and the TUC in Wales were in favour of an elected assembly, as were the leading members of the government. So were the Liberals, while Plaid Cymru, at its annual party conference, decided after much earnest debate to campaign for this modest version of devolution on the grounds that this was at least half a loaf compared with the 'no bread' of unionism. Almost all Welsh Conservatives were strongly anti-devolutionist; more dangerously for the government, so were a significant, though unquantifiable, number of its own Labour supporters in the south. Nevertheless, the referendum could provide a unique and crucial test of how seriously, and with what degree of commitment, the Welsh people

[27] Vernon Bogdanor, *Devolution* (Oxford, 1979), pp. 176–81. This book is an admirably fair-minded treatment of a complex subject.

embraced the prospect of controlling, to a modest degree, their own political destiny.

And yet the great debate never got off the ground. The devolution campaign was handicapped by severe wintry weather and by much greater concern with industrial disputes by public service workers. In addition to an all-party 'Yes to the assembly' campaign, the Labour Party and the Welsh TUC launched their own crusade to try to persuade Welsh opinion of the merits of the devolution proposals. Government spokesmen, headed by the Prime Minister and the Secretary for Wales, John Morris, urged that the assembly would be a major advance in local democracy, that it would have significant powers through taking over the social functions of the Welsh Office, and that it would control a budget, in the first instance, of £1,430,000, including expenditure in Wales by nominated bodies as well as by the Welsh Office itself. Less wisely, pro-assembly spokesmen tried to argue that devolution would assist employment and industrial expansion in Wales by giving new force to the Development Agency and lending Wales a stronger voice in government at the highest level.

But it was the opponents of the assembly who dominated the debate throughout. They included virtually all the Conservatives in Wales (it was striking that their party gained in public support in the opinion polls held in Wales between January and March 1979). They also numbered six dissident south Wales Labour MPs, of whom Leo Abse (Pontypool) and Neil Kinnock (Bedwellty), both from Gwent, were the most prominent. The right and the socialist left thus joined forces in savaging the government's proposals for executive devolution. Several factors seem to have swayed opinion against the proposed assembly. There was some fear, voiced both by Labour MPs and by the CBI in Wales, that governmental economic assistance, including allocations from the Consolidated Fund, would be obstructed by the creation of an intermediate body which might create new friction between Westminster and Wales. There was much criticism of the cost of creating another tier of government on top of the county and district councils remodelled in 1973; critics such as Leo Abse hinted darkly of the prospects of further corruption that might now open up. Another theme that emerged was the perennial one of alarm that a new assembly and its attendant civil service might be run by a Welsh-speaking élite from the rural areas. The force of this was far from clear since any assembly would be overwhelmingly dominated by the anglicized urban population of the south. Nevertheless, the same kind of social and cultural divisions that had arisen during the *Cymru Fydd* crisis at the end of the previous century loomed up again during the devolution campaign. As a result of these factors, added to the government's increased unpopularity generally after a winter of industrial discontent, it was not surprising that the opinion polls repeatedly showed large and increasing majorities against the assembly among the Welsh electors.

The polling on 1 March bore this out all too clearly. While the Scots that day did produce a narrow majority in favour of a Scottish assembly (amongst those who actually voted), in Wales the results were overwhelmingly negative. In all, only 243,048 voted in favour of the assembly (11.8 per cent of the total electorate) while 956,330 (46.5 per cent of the electorate) voted against. Every one of the eight counties in Wales voted strongly 'No'. The 'forty per cent' rule was thus irrelevant. In Gwynedd, with a preponderantly Welsh-speaking population and two Plaid Cymru MPs, the proportion of the electorate in favour of the assembly was the highest in Wales at 21.8 per cent. But even here there was a two-to-one majority against the assembly (37,363 to 71,157). Gwynedd voters evidently feared domination by a socialist body far away in Cardiff. Elsewhere in Wales the majorities against devolution were increasingly massive, most of all in the anglicized south-east where only 7.7 per cent of the electors in South Glamorgan and 6.7 per cent in Gwent voted in favour. At one level, the entire devolution affair was a massive miscalculation of Welsh opinion by the government, especially of the views of Labour grass-roots party workers and trade unionists: it put the government's entire position at risk and seemed to make defeat at the next general election highly probable. At a more profound historical level, the devolution debate, tepid though it was, did serve to confirm both the cultural divisions within Wales, and the political and economic factors which made the Welsh highly reluctant to embrace anything that remotely resembled any form of separatism. Even a body as modest as the proposed Welsh assembly could be made to appear as the first step down the slippery slope to self-government; the Welsh were as resolute against this in 1979 as in 1896. However powerful their sense of cultural and historical identity, the Welsh were, in political and economic terms, strictly unionist. Welsh devolution was promptly wiped off the political agenda.

There were some possible by-products that could be salvaged, perhaps stronger collective powers for the county councils, perhaps a Welsh Select Committee in the House of Commons, perhaps greater powers for the Secretary of State. Even the Conservatives proposed, during the referendum campaign, that the Welsh Office might be given its own independent budget, much as the abortive assembly would have been, negotiated directly with the Treasury and free from the parameters of departmental financial control. But these reforms were unlikely to prove spectacular. The basic fact remained that, for the first time in the twentieth century, the Welsh had been offered a real prospect of power being transferred from Whitehall to themselves; when given the choice, they had thrown it out with contumely. Arguments about more democracy, more open government, and national identity cut little ice. The great devolution debate ended not with any kind of bang but with the most anti-climactic of whimpers.

The results of the referendums on devolution had repercussions far wider than Wales or Scotland. Indirectly, they helped to bring down the Labour government. The government's inability or unwillingness to proceed immediately with a Scottish assembly led the Scottish Nationalist MPs to withdraw their support from the Callaghan administration and to put down a motion of no confidence. The Conservatives promptly followed with a motion of their own. On 28 March, this Conservative motion was carried by the narrowest of margins—311 votes to 310—and thus a government fell on a vote of confidence for the first time since MacDonald's in 1924. James Callaghan at once dissolved parliament. It is notable, as a commentary on the contrasting traditions of nationalism in the two Celtic countries, that whereas all the Scottish nationalists voted against the Labour government, the three Plaid Cymru MPs still gave Labour their vote. The immediate cause of this was the government's willingness to speed up a bill to give substantial compensation to quarrymen suffering from silicosis or other lung diseases, or to their dependants. More profoundly, this episode may suggest the more deep-rooted radicalism of nationalists in Wales, compared with those north of Hadrian's Wall, and the traditional reluctance of spokesmen for Welsh sentiment to return a Tory government to power.

In the election campaign that ensued, devolution and specifically Welsh issues seldom intruded. Indeed, the election of May 1979 was the least Welsh in character since Labour had proclaimed the need for a Secretary of State back in 1964. The campaigns in Wales were largely projections of those conducted by the leaders of the major parties in London, with a heavy emphasis on the economic and social problems of Britain as a whole. Even Plaid Cymru's manifesto, *Dyfodol i Gymru/A Future for Wales*, devoted only two general sentences to Welsh self-government. Its contents otherwise focused on economic questions and on the successful constituency work of the three Plaid Cymru MPs. Even Plaid Cymru had to play down the issue of political independence in the light of the crushing defeat of the proposed Welsh assembly.

The major features of the election results in 1979 were a further erosion of Labour's strength in north and central Wales, and a continued advance for the Conservatives. While Labour still finished up with twenty-one Welsh seats, as against eleven for the Conservatives, two for Plaid Cymru, one for the Liberals, and the Speaker, there was a swing of 4.8 per cent to the Conservatives in the total Welsh vote. The Conservatives made three gains to register their highest tally of Welsh seats for fifty years. They captured two from Labour—Brecon and Radnor, and, much more surprisingly, Anglesey, where a young Sussex barrister achieved a swing of over 12 per cent in this Welsh-speaking constituency, while Labour suffered from the retirement of Cledwyn Hughes. The Conservatives also won Montgomeryshire, a Liberal seat continuously since Rendel's historic triumph in 1880. It was possible now to travel from Holyhead to Chepstow, without leaving Tory territory. The total Liberal vote again declined, and they were left with Cardiganshire as their only Welsh seat. Plaid Cymru held on to their two Gwynedd seats, but elsewhere their vote fell away sharply. Their total of 132,544 votes was well down on 1974, while their share of the poll fell from 10.8 per cent to 7.6. Their challenge to Labour in the industrial valleys seemed to have petered out. This was confirmed in the local district elections (held on the same day) where Plaid Cymru suffered huge losses, especially in Merthyr where they comprehensively lost control to Labour. Most disappointing of all, one of their three parliamentary seats was captured. Gwynfor Evans, their president, again losing Carmarthen to Labour. Although devolution played little part in the election, it may have cost Labour votes in Anglesey, and the Liberals in Montgomeryshire. The 1979 general election seemed to mark the end of a distinct chapter in Welsh political history, with nationalism in full retreat, devolution in the shadows, Labour struggling, and a new Conservative government under Mrs Thatcher, in which Nicholas Edwards (Pembroke) became Secretary of State. Perhaps Wales was, in some respects, simply becoming less Welsh. At all events, the national upsurge heralded in the sixties by the appointment of a Secretary of State and the Plaid Cymru revival seemed to have beaten itself out. This election, therefore, is an appropriate point at which to bring consideration of recent Welsh politics to an end.

The significance of the relative nationalist upsurge in Wales after 1960 is peculiarly hard for the historian to assess. In many ways, it was largely ephemeral, the product of the temporary and purely local discontents at by-elections which tended to subside when the government of Britain generally was at issue. The prospects of the Welsh voting for anything that resembled separation from England seemed as remote as ever, after the shatteringly conclusive referendum on devolution. The SNP showed a marked loss of momentum in Scotland after 1974. In the 1979 general election, the Scottish Nationalists saw their tally of MPs fall from eleven to two. Plaid Cymru seemed in equally parlous state. Even Saunders Lewis now denounced it. Much of the nationalism of post-1960 seemed in any case peculiarly inbred. It attracted boredom or open hostility from the general mass of the Welsh population, especially those in urban and industrial communities in the south-east. Plaid Cymru's essential constituency still seemed to be the world of Welsh speakers, and that was contracting steadily, with only the fastnesses of Gwynedd remaining.

Nevertheless, the nationalist upsurge was too forceful and too sustained to be brushed aside as a temporary, negative reaction to the British parties and to London-based institutions. It was part of a wider uncertainty or disaffection with established forms of government and accepted values, general throughout Britain during the economic troubles of the sixties and seventies, a period which saw party membership and interest in politics (as conventionally interpreted) go into decline. Without doubt, the effect of the combined forces of fhe Welsh Language Society and of a revived Plaid Cymru had galvanized Welsh life since 1962. The Welsh-language movement had helped promote a new seriousness of approach by gaining recognition for the native language for official purposes. By the end of the seventies, official or civil service opposition to Welsh forms and television licences had ended. So, too, was the use of Welsh in town names and road signs, after a committee under the chairmanship of the former Liberal MP, Roderic Bowen, had reported favourably in November 1972. A twelve-strong committee was appointed in September 1973, under the chairmanship of a London Welsh solicitor, Ben G. Jones, to inquire into the general health and use of the language. There was in most areas of life, from the most obscure official notice boards or railway platforms, to official ceremonial, far more sensitivity towards the place of the language. These victories were, in the main, achieved with a fair amount of goodwill—the more so, perhaps, as the activities of the Welsh Language Society became more intermittent, and university students in Wales, as elsewhere, began to turn away from quasi-political demonstration to more formal patterns of academic life.

More generally, Welsh life had been reinvigorated through the rise of nationalism and the debate on devolution that followed the Kilbrandon Report. No longer did Welsh and Scottish issues attract the patronizing indifference that they had so often done prior to 1964. The teaching of Welsh in schools had made steady progress. The government had given its approval to a new Welsh-language television channel, scheduled for 1982. Radio and television programmes in both languages emphasized national themes. The most unexpected of bodies now proclaimed their Welshness, notably the newly-formed Welsh TUC. The debate on Welshness and the future of Welsh government was a passionate one in the late 1970s. It was clearly destined to continue (if perhaps less passionately) in years to come. Many questions were inevitably left unanswered by the result of the devolution referendum. But at least the debate was a peaceful and civilized one. Wales at no time manifested the communal violence of Northern Ireland. Its two linguistic communities lived side by side in comparative (though not invariable) amity. No bomb had been exploded in Wales since 1969. The 'Quebec situation' did not arise. The 'Welsh extremist' attracted less attention—or rather, his 'extremism' remained verbal only. Despite the failure of the Welsh Devolution Bill, it had surely helped to defuse and moderate some of the communal tensions thrown up by the nationalist upsurge. It enabled the Welsh to look at themselves and their predicament calmly, constructively, and in a mood of goodwill and peace. Whether this would survive in the 1980s, however, following renewed anger over 'second homes' and a Welsh television channel, remained to be seen. The dilemmas of nationalism remained.

CHAPTER 14

CONCLUSION

The pattern of change in Wales in the hundred years from the general election of 1880 to that of 1979 was bewildering and confusing. In that span of time, the land underwent successively an upsurge of political and economic advance, and of patriotic consciousness; a shattering collapse in its economic fabric with social despair and new cultural tension; and, finally, a period of economic rehabilitation and renewal in which the awareness of nationhood flourished anew, although with very different symbols and in very different circumstances from the earlier reawakening before 1914. A considerable gulf lay between the nationalism of Owen M. Edwards and of Saunders Lewis. There were key watersheds which stand out as marking off specific phases in the evolution of Wales. The First World War is perhaps the most important in some ways, with its traumatic consequences for the politics, the social structure, and the moral values of the Welsh people. The economic depression, mass unemployment, and emigration of the twenties and thirties form another, destroying as they did the optimism and the seemingly limit-less economic progress of the pre-war years, especially in the mining valleys of the south, and creating a new mood of class bitterness and desperation. The profound changes in the industrial base and the social structure and *mores* in the fifties and sixties provide yet another, creating new uncertainties and challenging and partially undermining the old sanctions. All in all, for Wales as for so much of the European world, the transition from the late nineteenth century to the late twentieth was one of extra-ordinary complexity. The Wales of Tom Ellis and John Morris-Jones in the 1880s was scarcely recognizable in terms of the more homogeneous, angli-cized, and secular society which emerged in the aftermath of war after 1945. Some of the characteristic features of Welsh society survived throughout the period—the national *eisteddfod*, the chapels, the educational and cultural forces associated with the Welsh language, the warm attachment to local community life. But they were surviving with difficulty in a world which was rapidly leaving old landmarks far behind.

In this vortex of revolutionary upheaval, there are, perhaps, two elements of continuity that provide some kind of unity in the evolution of the Welsh nation in this period. The first was common to Britain generally in the hundred years under review, though it had special implications and aspects peculiar to Wales. This was the transformation of the fabric of authority and of social and political leadership. Here, the forces of change since the eighties are striking indeed. In the late Victorian era, Wales retained, especially in that rural heartland which comprised by far the largest part of its geographical territory, many of those 'feudal' aspects which had been condemned by Henry Richard, Samuel Roberts, and other radicals for a generation past. The land was still largely dominated, at the levels of local government and social authority (and, to some degree, until 1885 and the democratizing of the franchise, at the parliamentary level as well) by the same landed class, Anglican, anglicized, alienated in basic respects from the broad mass of society, that had ruled Wales since the days of the Tudors. Traditions of prescription and of deference in the Burkeian mould, awed obedience to the influence and majesty of the *plastŷ* which had ruled over rural (and, to some extent, industrial) society, survived in full measure, despite the liberating and revolutionary effects of the coming of industry.

The first transformation in this respect, then, was the complete overthrow of this pattern of social authority in the years between 1880 and 1914. The advent of democracy had extraordinary effects upon the socio-political structure of Wales. Through the extension of the francise in 1884, through the creation of popularly-elected councils in 1888, through the rise of a popular radical mass movement bent on civic and religious equality, linked with the chapels and with its superstructure in the Welsh Party that emerged in the House of Commons, a new Liberal élite of leadership was created. By 1914, in rural and industrial areas alike, the old deference was a thing of the past. After the first 'cracking of the ice' noted in 1868, the surging currents of democracy were sweeping through unchecked. New groups of industrialists and manufacturers, shopkeepers and solicitors, academics and journalists, tenant farmers and nonconformist ministers had taken over the citadel of power, at every level from Westminster to the local magistrate's bench. In addition, during the years of the Edwardian renaissance up to 1914, with the rise of Lloyd George as the voice and the tribune of the new Wales, this Liberal ascendancy was associated with a remarkable period of cultural vitality, and a rare flowering in literature and the arts. There was an integrated character, socially, culturally, and politically, about Liberal Wales up to 1914 which was deeply impressive and made this a halcyon era in fundamental respects. It left legacies such as the national university and the 'county' schools which remained to shape the life of the nation for generations to come.

After the First World War there was an immense change. The growth of mass trade unions, such as the South Wales Miners' Federation, had been clearly heralded before 1914. The great strikes of the period from 1898 to 1912 in the coalfield, the growing militancy and quasi-syndicalism of rank-and-file miners, the energing strength of the Labour Party and of specifically socialist bodies such as the ILP, marked a fundamental challenge to the largely middle-class élite that dominated the Liberal years before the war. After 1918, especially with the cohesive class effects of the depression and mass unemployment, a new Labour élite now emerged. By the thirties, south Wales was even more totally under the control of a new Labour/trade-union ascendancy, based on local government and trade-union branches, on the world of adult education and of the constituency Labour Party, than it had been under Liberal domination in the past. Only gradually did this new Labour élite, with Aneurin Bevan as its symbol just as clearly as Lloyd George had symbolized the radicalism of pre-1914, penetrate the rural areas. It was slow to conquer Cardiff, Newport, and Swansea, the cosmopolitan ports of the southern coastal fringe, as well. But the entire political and social structure of south Wales looked and sounded very different by the advent of another world war in 1939. After 1945, the Labour ascendancy increasingly penetrated the rural outposts of north, mid- and south-west Wales. A change in the fabric of capitalism, the new polarization between capital and labour, the new intensity of class-consciousness, had had inevitable consequences for the political and social face of Wales.

From the late 1940s, this Labour élite began to change organically in its turn. While the Labour Party and the trade unions remained immensely powerful until the end of the seventies, they were evolving in their composition. They were less obviously related to traditional working-class groups such as the miners and steelworkers, and were a reflection of a more classless, broadly-based society. There were new challenges, too, not only from Plaid Cymru and cultural nationalists, but also from within the Labour world, and increasingly from a reviving Conservative Party, coming from critics who resented the entrenched, monopolistic power of an ageing Labour Party in the valleys, with its occasional abuses. These critics denounced the Labour ascendancy almost as fervently as Labour itself had once attacked the monolithic Liberal ascendancy before 1914. This factor should not be exaggerated. The May 1979 general election confirmed that Labour remained the dominant element in the social and political life of Wales. So did the European elections a month later, when Labour captured three seats out of four in Wales, despite a low poll. But at the dawn of the 1980s there seemed at least a possibility that the Labour ascendancy might eventually go the way of ossification and decline as had the Liberalism of the past, though how rapidly, and in favour of what combination of forces, it was difficult to predict.

These changes in the pattern of authority are one readily detectable thread in these hundred years. In general, they were paralleled by movements in Britain during the same period, although the very blanket dominance, first of Liberalism, then of Labour, was far more overwhelming in Wales than in either England or even Scotland. The other element of continuity is much more specific to the principality—the emerging consciousness of nationhood from the 1880s onwards, in some respects more acute and strident in the 1970s than a hundred years earlier. Here again, was a central feature of modern Wales—perhaps the crucial feature—which developed considerably in the course of the period surveyed here.

Before 1914, cultural nationalism received enormous new impetus. Partly, this was through the very impact of mass democracy which galvanized the Welsh chapels, newspapers, and cultural festivals into new life. Partly, too, it was a response to the awareness of the importance of public education at all levels, from the elementary schools to the university, as a force for promoting new ideas and social mobility. The growth of the movement for higher education, the founding of the 'county' schools and the creation of the national, federal university in 1893, had powerful effects upon the dawning of national consciousness. Most important of all was the extraordinary flowering of Welsh poetry and literary and musical culture generally from the 1890s until (and, indeed, well after) the First World War. This gave new intellectual toughness and aesthetic distinction to Welsh as a literary medium, and new stature to national figures like John Morris-Jones and Owen M. Edwards. It was to give self-confidence to the commitment to Welsh-language culture before the First World War which is highly impressive, and lent cultural nationalism a depth unimaginable in the middle decades of the nineteenth century.

Only to a limited extent, however, did this cultural nationalism attain political form. The *Cymru Fydd* débâcle of 1896 over Welsh home rule showed the emergent division between the society of the rural hinterland and of the industrial south, especially of the cosmopolitan Anglo-Welsh ports of the seaboard. In the main, nationalism was proclaimed before 1914 by men who were part of the Liberal-nonconformist élite of their generation. They saw the advancement of the Welsh nation within the context of a wider process of liberalization and social equality within the United Kingdom. Wales wanted its place in the sun. Unlike the Irish, whose nationalism became ever more militant and political, even republican, in the years up to 1916, the Welsh were content with national equality. Indeed, by 1914, with Lloyd George dominant in the Cabinet, the new vitality of the Welsh economy in the commercial and industrial life of Britain and the Empire, and the growing recognition of the value and the validity of the Welsh language, that equality appeared largely to have been attained. The badge of inferiority associated with Wales, by contrast with Scotland, for so much of the period from the early Tudors down to the later nineteenth century, had finally disappeared. There was simply no need to pursue the chimera of Welsh home rule when so much progress was so easily obtainable within the fabric of the union and the empire.

After the First World War, and for a prolonged period down to the 1960s, the awareness of nationhood did not greatly advance beyond the parameters laid down before 1914. Welsh culture remained vigorous at least down to the Second World War. It produced much distinguished writing, including less familiar art forms such as the drama and the novel. But it was set against a background of growing desperation about the fate of the language, as the statistics unfolded a remorseless story of relative decline, especially as far as the younger generation were concerned. The struggle for survival, for preventing the native language from falling into the virtual extinction of Manx or Cornish, subsumed all else in the minds of many patriots. Socially, economically, and politically, the unemployment and industrial stagnation of the twenties and thirties, with all the social misery involved, served to bind Wales, especially the working-class trade unions, ever more closely to England. It was through nationwide policies to provide stimulus to the economic development of the 'depressed areas', through centrally-conceived planning, through nationwide solidarity within the trade union and labour movement that the salvation of Wales appeared to lie, whatever the cultural cost.

The trade unions, and the Labour Party in particular, adhered to an ever more rigid centralism in their attitude towards economic policy and to the fabric of government. Proposals for the most limited form of devolution, certainly the idea of a Secretaryship of State for Wales, were resisted by the leadership of the Labour Party as sternly as by union-minded Conservatives. The decline of the Liberal Party, remorseless and continual from 1918 onwards, weakened still further the influence of Welsh national awareness in British politics and policy-making. The rise of the struggling Plaid Cymru, gestures like the bombing at Pen-y-berth in 1936, seemed at best an idealistic diversion from the realities of life, a hopeless resistance to the inevitable centralizing pressures of the twentieth century, which was brushed aside by the big battalions of the political parties, leaders of industry, and the trade unions. Political nationalism was scarcely a factor in the history of Wales in the inter-war years. Nor, indeed, did the mood greatly change in the period from 1945 to the early sixties. The ascendancy of a centrally-minded Labour Party (none being more centralist than Aneurin Bevan) became more deep-rooted than ever, with its gradual penetration into the rural areas, in the wake of the erosion of the older Liberalism. More generally, the vogue for planning on the Keynesian or 'Butskellite' models in the forties, the affluence of the fifties which swept Wales into a wider tide of consumer-led conformism and standardization made political pressure for some kind of national direction of Welsh life appear irrelevant or out of date. Meanwhile, the rise of a distinguished school of Anglo-Welsh poets and novelists showed that Welsh consciousness could flourish quite independently of political separatism or even of the language itself.

But it is an essential facet of modern Welsh history that the idea of nationhood, including the demand for self-government, never disappeared. It was always latent, ready to be rekindled. It was present even in segments of the trade-union movement, for instance in the frequent emergence from 1910 onwards of locally-based syndicalist pressures or rank-and-file movements on behalf of industrial self-government or devolution as an alternative to the nationalization of basic industries. In the very different society of the 1960s, Welsh people now showed a new passion towards the fate of their language and their culture. There was growing pressure—and much success—in getting a London-based, London-minded governmental machine to take seriously demands for greater status for the language in official business, in social communication, in broadcasting, and, most crucially, in the nation's schools. Politically, it was evident that nationalism remained a vibrant force, though perhaps less so than in Scotland. There was the resurgence of Plaid Cymru, gathering momentum in the later sixties as some disillusion set in with the Labour Party, and indeed with the British political system generally at a time of economic difficulties. There were signs now of that nationalism being socially more broadly-based. The folk-consciousness of pre-1914, treasured largely by scholars and *literati*, the mainly intellectual, rural-orientated nationalism of Plaid Cymru in the thirties became subsumed in a wider concern to preserve the Welsh identity, for reasons of economic survival as well as of cultural diversity. In the 1970s, Welsh nationalism became one compelling way of expressing anxiety about the course of economic manage-ment and industrial relations, a way of cutting down massive problems to a local, human scale, of trying to give new life to Welsh society as well as preserving the old cultural heritage. The Labour Party and, to a much lesser degree, the Conservatives, were noticeably more aware of the need to combine central planning with some form of devolution, of the importance of extending popular self-government (especially when the levers of power lay in Brussels as much as in London), and of taking full account of cultural pluralism within a framework of economic integration. Unity did not mean uniformity, as the very survival of Wales, against all the odds, bore witness.

The importance to be attached to the sense of Welsh nationality in the later twentieth century was a theme of much dispute, and this was likely to continue long beyond the abortive referendum on devolution in 1979. Certainly it seemed different in quality now from the 'nationalism' avowed by the Liberal élite before 1914, even though there were still important points of contact, through the nonconformist chapels and in other ways, between that era and the period of a more assertive Plaid Cymru. Welsh nationalism on the whole was a peaceful, gradualist movement. It had to combat serious forces for division, social and cultural as well as geographic, within Wales itself. It certainly took a different form from nationalism in Ireland since it was clear that, down to the end of the 1970s, the overwhelming bulk of the Welsh people, including many who regularly voted for Plaid Cymru, really wanted more attention for Wales from the London government, more advance factories, investment grants, and the like, not the adventure and perils of isolation. In any case, if unity was strength, isolation could well mean impotence.

Welsh national feeling was also very different from that of Scotland, despite the spurious similarity implied in nationalist successes in by-elections in the two countries from 1966 onwards. Welsh nationalism was far more concerned with cultural and linguistic aspects, with the preservation of a disappearing way of life, rather than building on to recognized institutions new ways of asserting distinctiveness from England. Wales, indeed, seemed less aggressive in its nationalism than Scotland, more willing to be placated and to let its call for home rule be killed by kindness. Perhaps, too, nationalism in Wales was more socially radical and intellectually adventurous than its Scottish counterpart, closer to working-class syndicalism or rural populism than to the Jacobite romanticism of the Scottish lairds which characterized some elements of the SNP. The MPs for Plaid Cymru looked with a far kindlier eye on the Labour government of 1974−9 than did those of the SNP: this suggested some vital differences between the political cultures of the two countries that they represented. The gulf between the Goidelic and the Brythonic variants of the Celt was still a real one.

A closer analogy for Welsh nationalism might be with the linguistic divide in Belgium between Flemings and Walloons, but even here there were many differences. A major one was that in Belgium it was the more local culture, that of the Flemings, which was traditionally dominant, while the French-speaking Walloons, who in any case tended to be socialist and anti-clerical, felt themselves to be oppressed. In Wales, of course, it was the linguistic minority which felt itself to be dominated, politically and socially. Nor does the comparison that has been made with the Liberation Front in Brittany or with the ETA movement in the Basque regions of Spain seem very fruitful.[1]

A better comparison might be with the province of French-speaking Quebec in Canada where the *Parti Québecois* achieved massive success in the early and mid-1970s and put forward a fierce demand for political separatism that many feared might undermine the unity of the dominion of Canada itself. There were fierce linguistic pressures here, too: the demands for fairer treatment for 'Francophones' in schooling, equal validity for the French language in law and government, and other cries had a familiar ring to visitors from Wales. But in Canada there was a long-standing provincial, federal constitution which gave the French-speaking Canadians a vital lever in pressing for a goal of independence. The post-1791 division into Lower and Upper Canada still remained a political and psychological reality. In Wales,

[1] Cf. Patricia Elton Mayo, *The Roots of Identity* (1974).

that constitutional leverage did not exist—indeed, a federal solution was explicitly rejected by all the members of the Kilbrandon Commission in 1973, and their verdict seemed to be confirmed by the Welsh voters. Nor did this leverage seem likely to materialize even if an elected assembly for Wales were ever created. The facts of economic integration and demographic change alone militated against it. In particular, there was the tendency for population and economic activity to be sucked after 1945 into the urban growth of the south-eastern axis between Newport and Cardiff, and of Deeside in the far north-east, linking the fortunes of an expanding proportion of the working population with their English or anglicized neighbours. Whereas René Levesque's *Parti Québecois* found substantial support from the provincial metropolis of Montreal, which remained overwhelmingly French-speaking for all its industry and finance, it seemed inconceivable that Plaid Cymru could make similar inroads into Cardiff or its immediate hinterland in the foreseeable future.

Even Quebec, then, did not provide any clear analogy with the Welsh question. National pressures in Wales remained *sui generis*, more subdued, a species of sub-nationalism more powerful than the regional feeling of, say the west of England or East Anglia, and with a vigorous cultural base, but less forceful than a full-blooded movement pressing for national liberation. The prospect of Wales joining the third-world nations of Africa and Asia in the United Nations (even such bogus states as the Ukraine or White Russia) as yet another small, isolated republic or dominion, remained utterly remote. Only some massive, unforeseeable change, such as a total collapse of the British and world economy, could perhaps transform a qualified, peripheral nationalism, essentially gradual in method and limited in demands, into something more significant.

Since, then, we are not talking of anything that closely resembles ETA in the Basque regions, a Croatian Ustasha in Yugoslavia, Sinn Fein in Ireland, or even the *Parti Québecois* in Canada—all movements of nationalist minorities that have provoked major and continuing crises in their respective countries—the question thus arises of how seriously to take the national awareness of Wales in this period. Some manifestations of Welshness have undoubtedly been matters of pomp and circumstance, and entirely ephemeral. The national euphoria of rugby internationals lasts for eighty minutes and little longer. The metropolitan pretensions of Cardiff as the capital city of Wales have significance in so far as many public institutions—the Welsh Office, the Arts Council, the Welsh Tourist Board, the University Registry, the Welsh BBC, Harlech Television, and the like—are located in one relatively compact area of the centre of the city. But the extent to which metropolitan status has made Cardiff as a city any less anglicized may well be debated. In 1979, Cardiff, was hardly a stronghold of devolutionist sentiment—very much the reverse, in fact. Its aspiration seemed to be rather a variant of the 'city regions' that surrounded Bristol in Avonside or Liverpool in Merseyside or Newcastle in Tyneside, supplying the services and many of the employment prospects for a quasi-colonized hinterland. Meanwhile, the mining valleys, the custodians of so much of the populist culture of Wales over the hundred years from 1880, were in visible transformation with the rapid running-down of the coal and steel industries, and their neighbourhoods and communities manifestly contracting. There was always the ritualistic aspect of events such as the investitures of Princes of Wales in 1911 and 1969, but these had little significant impact on the Welsh people. The Prince of Wales meant little to his nation, beyond a rousing chorus, and brief, air-lifted visits to the *eisteddfod* once a year. There was no conceivable analogy, say, with the role of the House of Orange and its relationship with the people of Holland over the centuries since the days of William the Silent. Creating a Prince of Wales was merely a way of neutralizing, perhaps trivializing, a real sense of national identity.

There is also the point, conveyed often enough in these pages, that some of the institutions long associated with the treasuring of Welsh aspirations and with the cultural heritage, underwent secular change. The nonconformist chapels gradually lost their dominant place in society in the course of these hundred years. The First World War marked one clear landmark in the decline of the pulpit and the *sêt fawr* as social leaders. Since then, the steady retreat of puritanism (so invigorating a process for Welsh and Anglo-Welsh literature) had profound weakening effects upon nonconformity, for such institutions as the 'Welsh Sunday' and, by extension, for older ideals of nationhood associated with the popular, extra-mural life of the chapels. The *eisteddfod*, too, became perhaps somewhat less central in the life of the people after 1914, despite the popular impact of its proceedings being televised. Local *eisteddfodau* lost much ground, despite some assistance from private patronage. The national university also became less closely associated with Welsh ideals, as the student population and much of the teaching staff increasingly came from outside the principality after 1945. In these vital respects, Welsh nationhood in the later twentieth century was a more anxious, apprehensive thing, cut off from many of its roots and its institutional base, by contrast with the almost unthinking confidence and serenity of the years of the national awakening between the eighties and 1914. It was certainly a nationhood often shaped by a profound sense of nostalgia, of the passing of a rewarding, culturally enriching way of life. The aspiration seemed too often to be that of *Cymru Fu* rather than of *Cymru Fydd*.

Nevertheless, it is impossible to survey the history of Wales in these hundred years without concluding, beyond all doubt, that the sense of separate national identity and distinctiveness from England, elusive and difficult to define though it might be, remained a powerful one. For many reasons, to some extent linguistic and cultural, to some extent the product of group consciousness and of kith-and-kin relationships (including among Welsh *emigrés*), the sense of Wales as an entity that comprehended north and south, rural and urban, border country and heartland. Anglo-Welsh and native speaker, remained intensely vigorous. The political implications of this remained confused. But there could be little doubt that Welsh nationality, like Scottish, remained a living force in the 1970s, even after the devolution referendum in 1979, a dormant giant ready perhaps to bestir itself and to crusade anew for the destiny of a nation. The idea of Wales was very much alive in the later twentieth century, more so than in 1880, when this book begins. In some ways, it was more firmly entrenched than ever in the past, with the broad tolerance of English-speaking Welshmen towards native traditions and the concern of the young with aspects of folk culture and national awareness. The force of modern mass communications and overseas travel brought the example of popular minority movements in other lands that much nearer.

After all, in many ways the crusade for Welsh nationhood had been a success story. In part, this was the result of the sympathy and the intelligence shown by successive British governments, Liberal, Conservative, and Labour, from the passage of the Welsh Intermediate Education Act of 1889 onwards. British governments began, early on, to realize that Welsh nationalism was different in quality from Irish, and that showing a proper respect for Wales and its cultural traditions was one way of shoring up the United Kingdom, not of launching it, through some mighty 'domino theory', into Gadarene-type separatism. Most of all, the successes of the Welsh national movement owed their origin to the idealism, intelligence, and determination of the Welsh themselves. Each phase of the national movement brought its own victories. Before 1914, there were institutions like the national museum, library, and above all the university. There was a distinct educational structure with the place of the Welsh language recognized within it. There were practical symbols of the Welsh reality, from the disestablishment of the Church to the immense vitality of the periodical press. The inter-war period in Britain was not a thriving time for movements concerned with the projection of nationhood. But, even here, from the ashes of depression, there survived a powerful sense that the centralist structure of the United Kingdom needed to be modified; that cultural distinctiveness alone demanded that Wales be treated as a separate economic planning unit; and that the political relationship between Wales and Westminster needed to be looked at anew. The years from 1962 saw a new recognition of the priorities current in Welsh life—new concern to protect the language, the creation of the Welsh Office, and inclusion of Welsh self-government, in however modest a form, as a major item of governmental legislation. The story was far from over even after the devolution referendum of 1979. New chapters would surely be written in the future, in response to the renewal of self-confidence and pride, of a sense of their own restless genius, amongst the Welsh people themselves.

For this reason alone—the continuing sense of nationhood during this period—the history of modern Wales forms a major theme for the historian. It became increasingly apparent during the late nineteenth and the twentieth centuries that Wales had its own traditions, values and priorities, that a Welsh community had survived and flourished despite the absence of a Welsh state. Further, the Welsh in many ways were becoming more aware of that history, an awareness rooted in reality and stripped of the old romantic fantasies that coloured much Welsh, like English, historical writing before 1914. There had been Welsh equivalents of the 'Norman yoke' theory which influenced late nineteenth-century Liberal historiography; there was the romantic idealization of the rural *werin*. But by 1970s this was much less current. A more durable and defensible concept of Welshness was being evolved, one based on social and economic realities. The factory worker in Cwmbran new town or the elderly resident in an anglicized coastal resort could respond to it, no less than the farmers or labourers or quarrymen in the rural areas, or the miners or steelworkers in the valleys of the south. Aided by modern techniques of mass communication—which made the Welsh BBC, for instance, crucially important in the transmission of ideas of national consciousness, in many ways replacing the force of the written word—a sense of the separate identity and of the unity of the nation was as deep-rooted as ever in the past.

More generally, consciousness of nationhood in Wales has become more relevant to Britain as a whole in the later twentieth century. For this reason, too, it affords a major theme for the chronicler of these recent times. After 1945, the loss of empire, the sense of economic and (more specifically) of comparative industrial decline, wrought powerful changes in the psyche of the British people. The sense of being a master race, the certainty that had once attached to English and imperial values, the unquestioned allegiance to Crown, parliament, and the political parties, the automatic deference to a hierarchy adminstered by a narrow public-school, Oxbridge élite, all steadily eroded. Britain became a less deferential society—and a less confident one. The abiding sense of national identity in Wales illustrates some key features in that process—the attachment to local communities, to local or native traditions; the revolt against centralization and bureaucracy; the emergence of modes of social organization other than those prescribed by a distant, once unchallengeable, now increasingly vulnerable authority in London. Welsh nationhood was more relevant to the dissolving certainties of later twentieth-century Britain, with the collapse of the old values and the doubts that surrounded established social and political structures, than it was for the crisis of the inter-war years, let alone the imperial heyday before 1914. For much of England, the dissolution and flux of the years after 1945 were sobering, even destructive. In Wales, they were to some degree liberating and invigorating, as new validity was restored to an ancient culture, and an immemorial attachment to locality, family, and race.

The eminent Yale historian, C. Vann Woodward, once upheld in unforgettable words the validity of his serving as a 'regional historian' of the American South.[2] The South, he wrote, was in some ways more in tune with the national experience of the United States of America in the twentieth century than was the industrial, poly-ethnic North. The South had known the bitterness of military defeat in the Civil War, and of psychological disillusion in the Reconstruction that followed it, with the need to cling, almost in despair, to old values and to rebuild a shattering society. To the United States generally, in the aftermath of the slump and mass unemployment after 1929, the pressures of the Cold War in the forties, and internal crises of conscience such as racial disturbances and the war in Vietnam in the sixties, the perspective and experience of the South were especially valuable. For, in Vann Woodward's phrase, 'history was something that had happened' to the South, in a painful fashion that the optimistic, nationalistic Yankee might find somewhat harder to understand. Of course, the history of modern Wales has been much more peaceable than that of the American southern states. Its main crisis, oppressive enough in all conscience but not tragic in the same sense, involved mass unemployment, emigration, and starvation in the thirties, but not military defeat and occupation of its territories by alien invaders. The perils undergone by the Welsh language were hardly comparable with the legacy of racist tension and bigotry which gave much of the American South and its people their sense of solidarity. *Twm Shon Cati* and Jim Crow were civilizations apart.

For all that, Wales, like Scotland indeed, also serves as a story of desperate survival against all the odds, of frequent failures and half-fulfilled aspirations, kept alive without self-destructive bitterness and ultimately with much success. In that sense, the experience of Wales and of the American South had some analogies, just as the agrarian, conservative ideology propounded by the twelve southern authors of *I'll Take My Stand* in 1930 parallels much of the writing of the early publicists of Plaid Cymru at the same period. The Welsh experience, like the Southern, induces a sense of humility, of the transitory, deceptive quality of political and economic achievements, of the fragility of a national culture treasured over the centuries by the common people. The Welsh experience, too, with its past setbacks and subsequent recovery of confidence in a very different social climate after 1945, may have more relevance for the history of Britain in the late twentieth century—clearly the history of a second-class power, at best—than may be the imperial path of ascendancy once trodden by the governing English. Amidst the cataract of evidence that illustrated British national decline, the Welsh might reflect that

    [2] C. Vann Woodward, 'The Irony of Southern History', originally published in *Journal of Southern History* xix (1953) and reprinted in *The Burden of Southern History* (Baton Rouge, Louisiana, 1960), pp. 167–91.

their social culture, still flourishing in its many forms from the hill farms of Gwynedd to the steel-works of Gwent, remained a living, distinctive part of the evolution of the British and the European world. That culture had survived and had been triumphantly renewed, against all the odds: for history was something that had happened to the Welsh in their part of the world.

BIBLIOGRAPHY

A comprehensive bibliography of the primary and secondary source materials relating to the history of Wales in the last hundred years would require another volume to itself. It would have to include a survey of much of the literature covering the history of Britain generally since 1880. I have sought here merely to provide some guidance to the reader by indicating the main manuscript and printed sources that proved useful in the writing of this book. I have confined myself, as far as possible, to materials of strictly Welsh interest, for the sake of brevity. There is, at the time of writing (winter of 1979), no generally satisfactory bibliographical aid that covers the whole of this period. The *Bibliography of the History of Wales* (Cardiff, 1962) is very useful but far from comprehensive, and does not really extend beyond 1914. Supplements were published in the *Bulletin of the Board of Celtic Studies* xx (May 1963) for publications in the years 1959–62, xxii (November 1966) for the years 1963–5, xxiii (November 1969) for the years 1966–8, and xxv (November 1972) for the years 1969–71. The *Bibliography* is now being completely revised and recast on a computerized basis by Mr Philip Jones of Aberystwyth, under the aegis of the History and Law Committee of the Board of Celtic Studies. Complete checklists of articles relating to the history of Wales are printed annually in the December issues of the *Welsh History Review*. The bibliographies in *Bibliotheca Celtica* are also helpful. H. J. Hanham (ed.), *Bibliography of British History, 1851–1914* (Oxford, 1976), chapter XI, has an excellent coverage of printed material on Welsh history down to 1914. G. H. Martin and Sylvia McIntyre (eds.), *A Bibliography of British and Irish Municipal History* (Leicester, 1972), includes the history of Wales. Frequent bibliographies of the sources for Welsh labour history appear in the journal *Llafur* (1972–   ), while Alun Morgan, *The South Wales Valleys in History: a guide to Literature* (Aberfan, 1975) is very useful. Joyce M. Bellamy and John Saville (eds.), *Dictionary of Labour Biography*, vols. i–v (London, 1972–9) append excellent guides to sources for their numerous Welsh entries. For Welsh language and literature, excellent bibliographies appear annually in *Studia Celtica*. Also valuable is Thomas Parry and Merfyn Morgan (eds.), *Llyfryddiaeth Llenyddiaeth Gymraeg* (Cardiff, 1976). A select bibliography on the language is given by W. T. R. Pryce in the *Bulletin of the Board of Celtic Studies* xxviii (November 1978). For Anglo-Welsh literature, see Brynmor Jones, *A Bibliography of Anglo-Welsh Literature, 1900–1965* (Cardiff, 1970). The *Annual Reports* of the National Library of Wales and of the National Museum are of the greatest importance, not least for the visual arts. Admirable checklists on most aspects of Welsh history are provided by David Lewis Jones in the *Welsh History Review*, June 1971 (for theses up to 1970), June 1974 (for theses, 1970–2), and June 1976 (for theses, 1973–6).

A. MANUSCRIPTS

Asquith Papers (Bodleian Library, Oxford)
C. E. Breese Papers (National Library of Wales, Aberystwyth (NLW))
Campbell-Bannerman Papers (British Library (BL))
'Cochfarf' Papers: papers of Edward Thomas, 'Cochfarf' (Cardiff Public Library)
Coetmor Papers: papers of W. J. Parry (University College of North Wales, Bangor)
    (UCNW))
Cwrtmawr Papers: papers of J. H. Davies (NLW)
Dalton Papers (London School of Economics library (LSE))
D. R. Daniel Papers (NLW)
Lord Davies of Llandinam Papers (NLW)
Ellis W. Davies Papers (NLW)
G. M. Ll. Davies Papers (NLW)
T. Huws Davies Reports (NLW)
Watkin Davies Papers (NLW)
T. E. Ellis Papers (NLW)
H. Tobit Evans Papers (NLW)
Sir Samuel T. Evans Papers (NLW)
Sir Vincent Evans Papers (NLW)
H. A. L. Fisher Papers (Bodleian Library)
Frondirion Papers: papers of E. W. Evans (NLW)
H. C. Fryer Papers (NLW)
Thomas Gee Papers (NLW)
Herbert, Viscount Gladstone Papers (BL)
William Ewart Gladstone Papers (BL)
Glansevern Papers: papers of A. C. Humphreys-Owen (NLW)
Sir Ellis Griffith Papers (NLW)
James Griffiths Papers (NLW)
J. M. Howell collection (NLW)
Independent Labour Party: NAC minutes (LSE)
E. T. John Papers (NLW)
Revd Josiah T. Jones Papers (NLW)
Thomas Jones Papers (NLW: courtesy of Lady White)
William Jones Papers (UCNW)
Labour Party archives: correspondence files and NEC minutes (Transport House)
A. Bonar Law Papers (House of Lords Record Office (HLRO))
J. Herbert Lewis Papers (NLW)
J. Herbert Lewis Papers (privately owned: courtesy of Mrs K. Idwal Jones)
Liberation Society minutes: microfilm (University College of Swansea)
Sir John Lloyd Papers (UCNW)
Earl Lloyd-George of Dwyfor Papers (HLRO)
Earl Lloyd-George of Dwyfor Papers (NLW)
Lady Megan Lloyd George Papers (NLW)
Ramsay MacDonald Papers (Public Record Office)
W. H. Mainwaring Papers (NLW: courtesy of Mrs J. Tudge)
Milner Papers (Bodleian Library)
R. Hopkin Morris Papers (NLW)
Sir John Morris-Jones Papers (UCNW)
North Wales Liberal Federation minute book, 1887–92 (NLW)

Bishop John Owen Papers (privately owned: courtesy of the late Miss Eluned Owen)
W. J. Parry Papers (NLW)
Lord Pontypridd Papers (Cardiff Public Library)
Rendel Papers (NLW)
Henry Richard Papers (NLW)
D. M. Richards Papers (NLW)
J. H. Richards Papers (privately owned: courtesy of the late Mrs Haslett)
J. Bryn Roberts Papers (NLW)
J. T. Roberts letter-book (Gwynedd Record Office, Caernarfon)
Marquess of Salisbury Papers (Christ Church library, Oxford)
D. A. Thomas Papers (NLW)
D. Lleufer Thomas Papers (NLW)
J. J. Vaughan Papers (Glamorgan Record Office, Cardiff)
Sir H. Hussey Vivian Papers (NLW)
Webb Papers (LSE)
Zimmern Papers (Bodleian Library)

In addition, the following classes of the Public Records were consulted:
CAB 21: Cabinet Registered Files
CAB 23: Cabinet Minutes to 1939
CAB 24: Cabinet Papers
CAB 26: Home Affairs Committee
CAB 27: Cabinet Committees
CAB 128: Cabinet Minutes, 1945–
CAB 129: Cabinet Papers, 1945–
ED 35: Board of Education Papers
ED 91: Board of Education files
HO 45: Home Office Papers

The above section does not include scores of smaller items consulted at the National Library of Wales, the Public Record Office and elsewhere.

B. OFFICIAL PAPERS (in chronological sequence)

Hansard, *Parliamentary Debates,* Third Series
Parliamentary Debates, Fourth and Fifth Series
Censuses of England and Wales, 1871–1971
Return of Owners of Land, 1873. England and Wales (C. 1097), H.C., 1874, lxii
Report of the Committee appointed to inquire into the Condition of Higher Education in Wales (C. 3047), H.C., 1881, xxxiii
Second Report of the Royal Commission on the Depression in Trade and Industry (C. 4715), H.C., 1886, xxi, xxii
Report of the Commissioners appointed to inquire into the operation of the Sunday Closing (Wales) Act, 1881 (C. 5994), H.C., 1890, xl
Evidence and Report of the Royal Commission on Labour (C. 6708, 6795), H.C., 1892, xxxiv, xxxvi
Evidence, Report and Appendices of the Royal Commission on Land in Wales and Monmouthshire:
    Evidence, vols 1 and 2 (C. 7439), H.C., 1894, xxxvi, xxxvii
    Evidence, vols 3 and 4 (C. 7661, 7757), H.C., 1895, xl, xli

Evidence, Report and Appendices, Index (C. 8242, 8221, 8222), H.C., 1896, xxxiii, xxxiv, xxxv

Report of the Board of Education on the Administration of Schools under the Welsh Intermediate Education Act of 1889, H.C., 1901, xxi, 244, 359

Report of the Select Committee on Private Legislation Procedure (Wales), H.C., 1904, vi, 409

List of Public Elementary Schools in Wales on 1 August 1906 (Cd. 3640), H.C., 1907, lxiii

Royal Commission on the Poor Laws: Appendix and Minutes of Evidence (Cd. 4626, 4888), H.C., 1909, xxxix, 635 and xli, 983

Report, Minutes of Evidence and Appendices of the Royal Commission appointed to inquire into the Church and other Religious Bodies in Wales:
Vol. 1 Report (Cd. 5432), H.C., 1910, xiv
Vols 2–4 Minutes of Evidence (Cd. 5433–5), H.C., 1910, xv-xvii
Vols 5–6 Appendices (Cd. 5436–7), H.C., 1910, xviii

Report of H.M. Inspectors of Mines for the Year 1910 (South Wales District) (Cd. 5676), H.C., 1911, xxxv, 335

Report and Correspondence on Disturbances in connection with the South Wales Colliery Strikes (Cd. 5568), H.C., 1911, lxiv

Report of the Departmental Committee on the National Medical School for Wales at Cardiff, H.C., 1916, viii

Report and Minutes of Evidence of the Royal Commission on the University of Wales:
First Report and Minutes (Cd. 8500, 8507), H.C., 1917–18, xii
Second Report and Minutes (Cd. 8698, 8699), H.C., 1917–18, xii
Final Report and Minutes (Cd. 8991, 8993), H.C., 1918, xiv

Report of the Commission appointed to inquire into Industrial Unrest (Cd. 8662), H.C., 1917–18, xv

Report and Minutes of Evidence of the Royal Commission on the Coal Industry (Cmd. 359, 360), H.C., 1919, xi, xii

A Letter from the Speaker to the Prime Minister (on Devolution) (Cmd. 692), H.C., 1920, xiii

First Report of the Welsh Consultative Council on Medical and Allied Services in Wales (Cd. 703), H.C., 1920, xvii

Report of the Departmental Committee on the organisation of Secondary Education in Wales (Cmd. 967), H.C., 1920, xv

Report on the Administration of the Welsh Board of Health (Cmd. 913), H.C., 1920, xvii, 535

Report of the Committee inquiring into the Distribution and Location of houses erected in the South Wales Coalfield (non-parl.), H.M.S.O., 1921

Report and Minutes of Evidence of the Royal Commission on the Coal Industry (Cmd. 2600), H.C., 1926, xiv

Report of the Board of Guardians on the Bedwellty Union for the period ending 30 September 1927 (Cmd. 2976), H.C., 1927, xi, 111

Report of the Board of Guardians for the period ending June 1928 (Cmd. 3141), H.C., 1928, xii, 133

Report of the Departmental Committee on Welsh in Education and Life (non-parl.), H.M.S.O., 1927

Report of the Ministry of Health on the Investigation into the South Wales Coalfield (Cmd. 3272), H.C., 1928–9, viii, 689

Report of the Departmental Committee appointed to inquire into Public Education in Wales and Monmouthshire in relation to the needs of Rural Areas (non-parl.), H.M.S.O., 1930

Report on the Educational Problems of the South Wales Coalfield (non-parl.), H.M.S.O., 1931

Industrial Survey of South Wales (non-parl.), H.M.S.O., 1932

Second Industrial Survey of South Wales (non-parl.), 3 vols, 1937

Investigation into Certain Depressed Areas (Cmd. 4728), H.C., 1933–4, xiii, 313

First Report of the Commission for the Special Areas (Cmd. 4957), H.C., 1934–5, x, 149

Second Report of the Commission for the Special Areas (Cmd. 5090), H.C., 1935–6, xiii, 149

Report of the Commission of Inquiry into the Status of Merthyr Tydfil as a County Borough (Cmd. 5039), H.C., 1935–6, xiv, 1

Report on Maternal Mortality in Wales (Cmd. 5423), H.C., 1936–7, xi, 367

Third Report of the Commission for the Special Areas (Cmd. 5303), H.C., 1936–7 xii, 661

Report on the causes of the explosion at Gresford Colliery (Cmd. 5358), H.C., 1936–7, xiii, 733

Fourth Report of the Commission for the Special Areas (Cmd. 5595), H.C., 1937–8, xii, 787

Fifth Report of the Commission for the Special Areas (Cmd. 5896), H.C., 1938–9, xii, 221

Report of the Committee on the Anti-Tuberculosis service in Wales and Monmouthshire (non-parl.), H.M.S.O., 1939

First Interim Report of the Welsh Reconstruction Advisory Council (non-parl.), H.M.S.O., 1944

Report from the Working Party on persons suspended from the South Wales mining industry on account of silicosis and pneumoconiosis (Cmd. 6719), H.C., 1945–6, xx, 205

Report of Government Action in Wales and Monmouthshire (Cmd. 6938), H.C., 1945–6, xx, 763

Report on the Welsh Slate Industry (non-parl.), H.M.S.O., 1947

Report of the Central Advisory Council on the future of Secondary Education in Wales (non-parl.), H.M.S.O., 1949

Report on the South Wales Outline Plan (non-parl.), H.M.S.O., 1949

The Council for Wales and Monmouthshire: a memorandum on its activities (Cmd. 8066), H.C., 1950, xix, 883

Report of the Committee on Welsh Language Publishing (Cmd. 8661), H.C., 1951–2, xviii, 1095

The Council for Wales and Monmouthshire: Second Memorandum on its activities (Cmd. 8844), H.C., 1952–3, xxiv, 875

Report of the Central Advisory Council on the place of Welsh and English in the Schools of Wales (non-parl.), H.M.S.O., 1953

The Council for Wales and Monmouthshire: reports of the Rural Development Panel (Cmd. 9014), H.C., 1953–4, xxvi, 867

Annual Report of the Iron and Steel Board for the period July 1953–December 1954, H.C., 1954–5, vi, 138, 311

The Council for Wales and Monmouthshire: report on the South Wales Ports (Cmd.

9359), H.C., 1954–5, vii, 565

Reports of the Welsh Agriculture Land Sub-Commission: Mid-Wales Investigation Report (Cmd. 9631, 9809), H.C., 1955–6, x, 471, and xxxvi, 407

Report of the Committee of Inquiry into Welsh Broadcasting (Cmnd. 39), H.C., 1956–7, ix, 169

The Council for Wales and Monmouthshire: Third Memorandum on its activities (Cmnd. 53), H.C., 1956–7, xxvi, 991

The Council for Wales and Monmouthshire: Text of letter addressed by the Prime Minister to the Chairman (Cmnd. 334), H.C., 1957–8, xxiv, 1177

Report of the Committee on the Technical Problems of Welsh Agriculture (non-parl.), H.M.S.O., 1958

Report on the proposals to construct a Nuclear Power station at Trawsfynydd (non-parl.), H.M.S.O., 1958

The Council for Wales and Monmouthshire: Fourth Memorandum on its activities (Cmnd. 631), H.C., 1958–9, xxv, 1455

Report on Education in Rural Wales (non-parl.), H.M.S.O., 1960

Report of a working party on a Welsh Agricultural College (non-parl.), H.M.S.O., 1960

Report of Government Action and Developments in Wales and Monmouthshire (Cmnd. 1293), H.C., 1960–1, xxi, 633

Report of the Welsh Advisory Water Committee on the Water Resources of Wales (Cmnd. 1331), H.C., 1960–1, xxi, 753

Housing in England and Wales (Cmnd. 1290), H.C., 1960–1, xxvii, 513

Report of the Committee on Broadcasting (Cmnd. 1819), H.C., 1961–2, ix, 613

The Council for Wales and Monmouthshire: Report on Rural Transport Problems in Wales (Cmnd. 1821), H.C., 1961–2, xxiv, 635

Report and Proposals of the Local Government Commission for Wales (non-parl.), H.M.S.O., 1963

The Council for Wales and Monmouthshire: report on the Welsh Language today (Cmnd. 2198), H.C., 1963–4, xx, 461

Depopulation in Mid-Wales (non-parl.), H.M.S.O., 1964

The Legal Status of the Welsh Language: Report of the Committee (Cmnd. 2785), H.C., 1964–5, xxiii, 877

Wales, 1965 (Cmnd. 2918), H.C., 1965–6, vii, 635

Wales: the Way Ahead (Cmnd, 3334), H.C., 1967, lix, 915

Local Government in Wales (Cmnd. 3340), H.C., 1967, lix, 879

Primary Education in Wales (non-parl.), H.M.S.O., 1968

Welsh Grand Committee: Minutes of Proceedings: Local Government Reorganisation in Glamorgan and Monmouthshire, H.C., 1969–70, xviii, 181

The Welsh Council: a Strategy for Rural Wales (non-parl.), H.M.S.O., 1971

Report and Memoranda of the Royal Commission on the Constitution (Cmnd. 5460), H.C., 1973–4, xi

Democracy and Devolution (Cmnd. 5732), H.C., 1974, v, 85

Our Changing Democracy: Devolution in Scotland and Wales (Cmnd. 6348), H.C., 1975–6, xiv

Devolution to Scotland and Wales: Supplementary Statement (Cmnd. 6585), H.C., 1976

Devolution: Financing the Devolved Services (Cmnd. 6890), H.C., 1976–7, xi, 291

A Future for the Welsh Language (non-parl.), H.M.S.O., 1978

Publishing in the Welsh Language (non-parl.), H.M.S.O., 1978
'Examination Achievement in Wales' (discussion paper prepared by Welsh Education Office, February 1978)

In addition, use was made of the following:
Annual Reports of the Committee of Council on Education (to 1899)
Annual Reports of the Board of Education (1899–1944)
Annual Reports of the Ministry of Education (1945–   )
Annual Reports of the Ministry of Health (1920–   )
Annual Reports of the Ministry of Labour (1920–   )
Annual Reports of the Welsh Office (1965–   )
Digest of Welsh Statistics (1954–   )

C. NEWSPAPERS AND PERIODICALS

1. Newspapers

English	Welsh
Daily News	*Aberdare Times*
Daily Telegraph	*Baner ac Amserau Cymru*
Financial Times	*Cambria Daily Leader*
Liverpool Daily Post	*Cambrian News*
Manchester Guardian (later the *Guardian*	*Cardiff Times*
	Carmarthen Times
Observer	*Carnarvon and Denbigh Herald*
Sunday Times	*Y Cymro*
The Times	*Y Genedl Gymreig*
	Glamorgan Free Press
	Yr Herald Cymraeg
	Labour Voice
	Llais Llafur
	Merthyr Express
	Mumbles Weekly Press and Gower News
	North Wales Observer and Express
	Rhondda Leader
	Rhondda Socialist
	Seren Cymru
	South Wales Daily News (*South Wales News* from 1919)
	South Wales Echo
	Tarian y Gweithiwr
	Y Tyst a'r Dydd
	Western Mail

2. Periodicals

English	Welsh
British Medical Journal	*Anglo-Welsh Review*
British Weekly	*Arolwg*
Church Times	*Y Beirniad*
Contemporary Review	*Cwrs y Byd*

The Economist
ILP News
Labour Leader
Lancet
Liberal Magazine
Life and Letters Today
Local Government Journal
New Statesman
Nineteenth Century and After
Punch
Radio Times
Socialist Review
Spectator

Cymru
Cymru Fydd (1888–91)
Cymru'r Plant
Y Ddraig Goch
Y Deyrnas
Y Dinesydd
Dock Leaves
Y Ddinas
Efrydiau Athronyddol
Y Geninen
Y Gwerinwr: Monthly Democrat
Labour Pioneer
Y Llenor (1922–51)
Lleufer
Merthyr Pioneer
Nationalist
Planet
Plebs
Poetry Wales
Tafod y Ddraig
Taliesin
Y Traethodydd
Yr Undebwr
Wales (1894–7: ed. by O. M. Edwards)
Wales (1911–14: ed. by J. Hugh Edwards)
Wales (1937–60: ed. by Keidrich Rhys)
Y Wawr
Welsh Anvil
Welsh Journal of Agriculture
The Welsh Leader
Welsh Music
Welsh Nationalist
Welsh Outlook (1914–34)
Welsh Outlook (1965)
Welsh Review (1891–3)
Welsh Review (1939–48)
Young Wales
Ysgrifau Beirniadol

D. REPORTS AND WORKS OF REFERENCE

1. Reports

Annual Reports of the following organizations:

Baptist Church
British Broadcasting Corporation
Calvinistic Methodist Church
Congregational Church
Independent Labour Party
Iron and Steel Board

Labour Party
Liberal Party
National Coal Board
National Eisteddfod
National Library of Wales
National Museum of Wales
National Union of Conservative and Unionist Associations
University of Wales (including constituent colleges)
Welsh Arts Council
Welsh Church Congress
Welsh Housing and Development Association
Welsh Labour Party
Wesleyan Methodist Church

2. Works of Reference
(place of publication London, unless othewise stated)

Annual Abstract of Statistics
Annual Register
Burke's Landed Gentry
Burke's Peerage, Baronetage and Knightage
Butler, D. E., and Richard Rose, *The British General Election of 1959* (1960)
—, and Anthony King, *The British General Election of 1964* (1965)
—— *The British General Election of 1966* (1966)
—, and M. Pinto-Duschinsky, *The British General Election of 1970* (1970)
—— and D. Kavanagh, *The British General Election of February 1974* (1974)
—— *The British General Election of October 1974* (1975)
Craig, F. W. S, *British Electoral Facts, 1885–1975* (1976 edition)
—— *British Parliamentary Election Results, 1918–1949* (Glasgow, 1969)
—— *British Parliamentary Election Statistics, 1918–1968* (Glasgow, 1968)
—— *British General Election Manifestos, 1918–1966* (Chichester, 1970)
—— *Minor Parties and British Parliamentary Elections, 1885–1974* (1975)
Dictionary of National Biography
Dictionary of Welsh Biography down to 1940 (1959, with Welsh-language supplement for 1941–50 (1970))
Dod's Parliamentary Companion
Ford, P. and G., *A Breviate of Parliamentary Papers, 1900–16* (Oxford, 1957)
—— *A Breviate of Parliamentary Papers, 1917–39* (Oxford, 1951)
—— *A Breviate of Parliamentary Papers, 1940–54* (Oxford, 1961)
The Herald Book of Labour Members (1923)
Industrial Directory of Wales
Mitchell, B. R., and Deane, Phyllis, *Abstract of British Economic Statistics* (Cambridge, 1962)
—— *The British Economy: Key Statistics, 1900–1966* (Cambridge, 1967)
Roberts, T. R., *A Dictionary of Eminent Welshmen* (Cardiff, 1908)
South Wales Coal Annual
South Wales Industrial Review
South Wales Ports Handbook
Statesmen's Year Book
The Times: the New Parliament, 1880–1974

Who's Who in Wales (1st ed., 1920; 2nd ed., 1933; 3rd ed., 1937)
Who was Who

E. SECONDARY WORKS
(place of publication London unless otherwise stated)

1. General Works

Bowen, E. G., *Wales: a Physical, Historical and Regional Geography* (Cardiff, 2nd ed., 1967)

Coupland, R., *Welsh and Scottish Nationalism* (1954)

Jenkins, R. T., 'The Development of Nationalism in Wales', *Sociological Review* (1935)

Jones, Brinley (ed.), *Anatomy of Wales* (Cardiff, 1972)

Morgan, Kenneth O., 'Welsh Nationalism: the Historical Background', *Jnl. of Contemporary History* 6, No. 1 (January 1971)

Morgan, Prys, *Background to Wales* (Llandybïe, 1968)

Morgan, W. J., *The Welsh Dilemma* (Swansea, 1973)

Rees, I. Bowen, *The Welsh Political Tradition* (1961)

Rees, J. F., *The Problem of Wales and other Essays* (Cardiff, 1963)

Rees, William, *Historical Atlas of Wales* (1959)

Roderick, A. J. (ed.), *Wales through the Ages*, ii (Llandybïe, 1960)

Thomas, D. (ed.), *Wales: a new Study* (Newton Abbot, 1977)

Williams, David, *A History of Modern Wales* (1950)

Williams, Glanmor, 'The Idea of Nationality in Wales', *Cambridge Jnl.* (1953)

—— *Religion, Language and Nationality in Wales* (Cardiff, 1979)

Williams, Gwyn A., 'Twf Hanesyddol y Syniad o Genedl yng Nghymru', *Efrydiau Athronyddol* xxiv (1961)

2. Politics, 1880–1914

Awbery, Stan, *Labour's Early Struggles in Swansea* (Swansea, 1949)

Barker, Michael, *Gladstone and Radicalism* (Hassocks, 1975)

Bealey, F., and Henry Pelling, *Labour and Politics, 1900–1906* (1958)

Brown, K. D. (ed.), *Essays in Anti-Labour History* (1974)

Davies, A. T., *The Lloyd George I Knew* (1948)

Davies, Ivor, *Top Sawyer* (1938)

Davies, Watkin, *Lloyd George, 1863–1914* (1939)

Edwards, J. Hugh, *The Life of David Lloyd George,* 4 vols (with vol. 5 by Saxon Mills, 1913–24)

Edwards, Wil John, *From the Valleys I Came* (1956)

Ellis, Thomas E., *Speeches and Addresses* (Wrexham, 1912)

Ellis, Thomas I., *Ellis Griffith* (Llandybïe, 1969)

—— *Thomas Edward Ellis: Cofiant,* 2 vols (Liverpool, 1944–8)

Evans, Beriah Gwynfe, *Dafydd Dafis: sef Hunangofiant Ymgeisydd Seneddol* (Wrexham, 1898)

—— *The Life Romance of David Lloyd George* (1915)

Fox, Kenneth O., 'Labour and Merthyr's Khaki Election of 1900', *Welsh History Review,* vol. 2, No. 4 (December 1965)

George, W. R. P., *The Making of Lloyd George* (1975)

George, William, *Cymru Fydd: Hanes y Mudiad Cenedlaethol Cyntaf* (Liverpool, 1945)

—— *My Brother and I* (1958)

Gregory, R. G., *The Miners and British Politics, 1906–1914* (Oxford, 1968)

Griffith-Boscawen, A. S. T., *Fourteen Years in Parliament* (1907)

—— *Memories* (1925)

Grigg, John, *The Young Lloyd George* (1973)

—— *The People's Champion* (1978)

Hanham, H. J., *Elections and Party Management* (1959)

Hughes, Emrys, *Keir Hardie* (1956)

Jones, E. Pan, *Oes a Gwaith Michael Daniel Jones* (Caernarfon, 1903)

Jones, I. Gwynedd, *Health, Wealth and Politics in Victorian Wales* (Swansea, 1979)

Jones, K. Idwal, *Syr Herbert Lewis, 1858–1933* (Aberystwyth, 1958)

Jones, T. Gwynn, *Cofiant Emrys ap Iwan* (Caernarfon, 1912)

—— *Cofiant Thomas Gee* (Denbigh, 1913)

Jones-Evans, Peris, 'Evan Pan Jones – Land Reformer', *Welsh History Review*, vol. 4, No. 2 (December 1968)

Jones-Roberts, K. W., 'D. R. Daniel', *Jnl. Merioneth Hist. and Record Society* (1965)

Koss, Stephen, *Asquith* (1976)

Lambert, W. R., 'Thomas Williams, Gwaelod-y-Garth', *Glamorgan Historian* xi (1975)

—— 'The Welsh Sunday Closing Act, 1881', *Welsh History Review*, vol. 6, No. 2 (December 1972)

Masterman, Neville C., *The Forerunner* (Llandybïe, 1972)

Miall, C. S., *Henry Richard M.P.* (1889)

Morgan, J. Vyrnwy, *The Life of D. A. Thomas, Viscount Rhondda* (1918)

—— (ed.), *Welsh Political and Educational Leaders in the Nineteenth Century* (1908)

Morgan, Kenneth O., 'Cardiganshire Politics: the Liberal Ascendancy, 1885–1923', *Ceredigion* v, No. 4 (1967)

—— 'D. A. Thomas: the Industrialist as Politician', *Glamorgan Historian* iii (1966)

—— 'Democratic Politics in Glamorgan', *Morgannwg* iv (1960)

—— 'Gladstone and Wales', *Welsh History Review*, vol. 1, No. 1 (1960)

—— 'The Gower Election of 1906', *Gower* xii (1959)

—— *Keir Hardie: Radical and Socialist* (1975)

—— 'The Khaki Election in Gower', *Gower* xiii (1960)

—— 'Labour's Early Struggles in South Wales: some New Evidence, 1900–1908', *Nat. Lib. Wales Jnl.* xvii, No. 4 (Winter 1972)

—— 'Liberals, Nationalists and Mr. Gladstone', *Trans. Hon. Soc. Cymmrodorion* (1960)

—— 'The Liberal Unionists in Wales', *Nat. Lib. Wales Jnl.* xvi, No. 2 (Winter 1969)

—— *Lloyd George* (1974)

—— 'Lloyd George and the Historians', *Trans. Hon. Soc. Cymmrodorion* (1972)

—— 'Wales and the Boer War – a Reply', *Welsh History Review*, vol. 4, No. 4 (December 1969)

—— *Wales in British Politics, 1868–1922* (Cardiff, 3rd ed., 1980)

—— (ed.), *Lloyd George: Family Letters, 1885–1936* (Oxford and Cardiff, 1973)

Nelmes, G. V., 'Stuart Rendel and Welsh Liberal Political Organisations in the late Nineteenth Century', *Welsh History Review*, vol. 9, No. 4 (December 1979)

Owen, Frank, *Tempestuous Journey* (1954)

Parcq, Herbert du, *The Life of David Lloyd George,* 4 vols (1912)

Parry, Cyril, 'Gwynedd Politics: the Rise of a Labour Party', *Welsh History Review,* vol. 6, No. 3 (June 1973)

—— *The Radical Tradition in Welsh Politics* (Hull, 1970)

Pelling, Henry, *The Origins of the Labour Party, 1880–1900* (1954)

—— *The Social Geography of British Elections, 1885–1910* (1967)

—— 'Wales and the Boer War', *Welsh History Review*, vol. 4, No. 4 (December 1969)

Price, R. Emyr, 'Lloyd George and the Caernarvon Boroughs By-Election of 1890', *Caernarvonshire Hist. Soc. Trans.* xxxvi (1975)

—— 'Lloyd George and Merioneth Politics, 1885, 1886', *Jnl. Merioneth Hist. and Record Soc.* vii, No. 3 (1975)

—— 'Lloyd George's pre-parliamentary Political Career' (unpublished Bangor M.A. thesis, 1974)

—— 'Newyddiadur Cyntaf David Lloyd George', *Jnl. Welsh Bibliographical Society* xi (1975)

Rathbone, Eleanor, *William Rathbone* (1905)

Rhondda, Viscountess, and others, *The Life of D. A. Thomas, Viscount Rhondda* (1921)

Richard, Henry, *Letters and Essays on Wales* (1884)

Rowland, Peter, *Lloyd George* (1976)

Smith, Samuel, *My Life Story* (1902)

Spender, J. A., *Sir Robert Hudson: a Memoir* (1930)

Williams, Glanmor (ed.), *Merthyr Politics: the Making of a Working-Class Tradition* (Cardiff, 1966)

3. Politics, 1914–1945

Bayliss, Gwyn M., 'The Outsider: Aspects of the Political Career of Sir Alfred Mond, First Viscount Melchett' (unpublished Swansea Ph.D. thesis, 1969)

Cook, C. P., 'Wales and the General Election of 1923', *Welsh History Review,* vol. 4, No. 2 (December 1969)

David, Edward, 'Charles Masterman and the Swansea District By-Election of 1915', *Welsh History Review,* vol. 4, No. 3 (June 1970)

Davies, D. H., 'The Welsh Nationalist Party, 1925–1945' (unpublished Cardiff M.Sc. (Econ.) thesis, 1979)

Davies, D. J., *The Economics of Welsh Self-Government* (Caernarfon, 1931)

Daniel, J. E., *Welsh Nationalism: What it Stands for* (1937)

Egan, David, 'The Swansea Conference of the British Council of Soldiers' and Workers' Delegates, July 1917', *Llafur,* vol. 1, No. 4 (Summer 1975)

Evans, T. J., *Rhys Hopkin Morris* (Llandysul, 1957)

Foot, Michael, *Aneurin Bevan,* 2 vols (1962 and 1973)

Francis, Hywel, 'Welsh Miners and the Spanish Civil War', *Jnl. of Contemporary History,* v, No. 3 (1970)

Griffiths, E. H. *Heddychwr Mawr Cymru,* 2 vols (Caernarfon, 1967–8)

Griffiths, James, *Pages from Memory* (1969)

Hopkin, Deian, 'Patriots and Pacifists in Wales, 1914–18', *Llafur,* vol. 1, No. 3 (May 1974)

—— 'The Merthyr Pioneer', *Llafur,* vol. 2, No. 4 (Spring 1979)

Humphreys, E. Morgan, *Gwŷr Enwog Gynt* (Aberystwyth, 1950)
—— *Gwŷr Enwog Gynt:* yr Ail Gyfres (Aberystwyth, 1953)
John, E. T., *Wales: its Politics and Economics* (Cardiff, 1919)
Jones, Goronwy J., *Wales and the Quest for Peace* (Cardiff, 1970)
Jones, W. Hughes, *Wales Drops the Pilots* (1937)
—— *A Challenge to Wales* (Caernarfon, 1938)
Kinnear, M., *The Fall of Lloyd George: the Political Crisis of 1922* (1973)
Lewis, Saunders, *Egwyddorion Cenedlaetholdeb* (1926)
Morgan, Kenneth O., *Consensus and Disunity: the Lloyd George Coalition Government of 1918–1922* (Oxford, 1979)
—— 'The New Liberalism and the Challenge of Labour: the Welsh Experience, 1885–1929', *Welsh History Review*, vol. 6, No. 3 (June 1973)
—— 'Twilight of Welsh Liberalism: Lloyd George and the Wee Frees, 1918–1935', *Bull. Bd. of Celtic Studies* xii, part IV (May 1968)
Morris, Rhys Hopkin, *Welsh Politics* (1927)
Morris-Jones, Sir Henry, *Doctor in the Whips' Room* (1955)
Mowat, C. L., *Britain between the Wars, 1918–1940* (1955)
Nicholas, Islwyn ap, *Heretic at Large* (Llandysul, 1978)
Nicholson, Ivor and Lloyd Williams, *Wales: its part in the War* (1919)
Pelling, Henry, *The British Communist Party* (1958)
Roberts. David M., 'Clement Davies and the fall of Neville Chamberlain, 1939–40', *Welsh History Review*, vol. 8, No. 2 (December 1976)
—— 'Clement Davies and the Liberal Party, 1929–1956' (unpublished Aberystwyth M.A. thesis, 1976)
Rowlands, E. W., 'Etholiad Gyffredinol Môn yn 1918', *Anglesey Antiquarian and Field Club Trans.* (1976–7)
Smith, J. Beverley and others, *James Griffiths and his Times* (Cardiff, 1977)
Stead, Peter, 'Vernon Hartshorn', *Glamorgan Historian* vi (1970)
Taylor, A. J. P., *English History, 1914–1945* (Oxford, 1965)
—— (ed.), *Lloyd George: Twelve Essays* (1971)
Zimmern, Sir A., *My Impressions of Wales* (1927)

4. Politics, 1945–1980

Balsom, D., 'The nature and distribution of support for Plaid Cymru' (ECPR Joint Workshop Paper, April 1979)
Davies, D. J., *Towards an Economic Democracy* (Cardiff, 1949)
Davies, E. Hudson, 'Welsh Nationalism', *Pol. Quarterly* (July–September 1968)
Davies, G. Prys, *A Central Council for Wales* (Aberystwyth, 1963)
Davies, W. Pennar, *Saunders Lewis: ei Feddwl a'i Waith* (Denbigh, 1950)
Edwards, Huw T., *Hewn from the Rock* (Cardiff, 1967)
Edwards, Owen Dudley and others, *Celtic Nationalism* (1968)
Ellis, P. Berresford, *Wales – a Nation again* (1968)
Evans, Gwynfor, *Aros Mae* (Swansea, 1971)
—— *Rhagom i Ryddid* (Bangor, 1964)
—— *Wales can Win* (Llandybïe, 1973)
Fishlock, Trevor, *Wales and the Welsh* (1972)
Griffiths, Bruce, *Saunders Lewis* (Cardiff, 1979)
Griffiths, James, *Pages from Memory* (1969)

Harvie, Christopher, *Scotland and Nationalism* (1977)

Hechter, M., *Internal Colonialism* (1975)

Jones, J. Barry, 'The Welsh Labour Party and Devolution' (Political Studies Assn. Work Group paper, 1977)

Jones, J. E., *Tros Gymru* (Cardiff, 1970)

Jones, J. R., *Prydeindod* (Llandybïe, 1966)

Kolinsky, M. (ed.), *Divided Loyalties* (Manchester, 1978)

Lewis, Robyn, *Second-Class Citizen* (Llandysul, 1969)

Lloyd, D. M. (ed.), *The Historical Basis of Welsh Nationalism* (Cardiff, 1950)

Lort-Phillips, P., *The Future of Wales* (Carmarthen, 1961)

Mayo, Patricia Elton, *The Roots of Identity* (1974)

Michie, A., and S. Hoggart, *The Pact* (1978)

Morgan, Alun, 'The 1970 Parliamentary Election at Merthyr Tydfil', *Morgannwg*, xxii (1978)

Morgan, Gerald, *The Dragon's Tongue* (Cardiff, 1966)

Morgan, Janet (ed.), *Richard Crossman: the Diaries of a Cabinet Minister,* vols i–iii (1975–7)

Philip, Alan Butt, *The Welsh Question: Nationalism in Welsh Politics, 1945–1970* (Cardiff, 1975)

Rawkins, P. M., 'Minority Nationalism' (unpublished Toronto Ph.D. thesis, 1976)

Smith, J. B. and others, *James Griffiths and his Times* (Cardiff, 1978)

Thomas, Ned, *The Welsh Extremist* (1970)

Thomas, Colin H., 'Non-Violence and the Development of the Welsh Language Society, 1962–c. 1974', *Welsh History Review,* vol. 8, No. 4 (December 1977)

Note: Subsections 2, 3, and 4 do not include contemporary tracts, pamphlets, leaflets, or other ephemeral political literature produced by the political parties and other bodies, of which there is a vast bulk.

5. Economic and Social

Arnot, R. Page, *South Wales Miners, 1898–1914* (1967)

—— *South Wales Miners, 1914–1926* (1976)

Ashby, A. W., and I. L. Evans, *Agriculture of Wales and Monmouthshire* (Cardiff, 1949)

Balchin, W. G. V. (ed.), *Swansea and its Region* (Swansea, 1971)

Ballard, P. H., and E. Jones (eds.), *The Valleys Call* (Ferndale, 1975)

Barclay, M., ' "The Slaves of the Lamp": the Aberdare Miners' Strike, 1910', *Llafur,* vol. 2, No. 3 (Summer 1978)

Beacham, Arthur, *Depopulation in Mid-Wales* (1964)

Bollom, C., *Attitudes and Second Homes in Rural Wales* (Cardiff, 1978)

Brennan, T., E. Cooney and H. Pollins, *Social Change in South-West Wales* (1954)

Burn, D., *The Steel Industry, 1939–1959* (Cambridge, 1961)

Carter, M., and W. K. D. Davies (eds.), *Urban essays* (1970)

Colyer, R. J., 'The Pryse Family of Gogerddan and the Decline of a Great Estate, 1800–1960', *Welsh History Review,* vol. 9, No. 4 (December 1979)

Coombes, B. L., *These Poor Hands* (1939)

Daunton, M. J., 'The Cardiff Coal Trimmers' Union, 1888–1914', *Llafur,* vol. 2, No. 3 (Summer 1978)

—— *Coal Metropolis: Cardiff, 1870–1914* (Leicester, 1977)

—— 'Jack Ashore: Seamen in Cardiff before 1914', *Welsh History Review*, vol. 9, No. 2 (December 1978)

Davies, E. T., *Religion in the Industrial Revolution in South Wales* (Cardiff, 1965)

Davies, Elwyn, and A. D. Rees (eds.), *Welsh Rural Communities* (Cardiff, 1950)

Davies, John, 'The End of the Great Estates and the Rise of Freehold Farming in Wales', *Welsh History Review*, vol. 7, No. 2 (December 1974)

Davies, P., 'The Making of A. J. Cook', *Llafur*, vol. 2, No. 3 (Summer 1978)

Dunbabin, J. P. D. and others, *Rural Discontent in Nineteenth-Century Britain* (1974)

Edwards, Ness, *The History of the South Wales Miners* (1926)

—— *History of the South Wales Miners' Federation*, vol. i (1938)

Egan, David, 'The Unofficial Reform Committee and the *Miners' Next Step*', *Llafur*, vol. 2, No. 3 (Summer 1978)

Emmett, Isobel, *A North Wales Village* (1964)

Evans, Eric Wyn, *Mabon* (Cardiff, 1959)

—— *The Miners of South Wales* (Cardiff, 1961)

Francis, Hywel, 'The Anthracite Strike and the Disturbances of 1925', *Llafur*, vol. 1, No. 2 (May 1973)

Frankenburg, R. (ed.), *Communities in Britain* (1966)

Gidwell, D. I., 'Philosophy and Geology in Conflict', *Llafur*, vol. 1, No. 4 (Summer 1975)

Hare, A. E. C., *The Anthracite Coal Industry of the Swansea District* (Swansea, 1940)

Hodge, John, *Workman's Cottage to Windsor Castle* (1931)

Hodges, Frank, *My Adventures as a Labour Leader* (1925)

Holloway, F. W., 'Industrial Flintshire in the Interwar Years' (unpublished Aberystwyth M.A. thesis, 1979)

Holmes, G. M., 'The South Wales Coal Industry, 1850–1914', *Trans. Hon. Soc. Cymmrodorion* (1976)

Hopkins, K. S. (ed.), *Rhondda: Past and Future* (Ferndale, 1975)

Horner, Arthur, *Incorrigible Rebel* (1960)

Howell, David, 'The Impact of Railways on Agricultural Development in Nineteenth Century Wales', *Welsh History Review*, vol. 7, No. 1 (June 1974)

—— *Land and People in Nineteenth-Century Wales* (1977)

Humphrys, Graham, *Industrial Britain: South Wales* (Newton Abbot, 1972)

Jenkins, David, *The Agricultural Community in South-West Wales* (Cardiff, 1971)

Jevons, H. S., *The British Coal Trade* (1915)

John, Brian, *Pembrokeshire* (Newton Abbot, 1976)

Jones, Emyr, *Canrif y Chwarelwr* (Denbigh, 1964)

Jones, Ieuan Gwynedd (ed.), *Aberystwyth, 1277–1977* (Aberystwyth, 1977)

Jones, Lewis, *Cwmardy* (1937)

—— *We Live* (1939)

Jones, P. N., *Colliery Settlement in the South Wales Coalfield, 1850 to 1926* (Hull, 1969)

Jones, R. Merfyn, 'The North Wales Quarrymen's Union, 1874–1900', *Caernarvonshire Hist. Soc. Trans.* xxxv (1974)

Jones, Thomas, *Rhymney Memories* (Newtown, 1938)

Lewis, E. D., *The Rhondda Valleys* (1959)

Lewis, Richard, 'The South Wales Miners and the Ruskin College Strike of 1909', *Llafur*, vol. 2, No. 1 (Spring 1976)

Lewis, W. J., *Leadmining in Wales* (Cardiff, 1967)

Lambert, W. R., 'Drink and Work-Discipline in Industrial South Wales', *Welsh History Review,* vol. 7, No. 3 (June 1975)

Lindsay, Jean, *A History of the North Wales Slate Industry* (Newton Abbot, 1974)

Llafur, vol. 2, No. 2 (Spring 1977) – special number on General Strike

Lloyd, Sir J. E. (ed.), *A History of Carmarthenshire,* vol. ii (1939)

Lloyd, Wynne, *Trade and Transport* (Swansea, 1940)

Macready, General Sir Nevil, *Annals of an Active Life,* 2 vols. (1924).

Manners, Gerald (ed.), *South Wales in the Sixties* (1964)

Marquand, Hilary, *Second Industrial Survey of South Wales,* 3 vols (Cardiff, 1937)

—— *South Wales Needs a Plan* (1936)

Minchinton, W. E., *The British Tinplate Industry* (Oxford, 1957)

—— (ed.), *Industrial South Wales, 1750–1914* (1969)

Morgan, J. Vyrnwy, *Wales and the War* (1916)

Morgan, Kenneth O., 'Socialism and Syndicalism: the Welsh Miners' Debate, 1912', *Soc. for the Study of Labour History,* Bulletin No. 30 (Spring 1975), pp. 22–36.

Morris, J. H. and L. J. Williams, *The South Wales Coal Industry, 1841 to 1875* (Cardiff, 1958)

Nevin, E., 'The Growth of the Welsh Economy', *Trans. Hon. Soc. Cymmrodorion* (1966, part I)

—— A. R. Roe, and J. I. Round, *Structure of the Welsh Economy* (Cardiff, 1966)

Parry, W. J., *The Penrhyn Lock-Out* (1901)

Parry-Jones, D., *Welsh Country Upbringing* (1948)

Percival, Geoffrey, 'The Government's Industrial Estates in Wales, 1936–1975' (Welsh Development Agency publication, 1978)

Pride, Emrys, 'The Economic Province of Wales', *Trans. Hon. Soc. Cymmrodorion* (1969, part I)

Rees, Alwyn D., *Life in a Welsh Countryside* (Cardiff, 1950)

Rees, G. L. and others, *Survey of the Welsh Economy* (1974)

Rees, Sir J. F. and others, *The Cardiff Region* (Cardiff, 1960)

Richards, P. S., 'Viscose Rayon Manufacture on Deeside', *Flintshire Hist. Soc.* (1967–8)

Rogers, J. Emlyn, 'North Wales Trade Unionism', *Trans. Denbighshire Hist. Soc.* xii (1963)–xxiii (1974)

Rosser, C. and C. Harris, *The Family and Social Change: a study of Family and Kinship in a South Wales Town* (1965)

Smith, David, 'The Reorganization of the South Wales Miners' Federation, 1927–39' (unpublished Swansea Ph.D. thesis, 1976)

—— 'The Struggle against Company Unionism in the South Wales Coalfield, 1926–1939', *Welsh History Review,* vol. 6, No. 3 (June 1973)

Stead, Peter, 'Schools in Glamorgan Society before 1914', *Morgannwg* xix (1975)

—— 'The Swansea of Dylan Thomas', *Remembering Dylan Thomas* (Swansea, 1978)

—— 'Working-Class Leadership in South Wales, 1900–1920', *Welsh History Review,* vol. 6, No. 3 (June 1973)

Thomas, Brinley (ed.), *The Welsh Economy* (Cardiff, 1962)

Thomas, D. A., 'The Coal Industry' in Harold Cox (ed.), *British Industries under Free Trade* (1903)

—— *The Growth and Direction of our Foreign Trade in Coal during the last Half Century* (1903)

—— *The Industrial Struggle in Mid-Rhondda* (Cardiff, 1911)

—— *Some Notes on the Present State of the Coal Trade in the United Kingdom with special reference to that of South Wales and Monmouthshire* (1896)

Thomas, D. Lleufer, *Labour Unions in South Wales* (Swansea, 1901)

Thomas, P. S., *Industrial Relations* (Swansea, 1940)

Vaughan, H. M., *The South Wales Squires* (1926)

Vincent, J. E., *The Land Question in North Wales* (1896)

—— *The Land Question in South Wales* (1897)

—— *Tenancy in Wales* (1889)

Walters, Rhodri, 'Labour Productivity in the South Wales Steam-Coal Industry, 1870–1914', *Econ. Hist. Rev.* xxviii, No. 2 (1975)

Wilkins, C., *History of Merthyr Tydfil* (1908)

Williams, D. T., *The Economic Development of Swansea . . . to 1921* (Swansea, 1940)

Williams, Glyn (ed.), *Social and Cultural Change in Contemporary Wales* (1978)

Williams, J. Roose, *Quarryman's Champion* (Denbigh, 1978)

Williams, L. J., 'The Coalowners of South Wales, 1873–80: Problems of Unity', *Welsh History Review,* vol. 8, No. 1 (June 1976), pp. 75–93.

—— 'The Great Miners' Strike of 1898 in South Wales,' *Morgannwg* ix (1965)

—— 'The New Unionism in Wales', *Welsh History Review*, vol. 1, No. 4

—— 'The Road to Tonypandy', *Llafur*, vol. 1, No. 2 (May 1973)

Williams, Moelwyn, *The South Wales Landscape* (1975)

Williams, Siân Rhiannon, 'The Bedwellty Board of Guardians and the Default Act of 1927', *Llafur,* vol. 2, No. 4 (Spring 1979)

Woodhouse, M. G., 'Rank-and-file Movements among the Miners of South Wales, 1910–1926' (unpublished Oxford D.Phil. thesis, 1970)

Forthcoming works are Hywel Francis and David Smith, *The Fed: a History of the South Wales Miners in the Twentieth Century* (1980), and R. Merfyn Jones, *The North Wales Quarrymen's Union* (Cardiff, 1980)

6. Constitutional and Administrative

Ambrose, G. P., *Monmouthshire County Council, 1888–1974* (Newport, 1974)

Birch, A. H., *Political Integration and Disintegration in the British Isles* (1977)

Bogdanor, Vernon, *Devolution* (Oxford, 1979)

Borthwick, R., 'The Welsh Grand Committee', *Parliamentary Affairs* (Summer 1968)

Chappell, E. L., *The Government of Wales* (1943)

Evans, L. Wynne, 'The Genesis of the Welsh Department, Board of Education, 1906–7', *Trans. Hon. Soc. Cymmrodorion* (1969, part II)

Gibson, E. L., 'A Study of the Council for Wales and Monmouthshire, 1948–1966' (unpublished Aberystwyth M.A. thesis, 1968)

Gowan, Ivor, 'Government in Wales in the Twentieth Century', in J. A. Andrews (ed.), *Welsh Studies in Public Law* (Cardiff, 1970)

Jones, Thomas, *A Diary with Letters* (Oxford, 1954)

—— *Leeks and Daffodils* (Newtown, 1942)

—— *Whitehall Diary,* vols. i and ii, ed. by K. Middlemas (Oxford, 1969)

—— *Welsh Broth* (1952)

Madgwick, Peter and others, *The Politics of Rural Wales* (1973)

Osmond, John, *The Centralist Enemy* (Swansea, 1974)

—— *Creative Conflict* (1978)

Randall, P. J., 'The Development of Administrative Decentralisation in Wales 1907 to 1964' (unpublished Cardiff M.Sc. thesis, 1969)

—— 'The Origins and Establishment of the Welsh Department of Education', *Welsh History Review*, vol. 7, No. 4 (June 1975)

—— 'Wales in the Structure of Central Government', *Public Administration* (Autumn 1972)

Rees, I. Bowen, *Government by Community* (1971)

Roberts, Glyn, *The Municipal Development of the Borough of Swansea to 1900* (Cardiff, 1940)

Rowlands, Edward, 'The Politics of Regional Administration: the Establishment of the Welsh Office', *Public Administration* (Autumn 1972)

Trice, J. E., 'Welsh Local Government Reform—an Assessment of Ad hoc Administrative Reform', *Public Law* (Autumn 1970)

Watkins, Sir Percy, *A Welshman Remembers* (Cardiff, 1944)

7. Religion

Bell, P. M. H., *Irish and Welsh Disestablishment* (1969)

Davies, E. T., *Religion in the Industrial Revolution in South Wales* (Cardiff, 1965)

Davies, E. Tegla, 'Welsh Wesleyan Methodism', in *The Methodist Church: its Origins, Divisions and Reunion* (1932)

Davies, T. Eirug (ed.), *Y Prifathro Thomas Rees: ei fywyd a'i Waith* (Llandysul, 1939)

Day, G. and M. Fitton, 'Religion and Social Status in Rural Wales', *Sociological Review* 23, No. 4 (November 1975)

Edwards, Archbishop A. G., *Landmarks in the History of the Welsh Church* (1912)
—— *Memories* (1927)

Evans, Eifion, *The Welsh Revival of 1904* (1969)

Evans, E. Keri, and W. Pari Huws, *Y Parch. David Adams, B.A., D.D.* (Liverpool, 1924)

de Fursac, J. Rogues, *Un mouvement mystique contemporain: le reveil religieux du pays de Galles (1904–1905)* (Paris, 1907)

Green, C. A. H., *Disestablishment and Disendowment: the Experience of the Church in Wales* (1935)

Hughes, R. R., *Y Parchedig John Williams, D.D., Brynsiencyn* (Caernarfon, 1929)

Jones, Bobi, *Llên Cymru a Chrefydd* (Swansea, 1977)

Jones, G. Hartwell, *A Celt looks at the World* (1946)

Jones, R. Tudur, *Hanes Annibyniaeth Cymru* (Swansea, 1966)

Jones, R. W., *John Puleston Jones* (Caernarfon, 1929)

Knox, R. Buick, *Voices from the Past* (Llandysul, 1969)

Koss, Stephen, *Nonconformity in Modern British Politics* (1975)

Lewis, H. Elfed, *Cofiant y Parchedig E. Herber Evans* (Wrexham, 1901)

Lerry, George, *Alfred George Edwards, Archbishop of Wales* (Oswestry, 1940)

Morgan, J. Vyrnwy (ed.), *Welsh Religious Leaders in the Victorian Era* (1905)

Morgan, Kenneth O., *Freedom or Sacrilege?* (Cardiff, 1966)

Owen, Eluned E., *The Early Life of Bishop Owen* (Llandysul, 1958)
—— *The Later Life of Bishop Owen* (Llandysul, 1961)

Rees, J. Machreth, and J. Owen, *Cofiant y Parchedig John Thomas D.D.* (Liverpool, 1898)

Rees, Thomas, *History of Protestant Nonconformity in Wales* (2nd ed., 1883)

Stead, W. T., *The Revival of the West* (1905)

Walker, David (ed.), *A History of the Church in Wales* (Cardiff, 1976)

—— 'The Welsh Church and Disestablishment', *Modern Churchman* xiv, No. 2.

Williams, C. R., 'The Welsh Religious Revival of 1904–5', *British Jnl. of Sociology* (1952)

Note: The above section does not include pamphlets and other emphemeral material produced during the disestablishment controversy, which can be weighed by the ton.

8. Education

Davies, J. A., *Education in a Welsh Rural County, 1870–1913* (Cardiff, 1913)

Davies, W. Cadwaladr, and W. Lewis Jones, *The University of Wales* (1905)

Ellis, E. L., *The University College of Wales, Aberystwyth, 1872–1972* (Cardiff, 1972)

Ellis, T. I., *The Development of Higher Education in Wales* (Wrexham, 1935)

—— *John Humphreys Davies* (Swansea, 1964)

—— (ed.), *The Letters of Thomas Charles Edwards,* 2 vols (Aberystwyth, 1952–3)

Evans, D. Emrys, *The University of Wales* (Cardiff, 1953)

Evans, L. Wynne, *Studies in Welsh Education* (1974)

Griffiths, S., 'The Welsh Intermediate Education Act and Cardiganshire', *Ceredigion* viii, No. 1 (1976)

Hetherington, H. J., *The Life and Letters of Sir Henry Jones,* 2 vols (1924)

James, D. Geraint, 'Sir Isambard Owen', *Trans. Hon. Soc. Cymmrodorion* (1976)

Jones, Gareth E., 'A study of the influence of Central Institutions on the Development of Secondary Education in Wales, 1914–1944' (unpublished Swansea Ph.D. thesis, 1978)

Jones, Sir Henry, *Old Memories* (1923)

Jones, K. Viriamu, *The Life of J. Viriamu Jones* (1915)

Jones, P. Mansell, *How they educated Jones* (1974)

Jones, W. R., *Bilingualism in Welsh Education* (Cardiff, 1976)

Kekewich, Sir George, *The Education Department and After* (1920)

Khlief, B. B., 'Cultural Regeneration and the School: an Anthropological Study of Welsh-Medium Schools in Wales', *Int. Rev. of Education,* 22, No. 2 (1978)

Lloyd, J. E. (ed.), *Sir Harry Reichel* (Cardiff, 1934)

Masterman, Neville C., *J. Viriamu Jones, 1856–1901: Pioneer of the Modern University* (Llandybïe, 1958)

Morgan, Iwan (ed.), *The College by the Sea* (Aberystwyth, 1928)

Pierce, G. O., '"The Coercion of Wales Act"; 1904', in H. Hearder and H. R. Loyn (eds.), *British Government and Administration* (Cardiff, 1974)

—— *A Matter of Primary Urgency* (Cardiff, 1979)

Price, D. T. W., *The History of St. David's College, Lampeter,* vol. 1 (Cardiff, 1977)

Stead, Peter, *Coleg Harlech: the First Fifty Years* (Cardiff, 1977)

—— 'Schools and Society in Glamorgan before 1914', *Morgannwg* xix (1975)

Stephen, E., *History of Education in Merthyr, 1840–1912* (Merthyr, n.d.)

Williams, David, *Thomas Francis Roberts* (Cardiff, 1961)

Williams, Glanmor, 'Some reflections on the Gittins Report', in *Aspects of Primary Education: the Challenge of Gittins* (1970)

—— and others, *Pioneers of Welsh Education* (Swansea, 1964)

Williams, Jac L., *Ysgrifau ar Addysg* (Llandysul, 1966)

9. Welsh Language

Bell, H. Idris, *The Crisis of our Time and other Papers* (Llandybïe, 1954)

Betts, Clive, *Culture in Crisis* (Upton, Wirral, 1976)

Bowen E. G. and Harold Carter, 'Preliminary Observations on the Distribution of the Welsh Language at the 1971 Census', *Geographical Jnl.* cxl (1974)

Davies, Cassie, *Undeb Cymru Fydd* (Denbigh, 1960)

Davies, Elwyn, and H. Lewis (eds.), *Celtic Studies in Wales* (Cardiff, 1963)

Davies, Gwennant, *The Story of the Urdd* (Aberystwyth, 1973)

Edwards, Hywel Teifi, *Yr Eisteddfod* (1976)

Foster, Idris, 'Sir Ifor Williams', *Proc. of the British Academy* liii (1967)

Griffith, R. E., *Urdd Gobaith Cymru* (Aberystwyth, 3 vols, 1971–3)

Jones, R. Gerallt, *A Bid for Unity* (Denbigh, 1971)

Jones, Thomas (ed.), *Astudiaethau Amrywiol* (Cardiff, 1968)

Le Calvez, A., *Un cas de bilingualisme: le pays de Galles* (Lannion, 1970)

Lewis, G., 'The Attitude to Language among bi-lingual Children and Adults in Wales', *Int. Jnl. of Sociology of Language* 4 (1975)

Lewis, J. Parry, 'The Anglicization of Glamorgan', *Morgannwg* iv (1960)

Lewis, Saunders, *Tynged yr Iaith* (Cardiff, 1962)

Morgan, Gerald, *The Dragon's Tongue* (Cardiff, 1966)

Price, Glanville, *The Present Position of Minority Languages in Western Europe: a selective Bibliography* (Cardiff, 1969, with supplements in the periodical *Orbis*)

Pryce, W. T. R., 'Wales as a Culture Region', *Trans. Hon. Soc. Cymmrodorion* (1978)

—— 'Welsh and English in Wales, 1750–1971: a spatial analysis based on the Linguistic Affiliation of Parochial Communities', *Bull. Bd. Celtic Studies* xxviii, part I (November 1978)

Roberts, Brynley, 'Syr Edward Anwyl', *Trans. Hoc. Soc. Cymmrodorion* (1968, part I)

Stephens, Meic (ed.), *The Welsh Language Today* (Llandysul, 1973)

Thomas, Alun R., *The Linguistic Geography of Wales* (Cardiff, 1973)

Thomas, J. Gareth, 'The Geographical Distribution of the Welsh Language', *Geog. Jnl.* 122 (1956)

Williams, D. Trevor, 'Linguistic Divides in North Wales', *Arch. Camb.* xci (1936)

—— 'Linguistic Divides in South Wales', *Arch. Camb* xc (1935)

—— 'A Linguistic Map of Wales', *Geog. Jnl.* 89 (1937)

Williams, Glyn (ed.), *Social and Cultural Change in Contemporary Wales* (1978)

For the language, the reader should also consult articles in *Bibliotheca Celtica, Studia Celtica, Llên Cymru,* and the *Bulletin of the Board of Celtic Studies* (Language and Literature section), together with such periodicals as *Y Geninen, Y Llenor* and *Y Traethodydd.*

10. Welsh Literature

Adams, S., and G. R. Hughes (eds.), *Triskel One* (Llandybïe, 1971) and *Triskel Two* (Llandybïe, 1973)

Bell, H. Idris, 'The Welsh Literary Renascence of the Twentieth Century', *Proc. of British Academy* xxxix (1953)

Bowen, Geraint (ed.), *Y Traddodiad Rhyddiaith yn yr Ugeinfed Ganrif* (Llandysul, 1976)

Conran, Anthony (ed.), *Penguin Book of Welsh Verse* (1967)

Davies, Sir Alfred T., *'O.M.': a Memoir* (1946)

Davies, Aneurin Talfan (ed.), *Gwŷr Llên* (Cardiff, 1948)

Davies, Pennar, *Saunders Lewis: ei feddwl a'i Waith* (Denbigh, 1950)

Davies, W. Beynon, *Thomas Gwynn Jones* (Cardiff, 1970)

Foster, Idris (ed.), *Cyfrol Deyrnged Syr Thomas Parry-Williams* (National Eisteddfod, 1967)

Griffiths, Bruce, *Saunders Lewis** (Cardiff, 1979)

Griffiths, J. Gwyn, *D. J. Williams: Cyfrol Deyrnged* (Llandysul, 1965)

Gruffydd, R. Geraint (ed.), *Meistri'r Canrifoedd* (Cardiff, 1973)

Gruffydd, W. J., *Hen Atgofion* (Aberystwyth, 1936)

—— *Owen Morgan Edwards: Cofiant,* vol. i (Aberystwyth, 1936)

Jenkins, Dafydd, *D. J. Williams** (Cardiff, 1973)

Jenkins, David, *Thomas Gwynn Jones* (Denbigh, 1973)

Jenkins, R. T., *Edrych yn Ôl* (Cardiff, 1968)

Jones, Alun R., and Gwyn Thomas (eds.), *Presenting Saunders Lewis* (Cardiff, 1973)

Jones, Bedwyr Lewis, *R. Williams Parry** (Cardiff, 1972)

Jones, Bobi (ed.), *Kate Roberts: Cyfrol Deyrnged* (Denbigh, 1969)

Jones, Gwilym Arthur, *Bywyd a Gwaith Owen Morgan Edwards* (Aberystwyth, 1958)

Jones, R. Gerallt (ed.), *Poetry of Wales, 1930–1970* (Llandysul, 1974)

—— *T. H. Parry-Williams** (Cardiff, 1978)

Jones, R. M., *Llenyddiaeth Gymraeg, 1936–1972* (Llandybïe, 1972)

Jones, Thomas (ed.), *Astudiaethau Amrywiol* (Cardiff, 1968)

Lewis, Saunders, *Canlyn Arthur* (Aberystwyth, 1958)

—— *An Introduction to Contemporary Welsh Literature* (Wrexham, 1926)

Lloyd, D. Myrddin (trans), *W. J. Gruffydd: the Years of the Locust* (Llandysul, 1976)

Lloyd, D. Tecwyn, and G. Rees Hughes (eds.), *Saunders Lewis* (Llandybïe, 1975)

Llywelyn-Williams, Alun, *Y nos, y niwl a'r ynys: Agweddau ar y Profiad Rhamantaidd yng Nghymru, 1890–1914* (Cardiff, 1960)

—— *R. T. Jenkins** (Cardiff, 1977)

—— *Yn Nes na'r Hanesydd?* (Denbigh, 1972)

Meredith, J. E., *Gwenallt: Bardd Crefyddol* (Llandysul, 1974)

Morgan, Derec Llwyd, *Kate Roberts** (Cardiff, 1974)

Morgan, Dyfnallt, *D. Gwenallt Jones** (Cardiff, 1972)

—— *Rhyw Hanner Ieuenctid* (Swansea, 1971)

Morgan, Gerald (ed.), *This World of Wales* (Cardiff, 1968)

Morgan, T. J., *W. J. Gruffydd** (Cardiff, 1970)

Nicholas, James, *Waldo Williams** (Cardiff, 1975)

—— (ed.), *Waldo—Cyfrol Deyrnged* (Cardiff, 1977)

Owen, Dafydd, *Cynan* (Cardiff, 1979)

Parry, T. Emrys, *Barddoniaeth Robert Williams Parry* (Denbigh, 1973)

Parry, Thomas, *A History of Welsh Literature* (trans. H. Idris Bell, Oxford, 1955)

—— *John Morris-Jones* (Cardiff, 1958)

—— *Llenyddiaeth Gymraeg, 1900–45* (Liverpool, 1945)

—— (ed.), *Oxford Book of Welsh Verse* (Oxford, 1962)

Parry, Thomas and Merfyn Morgan (eds.), *Llyfryddiaeth Llenyddiaeth Gymraeg* (Cardiff, 1976)

Parry-Williams, T. H., *Syr John Rhŷs* (Cardiff, 1954)

Rees, Edward T., *T. Rowland Hughes: Cofiant* (Llandysul, 1968)

Rowlands, John, *T. Rowland Hughes** (Cardiff, 1975)

Smith, J. Beverley, 'John Gwili Jenkins, 1872–1936', *Trans. Hon. Soc. Cymmrodorion* (1974–5)

Thomas, David, *Silyn* (Liverpool, 1956)

Triskel Two (Llandybïe, 1973)

Williams, Gwyn, *An Introduction to Welsh Literature* (Cardiff, 1978)

Williams, J. E. Caerwyn (ed.), *Literature in Celtic Countries* (Cardiff, 1971)

—— 'Syr John Morris-Jones', *Trans. Hon. Soc. Cymmrodorion* (1965, part I, and 196, part II)

The best way of approaching Welsh-language literature is through periodicals such as *Y Beirniad, Y Genhinen, Y Llenor, Lleufer, Y Traethodydd* and *Ysgrifau Beirniadol* (listed in section C, 2 above), and, of course, the other writings of the poets and prose authors in question. The University of Wales Press series, 'Writers of Wales', is excellent: its volumes are asterisked above.

11. Anglo-Welsh Literature

Adam, G. F., *Three Contemporary Anglo-Welsh Novelists* (Berne, 1948)

Adams, S., and G. R. Hughes (eds.), *Triskel One: Essays on Welsh and Anglo-Welsh Literature* (Llandybïe, 1971); *Triskel Two* (Llandybïe, 1973)

——, and R. Mathias (eds.), *The Shining Pyramid and Other Stories by Welsh Authors* (Llandysul, 1970)

Dale-Jones, D., *Emlyn Williams** (Cardiff, 1979)

Davies, Walford, *Dylan Thomas** (Cardiff, 1972)

—— (ed.) *Dylan Thomas: New Critical Essays* (1972)

Edwards, Keri, *Jack Jones** (Cardiff, 1974)

Evans, George Ewart (ed.), *Welsh Short Stories* (1959)

Ferris, Paul, *Dylan Thomas* (1978)

FitzGibbon, Constantine, *The Life of Dylan Thomas* (1965)

—— (ed.), *Selected Letters of Dylan Thomas* (1966)

Garlick, Raymond, 'Is there an Anglo-Welsh Literature?' in Williams, J. E. Caerwyn (ed.), *Literature in Celtic Countries* (Cardiff, 1971)

—— *An Introduction to Anglo-Welsh Literature** (Cardiff, 1970; 2nd ed. 1972)

Griffiths, Bryn (ed.), *Welsh Voices* (1967)

Hockey, L., *W. H. Davies** (Cardiff, 1971)

Hooker, J., *John Cowper Powys** (Cardiff, 1973)

Jenkins, I., *Idris Davies** (Cardiff, 1972)

John, Alun, *Alun Lewis** (Cardiff, 1970)

Jones, Glyn, 'The Second Flowering' in *British Poetry Since 1960* (Oxford, 1972)

—— *The Dragon Has Two Tongues* (1968)

Jones, Gwyn, *The First Forty Years: Some Notes on Anglo-Welsh Literature* (Cardiff, 1957)

—— (ed.), *Oxford Book of Welsh Verse in English* (Oxford, 1977)

—— *Being and Belonging* (Cardiff, 1977)

——, and Islwyn Ffowc Elis (eds.), *Twenty-Five Welsh Short Stories* (Oxford, 1971)

Lewis, Saunders, *Is There an Anglo-Welsh Literature?* (Cardiff, 1939)

Mathias, Roland, 'Thin Spring and Tributary: Welshmen Writing in English' in Jones, R. Brinley (ed.), *Anatomy of Wales* (Cardiff, 1972)

—— *Vernon Watkins** (Cardiff, 1974)

Michael, D. P. M., *Arthur Machen** (Cardiff, 1971)

Michael, Ian, *Gwyn Thomas** (Cardiff, 1977)

Morgan, Gerald (ed.), *This World of Wales: An Anthology of Anglo-Welsh Poetry from the Seventeenth to the Twentieth Century* (Cardiff, 1968)

Norris, Leslie, *Glyn Jones** (Cardiff, 1973)

Poetry Wales: special number on R. S. Thomas (Spring 1972)

Price, Cecil, *Gwyn Jones** (Cardiff, 1976)

Rees, David, *Rhys Davies** (Cardiff, 1975)

Rhys, Keidrych (ed.) *Modern Welsh Poetry* (1944)

Richards, Alun (ed.), *Penguin Book of Welsh Short Stories* (Harmondsworth, 1976)

Thomas, R. George, *R. S. Thomas* (1964)

Watkins, Gwen, and Ruth Pryor (eds.), *That I Was Born in Wales* (Cardiff, 1976)

Williams, John Stuart, and Stephens, Meic (eds.), *The Lilting House: An Anthology of Anglo-Welsh Poetry 1917–1967* (London and Llandybïe, 1969)

Williams, Trevor L., *Caradoc Evans** (Cardiff, 1970)

Anglo-Welsh Literature can also be approached through such periodicals as *Wales* (1937–40, 1943–9, 1958–60), *The Welsh Review* (1939–48), *Dock Leaves* (1949–57), *The Anglo-Welsh Review* (1957–), *Poetry Wales* (1965–), and *Planet* (1970–9), all listed in section C, 2 above, and, of course, through the other writings of the poets and prose authors in question. Volumes asterisked in the main list above are in the University of Wales Press 'Writers of Wales' series, which should be consulted for other and forthcoming titles and as a joint context for the treatment also of Welsh-language writers.

12. Other Arts and Broadcasting

Bell, David, *The Artist in Wales* (1957)

Bowen, H. (ed.), *Architecture in Wales* (Cardiff, 1966–9)

Boyd, M., *William Mathias** (Cardiff, 1978)

Briggs, Asa, *The History of Broadcasting in the United Kingdom,* vols i–iv (Oxford, 1961–79)

Chappell, Edgar L., *Cardiff's Civic Centre* (Cardiff, 1946)

Cleaver, Emrys, *Musicians of Wales* (Ruthin, 1968)

Colles, H. C., *Walford Davies* (Oxford, 1942)

Crossley-Holland, P. (ed.), *Music in Wales* (1948)

Deane, B., *Alun Hoddinot** (Cardiff, 1978)

Dunthorne, K. (ed.), *Artists exhibited in Wales, 1945–74* (Cardiff, 1976)

Edwards, Owain T., *Joseph Parry* (Cardiff, 1970)

Evans, E. Keri, *Cofiant Dr. Joseph Parry* (Cardiff, 1921)

Graham, J., *A Century of Welsh Music* (1923)

Griffith, R. D., *Hanes Canu Cynulleidfaol Cymru* (Cardiff, 1948)

Hilling, John B., *Cardiff and the Valleys* (1973)

—— *The Historic Architecture of Wales* (Cardiff, 1976)

—— *Plans and Prospects – Architecture in Wales, 1780–1914* (Cardiff, 1975)

Hughes, Glyn Tegai and others (eds.), *Gregynog* (Cardiff, 1977)

Jones, R. E., *David Wynne** (Cardiff, 1979)

Lewis, Idris, *Cerddoriaeth yng Nghymru* (Liverpool, 1947)

Mullins, E., *Joseph Herman* (1967)

Parrott, H. Ian, *The Spiritual Pilgrims* (Narberth, 1969)

Rees, T. Mardy, *Welsh Artists* (Caernarfon, 1912)

Rowan, Eric, *Art in Wales, 1850–1975* (Cardiff, 1978)

Smith, J. Sutcliffe, *Impressions of Music in Wales* (Penmaenmawr, 1948)

Stephens, Meic (ed.), *The Arts in Wales, 1950–1975* (Cardiff, 1979)

—— (ed.), *Artists in Wales,* i–iii (Llandysul, 1971–77)

Thompson, D., *Ceri Richards* (1963)

Webster, J. R., *Ceri Richards* (Cardiff, 1961)

—— '"For Wales – see England"; the Artist in Wales', in B. Jones (ed.), *Anatomy of Wales* (Cardiff, 1972)

—— *Joseph Herman* (Cardiff, 1962)

Williams, W. S. Gwynn, *Welsh National Music and Dance* (?1933)

Wright, Kenneth, *Gentle are its Songs* (1973)

Young, Percy, *A History of British Music* (1967)

Volumes asterisked above are in the University of Wales Press 'Composers of Wales' series which should be consulted for other, forthcoming titles. Music in Wales can also be approached in the Guild for the Promotion of Welsh Music's journal, *Welsh Music* (1947–   ).

13. Sport

Billott, John, *The History of Welsh International Rugby* (Ferndale, 1970)

Collins, W. J. T., *Rugby Recollections* (Newport, 1948)

Edwards, Gareth, *Gareth: an Autobiography* (1978)

Jenkins, Geraint H., *Cewri Pêl-Droed yng Nghymru* (Llandysul, 1977)

Thomas, J. B. G., and Rowe Harding (eds.), *Rugby in Wales* (Llandybïe, 1970)

Wooller, Wilfrid, *The History of Glamorgan Cricket* (1971)

An official history of the Welsh Rugby Union is currently being prepared by David Smith and Gareth Williams for the centenary in 1980.

INDEX